Information Security and Cryptography

Information Security – protecting information in potentially hostile environments – is a crucial factor in the growth of information-based processes in industry, business, and administration. Cryptography is a key technology for achieving information security in communications, computer systems, electronic commerce, and in the emerging information society.

Springer's Information Security & Cryptography (IS&C) book series covers all relevant topics, ranging from theory to advanced applications. The intended audience includes students, researchers and practitioners.

Michele Ciampi · Luisa Siniscalchi

Round and Computational Efficiency of Multi-party Protocols

Springer

Michele Ciampi
School of Informatics
University of Edinburgh
Edinburgh, UK

Luisa Siniscalchi
Technical University of Denmark
Copenhagen, Denmark

ISSN 1619-7100 ISSN 2197-845X (electronic)
Information Security and Cryptography
ISBN 978-3-031-92373-9 ISBN 978-3-031-92374-6 (eBook)
https://doi.org/10.1007/978-3-031-92374-6

This Springer imprint is published by the registered company Springer Nature Switzerland AG
The registered company address is: Gewerbestrasse 11, 6330 Cham, Switzerland

To our families.

Preface

A cryptographic protocol is defined by the behavior of the involved parties and the messages that those parties send to each other. Besides the functionality and the security that a cryptographic protocol provides, it is also important that the protocol is *efficient*. In this document, we focus on efficiency parameters related to the computational and round complexity. We are interested in the computational cost that the parties involved in the protocol have to incur and how many interactions between the parties are required to securely implement a certain cryptographic functionality. Another important aspect of a cryptographic protocol is related to the computational assumptions. This document aims to show how some fundamental cryptographic multi-party functionalities can be designed requiring minimal interaction while relying on standard and well-understood cryptographic assumptions. The core technical focus of the document is in the design of protocols that do not require any setup assumption. Hence, we will face the common issue that occurs in such a context, in relation to the design of simulators and security reductions that crucially require to *rewind* the adversary. We believe that this document is particularly suitable for readers interested in understanding the challenges that need to be faced when designing and proving the security of cryptographic protocols in such a challenging but fascinating setting.

The document is divided into three main parts. In the first part, we consider *secure multi-party computation* (MPC), a cryptographic paradigm. In this we can consider, for example, two parties (but more than two can be considered), Alice and Bob, willing to compute the output of a function f given x and y as their inputs, respectively. Moreover, each party wants to keep the input secret while allowing the other party to learn $f(x, y)$. As a first result, we show how to design a secure two-party computation (2PC) protocol with black box simulation, secure under standard and generic assumptions, with optimal round complexity in the simultaneous message exchange model. In the simultaneous message exchange model, both parties can send a message in each round. We then show how to obtain the same results, but in the multi-party setting, for the case of the coin-tossing functionality. In this part, we will also introduce and construct a special proof system, that is instrumental for the design of both the coin-tossing protocol, and the mentioned 2PC protocol.

We also consider the relaxed setting where adversaries are instead forced to follow the protocol description (i.e., *semi-honest* or *honest-but-curious* adversary), for the case where parties want to compute the *Set-Membership* functionality. Such a functionality allows checking whether an element belongs to a set or not. The protocol we propose provides good performance in terms of communication and computational complexity (i.e., a practical construction compared to the previous results).

In the second part of the document considers the problem of designing round-efficient *non-malleable commitments* from generic assumptions. A commitment scheme allows the sender to send an encrypted message, called commitment, in such a way that the message inside the commitment cannot be opened until the *opening* information is provided by the sender. Moreover, there is a unique way in which the commitment can be open. In this document, we consider the case in which the sender sends the commitment (e.g., through a computer network) that can be actively tampered with by the adversary. In this setting, the adversary can catch the commitment C and modify it, thus obtaining a new commitment C' that contains a message related to the content of C. A non-malleable commitment scheme prevents such an attack, and the schemes we propose can be proved secure even in the case that the adversary can eavesdrop on multiple commitments and in turn, compute and send multiple commitments. In particular, we show how to obtain a four-round protocol relying on one-way functions, and a three-round scheme relying on sub-exponentially hard one-way permutations.

The last part of the document concerns *proof systems*. Let us consider an $\mathcal{NP}$-language, like the language of graph Hamiltonicity. A proof system allows an entity called *prover* to prove that a certain graph (instance) contains a Hamiltonian cycle (witness) to another entity called *verifier*. A proof system can be easily instantiated in one round by letting the prover send the cycle to the verifier. What we want though, is a protocol in which the prover can convince the verifier that a certain graph belongs to the language of Graph Hamiltonicity, in such a way that no information about the cycle is leaked to the verifier. This kind of proof systems are called *zero knowledge*. We show a non-interactive zero-knowledge proof system, under the assumption that both prover and verifier have access to some honestly generated *common reference string* (CRS). The provided construction is practical, and makes minimal use of the heuristic assumption of the so-called *random oracle*. This is also the only construction we propose that relies on some form of setup (i.e., the CRS and the random oracle). We consider also the scenario in which the prover and verifier do not have access to any honestly generated information nor the random oracle, and study the notion of *witness indistinguishability*. This notion considers instances that admit more than one witness, e.g. graphs that admit two distinct Hamiltonian cycles (as for the notion of zero knowledge, the notion of witness indistinguishability makes sense for all the languages in $\mathcal{NP}$, but for ease of exposition we keep focusing our attention of the language of graph Hamiltonicity). The security notion of witness-indistinguishability ensures that a verifier, upon receiving a proof from a prover, is not able to figure out which one of the two Hamiltonian cycles has been used by the prover to compute the proof. Even though the notion of witness indistinguishability is weaker than the notion of zero knowledge, witness indistinguishability is widely used in many cryptographic applications. Moreover, given that a witness-indistinguishable protocol can be constructed using just three rounds of communication compared to the four rounds required to obtain zero knowledge (with black-box simulation), the use of zero-knowledge as a building block to construct a protocol with an optimal number of rounds is sometimes prohibitive and witness indistinguishabile proofs are prefered. Always in order to provide suitable building block to construct more advanced cryptographic protocols with a nice round complexity, a useful property is the so-called *delayed-input* property. This property allows the prover to compute all but the last round of the protocol without knowing the instance or the witness. Also, the delayed-input property allows the verifier to interact with the prover without knowing the instance at all (i.e. the verifier needs the instance just to decide whether to accept or not the proof received by the prover). We show how to design efficient delayed-input witness-indistinguishable proof systems that consist of just three rounds of communication, and formally argue about the security of these protocols in the case where the inputs are adaptively chosen by the adversary (instead of being statically chosen as in the standard notion of witness indistinguishability).

Edinburgh, UK
Copenhagen, Denmark
March 2025

Michele Ciampi
Luisa Siniscalchi

Declarations This book contains a cohesive collection of extended versions of results that appeared in the following works:

- [52] Michele Ciampi, Giuseppe Persiano, Alessandra Scafuro, Luisa Siniscalchi, and Ivan Visconti. Improved OR-composition of sigma-protocols. *Theory of Cryptography—13th International Conference, TCC 2016-A*
- [53] Michele Ciampi, Giuseppe Persiano, Alessandra Scafuro, Luisa Siniscalchi, and Ivan Visconti. Online/offline OR composition of sigma protocols. *Advances in Cryptology—EUROCRYPT 2016—35th Annual International Conference on the Theory and Applications of Cryptographic Techniques*
- [54] Michele Ciampi, Giuseppe Persiano, Luisa Siniscalchi, and Ivan Visconti. A transform for NIZK almost as efficient and general as the Fiat-Shamir transform without programmable random oracles. *Theory of Cryptography—13th International Conference, TCC 2016-A*
- [46] Michele Ciampi, Rafail Ostrovsky, Luisa Siniscalchi, and Ivan Visconti. Concurrent non-malleable commitments (and more) in three rounds. *Advances in Cryptology—CRYPTO 2016—36th Annual International Cryptology Conference*
- [48] Michele Ciampi, Rafail Ostrovsky, Luisa Siniscalchi, and Ivan Visconti. Four-round concurrent non-malleable commitments from one-way functions. *Advances in Cryptology—CRYPTO 2017—37th Annual International Cryptology Conference*
- [49] Michele Ciampi, Rafail Ostrovsky, Luisa Siniscalchi, and Ivan Visconti. Round-optimal secure two-party computation from trapdoor permutations. *Theory of Cryptography—15th International Conference, TCC 2017*
- [47] Michele Ciampi, Rafail Ostrovsky, Luisa Siniscalchi, and Ivan Visconti. Delayed-input non-malleable zero knowledge and multi-party coin tossing in four rounds. *Theory of Cryptography—15th International Conference, TCC 2017*
- [44] Michele Ciampi and Claudio Orlandi. Combining private set-intersection with secure two-party computation. *Security and Cryptography for Networks—11th International Conference, SCN 2018*

Competing Interests The authors have no competing interests to declare that are relevant to the content of this manuscript.

Contents

Chapter 1
Introduction

1.1 Secure Multi-party Computation

Designing protocols for secure computation [90, 192] that requires minimal interaction between the parties has been a long-standing open problem. For the two-party case, the work of Katz and Ostrovsky [124] demonstrated that 5 rounds are both necessary and sufficient, with black-box simulation, when both parties need to obtain the output. Their construction relies on the use of trapdoor permutations.[1] In a follow-up work, Ostrovsky et al. [161] showed that a black-box use of trapdoor permutations is sufficient for obtaining the above round-optimal construction.

The work of Garg et al. [84] revisited the lower bound of [124] when the communication channel allows both players to send messages in the same round: *simultaneous message exchange model*. Focusing on this model, Garg et al. showed that 4 rounds are necessary to build a secure two-party computation (2PC) protocol for every functionality with black-box simulation. In the same work they also designed a 4-round secure 2PC protocol for every functionality. However their construction compared to the one of [124] relies on much stronger complexity assumptions: 3-round 3-robust [179] parallel non-malleable commitment scheme. According to [179], such commitment scheme can be constructed either through non-falsifiable assumptions (i.e., using the construction of [163]) or through sub-exponentially-strong assumptions (i.e., using the construction of [46]). Moreover in [7, 106] the authors showed how to construct a 4-round protocol to securely compute every functionality for the

[1] The actual assumption is *enhanced* trapdoor permutations, but for simplicity, we will omit the word *enhanced* assuming it implicitly.

M. Ciampi and L. Siniscalchi, *Round and Computational Efficiency of Multi-party Protocols*, Information Security and Cryptography,
https://doi.org/10.1007/978-3-031-92374-6_1

multi-party case under the Decisional Diffie-Hellman (DDH) assumption for the case of [106] and under the LWE+DDH assumptions for the case of [7].

We then try to answer the following interesting question:

Question: *is there a 4-round construction for secure 2PC for any functionality in the simultaneous message exchange model, assuming trapdoor permutations?*

We show a positive answer to this question by designing a secure two-party computation protocol relying on a special 4-round oblivious transfer that has interesting (parallel-)composition properties, and on a novel 4-round non-malleable zero-knowledge argument.

One core tool that will be used to design the 2PC protocols is a 4-round non-malleable zero-knowledge (NMZK) argument. The novel feature of this 4-round NMZK is its *delayed-input* feature. This feature guarantees that the first three rounds of the protocol are independent of the theorem and the witness. This feature has proven to be particularly useful when composing protocols in a round-preserving way. We will also show that such a NMZK protocol can be used to also design a 4-round multi-party protocol to realize the coin-tossing functionality.

More Related Works

A sequence of works tried to match the same lower bound for the multi-party setting in the case of general functinoalities [4, 27], and finally [8, 107] showed the first four-round protocols based on polynomial time number theoretic assumptions. This result was later improved in [42] proposing a four-round scheme based on maliciously secure oblivious transfer (OT). The question has also been investigated with respect to the black-box use of the underlying cryptographic primitives.

Ishai, Khurana, Sahai, and Srinivasan [116] proposed a five-round protocol that makes *black-box* use of secure oblivious transfer and public-key encryption (PKE) with pseudorandom public keys. This result was later improved in [117] where the same authors construct a (black-box) four-round protocol, requiring sub-exponential security of the underlying assumptions. In a concurrent and independent work [50], authors propose a black-box protocol that requires polynomial-time assumptions but only realizes a restricted set of functionalities (i.e., input-less functionalities). In [51], the authors show a round optimal protocol relying in a black-box way on two-round oblivious transfer with statistical sender security.

Results in the Semi-honest Setting

All the results mentioned so far will be proven secure in the malicious setting (where the adversary can arbitrarily misbehave). In the first part of the document, we will also consider the *semi-honest* model and *Private-Set Intersection (PSI)*, one of the most popular and practically relevant secure two-party computation tasks. Designing special-purpose PSI protocols (which are more efficient than generic 2PC solutions) is a very active line of research. In particular, a long line of work has proposed PSI protocols based on oblivious transfer (OT) which, thanks to advances in OT-extension techniques, is nowadays a very cheap cryptographic building block. Unfortunately, most protocols cannot be plugged into larger 2PC applications since in these protocols one party (by design) learns the output of the intersection. Therefore, it is not possible to perform secure *post-processing* of the output of the PSI protocol. We show an efficient OT-based PSI protocol that produces an "encrypted" output that can, therefore, be later used as an input to other 2PC protocols. In particular, the protocol can be used in combination with all common approaches to 2PC including garbled circuits, secret sharing, and homomorphic encryption. Thus, the protocol can be combined with the right 2PC techniques to achieve more efficient protocols for computations of the form $z = f(X \cap Y)$ for arbitrary functions f.

1.2 Non-malleable Commitments

Commitment schemes are a fundamental primitive in Cryptography. Here we consider the intriguing question of constructing round-efficient schemes that remain secure even against man-in-the-middle (MiM) attacks: *non-malleable (NM) commitments* [70].

Non-malleable Commitments. The round complexity of commitment schemes in the stand-alone setting is nowadays well understood. Non-interactive commitments can be constructed assuming the existence of 1-to-1 one-way functions (OWFs) [88]; 2-round commitments can be constructed assuming the existence of OWFs only. Moreover, non-interactive commitments do not exist if one relies on the black-box use of OWFs only [145]. Instead, the round complexity of NM commitments after ~30 years of research remains a fascinating open question, in particular when taking into account the required computational assumptions. The original construction of [70] required a logarithmic number of rounds and the sole use of OWFs. Then, through a long sequence of very exciting positive results [11, 94, 95, 135, 136, 138, 168–173, 191], the above open question has been in part solved by obtaining a constant-round[2] (even concurrent) NM commitment scheme by using any OWF in a black-box fashion. On the negative side, Pass [167] proved the impossibility for constructing non-malleable commitments using 2 rounds of communication or less, via a black-box reduction to any *standard* polynomial intractability assumptions[3] when security is proved through a black-box reduction to polynomial-time hardness assumptions.

Concurrent Non-malleable Commitments from Polynomial-Time Assumptions

A main common issue for round-efficient non-malleable commitments is that typically a security proof requires some simulation on the left and extraction on the

[2] The construction of [95] can be compressed to 6 rounds (see [99]).

[3] If instead one relies on non-standard assumptions or trusted setups (e.g., using trusted parameters, working in the random oracle model, relying on the existence of NM OWFs) then there exist non-interactive NM commitments [64, 163].

right that should not interfere with each other. Indeed, a known paradigm introduced by Pass [166] proposes to have in a protocol multiple potential rewind slots so that extraction and simulation can both be run in 2 independent sequential steps. On the negative side, the use of multiple rewind slots increases the round complexity of the protocol (i.e., two slots require at least 5 rounds).

This multiple rewind-slot technique has been bypassed in [99] but only for the (simpler) one-one case (i.e., just one sender and one receiver). In particular, Goyal et al. [99] showed a *one-one* 4-round NM commitment scheme based on OWFs only. The work of Goyal et al. [97] exploited the use of the NM codes in the split-state model of Aggarwal et al., [2] to show a 3-round one-one NM commitment scheme based on the black-box use of any 1-to-1 OWF that is secure against super-polynomial time adversaries. In this document, we show how to break the multiple-slot barrier for concurrent NM commitments by showing a 4-round scheme based on the sole existence of OWFs.

More specifically, we consider the following four contributions.

Non-malleable commitments w.r.t. non-aborting adversaries. We prove that a subprotocol of [99] is a 4-round statistically binding concurrent NM commitment scheme from OWFs (resp. a 3-round perfectly binding concurrent NM commitment scheme from 1-to-1 OWFs), if the adversary is restricted to playing well-formed commitments in the right sessions when receiving well-formed commitments from the left sessions. We refer to this weaker security notion as *concurrent weak non-malleability (wNM)*.

Simulation-Witness-Independence. We define a security notion for argument systems w.r.t. man-in-the-middle attacks that we refer to as simulation-witness-independence (SimWI). This security notion seemingly is not implied by previous notions such as simulation-extractability/soundness and strong non-malleable witness indistinguishability.

4-Round One-Many SimWI from OWFs. We then construct a 4-round one-many SimWI argument of knowledge for same specific languages by relying on OWFs only. This construction circumvents the major problem caused by the need to rewind on the left to simulate and on the right to extract when there is only one available slot.

Concurrent wNM + One-Many SimWI $\Rightarrow$ 4-Round Concurrent NM Commitments. We present a paradigm consisting of combining the above two notions in a protocol that runs in parallel , the concurrent wNM commitment scheme, and the one-many SimWI argument of knowledge. Hence, we upgrade concurrent wNM to full-fledged concurrent non-malleability without any penalization in rounds and assumptions.

Going Below Three-Rounds

In this part of the document, we also show how to obtain the same result in three rounds only but relying on sub-exponentiality secure one-way permutations.

More Related Works

Khurana [127] showed how to obtain a 3-round (which is optimal for the case of polynomial-time assumptions [167]) non-malleable commitment scheme based on specific number-theoretic assumptions, and to [98] where the authors proposed a round optimal scheme based on one-to-one OWFs (the scheme only enjoys one-one non-malleability). In [45], the authors show another 4-round construction (still only one-one non-malleable) but relying in a black-box way on one-way permutations. In [129, 137] the authors show how to go below the three-round barrier in the concurrent setting, relying on a combination of sub-exponentially secure complexity assumptions.

1.3 Efficient and Delayed-Input Proof System

Proofs of partial knowledge allow a prover to prove knowledge of witnesses for k out of n instances of $\mathcal{NP}$ languages. Cramer, Damgård, and Schoenmakers [57] provided an efficient construction of a 3-round public-coin witness-indistinguishable (k, n)-proof of partial knowledge for any $\mathcal{NP}$ language, by cleverly combining n executions of Σ-protocols for that language. This transform assumes that all n instances are fully specified before the proof starts, and thus directly rules out the possibility of choosing some of the instances after the first round.

We show a transform where one of the instances can be specified in the last round is provided. In particular, we propose a $(1, 2)$-proofs of partial knowledge with the additional feature that one instance is defined in the last round and could be *adaptively* chosen by the adversarial verifier (in the witness-indistinguishability security game). This property is also referred to as *adaptive-input witness-indistinguishability*.

We then consider the more general case of constructing an efficient (k, n)-proof of partial knowledge where knowledge of *all n* instances can be postponed. Indeed, this property is achieved only by inefficient constructions requiring $\mathcal{NP}$ reductions [133].

In particular, we focus on the question of achieving *adaptive-input* proofs of partial knowledge. We provide through a transform an efficient construction of a 3-round public-coin witness-indistinguishable (k, n)-proof of partial knowledge where *all* instances can be decided in the third round. This construction enjoys *adaptive-input* witness indistinguishability. Additionally, we show how to maintain the proof of knowledge property even in the setting where the adversarial prover selects instances adaptively to the message of the verifier: *adaptive PoK*. We show this by means of a transform, that on input a sigma-protocol belonging to the widely used class of (non-adaptive) proofs of knowledge described in [56, 146], returns an adaptive PoK. Since knowledge of instances and witnesses is not needed before the last round, we have that the first round can be precomputed and in the online/offline setting, our performance is similar to the one of [57].

This transform relies on the DDH assumption (in contrast to the (1,2)-proof of partial knowledge mentioned above).

Efficient Non-interactive Zero-Knowledge

In the last part of this document, we study the Fiat-Shamir (FS) transform. This transform uses a hash function to generate, without any further overhead, non-interactive zero-knowledge (NIZK) argument systems from constant-round public-coin honest-verifier zero-knowledge (public-coin HVZK) proof systems. In the proof of zero knowledge, the hash function is modeled as a *programmable* random oracle (PRO). In TCC 2015, Lindell [141] embarked on the challenging task of obtaining a similar transform with improved heuristic security. Lindell showed that, for several interesting and practical languages, there exists an efficient transform in the *non-programmable* random oracle (NPRO) model that also uses a common reference string (CRS). A major contribution of Lindell's transform is that zero-knowledge is proved without random oracles and this is an important step toward achieving efficient NIZK arguments in the CRS model without random oracles.

We then propose a transform that aims at improving the efficiency of Lindell's transform. Indeed, the transformation we show is almost as efficient as the FS transform and can be applied to a broad class of public-coin HVZK proof systems. The transform requires a CRS and an NPRO in the proof of soundness, similar to Lindell's transform.

Chapter 2
Preliminar Definitions

2.1 Notation

We denote the security parameter by λ and use "$||$" as concatenation operator (i.e., if a and b are two strings then by $a||b$ we denote the concatenation of a and b). For a finite set Q, $x \leftarrow Q$ denotes a sampling of x from Q with uniform distribution. We use the abbreviation PPT that stands for probabilistic polynomial time. We use $\mathsf{poly}(\cdot)$ to indicate a generic polynomial function.

A *polynomial-time relation* Rel (or *polynomial relation*, in short) is a subset of $\{0,1\}^* \times \{0,1\}^*$ such that membership of (x, w) in Rel can be decided in time polynomial in $|x|$. For $(x, w) \in \mathsf{Rel}$, we call x the *instance* and w a *witness* for x. For a polynomial-time relation Rel, we define the $\mathcal{NP}$-language L_{Rel} as $L_{\mathsf{Rel}} = \{x | \exists w : (x, w) \in \mathsf{Rel}\}$. Analogously, unless otherwise specified, for an $\mathcal{NP}$-language L we denote by $\mathsf{Rel}_{\mathsf{L}}$ the corresponding polynomial-time relation (that is, $\mathsf{Rel}_{\mathsf{L}}$ is such that $L = L_{\mathsf{Rel}_{\mathsf{L}}}$). We denote by $\hat{L}$ the language that includes both L and all well formed instances that do not have a witness. Moreover we require that membership in $\hat{L}$ can be tested in polynomial time. We implicitly assume that a PPT algorithm that is supposed to receive an instance in $\hat{L}$ will abort immediately if the instance does not belong to $\hat{L}$.

Let A and B be two interactive probabilistic algorithms. We denote by $\langle A(\alpha), B(\beta)\rangle(\gamma)$ the distribution of B's output after running on private input β with A using private input α, both running on common input γ. Typically, one of the two algorithms receives 1^λ as input. A *transcript* of $\langle A(\alpha), B(\beta)\rangle(\gamma)$ consists of the messages exchanged during an execution where A receives a private input α, B receives a private input β and both A and B receive a common input γ. Moreover, we will refer to the *view* of A (resp. B) as the messages it received during the execution of $\langle A(\alpha), B(\beta)\rangle(\gamma)$, along with its randomness and its input. We say that a protocol (A, B) is public coin if B sends to A random bits only. When it is necessary to refer to the randomness r used by and algorithm A we use the following notation: $A(\cdot; r)$.

M. Ciampi and L. Siniscalchi, *Round and Computational Efficiency of Multi-party Protocols*, Information Security and Cryptography,
https://doi.org/10.1007/978-3-031-92374-6_2

2.2 Proof Systems

Definition 2.1 (*Proof/argument system*) A pair of PPT interactive algorithms $\Pi = (\mathcal{P}, \mathcal{V})$ constitutes a *proof system* (resp., an *argument system*) for an $\mathcal{NP}$-language L, if the following conditions hold:

Completeness: For every $x \in L$ and w such that $(x, w) \in \mathsf{Rel_L}$, it holds that

$$\text{Prob}[\ \langle \mathcal{P}(w), \mathcal{V}\rangle(x) = 1\ ] = 1.$$

Soundness: For every interactive (resp., PPT interactive) algorithm $\mathcal{P}^\star$, there exists a negligible function ν such that for every $x \notin L$ and every z:

$$\text{Prob}\left[\ \langle \mathcal{P}^\star(z), \mathcal{V}\rangle(x) = 1\ \right] < \nu(|x|).$$

A proof/argument system $\Pi = (\mathcal{P}, \mathcal{V})$ for an $\mathcal{NP}$-language L enjoys *delayed-input* completeness if $\mathcal{P}$ needs x and w only to compute the last round and $\mathcal{V}$ needs x only to compute the output. Before that, $\mathcal{P}$ and $\mathcal{V}$ run having as input only the size of x. The notion of delayed-input completeness was defined in [52]. We say that the transcript τ of an execution $b = \langle \mathcal{P}(z), \mathcal{V}\rangle(x)$ is *accepting* if $b = 1$.

Definition 2.2 (*Computational indistinguishability*) Let $X = \{X_\lambda\}_{\lambda\in\mathbb{N}}$ and $Y = \{Y_\lambda\}_{\lambda\in\mathbb{N}}$ be ensembles, where X_λ's and Y_λ's are probability distribution over $\{0, 1\}^l$, for same $l = \mathsf{poly}(\lambda)$. We say that $X = \{X_\lambda\}_{\lambda\in\mathbb{N}}$ and $Y = \{Y_\lambda\}_{\lambda\in\mathbb{N}}$ are *computationally indistinguishable*, denoted $X \approx Y$, if for every PPT distinguisher $\mathcal{D}$ there exists a negligible function ν such that for sufficiently large $\lambda \in \mathbb{N}$,

$$\left|\text{Prob}\left[\ t \leftarrow X_\lambda : \mathcal{D}(1^\lambda, t) = 1\ \right] - \text{Prob}\left[\ t \leftarrow Y_\lambda : \mathcal{D}(1^\lambda, t) = 1\ \right]\right| < \nu(\lambda).$$

We note that in the usual case where $|X_\lambda| = \Omega(\lambda)$ and λ can be derived from a sample of X_λ, it is possible to omit the auxiliary input 1^λ. We also use the definition of *Statistical Indistinguishability*. This definition is the same as Definition 2.2 with the only difference that the distinguisher $\mathcal{D}$ is unbounded. In this case use $X \equiv_s Y$ to denote that two ensembles are statistically indistinguishable.

Definition 2.3 (*Proof of Knowledge* [62]) A pair $(\mathcal{P}, \mathcal{V})$ of PPT interactive machines is a *proof of knowledge with knowledge error* $k(\cdot)$ for polynomial-time relation Rel if the following properties hold:

- *Completeness*. For every $(x, w) \in \mathsf{Rel}$, it holds that

$$\text{Prob}[\ \langle \mathcal{P}(w), \mathcal{V}\rangle(x) = 1\ ] = 1.$$

- *Knowledge Soundness*: there exists a probabilistic oracle machine $\mathsf{Extract}$, called the *extractor*, such that for every interactive machine $\mathcal{P}^\star$ and for every input x accepted by $\mathcal{V}$ when interacting with $\mathcal{P}^\star$ with probability $\epsilon(x) > k(x)$, $\mathsf{Extract}^{\mathcal{P}^\star}(x)$ outputs a witness w for x. Moreover, the expected number of steps performed by $\mathsf{Extract}$ is bounded by $\mathtt{poly}(|x|)/(\epsilon(x) - k(x))$.

In the security proofs we make use of the following observation. An interactive protocol Π that enjoys the property of completeness and PoK (AoK) with negligible soundness error is a proof (an argument) system. Indeed suppose by contradiction that is not. By the definition of PoK (AoK) it is possible to extract the witness for every theorem $x \in \{0, 1\}^\lambda$ proved by $\mathcal{P}^\star$ with probability greater than negligible; contradiction.

Definition 2.4 (*Witness Indistinguishable (WI)*) An argument/proof system $\Pi = (\mathcal{P}, \mathcal{V})$, is *Witness Indistinguishable (WI)* for a relation Rel if, for every malicious PPT verifier $\mathcal{V}^\star$, there exists a negligible function ν such that for all x, w, w' such that $(x, w) \in \mathsf{Rel}$ and $(x, w') \in \mathsf{Rel}$ it holds that

$$\left|\mathrm{Prob}\left[\, \langle \mathcal{P}(w), \mathcal{V}^\star\rangle(x) = 1 \,\right] - \mathrm{Prob}\left[\, \langle \mathcal{P}(w'), \mathcal{V}^\star\rangle(x) = 1 \,\right]\right| < \nu(|x|).$$

The notion of a *perfect* WI argument/proof system is obtained by requiring that $\nu(|x|) = 0$.

2.3 Three Rounds and Public Coins

We present a generalization of the classical notion of a Σ-protocol.

Definition 2.5 Let $t \geq 2$ and $t \in \mathbb{N}$. A protocol $(\mathcal{P}, \mathcal{V})$ is a *t-Σ -protocol* for polynomial-time relation Rel if it enjoys the following properties:

- *Completeness*. For every $(x, w) \in \mathsf{Rel}$, it holds that

$$\mathrm{Prob}\left[\, \langle \mathcal{P}(w), \mathcal{V}\rangle(x) = 1 \,\right] = 1.$$

- *t -Special Soundness*. There exists a PPT algorithm $\mathsf{Extract}$ that, on input x and t transcripts such that any two of them constitute a collision for x, outputs a witness w for x.
- *Special Honest Verifier Zero Knowledge (SHVZK)*. There exists a PPT *simulator* algorithm Sim that, on input an instance $x \in L$ and a challenge c, outputs (a, z) such that (a, c, z) has the same distribution of transcripts obtained when $\mathcal{V}$ sends c as challenge and $\mathcal{P}$ runs on common input x and any private input w such that $(x, w) \in \mathsf{Rel}$.

It is easy to observe that the notion of a 2-Σ-protocol coincides with the notion of a Σ-protocol as introduced by [57]. Indeed, we will refer to 2-special soundness as special soundness, thus conforming with the terminology of [57]. We also stress that SHVZK as defined above corresponds to the notion of *Perfect* SHVZK as distinct from *Computational* SHVZK. This latter notion has also been studied in the literature in the context of Σ-protocols [82] but it will not be considered here.

SHVZK is a weaker requirement than Zero Knowledge; nonetheless, it implies non-trivial security against adversarial verifiers, as stated below.

Theorem 2.1 **([57])** *Let* Π *be a protocol that enjoys completeness and SHVZK for relation* Rel. *Then* Π *is Perfect WI.*

In a t-Σ-protocol security for $\mathcal{P}$ is unconditional. The following result implies instead that the challenge length acts as a security parameter for $\mathcal{V}$.

Theorem 2.2 *Let* Π *be a protocol for polynomial-time relation* Rel *that is* t*-special sound for some* t*, where* t *is polynomially bounded in the length of the challenge of* Π. *Then* Π *is a proof of knowledge with knowledge error negligible in the challenge length.*

Proof The proof of this theorem strictly follows the proof of [62, Theorem 1] where it is showed that: if Π is 2-special sound then Π is a proof of knowledge with knowledge error negligible in the challenge length. Indeed, the same arguments of [62, Theorem 1] hold for the case where t is greater than 2 and polynomially bounded. □

In this book we also consider the notion of optimal soundness which is defined as follows.

Definition 2.6 A 3-round public-coin proof system $\Pi_L = (\mathcal{P}_L, \mathcal{V}_L)$ for language L with challenge length l enjoys *optimal soundness* if for every $x \notin L$ and for every first-round message a there is at most one challenge $e \in \{0, 1\}^l$ for which there exists a third-round message z such that (a, e, z) is accepting for x.

Note that any 3-round public-coin optimally sound proof system with challenge length l has soundness error 2^{-l} [150].

It is easy to see that Σ-protocols enjoy optimal soundness. The converse, however, is not true. See Sect. 10.7 for an example of an optimal-sound 3-round public-coin proof system that does not enjoy special soundness (and is special perfect HVZK).

2.3.1 Delayed-Input Protocols

In this section, we present the notion of a *delayed-input* three-round public-coin protocol and give security notions both for the prover and the verifier.

Definition 2.7 (*Delayed-input* [52]) A *delayed-input* protocol for a polynomial-time relation Rel is a protocol $(\mathcal{P}, \mathcal{V})$ in which the first message of $\mathcal{P}$ can be computed on input the length ℓ of the future common input in unary notation.

For simplicity, we will drop input 1^ℓ when describing the prover of a delayed-input protocol.

Since in a delayed-input protocol the input might not be fixed at the onset of the protocol, it could be adversarially chosen by the prover or by the verifier based on the exchanged messages. For example, the special soundness of a Σ-protocol guarantees extraction from collisions only if the transcripts are accepting for the same input. However when the statement to be proved is chosen adaptively by the prover depending on the challenge received, special soundness does not guarantee extraction. We thus introduce a stronger notion that we call *adaptive-input t-special soundness*. Roughly speaking, we require that it is possible to extract witnesses from a collision even if the t accepting transcripts are for different inputs.

Definition 2.8 A delayed-input protocol Π for relation Rel enjoys *adaptive-input t-special soundness* if there exists an efficient algorithm that, on input accepting transcripts $((a, c_1, z_1), \ldots, (a, c_t, z_t))$ for inputs $x_1, \ldots, x_t$, respectively, with $c_i \neq c_j$ for $1 \leq i < j \leq t$, outputs witnesses $(w_1, \ldots, w_t)$ such that $(x_i, w_i) \in \mathsf{Rel}$ for $i = 1, \ldots, t$.

Adaptive-input 2-special soundness is closely related to the notion of an *adaptive-input proof of knowledge*. A protocol $\Pi = (\mathcal{P}, \mathcal{V})$ for relation Rel is an adaptive-input proof of knowledge if the proof of knowledge property holds even if the adversarial prover $\mathcal{P}^\star$ can choose the statement adaptively. Let ℓ be the maximum length of the instance of L_{Rel}. To formally define this concept, we introduce, for every adversarial prover $\mathcal{P}^\star$, the family $\mathsf{aPoK}^{\mathcal{P}^\star} = \{\mathsf{aPoK}_\ell^{\mathcal{P}^\star}\}_\ell$ of probability distributions over $\{0, 1\}^\ell \cup \{\perp\}$. Distribution $\mathsf{aPoK}_\ell^{\mathcal{P}^\star}$ assigns to $x \in \{0, 1\}^\ell$ the probability that $\mathcal{P}^\star$ concludes an accepting interaction with the honest verifier $\mathcal{V}$ for input x; the symbol $\perp$ is instead assigned the probability that $\mathcal{V}$ rejects an interaction with $\mathcal{P}^\star$.

Definition 2.9 A delayed-input protocol $\Pi = (\mathcal{P}, \mathcal{V})$ is an *adaptive-input proof of knowledge with knowledge error $\kappa(\cdot)$* for Rel if there exists an oracle machine $\mathsf{AExtract}$ such that, for all adversarial provers $\mathcal{P}^\star$ with $\mathrm{Prob}\left[\langle \mathcal{P}^\star, \mathcal{V}\rangle(1^\ell) = 1\right] = p(\ell) > \kappa(\ell)$, $\mathsf{AExtract}^{\mathcal{P}^\star}(1^\ell)$ outputs pairs (x, w) with $x \in \{0, 1\}^\star \cup \{\perp\}$ and

- whenever $x \neq \perp$, it holds that $(x, w) \in \mathsf{Rel}$;
- the family of probability distributions of the first output of $\mathsf{AExtract}^{\mathcal{P}^\star}$ is perfectly close to $\mathsf{aPoK}^{\mathcal{P}^\star}$;
- there exists a constant c such that $\mathsf{AExtract}^{\mathcal{P}^\star}$ stops within expected number of steps $\frac{\ell^c}{p(\ell) - \kappa(\ell)}$.

We have the following theorem.

Theorem 2.3 *Let Π be a delayed-input protocol with challenge length λ. If, for some $t = \mathsf{poly}(\lambda)$, Π is an adaptive-input t-special sound protocol for relation Rel then Π is an adaptive-input proof of knowledge with knowledge error $\kappa(\ell) = (t - 1)2^{-\lambda}$ where ℓ denotes the maximum length of the instances of L_{Rel}.*

Proof We start by giving the proof for $t = 2$.

In order to prove that Π is an adaptive-input PoK for Rel, we consider the following $\mathsf{AExtract}^{\mathcal{P}^\star}$. $\mathsf{AExtract}^{\mathcal{P}^\star}$, upon receiving a from $\mathcal{P}^\star$, picks and sends a random challenge $c \leftarrow \{0, 1\}^\lambda$ to $\mathcal{P}^\star$. Upon receiving z and the theorem x, $\mathsf{AExtract}$ checks if (a, c, z) is accepting for x. If $\mathcal{V}$ rejects, $\mathsf{AExtract}$ outputs $\perp$ and stops, otherwise it continues as follows. The extractor $\mathsf{AExtract}^{\mathcal{P}^\star}$ now rewinds $\mathcal{P}^\star$ by sending a new challenge $c' \leftarrow \{0, 1\}^\lambda$, with $c \neq c'$, until another accepting transcript (a, c', z'), with respect to a potentially different input x', is provided by $\mathcal{P}^\star$. We now analyze the running time of $\mathsf{AExtract}$. Let $p^\star(\ell) > 2^{-\lambda}$ be the probability that $\mathcal{P}^\star$ provides an accepting transcript for a challenge of length λ. Then the probability that, for a randomly selected challenge $c' \neq c$, $\mathcal{P}^\star$ provides an accepting transcript (a, c', z') conditioned on the fact that (a, c, z) is accepting is $p^\star(\ell) - 2^{-\lambda}$. Therefore the expected number of rewinds is $\frac{1}{p^\star(\ell)-2^{-\lambda}}$.

We now observe that the two accepting transcripts obtained by $\mathsf{AExtract}^{\mathcal{P}^\star}$ share the same first round and have different challenges, therefore by the adaptive-input 2-special soundness of Π the witness for x and x' can be computed in time $\mathsf{poly}(\lambda)$. At this point $\mathsf{AExtract}^{\mathcal{P}^\star}$ just outputs x and w such that $(x, w) \in \mathsf{Rel}$. The above arguments are sufficient to conclude proof for the case where $t = 2$.

The proof for $t > 2$ follows similar arguments, with the difference that once that $\mathsf{AExtract}^{\mathcal{P}^\star}$ has received an accepting transcript from $\mathcal{P}^\star$, he needs to do $\frac{1}{p^\star(\ell)-(t-1)\cdot 2^{-\lambda}}$ rewinds to obtain another accepting transcript. In order to rely on the adaptive-input t-special soundness of Π, t accepting transcripts that share the same first round needs to be extracted by $\mathsf{AExtract}^{\mathcal{P}^\star}$, therefore the above process needs to be executed up to $t - 1$ times. That is, the expected number of rewinds that $\mathsf{AExtract}^{\mathcal{P}^\star}$ needs to do is $\frac{t-1}{p^\star(\ell)-(t-1)\cdot 2^{-\lambda}}$. The proof ends with the observation that $t = \mathsf{poly}(\ell)$. □

The notion of *adaptive-input WI* formalizes security of the prover with respect to an adversarial verifier $\mathcal{A}$ that adaptively chooses the input instance to the protocol; that is, after seeing the first message of the prover. We consider the computational version of this notion and therefore protocols will have a security parameter λ for the prover. More specifically, for a delayed-input protocol Π, we consider game $\mathsf{ExpAWI}_{\Pi,\mathcal{A}}$ between a challenger C and an adversary $\mathcal{A}$ in which the instance x and two witnesses w_0 and w_1 for x are chosen by $\mathcal{A}$ *after* seeing the first message of the protocol played by the challenger. The challenger then continues the game by randomly selecting one of the two witnesses, w_b, and by computing the third message by running the prover's algorithm on input the instance x, the selected witness w_b and the challenge received from the adversary. The adversary wins the game if she can guess which of the two witnesses was used by the challenger.

We now define the adaptive-input WI experiment $\mathsf{ExpAWI}_{\Pi,\mathcal{A}}(\lambda, \mathsf{aux})$. This experiment is parameterized by a delayed-input protocol $\Pi = (\mathcal{P}, \mathcal{V})$ for a relation Rel and by PPT adversary $\mathcal{A}$. The experiment has as input the security parameter λ and auxiliary information aux for $\mathcal{A}$.

$\mathsf{ExpAWI}_{\Pi,\mathcal{A}}(\lambda, \mathsf{aux})$:

1. C randomly selects coin tosses r and runs $\mathcal{P}$ on input $(1^\lambda; r)$ to obtain a;
2. $\mathcal{A}$, on input a and aux, outputs instance x, witnesses w_0 and w_1 such that $(x, w_0), (x, w_1) \in \mathsf{Rel}$, challenge c and internal state $\mathtt{state}$;
3. C randomly selects $b \leftarrow \{0, 1\}$ and runs $\mathcal{P}$ on input (x, w_b, c) and the randomness used at the first round thus obtaining z;
4. $b' \leftarrow \mathcal{A}((a, c, z), \mathsf{aux}, \mathtt{state})$;
5. if $b = b'$ then output 1 else output 0.

We set $\mathsf{AdvAWI}_{\Pi,\mathcal{A}}(\lambda, \mathsf{aux}) = \left|\text{Prob}\left[\,\mathsf{ExpAWI}_{\Pi,\mathcal{A}}(\lambda, \mathsf{aux}) = 1\,\right] - \frac{1}{2}\right|$.

Definition 2.10 (*Adaptive-Input Witness Indistinguishability*) A delayed-input protocol Π is *adaptive-input WI* if for every PPT adversary $\mathcal{A}$ there exists a negligible function ν such that for any $\mathsf{aux} \in \{0, 1\}^*$ it holds that $\mathsf{AdvAWI}_{\Pi,\mathcal{A}}(\lambda, \mathsf{aux}) \leq \nu(\lambda)$.

2.3.2 Challenge Length of Σ-Protocols

In this section, we show how one can reduce or stretch the size of the challenge in a Σ-protocol and in a t-Σ-protocol.

Challenge-length amplification.

The challenge of a Σ-protocol can be extended through parallel repetition.

Lemma 2.1 ([57, 62]) *Let Π be a Σ-protocol (resp. t-Σ-protocol) for relation* Rel *and challenge length l. Running Π k-times in parallel for the same instance x corresponds to running Σ-protocol (resp. t-Σ-protocol) for* Rel *with challenge length $k \cdot l$.*

Challenge-length reduction.

Lemma 2.2 ([62]) *Given a Σ-protocol of challenge length l for the relation* Rel*, is possible to construct a Σ-protocol, for the same relation* Rel *with challenge length l' where $l' < l$.*

We now show that Lemma 2.2 it is true even when we consider a t-Σ-protocol.

Lemma 2.3 *For any t-Σ-protocol $\Pi = (\mathcal{P}, \mathcal{V})$, for a relation* Rel *with challenge length l, simulator* Sim*, and the associated triple (P_1, P_2, V), there exists a t-Σ-protocol $\Pi' = (\mathcal{P}', \mathcal{V}')$, for the same relation* Rel*, with challenge length l', where $l' < l$ and with the same efficiency.*

Proof We show Π' by presenting the associated triple $(P_1', P_2', \mathsf{V}')$ of efficient PPT algorithms.

1. P_1' on input (x, w) and randomness R_1 computes and outputs $a \leftarrow P_1(x, w; R_1)$.
2. P_2' on input (x, w), $c \in \{0, 1\}^{l'}$, R_1 and randomness R_2, parses R_2 as (pad, R_2') where pad is an $(l - l')$-bit string, sets $c' = c||pad$, computes $z \leftarrow P_2(x, w, R_1, c'; R_2')$ and outputs $z' = (z, pad)$.
3. V' on input $x, a, z' = (z, pad)$ and c, outputs the output of $\mathsf{V}(a, c||pad, z)$.

Completeness follows directly from the completeness of Π.

HVZK
We can consider the simulator Sim', that on input x runs as follows:

- runs $(a, c, z) \leftarrow \mathsf{Sim}(x)$;
- sets pad equal to the last $l - l'$ bits of c, and sets c' equal to the fist l' bits of c;
- outputs $(a, c', (z, pad))$.

Special soundness follows directly from the special soundness of Π. □

From Lemmas 2.1, 2.2 and 2.3, we can claim the following theorem.

Theorem 2.4 *Suppose that relation* Rel *has a* Σ*-protocol (*t*-*Σ*-protocol)* Π*. Then, for any challenge length* l*,* Rel *admits a* Σ*-protocol (*t*-*Σ*-protocol)* Π' *with challenge length* l'*. If* $l' \leq l$ *than* Π' *is almost as efficient as* Π*. Otherwise the communication and computation complexities of* Π' *are* l'/l *times the ones of* Π*.*

2.3.3 3-Round Public-Coin HVZK Proofs for OR Composition of Statements

In this section we recall the construction of [57] that starts from a HVZK 3-round public-coin proof system Π_L for an $\mathcal{NP}$-language L and constructs a HVZK 3-round public-coin proof system $\Pi_{L \vee L}$ for the "OR" language of L; that is the $\mathcal{NP}$-language

$$L \vee L = \{(x_0, x_1) : x_0 \in L \vee x_1 \in L\}.$$

Below we give the descriptions of the prover $\mathcal{P}_{L \vee L}$ and of the verifier $\mathcal{V}_{L \vee L}$ of $\Pi_{L \vee L}$. In the description, we let Sim denote the simulator for Π_L and l denote the challenge length of Π_L. We also let $b \in \{0, 1\}$ be such that w is a witness for $x_b \in L$; that is, $(x_b, w) \in \mathsf{Rel}_L$.

Common input: instances x_0, x_1 for an $\mathcal{NP}$-language L.
Private input of $\mathcal{P}_{L \vee L}$: w s.t $(x_0, x_1, w) \in \hat{\mathsf{Rel}}_{L \vee L}$. where

$$\hat{\mathsf{Rel}}_{L \vee L} = \left\{((x_0, x_1), w) : \left((x_0, w) \in \mathsf{Rel}_L \wedge x_1 \in \hat{L}\right) \vee \left((x_1, w) \in \mathsf{Rel}_L \wedge x_0 \in \hat{L}\right)\right\}.$$

The protocol $\Pi_{L\vee L}$:

1. $\mathcal{P}_{L\vee L}$ computes $a_b \leftarrow \mathcal{P}_L(x_b, w)$, $(a_{1-b}, e_{1-b}, z_{1-b}) \leftarrow \mathsf{Sim}(x_{1-b})$ and sends (a_0, a_1) to $\mathcal{V}_{L\vee L}$.
2. $\mathcal{V}_{L\vee L}$ chooses at random challenge $e \leftarrow \{0,1\}^l$ and sends e to $\mathcal{P}_{L\vee L}$.
3. $\mathcal{P}_{L\vee L}$ sets $e_b = e \oplus e_{1-b}$, computes $z_b \leftarrow \mathcal{P}_L(x_b, w, a_b, e_b)$ and outputs $\big((e_0, e_1), (z_0, z_1)\big)$.
4. $\mathcal{V}_{L\vee L}\big((x_0, x_1), (a_0, a_1), e, ((e_0, e_1), (z_0, z_1))\big)$. $\mathcal{V}_{L\vee L}$ accepts if and only if $e = e_0 \oplus e_1$ and $\mathcal{V}_L(x_0, a_0, e_0, z_0) = 1$ and $\mathcal{V}_L(x_1, a_1, e_1, z_1) = 1$.

Theorem 2.5 ([57, 82]) *If Π_L is a HVZK 3-round public-coin proof system with optimal soundness for $\mathcal{NP}$-language L then $\Pi_{L\vee L}$ is a HVZK 3-round public-coin proof system with optimal soundness for $\mathcal{NP}$-language $L \vee L$ and is WI for polynomial-time relation*

$$\mathsf{Rel}_{L\vee L} = \big\{((x_0, x_1), w) : \big((x_0, w) \in \mathsf{Rel}_L \wedge x_1 \in L\big) \vee \big((x_1, w) \in \mathsf{Rel}_L \wedge x_0 \in L\big)\big\}.$$

Moreover if Π_L is perfect HVZK then $\Pi_{L\vee L}$ is perfect WI for polynomial-time relation $\hat{\mathsf{Rel}}_{L\vee L}$

We remark that results of [57, 82] are known to hold for Σ-protocols, but in the proof of WI they use only HVZK. Therefore their results also hold starting from a HVZK 3-round public-coin proof system with optimal soundness (and not necessarily special soundness) that we consider in the above theorem. Indeed we observe that $\Pi_{L\vee L}$ has optimal soundness for the following reason. Suppose that $\Pi_{L\vee L}$ does not enjoy optimal soundness. This means that for a false instance and the same first round (a_0, a_1) there are two accepting conversation, namely:

$$\Big((a_0, a_1), e, ((e_0, e_1), (z_0, z_1))\Big), \Big((a_0, a_1), e', ((e_0', e_1'), (z_0', z_1'))\Big)$$

with $e \neq e'$. Then it must be the case that for some $b = 0$ or $b = 1$, $e_b \neq e_b'$ and then (a_b, e_b, z_b) (a_b, e_b', z_b') are two accepting transcripts with the same first round for the protocol Π_L, and thus the optimal soundness of Π_L is violated.

It is possible to extend the above construction to handle two different $\mathcal{NP}$-languages L_0, L_1 that admit HVZK 3-round public-coin proof system with optimal soundness. Indeed by Theorem 2.4, we can assume, without loss of generality, that L_0 and L_1 have 3-round public-coin proof systems Π_{L_0} and Π_{L_1} with the same challenge length.

Assuming that L_0 and L_1 have 3-round public-coin proof systems Π_{L_0} and Π_{L_1} that are HVZK and have optimal soundness with the same challenge length. We can apply the same construction outlined above to obtain a 3-round public-coin proof system $\Pi_{L_0\vee L_1}$ that enjoys HVZK and has optimal soundness for relation

$\hat{\mathsf{Rel}}_{L_0\vee L_1} = \Big\{\big((x_0, x_1), w\big) : \big((x_0, w) \in \mathsf{Rel}_{L_0} \wedge x_1 \in \hat{L}_1\big) \vee \big((x_1, w) \in \mathsf{Rel}_{L_1} \wedge x_0 \in \hat{L}_0\big)\Big\}$.

We have the following theorem.

Theorem 2.6 *If Π_{L_0} and Π_{L_1} are HVZK 3-round public-coin proof systems with optimal soundness for $\mathcal{NP}$-languages L_0 and L_1 then $\Pi_{L_0 \vee L_1}$ is a HVZK 3-round public-coin proof system with optimal soundness for the for $\mathcal{NP}$-language*

$$L_0 \vee L_1 = \{(x_0, x_1) : x_0 \in L_0 \vee x_1 \in L_1\}$$

and is WI for polynomial-time relation

$$\mathsf{Rel}_{L_0 \vee L_1} = \Big\{((x_0, x_1), w) : \big((x_0, w) \in \mathsf{Rel}_{L_0} \wedge x_1 \in L_1\big) \vee \big((x_1, w) \in \mathsf{Rel}_{L_1} \wedge x_0 \in L_0\big)\Big\}.$$

Moreover, if Π_{L_0} and Π_{L_1} are perfect then $\Pi_{L_0 \vee L_1}$ is perfect WI for polynomial-time relation $\hat{\mathsf{Rel}}_{L \vee L}$.

2.4 Commitment Schemes

Definition 2.11 (*Commitment Scheme*) Given a security parameter 1^λ, a commitment scheme (Sen, Rec) is a two-phase protocol between two PPT interactive algorithms, a sender Sen and a receiver Rec. In the commitment phase Sen on input a message m interacts with Rec to produce a commitment $\mathtt{com}$. In the decommitment phase, Sen sends to Rec a decommitment information $\mathtt{d}$ such that Rec accepts m as the commitment of $\mathtt{com}$.

Formally, we say that $\mathsf{CS} = (\mathsf{Sen}, \mathsf{Rec})$ is a perfectly binding commitment scheme if the following properties hold:

Correctness:

- Commitment phase. Let $\mathtt{com}$ be the commitment of the message m (i.e., $\mathtt{com}$ is the transcript of an execution of $\mathsf{CS} = (\mathsf{Sen}, \mathsf{Rec})$ where Sen runs on input a message m). Let $\mathtt{d}$ be the private output of Sen in this phase.
- Decommitment phase.[1] Rec on input m and $\mathtt{d}$ accepts m as decommitment of $\mathtt{com}$.

Hiding: for a PPT adversary $\mathcal{A}$ and a randomly chosen bit $b \in \{0, 1\}$, consider the following hiding experiment $\mathsf{ExpHiding}^b_{\mathcal{A},\mathsf{CS}}(\lambda)$:

- Upon input 1^λ, the adversary $\mathcal{A}$ outputs a pair of messages m_0, m_1 that are of the same length.
- Sen on input the message m_b interacts with $\mathcal{A}$ to produce a commitment of m_b.
- $\mathcal{A}$ outputs a bit b' and this is the output of the experiment.

[1] We consider a non-interactive decommitment phase only.

For any PPT adversary $\mathcal{A}$, there exist a negligible function ν, such that:

$$\Big|\text{Prob}\left[\,\mathsf{ExpHiding}^0_{\mathcal{A},\mathtt{CS}}(\lambda) = 1\,\right] - \text{Prob}\left[\,\mathsf{ExpHiding}^1_{\mathcal{A},\mathtt{CS}}(\lambda) = 1\,\right]\Big| < \nu(\lambda).$$

Binding: for every commitment $\mathtt{com}$ generated during the commitment phase by a possibly malicious unbounded sender $\mathsf{Sen}^\star$ interacting with an honest receiver Rec, there exists at most one message m that Rec accepts as decommitment of $\mathtt{com}$.

We also consider the definition of a commitment scheme where the hiding property still holds against an adversary $\mathcal{A}$ running in time bounded by $T = 2^{\lambda^\alpha}$ for some positive constant $\alpha < 1$. In this case we will say that a commitment scheme is T-hiding. We will also say that a commitment scheme is $\tilde{T}$-breakable to specify that an algorithm running in time $\tilde{T} = 2^{\lambda^\beta}$, for some positive constant $\beta < 1$, recovers the (if any) only message that can be successfully decommitment.

In the rest of the work we also use a non-interactive commitment schemes, with secure parameter λ. In this case we consider a commitment scheme as a pair of PPT algorithms (NISen, NIRec) where

- NISen takes as input $(m; \sigma)$, where $m \in \{0, 1\}^{\mathsf{poly}(\lambda)}$ is the message to be committed and $\sigma \leftarrow \{0, 1\}^\lambda$ is randomness, and outputs the commitment $\mathtt{com}$ and the decommitment $\mathtt{dec}$;
- NIRec takes as input $(\mathtt{dec}, \mathtt{com}, m)$ and outputs 1 if it accepts m as a decommitment of $\mathtt{com}$ and 0 otherwise.

3-Round extractable commitment schemes. Informally, a 3-round commitment scheme is extractable if there exists an efficient extractor that having black-box access to any efficient malicious sender ExSen* that successfully performs the commitment phase, outputs the only committed string that can be successfully decommitted.

Definition 2.12 (*Extractable Commitment Scheme* [95]) A 3-round perfectly (resp. statistically) binding commitment scheme $\mathtt{ExCS} = (\text{ExSen}, \text{ExRec})$ is an *extractable commitment scheme* if given oracle access to any malicious sender ExSen*, there exists an expected PPT extractor $\mathtt{ExtCom}$ that outputs a pair $(\tau, \sigma^\star)$ such that the following properties hold:

- **Simulatability:** τ is identically distributed to the view of ExSen* (when interacting with an honest ExRec) in the commitment phase.
- **Extractability:** the probability that there exists a decommitment of τ to a message m', where $m \neq m'$ is 0 (resp. negligible).

If the definition holds only against honest sender, then we said that the commitment scheme is *honest extractable*.

2.4.1 Non-malleable Commitment Schemes

Here we follow [138].[2] Let $\Pi = (\mathsf{Sen}, \mathsf{Rec})$ be a statistically binding commitment scheme. Consider MiM adversaries that are participating in left and right sessions in which $\mathsf{poly}(\lambda)$ commitments take place. We compare between a MiM and a simulated execution. In the MiM execution the adversary $\mathcal{A}$, with auxiliary information z, is simultaneously participating in $\mathsf{poly}(\lambda)$ left and right sessions. In the left sessions the MiM adversary $\mathcal{A}$ interacts with Sen receiving commitments to values $m_1, \ldots, m_{\mathsf{poly}(\lambda)}$ using identities $\mathtt{id}_1, \ldots, \mathtt{id}_{\mathsf{poly}(\lambda)}$ of its choice. In the right session $\mathcal{A}$ interacts with Rec attempting to commit to a sequence of related values $\tilde{m}_1, \ldots, \tilde{m}_{\mathsf{poly}(\lambda)}$ again using identities of its choice $\tilde{\mathtt{id}}_1, \ldots, \tilde{\mathtt{id}}_{\mathsf{poly}}(\lambda)$. If any of the right commitments is invalid, or undefined, its value is set to $\perp$. For any i such that $\tilde{\mathtt{id}}_i = \mathtt{id}_j$ for some j, set $\tilde{m}_i =\perp$ (i.e., any commitment where the adversary uses the same identity of one of the honest senders is considered invalid). Let $\mathsf{mim}_{\Pi}^{\mathcal{A}, m_1, \ldots, m_{\mathsf{poly}(\lambda)}}(z)$ denote a random variable that describes the values $\tilde{m}_1, \ldots, \tilde{m}_{\mathsf{poly}(\lambda)}$ and the view of $\mathcal{A}$, in the above experiment. In the simulated execution, an efficient simulator S directly interacts with Rec. Let $\mathsf{sim}_{\Pi}^{S}(1^\lambda, z)$ denote the random variable describing the values $\tilde{m}_1, \ldots, \tilde{m}_{\mathsf{poly}(\lambda)}$ committed by S, and the output view of S; whenever the view contains in the i-th right session the same identity of any of the identities of the left session, then $\tilde{m}_i$ is set to $\perp$.

In all the work, we denote by $\tilde{\delta}$ a value associated with the right session (where the adversary $\mathcal{A}$ plays with a receiver NMRec) where δ is the corresponding value in the left session. For example, the sender commits to v in the left session while $\mathcal{A}$ commits to $\tilde{v}$ in the right session.

Definition 2.13 (*Concurrent NM commitment scheme* [138]) A commitment scheme is *concurrent NM with respect to commitment* (or a many-many NM commitment scheme) if, for every PPT concurrent MiM adversary $\mathcal{A}$, there exists a PPT simulator S such that for all $m_i \in \{0, 1\}^{\mathsf{poly}(\lambda)}$ for $i = \{1, \ldots, \mathsf{poly}(\lambda)\}$ the following ensembles are computationally indistinguishable:

$$\{\mathsf{mim}_{\Pi}^{\mathcal{A}, m_1, \ldots, m_{\mathsf{poly}(\lambda)}}(z)\}_{z \in \{0,1\}^\star} \approx \{\mathsf{sim}_{\Pi}^{S}(1^\lambda, z)\}_{z \in \{0,1\}^\star}.$$

As in [138] we also consider relaxed notions of concurrent non-malleability: one-many and one-one NM commitment schemes. In a one-many NM commitment scheme, $\mathcal{A}$ participates in one left and polynomially many right sessions. In a one-one (i.e., a stand-alone secure) NM commitment scheme, we consider only adversaries $\mathcal{A}$ that participate in one left and one right session.

We will make use of the following proposition of [138].

Proposition 2.1 *Let* $(\mathsf{Sen}, \mathsf{Rec})$ *be a one-many NM commitment scheme. Then,* $(\mathsf{Sen}, \mathsf{Rec})$ *is also a concurrent (i.e., many-many) NM commitment scheme.*

---

[2] We will consider only NM commitments w.r.t. commitments.

Definition 2.14 (*weak NM commitment scheme*) A commitment scheme is *weak* one-one (resp., one-many) non-malleable if it is a one-one (resp., one-many) NM commitment scheme with respect to MiM adversary that when receiving a well formed commitment in the left session, except with negligible probability computes well formed commitments (i.e., the computed commitments can be opened to messages $\neq \bot$) in the right sessions.

Following [99], we assume that identities are known before the protocol begins, though strictly speaking this is not necessary, as the identities do not appear in the protocol until after the first committer message. The MiM can choose his identity adversarially as long as it differs from the identities used by honest senders. As already observed in previous work, when the identity is selected by the sender the id-based definitions guarantee non-malleability as long as the MiM does not behave like a proxy (an unavoidable attack). Indeed the sender can pick as `id` the public key of a signature scheme signing the transcript. The MiM will have to use a different `id` or to break the signature scheme.

Definition 2.15 (*synchronous NM commitment scheme*) A commitment scheme is *synchronous* one-one (resp., one-many) non-malleable if it is one-one (resp., one-many) NM with respect to synchronous MiM adversaries.[3]

We also consider the definition of a NM commitment scheme secure against a MIM $\mathcal{A}$ running in time bounded by $T = 2^{\lambda^\alpha}$ for some positive constant $\alpha < 1$. In this case we will say that a commitment scheme is T-non-malleable. We will also say that an NM commitment scheme is $\tilde{T}$-breakable to specify that an algorithm which runs in time $\tilde{T} = 2^{\lambda^\beta}$, for some positive constant $\beta < 1$, can maul the committed message.

We consider a 4-round synchronous honest-extractable non-malleable commitment. That is, a commitment scheme that enjoys (1) non-malleability only against synchronous adversaries, (2) is extractable w.r.t. honest sender (honest-extractable) and 3) is public-coin. The non-malleable commitment Π provided in Fig. 2 of [97] enjoys non-malleability against synchronous adversary (as proved in Theorem 1 of [97]), is public-coin and can be instantiated in 4 rounds relying on OWFs (the protocol can be squeezed to 3 rounds using OWPs). Also, as stated in Sect. 5 of [97], given a commitment computed by the sender of Π one can rewind the sender in order to obtain a new accepting transcript with the same first round (resp., first two rounds if we consider the instantiation that relies on OWFs) in order to extract a message m. Moreover, if the sender is honest, then it is possible to claim that m is the actual message committed by the sender. We remark that in this case we do not require any form of extractability against malicious senders.

---

[3] Following [135] we say that a MiM is *synchronous* if it "aligns" the left and the right sessions; that is, whenever it receives message i on the left, it directly sends message i on the right, and vice versa.

2.4.2 T-Instance-Dependent Trapdoor Commitment

2-Round Instance-Dependent Trapdoor Commitments.

Here we define a special commitment scheme based on an $\mathcal{NP}$-language L where sender and receiver also receive as input an instance x. While correctness and computational hiding hold for any x, we require that statistical binding holds for $x \notin L$ and moreover knowledge of a witness for $x \in L$ allows to equivocate. Finally, we require that a commitment along with two valid openings to different messages allows to compute the witness for $x \in L$. We recall that $\hat{L}$ denotes the language that includes L and all well formed instances that are not in L.

Definition 2.16 (*2-Round Instance-Dependent Trapdoor Commitments*) Let 1^λ be the security parameter, L be an $\mathcal{NP}$-language and $\mathsf{Rel_L}$ be the corresponding $\mathcal{NP}$-relation. A triple of PPT algorithms $\mathsf{TC} = (\mathsf{Sen}, \mathsf{Rec}, \mathsf{TFake})$ is a 2-Round Instance-Dependent Trapdoor Commitment scheme if the following properties hold.

Correctness. In the 1st round, Rec on input 1^λ and $x \in \hat{L}$ outputs ρ. In the 2nd round Sen on input the message m, 1^λ, ρ and $x \in L$ outputs $(\mathtt{com}, \mathtt{dec})$. We will refer to the pair $(\rho, \mathtt{com})$ as the commitment of m. Moreover we will refer to the execution of the above two rounds including the exchange of the corresponding two messages as the commitment phase. Then Rec on input m, x, $\mathtt{com}$, $\mathtt{dec}$ and the private coins used to generate ρ in the commitment phase outputs 1. We will refer to the execution of this last round including the exchange of $\mathtt{dec}$ as the decommitment phase. Notice that an adversarial sender $\mathsf{Sen}^\star$ could deviate from the behavior of Sen when computing and sending $\mathtt{com}$ and $\mathtt{dec}$ for an instance $x \in \hat{L}$. As a consequence Rec could output 0 in the decommitment phase. We will say that $\mathtt{dec}$ is a valid decommitment of $(\rho, \mathtt{com})$ to m for an instance $x \in \hat{L}$, if Rec outputs 1.

Hiding. Given a PPT adversary $\mathcal{A}$, consider the following hiding experiment $\mathsf{ExpHiding}^b_{\mathcal{A},\mathsf{TC}}(\lambda, x)$ for $b = 0, 1$ and $x \in \hat{L}_R$:

- On input 1^λ and x, $\mathcal{A}$ outputs a message m, along with ρ.
- The challenger on input x, m, ρ, b works as follows: if $b = 0$ then it runs Sen on input m, x and ρ, obtaining a pair $(\mathtt{com}, \mathtt{dec})$, otherwise it runs TFake on input x and ρ, obtaining a pair $(\mathtt{com}, \mathtt{aux})$. The challenger outputs $\mathtt{com}$.
- $\mathcal{A}$ on input $\mathtt{com}$ outputs a bit b' and this is the output of the experiment.

  We say that *hiding* holds if for any PPT adversary $\mathcal{A}$ there exist a negligible function ν, s.t.:

$$\left|\text{Prob}\left[\mathsf{ExpHiding}^0_{\mathcal{A},\mathsf{TC}}(\lambda, x) = 1\right] - \text{Prob}\left[\mathsf{ExpHiding}^1_{\mathcal{A},\mathsf{TC}}(\lambda, x) = 1\right]\right| < \nu(\lambda).$$

Special Binding. There exists a PPT algorithm that on input a commitment $(\rho, \mathtt{com})$, the private coins used by Rec to compute ρ, and two valid decommitments $(\mathtt{dec}, \mathtt{dec}')$ of $(\rho, \mathtt{com})$ to two different messages m and m', outputs w s.t. $(x, w) \in \mathsf{Rel_L}$ with overwhelming probability.

Instance-Dependent Binding. For every malicious unbounded sender $\mathsf{Sen}^\star$ there exists a negligible function ν s.t. for a commitment $(\rho, \mathtt{com})$ $\mathsf{Sen}^\star$, with probability at most $\nu(\lambda)$, outputs two decommitments (m_0, d_0) and (m_1, d_1) with $m_0 \neq m_1$ s.t. Rec on input the private coins used to compute ρ and $x \notin L$ accepts both decommitments.

Trapdoorness. For any PPT adversary $\mathcal{A}$ there exist a negligible function ν, s.t. for all $x \in L$ it holds that

$$\left|\text{Prob}\left[\,\mathsf{ExpCom}_{\mathcal{A},\mathsf{TC}}(\lambda, x) = 1\,\right] - \text{Prob}\left[\,\mathsf{ExpTrapdoor}_{\mathcal{A},\mathsf{TC}}(\lambda, x) = 1\,\right]\right| < \nu(\lambda)$$

where $\mathsf{ExpCom}_{\mathcal{A},\mathsf{TC}}(\lambda, x)$ and $\mathsf{ExpTrapdoor}_{\mathcal{A},\mathsf{TC}}(\lambda, x)$ are defined below.[4]

$\mathsf{ExpCom}_{\mathcal{A},\mathsf{TC}}(\lambda, x)$:	$\mathsf{ExpTrapdoor}_{\mathcal{A},\mathsf{TC}}(\lambda, x)$:
–On input 1^λ and x, $\mathcal{A}$ outputs (ρ, m). –Sen on input 1^λ, x, m and ρ, outputs $(\mathtt{com}, \mathtt{dec})$. –$\mathcal{A}$ on input $(\mathtt{com}, \mathtt{dec})$ outputs a bit b and this is the output of the experiment.	–On input 1^λ and x, $\mathcal{A}$ outputs (ρ, m). –TFake on input 1^λ, x and ρ, outputs $(\mathtt{com}, \mathtt{aux})$. –$\mathsf{TFake}$ on input $\mathtt{tk}$ s.t. $(x, \mathtt{tk}) \in \mathsf{Rel_L}$, x, ρ, $\mathtt{com}$, $\mathtt{aux}$ and m outputs $\mathtt{dec}$. –$\mathcal{A}$ on input $(\mathtt{com}, \mathtt{dec})$ outputs a bit b and this is the output of the experiment.

In this work, we consider also a non-interactive version of Instance-Dependent Trapdoor Commitments. The only difference in the definition is that the first round sent by the receiver to the sender just disappears. In this case we use the following simplified notation.

- Commitment phase. $(\mathtt{com}, \mathtt{dec}) \leftarrow \mathsf{Sen}(m, 1^\lambda, x)$ denotes that $\mathtt{com}$ is the commitment of the message m and $\mathtt{dec}$ represents the corresponding decommitment information.
- Decommitment phase. $1 \leftarrow \mathsf{Rec}(m, x, \mathtt{com}, \mathtt{dec})$.
- Trapdoor algorithms. $(\mathtt{com}, \mathtt{aux}) \leftarrow \mathsf{TFake}(1^\lambda, x), \mathtt{dec} \leftarrow \mathsf{TFake}(\mathtt{tk}, x, \mathtt{com}, \mathtt{aux}, m)$ with $(x, \mathtt{tk}) \in \mathsf{Rel_L}$.

In the rest of the work, we say that the sender uses the *honest procedure* when he computes the commitment $\mathtt{com}$ of a message m along with the decommitment information $\mathtt{dec}$ running Sen. Instead, the sender uses *trapdoor procedure* when he computes $\mathtt{com}$ and $\mathtt{dec}$ running TFake.

---

[4] We assume wlog that $\mathcal{A}$ is stateful.

OWFs $\Rightarrow$ 2-round instance-dependent trapdoor commitments for any $\mathcal{NP}$ language.

Here we recall the construction $(\mathsf{Sen_H}, \mathsf{Rec_H}, \mathsf{TFake_H})$ of [78] for Hamiltonian graphs already considered in [160] that satisfies Def. 2.16 and requires OWFs only.

$\mathsf{Sen_H}$ and $\mathsf{Rec_H}$ run as follows.

- $\mathsf{Rec_H} \rightarrow \mathsf{Sen_H}$. $\mathsf{Rec_H}$ on input a graph G with n nodes computes and sends ρ to the sender, where ρ is the 1st round of a two-round statistically binding commitment scheme from OWFs of [154].
- $\mathsf{Sen_H}$ on input a bit b, ρ and a graph G with n nodes works as follows. If $b = 0$ then $\mathsf{Sen_H}$ picks a random permutation π and computes and sends the 2nd round of the statistically binding commitment using ρ as 1st round and committing one-by-one to all bits of the adjacency matrix of $\pi(G)$. If instead $b = 1$, then $\mathsf{Sen_H}$ computes and sends the 2nd round of the statistically binding commitment, using ρ as 1st round and committing to all bits of the adjacency matrix of a a graph that consists of a random cycle H of n nodes. In both cases, $(\rho, \mathtt{com} = (\mathtt{com}_1, \ldots, \mathtt{com}_{n^2}))$ corresponds to the commitment of b. In the 1st case $\mathtt{dec}$ corresponds to the randomness used by $\mathsf{Sen_H}$, while in the 2nd case $\mathtt{dec}$ corresponds to the decommitments of those n edges in the adjacency matrix that correspond to the cycle.
- $\mathsf{Rec_H}$ on input a bit b, a graph G with n nodes, $\mathtt{dec}$ and $\mathtt{com}$ works as follows. If $b = 0$ then $\mathsf{Rec_H}$ verifies that $\mathtt{com}$ is a commitment of the adjacency matrix of $\pi(G)$ where both π and the decommitments of the adjacency matrix are taken from $\mathtt{dec}$. If instead $b = 1$ then $\mathsf{Rec_H}$ verifies that the decommitted edges in $\mathtt{dec}$ correspond to a cycle that was committed in $(\rho, \mathtt{com})$.
- $\mathsf{TFake_H}$ runs $\mathsf{Sen_H}$ on input ρ, a graph G with n nodes and $b = 0$ therefore obtaining $(\mathtt{com}, \mathtt{dec})$. Then $\mathsf{TFake_H}$ on input 0 and a cycle in G outputs $\mathtt{dec}$. Instead on input 1 and a cycle in G, $\mathsf{TFake_H}$ outputs the decommitments of the edges committed in $(\rho, \mathtt{com})$ corresponding to a cycle in $\pi(G)$ where π was the permutation selected to compute $\mathtt{com}$.

It is easy to see that the above construction is a 2-round instance-dependent trapdoor commitment scheme from OWFs. While the construction can be used to commit to a bit, we will use this construction to commit to strings by implicitly assuming that the above steps are repeated in parallel for each bit of the string. Moreover, note that since Hamiltonicity is an $\mathcal{NP}$-complete language, the above construction works for any $\mathcal{NP}$-language through $\mathcal{NP}$ reductions. For simplicity, we will omit the $\mathcal{NP}$ reduction therefore assuming that the above scheme works directly on a given $\mathcal{NP}$-language L. We also observe that if a non-interactive statistically binding commitment scheme is used in the above construction, then we obtain an instance-dependent trapdoor commitment where the commitment phase is non-interactive as well. We also recall that non-interactive statistically binding commitment scheme can be constructed from one-to-one OWFs.

2.5 Delayed-Input Non-malleable Zero Knowledge

Delayed-Input non-malleable zero knowledge. Following [134] we use a definition that gives to the adversary the power of adaptive-input selection. More precisely, in [134] the adversary selects the instance and a Turing machine outputs the witness in exponential time. Here we slightly deviate (similarly to [183]) by (1) requiring the adversary to output also the witness and (2) allowing the adversary to make this choice at the last round. This choice is due to the application where delayed-input non-malleable zero knowledge is used. Indeed we will show that this definition is enough for our propose.

Let $\Pi = (\mathcal{P}, \mathcal{V})$ be a delayed-input interactive argument system for a $\mathcal{NP}$-language L with witness relation $\mathsf{Rel}_{\mathsf{L}}$. Consider a PPT MiM adversary $\mathcal{A}$ that is simultaneously participating in one left session and $\mathsf{poly}(\lambda)$ right sessions. Before the execution starts, $\mathcal{P}$, $\mathcal{V}$ and $\mathcal{A}$ receive as a common input the security parameter in unary 1^λ. Additionally $\mathcal{A}$ receives as auxiliary input $z \in \{0, 1\}^\star$.[5] In the left session $\mathcal{A}$ verifies the validity of a statement x (chosen adaptively in the last round of Π) by interacting with $\mathcal{P}$ using identity $\mathtt{id}$ of his choice. In the right sessions $\mathcal{A}$ proves the validity of the statements $\tilde{x}_1 \ldots, \tilde{x}_{\mathsf{poly}(\lambda)}$ (chosen adaptively in the last round of Π) to the honest verifiers $\mathcal{V}_1, \ldots, \mathcal{V}_{\mathsf{poly}(\lambda)}$, using identities $\tilde{\mathtt{id}}_1, \ldots, \tilde{\mathtt{id}}_{\mathsf{poly}(\lambda)}$ of his choice.

More precisely in the left session $\mathcal{A}$, before the last round of Π is executed, adaptively selects the statement x to be proved and the witness w, s.t. $(x, w) \in \mathsf{Rel}_{\mathsf{L}}$, and sends them to $\mathcal{P}$.[6]

Let $\mathsf{View}^{\mathcal{A}}(1^\lambda, z)$ denote a random variable that describes the view of $\mathcal{A}$ in the above experiment.

Definition 2.17 (*Delayed-Input NMZK*) A delayed-input argument system $\Pi = (\mathcal{P}, \mathcal{V})$ for an $\mathcal{NP}$-language L with witness relation $\mathsf{Rel}_{\mathsf{L}}$ is delayed-input non-malleable zero knowledge (NMZK) if for any MiM adversary $\mathcal{A}$ that participates in one left session and $\mathsf{poly}(\lambda)$ right sessions, there exists a expected PPT machine $S(1^\lambda, z)$ such that

1. The probability ensembles $\{S^1(1^\lambda, z)\}_{\lambda \in \mathbb{N}, z \in \{0,1\}^\star}$ and $\{\mathsf{View}^{\mathcal{A}}(1^\lambda, z)\}_{\lambda \in \mathbb{N}, z \in \{0,1\}^\star}$ are computationally indistinguishable over λ, where $S^1(1^\lambda, z)$ denotes the first output of $S(1^\lambda, z)$.
2. Let $(\mathsf{View}, w_1, \ldots, w_{\mathsf{poly}(\lambda)})$ denote the output of $S(1^\lambda, z)$, for some $z \in \{0, 1\}^\star$. Let $\tilde{x}_1, \ldots, \tilde{x}_{\mathsf{poly}(\lambda)}$ be the right-session statements appearing in View and let $\mathtt{id}$ and $\tilde{\mathtt{id}}_1, \ldots, \tilde{\mathtt{id}}_{\mathsf{poly}(\lambda)}$ be respectively the identities used in the left and right sessions appearing in View. Then for every $i \in \{1, \ldots, \mathsf{poly}(\lambda)\}$, if the i-th right session is accepting and $\mathtt{id} \neq \tilde{\mathtt{id}}_i$, then $\tilde{w}_i$ is s.t. $(\tilde{x}_i, \tilde{w}_i) \in \mathsf{Rel}_{\mathsf{L}}$.

---

[5] We denote by $\tilde{\delta}$ a value associated with the right session where δ is the corresponding value in the left session.

[6] The witness w sent by $\mathcal{A}$ will be just ignored by the simulator.

The above definition of NMZK allows the adversary to select statements adaptively in the last round both in left and in the right sessions. Therefore any argument system that is NMZK according to the above definition enjoys also adaptive-input argument of knowledge. We also consider the notion of *many-many synchronous delayed-input NMZK*, that is equal to the notion of delayed-input NMZK except that polynomially many left and right sessions are played in parallel.

2.6 Two-Party Computation

Here we recall some useful definitions for one of our applications. The Multi-Party Computation (MPC) protocol for coin tossing is secure in the same model used in [84], therefore some definitions are taken almost verbatim from [84]. Always following Garg et al. we only recall the security definition for the two-party case. The description naturally extends to multi-party cases as well (details can be found in [85]).

Two-Party Protocol. A two-party protocol problem is cast by specifying a random process that maps pairs of inputs to pairs of outputs (one for each party). We refer to such a process as a functionality and denote it $F : \{0, 1\}^* \times \{0, 1\}^* \rightarrow \{0, 1\}^* \times \{0, 1\}^*$ where $F = (F_1, F_2)$. That is, for every pair of inputs (x, y), the output-pair is a random variable $(F_1(x, y), F_2(x, y))$ ranging over pairs of strings. The first party (with input x) wishes to obtain $F_1(x, y)$ and the second party (with input y) wishes to obtain $F_2(x, y)$.

Adversarial Behavior. Loosely speaking, the aim of a secure two-party protocol is to protect an honest party against dishonest behavior by the other party. We consider malicious adversaries who may arbitrarily deviate from the specified protocol. When considering malicious adversaries, there are certain undesirable actions that cannot be prevented. Specifically, a party may refuse to participate in the protocol, may substitute its local input (and use instead a different input), and may abort the protocol prematurely. One ramification of the adversary's ability to abort is that it is impossible to achieve fairness. That is, the adversary may obtain its output while the honest party does not. In this work, we consider a static corruption model, where one of the parties is adversarial and the other is honest, and this is fixed before the execution begins.

Communication Channel. We consider a secure simultaneous message exchange channel in which all parties can simultaneously send messages over the channel at the same communication round but allowing a rushing adversary. Moreover, we assume an asynchronous network[7] where the communication is open and delivery of messages are not guaranteed. For simplicity, we assume that the delivered messages are authenticated. This can be achieved using standard methods.

Execution in the Ideal Model. An ideal execution proceeds as follows. Each party obtains an input, denoted w ($w = x$ for P_1, and $w = y$ for P_2). An honest party

[7] The fact that the network is asynchronous means that the messages are not necessarily delivered in the order in which they are sent.

always sends w to the trusted party. A malicious party may, depending on w, either abort or send some $w' \in \{0, 1\}^{|w|}$ to the trusted party. In case it has obtained an input pair (x, y), the trusted party first replies to the first party with $F_1(x, y)$. Otherwise (i.e., in case it receives only one valid input), the trusted party replies to both parties with a special symbol $\perp$. In case the first party is malicious it may, depending on its input and the trusted party's answer, decide to stop the trusted party by sending it $\perp$ after receiving its output. In this case the trusted party sends $\perp$ to the second party. Otherwise (i.e., if not stopped), the trusted party sends $F_2(x, y)$ to the second party. Outputs: An honest party always outputs the message it has obtained from the trusted party. A malicious party may output an arbitrary (probabilistic polynomial-time computable) function of its initial input and the message obtained from the trusted party.

Let $F : \{0, 1\}^* \times \{0, 1\}^* \rightarrow \{0, 1\}^* \times \{0, 1\}^*$ be a functionality where $F = (F_1, F_2)$ and let $S = (S_1, S_2)$ be a pair of non-uniform probabilistic expected polynomial-time machines (representing parties in the ideal model). Such a pair is admissible if for at least one $i \in \{0, 1\}$ we have that S_i is honest (i.e., follows the honest party instructions in the above-described ideal execution). Then, the joint execution of F under S in the ideal model (on input pair (x, y) and security parameter λ), denoted $\mathsf{IDEAL}_{F,S(z)}(1^\lambda, x, y)$ is defined as the output pair of S_1 and S_2 from the above ideal execution.

Execution in the Real Model. We next consider the real model in which a real (two-party) protocol is executed (and there exists no trusted third party). In this case, a malicious party may follow an arbitrary feasible strategy; that is, any strategy implementable by non-uniform probabilistic polynomial-time machines. In particular, the malicious party may abort the execution at any point in time (and when this happens prematurely, the other party is left with no output). Let F be as above and let Π be a two-party protocol for computing F. Furthermore, let $A = (A_1, A_2)$ be a pair of non-uniform probabilistic polynomial-time machines (representing parties in the real model). Such a pair is admissible if for at least one $i \in \{0, 1\}$ we have that A_i is honest (i.e., follows the strategy specified by Π). Then, the joint execution of Π under A in the real model, denoted $\mathsf{REAL}_{\Pi,\mathcal{A}(z)}(1^\lambda)$, is defined as the output pair of A_1 and A_2 resulting from the protocol interaction.

Definition 2.18 (*Secure Two-Party Computation*) Let F and Π be as above. Protocol Π is said to securely compute F (in the malicious model) if for every pair of admissible non-uniform probabilistic polynomial-time machines $A = (A_1, A_2)$ that run with auxiliary input z for the real model, there exists a pair of admissible non-uniform probabilistic expected polynomial-time machines $S = (S_1, S_2)$ (that use z as auxiliary input) for the ideal model, such that

$$\mathsf{REAL}_{\Pi,\mathcal{A}(z)}(1^\lambda) \approx \mathsf{IDEAL}_{f,S(z)}(1^\lambda).$$

Multi-party Coin Tossing Protocol [95].

Coin tossing allows parties to generate a common unbiased random string. Let Π_{MCF} be a synchronized multi-party coin tossing protocol, let $\mathcal{A}$ denote the real-world adversary running on auxiliary inputs z, and let S be the ideal-world adversary (the simulator). We then denote by $\mathsf{REAL}_{\Pi_{\mathsf{MCF}},\mathcal{A}(z)}(1^\lambda)$ the random variable consisting of the output of $\mathcal{A}$ and the outputs of all parties. We denote by $\mathsf{IDEAL}_{f_{\mathsf{CT}},S(z)}(1^\lambda)$ the analogous output of S and honest parties after an ideal execution with a trusted party computing the n-ary function $f_{\mathsf{CT}} : (1^\lambda)^n \rightarrow \{0, 1\}^\lambda$, where each party has only the security parameter k as its input and the output of f_{CT} is uniformly and independently chosen from $\{0, 1\}^\lambda$.

Definition 2.19 (*Secure Multi-party Coin Tossing*) Let f_{CT} and Π_{MCF} be as above. Protocol Π_{MCF} is said to securely compute f_{CT} (in the malicious model) if for every pair of admissible non-uniform probabilistic polynomial-time machine $\mathcal{A}$ that run with auxiliary input z for the real model, there exists a pair of admissible non-uniform probabilistic expected polynomial-time machines S (that use z as auxiliary input) for the ideal model, such that

$$\mathsf{REAL}_{\Pi_{\mathsf{MCF}},\mathcal{A}(z)}(1^\lambda) \approx \mathsf{IDEAL}_{f_{\mathsf{CT}},S(z)}(1^\lambda).$$

2.7 Number-Theoretic Assumptions

We define *group generator* algorithms to be probabilistic polynomial-time algorithms that take as input security parameter 1^λ and output $(\mathcal{G}, q, g)$, where $\mathcal{G}$ is (the description of) a cyclic group of order q and g is a generator of $\mathcal{G}$. We assume that membership in $\mathcal{G}$ and its group operations can be performed in time polynomial in the length of q and that there is an efficient procedure to randomly select elements from $\mathcal{G}$. Moreover, with a slight abuse of notation, we will use $\mathcal{G}$ to denote the group and its description.

2.7.1 *The DLog Assumption*

Assumption 1 (*Sub-exponetial DLog Assumption*) There exists a constant α such that for every probabilistic algorithm A running in time 2^{λ^α} the following probability is a negligible function of λ

$$\mathrm{Prob}\left[\, (\mathcal{G}, q, g) \leftarrow \mathsf{GG}(1^\lambda); y \leftarrow \mathbb{Z}_q : A(g^y) = y \,\right].$$

Assumption 2 (*Strong DLog Assumption* [29]) Consider a pair of probabilistic algorithms (A_0, A_1) such that A_0, on input 1^λ, outputs $(\mathcal{G}, q, g)$, where $\mathcal{G}$ is the group of the quadratic residues modulo p, where p is prime, $p = 2q + 1$, q is a λ-bit prime and $g \in \mathcal{G}$, along with some auxiliary information $\mathtt{aux}$. There exists a constant α such that for any such pair (A_0, A_1) running in time 2^{λ^α} the following probability is a negligible function of λ:

$$\text{Prob}\left[\,((\mathcal{G}, q, g), \mathtt{aux}) \leftarrow A_0(1^\lambda);\ y \leftarrow \mathbb{Z}_q : A_1(g^y, \mathtt{aux}) = y\,\right].$$

2.7.2 The DDH Assumption

Let $\mathcal{G}$ be a cyclic group, g generator of $\mathcal{G}$ and let A, B and X be elements of $\mathcal{G}$. We say that (g, A, B, X) is a *Diffie-Hellman tuple* (a *DH tuple*, in short) if $A = g^\alpha$, $B = g^\beta$ for some integers $0 \le \alpha, \beta \le |\mathcal{G}| - 1$ and $X = g^{\alpha\beta}$. If this is not the case, the tuple is called *non-DH*. To verify that a tuple is DH, it is sufficient to have the discrete log α of A to the base g and then to check that $X = B^\alpha$. We thus define the polynomial-time relation $\mathsf{DH} = \{((g, A, B, X), \alpha) : A = g^\alpha \text{ and } X = B^\alpha\}$ of the DH tuples.

The *Decisional Diffie-Hellman* assumption (the DDH assumption) posits the hardness of distinguishing a randomly selected DH tuple from a randomly selected non-DH tuple with respect to a *group generator* algorithm. For sake of concreteness, we consider the specific group generator GG that, on input 1^λ, randomly selects a λ-bit prime p such that $q = (p-1)/2$ is also prime and outputs the (description of the) order q group $\mathcal{G}$ of the quadratic residues modulo p along with a random generator g of $\mathcal{G}$.

Assumption 3 (*DDH Assumption*) For every probabilistic polynomial-time algorithm $\mathcal{A}$ there exists a negligible function ν s.t.

$$\Big|\text{Prob}\left[\,(\mathcal{G}, q, g) \leftarrow \mathsf{GG}(1^\lambda); \alpha, \beta, \gamma \leftarrow \mathbb{Z}_q : \mathcal{A}((\mathcal{G}, q, g), g^\alpha, g^\beta, g^\gamma) = 1\,\right] -$$
$$\text{Prob}\left[\,(\mathcal{G}, q, g) \leftarrow \mathsf{GG}(1^\lambda); \alpha, \beta, \gamma \leftarrow \mathbb{Z}_q : \mathcal{A}((\mathcal{G}, q, g), g^\alpha, g^\beta, g^{\alpha\beta}) = 1\,\right]\Big| \le \nu(\lambda).$$

Assumption 4 (*Strong DDH Assumption*) Consider a pair of probabilistic algorithms (A_0, A_1) such that A_0, on input 1^λ, outputs $(\mathcal{G}, q, g)$, where $\mathcal{G}$ is the group of the quadratic residues modulo p, where p is prime, $p = 2q + 1$, q is a λ-bit prime and $g \in \mathcal{G}$, along with some auxiliary information $\mathtt{aux}$. There exists a constant α such that, for any such pair (A_0, A_1) running in time 2^{λ^α}, the following is a negligible function of λ

$$\begin{aligned}\Big|\text{Prob}\big[\{((\mathcal{G}, q, g), \mathtt{aux}) \leftarrow A_0(1^\lambda); x, y, z \leftarrow \mathbb{Z}_q :\\ A_1((\mathcal{G}, q, g), g^x, g^y, g^z, \mathtt{aux}) = 1\big] -\\ \text{Prob}\big[((\mathcal{G}, q, g), \mathtt{aux}) \leftarrow A_0(1^\lambda); x, y, z \leftarrow \mathbb{Z}_q :\\ A_1((\mathcal{G}, q, g), g^x, g^y, g^{xy}, \mathtt{aux}) = 1\big]\Big|\end{aligned}$$

1-non-DDH.

We define polynomial time relation $\mathsf{1nDH}$ as $\mathsf{1nDH} = \{((g, A, B, X), \alpha) : A = g^\alpha \text{ and } X = g \cdot B^\alpha\}$. Thus a *1-non-DH* tuple is a tuple $T = (g, A, B, X)$ such that $A = g^\alpha$, $B = g^\beta$ and

$$X = g \cdot B^\alpha = g^{\alpha \cdot \beta + 1}$$

Under the DDH assumption random 1-non-DH tuples are indistinguishable from random non-DH tuple. Indeed, let $T = (g, A, B, X)$ be any tuple and consider tuple $T' = (g, A, B, g \cdot X)$. Then we have that if T is a randomly selected DH tuple, then T' is a randomly selected 1-non-DH tuple; whereas, if T is a randomly selected non-DH tuple then T' is statistically close to a randomly selected non-DH tuple. Indeed, it is possible to prove that, under the DDH assumption, randomly selected 1-non-DH tuples are indistinguishable from randomly selected DH tuples. We can thus state the following lemma (first proved as Lemma 3.1 in [110]).

Lemma 2.4 ([110]) *Under the DDH assumption, for every probabilistic polynomial-time algorithm $\mathcal{A}$ there exists a negligible function ν s.t.*

$$\Big|Prob\Big[\,(\mathcal{G}, q, g) \leftarrow \mathsf{GG}(1^\lambda); \alpha, \beta \leftarrow \mathbb{Z}_q : \mathcal{A}((\mathcal{G}, q, g), g^\alpha, g^\beta, g^{\alpha\beta+1}) = 1\,\Big] -$$
$$Prob\Big[\,(\mathcal{G}, q, g) \leftarrow \mathsf{GG}(1^\lambda); \alpha, \beta \leftarrow \mathbb{Z}_q : \mathcal{A}((\mathcal{G}, q, g), g^\alpha, g^\beta, g^{\alpha\beta}) = 1\,\Big]\Big| \leq \nu(\lambda).$$

Sigma-Protocol for $\mathsf{1nDH}$ Tuples.

A Σ-protocol Π_k^{1nDH} for the threshold relation of $\mathsf{1nDH}$ can be constructed based on the Σ-protocol Π^{DDH} of [57] to prove that k out of n tuples are DDH tuples as follows. Specifically, let $\mathsf{1nDH}_k$ be the threshold relation for $\mathsf{1nDH}$ defined as follows:

$$\mathsf{1nDH}_k = \Big\{\Big(((g_1, A_1, B_1, X_1), \ldots, (g_n, A_n, B_n, X_n)), ((\alpha_1, b_1) \ldots, (\alpha_k, b_k))\Big) :$$
$$1 \leq b_1 < \cdots < b_k \leq n \text{ and } A_{b_i} = g_{b_i}^{\alpha_i} \text{ and } X_{b_i} = g_{b_i} \cdot B_{b_i}^{\alpha_i}, \text{ for } i = 1, \ldots, k\Big\}.$$

We construct Σ-protocol $\Pi_k^{\mathsf{1nDH}} = (\mathcal{P}_k^{\mathsf{1nDH}}, \mathcal{V}_k^{\mathsf{1nDH}})$ as follows. On input tuples $(g_1, A_1, B_1, X_1), \ldots, (g_n, A_n, B_n, X_n)$, $\mathcal{P}_k^{\mathsf{1nDH}}$ and $\mathcal{V}_k^{\mathsf{1nDH}}$ construct tuples $(g_1, A_1, B_1, Y_1), \ldots, (g_n, A_n, B_n, Y_n)$ by setting $Y_i = X_i / g_i$, for $i = 1, \ldots, n$. Then, $\mathcal{P}_k^{\mathsf{1nDH}}$ and $\mathcal{V}_k^{\mathsf{1nDH}}$ simply run Σ-protocol Π^{DDH} on input the theorem $(g_1, A_1, B_1, Y_1), \ldots, (g_n, A_n, B_n, Y_n)$.

Theorem 2.7 *Protocol Π_k^{1nDH} is a Σ-protocol for the threshold relation, $\mathsf{1nDH}_k$, of $\mathsf{1nDH}$.*

Proof The completeness follows from the completeness of Π^{DDH} and from the fact that $\mathcal{G}$ is a cyclic group with generator g. The special-soundness of Π^{1nDH} follows from the special soundness of Π^{DDH}. Indeed, a collision for Π^{1nDH} represents a collision for Π^{DDH} as well. Thus, the witnesses for k of the constructed tuples can be extracted. This part of the proof ends with the observation that k witnesses for the constructed tuples correspond to k witnesses for the input tuples.

If at least k of the input tuples are 1-non-DH then at least k of the *constructed* tuples (g_i, A_i, B_i, Y_i) are DH and the prover has a witness for it. On the other hand, if fewer than k of the input tuples are 1-non-DH then the constructed tuples contain fewer than k DH tuples.

The SHVZK property follows directly from the same property of Π^{DDH}. □

Part I
Secure Multi-party Computation

Chapter 3
Round Optimal Two-Party Computation

3.1 Introduction

In [84], the authors show that in the simultaneous message model, there are functionalities that cannot be realized while making use of less than four rounds of communication. Along with this lower bound, [84] also provided a construction for 2PC that needs a 3-round 3-robust parallel non-malleable commitment, and constructing this primitive from standard polynomial-time assumptions is still an open problem. We circumvent the use of this primitive through a different approach. As done in [84], we start considering the 4-round 2PC protocol of [124] (KO protocol) that works only for those functionalities where only one player receives the output (we recall that the KO protocols do not assume the existence of a simultaneous message exchange channel). Then, as in [84] we consider two simultaneous executions of the KO protocol to make both parties able to obtain the output *assuming the existence of a simultaneous message exchange channel*. We describe now the KO protocol and then we explain how we manage to avoid 3-round 3-robust parallel non-malleable commitments.

The 4-Round KO Protocol. Following Fig. 3.1, at a very high level the KO protocol between the players P_1 and P_2, where only P_1 gets the output, works as follows. Let f be the function that P_1 and P_2 want to compute. In the second round, P_2 generates, using his input, a Yao's garbled circuit C for the function f with the associated labels L. Then P_2 commits to C using a commitment scheme that is binding if P_2 runs the honest committer procedure. This commitment scheme, however, admits also an indistinguishable equivocal commitment procedure that allows later to open the equivocal commitment as any message. Let $\mathtt{com}_0$ be such commitment. In addition, P_2 commits to L using a statistically binding commitment scheme. Let $\mathtt{com}_1$ be such commitment. In the last round P_2 sends the opening of the equivocal commitment to the message C. Furthermore, using L as input, P_2 in the 2nd and in the 4th round runs as a sender of a specific 4-round oblivious transfer protocol KOOT that is secure against a malicious receiver and secure against a semi-honest sender. Finally, in

M. Ciampi and L. Siniscalchi, *Round and Computational Efficiency of Multi-party Protocols*, Information Security and Cryptography,
https://doi.org/10.1007/978-3-031-92374-6_3

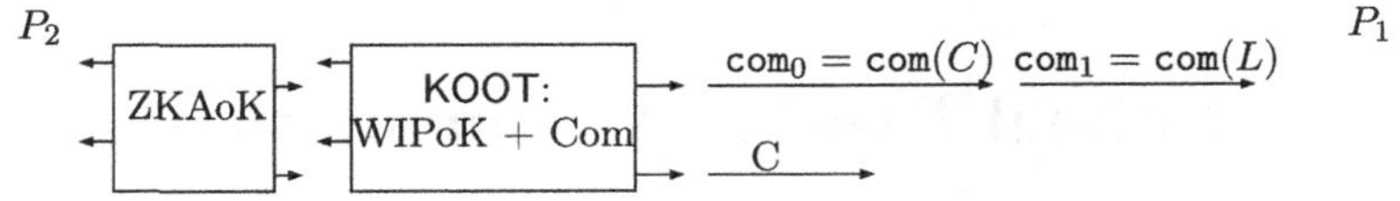

Fig. 3.1 The 4-round KO protocol from trapdoor permutations for functionalities where only one player receives the output

parallel with KOOT, P_2 computes a specific delayed-input zero-knowledge argument of knowledge (ZKAoK) to prove that the labels L committed in $\mathtt{com}_1$ correspond to the ones used in KOOT, and that $\mathtt{com}_0$ is binding since it has been been computed running the honest committer on input some randomness and some message. P_1 plays as a receiver of KOOT to obtain the labels associated with his input and computes the output of the two-party computation by running C on input the received labels. Moreover P_1 acts as a verifier for the ZKAoK where P_2 acts as a prover.

The 4-Round Protocol of Garg et al. To allow both parties to get the output in 4 rounds using a simultaneous message exchange channel, [84] first considers two simultaneous executions of the KO protocol (Fig. 3.2). Such natural approach yields to the following two problems (as stated in [84]): (1) nothing prevents an adversary from using two different inputs in the two executions of the KO protocol; (2) an adversary could adapt his input based on the input of the other party, for instance the adversary could simply forward the messages that he receives from the honest party. To address the first problem the authors of [84] add another statement to the ZKAoK where the player P_j (with $j = 1, 2$) proves that both executions of the KO protocol use the same input. The second problem is solved in [84] by using a 3-round 3-robust non-malleable commitment to construct KOOT and the ZKAoK in such a way that the input used by the honest party in KOOT cannot be mauled by the malicious party. The 3-robustness is required to avoid rewinding issues in the security proof. Indeed, in parallel with the 3-round 3-robust non-malleable commitment a WIPoK is executed in KOOT. At some point the security proof of [84] needs to rely on the witness-indistinguishability property of the WIPoK while the simulator of the ZKAoK is run. The simulator for the ZKAoK rewinds the adversary from the third to the second round, therefore rewinding also the challenger of the WIPoK of the reduction. To solve this problem [84, 179] rely on the stronger security of a 3-round 3-robust parallel non-malleable commitment scheme. Unfortunately, constructing this tool with standard polynomial-time assumptions is still an open question.

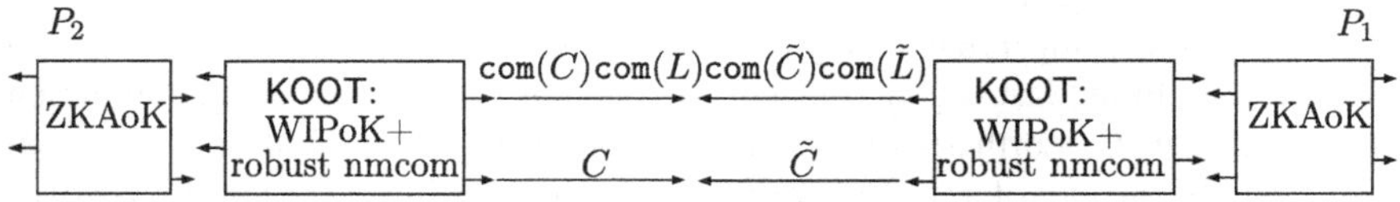

Fig. 3.2 The 4-round protocol of [84] for any functionality assuming 3-round 3-robust parallel non-malleable commitments in the simultaneous message exchange model

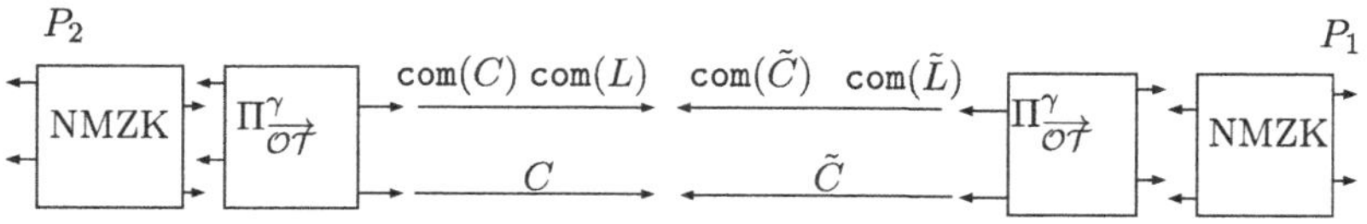

Fig. 3.3 4-round protocol for any functionality assuming trapdoor permutations in the simultaneous message exchange model

A 4-Round Protocol. The approach (that is summarized in Fig. 3.3), to solve problems 1 and 2 listed above using standard polynomial-time assumption (trapdoor permutations), we replace the ZKAoK and KOOT (that uses the 3-round 3-robust parallel commitment scheme) with the following two tools. (1) A 4-round delayed-input non-malleable zero-knowledge (NMZK) argument of knowledge (AoK) NMZK from one-way functions (OWFs) (we will show how to design such protocol in Chap. 4) (the theorem proved by NMZK is roughly the same as the theorem proved ZKAoK of [84]). (2) A special OT protocol $\Pi^{\gamma}_{\overrightarrow{OT}}$ that is *one-sided* simulatable [161]. In this security notion for OT it is not required the existence of a simulator against a malicious sender, but only that a malicious sender cannot distinguish whether the honest receiver uses his real input or a fixed input (e.g., a string of 0s). Moreover some security against a malicious sender still holds even if the adversary can perform a mild form of "rewinds" against the receiver, and the security against a malicious receiver holds even when an interactive primitive (like a WIPoK) is run in parallel (more details about the security provided by $\Pi^{\gamma}_{\overrightarrow{OT}}$ will be provided later).

Security Proof. We exploit immediately the major differences with [84]. Indeed we start the security proof with a hybrid experiment where the simulator of NMZK is used, and we are guaranteed that the malicious party is behaving honestly by the non-malleability/extractability of NMZK. In the next hybrid experiment we use the simulator of the OT protocol $\Pi^{\gamma}_{\overrightarrow{OT}}$ thus extracting the input from the adversary. In the rest of the hybrid experiments we remove the input of the honest party, and use the input extracted via $\Pi^{\gamma}_{\overrightarrow{OT}}$ to complete the interaction against the adversary. An important difference with the approach used in [84] is that in all the steps of the security proof the simulator-extractor of NMZK is used to check every time that the adversary is using the same input in both the executions of the KO protocol even though the adversary is receiving a simulated NMZK of a false statement. More precisely, every time that we change something, obtaining a new hybrid experiment, we prove that: (1) the output distributions of the experiments are indistinguishable; (2) the malicious party is behaving honestly (the statement proved by the NMZK given by the adversary is true). We will show that if one of these two invariants does not hold, then we can make a reduction that breaks a cryptographic primitive.

The Need of a Special 4-Round OT Protocol. Interestingly, the security proof has to address a major issue. After we switch to the simulator of the NMZK, we have that in some hybrid experiment H_i, we need to change the input of the receiver of $\Pi^{\gamma}_{\overrightarrow{OT}}$ (following the approach used in the security proof of the KO protocol). To demonstrate the indistinguishability between H_i and H_{i-1} we want to rely on the security of $\Pi^{\gamma}_{\overrightarrow{\mathcal{OT}}}$ against a malicious sender. Therefore we construct an adversarial sender $\mathcal{A}_{\mathcal{OT}}$ of $\Pi^{\gamma}_{\overrightarrow{\mathcal{OT}}}$. $\mathcal{A}_{\mathcal{OT}}$ acts as a proxy for the messages of $\Pi^{\gamma}_{\overrightarrow{\mathcal{OT}}}$ and internally computes the other messages of the protocol. In particular, the 1st and the 3rd rounds of $\Pi^{\gamma}_{\overrightarrow{\mathcal{OT}}}$ are given by the challenger (that acts as a receiver of $\Pi^{\gamma}_{\overrightarrow{\mathcal{OT}}}$), and the 2nd and the 4th messages of $\Pi^{\gamma}_{\overrightarrow{\mathcal{OT}}}$ are given by the malicious party. Furthermore, to compute the other messages of the 2PC protocol $\mathcal{A}_{\mathcal{OT}}$ needs to run the simulator-extractor of NMZK that, and this requires to rewind from the 3rd to the 2nd round. This means that $\mathcal{A}_{\mathcal{OT}}$ needs to complete a 3rd round of $\Pi^{\gamma}_{\overrightarrow{\mathcal{OT}}}$, for every different 2nd round that it receives (this is due to the rewinds made by the simulator of NMZK that are emulated by $\mathcal{A}_{\mathcal{OT}}$). We observe that since the challenger cannot be rewound, $\mathcal{A}_{\mathcal{OT}}$ needs a strategy to answer to these multiple queries w.r.t. $\Pi^{\gamma}_{\overrightarrow{\mathcal{OT}}}$ without knowing the randomness and the input used by the challenger so far. For these reasons we need $\Pi^{\gamma}_{\overrightarrow{\mathcal{OT}}}$ to enjoy an additional property: the *replayability* of the 3rd round. More precisely, given the messages computed by an honest receiver, the third round can be indistinguishability used to answer to any second round of $\Pi^{\gamma}_{\overrightarrow{\mathcal{OT}}}$ sent by a malicious sender. Another issue is that the idea of the security proof explained so far relies on the simulator-extractor of NMZK and this simulator rewinds also from the 4th to the 3rd round. The rewinds made by the simulator-extractor allow a malicious receiver to ask for different 3rd rounds of $\Pi^{\gamma}_{\overrightarrow{\mathcal{OT}}}$. Therefore we need $\Pi^{\gamma}_{\overrightarrow{\mathcal{OT}}}$ to be also secure against a more powerful malicious receiver that can send multiple (up to a polynomial γ) third rounds to the honest sender. As far as we know the literature does not provide an OT with the properties that we require, so we also provide an OT protocol with these additional features. This clearly is of independent interest.

3.2 Special One-Sided Simulatable OT

One of the main building blocks of the 2PC protocol is an OT protocol $\Pi^{\gamma}_{\mathcal{OT}} = (S_{\mathcal{OT}}, R_{\mathcal{OT}})$ one-sided simulatable.[1] $\Pi^{\gamma}_{\mathcal{OT}}$ has four rounds where the first (ot_1) and the third (ot_3) rounds are played by the receiver, and the remaining rounds (ot_2 and ot_4) are played by the sender. In addition $\Pi^{\gamma}_{\mathcal{OT}}$ enjoys the following two additional properties.

1. *Replayable third round.* Let $(\mathsf{ot}_1, \mathsf{ot}_2, \mathsf{ot}_3, \mathsf{ot}_4)$ be the messages exchanged by an honest receiver and a malicious sender during an execution of $\Pi^{\gamma}_{\mathcal{OT}}$. For any honestly computed ot'_2, we have that $(\mathsf{ot}_1, \mathsf{ot}_2, \mathsf{ot}_3)$ and $(\mathsf{ot}_1, \mathsf{ot}'_2, \mathsf{ot}_3)$ are identically distributed. Roughly, we are requiring that the third round can be reused to answer to any second round ot'_2 sent by a malicious sender.

---

[1] In the 2PC protocol we will actually use $\Pi^{\gamma}_{\overrightarrow{\mathcal{OT}}}$ that roughly corresponds to parallel executions of $\Pi^{\gamma}_{\mathcal{OT}}$. More details will be provided later.

2. *Repeatability.* We require $\Pi^{\gamma}_{\mathcal{OT}}$ to be secure against a malicious receiver $R^{\star}$ even when the last two rounds of $\Pi^{\gamma}_{\mathcal{OT}}$ can be repeated multiple times. More precisely a 4-round OT protocol that is secure in this setting can be seen as an OT protocol of $2 + 2\gamma$ rounds, with $\gamma \in \{1, \ldots, \mathsf{poly}(\lambda)\}$ where λ represents the security parameter. In this protocol $R^{\star}$, upon receiving the 4th round, can continue the execution with $S_{\mathcal{OT}}$ by sending a freshly generated third round of $\Pi^{\gamma}_{\mathcal{OT}}$ up to a total of γ 3rd rounds.
   Roughly, we require that the output of such $R^{\star}$ that runs $\Pi^{\gamma}_{\mathcal{OT}}$ against an honest sender can be simulated by an efficient simulator Sim that has only access to the ideal world functionality $F_{\mathcal{OT}}$ and oracle access to $R^{\star}$.

The security of $\Pi^{\gamma}_{\mathcal{OT}}$ is based on the existence of trapdoor permutations.

Techniques.

To construct $\Pi^{\gamma}_{\mathcal{OT}}$ we use as a starting point the following basic 3-round semi-honest OT Π_{sh} based on trapdoor permutations (TDPs) of [73, 124]. Let $l_0, l_1 \in \{0, 1\}^{\lambda}$ be the input of the sender S and b be the input bit of the receiver R.

1. The sender S chooses a trapdoor permutation $(f, f^{-1}) \leftarrow \mathsf{Gen}(1^{\lambda})$ and sends f to the receiver R.
2. R chooses $x \leftarrow \{0, 1\}^{\lambda}$ and $z_{1-b} \leftarrow \{0, 1\}^{\lambda}$, computes $z_b = f(x)$ and sends (z_0, z_1).
3. For $c = 0, 1$ S computes and sends $w_c = l_c \oplus \mathsf{hc}(f^{-1}(z_c))$

where $\mathsf{hc}(\cdot)$ is a hardcore bit of f. If the parties follow the protocol (i.e., in the semi-honest setting) then S cannot learn the receiver's input (the bit b) as both z_0 and z_1 are random strings. Also, due to the security of the TDP f, R cannot distinguish w_{1-b} from random as long as z_{1-b} is randomly chosen. If we consider a fully malicious receiver $R^{\star}$ then this protocol is not secure anymore. Indeed $R^{\star}$ could just compute $z_{1-b} = f(y)$ picking a random $y \leftarrow \{0, 1\}^{\lambda}$. In this way $R^{\star}$ can retrieve both the inputs of the sender l_0 and l_1. In [124] the authors solve this problem by having the parties engage in a coin-flipping protocol such that the receiver is forced to set at least one between z_0 and z_1 to a random string. This is done by forcing the receiver to commit to two strings (r_0, r_1) in the first round (for the coin-flipping) and providing a witness-indistinguishable proof of knowledge (WIPoK) that either $z_0 = r_0 \oplus r'_0$ or $z_1 = r_1 \oplus r'_1$ where r'_0 and r'_1 are random strings sent by the sender in the second round. The resulting protocol, as observed in [161], leaks no information to S about R's input. Moreover the soundness of the WIPoK forces a malicious $R^{\star}$ to behave honestly, and the PoK allows to extract the input from the adversary in the simulation. Therefore the protocol constructed in [124] is one-sided simulatable. Unfortunately this approach is not sufficient to have an OT protocol that has a *replayable* third round. This is due to the added WIPoK. More precisely, the receiver has to execute a WIPoK (acting as a prover) in the first three rounds. There is no 3-round WIPoK such that given an accepting transcript (a, c, z) one can efficiently compute multiple accepting transcripts w.r.t. different second rounds without knowing the randomness used to compute a. This is the reason why we need to use a different approach to construct an OT protocol simulation-based secure against a malicious receiver that also has a replayable 3rd round.

The construction: $\Pi^{\gamma}_{\mathcal{OT}}$.

We start by considering a trick proposed in [161]. In [161] the authors construct a 4-round black-box OT starting from Π_{sh}. In order to force the receiver to compute a random z_{b-1}, in the first round R sends two commitments c_0 and c_1 such that $c_b = \mathsf{Eqcom}(\cdot)$, $c_{1-b} = \mathsf{Eqcom}(r_{1-b})$. Eqcom is a commitment scheme that is binding if the committer runs the honest committer procedure; however, this commitment scheme admits also an indistinguishable equivocal commitment procedure that allows later to open the equivocal commitment as any message. R then proves using a special WIPoK that either c_0 or c_1 is computed using the honest procedure (i.e., at least one of these commitments is binding). Then S in the second round computes $r'_0 \leftarrow \{0,1\}^\lambda$, $r'_1 \leftarrow \{0,1\}^\lambda$ and two TDPs f_0, f_1 with the respective trapdoor and sends (r'_0, r'_1, f_0, f_1) to R. R, upon receiving (r'_0, r'_1, f_0, f_1), picks $x \leftarrow \{0,1\}^\lambda$, computes $r_b = f_b(x) \oplus r'_b$ and sends the opening of c_{1-b} to the message r_{1-b} and the opening of c_b to the message r_b. At this point the sender computes and sends $w_0 = l_0 \oplus \mathsf{hc}(f_0^{-1}(r_0 \oplus r'_0))$, $w_1 = l_1 \oplus \mathsf{hc}(f_1^{-1}(r_1 \oplus r'_1))$. Since at least one between c_0 and c_1 is binding (due to the WIPoK), a malicious receiver can retrieve only one of the sender's input l_b. We observe that this OT protocol is still not sufficient for our purpose due to the WIPoK used by the receiver (i.e., the 3rd round is not *replayable*). Moreover, we cannot remove the WIPoK, otherwise a malicious receiver could compute both c_0 and c_1 using the equivocal procedure thus obtaining l_0 and l_1. The solution is to replace the WIPoK with some primitives that make replayable the 3rd round, still allowing the receiver to prove that at least one of the commitments sent in the first round is binding. The key idea is to use a combination of instance-dependent trapdoor commitment (IDTCom) and non-interactive commitment schemes. An IDTCom is defined over an instance x that could belong to the $\mathcal{NP}$-language L or not. If $x \notin L$ then the IDTCom is perfectly binding, otherwise It is equivocal and the trapdoor information is represented by the witness w for x. The protocol is described as follows. R sends an IDTCom $\mathtt{tcom}_0$ of r_0 and an IDTCom $\mathtt{tcom}_1$ of r_1. In both cases the instance used is $\mathtt{com}$, a perfectly binding commitment of the bit b. The $\mathcal{NP}$-language used to compute $\mathtt{tcom}_0$ consists of all valid perfectly binding commitments of the message 0, while the $\mathcal{NP}$-language used to compute $\mathtt{tcom}_1$ consists of all valid perfectly binding commitments of the message 1.

This means that $\mathtt{tcom}_b$ can be opened to any value[2] and $\mathtt{tcom}_{1-b}$ is perfectly binding (we recall that b is the input of the receiver). It is important to observe that due to the binding property of $\mathtt{com}$ it could be that both $\mathtt{tcom}_0$ and $\mathtt{tcom}_1$ are binding, but it can never happen that they are both equivocal. Now we can replace the two commitments and the WIPoK used in [161] with $\mathtt{tcom}_0$, $\mathtt{tcom}_1$ and $\mathtt{com}(b)$ that are sent in the first round. The rest of the protocol stays the same as in [161]

[2] The decommitment information of $\mathtt{com}$ represents the trapdoor of the IDTCom $\mathtt{tcom}_b$.

with the difference that in the third round the openings to the messages r_0 and r_1 are w.r.t. $\mathtt{tcom}_0$ and $\mathtt{tcom}_1$. What remains to observe is that when a receiver provides a valid third round of this protocol then the same message can be used to answer all second rounds. Indeed, a well formed third round is accepting if and only if the opening w.r.t. $\mathtt{tcom}_0$ and $\mathtt{tcom}_1$ are well computed. Therefore, whether the third round is accepting or not does not depend on the second round sent by the sender.

Intuitively this protocol is also already secure when we consider a malicious receiver that can send multiple third rounds up to a total of γ 3rd rounds, thus obtaining an OT protocol of $2 + 2\gamma$ rounds (repeatability). This is because, even though a malicious receiver obtains multiple fourth rounds in response to multiple third rounds sent by $R^\star$, no information about the input of the sender is leaked. Indeed, in $\Pi^{\gamma}_{\mathcal{OT}}$, the input of the receiver is fixed in the first round (only one between $\mathtt{tcom}_0$ and $\mathtt{tcom}_1$ can be equivocal). Therefore the security of the TDP ensures that only l_b can be obtained by $R^\star$ independently of what he does in the third round.

We finally point out that the OT protocol that we need has to allow parties to use strings instead of bits as input. More precisely the sender's input is represented by $(l^1_0, l^1_1, \dots, l^m_0, l^m_1)$ where each l^i_b is an λ-bit length string (for $i = 1, \dots, m$ and $b = 0, 1$), while the input of the receiver is λ-bit length string.

This is achieved in two steps. First we construct an OT protocol where the sender's input is represented by just two m-bit strings l_0 and l_1 and the receiver's input is still a bit. We obtain this protocol by just using in $\Pi^{\gamma}_{\mathcal{OT}}$ a vector of m hard-core bits instead of just a single hard core bit following the approach of [84, 124]. Then we consider m parallel execution of this modified $\Pi^{\gamma}_{\mathcal{OT}}$ (where the sender uses a pair of strings as input) thus obtaining $\Pi^{\gamma}_{\overrightarrow{\mathcal{OT}}}$.

3.3 Definitions and Tools

Definition 3.1 (*Yao's garbled circuit*) We view Yao's garbled circuit scheme as a tuple of PPT algorithms (GenGC, EvalGC) where GenGC is the generation procedure which generates a garbled circuit for a circuit $\mathsf{GC_y}$ along with labels, and EvalGC is the evaluation procedure which evaluates the circuit on the correct labels. Each individual wire i of the circuit is assigned two labels, namely $Z_{i,0}, Z_{i,1}$. More specifically, the two algorithms have the following format:

- $(Z_{1,0}, Z_{1,1}, \dots, Z_{\lambda,0}, Z_{\lambda,1}, \mathsf{GC_y}) \leftarrow \mathsf{GenGC}(1^\lambda, F, y)$: GenGC takes as input a security parameter λ, a circuit F and a string $y \in \{0, 1\}^\lambda$. It outputs a garbled circuit $\mathsf{GC_y}$ along with the set of all input-wire labels $\{Z_{1,b}, \dots, Z_{\lambda,b}\}_{b\in\{0,1\}}$. The garbled circuit may be viewed as representing the function $F(\cdot, y)$.
- $v = \mathsf{EvalGC}(\mathsf{GC_y}, Z_{1,x_1}, \dots, Z_{\lambda,x_\lambda})$: Given a garbled circuit $\mathsf{GC_y}$ and a set of input-wire labels Z_{i,x_i} where $x_i \in \{0, 1\}$ for $i = 1, \dots, \lambda$, EvalGC outputs either an invalid symbol $\bot$, or a value $v = F(x, y)$.

The following properties are required.

Correctness. Prob$\left[\ F(x,y) = \mathsf{EvalGC}(\mathsf{GC_y}, Z_{1,x_1}, \ldots, Z_{\lambda,x_\lambda})\ \right] = 1$.

Security. There exists a PPT simulator SimGC such that for any (F, x) and uniformly random labels $Z_{1,x_1}, \ldots, Z_{\lambda,x_\lambda}$, it holds that:

$$(\mathsf{GC_y}, Z_{1,x_1}, \ldots, Z_{\lambda,x_\lambda}) \approx \mathsf{SimGC}(1^\lambda, F, x, v)$$

where $(Z_{1,0}, Z_{1,1}, \ldots, Z_{\lambda,0}, Z_{\lambda,1}, \mathsf{GC_y}) \leftarrow \mathsf{GenGC}(1^\lambda, F, y)$ and $v = F(x, y)$.

Definition 3.2 (*Trapdoor Permutation*) Let $\mathcal{F}$ be a triple of PPT algorithms (Gen, Eval, Invert) such that if $\mathsf{Gen}(1^\lambda)$ outputs a pair $(f, \mathtt{td})$, then $\mathsf{Eval}(f, \cdot)$ is a permutation over $\{0, 1\}^\lambda$ and Invert $(f, \mathtt{td}, \cdot)$ is its inverse. $\mathcal{F}$ is a trapdoor permutation such that for all PPT adversaries $\mathcal{A}$:

$$\text{Prob}\left[\ (f, \mathtt{td}) \leftarrow \mathsf{Gen}(1^\lambda);\ y \leftarrow \{0,1\}^\lambda, x \leftarrow \mathcal{A}(f, y) : \mathsf{Eval}(f, x) = y\ \right] \leq \nu(\lambda).$$

For convenience, we drop $(f, \mathtt{td})$ from the notation, and write $f(\cdot)$, $f^{-1}(\cdot)$ to denote algorithms $\mathsf{Eval}(f, \cdot)$, $\mathsf{Invert}(f, \mathtt{td}, \cdot)$ respectively, when f, $\mathtt{td}$ are clear from the context. Following [84, 124] we assume that $\mathcal{F}$ satisfies (a weak variant of) "certifiability": namely, given some f it is possible to decide in polynomial time whether $\mathsf{Eval}(f, \cdot)$ is a permutation over $\{0, 1\}^\lambda$. Let hc be the hardcore bit function for λ bits for the family $\mathcal{F}$. λ hardcore bits are obtained from a single-bit hardcore function h and $f \in \mathcal{F}$ as follows: $\mathsf{hc}(z) = h(z)||h(f(z))|| \ldots ||h(f^{\lambda-1}(z))$. Informally, $\mathsf{hc}(z)$ looks pseudorandom given $f^\lambda(z)$.[3]

3.3.1 Oblivious Transfer

Here we follow [161]. Oblivious Transfer (OT) is a two-party functionality $F_{\mathcal{OT}}$, in which a sender S holds a pair of strings (l_0, l_1), and a receiver R holds a bit b, and wants to obtain the string l_b. The security requirement for the $F_{\mathcal{OT}}$ functionality is that any malicious receiver does not learn anything about the string l_{1-b} and any malicious sender does not learn which string has been transferred. This security requirement is formalized via the ideal/real world paradigm. In the ideal world, the functionality is implemented by a trusted party that takes the inputs from S and R and provides the output to R and is therefore secure by definition. A real world protocol Π securely realizes the ideal $F_{\mathcal{OT}}$ functionalities, if the following two conditions hold. (a) Security against a malicious receiver: the output of any malicious receiver $R^\star$ running one execution of Π with an honest sender S can be simulated by a PPT simulator Sim that has only access to the ideal world functionality $F_{\mathcal{OT}}$ and oracle access to $R^\star$. (b) Security against a malicious sender. The joint view of the output of any malicious sender $S^\star$ running one execution of Π with R and the output of R can be simulated by a PPT simulator Sim that has only access to the ideal world functionality

[3] $f^\lambda(z)$ means the λ-th iteration of applying f on z.

Functionality $F_{\mathcal{OT}}$

$F_{\mathcal{OT}}$ running with a sender S a receiver R and an adversary Sim proceeds as follows:

- Upon receiving a message (send, l_0, l_1, S, R) from S where each $l_0, l_1 \in \{0,1\}^\lambda$, record the tuple (l_0, l_1) and send send to R and Sim. Ignore any subsequent send messages.
- Upon receiving a message (receive, b) from R, where $b \in \{0,1\}$ send l_b to R and receive to S and Sim and halt. (If no (send, $\cdot$) message was previously sent, do nothing).

Fig. 3.4 The oblivious transfer functionality $F_{\mathcal{OT}}$

functionality $F_{\mathcal{OT}}$ and oracle access to $S^\star$. We consider a weaker definition of $F_{\mathcal{OT}}$ that is called one-sided simulatable $F_{\mathcal{OT}}$, in which we do not demand the existence of a simulator against a malicious sender, but we only require that a malicious sender cannot distinguish whether the honest receiver is playing with bit 0 or 1. A bit more formally, we require that for any PPT malicious sender $S^\star$ the view of $S^\star$ executing Π with the R playing with bit 0 is computationally indistinguishable from the view of $S^\star$ where R is playing with bit 1. Finally, we consider the $F^m_{\mathcal{OT}}$ functionality where the sender S and the receiver R run m executions of OT in parallel. The formal definitions of one-sided secure $F_{\mathcal{OT}}$ and one-sided secure $F^m_{\mathcal{OT}}$ follow.

Definition 3.3 ([161]) Let $F_{\mathcal{OT}}$ be the Oblivious Transfer functionality as shown in Fig. 3.4. We say that a protocol Π securely computes $F_{\mathcal{OT}}$ with one-sided simulation if the following holds:

1. For every non-uniform PPT adversary $R^\star$ controlling the receiver in the real model, there exists a non-uniform PPT adversary Sim for the ideal model such that

$$\{\mathsf{REAL}_{\Pi,R^\star(z)}(1^\lambda)\}_{z\in\{0,1\}^\lambda} \approx \mathsf{IDEAL}_{F_{\mathcal{OT}},\mathsf{Sim}(z)}(1^\lambda)\}_{z\in\{0,1\}^\lambda}$$

   where $\mathsf{REAL}_{\Pi,R^\star(z)}(1^\lambda)$ denotes the distribution of the output of the adversary $R^\star$ (controlling the receiver) after a real execution of protocol Π, where the sender S has inputs l_0, l_1 and the receiver has input b. $\mathsf{IDEAL}_{f,\mathsf{Sim}(z)}(1^\lambda)$ denotes the analogous distribution in an ideal execution with a trusted party that computes $F_{\mathcal{OT}}$ for the parties and hands the output to the receiver.
2. For every non-uniform PPT adversary $S^\star$ controlling the sender it holds that

$$\{\mathsf{View}^R_{\Pi,S^\star(z)}(l_0, l_1, 0)\}_{z\in\{0,1\}^\star} \approx \{\mathsf{View}^R_{\Pi,S^\star(z)}(l_0, l_1, 1)\}_{z\in\{0,1\}^\star}$$

   where $\mathsf{View}^R_{\Pi,S^\star(z)}$ denotes the view of adversary $S^\star$ after a real execution of protocol Π with the honest receiver R.

Definition 3.4 (*Parallel oblivious transfer functionality* $F^m_{\mathcal{OT}}$ [161]) The parallel Oblivious Transfer Functionality $F^m_{\mathcal{OT}}$ is identical to the functionality $F_{\mathcal{OT}}$, with the difference that takes in input m pairs of string from S $(l^1_0, l^1_1, \dots, l^m_0, l^m_1)$ (whereas $F_{\mathcal{OT}}$ takes just one pair of strings from S) and m bits from R, $b_1, \dots, b_m$ (whereas $F_{\mathcal{OT}}$ takes one bit from R) and outputs to the receiver values $(l^1_{b_1}, \dots, l^m_{b_m})$ while the sender receives nothing.

Definition 3.5 ([161]) Let F^m_{OT} be the Oblivious Transfer functionality as described in Definition 3.4. We say that a protocol Π securely computes F^m_{OT} with one-sided simulation if the following holds:

1. For every non-uniform PPT adversary $R^\star$ controlling the receiver in the real model, there exists a non-uniform PPT adversary Sim for the ideal model such that for every $x_1 \in \{0, 1\}, \ldots, x_m \in \{0, 1\}$

$$\{\mathsf{REAL}_{\Pi,R^\star(z)}(1^\lambda, (l_0^1, l_1^1, \ldots, l_0^m, l_1^m), (x_1, \ldots, x_m))\} \approx$$
$$\mathsf{IDEAL}_{F^m_{OT},\mathsf{Sim}(z)}(1^\lambda), (l_0^1, l_1^1, \ldots, l_0^m, l_1^m), (x_1, \ldots, x_m))\}_{z\in\{0,1\}^\lambda}$$

   where $\mathsf{REAL}_{\Pi,R^\star(z)}(1^\lambda)$ denotes the distribution of the output of the adversary $R^\star$ (controlling the receiver) after a real execution of protocol Π, where the sender S has inputs $(l_0^1, l_1^1, \ldots, l_0^m, l_1^m)$ and the receiver has input $(x_1, \ldots, x_m)$. $\mathsf{IDEAL}_{f,\mathsf{Sim}(z)}(1^\lambda)$ denotes the analogous distribution in an ideal execution with a trusted party that computes F^m_{OT} for the parties and hands the output to the receiver.
2. For every non-uniform PPT adversary $S^\star$ controlling the sender it holds that for every $x_1 \in \{0, 1\}, \ldots, x_m \in \{0, 1\}$ and for every $y_1 \in \{0, 1\}, \ldots, y_m \in \{0, 1\}$:

$$\{\mathsf{View}^R_{\Pi,S^\star(z)}((l_0^1, l_1^1, \ldots, l_0^m, l_1^m), (x_1, \ldots, x_m))\}_{z\in\{0,1\}^\star} \approx$$
$$\{\mathsf{View}^R_{\Pi,S^\star(z)}((l_0^1, l_1^1, \ldots, l_0^m, l_1^m), (y_1, \ldots, y_m))\}_{z\in\{0,1\}^\star}$$

   where $\mathsf{View}^R_{\Pi,S^\star(z)}$ denotes the view of adversary $S^\star$ after a real execution of protocol Π with the honest receiver R.

We remark that in this notions of OT we do not suppose the existence of a simultaneous message exchange channel.

3.4 The OT Protocol $\Pi^\gamma_{OT} = (S_{OT}, R_{OT})$

We use the following tools.

1. A non-interactive perfectly binding, computationally hiding commitment scheme $\mathsf{PBCOM} = (\mathsf{Com}, \mathsf{Dec})$.
2. A trapdoor permutation $\mathcal{F} = (\mathsf{Gen}, \mathsf{Eval}, \mathsf{Invert})$[4] with the hardcore bit function for λ bits $\mathsf{hc}(\cdot)$ (see Definition 3.2).
3. A non-interactive IDTC scheme $\mathsf{TC}_0 = (\mathsf{Sen}_0, \mathsf{Rec}_0, \mathsf{TFake}_0)$ for the $\mathcal{NP}$-language $L_0 = \{\mathtt{com} : \exists\, \mathtt{dec} \text{ s.t. } \mathsf{Dec}(\mathtt{com}, \mathtt{dec}, 0) = 1\}$.

[4] We recall that for convenience, we drop $(f, \mathtt{td})$ from the notation, and write $f(\cdot)$, $f^{-1}(\cdot)$ to denote algorithms $\mathsf{Eval}(f, \cdot)$, $\mathsf{Invert}(f, \mathtt{td}, \cdot)$ respectively, when f, $\mathtt{td}$ are clear from the context. Also we omit the generalization to a family of TDPs.

4. A non-interactive IDTC scheme $\mathsf{TC}_1 = (\mathsf{Sen}_1, \mathsf{Rec}_1, \mathsf{TFake}_1)$ for the $\mathcal{NP}$-language $L_1 = \{\mathtt{com} : \exists\ \mathtt{dec}\ \text{s.t.}\ \mathsf{Dec}(\mathtt{com}, \mathtt{dec}, 1) = 1\}$.

Let $b \in \{0, 1\}$ be the input of $R_{\mathcal{OT}}$ and $l_0, l_1 \in \{0, 1\}^{\lambda}$ be the input of $S_{\mathcal{OT}}$, we now give the description of the protocol following Fig. 3.5.

In the **first round** $R_{\mathcal{OT}}$ runs Com on input the message to be committed b in order to obtain the pair $(\mathtt{com}, \mathtt{dec})$. On input the instance $\mathtt{com}$ and a random string r^1_{b-1}, $R_{\mathcal{OT}}$ runs Sen_{1-b} in order to compute the pair $(\mathtt{tcom}_{1-b}, \mathtt{tdec}_{1-b})$. We observe that the *Instance-Dependent Binding* property of the IDTCs, the description of the $\mathcal{NP}$-language L_{1-b} and the fact that in $\mathtt{com}$ the bit b has been committed, ensure that $\mathtt{tcom}_{1-b}$ can be opened only to the value r^1_{b-1}.[5] $R_{\mathcal{OT}}$ runs the trapdoor procedure of the IDTC scheme TC_b. More precisely $R_{\mathcal{OT}}$ runs TFake_b on input the instance $\mathtt{com}$ to compute the pair $(\mathtt{tcom}_b, \mathtt{aux})$. In this case $\mathtt{tcom}_b$ can be equivocated to any message using the trapdoor (the opening information of $\mathtt{com}$), due to the trapdoorness of the IDTC, the description of the $\mathcal{NP}$-language L_b and the message committed in $\mathtt{com}$ (that is represented by the bit b). $R_{\mathcal{OT}}$ sends $\mathtt{tcom}_0$, $\mathtt{tcom}_1$ and $\mathtt{com}$ to $S_{\mathcal{OT}}$.

In the **second round** $S_{\mathcal{OT}}$ picks two random strings R_0, R_1 and two trapdoor permutations $(f_{0,1}, f_{1,1})$ along with their trapdoors $(f^{-1}_{0,1}, f^{-1}_{1,1})$. Then $S_{\mathcal{OT}}$ sends R_0, R_1, $f_{0,1}$ and $f_{1,1}$ to $R_{\mathcal{OT}}$.

In the **third round** $R_{\mathcal{OT}}$ checks whether or not $f_{0,1}$ and $f_{1,1}$ are valid trapdoor permutations. In the negative case $R_{\mathcal{OT}}$ aborts, otherwise $R_{\mathcal{OT}}$ continues with the following steps. $R_{\mathcal{OT}}$ picks a random string z'_1 and computes $z_1 = f_{b,1}(z'_1)$. $R_{\mathcal{OT}}$ now computes $r^1_b = z_1 \oplus R_b$ and runs TFake_b on input $\mathtt{dec}$, $\mathtt{com}$, $\mathtt{tcom}_b$, $\mathtt{aux}$ and r^1_b in order to obtain the equivocal opening $\mathtt{tdec}_b$ of the commitment $\mathtt{tcom}_b$ to the message r^1_b. $R_{\mathcal{OT}}$ renames r_b to r^1_b and $\mathtt{tdec}_b$ to $\mathtt{tdec}^1_b$ and sends to $S_{\mathcal{OT}}$ $(\mathtt{tdec}^1_0, r^1_0)$ and $(\mathtt{tdec}^1_1, r^1_1)$.

In the **fourth round** $S_{\mathcal{OT}}$ checks whether or not $(\mathtt{tdec}^1_0, r^1_0)$ and $(\mathtt{tdec}^1_1, r^1_1)$ are valid openings w.r.t. $\mathtt{tcom}_0$ and $\mathtt{tcom}_1$. In the negative case $S_{\mathcal{OT}}$ aborts, otherwise $S_{\mathcal{OT}}$ computes $W^1_0 = l_0 \oplus \mathsf{hc}(f^{-\lambda}_{0,1}(r^1_0 \oplus R_0))$ and $W^1_1 = l_1 \oplus \mathsf{hc}(f^{-\lambda}_{1,1}(r^1_1 \oplus R_1))$. Informally $S_{\mathcal{OT}}$ encrypts his inputs l_0 and l_1 through a one-time pad using as a secret key the pre-image of $r^1_0 \oplus R_0$ for l_0 and the pre-image of $r^1_1 \oplus R_1$ for l_1. $S_{\mathcal{OT}}$ also computes two trapdoor permutations $(f_{0,2}, f_{1,2})$ along with their trapdoors $(f^{-1}_{0,2}, f^{-1}_{1,2})$ and sends $(W^1_0, W^1_1, f_{0,2}, f_{1,2})$ to $R_{\mathcal{OT}}$. At this point the third and the fourth rounds are repeated up to $\gamma - 1$ times using fresh randomness as shown in Fig. 3.5. In the last round, no trapdoor permutations are needed/sent.

We observe that a malicious sender $S^{\star}_{\mathcal{OT}}$ could easily understand the input bit of $R_{\mathcal{OT}}$ when $\gamma > 1$. This is not a problem since for the application we need to prove the security of $\Pi^{\gamma}_{\mathcal{OT}}$ to hold against malicious sender only for $\gamma = 1$. We only consider $\gamma = \mathsf{poly}(\lambda)$ when proving the security of $\Pi^{\gamma}_{\mathcal{OT}}$ against malicious receiver.

In the **output phase**, $R_{\mathcal{OT}}$ computes and outputs $l_b = W^1_b \oplus \mathsf{hc}(z'_1)$. That is, $R_{\mathcal{OT}}$ just uses the information gained in the fourth round to compute the output. It is important to observe that $R_{\mathcal{OT}}$ can correctly and efficiently compute the output because

---

[5] $\mathtt{com}$ does not belong to the $\mathcal{NP}$-language L_{b-1}, therefore $\mathtt{tcom}_{1-b}$ is a perfectly binding commitment.

$R_{\mathcal{OT}}(b)$		$S_{\mathcal{OT}}(l_0, l_1)$
$(\mathtt{com}, \mathtt{dec}) \leftarrow \mathsf{Com}(1^\lambda, b)$; $(\mathtt{tcom}_b, \mathtt{aux}) \leftarrow \mathsf{TFake}_b(1^\lambda, \mathtt{com})$; $r_{1-b} \leftarrow \{0,1\}^\lambda$; $(\mathtt{tcom}_{1-b}, \mathtt{tdec}_{1-b}) \leftarrow \mathsf{Sen}_{1-b}(1^\lambda, r_{1-b}, \mathtt{com})$.		
	$\mathtt{com}, \mathtt{tcom}_0, \mathtt{tcom}_1$ $\longrightarrow$	
		$R_0 \leftarrow \{0,1\}^\lambda$; $R_1 \leftarrow \{0,1\}^\lambda$; $(f_{0,1}, f_{0,1}^{-1}) \leftarrow \mathsf{Gen}(1^\lambda)$; $(f_{1,1}, f_{1,1}^{-1}) \leftarrow \mathsf{Gen}(1^\lambda)$.
	$R_0, R_1, f_{0,1}, f_{1,1}$ $\longleftarrow$	
$z'_1 \leftarrow \{0,1\}^\lambda$; $z_1 = f_{b,1}^\lambda(z'_1)$; $r_b^1 = z_1 \oplus R_b$; $\mathtt{tdec}_b^1 \leftarrow \mathsf{TFake}_b(\mathtt{dec}, \mathtt{com}, \mathtt{tcom}_b, \mathtt{aux}, r_b^1)$; $\mathtt{tdec}_{1-b}^1 = \mathtt{tdec}_{1-b}, r_{1-b}^1 = r_{1-b}$.		
	$(\mathtt{tdec}_0^1, r_0^1), (\mathtt{tdec}_1^1, r_1^1)$ $\longrightarrow$	
		$(f_{0,2}, f_{0,2}^{-1}) \leftarrow \mathsf{Gen}(1^\lambda)$; $(f_{1,2}, f_{1,2}^{-1}) \leftarrow \mathsf{Gen}(1^\lambda)$; $W_0^1 = l_0 \oplus \mathsf{hc}(f_{0,1}^{-\lambda}(r_0^1 \oplus R_0))$; $W_1^1 = l_1 \oplus \mathsf{hc}(f_{1,1}^{-\lambda}(r_1^1 \oplus R_1))$.
	$W_0^1, W_1^1, f_{0,2}, f_{1,2}$ $\longleftarrow$	
$z'_2 \leftarrow \{0,1\}^\lambda$; $z_2 = f_{b,2}^\lambda(z'_2)$; $r_b^2 = z_2 \oplus R_b$; $\mathtt{tdec}_b^2 \leftarrow \mathsf{TFake}_b(\mathtt{dec}, \mathtt{com}, \mathtt{tcom}_b, \mathtt{aux}, r_b^2)$; $\mathtt{tdec}_{1-b}^2 = \mathtt{tdec}_{1-b}, r_{1-b}^2 = r_{1-b}$.		
	$(\mathtt{tdec}_0^2, r_0^2), (\mathtt{tdec}_1^2, r_1^2)$ $\longrightarrow$	
		$(f_{0,3}, f_{0,3}^{-1}) \leftarrow \mathsf{Gen}(1^\lambda)$; $(f_{1,3}, f_{1,3}^{-1}) \leftarrow \mathsf{Gen}(1^\lambda)$; $W_0^2 = l_0 \oplus \mathsf{hc}(f_{0,2}^{-\lambda}(r_0^2 \oplus R_0))$; $W_1^2 = l_1 \oplus \mathsf{hc}(f_{1,2}^{-\lambda}(r_1^2 \oplus R_1))$.
	$W_0^2, W_1^2, f_{0,3}, f_{1,3}$ $\longleftarrow$	
	$\vdots$	
	$(\mathtt{tdec}_0^\gamma, r_0^\gamma), (\mathtt{tdec}_1^\gamma, r_1^\gamma)$ $\longrightarrow$	
	W_0^γ, W_1^γ $\longleftarrow$	
Output $l_b = W_b^1 \oplus \mathsf{hc}(z'_1)$.		

Fig. 3.5 Description of $\Pi_{\mathcal{OT}}^\gamma$.

$z' = r_b^1 \oplus R_b$. Moreover $R_{\mathcal{OT}}$ cannot compute l_{1-b} because he has no way to change the value committed in $\mathtt{tcom}_{1-b}$ and invert the TDP since it is supposed to be hard without having the trapdoor.

In order to construct the protocol for two-party computation in the simultaneous message exchange model we need to consider an extended version of $\Pi_{\mathcal{OT}}^\gamma$, that we denote by $\Pi_{\overrightarrow{\mathcal{OT}}}^\gamma = (S_{\overrightarrow{\mathcal{OT}}}, R_{\overrightarrow{\mathcal{OT}}})$. In $\Pi_{\overrightarrow{\mathcal{OT}}}^\gamma$ the $S_{\overrightarrow{\mathcal{OT}}}$'s input is represented by m pairs

$(l_0^1, l_1^1, \ldots, l_0^m, l_1^m)$ and the $R_{\overrightarrow{\mathcal{OT}}}$'s input is represented by the sequence $b_1, \ldots, b_m$ with $b_i \in \{0, 1\}$ for all $i = 1, \ldots, m$. In this case the output of $R_{\overrightarrow{\mathcal{OT}}}$ is $(l_{b_1}, \ldots, l_{b_m})$. We construct $\Pi^{\gamma}_{\overrightarrow{\mathcal{OT}}} = (S_{\overrightarrow{\mathcal{OT}}}, R_{\overrightarrow{\mathcal{OT}}})$ by simply considering m parallel iterations of $\Pi^{\gamma}_{\mathcal{OT}}$ and then we prove that it securely computes $F^m_{\mathcal{OT}}$ with one-sided simulation (see Definition 3.5).

Proof Sketch.

The security proof of $\Pi^{\gamma}_{\mathcal{OT}}$ is divided in two parts. In the former, we prove the security against a malicious sender with $\gamma = 1$ and in the latter we prove the security of $\Pi^{\gamma}_{\mathcal{OT}}$ against a malicious receiver with $\gamma = \mathsf{poly}(\lambda)$. In order to prove the security against malicious sender we recall that for the definition of one-sided simulation, it is just needed that no information about R's input is leaked to $S^\star$. We consider the experiment H_0 where R's input is 0 and the experiment H_1 where R's input is 1 and we prove that $S^\star$ cannot distinguish between H_0 and H_1. More precisely we consider the experiment H^a where $\mathtt{tcom}_0$ and the corresponding opening is computed without using the trapdoor (the randomness of $\mathtt{com}$) and relying on the trapdoorness of the IDTCom TC_0 we prove that $H_0 \approx H^a$. Then we consider the experiment H^b where the value committed in $\mathtt{com}$ goes from 0 to 1 and prove that $H^a \approx H^b$ due to the hiding of $\mathtt{com}$. We observe that this reduction can be made because to compute both H^a and H^b the opening information of $\mathtt{com}$ are not required anymore. The proof ends with the observation that $H^b \approx H_1$ due to the trapdoorness of the IDTCom TC_1.

To prove the security against a malicious receiver $R^\star$ we need to show a simulator Sim. Sim rewinds $R^\star$ from the third to the second round by sending every time freshly generated R_0 and R_1. Sim then checks whether the values r_0^1 and r_1^1 change during the rewinds. We recall that $\mathtt{com}$ is a perfectly binding commitment, therefore only one between $\mathtt{tcom}_0$ and $\mathtt{tcom}_1$ can be opened to multiple values using the trapdoor procedure ($\mathtt{com}$ can belong only to one of the $\mathcal{NP}$-languages L_0 and L_1). Moreover, intuitively, the only way that $R^\star$ can compute the output is by equivocating one between $\mathtt{tcom}_0$ and $\mathtt{tcom}_1$ based on the values R_0, R_1 received in the second round. This means that if during the rewinds the value opened w.r.t. $\mathtt{tcom}_b$ changes, then the input that $R^\star$ is using is b. Therefore the simulator can call the ideal functionality thus obtaining l_b. At this point Sim uses l_b to compute W_b^1 according to the description of $\Pi^{\gamma}_{\mathcal{OT}}$ and sets W_{1-b}^1 to a random string.

Moreover Sim will use the same strategy used to compute W_b^1 and W_{1-b}^1 to compute, respectively W_b^i and W_{1-b}^i for $i = 2, \ldots, \gamma$. In case during the rewinds the value r_0^1, r_1^1 stay the same, then Sim sets both W_0^1 and W_1^1 to random strings. We observe that $R^\star$ could detect that now W_0^1 and W_1^1 are computed in a different way, but this would violate the security of the TDPs.

Theorem 3.1 *Assuming TDPs, for any $\gamma > 0$ $\Pi^{\gamma}_{\overrightarrow{\mathcal{OT}}}$ securely computes $F^m_{\mathcal{OT}}$ with one-sided simulation. Moreover the third round is* replayable.

Proof We first observe that in the third round of $\Pi^{\gamma}_{\mathcal{OT}}$ only the opening information for the IDTCs $\mathtt{tcom}_0$ and $\mathtt{tcom}_1$ are sent. Therefore once a valid third round is received, it is possible to replay it to answer to many second rounds sent by a malicious sender. Roughly, whether the third round of $\Pi^{\gamma}_{\mathcal{OT}}$ is accepting or not is independent of what a malicious sender sends in the second round. Therefore we have proved that $\Pi^{\gamma}_{\mathcal{OT}}$ has a *replayable* third round. In order to prove that $\Pi^{\gamma}_{\mathcal{OT}}$ is one-sided simulatable secure for $F_{\mathcal{OT}}$ (see Definition 3.3) we divide the security proof in two parts; the former proves the security against a malicious sender, and the latter proves the security against a malicious receiver. More precisely we prove that $\Pi^{\gamma}_{\mathcal{OT}}$ is secure against a malicious receiver for an arbitrary chosen $\gamma = \mathsf{poly}(\lambda)$, and is secure against a malicious sender for $\gamma = 1$ (i.e., when just the first four rounds of the protocol are executed).

Security Against a Malicious Sender.

In this case, we just need to prove that the output of $S^{\star}_{\mathcal{OT}}$ of the execution of $\Pi^{\gamma}_{\mathcal{OT}}$ when $R_{\mathcal{OT}}$ interacts with $S^{\star}_{\mathcal{OT}}$ using $b = 0$ as input is computationally indistinguishable from when $R_{\mathcal{OT}}$ uses $b = 1$ as input. The differences between these two hybrid experiments consist of the message committed in $\mathtt{com}$ and how the IDTCs are computed. More precisely, in the first experiment, when $b = 0$ is used as input, $\mathtt{tcom}_0$ and the corresponding opening $(\mathtt{tdec}^1_0, r^1_0)$ are computed using the trapdoor procedure (in this case the message committed in $\mathtt{com}$ is 0), while $\mathtt{tcom}_1$ and $(\mathtt{tdec}^1_1, r^1_1)$ are computed using the *honest* procedure. In the second experiment, $\mathtt{tcom}_0$ and the respective opening $(\mathtt{tdec}^1_0, r^1_0)$ are computed using the honest procedure, while $\mathtt{tcom}_1$ and $(\mathtt{tdec}^1_1, r^1_1)$ are computed using the trapdoor procedure of the IDTC scheme. To prove the indistinguishability between these two experiments, we proceed via hybrid arguments. The first hybrid experiment $\mathcal{H}_1$ is equal to when $R_{\mathcal{OT}}$ interacts with $S^{\star}_{\mathcal{OT}}$ according to $\Pi^{\gamma}_{\mathcal{OT}}$ when $b = 0$ is used as input. In $\mathcal{H}_2$ the honest procedure of IDTC is used instead of the trapdoor one to compute $\mathtt{tcom}_0$ and the opening $(\mathtt{tdec}^1_0, r^1_0)$. We observe that in $\mathcal{H}_2$ both the IDTCs are computed using the honest procedure, therefore no trapdoor information (i.e., the randomness used to compute $\mathtt{com}$) is required. The computational-indistinguishability between $\mathcal{H}_1$ and $\mathcal{H}_2$ comes from the trapdoorness of the IDTC TC_0. In $\mathcal{H}_3$ the value committed in $\mathtt{com}$ goes from 0 to 1. $\mathcal{H}_2$ and $\mathcal{H}_3$ are indistinguishable due to the hiding of PBCOM. It is important to observe that a reduction to the hiding of PBCOM is possible because the randomness used to compute $\mathtt{com}$ is no longer used in the protocol execution to run one of the IDTCs. In the last hybrid experiment $\mathcal{H}_4$ the trapdoor procedure is used to compute $\mathtt{tcom}_1$ and the opening $(\mathtt{tdec}^1_1, r^1_1)$. We observe that it is possible to run the trapdoor procedure for TC_1 because the message committed in $\mathtt{com}$ is 1. The indistinguishability between $\mathcal{H}_3$ and $\mathcal{H}_4$ comes from the trapdoorness of the IDTC. The observation that $\mathcal{H}_4$ corresponds to the experiment where the honest receiver executes $\Pi^{\gamma}_{\mathcal{OT}}$ using $b = 1$ as input concludes the security proof.

Security Against a Malicious Receiver.

To prove that $\Pi^{\gamma}_{\mathcal{OT}}$ is simulation-based secure against malicious receiver $R^{\star}_{\mathcal{OT}}$ we need to show a PPT simulator Sim that, having only access to the ideal world functionality $F_{\mathcal{OT}}$, can simulate the output of any malicious $R^{\star}_{\mathcal{OT}}$ running one execution of $\Pi^{\gamma}_{\mathcal{OT}}$ with an honest sender $S_{\mathcal{OT}}$. The simulator Sim works as follows. Having oracle access to $R^{\star}_{\mathcal{OT}}$, Sim runs as a sender in $\Pi^{\gamma}_{\mathcal{OT}}$ by sending two random strings R_0 and R_1 and the pair of TDPs $f_{0,1}$ and $f_{1,1}$ in the second round. Let $(\mathtt{tdec}^1_0, r^1_0)$, $(\mathtt{tdec}^1_1, r^1_1)$ be the messages sent in the third round by $R^{\star}_{\mathcal{OT}}$. Now Sim rewinds $R^{\star}_{\mathcal{OT}}$ by sending two fresh random strings $\overline{R}_0$ and $\overline{R}_1$ such that $\overline{R}_0 \neq R_0$ and $\overline{R}_1 \neq R_1$.

Let $(\overline{\mathtt{tdec}}^1_0, \overline{r}^1_0)$, $(\overline{\mathtt{tdec}}^1_1, \overline{r}^1_1)$ be the messages sent in the third round by $R^{\star}_{\mathcal{OT}}$ after this rewind, then there are only two things that can happen[6]:

1. $r^1_{b^\star} \neq \overline{r}^1_{b^\star}$ and $r^1_{1-b^\star} = \overline{r}^1_{1-b^\star}$ for some $b^\star \in \{0, 1\}$ or
2. $r^1_0 = \overline{r}^1_0$ and $r^1_1 = \overline{r}^1_1$.

More precisely, due to the perfect binding of PBCOM at most one between $\mathtt{tcom}_0$ and $\mathtt{tcom}_1$ can be opened to a different message. Therefore $R^{\star}_{\mathcal{OT}}$ can either open both $\mathtt{tcom}_0$ and $\mathtt{tcom}_1$ to the same messages r^1_0 and r^1_1, or change in the opening of at most one of them. This yields to the following important observation. If one among r^1_0 and r^1_1 changes during the rewind, let us say $r_{b^\star}$ for $b^\star \in \{0, 1\}$ (case 1), then the input bit used by $R^{\star}_{\mathcal{OT}}$ has to be $b^\star$. Indeed, we recall that the only efficient way (i.e., without inverting the TDP) for a receiver to get the output is to equivocate one of the IDTCs to compute the inverse of one between $R_0 \oplus r^1_0$ and $R_1 \oplus r^1_1$ (a formal argument will follow). Therefore the simulator invokes the ideal world functionality $F_{\mathcal{OT}}$ using $b^\star$ as input, and upon receiving $l_{b^\star}$ computes $W^1_{b^\star} = l_{b^\star} \oplus \mathsf{hc}(f^{-\lambda}_{b^\star,1}(r^1_{b^\star} \oplus R_{b^\star}))$ and sets $W^1_{1-b^\star}$ to a random string. Then sends W^1_0 and W^1_1 with two freshly generated TDPs $f_{0,2}$, $f_{1,2}$ (according to the description of $\Pi^{\gamma}_{\mathcal{OT}}$ given in Fig. 3.5) to $R^{\star}_{\mathcal{OT}}$. Let us now consider the case where the opening of $\mathtt{tcom}_0$ and $\mathtt{tcom}_1$ stay the same after the rewinding procedure (case two). In this case, Sim comes back to the main thread and sets both W^1_0 and W^1_1 to a random string. Intuitively if $R^{\star}_{\mathcal{OT}}$ does not change neither r^1_0 nor r^1_1 after the rewind, then his behavior is not adaptive on the second round sent by Sim. Therefore, he will be able to compute the inverse of neither $R_0 \oplus r^1_0$ nor $R_1 \oplus r^1_1$. That is, both $R_0 \oplus r^1_0$ and $R_1 \oplus r^1_1$ would be the results of the execution of two coin-flipping protocols, therefore both of them are difficult to invert without knowing the trapdoors of the TDPs. This implies that $R^{\star}_{\mathcal{OT}}$ has no efficient way to tell apart whether W^1_0 and W^1_1 are random strings or not.

Completed the fourth round, for $i = 2, \ldots, \gamma$, Sim continues the interaction with $R^{\star}_{\mathcal{OT}}$ by always setting both W^i_0 and W^i_1 to a random string when $r^1_0 = r^i_0$ and $r^1_1 = r^i_1$, and using the following strategy when $r^1_{b^\star} \neq r^i_{b^\star}$ and $r^1_{1-b^\star} = r^i_{1-b^\star}$ for some $b^\star \in \{0, 1\}$. Sim invokes the ideal world functionality $F_{\mathcal{OT}}$ using $b^\star$ as input, and upon receiving $l_{b^\star}$ computes $W^i_{b^\star} = l_{b^\star} \oplus \mathsf{hc}(f^{-\lambda}_{b^\star,i}(r^i_{b^\star} \oplus R_{b^\star}))$, sets $W^i_{1-b^\star}$ to a random

[6] $R^{\star}_{\mathcal{OT}}$ could also abort after the rewind. In this case we use the following standard argument. If p is the probability of $R^{\star}_{\mathcal{OT}}$ of giving an accepting third round, λ/p rewinds are made until $R^{\star}_{\mathcal{OT}}$ gives another answer.

string and sends with them two freshly generated TDPs $f_{0,i+1}, f_{1,i+1}$ to $R^\star_{\mathcal{OT}}$. When the interaction against $R^\star_{\mathcal{OT}}$ is over, Sim stops and outputs what $R^\star_{\mathcal{OT}}$ outputs. We observe that the simulator needs to invoke the ideal world functionality just once. Indeed, we recall that only one of the IDTCs can be equivocated, therefore once the bit $b^\star$ is decided (using the strategy described before) it cannot change during the simulation. The last thing that remains to observe is that it could happen that Sim never needs to invoke the ideal world functionality in the case that: (1) during the rewind the values (r^1_0, r^1_1) stay the same; (2) $r^i_b = r^j_b$ for all $i, j \in \{1, \ldots, \gamma\}$ and all $b = \{0, 1\}$. In this case Sim, even though it does not need to query the ideal functionality to internally complete an interaction with $R^\star_{\mathcal{OT}}$ we assume, without loss of generality, that Sim invokes the ideal functionality by using a random bit $b^\star \in \{0, 1\}$.

We formally prove that the output of Sim is computationally indistinguishable from the output of $R^\star_{\mathcal{OT}}$ in the real world execution for every $\gamma = \mathsf{poly}(\lambda)$. The proof goes through hybrid arguments starting from the real world execution. We gradually modify the real world execution until the input of the honest party is not needed anymore, such that the final hybrid would represent the simulator for the ideal world. We denote by $\mathsf{OUT}_{\mathcal{H}_i, R^\star_{\mathcal{OT}}(z)}(1^\lambda)$ the output distribution of $R^\star_{\mathcal{OT}}$ in the hybrid experiment $\mathcal{H}_i$.

- $\mathcal{H}_0$ is identical to the real execution. More precisely $\mathcal{H}_0$ runs $R^\star_{\mathcal{OT}}$ using fresh randomness and interacts with it as the honest sender would do on input (l_0, l_1).
- $\mathcal{H}_0^{\mathsf{rew}}$ proceeds according to $\mathcal{H}_0$ with the difference that $R^\star_{\mathcal{OT}}$ is rewound up to the second round by receiving two fresh random strings $\overline{R}_0$ and $\overline{R}_1$. This process is repeated until $R^\star_{\mathcal{OT}}$ completes the third round again (every time using different randomness). More precisely, if $R^\star_{\mathcal{OT}}$ aborts after the rewind then a fresh second round is sent up to λ/p times, where p is the probability of $R^\star_{\mathcal{OT}}$ of completing the third round in $\mathcal{H}_0$. If $p = \mathsf{poly}(\lambda)$ then the expected running time of $\mathcal{H}_0^{\mathsf{rew}}$ is $\mathsf{poly}(\lambda)$ and its output is statistically close to the output of $\mathcal{H}_0$. When the third round is completed, the hybrid experiment comes back to the main thread and continues according to $\mathcal{H}_0$
- $\mathcal{H}_1$ proceeds according to $\mathcal{H}_0^{\mathsf{rew}}$ with the difference that after the rewinds it executes the following steps. Let r^1_0 and r^1_1 be the messages opened by $R^\star_{\mathcal{OT}}$ in the third round of the main thread and $\overline{r}^1_0$ and $\overline{r}^1_1$ be the messages opened during the rewind.

We distinguish two cases that could happen:

1. $r^1_0 = \overline{r}^1_0$ and $r^1_1 = \overline{r}^1_1$ or
2. $r^1_{b^\star} \neq \overline{r}^1_{b^\star}$ and $\overline{r}^1_{1-b^\star} = r^1_{1-b^\star}$ for some $b^\star \in \{0, 1\}$.

In this hybrid we assume that the first case happens with non-negligible probability. After the rewind $\mathcal{H}_1$ goes back to the main thread, and to compute the fourth round, picks $W^1_0 \leftarrow \{0, 1\}^\lambda$ computes $W^1_1 = l_1 \oplus \mathsf{hc}(f^{-\lambda}_{1,1}(r^1_1 \oplus R_1)), (f_{0,2}, f^{-1}_{0,2}) \leftarrow \mathsf{Gen}(1^\lambda), (f_{1,2}, f^{-1}_{1,2}) \leftarrow \mathsf{Gen}(1^\lambda)$ and sends $(W^1_0, W^1_1, f_{0,2}, f_{1,2})$ to $R^\star_{\mathcal{OT}}$. Then the experiment continues according to $\mathcal{H}_0$. Roughly, the difference between $\mathcal{H}_0$ and $\mathcal{H}_1$ is that in the latter hybrid experiment W^1_0 is a random string whereas in $\mathcal{H}_1$ $W^1_0 = l_0 \oplus \mathsf{hc}(f^{-\lambda}_{0,1}(r^1_0 \oplus R_0))$.

We now prove that the indistinguishability between $\mathcal{H}_0$ and $\mathcal{H}_1$ comes from the security of the hardcore bit function for λ bits hc for the TDP $\mathcal{F}$. More precisely, assuming by contradiction that the outputs of $\mathcal{H}_0$ and $\mathcal{H}_1$ are distinguishable we construct and adversary $\mathcal{A}^{\mathcal{F}}$ that distinguishes between the output of $\mathsf{hc}(x)$ and a random string of λ bits having as input $f^{\lambda}(x)$. Consider an execution where $R_{\mathcal{OT}}^{\star}$ has non-negligible advantage in distinguishing $\mathcal{H}_0^{\mathsf{rew}}$ from $\mathcal{H}_1$ and consider the randomness ρ used by $R_{\mathcal{OT}}^{\star}$ and the first round computed by $R_{\mathcal{OT}}^{\star}$ in this execution, let us say $\mathtt{com}, \mathtt{tcom}_0, \mathtt{tcom}_1$. $\mathcal{A}^{\mathcal{F}}$, on input the randomness ρ, the messages r_0^1 and r_1^1 executes the following steps.

1. Start $R_{\mathcal{OT}}^{\star}$ with randomness ρ.
2. Let $(f, H, f^{\lambda}(x))$ be the challenge. Upon receiving the first round $(\mathtt{com}, \mathtt{tcom}_0, \mathtt{tcom}_1)$ by $R_{\mathcal{OT}}^{\star}$, compute $R_0 = r_0^1 \oplus f^{\lambda}(x)$, pick a random string R_1, compute $(f_{1,1}, f_{1,1}^{-1}) \leftarrow \mathsf{Gen}(1^{\lambda})$, set $f_{0,1} = f$ and sends $R_0, R_1, f_{0,1}, f_{1,1}$ to $R_{\mathcal{OT}}^{\star}$.
3. Upon receiving $(\mathtt{tdec}_0^1, r_0^1), (\mathtt{tdec}_1^1, r_1^1)$ compute $W_0^1 = l_0 \oplus H$, $W_1^1 = l_1 \oplus \mathsf{hc}(f_{1,1}^{-\lambda}(r_1^1 \oplus R_1))$, $(f_{0,2}, f_{0,2}^{-1}) \leftarrow \mathsf{Gen}(1^{\lambda})$, $(f_{1,2}, f_{1,2}^{-1}) \leftarrow \mathsf{Gen}(1^{\lambda})$ and send $(W_0^1, W_1^1, f_{0,2}, f_{1,2})$.[7]
4. Continue the interaction with $R_{\mathcal{OT}}^{\star}$ according to $\mathcal{H}_1$ (and $\mathcal{H}_0^{\mathsf{rew}}$) and output what $R_{\mathcal{OT}}^{\star}$ outputs.

This part of the security proof ends with the observation that if $H = \mathsf{hc}(x)$ then $R_{\mathcal{OT}}^{\star}$ acts as in $\mathcal{H}_0^{\mathsf{rew}}$, otherwise $R_{\mathcal{OT}}^{\star}$ acts as in $\mathcal{H}_1$.

- $\mathcal{H}_2$ proceeds according to $\mathcal{H}_1$ with the difference that both W_0 and W_1 are set to random strings. Also in this case the indistinguishability between $\mathcal{H}_1$ and $\mathcal{H}_2$ comes from the security of the hardcore bit function for λ bits hc for the family $\mathcal{F}$ (the same arguments of the previous security proof can be used to prove the indistinguishability between $\mathcal{H}_2$ and $\mathcal{H}_1$).
- $\mathcal{H}_3$ In this hybrid experiment we consider the case where after the rewind, with non-negligible probability, $r_{b^\star}^1 \neq \overline{r}_{b^\star}^1$ and $\overline{r}_{1-b^\star}^1 = r_{1-b^\star}^1$ for some $b^\star \in \{0, 1\}$.

In this case, in the main thread, the hybrid experiment computes $W_{b^\star}^1 = l_{b^\star} \oplus \mathsf{hc}(f_{b^\star,1}^{-\lambda}(r_{b^\star}^1 \oplus R_{b^\star}))$, picks $W_{1-b^\star}^1 \leftarrow \{0,1\}^\star$ sends W_0^1, W_1^1 with two freshly generated TDPs $f_{0,2}, f_{1,2}$. $\mathcal{H}_3$ now continues the interaction with $R_{\mathcal{OT}}^{\star}$ according to $\mathcal{H}_2$. The indistinguishability between $\mathcal{H}_2$ and $\mathcal{H}_3$ comes from the security of the hardcore bit function for λ bits hc for the TDP $\mathcal{F}$. More precisely, assuming by contradiction that $\mathcal{H}_2$ and $\mathcal{H}_3$ are distinguishable, we construct and adversary $\mathcal{A}^{\mathcal{F}}$ that distinguishes between the output of $\mathsf{hc}(x)$ and a random string of λ bits having as input $f^{\lambda}(x)$. Consider an execution where $R_{\mathcal{OT}}^{\star}$ has non-negligible advantage in distinguish $\mathcal{H}_2$ from $\mathcal{H}_3$ and consider the randomness ρ used by $R_{\mathcal{OT}}^{\star}$ and the first round computed

[7] Observe that $R_{\mathcal{OT}}^{\star}$ could send values different from r_0^1 and r_1^1 in the third round. In this case $\mathcal{A}^{\mathcal{F}}$ just recomputes the second round using fresh randomness and asking another challenge $\overline{f}, \overline{H}, \overline{f}^{\lambda}(x)$ to the challenger until in the third round the messages r_0^1 and r_1^1 are received again. This allows $\mathcal{A}^{\mathcal{F}}$ to break the security of $\overline{f}$ because we are assuming that in this experiment $R_{\mathcal{OT}}^{\star}$ opens, with non-negligible probability, $\mathtt{tcom}_0$ to r_0^1 and $\mathtt{tcom}_1$ to r_1^1.

in this execution, let us say $\texttt{com}, \texttt{tcom}_0, \texttt{tcom}_1$. $\mathcal{A}^{\mathcal{F}}$, on input the randomness ρ, the message $b^\star$ committed in $\texttt{com}$ and the message $r^1_{1-b^\star}$ committed $\texttt{tcom}_{1-b^\star}$, $\mathcal{A}^{\mathcal{F}}$ executes the following steps.

1. Start $R^\star_{\mathcal{OT}}$ with randomness ρ.
2. Let $(f, H, f^\lambda(x))$ be the challenge. Upon receiving the first round $(\texttt{com}, \texttt{tcom}_0, \texttt{tcom}_1)$ by $R^\star_{\mathcal{OT}}$, compute $R_{1-b^\star} = r^1_{1-b^\star} \oplus f^\lambda(x)$, pick a random string $R_{b^\star}$, computes $(f_{b^\star,1}, f^{-1}_{b^\star,1}) \leftarrow \mathsf{Gen}(1^\lambda)$, sets $f_{1-b^\star,1} = f$ and send $(R_0, R_1, f_{0,1}, f_{1,1})$ to $R^\star_{\mathcal{OT}}$.
3. Upon receiving $(\texttt{tdec}^1_0, r^1_0), (\texttt{tdec}^1_1, r^1_1)$ compute $W^1_{1-b^\star} = l_{1-b^\star} \oplus H$, $W^1_{b^\star} = l_{b^\star} \oplus \mathsf{hc}(f^{-\lambda}_{b^\star,1}(r^1_{b^\star} \oplus R_{b^\star}))$, $(f_{0,2}, f^{-1}_{0,2}) \leftarrow \mathsf{Gen}(1^\lambda)$, $(f_{1,2}, f^{-1}_{1,2}) \leftarrow \mathsf{Gen}(1^\lambda)$ and send $(W^1_0, W^1_1, f_{0,2}, f_{1,2})$.
4. Continue the interaction with $R^\star_{\mathcal{OT}}$ according to $\mathcal{H}_2$ (and $\mathcal{H}_3$) and output what $R^\star_{\mathcal{OT}}$ outputs.

This part of the security proof ends with the observation that if $H = \mathsf{hc}(x)$ then $R^\star_{\mathcal{OT}}$ acts as in $\mathcal{H}_2$, otherwise he acts as in $\mathcal{H}_3$.

– $\mathcal{H}^j_3$ proceeds according to $\mathcal{H}_3$ with the differences that for $i = 2, \ldots, j$

1. if $r^i_{b^\star} \neq r^1_{b^\star}$ for some $b^\star \in \{0, 1\}$ then $\mathcal{H}^j_3$ picks $W^i_{1-b^\star} \leftarrow \{0, 1\}^\lambda$, computes $W^i_{b^\star} = l_{b^\star} \oplus \mathsf{hc}(f^{-\lambda}_{b^\star,i}(r^i_{b^\star} \oplus R_{b^\star}))$ and sends W^i_0, W^i_i with two freshly generated TDPs $f_{0,i+1}, f_{1,i+1}$ to $R^\star_{\mathcal{OT}}$ otherwise
2. $\mathcal{H}^j_3$ picks $W^i_0 \leftarrow \{0, 1\}^\lambda$ and $W^i_1 \leftarrow \{0, 1\}^\lambda$ and sends W^i_0, W^i_1 with two freshly generated TDPs $f_{0,i+1}, f_{1,i+1}$ to $R^\star_{\mathcal{OT}}$.

Roughly speaking, if $R^\star_{\mathcal{OT}}$ changes the opened message w.r.t. $\texttt{tcom}_{b^\star}$, then $W^i_{b^\star}$ is correctly computed and $W^i_{1-b^\star}$ is sets to a random string. Otherwise, if the opening of $\texttt{tcom}_0$ and $\texttt{tcom}_1$ stay the same as in the third round, then both W^i_0 and W^i_1 are random strings (for $i = 2, \ldots, j$). We show that $\mathsf{OUT}_{\mathcal{H}^{j-1}_3, R^\star_{\mathcal{OT}}(z)}(1^\lambda) \approx \mathsf{OUT}_{\mathcal{H}^j_3, R^\star_{\mathcal{OT}}(z)}(1^\lambda)$ in two steps. In the first step we show that the indistinguishability between these two hybrid experiments holds for the first case (when $r^i_{b^\star} \neq r^1_{b^\star}$ for some bit $b^\star$), and in the second step we show that the same holds when $r^i_0 = r^1_0$ and $r^i_1 = r^1_1$.

We first recall that if $r^i_{b^\star} \neq r^1_{b^\star}$, then $\texttt{tcom}_{1-b^\star}$ is perfectly binding, therefore we have that $r^i_{1-b^\star} = r^1_{1-b^\star}$. Assuming by contradiction that $\mathcal{H}^{j-1}_3$ and $\mathcal{H}^j_3$ are distinguishable then we construct and adversary $\mathcal{A}^{\mathcal{F}}$ that distinguishes between the output of $\mathsf{hc}(x)$ and a random string of λ bits having as input $f^\lambda(x)$. Consider an execution where $R^\star_{\mathcal{OT}}$ has non-negligible advantage in distinguishing $\mathcal{H}^{j-1}_3$ from $\mathcal{H}^j_3$ and consider the randomness ρ used by $R^\star_{\mathcal{OT}}$ and the first round computed by $R^\star_{\mathcal{OT}}$ in this execution, let us say $\texttt{com}, \texttt{tcom}_0, \texttt{tcom}_1$. $\mathcal{A}^{\mathcal{F}}$, on input the randomness ρ, the message $b^\star$ committed in $\texttt{com}$ and the message $r^1_{1-b^\star}$ committed $\texttt{tcom}_{1-b^\star}$, executes the following steps.

1. Start $R^{\star}_{\mathcal{OT}}$ with randomness ρ.
2. Let $f, H, f^{\lambda}(x)$ be the challenge. Upon receiving the first round ($\mathtt{com}$, $\mathtt{tcom}_0$, $\mathtt{tcom}_1$) by $R^{\star}_{\mathcal{OT}}$, compute $R_{1-b^\star} = r^1_{1-b^\star} \oplus f^{\lambda}(x)$, pick a random string $R_{b^\star}$, compute $(f_{0,1}, f^{-1}_{0,1}) \leftarrow \mathsf{Gen}(1^\lambda)$ and $(f_{1,1}, f^{-1}_{1,1}) \leftarrow \mathsf{Gen}(1^\lambda)$ send $R_0, R_1, f_{0,1}, f_{1,1}$ to $R^{\star}_{\mathcal{OT}}$.
3. Continue the interaction with $R^{\star}_{\mathcal{OT}}$ according to $\mathcal{H}^{j-1}_3$ using $f_{1-b^\star,j} = f$ instead of using the generation function $\mathsf{Gen}(\cdot)$ when it is required.
4. Upon receiving $(\mathtt{tdec}^j_0, r^j_0)$, $(\mathtt{tdec}^j_1, r^j_1)$ compute $W^j_{1-b^\star} = l_{1-b^\star} \oplus H$,[8] $W^j_{b^\star} = l_{b^\star} \oplus \mathsf{hc}(f^{-\lambda}_{b^\star,j}(r^j_{b^\star} \oplus R_{b^\star}))$, $(f_{0,j+1}, f^{-1}_{0,j+1}) \leftarrow \mathsf{Gen}(1^\lambda)$, $(f_{1,j+1}, f^{-1}_{1,j+1}) \leftarrow \mathsf{Gen}(1^\lambda)$ and sends $(W^{j+1}_0, W^{j+1}_1, f_{0,j+1}, f_{1,j+1})$.
5. Continue the interaction with $R^{\star}_{\mathcal{OT}}$ according to $\mathcal{H}^{j-1}_3$ (and $\mathcal{H}^j_3$) and output what $R^{\star}_{\mathcal{OT}}$ outputs.

This step of the security proof ends with the observation that if $H = \mathsf{hc}(x)$ then $R^{\star}_{\mathcal{OT}}$ acts as in $\mathcal{H}^{j-1}_3$, otherwise he acts as in $\mathcal{H}^j_3$.

The second step of the security proof is almost identical to the proof used to argue the indistinguishability between the outputs of $\mathcal{H}_0$ and $\mathcal{H}_2$.

The entire security proof is almost over, indeed the output of $\mathcal{H}^{\gamma}_3$ corresponds to the output of the simulator Sim and $\mathsf{OUT}_{\mathcal{H}_3, R^{\star}_{\mathcal{OT}}(z)}(1^\lambda) = \mathsf{OUT}_{\mathcal{H}^1_3, R^{\star}_{\mathcal{OT}}(z)}(1^\lambda) \approx \mathsf{OUT}_{\mathcal{H}^2_3, R^{\star}_{\mathcal{OT}}(z)}(1^\lambda) \cdots \approx \mathsf{OUT}_{\mathcal{H}^{\gamma}_3, R^{\star}_{\mathcal{OT}}(z)}(1^\lambda)$. Therefore we can claim that the output of $\mathcal{H}_0$ is indistinguishable from the output of Sim when at most one between l_0 and l_1 is used.

□

Theorem 3.2 *Assuming TDPs, for any $\gamma > 0$ $\Pi^{\gamma}_{\overrightarrow{\mathcal{OT}}}$ securely computes $F^m_{\mathcal{OT}}$ with one-sided simulation. Moreover, the third round is* replayable.

Proof The third round of $\Pi^{\gamma}_{\overrightarrow{\mathcal{OT}}}$ is *replayable* due to the same arguments used in the security proof of Theorem 3.1. We now prove that $\Pi^{\gamma}_{\overrightarrow{\mathcal{OT}}}$ securely computes $F^m_{\mathcal{OT}}$ with one-sided simulation according to Definition 3.5. More precisely, to prove the security against the malicious sender $S^{\star}_{\overrightarrow{\mathcal{OT}}}$ we start by consider the execution $\mathcal{H}_0$ that correspond to the real execution where the input $b_1, \ldots, b_m$ is used by the receiver and then we consider the experiment $\mathcal{H}_i$ where the input used by the receiver is $1 - b_1, \ldots, 1 - b_i, b_{i+1}, \ldots, b_m$. Suppose now by contradiction that the output distributions of $\mathcal{H}_i$ and $\mathcal{H}_{i+1}$ (for some $i \in \{1, m-1\}$) are distinguishable, then we can construct a malicious sender $S^{\star}_{\mathcal{OT}}$ that breaks the security of $\Pi^{\gamma}_{\mathcal{OT}}$ against malicious sender. This allows us to claim that the output distribution of $\mathcal{H}_0$ is indistinguishable from the output distribution of $\mathcal{H}_m$. A similar proof can be made when the malicious party is the receiver. More precisely, we start by consider the execution $\mathcal{H}_0$ that correspond to the real execution where the input $((l^1_0, l^1_1), \ldots, (l^m_0, l^m_1))$ is used by the sender and then we consider the experiment $\mathcal{H}_i$ where the simulator instead of the honest sender procedure is used in the first i parallel executions of $\Pi^{\gamma}_{\mathcal{OT}}$.

[8] It is important to observe that $r^1_{b^\star} = r^j_{b^\star}$.

Supposing by contradiction that the output distributions of $\mathcal{H}_i$ and $\mathcal{H}_{i+1}$ (for some $i \in \{1, m-1\}$) are distinguishable, then we can construct a malicious receiver $R^{\star}_{\mathcal{OT}}$ that breaks the security of $\Pi^{\gamma}_{\mathcal{OT}}$ against malicious sender. We observe that in $\mathcal{H}_i$ in the first i parallel executions of $\Pi^{\gamma}_{\mathcal{OT}}$ the simulator Sim is used and this could disturb the reduction to the security of $\Pi^{\gamma}_{\mathcal{OT}}$ when proving that the output distribution of $\mathcal{H}_i$ is indistinguishable from the output distribution of $\mathcal{H}_{i+1}$. To conclude the security proof we just need to show that Sim's behavior does not disturb the reduction. As described in the security proof of $\Pi^{\gamma}_{\mathcal{OT}}$, the simulation made by Sim roughly works by rewinding from the third to the second round, while from the fourth round onwards Sim works straight line. An important feature enjoyed by Sim is that he maintains the main thread. Let $\mathcal{C}^{\mathcal{OT}}$ be the challenger of $\Pi^{\gamma}_{\mathcal{OT}}$ against malicious receiver, our adversary $R^{\star}_{\mathcal{OT}}$ works as follows.

1. Upon receiving the first round of $\Pi^{\gamma}_{\overrightarrow{\mathcal{OT}}}$ from $R^{\star}_{\overrightarrow{\mathcal{OT}}}$, forward the $(i+1)$-th component ot_1 to $\mathcal{C}^{\mathcal{OT}}$.[9]
2. Upon receiving ot_2 from $\mathcal{C}^{\mathcal{OT}}$ interacts against $R^{\star}_{\overrightarrow{\mathcal{OT}}}$ by computing the second round of $\Pi^{\gamma}_{\overrightarrow{\mathcal{OT}}}$ according to $\mathcal{H}_i$ ($\mathcal{H}_{i+1}$) with the difference that in the $(i+1)$-th position the value ot_2 is used.
3. Upon receiving the third round of $\Pi^{\gamma}_{\overrightarrow{\mathcal{OT}}}$ from $R^{\star}_{\overrightarrow{\mathcal{OT}}}$, forward the $(i+1)$-th component ot_3 to $\mathcal{C}^{\mathcal{OT}}$.
4. Upon receiving ot_4 from $\mathcal{C}^{\mathcal{OT}}$ interacts against $R^{\star}_{\overrightarrow{\mathcal{OT}}}$ by computing the fourth round of $\Pi^{\gamma}_{\overrightarrow{\mathcal{OT}}}$ according to $\mathcal{H}_i$ ($\mathcal{H}_{i+1}$) with the difference that in the $(i+1)$-th position the value ot_4 is used.
5. for $i = 2, \ldots, \gamma$ follow the strategy described in step 3 and 4 and output what $R^{\star}_{\overrightarrow{\mathcal{OT}}}$ outputs.

We recall that in $\mathcal{H}_i$ (as well as in $\mathcal{H}_{i+1}$) in the first i execution of $\Pi^{\gamma}_{\mathcal{OT}}$ the simulator is used, therefore a rewind is made from the third to the second round. During the rewinds, $R^{\star}_{\mathcal{OT}}$ can forward to $R^{\star}_{\overrightarrow{\mathcal{OT}}}$ the same second round ot_2. Moreover, due to the main thread property enjoyed by Sim, after the rewind $R^{\star}_{\mathcal{OT}}$ can continue the interaction against $R^{\star}_{\overrightarrow{\mathcal{OT}}}$ without rewind $\mathcal{C}^{\star}$. Indeed if Sim does not maintain the main thread then, even though the same ot_2 is used during the rewind, $R^{\star}_{\overrightarrow{\mathcal{OT}}}$ could send a different ot_3 making impossible to efficiently continue the reduction. □

[9] We recall that $\Pi^{\gamma}_{\overrightarrow{\mathcal{OT}}}$ is constructed by executing in parallel m instantiations of $\Pi^{\gamma}_{\mathcal{OT}}$, therefore in this reduction we are just replacing the $(i+1)$-th component of every rounds sent to $R^{\star}_{\overrightarrow{\mathcal{OT}}}$ with the value received by $\mathcal{C}^{\mathcal{OT}}$. Vice versa, we forward to $\mathcal{C}^{\star}$ the $(i+1)$-th component of the rounds received from $R^{\star}_{\overrightarrow{\mathcal{OT}}}$.

3.5 Secure 2PC in the Simultaneous Message Exchange Model

Overview of the Protocol $\Pi_{2\mathcal{PC}} = (P_1, P_2)$.

In this section, we give an high-level overview of the 4-round 2PC protocol $\Pi_{2\mathcal{PC}} = (P_1, P_2)$ for every functionality $F = (F_1, F_2)$ in the simultaneous message exchange model. $\Pi_{2\mathcal{PC}}$ consists of two simultaneous symmetric executions of the same subprotocol in which only one party learns the output. We indicate as left execution the execution of the protocol where P_1 learns the output and as right execution the execution of the protocol where P_2 learns the output. In Fig. 3.6 we provide the high level description of the left execution of $\Pi_{2\mathcal{PC}}$. We denoted by (m_1, m_2, m_3, m_4) the messages played in the left execution where (m_1, m_3) are sent by P_1 and (m_2, m_4) are sent by P_2. Likewise, in the right execution of the protocol the messages are denoted by $(\tilde{m}_1, \tilde{m}_2, \tilde{m}_3, \tilde{m}_4)$ where $(\tilde{m}_1, \tilde{m}_3)$ are sent by P_2 and $(\tilde{m}_2, \tilde{m}_4)$ are sent by P_1. Therefore, messages $(m_j, \tilde{m}_j)$ are exchanged simultaneously in the j-th round, for $j \in \{1, \ldots, 4\}$. The construction uses the following tools.

- A non-interactive perfectly binding computationally hiding commitment scheme $\mathsf{PBCOM} = (\mathsf{Com}, \mathsf{Dec})$.
- A Yao's garbled circuit scheme $(\mathsf{GenGC}, \mathsf{EvalGC})$ with simulator SimGC.
- A protocol $\Pi^{\gamma}_{\overrightarrow{\mathcal{OT}}} = (S_{\overrightarrow{\mathcal{OT}}}, R_{\overrightarrow{\mathcal{OT}}})$ that securely computes $F^{m}_{\mathcal{OT}}$ with one-sided simulation.
- A 4-round delayed-input NMZK AoK $\mathsf{NMZK} = (\mathcal{P}_{\mathsf{NMZK}}, \mathcal{V}_{\mathsf{NMZK}})$ for the $\mathcal{NP}$-language L_{NMZK} that will be specified later (see Sect. 3.5.1 for the formal definition of L_{NMZK}).

In Fig. 3.6, we propose the high-level description of the left execution of $\Pi_{2\mathcal{PC}}$ where P_1 runs on input $x \in \{0, 1\}^{\lambda}$ and P_2 on input $y \in \{0, 1\}^{\lambda}$.

3.5.1 *Formal Description of* $\Pi_{2\mathcal{PC}} = (P_1, P_2)$

We first start by defining the following $\mathcal{NP}$-language

$$
\begin{aligned}
L_{\mathsf{NMZK}} = \Big\{ \big(\mathtt{com}_{\mathsf{GC}}, \mathtt{com}_{\mathsf{L}}, \mathsf{GC}, (\mathsf{ot}^1, \mathsf{ot}^2, \mathsf{ot}^3, \mathsf{ot}^4)\big) :&\\
\exists (\mathtt{dec}_{\mathsf{GC}}, \mathtt{dec}_{\mathsf{L}}, \mathsf{input}, \alpha, \beta, \omega) \text{ s.t.}&\\
\big((Z_{1,0}, Z_{1,1}, \ldots, Z_{\lambda,0}, Z_{\lambda,1}, \mathsf{GC}) \leftarrow \mathsf{GenGC}(1^{\lambda}, F_1, \mathsf{input}; \omega)\big) \text{ AND}&\\
\big(\mathsf{Dec}(\mathtt{com}_{\mathsf{L}}, \mathtt{dec}_{\mathsf{L}}, Z_{1,0}||Z_{1,1}||, \ldots, ||Z_{\lambda,0}||Z_{\lambda,1}) = 1\big) \text{ AND}&\\
\big(\mathsf{ot}^1 \text{ and } \mathsf{ot}^3 \text{are obtained by running } R_{\overrightarrow{\mathcal{OT}}} \text{ on input } (1^{\lambda}, \mathsf{input}, \alpha)\big) \text{ AND}&\\
\big(\tilde{\mathsf{ot}}^2 \text{ and } \tilde{\mathsf{ot}}^4 \text{ are obtained by running } S_{\overrightarrow{\mathcal{OT}}} \text{ on input}&\\
(1^{\lambda}, Z_{1,0}, Z_{1,1}, \ldots, Z_{\lambda,0}, Z_{\lambda,1}, \beta)\big)\Big\}.&
\end{aligned}
$$

$P_1(x)$		$P_2(y)$
Run $R_{\overrightarrow{\mathcal{OT}}}$ on input 1^λ, x and randomness α to get ot^1; Run $\mathcal{V}_{\mathsf{NMZK}}$ on input 1^λ to get nmzk^1.		
	$m_1 = (\mathsf{ot}^1, \mathsf{nmzk}^1)$ $\longrightarrow$	
		$(Z_{1,0}, Z_{1,1}, \dots, Z_{\lambda,0}, Z_{\lambda,1}, \mathsf{GC_y}) \leftarrow \mathsf{GenGC}(1^\lambda, F_1, y; \omega)$; $(\mathsf{com_L}, \mathsf{dec_L}) \leftarrow \mathsf{Com}(Z_{1,0}\vert\vert Z_{1,1}\vert\vert, \dots, \vert\vert Z_{\lambda,1})$; $(\mathsf{com_{GC_y}}, \mathsf{dec_{GC_y}}) \leftarrow \mathsf{Com}(\mathsf{GC_y})$; Run $S_{\overrightarrow{\mathcal{OT}}}$ on input 1^λ, ot^1, $(Z_{1,0}, Z_{1,1}, \dots, Z_{\lambda,0}, Z_{\lambda,1})$ and randomness β to get ot^2; Run $\mathcal{P}_{\mathsf{NMZK}}$ on input 1^λ and nmzk^1 to get nmzk^2.
	$m_2 = (\mathsf{com_L}, \mathsf{ot}^2, \mathsf{com_{GC_y}}, \mathsf{nmzk}^2)$ $\longleftarrow$	
Run $R_{\overrightarrow{\mathcal{OT}}}$ on input ot^2 to get ot^3; Run $\mathcal{V}_{\mathsf{NMZK}}$ on input nmzk^2 to get nmzk^3.		
	$m_3 = (\mathsf{c}_0, \mathsf{z}_0, \mathsf{c}_1, \mathsf{z}_1, \mathsf{ot}^3, \mathsf{nmzk}^3)$ $\longrightarrow$	
		Run $S_{\overrightarrow{\mathcal{OT}}}$ on input ot^3 to get ot^4; Run $\mathcal{P}_{\mathsf{NMZK}}$ on input nmzk^3, stm[a] and w_{stm}[b] to get nmzk^4.
	$m_4 = (\mathsf{ot}^4, \mathsf{GC_y}, \mathsf{nmzk}^4)$ $\longleftarrow$	
Run $R_{\overrightarrow{\mathcal{OT}}}$ in input ot^4 thus obtaining $Z_{1,x_1}, \dots, Z_{\lambda,x_\lambda}$; If $\mathcal{V}_{\mathsf{NMZK}}$ on input nmzk^4 and stm outputs 1 output $v = \mathsf{EvalGC}(\mathsf{GC_y}, Z_{1,x_1}, \dots, Z_{\lambda,x_\lambda})$; otherwise output $\bot$.		

[a] Informally, NMZK proves that: 1) P_2 has performed both oblivious transfers correctly using the same input y; 2) the Yao's gabled circuit $\mathsf{GC_y}$ is correctly computed and 3) the value $\mathsf{GC_y}$ sent in the last round represents the message committed in $\mathsf{com_{GC_y}}$.

[b] w_{stm} is s.t. $(\mathsf{stm}, w_{\mathsf{stm}}) \in \mathsf{Rel}_{\mathsf{L_{NMZK}}}$.

Fig. 3.6 High-level description of the left execution of $\Pi_{2\mathcal{PC}}$

The NMZK AoK NMZK used in our protocol is for the $\mathcal{NP}$-language L_{NMZK} described above. Now we are ready to describe our protocol $\Pi_{2\mathcal{PC}} = (P_1, P_2)$ in a formal way.

Protocol $\Pi_{2\mathcal{PC}} = (P_1, P_2)$

Common input: security parameter λ and instance length ℓ_{NMZK} of the statement of the NMZK.

P_1's input: $x \in \{0, 1\}^\lambda$, *P_2's input:* $y \in \{0, 1\}^\lambda$.

Round 1. In this round P_1 sends the message m_1 and P_2 the message $\tilde{m}_1$. The steps computed by P_1 to construct m_1 are the following.

1. Run $\mathcal{V}_{\mathsf{NMZK}}$ on input the security parameter 1^λ and ℓ_{NMZK} thus obtaining the first round nmzk^1 of NMZK.
2. Run $R_{\overrightarrow{OT}}$ on input 1^λ, x and the randomness α thus obtaining the first round ot^1 of $\Pi^{\gamma}_{\overrightarrow{OT}}$.
3. Set $m_1 = (\mathsf{nmzk}^1, \mathsf{ot}^1)$ and send m_1 to P_2.

Likewise, P_2 performs the same actions of P_1 constructing message $\tilde{m}_1 = (\tilde{\mathsf{nmzk}}^1, \tilde{\mathsf{ot}}^1)$.

Round 2. In this round P_2 sends the message m_2 and P_1 the message $\tilde{m}_2$. The steps computed by P_2 to construct m_2 are the following.

1. Compute $(Z_{1,0}, Z_{1,1}, \ldots, Z_{\lambda,0}, Z_{\lambda,1}, \mathsf{GC_y}) \leftarrow \mathsf{GenGC}(1^\lambda, F_2, y; \omega)$.
2. Compute $(\mathtt{com}_{\mathsf{GC_y}}, \mathtt{dec}_{\mathsf{GC_y}}) \leftarrow \mathsf{Com}(\mathsf{GC_y})$ and $(\mathtt{com}_{\mathsf{L}}, \mathtt{dec}_{\mathsf{L}}) \leftarrow \mathsf{Com}(Z_{1,0}||Z_{1,1}||, \ldots, ||Z_{\lambda,0}||Z_{\lambda,1})$.[10]
3. Run $\mathcal{P}_{\mathsf{NMZK}}$ on input 1^λ and nmzk^1 thus obtaining the second round nmzk^2 of NMZK.
4. Run $S_{\overrightarrow{OT}}$ on input 1^λ, $Z_{1,0}, Z_{1,1}, \ldots, Z_{\lambda,0}, Z_{\lambda,1}$, ot^1 and the randomness β thus obtaining the second round ot^2 of $\Pi^{\gamma}_{\overrightarrow{OT}}$.
5. Set $m_2 = (\mathsf{ot}^2, \mathtt{com}_{\mathsf{L}}, \mathtt{com}_{\mathsf{GC_y}}, \mathsf{nmzk}^2)$ and send m_2 to P_1.

Likewise, P_2 performs the same actions of P_1 constructing message $\tilde{m}_2 = (\tilde{\mathsf{ot}}^2, \tilde{\mathtt{com}}_{\mathsf{L}}, \tilde{\mathtt{com}}_{\tilde{\mathsf{GC}}_x}, \tilde{\mathsf{nmzk}}^2)$.

Round 3. In this round P_1 sends the message m_3 and P_2 the message $\tilde{m}_3$. The steps computed by P_1 to construct m_3 are the following.

1. Run $\mathcal{V}_{\mathsf{NMZK}}$ on input nmzk^2 thus obtaining the third round nmzk^3 of NMZK.
2. Run $R_{\overrightarrow{OT}}$ on input ot^2 thus obtaining the third round ot^3 of $\Pi^{\gamma}_{\overrightarrow{OT}}$.
3. Set $m_3 = (\mathsf{nmzk}^3, \mathsf{ot}^3)$ and send m_3 to P_2.

Likewise, P_2 performs the same actions of P_1 constructing message $\tilde{m}_3 = (\tilde{\mathsf{nmzk}}^3, \tilde{\mathsf{ot}}^3)$.

Round 4. In this round P_2 sends the message m_4 and P_1 the message $\tilde{m}_4$. The steps computed by P_2 to construct m_4 are the following.

1. Run $S_{\overrightarrow{OT}}$ on input ot^3, thus obtaining the fourth round ot^4 of $\Pi^{\gamma}_{\overrightarrow{OT}}$.
2. Set $\mathtt{stm} = (\mathtt{com}_{\mathsf{GC_y}}, \mathtt{com}_{\mathsf{L}}, \mathsf{GC_y}, \tilde{\mathsf{ot}}_1, \mathsf{ot}_2, \tilde{\mathsf{ot}}_3, \mathsf{ot}_4)$ and $w_{\mathtt{stm}} = (\mathtt{dec}_{\mathsf{GC_y}}, \mathtt{dec}_{\mathsf{L}}, y, \tilde{\alpha}, \beta, \omega)$.
3. Run $\mathcal{P}_{\mathsf{NMZK}}$ on input nmzk^3, $\mathtt{stm}$ and $w_{\mathtt{stm}}$ thus obtaining the fourth round nmzk^4 of NMZK.
4. Set $m_4 = (\mathsf{nmzk}^4, \mathsf{ot}^4, \mathsf{GC_y})$ and send m_4 to P_1.

---

[10] Instead of one commitment for each label, P_2 commits to the concatenation of all the labels of the garbled circuit $\mathsf{GC_y}$.

Likewise, P_1 performs the same actions of P_2 constructing message $\tilde{m}_4 = (\tilde{\mathsf{nmzk}}^4, \tilde{\mathsf{ot}}^4, \tilde{\mathsf{GC}}_x)$.

Output Computation.

P_1**'s output:** P_1 checks if the transcript $(\mathsf{nmzk}^1, \mathsf{nmzk}^2, \mathsf{nmzk}^3, \mathsf{nmzk}^4)$ is accepting w.r.t. $\mathtt{stm}$. In the negative case P_1 outputs $\perp$, otherwise P_1 runs $R_{\overrightarrow{\mathcal{OT}}}$ on input ot^4 thus obtaining $Z_{1,x_1}, \ldots, Z_{\lambda,x_\lambda}$ and computes the output $v_1 = \mathsf{EvalGC}(\mathsf{GC_y}, Z_{1,x_1}, \ldots, Z_{\lambda,x_\lambda})$.

P_2**'s output:** P_2 checks if the transcript $\tilde{\mathsf{nmzk}}^1, \tilde{\mathsf{nmzk}}^2, \tilde{\mathsf{nmzk}}^3, \tilde{\mathsf{nmzk}}^4$ is accepting w.r.t. $\tilde{\mathtt{stm}}$. In the negative case P_2 outputs $\perp$, otherwise P_2 runs $R_{\overrightarrow{\mathcal{OT}}}$ on input $\tilde{\mathsf{ot}}^4$ thus obtaining $\tilde{Z}_{1,y_1}, \ldots, \tilde{Z}_{\lambda,y_\lambda}$ and computes the output $v_2 = \mathsf{EvalGC}(\tilde{\mathsf{GC}}_x, \tilde{Z}_{1,y_1}, \ldots, \tilde{Z}_{\lambda,y_\lambda})$.

High-Level Overview of the Security Proof. Due to the symmetrical nature of the protocol, it is sufficient to prove the security against one party (let this party be P_2). We start with the description of the simulator Sim. Sim starts the simulator of $\Pi^{\gamma}_{\overrightarrow{\mathcal{OT}}}$ $\mathsf{Sim}_{\mathcal{OT}}$ which outputs the input $y^\star$ used by the malicious party. Sim sends $y^\star$ to the ideal functionality F and receives back $(v_1, v_2) = \big(F_1(x, y^\star), F_2(x, y^\star)\big)$. Then, Sim computes $(\tilde{\mathsf{GC}}_\star, (\tilde{Z}_1, \ldots, \tilde{Z}_\lambda)) \leftarrow \mathsf{SimGC}(1^\lambda, F_2, y^\star, v_2)$ and answer to $\mathsf{Sim}_{\mathcal{OT}}$ using $(\tilde{Z}_1, \ldots, \tilde{Z}_\lambda)$ (we recall that Sim acts as the ideal functionality $F^m_{\mathcal{OT}}$ for $\mathsf{Sim}_{\mathcal{OT}}$). Moreover, instead of committing to the labels of Yao's garbled circuit, in the second round Sim commits to 0 and $\tilde{\mathsf{GC}}_\star$ is sent in the last round. Then Sim runs the simulator $\mathsf{Sim}_{\mathsf{NMZK}}$ of NMZK. For the messages of $\Pi_{\mathcal{OT}}$ where P_1 acts as the receiver, Sim runs $R_{\overrightarrow{\mathcal{OT}}}$ on input 0^λ instead of using x. If the adversary provides an accepting NMZK proof, then Sim instructs the ideal functionality to deliver the output to the ideal-world honest party, otherwise it instructs the honest party to abort.

In our security proof we proceed through a sequence of hybrid experiments, where the first one corresponds to the real-world execution and the final represents the execution of Sim in the ideal world. The core idea of our approach is to run the simulator of NMZK, while extracting the input from $P_2^\star$. By running the simulator of NMZK we are able to guarantee that the value extracted via $\mathsf{Sim}_{\mathcal{OT}}$ is correct, even though $P_2^\star$ is receiving proofs for a false statement. Indeed in each intermediate hybrid experiment that we will consider, also the extractor of NMZK is run in order to extract the witness for the theorem proved by $P_2^\star$. In this way, we can prove that the value extracted via $\mathsf{Sim}_{\mathcal{OT}}$ is consistent with the input that $P_2^\star$ is using in the other part of the protocol (e.g., in the construction of the garbled circuit and in the execution of $\Pi^{\gamma}_{\overrightarrow{\mathcal{OT}}}$ in which the adversary acts as a sender). For what we have discussed, the simulator of NMZK rewinds first from the third to the second round (to extract the trapdoor), and then from the fourth to the third round (to extract the witness for the statement proved by $P_2^\star$). We need to show that these rewinding procedures do not disturb the security proof when we rely on the security of $\Pi^{\gamma}_{\overrightarrow{\mathcal{OT}}}$. This is roughly the reason why we require the third round of $\Pi^{\gamma}_{\overrightarrow{\mathcal{OT}}}$ to be reusable and the security of $\Pi^{\gamma}_{\overrightarrow{\mathcal{OT}}}$ against malicious receiver to hold for any $\gamma = \mathsf{poly}(\lambda)$.

Theorem 3.3 *Assuming TDPs, $\Pi_{2\mathcal{PC}}$ securely computes every two-party functionality $F = (F_1, F_2)$ with black-box simulation.*

Proof In order to prove that $\Pi_{2\mathcal{PC}}$ securely computes $F = (F_1, F_2)$, we first observe that, due to the symmetrical nature of the protocol, it is sufficient to prove the security against one party (let this party be P_2). We now show that for every adversary $P_2^\star$, there exists an ideal-world adversary (simulator) Sim such that for all inputs x, y of equal length and security parameter λ:

$$\{\mathsf{REAL}_{\Pi_{2\mathcal{PC}}, P_2^\star(z)}(1^\lambda, x, y)\} \approx \{\mathsf{IDEAL}_{F, \mathsf{Sim}(z)}(1^\lambda, x, y)\}.$$

Our simulator Sim is the one shown in Sect. 3.5.1.

In our security proof we proceed through a series of hybrid experiments, where the first one corresponds to the execution of $\Pi_{2\mathcal{PC}}$ between P_1 and $P_2^\star$ (real-world execution). Then, we gradually modify this hybrid experiment until the input of the honest party is not needed anymore, such that the final hybrid would represent the simulator (simulated execution).

We now give the descriptions of the hybrid experiments and the corresponding security reductions. We denote the output of $P_2^\star$ and the output of the procedure that interacts against $P_2^\star$ on the behalf of P_1 in the hybrid experiment $\mathcal{H}_i$ with $\{\mathsf{OUT}_{\mathcal{H}_i, P_2^\star(z)}(1^\lambda, x, y)\}_{x\in\{0,1\}^\lambda, y\in\{0,1\}^\lambda}$.

- $\mathcal{H}_0$ corresponds to the real executions. More in detail, $\mathcal{H}_0$ runs $P_2^\star$ with a fresh randomness, and interacts with it as the honest player P_1 does using x as input. The output of the experiment is $P_2^\star$'s view and the output of P_1. Note that we are guarantee from the soundness of NMZK that $\mathsf{stm} \in L_{\mathsf{NMZK}}$, that is: (1)$P_2^\star$ uses the same input $y^\star$ in both the OT executions; (2) the garbled circuit committed in $\mathtt{com}_{\mathsf{GC_y}}$ and the corresponding labels committed in $\mathtt{com}_{\mathsf{L}}$ are computed using the input $y^\star$; (3) the garbled circuit sent in the last round is the one committed in $\mathtt{com}_{\mathsf{GC_y}}$. In the case the adversary does not complete the NMZK proof, then the above does not hold, but in that case the honest party would simply abort, not returning an output. Hence, the fact that the adversary does not use the same input $y^\star$ does not cause any problem.
- $\mathcal{H}_1$ proceeds in the same way of $\mathcal{H}_0$ except that the simulator $\mathsf{Sim}_{\mathsf{NMZK}}$ of NMZK is used in order to compute the messages of NMZK played by P_1. Note that $\mathsf{Sim}_{\mathsf{NMZK}}$ rewinds $P_2^\star$ from the 3rd to the 2nd round to extract the trapdoor. The indistinguishability between the output distribution of these two hybrids experiments holds from the property 1 of NMZK (see Definition 2.17). In this, and also in the next hybrids, we prove that Prob$[\ \mathsf{stm} \notin L_{\mathsf{NMZK}}\ ] \leq \nu(\lambda)$. That is, we prove that $P_2^\star$ behaves honestly across the hybrid experiments even though he is receiving a simulated proof w.r.t. NMZK and $\tilde{\mathsf{stm}}$ does not belong to L_{NMZK}. In this hybrid experiment, we can prove that if by contradiction this probability is non-negligible, then we can construct a reduction that breaks the property 2 of NMZK (see Definition 2.17). Indeed, in this hybrid experiment, the theorem that $P_2^\star$ receives belongs to L_{NMZK} and the simulator of $\mathsf{Sim}_{\mathsf{NMZK}}$ is used to compute

and accepting transcript w.r.t. NMZK. Therefore, relying on property 2 of Definition 2.17 we know that there exists a simulator that extracts the the witness for the statement stm proved by $P_2^\star$ with all but negligible probability.

- $\mathcal{H}_2$ proceeds in the same way of $\mathcal{H}_1$ except that the simulator of $\Pi^{\gamma}_{\overrightarrow{\mathcal{OT}}}$, $\mathsf{Sim}_{\mathcal{OT}}$, is used instead of the sender algorithm $S_{\overrightarrow{\mathcal{OT}}}$. We recall that $\mathsf{Sim}_{\mathcal{OT}}$ requires to interact with the ideal functionality $F^m_{\mathcal{OT}}$. In this case the hybrid experiment $\mathcal{H}_2$ acts on the behalf of the $F^m_{\mathcal{OT}}$ by answering to a query $y^\star$ made by $\mathsf{Sim}_{\mathcal{OT}}$ using the garbled circuit labels $(\tilde{Z}_{1,y_1^\star}, \ldots, \tilde{Z}_{\lambda,y_\lambda^\star})$. To compute the final output, if the adversary provides an accepting NMZK proof, then $\mathcal{H}_2$ runs the simulator-extractor $\mathsf{Sim}_{\mathsf{NMZK}}$, and if the input obtained from the extraction $\overline{y}^\star$ is such that $\overline{y}^\star = y^\star$, then returns $v_1 = F_1(x, y^\star)$, else it aborts. $\mathcal{H}_2$ aborts also in the case where the adversary does not send an accepting NMZK proof.
From the simulatable security against malicious receiver of $\Pi^{\gamma}_{\overrightarrow{\mathcal{OT}}}$ for every $\gamma = \mathsf{poly}(\lambda)$ follows that the output distributions of $\mathcal{H}_2$ and $\mathcal{H}_1$ are indistinguishable. Suppose by contradiction that this claim does not hold, then we can show a malicious receiver $R^\star_{\overrightarrow{\mathcal{OT}}}$ that breaks the simulatable security of $\Pi^{\gamma}_{\overrightarrow{\mathcal{OT}}}$ against a malicious receiver. In more detail, let $C_{\mathcal{OT}}$ be the challenger of $\Pi^{\gamma}_{\overrightarrow{\mathcal{OT}}}$. $R^\star_{\overrightarrow{\mathcal{OT}}}$ plays all the messages of $\Pi_{2\mathcal{PC}}$ as in $\mathcal{H}_1$ ($\mathcal{H}_2$) except for the messages of $\Pi^{\gamma}_{\overrightarrow{\mathcal{OT}}}$. For these messages $R^\star_{\overrightarrow{\mathcal{OT}}}$ acts as a proxy between $C_{\mathcal{OT}}$ and $P_2^\star$. In the end of the execution $R^\star_{\overrightarrow{\mathcal{OT}}}$ runs the distinguisher D that distinguishes $\{\mathsf{OUT}_{\mathcal{H}_1,P_2^\star(z)}(1^\lambda, x, y)\}$ from $\{\mathsf{OUT}_{\mathcal{H}_2,P_2^\star(z)}(1^\lambda, x, y)\}$ and outputs what D outputs. We observe that if $C_{\mathcal{OT}}$ acts as the simulator then $P_2^\star$ acts as in $\mathcal{H}_2$ otherwise he acts as in $\mathcal{H}_1$.
To argue that $\mathrm{Prob}[\ \mathsf{stm} \notin L_{\mathsf{NMZK}}\ ] \leq \nu(\lambda)$, as we mentioned, also in this hybrid experiment we use the simulator-extractor $\mathsf{Sim}_{\mathsf{NMZK}}$ to check whether the theorem proved by $P_2^\star$ is still true. If it is not the case, then we can construct a reduction to the simulatable security against malicious receiver of $\Pi^{\gamma}_{\overrightarrow{\mathcal{OT}}}$. Note that $\mathsf{Sim}_{\mathsf{NMZK}}$ rewinds from the 4th to the 3rd round to extract the witness $w_{\mathtt{stm}}$ for the statement $\mathtt{stm}$ proved by $P_2^\star$. These rewinds could cause $P_2^\star$ to ask multiple third rounds of OT $\tilde{\mathsf{ot}}_i^3$ $(i = 1, \ldots, \mathsf{poly}(\lambda))$. In this case $R^\star_{\overrightarrow{\mathcal{OT}}}$ can simply forward $\tilde{\mathsf{ot}}_i^3$ to $C_{\mathcal{OT}}$ and obtains from $C_{\mathcal{OT}}$ an additional $\tilde{\mathsf{ot}}_i^4$. This behavior of $R^\star_{\overrightarrow{\mathcal{OT}}}$ is allowed because $\Pi^{\gamma}_{\overrightarrow{\mathcal{OT}}}$ is simulatable secure against a malicious receiver even when the last two rounds of $\Pi^{\gamma}_{\overrightarrow{\mathcal{OT}}}$ are executed γ times (as stated in Theorem 3.1). Therefore, the reduction still works if we set γ to the expected number of rewinds that $\mathsf{Sim}_{\mathsf{NMZK}}$ could do. We observe that since we have proved that $\mathsf{stm} \in L_{\mathsf{NMZK}}$, then the value $y^\star$ queried by $\mathsf{Sim}_{\mathcal{OT}}$ corresponds to the input used by $P_2^\star$ in the overall execution of the protocol. That is, $P_2^\star$ uses $y^\star$ to both compute the garbled circuit and to complete the execution $\Pi^{\gamma}_{\overrightarrow{\mathcal{OT}}}$ in which she acts as a sender. On top of this observation, we obtain that in $\mathcal{H}_1$ the value $v_1 = F_1(x, y^\star)$ corresponds, with overwhelming probability, to the valued computed by running the garbled circuit GC_{y} received by $P_2^\star$ using as input the labels $Z_{1,x_1}, \ldots, Z_{\lambda,x_\lambda}$. As observed earlier, in the case

where the adversary does not provide an accepting NMZK proof, then the hybrid simply aborts (no output is computed on the behalf of the honest parties).

- $\mathcal{H}_3$ differs from $\mathcal{H}_2$ in the way the rounds of $\Pi^{\gamma}_{\overrightarrow{\mathcal{OT}}}$, where $P_2^\star$ acts as sender, are computed. More precisely, instead of using x as input, 0^λ is used. We recall that to compute the output we use the same strategy described in the previous hybrids. The indistinguishability between the output distributions of $\mathcal{H}_3$ and $\mathcal{H}_2$ comes from the security of $\Pi^{\gamma}_{\overrightarrow{\mathcal{OT}}}$ against malicious sender. Indeed, suppose by contradiction that it is not the case, then we can show a malicious sender $S^\star_{\overrightarrow{\mathcal{OT}}}$ that breaks the indistinguishability-based security of $\Pi^{\gamma}_{\overrightarrow{\mathcal{OT}}}$ against a malicious sender. In more detail, let $C_{\mathcal{OT}}$ be the challenger. $S^\star_{\overrightarrow{\mathcal{OT}}}$ plays all the messages of $\Pi_{2\mathcal{PC}}$ as in $\mathcal{H}_3$ ($\mathcal{H}_2$) except for the messages of OT where he acts as a receiver. For these messages $S^\star_{\overrightarrow{\mathcal{OT}}}$ plays as a proxy between $C_{\mathcal{OT}}$ and $P_2^\star$. At the end of the execution $S^\star_{\overrightarrow{\mathcal{OT}}}$ runs the distinguisher D that distinguishes $\{\mathsf{OUT}_{\mathcal{H}_2, P_2^\star(z)}(1^\lambda, x, y)\}$ from $\{\mathsf{OUT}_{\mathcal{H}_3, P_2^\star(z)}(1^\lambda, x, y)\}$ and outputs what D outputs. We observe that if $C_{\mathcal{OT}}$ computes the messages of $\Pi^{\gamma}_{\overrightarrow{\mathcal{OT}}}$ using the input 0^λ then $P_2^\star$ acts as in $\mathcal{H}_3$ otherwise he acts as in $\mathcal{H}_2$. In this security proof there is another subtlety. During the reduction $S^\star_{\overrightarrow{\mathcal{OT}}}$ runs $\mathsf{Sim}_{\mathsf{NMZK}}$ that rewinds from the third to the second round. This means that $P_2^\star$ could send multiple different second rounds ot_i^2 of OT (with $i = 1, \ldots, \mathsf{poly}(\lambda)$). $S^\star_{\overrightarrow{\mathcal{OT}}}$ cannot forward these other messages to $C_{\mathcal{OT}}$ (he cannot rewind the challenger). This is not a problem because the third round of $\Pi^{\gamma}_{\overrightarrow{\mathcal{OT}}}$ is replayable (as proved in Theorem 3.1). That is the round ot^3 received from the challenger can be used to answer any ot^2. To prove that $\text{Prob}[\ \mathsf{stm} \notin L_{\mathsf{NMZK}}\ ] \leq \nu(\lambda)$ we use the same arguments as before by observing that the rewinds made by the simulator-extractor from the fourth round to the third one do not affect the reduction.
- $\mathcal{H}_4$ proceeds in the same way of $\mathcal{H}_3$ except for the message committed in $\tilde{\mathsf{com}}_{\mathsf{L}}$. More precisely, instead of computing a commitment of the labels $(\tilde{Z}_{1,0}, \tilde{Z}_{1,1}, \ldots, \tilde{Z}_{\lambda,0}, \tilde{Z}_{\lambda,1})$, a commitment of $0^\lambda || \ldots || 0^\lambda$ is computed. The indistinguishability between the output distributions of $\mathcal{H}_3$ and $\mathcal{H}_4$ follows from the hiding of PBCOM. Moreover, $\text{Prob}[\ \mathsf{stm} \notin L_{\mathsf{NMZK}}\ ] \leq \nu(\lambda)$ in this hybrid experiment due to the same arguments used previously.
- $\mathcal{H}_5$ proceeds in the same way of $\mathcal{H}_4$ except for the message committed in $\tilde{\mathsf{com}}_{\mathsf{GC_y}}$: instead of computing a commitment of the Yao's garbled circuit $\tilde{\mathsf{GC}}_x$, a commitment of 0 is computed. The indistinguishability between the output distributions of $\mathcal{H}_4$ and $\mathcal{H}_5$ follows from the hiding of PBCOM. We have that $\text{Prob}[\ \mathsf{stm} \notin L_{\mathsf{NMZK}}\ ] \leq \nu(\lambda)$ in this hybrid experiment due to the same arguments used previously.
- $\mathcal{H}_6$ proceeds in the same way as $\mathcal{H}_5$ except that the simulator SimGC is run (instead of GenGC) to obtain the Yao's garbled circuit and the corresponding labels. In more detail, once $y^\star$ is obtained by $\mathsf{Sim}_{\mathcal{OT}}$ (in the third round), the ideal functionality F is invoked on input $y^\star$. Upon receiving $(v_1, v_2) = \big(F_1(x, y^\star), F_2(x, y^\star)\big)$ the hybrid experiment compute $(\tilde{\mathsf{GC}}_\star, \tilde{Z}_1, \ldots, \tilde{Z}_\lambda) \leftarrow \mathsf{SimGC}(1^\lambda, F_2, y^\star, v_2)$ and

replies to the query made by $\mathsf{Sim}_{\mathcal{OT}}$ with $(\tilde{Z}_1, \ldots, \tilde{Z}_\lambda)$. Furthermore, in the 4th round the simulated Yao's garbled circuit $\tilde{\mathsf{GC}}_\star$ is sent, instead of the one generated using GenGC. The indistinguishability between the output distributions of $\mathcal{H}_5$ and $\mathcal{H}_6$ follows from the security of Yao's garbled circuit. To prove that $\mathrm{Prob}[\ \mathsf{stm} \notin L_{\mathsf{NMZK}}\ ] \leq \nu(\lambda)$ we use the same arguments as before by observing that the rewinds made by the simulator-extractor from the fourth round to the third one do not affect the reduction.

The proof ends with the observation that $\mathcal{H}_6$ corresponds to the simulated execution with the simulator Sim.

□

Chapter 4
Multi-party Coin-Tossing and Non-malleable-Zero-Knowledge

4.1 Introduction

The first construction of NMZK was given by Dolev et al. in [70]. Later on, Barak in [11] showed the first constant-round construction. An improved construction was then given by Pass and Rosen in [169, 172]. The work of Goyal et al. [99] obtained the first round-optimal construction requiring only 4 rounds and one-way functions (OWFs). Their construction requires the instance and the witness to be known already when the prover plays his first round. Their definition is the standard one-one definition where the adversary opens two sessions, one with a prover and one with a verifier.

The fact that the instance and the witness need to be known already at the second round is an important limitation when NMZK is used as a subprotocol to prove statements about another subprotocol played in parallel. Moreover, the one-one security is an important limitation when NMZK is used in a multi-party scenario where several of such argument systems are played in parallel.

The above two limitations clearly raise the following natural and interesting questions:

Question 1: is there a 4-round delayed-input NMZK argument system?

Question 2: is there a 4-round many-many synchronous NMZK argument system?

Multi-party Coin-Flipping (MPCT).

In [125], Katz et al. obtained a constant-round secure MPC protocol using sub-exponential hardness assumptions. This result was then improved by Pass in [166] that showed how to get bounded-concurrent secure MPC for any functionality with standard assumptions. Further results of Goyal [94] and Goyal et al. [95] relied on better assumptions but with a round complexity still far from optimal.

The work of Garg et al. [84] makes a long jump ahead toward fully understanding the round complexity of secure MPCT. They show that the existence of a 3-round

M. Ciampi and L. Siniscalchi, *Round and Computational Efficiency of Multi-party Protocols*, Information Security and Cryptography,
https://doi.org/10.1007/978-3-031-92374-6_4

3-robust parallel non-malleable commitment scheme implies a 4-round protocol for secure MPCT for polynomially many coins with black-box simulation. Some candidate instantiations of such special commitment scheme are the one of Pass et al. [163] based on non-falsifiable assumptions, or the one of Ciampi et al. [46] (Chap. 6) based on sub-exponentially strong one-to-one one-way functions (see [84, 179] for more details). The achieved round complexity (i.e., 4 rounds) is proven optimal in [84] when the simulation black box and the number of bits in the output of the functionality is superlogarithmic.

The work of Ananth et al. [4] constructs a 4-round MPC protocol for any functionality assuming DDH w.r.t. superpolynomial-time adversaries. The above leaves open the following question.

Question 3: is there a 4-round secure MPCT protocol under standard assumptions?

4.1.1 Contributions of This Chapter

In this chapter, we show how to solve the above 3 problems. More precisely we present the following results:

1. a *delayed-input* 4-round one-*many* NMZK argument Π_{NMZK} from OWFs, therefore solving Question 1; moreover Π_{NMZK} is also a *delayed-input* many-many *synchronous* NMZK argument, therefore solving Question 2;
2. a 4-round MPCT protocol Π_{MPCT} from one-to-one OWFs, therefore solving Question 3.

The two constructions are not uncorrelated. Indeed Π_{MPCT} uses Π_{NMZK} as sub-protocol and exploits the special properties (e.g., delayed input, many-many synchronous) of Π_{NMZK}. Moreover, Π_{MPCT} makes use of a special proof of knowledge that offers additional security guarantees when played in parallel with other protocols. Designing such a proof of knowledge is an additional contribution that we show.

Interestingly, several years after the 4-round zero knowledge argument system from OWFs of [16], the same optimal round complexity and optimal complexity assumptions have been shown sufficient in this work for delayed-input NMZK and in [43] for resettably sound zero knowledge.

More details on the two constructions follow below.

4.1.2 MPCT from NMZK

A first main idea that allows us to bypass the strong requirements of the construction of [84] is that we avoid robust/non-malleable commitments and instead focus on non-malleable zero knowledge. Since we want a 4-round MPCT protocol, we need to rely on 4-round NMZK. The only known construction is the one of [99]. Unfortunately their NMZK argument system seems to be problematic to use in our design of a 4-round MPCT protocol. There are two main reasons. The first reason is that the construction of [99] uses the technique of secure computation in the head and therefore requires the instance already in the second round. This is often a problem when the NMZK argument is played in parallel with other subprotocols as in our construction. Indeed these additional subprotocols end in the 3rd or 4th round and typically[1] need to be strengthened by a zero-knowledge proof of correctness. The second reason is that in the setting of 4-round MPCT the adversary can play as a many-many synchronous man-in-the-middle (MiM), while the construction of [99] is proved one-one non-malleable only.

We therefore improve the state-of-the-art on NMZK constructing a delayed-input NMZK argument system. Our construction only needs one-way functions and is secure even when (a) there are polynomially many verifiers (i.e., it is a one-many NMZK argument), and (b) there are polynomially many provers and they are played in parallel. We will crucially use both the delayed-input property and security with multiple parallelized provers and verifiers in our secure MPCT construction. Our NMZK argument is also crucially used in [49].

4.1.3 *Overview of Our Delayed-Input Parallel NMZK Argument from OWFs*

Issues in Natural Constructions.

A natural construction of a NMZK argument consists of having: (1) a subprotocol (usually a witness-indistinguishable proof of knowledge) useful to extract a trapdoor from the verifier; (2) a non-malleable commitment of the witness for the statement to be proved; (3) a witness-indistinguishable proof of knowledge (WIPoK) to prove that either the committed message is a witness or the trapdoor is known. Combining the above 3 tools in parallel is necessary to obtain a 4-round construction.

The simulator for such a scheme would complete the transcript for the WIPoK by extracting the trapdoor from the verifier and committing to 0 in the non-malleable commitment.

Unfortunately it is not clear how to prove the security of this scheme when all subprotocols are squeezed into 4 rounds. The problem arises from the interactivity nature of the primitives involved, that are: a 3-round non-malleable commitment and two instantiations of a 3-round WIPoK. More precisely the non-malleable commitment is executed in parallel with a 3-round WIPoK Π. When in the security proof the trapdoor is used as witness of Π, the MiM could do the same and also commit to the message 0 in the non-malleable commitment. To detect this behavior, in

[1] Indeed, even the construction of [84] that makes use of a special non-malleable commitments requires also a delayed-input zero-knowledge argument.

order to break the WI of Π, the reduction should extract the message committed in the non-malleable commitment by rewinding it. This implies that also the WIPoK involved in the reduction must be rewound (we recall that these two subprotocols are executed in parallel). It is important to observe that if we allow the MiM to commit to the message 0 then the simulator has no way to extract a witness from the MiM (extraction is required by the definition of NMZK).

A Different Approach.

To overcome this problem, we follow the approach proposed in [48] relying on non-interactive primitives instead of 3-rounds WIPoK. In this way, in every security reduction to such primitives, it will be always possible to extract the message committed in the non-malleable commitment without interfering with the reduction. Therefore, similarly to [48], we construct this WIPoK relying on: statistically binding commitment, instance-dependent trapdoor commitments (IDTCom) and special honest-verifier zero knowledge (HVZK).

More in details, let $(\pi_1, \pi_2, \pi_3, \pi_4)$ be the transcript of a 4-round Special HVZK delayed-input[2] proof of knowledge (PoK) for the $\mathcal{NP}$-language L. We require the prover to send an IDTCom $\mathtt{tcom}_0$ of π_2 that is opened only in the last round, when π_4 is sent. The instance used for the IDTCom is the pair $(\mathtt{com}, 0)$ where $\mathtt{com}$ is a statistically binding commitment. This means that the commitment $\mathtt{tcom}_0$ (computed using IDTCom) can be opened to any value if $\mathtt{com}$ is a valid commitment of the message 0 and the decommitment information of $\mathtt{com}$ is known[3] ($\mathtt{tcom}_0$ is binding otherwise).

The actual transcript for such protocol therefore can be denoted by $(\pi_1, (\mathtt{tcom}_0, \mathtt{com}), \pi_3, (\pi_2, \mathtt{tdec}_0, \pi_4))$ where $\mathtt{com}$ is a valid commitment of the message 0 but the IDTCom is honestly computed (without using the decommitment information of $\mathtt{com}$ in order to open a message different from π_2).

Consider now an experiment where $\mathtt{com}$ is still a commitment of the message 0, but π_2 can be opened arbitrarily using the trapdoor procedure. If the output of this new experiment deviates from the previous one, we will have a reduction to the trapdoorness of the IDTCom. The reduction is not problematic since the challenger of the trapdoorness is non-interactive and just sends a pair (commitment, decommitment) that is either computed using the regular procedure or through the use of the trapdoor. Next, in another experiment we can replace the prover of the adaptive-input PoK with the special HVZK simulator that will compute π_2 and π_4 after having as input π_1 and π_3. Again, the output of this experiment will not deviate from the previous one otherwise we can show an adversary for the Special HVZK property. The reduction again is not problematic since the challenger of Special HVZK is non-interactive.

We observe that if the instance used to compute the IDTCom is false (i.e., the instance used is $(\mathtt{com}, 0)$ but $\mathtt{com}$ is not a commitment of 0) then the protocol described so far is a 3-round adaptive-input PoK for the language L.

---

[2] By *delayed-input* we mean that the witness and the instance are needed only to play the last round.

[3] The decommitment information of $\mathtt{com}$ represents the trapdoor of the IDTCom.

We consider now two instantiations of the protocol described above: Π_0 and Π_1. The instance used to run the IDTCom used in Π_0 is $(\mathtt{com}, 0)$ and the instance used to execute Π_1 is $(\mathtt{com}, 1)$. Basically, the instances used by Π_0 and Π_1 share the same value $\mathtt{com}$. We observe that $\mathtt{com}$ is a statistically binding commitment, therefore it could contain only one message out of 0 and 1. This means that the execution of both Π_0 and Π_1 represents an adaptive-input PoK for the language $L_{\mathsf{OR}} = L_0$ OR L_1. Indeed given that $\mathtt{com}$ is statistically binding, at least one out of the two IDTCom is binding too. Therefore rewinding our protocol using different challenges π_3^0 and π_3^1 yields the extraction of a least one witness. Let's call this protocol (i.e., Π_0 and Π_1 along with a shared $\mathtt{com}$) $\Pi_{\mathcal{WI}}$. We observe that $\Pi_{\mathcal{WI}}$ is still interactive like Π_0 and Π_1. However, if executed in parallel with an interactive protocol, the rewinds made to this protocol do not interfere with the security of $\Pi_{\mathcal{WI}}$. More precisely, it is possible to do all the reductions described above even though the third and the second rounds are rewound. Intuitively, this is true because all the primitive involved in the reductions are non-interactive, and so it is possible to rely on their security even in the case that some rewinds occur.

A NMZK Argument System: NMZK.

We run $\Pi_{\mathcal{WI}}$ in parallel with a 4-round public-coin honest-extractable one-one non-malleable commitment scheme Π_{nm}. The prover now runs $\Pi_{\mathcal{WI}}$ in order to prove either the validity of some $\mathcal{NP}$-statement, or that the non-malleable commitment computed using Π_{nm} contains a trapdoor. The simulator for NMZK works by extracting the trapdoor, then committing to it using the non-malleable commitment, and finally using the knowledge of both the trapdoor and the opening information used to compute the non-malleable commitment, as a witness for $\Pi_{\mathcal{WI}}$. The subprotocol for the trapdoor extraction follows also [48]. More precisely, the trapdoor is represented by the knowledge of two signatures under a verification key sent by the verifier in the 1st round. In order to allow the extraction of the trapdoor, we consider a verifier that sends a signature for a message chosen in the 2nd round by the prover.

On the Limited Non-malleability of the Commitment that is Needed in NMZK.

For our construction we use a 4-round public-coin one-one honest-extractable synchronous non-malleable commitment Π_{nm}. The *public-coin* requirement is due to the security reduction since we will have to simulate the last round of the receiver without knowing the randomness used to compute the previous round. Of course the public-coin property allows such a simulation. Just for simplicity we state our theorems requiring the public-coin property even though our approach can make use of a broader class of protocols. Moreover, we require the existence of a public-coin commitment scheme that is non-malleable only w.r.t. a specific limited adversary: one-one (that opens only one left and one right session) and synchronous (that she aligns the messages of the left sessions with the messages of the right sessions).

Defeating the Issues.

Using such limited non-malleable commitment we are able to prove that our protocol NMZK is one-many NMZK (synchronous many-many NMZK). This is done following the approach provided in [46] where a one-one non-malleable commitment Π_{nm} is used in order to construct a one-many (and then a many-many) non-malleable commitment. Indeed, in our protocol the simulator extracts the trapdoor,[4] and commits to it using the non-malleable commitment scheme. We need to prove that the MiM adversary does not do the same. Roughly, we are requiring only a specific, weaker form of non-malleability just in order to prevent such attack. Therefore, the reduction to the non-malleability of the underling commitment scheme isolates one right session and checks if the MiM has committed to the trapdoor or not. The distinguisher for the non-malleable commitment takes as input the committed message an checks if it corresponds to two signatures of two different messages for a given signature key.

The above approach works only with synchronous sessions. Indeed the non-malleable commitment that we use is secure only in the synchronous case. In order to deal with the asynchronous case we rely on the *honest-extractability* of Π_{nm}. An honest-extractable commitment scheme is a commitment scheme that guarantees the extraction only from honest senders. We recall that $\Pi_{\mathcal{WI}}$ is executed in parallel with Π_{nm} in order to ensure that the MiM either knows a witness for an $\mathcal{NP}$-statement $x \in L$ or the trapdoor has been *correctly* committed using Π_{nm}. For our propose, we only need to ensure that the MiM never commits to the trapdoor and uses it as a witness to execute $\Pi_{\mathcal{WI}}$ in the right sessions. In this way, we can rely on the adaptive-input PoK property of $\Pi_{\mathcal{WI}}$ in order to extract a witness for x even when the simulator is executed. We observe that if by contradiction the MiM (with non-negligible probability) is not using the witness for x to execute $\Pi_{\mathcal{WI}}$, we have that he honestly computes a commitment to the signatures using Π_{nm}. Therefore, we can extract the message committed by the MiM in order to break the hiding of Π_{nm}.[5]

From One-Many NMZK to Parallel Many-Many NMZK.

Fortunately, our scheme is also many-many NMZK when the sessions are parallelized. Indeed, the simulator can extract (simultaneously) the trapdoor from the right sessions, playing as described previously. The only substantial difference is that we need to use a many-one non-malleable commitment with all the properties listed above. Following the approach proposed in the security proof of Proposition 1 provided in [138], it is possible to claim that a synchronous (one-one) non-malleable commitment is also synchronous many-one non-malleable.

---

[4] The trapdoor for our protocol is represented by two signatures for a verification key chosen by the verifier.

[5] A rewind made in an asynchronous session does not interfere with (i.e., does not rewind) the challenger of the hiding of Π_{nm}. This part of the proof actually deals with more interesting subtleties. We refer the reader to the formal proof for more details.

We end this section by observing that a non-malleable commitment scheme that enjoys all the properties that we require is provided in [97][6] and relies on OWFs. Also the IDTCom, the Special HVZK adaptive-input PoK and the statistically binding commitment can be constructed assuming OWFs only.

A Special WIPoK Π_{OR}.

In order to construct our MPC coin-tossing protocol Π_{MPCT}, we also propose a generic approach for a special WIPoK Π_{OR} that can be nicely composed with other protocols in parallel in the same spirit of $\Pi_{\mathcal{WI}}$. The main difference with $\Pi_{\mathcal{WI}}$ is that our special WIPoK Π_{OR} can be used only when the theorem to be proved is known in the beginning of the protocol (which is sufficient for our MPC application).

In a nutshell, Π_{OR} takes two instantiations of the three-move Special HVZK PoK (like as in Blum's protocol [22]) and composes them via the OR composition proposed in [57] thus obtaining a WIPoK. Using this WIPoK a reduction can be successfully completed even when there are rewinds due to other protocols played in parallel.

In more detail, we combine together two executions of Blum's protocol by using the trick for composing two three-move Special HVZK PoKs Σ_0, Σ_1 to construct a three-move Special HVZK PoK for the $\mathcal{NP}$-language L_0 OR L_1 [57]. Let (x_0, x_1) be the compound statement to be proved, with $x_0 \in L_0$ and $x_1 \in L_1$, and let w_b be the witness for x_b. The protocol Π_{OR} proposed in [57] executes Σ_0 and Σ_1 (respectively for L_0 and L_1) in parallel, but after receiving the challenge c from the verifier, the prover can use as challenges for Σ_0 and Σ_1 every pair (c_0, c_1) s.t. $c_0 \oplus c_1 = c$. Therefore the prover could choose in advance one of the challenges to be used (e.g., c_{1-b}), and compute the other one by setting $c_b = c \oplus c_{1-b}$. In this way, the transcript for Σ_{1-b} can be computed using the Special HVZK simulator while the transcript for Σ_b is computed using the witness w_b. Thus the prover has the "freedom" of picking one out of two challenges before seeing c, but still being able to complete the executions of both Σ_0 and Σ_1 for every c. We will show that this "freedom" is sufficient to switch from the use of w_0 to the use of w_1 (in order to prove WI) even when it is required to answer to additional (and different) challenges $c^1, \ldots, c^{\mathsf{poly}(\lambda)}$ (i.e., when some rewinds occur). Indeed it is possible to switch the witness used (from w_0 to w_1) in two steps relying first on the Special HVZK of Σ_1, and then on the Special HVZK of Σ_0. More precisely we consider the hybrid experiment H^{w_0} as the experiment where in Π_{OR} the witness w_0 is used (analogously we define H^{w_1}). We now consider H^{w_0,w_1} that differs from H^{w_0} because both the witnesses w_0 and w_1 are used. We prove that H^{w_0} and H^{w_0,w_1} are indistinguishable due to the Special HVZK of Σ_1 even though Π_{OR} is rewound polynomially many times. The reduction works as follows. A challenge c_1 is chosen before the protocol Π_{OR} starts and the

[6] In order to ensure non-malleability against a non-synchronous adversary the construction of Goyal et al. modifies Π and uses assumptions w.r.t. a quasi-polynomial-time adversary. For our propose, we just need to use the basic protocol Π of [97] that relies on assumptions w.r.t. polynomial-time adversaries.

Special HVZK challenger is invoked thus obtaining (a_1, z_1). The transcript for Σ_0 is computed by the reduction using the witness w_0 in order to answer to the challenge $c_0^i = c^i \oplus c_1$ for $i = 1, \ldots, \mathsf{poly}(\lambda)$. We recall that we are in a setting where Π_{OR} could be rewound, and therefore the reduction needs to answer to multiple challenges. We observe that the reduction to the Special HVZK is not disturbed by these rewinds because c_1 can be kept fixed. The same arguments can be used to prove that H^{w_0,w_1} is computationally indistinguishable from H^{w_1}. We also notice that Π_{OR} remains a PoK [57].

4.1.4 4-Round Secure Multi-party Coin Tossing

The MPCT protocol will critically make use of our delayed-input synchronous many-many NMZK from OWFs, and of a special WIPoK Π_{OR}. Similarly to [84] our protocol consists of each party committing to a random string r, that is then sent in the clear in the last round. Moreover there will be a simulatable proof of correctness of the above commitment w.r.t. r, that is given to all parties independently. The output consists of the $\bigoplus$ of all opened strings. We now discuss in more detail the construction of a the special WIPoK Π_{OR} and the messages exchanged by a pair of parties P_1 and P_2 in our multi-party coin tossing protocol Π_{MCF}. The generalization to n players is straightforward and discussed in Sect. 4.3.1.

Informal Description of the Protocol.

P_1, using a perfectly binding computationally hiding commitment scheme, commits in the first round to a random string r_1 two times thus obtaining $\mathtt{com}_0, \mathtt{com}_1$. Moreover P_1 runs Π_{OR} in order to prove knowledge of either the message committed in $\mathtt{com}_0$ or the message committed in $\mathtt{com}_1$. In the last (fourth) round P_1 sends r_1. In parallel, an execution of a NMZK ensures that both $\mathtt{com}_0$ and $\mathtt{com}_1$ contain the same message r_1 (that is sent in the fourth round).[7] When P_1 receives the last round that contains r_2, P_1 computes and outputs $r_1 \oplus r_2$. P_2 symmetrically executes the same steps using as input r_2.

The simulator for Π_{MCF} runs the simulator of NMZK and extracts the input $r^\star$ from the malicious party using the PoK extractor of Π_{OR}. At this point, the simulator invokes the functionality thus obtaining r and plays in the last round $r_s = r \oplus r^\star$. Note that the values that the simulator commits in $\mathtt{com}_0$ and $\mathtt{com}_1$ are unrelated to r_s and this is possible because the NMZK is simulated. The extraction of the input from the adversary made by the simulator needs more attention. Indeed the security of NMZK will ensure that, even though the simulator cheats (he commits to a random string in both $\mathtt{com}_0$ and $\mathtt{com}_1$) the adversary cannot do the same. Therefore the only way he can complete an execution of Π_{MCF} consists of committing two times to $r^\star$ in the first round, and of sending the same value in the fourth round. This means that

[7] Notice here how crucial is the delayed-input property of the synchronous many-many NMZK.

the value extracted (in the third round) from the PoK extractor of Π_{OR} is the input of the malicious party.

Our security proof consists of showing the indistinguishability of a sequence of hybrid experiments where the first hybrid corresponds to the real-world experiment, and the last hybrid corresponds to the simulated experiment. The second hybrid experiment differs from the real game because the simulator of NMZK is used (instead of the honest prover). The simulator, in order to extract the trapdoor from the adversary, rewinds from the third to the second round, thus rewinding also Π_{OR}. Indeed the adversary, for every different second round of the NMZK could sent a different second round for Π_{OR}. This becomes a problem when we consider the hybrid experiment H_i where the witness for Π_{OR} changes. Due to the rewinds made by the simulator of the NMZK it is not clear how to rely on the security of the WI property of Π_{OR} (the challenger of WI would be rewound). This is the reason why we need to consider an intermediate hybrid experiment H^{w_0,w_1} where both witnesses of Π_{OR} can be used. Then we can prove the indistinguishability between H^{w_0,w_1} and H_i still relying on the Special HVZK of the sub-protocol used in Π_{OR} (which is Blum's protocol).

More Related Works on NMZK

Other works have focusing on optimizing the other aspects of non-malleable zero-knowledge (not just round complexity). In particular, [130] proposes a (constant-round) protocol based on one-way functions, which introduces new techniques to achieve efficiency while living in Minicrypt. In a later work [26], the authors show how to achieve the same results (with a reduced round, but still not optimal round complexity) by relying on black-box use of one-way functions.

4.2 4-Round Delayed-Input NMZK from OWFs

4.2.1 Overview of the Protocol

For our construction of a 4-round delayed-input non-malleable zero knowledge $\mathsf{NMZK} = (\mathcal{P}_{\mathsf{NMZK}}, \mathcal{V}_{\mathsf{NMZK}})$ we use the following tools.

1. A signature scheme $\Sigma = (\mathsf{Gen}, \mathsf{Sign}, \mathcal{V})$;
2. A 2-round statistically binding, computationally hiding commitment scheme $\mathsf{PBCOM} = (\mathsf{Com}, \mathsf{Dec})$.
3. A 4-round public-coin synchronous honest-extractable one-one non-malleable commitment scheme $\mathsf{NM} = (\mathcal{S}, \mathcal{R})$ that fixes the opening information in the second round.
4. A 2-round IDTC scheme $\mathsf{TC}_0 = (\mathsf{Sen}_0, \mathsf{Rec}_0, \mathsf{TFake}_0)$ for the $\mathcal{NP}$-language $L_0 = \{(\mathtt{com}, 0) : \exists\ \mathtt{dec}$ s.t. Dec accepts $\mathtt{dec}$ as a decommitment of $\mathtt{com}$ to $0\}$.

5. A 2-round IDTC scheme $\mathsf{TC}_1 = (\mathsf{Sen}_1, \mathsf{Rec}_1, \mathsf{TFake}_1)$ for the $\mathcal{NP}$-language $L_1 = \{(\mathtt{com}, 1) : \exists\ \mathtt{dec}$ s.t. Dec accepts $\mathtt{dec}$ as a decommitment of $\mathtt{com}$ to $1\}$.
6. A 4-round delayed-input public-coin Special HVZK $\mathsf{LS}_L = (\mathcal{P}_L, \mathcal{V}_L)$ for the $\mathcal{NP}$-language L that is adaptive-input PoK for the corresponding relation $\mathsf{Rel_L}$.
7. A 4-round delayed-input public-coin Special HVZK $\mathsf{LS_{nm}} = (\mathcal{P}_{\mathsf{nm}}, \mathcal{V}_{\mathsf{nm}})$ for the following $\mathcal{NP}$-language

$$L_{\mathsf{nm}} = \{(\mathsf{vk}, \tau = (\mathtt{id}, \mathsf{nm}_1, \mathsf{nm}_2, \mathsf{nm}_3, \mathsf{nm}_4), s_1 : \exists(\mathtt{dec}_{\mathsf{nm}}, s_0, \sigma_1, \mathtt{msg}_1, \sigma_2, \mathtt{msg}_2) \text{ s.t.}$$
$$\mathcal{V}(\mathsf{vk}, \mathtt{msg}_1, \sigma_1) = 1 \text{ AND } \mathcal{V}(\mathsf{vk}, \mathtt{msg}_2, \sigma_2) = 1 \text{ AND } \mathtt{msg}_1 \neq \mathtt{msg}_2 \text{ AND}$$
$$\mathcal{R} \text{ accepts } (\mathtt{id}, s_0, \mathtt{dec}_{\mathsf{nm}}) \text{ as a valid decommitment of } \tau \text{ AND } s_0 \oplus s_1 = \sigma_1 || \sigma_2\}$$

that is adaptive-input PoK for the corresponding relation $\mathsf{Rel}_{\mathsf{L_{nm}}}$.
Informally by running $\mathsf{LS_{nm}}$ one can prove that s_0 is committed using a non-malleable commitment and $s_0 \oplus s_1 = \sigma_1 || \sigma_2$. Moreover σ_1 and σ_2 are two signatures for two different messages w.r.t. the verification key vk.

4.2.1.1 Formal Protocol Description: NMZK

We now give a high-level description of our delayed-input non-malleable ZK protocol depicted in Fig. 4.1. For a formal description, see Fig. 4.2.

In the **first round** $\mathcal{V}_{\mathsf{NMZK}}$ computes a signature-verification key pair $(\mathsf{sk}, \mathsf{vk})$ and sends vk to $\mathcal{P}_{\mathsf{NMZK}}$. $\mathcal{V}_{\mathsf{NMZK}}$ computes and sends a (public coin) first rounds ls^1_L of LS_L and the first round $\mathsf{ls}^1_{\mathsf{nm}}$ of $\mathsf{LS_{nm}}$. $\mathcal{V}_{\mathsf{NMZK}}$ computes and sends a first rounds nm_1 of NM. Finally, $\mathcal{V}_{\mathsf{NMZK}}$ computes and sends a fresh first round of Naor's commitment for the remaining tools listed above involved in the construction. To not overburden the notation we omit these additional messages.

In the **second round** $\mathcal{P}_{\mathsf{NMZK}}$ runs Com on input the bit 1 thus obtaining $\mathtt{com}$, $\mathtt{dec}$ (where $\mathtt{com}$ represents the statistically binding commitment of the bit 1). $\mathcal{P}_{\mathsf{NMZK}}$ sends $\mathtt{com}$, computes ls^2_L by running $\mathcal{P}_L$ on input ls^1_L and commits to it using the 2-round IDTC scheme TC_0. More precisely, $\mathcal{P}_{\mathsf{NMZK}}$ runs Sen_0 on input the instance $(\mathtt{com}, 0)$ and the message to be committed ls^2_L in order to compute the pair $(\mathtt{tcom}_0, \mathtt{tdec}_0)$ and sends $\mathtt{tcom}_0$. We observe that the commitment $\mathtt{tcom}_0$ is binding because of the Instance-Dependent Binding property enjoyed by the IDTC scheme (the instance used to compute $\mathtt{tcom}_0$ is false, indeed $\mathtt{com}$ is a commitment of the bit 1). $\mathcal{P}_{\mathsf{NMZK}}$ now runs the trapdoor procedure of the IDTC scheme TC_1. More precisely, $\mathcal{P}_{\mathsf{NMZK}}$ runs TFake_1 on input the instance $(\mathtt{com}, 1)$ to compute the pair $(\mathtt{tcom}_1, \mathtt{aux})$ and then sends $\mathtt{tcom}_1$ to $\mathcal{V}_{\mathsf{NMZK}}$. In this case $\mathtt{tcom}_1$ can be equivocated to any message using the trapdoor (the opening information of $\mathtt{com}$) due to the trapdoorness of the IDTC scheme. $\mathcal{P}_{\mathsf{NMZK}}$ now starts the procedure to commit to a random message s_0 using the non-malleable commitment NM. So, he runs $\mathcal{S}$ on input s_0, the identity $\mathtt{id}$ and nm_1 thus obtaining $(\mathsf{nm}_2, \mathtt{dec}_{\mathsf{nm}})$ and then sends nm_2.[8] In addition, $\mathcal{P}_{\mathsf{NMZK}}$ sends a random message $\mathtt{msg}$.

---

[8] We recall that the decommitment information of the non-malleable commitment scheme can be computed together with the second (the first in this informal description) round of the protocol.

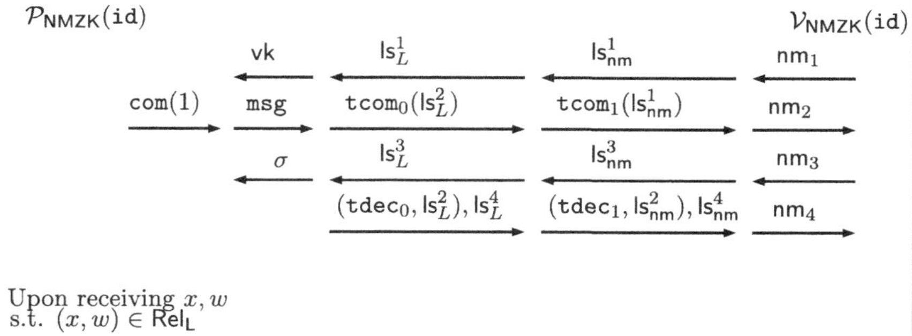

- com is the commitment of the bit 1 computed using PBCOM.
- vk is a a verification key of a signature scheme and σ is a valid signature of the message msg.
- $\tau_L = (\mathsf{ls}_L^1, \mathsf{ls}_L^2, \mathsf{ls}_L^3, \mathsf{ls}_L^4)$ is the transcript output from the honest prover procedure of LS_L proving knowledge of the witness for $x \in L$.
- $\mathtt{tcom}_0$ is the commitment of ls_L^2 computed using the honest sender procedure of the IDTC TC_0. $\mathtt{tdec}_0$ represents the decommitment information of $\mathtt{tcom}_0$.
- $\mathtt{tcom}_1$ is computed using the trapdoor procedure of TC_1. $\mathtt{tdec}_1$ represents the decommitment information (computed using the trapdoor procedure of TC_1) of $\mathtt{tcom}_1$ w.r.t. the message $\mathsf{ls}_{\mathsf{nm}}^2$.
- s_0, s_1 are random strings.
- $\tau = (\mathtt{id}, \mathsf{nm}_1, \mathsf{nm}_2, \mathsf{nm}_3, \mathsf{nm}_4)$ represents the transcript of $\langle \mathcal{S}(s_0), \mathcal{R}\rangle(\mathtt{id})$ that is, a commitment of the message s_0 computed using the synchronous honest-extractable one-one non-malleable commitment scheme NM.
- $\tau_{\mathsf{nm}} = (\mathsf{ls}_{\mathsf{nm}}^1, \mathsf{ls}_{\mathsf{nm}}^2, \mathsf{ls}_{\mathsf{nm}}^3, \mathsf{ls}_{\mathsf{nm}}^4)$ is the transcript output of a Special HVZK simulator of $\mathsf{LS}_{\mathsf{nm}}$ proving knowledge of a decommitment of τ to the message s_0 s.t. $s_0 \oplus s_1 = \sigma_1 || \sigma_2$ where σ_1, σ_2 are two signatures of two different messages w.r.t vk.

Fig. 4.1 Our 4-round delayed-input NMZK AoK

In the **third round** of the protocol $\mathcal{V}_{\mathsf{NMZK}}$, upon receiving msg, computes and sends a signature σ of msg by running $\mathsf{Sign}(\mathsf{sk}, \mathtt{msg})$. Also, $\mathcal{V}_{\mathsf{NMZK}}$ computes and sends all the (public coin) second rounds ls_L^3, $\mathsf{ls}_{\mathsf{nm}}^3$, nm_3 for the respective protocols LS_L, $\mathsf{LS}_{\mathsf{nm}}$ and NM.

In the **fourth round** $\mathcal{P}_{\mathsf{NMZK}}$ checks whether or not σ is a valid signature for msg w.r.t. the verification key vk. In the negative case $\mathcal{P}_{\mathsf{NMZK}}$ aborts, otherwise he continues with the following steps. Upon receiving the instance x to be proven and the witness w s.t. $(x, w) \in \mathsf{Rel_L}$, $\mathcal{P}_{\mathsf{NMZK}}$ completes the transcript for LS_L thus obtaining ls_L^4 by running the prover procedure $\mathcal{P}_L$ on input x, w and ls_L^3. At this point $\mathcal{P}_{\mathsf{NMZK}}$ can send the opening $(\mathtt{tdec}_0, \mathsf{ls}_L^2)$ for the commitment $\mathtt{tcom}_0$ computed in the second round, and completes an accepting transcript for LS_L for the instance x by sending ls_L^4.

$\mathcal{P}_{\mathsf{NMZK}}$ completes the commitment of s_0 by running $\mathcal{S}$ on input nm_3 thus obtaining nm_4 and sends nm_4. $\mathcal{P}_{\mathsf{NMZK}}$ picks a random string s_1, sets $x_{\mathsf{nm}} = (\mathsf{vk}, \mathtt{id}, (\mathsf{nm}_1, \mathsf{nm}_2, \mathsf{nm}_3, \mathsf{nm}_4), s_1)$ and runs the Special HVZK simulator of $\mathsf{LS}_{\mathsf{nm}}$

Common input: security parameter λ, identity $\mathtt{id} \in \{0,1\}^\lambda$, lengths for LS_L and $\mathsf{LS}_{\mathsf{nm}}$: ℓ_x, ℓ_{nm}.
Input to $\mathcal{P}_{\mathsf{NMZK}}$: (x, w) s.t. $(x, w) \in \mathsf{Rel_L}$, with (x, w) available only in the 4th round.
Commitment phase:

1. $\mathcal{V}_{\mathsf{NMZK}} \rightarrow \mathcal{P}_{\mathsf{NMZK}}$
   1. Run $(\mathsf{sk}, \mathsf{vk}) \leftarrow \mathsf{Gen}(1^\lambda)$.
   2. Run $\mathcal{V}_L$ on input 1^λ and ℓ_x thus obtaining the 1st round ls^1_L of LS_L.
   3. Run $\mathcal{V}_{\mathsf{nm}}$ on input 1^λ and ℓ_{nm} thus obtaining the 1st round $\mathsf{ls}^1_{\mathsf{nm}}$ of $\mathsf{LS}_{\mathsf{nm}}$.
   4. Run Dec on input 1^λ thus obtaining ρ.
   5. Run Rec_0 on input 1^λ thus obtaining ρ_0.
   6. Run Rec_1 on input 1^λ thus obtaining ρ_1.
   7. Run $\mathcal{R}$ on input 1^λ and $\mathtt{id}$ thus obtaining nm_1.
   8. Send $(\mathsf{vk}, \mathsf{ls}^1_L, \mathsf{ls}^1_{\mathsf{nm}}, \mathsf{nm}_1, \rho, \rho_0, \rho_1)$ to $\mathcal{P}_{\mathsf{NMZK}}$.
2. $\mathcal{P}_{\mathsf{NMZK}} \rightarrow \mathcal{V}_{\mathsf{NMZK}}$
   1. Run Com on input ρ and message 1 in order to compute the pair $(\mathtt{com}, \mathtt{dec})$.
   2. Run $\mathcal{P}_L$ on input 1^λ, ℓ_x and ls^1_L thus obtaining the 2nd round ls^2_L of LS_L.
   3. Run Sen_0 on input 1^λ, $((\rho, \mathtt{com}), 0)$, ρ_0 and message ls^2_L to compute the pair $(\mathtt{tcom}_0, \mathtt{tdec}_0)$.
   4. Run TFake_1 on input 1^λ, $((\rho, \mathtt{com}), 1), \rho_1$ to compute the pair $(\mathtt{tcom}_1, \mathtt{aux})$.
   5. Pick $s_0 \leftarrow \{0,1\}^\lambda$ and run $\mathcal{S}$ on input 1^λ, $\mathtt{id}$, nm_1, s_0 (in order to commit to the message s_0) thus obtaining nm_2.
   6. Pick a message $\mathtt{msg} \leftarrow \{0,1\}^\lambda$ and send $(\mathtt{com}, \mathtt{tcom}_0, \mathtt{tcom}_1, \mathtt{msg}, \mathsf{nm}_2)$ to $\mathcal{V}_{\mathsf{NMZK}}$.
3. $\mathcal{V}_{\mathsf{NMZK}} \rightarrow \mathcal{P}_{\mathsf{NMZK}}$
   1. Run $\mathcal{V}_L$ thus obtaining the 3rd round ls^3_L of LS_L.
   2. Run $\mathcal{V}_{\mathsf{nm}}$ thus obtaining the 3rd round $\mathsf{ls}^3_{\mathsf{nm}}$ of $\mathsf{LS}_{\mathsf{nm}}$.
   3. Run $\mathcal{R}$ thus obtaining nm_3 of NM.
   4. Run $\mathsf{Sign}(\mathsf{sk}, \mathtt{msg})$ to obtain a signature σ of $\mathtt{msg}$.
   5. Send $(\mathsf{ls}^3_L, \mathsf{ls}^3_{\mathsf{nm}}, \mathsf{nm}_3, \sigma)$ to $\mathcal{P}_{\mathsf{NMZK}}$.
4. $\mathcal{P}_{\mathsf{NMZK}} \rightarrow \mathcal{V}_{\mathsf{NMZK}}$
   1. If $\mathcal{V}(\mathsf{vk}, \mathtt{msg}, \sigma) \neq 1$ then abort, continue as follows otherwise.
   2. Run $\mathcal{P}_L$ on input x, w and ls^3_L thus obtaining the 4th round ls^4_L of LS_L.
   3. Run $\mathcal{S}$ on input nm_3 thus obtaining $(\mathsf{nm}_4, \mathsf{dec}_{\mathsf{nm}})$.
   4. Pick $s_1 \leftarrow \{0,1\}^\lambda$ and set $x_{\mathsf{nm}} = (\mathsf{vk}, \mathsf{nm}_1, \mathsf{nm}_2, \mathsf{nm}_3, \mathsf{nm}_4, s_1)$ and run the Special HVZK simulator of $\mathsf{LS}_{\mathsf{nm}}$ on input $(x_{\mathsf{nm}}, \mathsf{ls}^1_{\mathsf{nm}}, \mathsf{ls}^3_{\mathsf{nm}})$ thus obtaining $(\mathsf{ls}^2_{\mathsf{nm}}, \mathsf{ls}^4_{\mathsf{nm}})$.
   5. Run TFake_1 on input $\mathtt{tk} = (\mathtt{dec})$, ρ_1, $\mathtt{tcom}_1$, $\mathtt{aux}$ and $\mathsf{ls}^2_{\mathsf{nm}}$ to compute $\mathtt{tdec}_1$.
   6. Send $((\mathtt{tdec}_1, \mathsf{ls}^2_{\mathsf{nm}}), \mathsf{ls}^4_{\mathsf{nm}}, (\mathtt{tdec}_0, \mathsf{ls}^2_L), \mathsf{ls}^4_L, x, x_{\mathsf{nm}})$ to $\mathcal{V}_{\mathsf{NMZK}}$.
5. $\mathcal{V}_{\mathsf{NMZK}}$: output 1 iff the following conditions are satisfied.
   1. Rec_0 on input $(\rho_0, (\rho, \mathtt{com}), 0)$, $\mathtt{tcom}_0$, $\mathtt{tdec}_0$, ls^2_L accepts $(\mathsf{ls}^2_L, \mathtt{tdec}_0)$ as a decommitment of $\mathtt{tcom}_0$.
   2. Rec_1 on input $(\rho_1, (\rho, \mathtt{com}), 1)$, $\mathtt{tcom}_1$, $\mathtt{tdec}_1$, $\mathsf{ls}^2_{\mathsf{nm}}$ accepts $(\mathsf{ls}^2_{\mathsf{nm}}, \mathtt{tdec}_1)$ as a decommitment of $\mathtt{tcom}_1$.
   3. $(\mathsf{ls}^1_L, \mathsf{ls}^2_L, \mathsf{ls}^3_L, \mathsf{ls}^4_L)$ is accepting for $\mathcal{V}_L$ with respect to the instance x.
   4. $(\mathsf{ls}^1_{\mathsf{nm}}, \mathsf{ls}^2_{\mathsf{nm}}, \mathsf{ls}^3_{\mathsf{nm}}, \mathsf{ls}^4_{\mathsf{nm}})$ is accepting for $\mathcal{V}_{\mathsf{nm}}$ with respect to the instance x_{nm}.

Fig. 4.2 Formal construction of the delayed-input NMZK AoK

on input $(x_{\mathsf{nm}}, \mathsf{ls}^1_{\mathsf{nm}}, \mathsf{ls}^3_{\mathsf{nm}})$ thus obtaining $(\mathsf{ls}^2_{\mathsf{nm}}, \mathsf{ls}^4_{\mathsf{nm}})$. Now $\mathcal{P}_{\mathsf{NMZK}}$ opens the trapdoor commitment $\mathtt{tcom}_1$ to $\mathsf{ls}^2_{\mathsf{nm}}$. More precisely he runs TFake_1 on input $\mathtt{tk} = (\mathtt{dec})$, $\mathtt{tcom}_1$, $\mathtt{aux}$ and $\mathsf{ls}^2_{\mathsf{nm}}$ in order to compute $\mathtt{tdec}_1$ and sends $((\mathtt{tdec}_1, \mathsf{ls}^2_{\mathsf{nm}}), \mathsf{ls}^4_{\mathsf{nm}}, x_{\mathsf{nm}})$ to $\mathcal{V}_{\mathsf{NMZK}}$. We recall that $\mathtt{tcom}_1$ has been computed in *trapdoor mode* in the

second round of the protocol using the instance $(\mathtt{com}, 1)$, where $\mathtt{com}$ is a valid commitment of the bit 1.
The verifier $\mathcal{V}_{\mathsf{NMZK}}$ **accepts** x iff the following conditions are satisfied.

1. Rec_0 on input $(\mathtt{com}, 0), \mathtt{tcom}_0, (\mathtt{tdec}_0, \mathsf{ls}_L^2)$ accepts $(\mathsf{ls}_L^2, \mathtt{tdec}_0)$ as a decommitment of $\mathtt{tcom}_0$ (we recall that $(\mathtt{com}, 0)$ is the instance used to run the algorithms of the IDTC scheme TC_0).
2. Rec_1 on input $(\mathtt{com}, 1), \mathtt{tcom}_1, (\mathtt{tdec}_1, \mathsf{ls}_{\mathsf{nm}}^2)$ accepts $(\mathsf{ls}_{\mathsf{nm}}^2, \mathtt{tdec}_1)$ as a decommitment of $\mathtt{tcom}_1$ (we recall that $(\mathtt{com}, 1)$ is the instance used to run the algorithms of the IDTC scheme TC_1).
3. $(\mathsf{ls}_L^1, \mathsf{ls}_L^2, \mathsf{ls}_L^3, \mathsf{ls}_L^4)$ is accepting for $\mathcal{V}_L$ with respect to the instance x.
4. $(\mathsf{ls}_{\mathsf{nm}}^1, \mathsf{ls}_{\mathsf{nm}}^2, \mathsf{ls}_{\mathsf{nm}}^3, \mathsf{ls}_{\mathsf{nm}}^4)$ is accepting for $\mathcal{V}_{\mathsf{nm}}$ with respect to the instance x_{nm}.

The simulator extractor. Informally, the simulator $\mathsf{Sim}_{\mathsf{NMZK}}$ of our protocol interacts with the adversary $\mathcal{A}_{\mathsf{NMZK}}$ by emulating both the prover in the left session and polynomially many verifiers in the right sessions. In the left sessions $\mathsf{Sim}_{\mathsf{NMZK}}$ interacts with $\mathcal{A}_{\mathsf{NMZK}}$ as the honest verifiers do. While, in the right session for an instance $x \in L$ chosen adaptively by $\mathcal{A}_{\mathsf{NMZK}}$, $\mathsf{Sim}_{\mathsf{NMZK}}$ equivocates the commitment computed using TC_0, and runs the SHVZK simulator of LS_L to completes the transcript for LS_L w.r.t. the instance x. In order to use the trapdoor procedure of TC_0 the simulator has to commit to 0 in $\mathtt{com}$. In this way the commitment computed using TC_1 becomes statistically binding, therefore the transcript for $\mathsf{LS}_{\mathsf{nm}}$ needs to be computed using the honest prover procedure. We recall that the transcript for $\mathsf{LS}_{\mathsf{nm}}$ proves (in the sense of knowledge of a witness) that the message committed in NM contains a value s_0[9] such $s_0 \oplus s_1$ corresponds to two signatures (σ_1, σ_2)[10] of two different messages w.r.t. the verification key vk (s_1 is sent in clear in the fourth round). In order to compute these s_0 and s_1, $\mathsf{Sim}_{\mathsf{NMZK}}$ extracts two signatures for two different messages rewinding $\mathcal{A}_{\mathsf{NMZK}}$ from the third to the second round. We use this trick following [46] in order to avoid any additional requirement. Indeed if the sender of NM is delayed-input (i.e., the message to be committed can be decided in the last round), then $\mathsf{Sim}_{\mathsf{NMZK}}$ can simply compute the first round of NM, extract the signatures, and compute the last round of NM committing to the signatures. It is important to observe that even though the non-malleable commitment scheme of [97] fixes the message to be committed in the third round, there is no guarantee that the scheme is secure against an adversary that adaptively chooses the challenge messages in the last round of the non-malleability security game. Therefore, even though the completeness of our scheme would work without using the trick of [46], it would be unclear, in this case, how to prove the security of our scheme. A formal description of $\mathsf{Sim}_{\mathsf{NMZK}}$ can be found in the proof of Theorem 4.1.

The formal construction of our delayed-input NMZK AoK $\mathsf{NMZK} = (\mathcal{P}_{\mathsf{NMZK}}, \mathcal{V}_{\mathsf{NMZK}})$ is showed in Fig. 4.2. The security proof of our protocol follows below.

[9] For ease of exposition we will simply say that $\mathcal{A}_{\mathsf{NMZK}}$ commits to two signatures using NM.

[10] W.l.o.g. we assume that the signatures σ_1, σ_2 include the signed messages.

Theorem 4.1 *If OWFs exist, then* NMZK *is a delayed-input NMZK AoK for $\mathcal{NP}$.*

Proof We divide the security proof in two parts, proving that NMZK enjoys delayed-input completeness and non-malleable ZK; the proof of NMZK is divided in two additional lemmas, one for each of the two properties of Definition 2.17. Before that, we recall that $\mathsf{LS}_{\mathsf{nm}}$ and LS_L can be constructed from OWFs as well as Σ using [181]. The 4-round public-coin synchronous honest-extractable non-malleable commitment scheme NM can be instantiated from OWFs, as well as PBCOM [154]. We also observe that if PBCOM relies on OWFs, then also TC_0 and TC_1 can be constructed from OWFs (see [48]).

(Delayed-Input) Completeness. The completeness follows directly from the completeness of $\mathsf{LS}_{\mathsf{nm}}$ and LS_L, the correctness of PBCOM, NM, TC_0, TC_1 and the validity of Σ. We observe that, due to the delayed-input property of LS_L, the statement x and the respective witness w are needed by $\mathcal{P}_{\mathsf{NMZK}}$ only to compute the last round; therefore NMZK enjoys delayed-input completeness as well.

(Delayed-Input) NMZK. Following Definition 2.17 we start by describing how the simulator $\mathsf{Sim}_{\mathsf{NMZK}}$ for NMZK works. In the left session $\mathsf{Sim}_{\mathsf{NMZK}}$ interacts with the MiM adversary $\mathcal{A}_{\mathsf{NMZK}}$ in the following way. Upon receiving the first round, vk, ls_L^1, $\mathsf{ls}_{\mathsf{nm}}^1$, nm_1, ρ_0, ρ_1, ρ, from $\mathcal{A}_{\mathsf{NMZK}}$, $\mathsf{Sim}_{\mathsf{NMZK}}$ runs Com on input ρ and the message 0 in order to obtain $\mathtt{com}$, $\mathtt{dec}$. Furthermore, $\mathsf{Sim}_{\mathsf{NMZK}}$ on input $\mathsf{ls}_{\mathsf{nm}}^1$ computes $\mathsf{ls}_{\mathsf{nm}}^2$ by running $\mathcal{P}_{\mathsf{nm}}$ and commits to it using the IDTC scheme TC_1. More precisely, $\mathsf{Sim}_{\mathsf{NMZK}}$ runs Sen_1 on input the instance $((\rho, \mathtt{com}), 0)$, ρ_1 and message to be committed $\mathsf{ls}_{\mathsf{nm}}^2$ thus obtaining the pair $(\mathtt{tcom}_1, \mathtt{tdec}_1)$. Then $\mathsf{Sim}_{\mathsf{NMZK}}$ runs the trapdoor procedure of the IDTC scheme TC_0. That is, $\mathsf{Sim}_{\mathsf{NMZK}}$ runs TFake_0 on input the instance $((\rho, \mathtt{com}), 0)$ and ρ_0 thus obtaining the pair $(\mathtt{tcom}_0, \mathtt{aux})$. $\mathsf{Sim}_{\mathsf{NMZK}}$, in order to commit to a random message s_0 uses the scheme NM, runs $\mathcal{S}$ on input nm_1, the identity $\mathtt{id}$ and s_0 thus obtaining nm_2. $\mathsf{Sim}_{\mathsf{NMZK}}$ sends $\mathtt{tcom}_0$, $\mathtt{tcom}_1$, nm_2, $\mathtt{com}$ and a random message $\mathtt{msg}_1$ to $\mathcal{A}_{\mathsf{NMZK}}$.

Upon receiving the third round (ls_L^3, $\mathsf{ls}_{\mathsf{nm}}^3$, nm_3, σ_1) and the instance x to be proved from $\mathcal{A}_{\mathsf{NMZK}}$, the simulator checks whether or not σ_1 is a valid signature for $\mathtt{msg}_1$ w.r.t. the verification key vk. In the negative case $\mathsf{Sim}_{\mathsf{NMZK}}$ aborts, otherwise he rewinds $\mathcal{A}_{\mathsf{NMZK}}$ from the third to the second round in order to obtain a second signature σ_2 for a different message $\mathtt{msg}_2$. After the extraction of the signatures $\mathsf{Sim}_{\mathsf{NMZK}}$ returns to the execution that he started before the rewinding procedure (that we will denote as the main thread) and computes the fourth round as follows.[11]

$\mathsf{Sim}_{\mathsf{NMZK}}$ completes the commitment of s_0 by running $\mathcal{S}$ on input nm_3 thus obtaining (nm_4, $\mathtt{dec}_{\mathsf{nm}}$) and then sending nm_4. Furthermore, $\mathsf{Sim}_{\mathsf{NMZK}}$ sets s_1 s.t. $s_1 = (\sigma_1||\sigma_2) \oplus s_0$, $x_{\mathsf{nm}} = (\mathsf{vk}, \mathtt{id}, \mathsf{nm}_1, \mathsf{nm}_2, \mathsf{nm}_3, \mathsf{nm}_4, s_1)$, $w_{\mathsf{nm}} = (\mathtt{dec}_{\mathsf{nm}}, s_0, \sigma_1, \mathtt{msg}_1, \sigma_2, \mathtt{msg}_2)$ and completes the transcript for $\mathsf{LS}_{\mathsf{nm}}$ thus obtaining $\mathsf{ls}_{\mathsf{nm}}^4$ by running the prover procedure $\mathcal{P}_{\mathsf{nm}}$ on input x_{nm}, w_{nm} and $\mathsf{ls}_{\mathsf{nm}}^3$. Then the values $((\mathtt{tdec}_1, \mathsf{ls}_{\mathsf{nm}}^2), \mathsf{ls}_{\mathsf{nm}}^4, x_{\mathsf{nm}})$ are sent to $\mathcal{A}_{\mathsf{NMZK}}$. At this point $\mathsf{Sim}_{\mathsf{NMZK}}$ runs the SHVZK simulator of LS_L on input $(x, \mathsf{ls}_L^1, \mathsf{ls}_L^3)$ thus obtaining $(\mathsf{ls}_L^2, \mathsf{ls}_L^4)$. Then

[11] Note that it is possible to complete the main thread, due to the delayed-input of $\mathsf{LS}_{\mathsf{nm}}$, and to the fact that we do not need to change the first round of NM (that is, we do not need to change the committed message s_0) in order to have $x_{\mathsf{nm}} \in L_{\mathsf{nm}}$.

$\mathsf{Sim}_{\mathsf{NMZK}}$ opens, using the trapdoor procedure, the commitment $\mathtt{tcom}_0$ to ls_L^2. More precisely, $\mathsf{Sim}_{\mathsf{NMZK}}$ runs TFake_0 on input $\mathtt{tk} = (\mathtt{dec})$, ρ_0, $\mathtt{tcom}_0$, $\mathtt{aux}$ and ls_L^2 in order to compute $\mathtt{tdec}_0$ and sends $((\mathtt{tdec}_0, \mathsf{ls}_L^2), \mathsf{ls}_L^4, x)$ to $\mathcal{A}_{\mathsf{NMZK}}$.

At the end of the execution $\mathsf{Sim}_{\mathsf{NMZK}}$ outputs $\mathcal{A}_{\mathsf{NMZK}}$'s view in the main thread. Furthermore, he uses the extractor of LS_L to extract and output, from the $\mathsf{poly}(\lambda)$ right sessions, the witnesses $\tilde{w}_1, \ldots, \tilde{w}_{\mathsf{poly}(\lambda)}$ used by $\mathcal{A}_{\mathsf{NMZK}}$ to compute the transcript of LS_L (the witnesses correspond to statements $\tilde{x}_i$ proved by $\mathcal{A}_{\mathsf{NMZK}}$ in the i-th right session, for $i = 1, \ldots, \mathsf{poly}(\lambda)$).

Lemma 4.1 $\{\mathsf{Sim}_{\mathsf{NMZK}}{}^1(1^\lambda, z)\}_{\lambda\in\mathbb{N}, z\in\{0,1\}^*} \approx \{\mathsf{View}^{\mathcal{A}_{\mathsf{NMZK}}}(1^\lambda, z)\}_{\lambda\in\mathbb{N}, z\in\{0,1\}^*}$, *where* $\mathsf{Sim}_{\mathsf{NMZK}}{}^1(1^\lambda, z)$ *denotes the 1st output of* $\mathsf{Sim}_{\mathsf{NMZK}}$.

In order to prove the above lemma we consider the series of hybrid experiments described below. In the proof we denote with $\{\mathsf{View}_{\mathcal{H}_i}^{\mathcal{A}_{\mathsf{NMZK}}}(1^\lambda, z)\}_{\lambda\in\mathbb{N}, z\in\{0,1\}^*}$ the random variable that describes the view of $\mathcal{A}_{\mathsf{NMZK}}$ in the hybrid $\mathcal{H}_i(1^\lambda, z)$. Let p be the probability that in the real execution, $\mathcal{A}_{\mathsf{NMZK}}$ completes the left session.

- We start considering the hybrid experiment $\mathcal{H}_0(1^\lambda, z)$ in which in the left session $\mathcal{P}_{\mathsf{NMZK}}$ interacts with $\mathcal{A}_{\mathsf{NMZK}}$ and in the i-th right session $\mathcal{V}_{\mathsf{NMZK}i}$ interacts with $\mathcal{A}_{\mathsf{NMZK}}$, for $i = 1, \ldots, \mathsf{poly}(\lambda)$. Note that $\{\mathsf{View}_{\mathcal{H}_0}^{\mathcal{A}_{\mathsf{NMZK}}}(1^\lambda, z)\}_{\lambda\in\mathbb{N}, z\in\{0,1\}^*} = \{\mathsf{View}_{\mathsf{NMZK}}^{\mathcal{A}}(1^\lambda, z)\}_{\lambda\in\mathbb{N}, z\in\{0,1\}^*}$.
- The hybrid experiment $\mathcal{H}_1(1^\lambda, z)$ differs from $\mathcal{H}_0(1^\lambda, z)$ only in the fact that in the left session of $\mathcal{H}_1(1^\lambda, z)$ $\mathcal{A}_{\mathsf{NMZK}}$ is rewound from the third to the second round, in order to extract two signatures σ_1, σ_2 for two distinct messages $(\mathtt{msg}_1, \mathtt{msg}_2)$ w.r.t. a verification key vk. Note that after $1/p$ rewinds the probability of not obtaining a valid new signature is less than $1/2$. Therefore the probability that $\mathcal{A}_{\mathsf{NMZK}}$ does not give a second valid signature for a randomly chosen message after λ/p rewinds is negligible in λ. For the above reason the procedure of extraction of signatures of different messages in $\mathcal{H}_1(1^\lambda, z)$ succeeds except with negligible probability. Observe that the above deviation increases the abort probability of the experiment only by a negligible amount, therefore $\{\mathsf{View}_{\mathcal{H}_0}^{\mathcal{A}_{\mathsf{NMZK}}}(1^\lambda, z)\}_{\lambda\in\mathbb{N}, z\in\{0,1\}^*} \equiv_s \{\mathsf{View}_{\mathcal{H}_1}^{\mathcal{A}_{\mathsf{NMZK}}}(1^\lambda, z)\}_{\lambda\in\mathbb{N}, z\in\{0,1\}^*}$.
- The hybrid experiment $\mathcal{H}_2(1^\lambda, z)$ differs from $\mathcal{H}_1(1^\lambda, z)$ only in the message committed using NM. Indeed $\mathcal{P}_{\mathsf{NMZK}}$ commits using NM to two signatures σ_1, σ_2 of two distinct messages $(\mathtt{msg}_1, \mathtt{msg}_2)$ instead of a random message. In more details, $\mathcal{P}_{\mathsf{NMZK}}$ commits to a random string s_0 using NM and in the 4th round sets and sends $s_1 = (\sigma_1||\sigma_2) \oplus s_0$, instead of sending $s_1 \leftarrow \{0,1\}^\lambda$. Observe that the procedure to extract the signatures succeeds in $\mathcal{H}_2(1^\lambda, z)$ with overwhelming probability because the first three rounds are played exactly as in $\mathcal{H}_1(1^\lambda, z)$. Now we can claim that $\{\mathsf{View}_{\mathcal{H}_2}^{\mathcal{A}_{\mathsf{NMZK}}}(1^\lambda, z)\}_{\lambda\in\mathbb{N}, z\in\{0,1\}^*}$ and $\{\mathsf{View}_{\mathcal{H}_1}^{\mathcal{A}_{\mathsf{NMZK}}}(1^\lambda, z)\}_{\lambda\in\mathbb{N}, z\in\{0,1\}^*}$ are computationally indistinguishable by using the computational hiding property of NM. Suppose by contradiction that there exist an adversary $\mathcal{A}_{\mathsf{NMZK}}$ and a distinguisher $\mathcal{D}_{\mathsf{ZK}}$ such that $\mathcal{D}_{\mathsf{ZK}}$ distinguishes $\{\mathsf{View}_{\mathcal{H}_1}^{\mathcal{A}_{\mathsf{NMZK}}}(1^\lambda, z)\}_{\lambda\in\mathbb{N}, z\in\{0,1\}^*}$ from $\{\mathsf{View}_{\mathcal{H}_2}^{\mathcal{A}_{\mathsf{NMZK}}}(1^\lambda, z)\}_{\lambda\in\mathbb{N}, z\in\{0,1\}^*}$. Then we can construct an adversary $\mathcal{A}_{\mathsf{Hiding}}$ that breaks the computational hiding of NM in the following way. $\mathcal{A}_{\mathsf{Hiding}}$ sends to the

challenger of the hiding game C_{Hiding} two random messages (m_0, m_1). Then, in the left session $\mathcal{A}_{\text{Hiding}}$ acts as in $\mathcal{H}_2(1^\lambda, z)$ (and $\mathcal{H}_1(1^\lambda, z)$) except for messages of NM for which he acts as proxy between C_{Hiding} and $\mathcal{A}_{\text{NMZK}}$. When $\mathcal{A}_{\text{Hiding}}$ computes the last round of the left session he sets and sends $s_1 = \sigma_1||\sigma_2 \oplus m_0$. In the right sessions $\mathcal{A}_{\text{Hiding}}$ interacts with $\mathcal{A}_{\text{ZK}}$ acting as $\mathcal{V}_{\text{NMZK}}$ does. At the end of the execution $\mathcal{A}_{\text{Hiding}}$ runs $\mathcal{D}_{\text{ZK}}$ and outputs what $\mathcal{D}_{\text{ZK}}$ outputs. It easy to see that if C_{Hiding} commits to m_1 then, $\mathcal{A}_{\text{ZK}}$ acts as in $\mathcal{H}_1(1^\lambda, z)$, otherwise he acts as in $\mathcal{H}_2(1^\lambda, z)$. Note that the reduction to the hiding property of NM is possible because the rewinds to extract a second signature do not affect the execution with the challenger of NM that remains straight-line.

- The hybrid experiment $\mathcal{H}_3(1^\lambda, z)$ differs from $\mathcal{H}_2(1^\lambda, z)$ in the way the transcript of LS_{nm} is computed. More precisely, the prover $\mathcal{P}_{\text{nm}}$ of LS_{nm} is used to compute the messages $\mathsf{ls}^2_{\text{nm}}$ and $\mathsf{ls}^4_{\text{nm}}$ instead of the Special HVZK simulator. Note that due to the delayed-input property of LS_{nm} the statement $x_{\text{nm}} = (\mathsf{vk}, \mathsf{nm}_1, \mathsf{nm}_2, \mathsf{nm}_3, \mathsf{nm}_4, s_1)$ and the witness $w_{\text{nm}} = (\mathtt{dec}_{\text{nm}}, s_0, \sigma_1, \mathtt{msg}_1, \sigma_2, \mathtt{msg}_2)$ are needed by $\mathcal{P}_{\text{nm}}$ only to compute $\mathsf{ls}^4_{\text{nm}}$ and are not needed to compute $\mathsf{ls}^2_{\text{nm}}$. Observe that the procedure of extraction of the signatures succeeds in $\mathcal{H}_3(1^\lambda, z)$ with overwhelming probability because before that the 4th round of the left session is played the view of $\mathcal{A}_{\text{NMZK}}$ is identically distributed to the view of $\mathcal{H}_2(1^\lambda, z)$. From the Special HVZK of LS_{nm} it follows that $\{\mathsf{View}^{\mathcal{A}_{\text{NMZK}}}_{\mathcal{H}_2}(1^\lambda, z)\}_{\lambda\in\mathbb{N}, z\in\{0,1\}^*}$ and $\{\mathsf{View}^{\mathcal{A}_{\text{NMZK}}}_{\mathcal{H}_3}(1^\lambda, z)\}_{\lambda\in\mathbb{N}, z\in\{0,1\}^*}$ are computationally indistinguishable.
- The hybrid $\mathcal{H}_4(1^\lambda, z)$ differs from $\mathcal{H}_3(1^\lambda, z)$ in the way the commitment $(\rho_1, \mathtt{com}_1)$ of TC_1 and the corresponding decommitment information are computed. In more details, the values $\mathtt{tcom}_1, \mathtt{tdec}_1$ are computed by running Sen_1 instead of TFake_1. Observe that the procedure of extraction of the signatures succeeds in $\mathcal{H}_4(1^\lambda, z)$ with overwhelming probability otherwise we can break the hiding of TC_1. From the trapdoorness of TC_1 it follows that $\{\mathsf{View}^{\mathcal{A}_{\text{NMZK}}}_{\mathcal{H}_4}(1^\lambda, z)\}_{\lambda\in\mathbb{N}, z\in\{0,1\}^*}$ and $\{\mathsf{View}^{\mathcal{A}_{\text{NMZK}}}_{\mathcal{H}_3}(1^\lambda, z)\}_{\lambda\in\mathbb{N}, z\in\{0,1\}^*}$ are computationally indistinguishable.
- The hybrid $\mathcal{H}_5(1^\lambda, z)$ differs from $\mathcal{H}_4(1^\lambda, z)$ in the message committed using PBCOM. In the left session $\mathcal{P}_{\text{NMZK}}$ commits to 0 using PBCOM, instead of committing to 1. Observe that the procedure of extraction of the signatures succeeds in $\mathcal{H}_5(1^\lambda, z)$ with overwhelming probability otherwise we can break the hiding of PBCOM. From the hiding of PBCOM it also follows that $\{\mathsf{View}^{\mathcal{A}_{\text{NMZK}}}_{\mathcal{H}_5}(1^\lambda, z)\}_{\lambda\in\mathbb{N}, z\in\{0,1\}^*}$ and $\{\mathsf{View}^{\mathcal{A}_{\text{NMZK}}}_{\mathcal{H}_4}(1^\lambda, z)\}_{\lambda\in\mathbb{N}, z\in\{0,1\}^*}$ are computationally indistinguishable.
- The hybrid $\mathcal{H}_6(1^\lambda, z)$ differs from $\mathcal{H}_5(1^\lambda, z)$ in the way the commitment $(\rho_0, \mathtt{com}_0)$ of TC_0 and the corresponding decommitment information are computed. More precisely, TFake_0 is run to compute a commitment $(\rho_0, \mathtt{tcom}_0)$ and the corresponding decommitment information $\mathtt{tdec}_0$ with respect to the message ls^2_L. Observe that the procedure of extraction of the signatures succeeds in $\mathcal{H}_6(1^\lambda, z)$ with overwhelming probability otherwise we can break the hiding of TC_0. From the trapdoorness of the 2-round instance-dependent trapdoor commitment scheme TC_0 it follows that $\{\mathsf{View}^{\mathcal{A}_{\text{NMZK}}}_{\mathcal{H}_6}(1^\lambda, z)\}_{\lambda\in\mathbb{N}, z\in\{0,1\}^*}$ and $\{\mathsf{View}^{\mathcal{A}_{\text{NMZK}}}_{\mathcal{H}_5}(1^\lambda, z)\}_{\lambda\in\mathbb{N}, z\in\{0,1\}^*}$ are computationally indistinguishable.

- The hybrid $\mathcal{H}_7(1^\lambda, z)$ differs from $\mathcal{H}_6(1^\lambda, z)$ in the way the transcript of LS_L is computed. More precisely, the Special HVZK simulator of LS_L is used to compute the messages ls^2_L and ls^4_L instead of the honest prover procedure. Observe that the procedure of extraction of the signatures succeeds in $\mathcal{H}_7(1^\lambda, z)$ with overwhelming probability because before that the 4th round of the left session is played the view of $\mathcal{A}_{\mathsf{NMZK}}$ is identically distributed to the view that $\mathcal{A}_{\mathsf{NMZK}}$ has in $\mathcal{H}_6(1^\lambda, z)$. From the Special HVZK of LS_L it follows that $\{\mathsf{View}^{\mathcal{A}_{\mathsf{NMZK}}}_{\mathcal{H}_6}(1^\lambda, z)\}_{\lambda\in\mathbb{N}, z\in\{0,1\}^*}$ and $\{\mathsf{View}^{\mathcal{A}_{\mathsf{NMZK}}}_{\mathcal{H}_7}(1^\lambda, z)\}_{\lambda\in\mathbb{N}, z\in\{0,1\}^*}$ are computationally indistinguishable. Note that $\mathcal{H}_7(1^\lambda, z)$ corresponds to the simulated experiment, that is $\{\mathsf{View}^{\mathcal{A}_{\mathsf{NMZK}}}_{\mathcal{H}_7}(1^\lambda, z)\}_{\lambda\in\mathbb{N}, z\in\{0,1\}^*} = \{S^1(1^\lambda, z)\}_{\lambda\in\mathbb{N}, z\in\{0,1\}^*}$.

The proof ends with the observation that for all $\lambda \in \mathbb{N}$, $z \in \{0, 1\}^*$ it holds that: $\{\mathsf{View}^{\mathcal{A}}_{\mathsf{NMZK}}(1^\lambda, z)\}_{\lambda,z} = \{\mathsf{View}^{\mathcal{A}_{\mathsf{NMZK}}}_{\mathcal{H}_0}(1^\lambda, z)\}_{\lambda,z} \approx \cdots \approx \{\mathsf{View}^{\mathcal{A}_{\mathsf{NMZK}}}_{\mathcal{H}_7}(1^\lambda, z)\}_{\lambda,z} = \{S^1(1^\lambda, z)\}_{\lambda,z}$

Lemma 4.2 *Let* $\tilde{x}_1, \ldots, \tilde{x}_{\mathsf{poly}(\lambda)}$ *be the right-session statements appearing in* $\mathsf{View} = \mathsf{Sim_{NMZK}}^1(1^\lambda, z)$ *and let* $\mathtt{id}$ *be the identity of the left session and* $\tilde{\mathtt{id}}_1, \ldots, \tilde{\mathtt{id}}_{\mathsf{poly}(\lambda)}$ *be the identities of right sessions appearing in* View. *If the i-th right session is accepting and* $\mathtt{id} \neq \tilde{\mathtt{id}}_i$ *for* $i \in \{1, \ldots, \mathsf{poly}(\lambda)\}$, *then except with negligible probability, the second output of* $\mathsf{Sim_{NMZK}}(1^\lambda, z)$ *is* $\tilde{w}_i$ *such that* $(\tilde{x}_i, \tilde{w}_i) \in \mathsf{Rel_L}$ *for* $i \in \{1, \ldots, \mathsf{poly}(\lambda)\}$.

In order to simplify the security proof, here we actually consider the notion of *adaptive Special HVZK*, *adaptive trapdoorness* and *adaptive hiding* instead of Special HVZK, trapdoorness and hiding. The only difference between adaptive Special HVZK and the classical notion of Special HVZK is the following. Let $(\mathsf{ls}^1, \mathsf{ls}^3, x)$ be a challenge of the Special HVZK security game. The challenger of adaptive Special HVZK picks a random bit b and computes an accepting transcript $t = (\mathsf{ls}^1, \mathsf{ls}^2, \mathsf{ls}^3, \mathsf{ls}^4)$ for x. If $b = 0$ then t has been computed using the prover procedure, otherwise it has been computed using the Special HVZK simulator. The adversary, upon receiving t, either outputs his guess $b' \in \{0, 1\}$, or asks to receive another transcript t according to a new possible challenge $(\mathsf{ls}^{1'}, \mathsf{ls}^{3'}, x')$. The adversary can ask a polynomial number of transcripts according to different challenges before that he outputs b'. The adversary is successful if $\mathrm{Prob}\left[\ b = b'\ \right] - 1/2$ is non-negligible in the security parameter. It is easy to see that a protocol is Special HVZK iff it is adaptive Special HVZK.

Analogously, the only difference with the definition of trapdoorness given in Definition 2.16 and adaptive trapdoorness is the following. Let (x, ρ, m) and $\mathtt{tk}$ s.t. $(x, \mathtt{tk}) \in \mathsf{Rel}_{L_\Sigma}$ be the challenge message used by the adversary to interact with the challenger. The challenger of adaptive trapdoorness picks a random bit b and computes a commitment $\mathtt{com}$ and the corresponding decommitment information $(m, \mathtt{dec})$. If $b = 0$ then both $\mathtt{com}$ and $(m, \mathtt{dec})$ are computed using the trapdoor procedure TFake_Σ, otherwise they are computed using the honest procedure Sen_Σ. The adversary, upon receiving $\mathtt{com}$ and $(m, \mathtt{dec})$, either outputs his guess $b' \in \{0, 1\}$, or asks to start another interaction against the challenger by using possible different (x', ρ', m') and $\mathtt{tk}'$. Note that the adversary can start a polynomial number of other interactions using different (x', ρ', m') before he outputs b'. The adversary is successful if $\text{Prob}\left[\ b = b'\ \right] - 1/2$ is non-negligible in the security parameter. It is easy to see that a commitment scheme enjoys the adaptive trapdoorness property iff it enjoys the trapdoorness property.

Analogously, we define the notion of adaptive hiding. The only difference with the classical definition of hiding is the following. Let m_0 and m_1 be the challenge messages. The challenger of adaptive hiding picks a random bit b and computes the commitment of m_b. The adversary, upon receiving the commitment, either outputs his guess $b' \in \{0, 1\}$, or sends (m'_0, m'_1) and asks to receive a commitment of m'_b where (m'_0, m'_1) represents a new pair of challenge messages (the latter step can be executed up to a polynomial number of times). The adversary is successful if $\text{Prob}\left[\ b = b'\ \right] - 1/2$ is non-negligible in the security parameter. It is easy to see that a commitment scheme is hiding iff it is adaptive hiding. Let us now proceed with the security proof of Lemma 4.2. We start the proof assuming that the adversary is synchronous. In the end of the security proof we show how to deal with an asynchronous adversary as well.

We now consider the hybrid experiments $\mathcal{H}_7, \ldots, \mathcal{H}_0$ described in Lemma 4.1. We show that if the adversary completes at least one right session in $\mathcal{H}_7$ with non-negligible probability then, for each hybrid experiment $\mathcal{H}_i$ with $i = 0, \ldots, 7$ there exists a procedure that extracts (except with negligible probability) the signatures for one of the verification keys used in the right sessions, thus reaching a contradiction in $\mathcal{H}_0$.[12] In the hybrid experiments $\mathcal{H}_7, \ldots, \mathcal{H}_0$ we denote as the *main thread* the execution of the hybrid that comes before that the adversary is rewound.

- The hybrid experiment $\mathcal{H}_7$ corresponds to the simulated game. Assume by contradiction that Lemma 4.2 does not hold, then with non-negligible probability there exists a right session j that is accepting but the simulator $\mathsf{Sim}_{\mathsf{NMZK}}$ does not output a valid witness $\tilde{w}_j$ for the statement $\tilde{x}_j$ proved by the adversary.

Since the probability that the adversary provides an accepting transcript for $\tilde{x}_j$ is non-negligible then $\mathsf{Sim}_{\mathsf{NMZK}}$ rewinds the adversary by sending randomly generated third rounds for LS_L until another accepting transcript for NMZK is received.[13] Given that we are assuming (by contradiction) that $\mathsf{Sim}_{\mathsf{NMZK}}$ does not extract $\tilde{w}_j$, then the accepting transcript for $\tilde{x}_j$ contains, in the last round, a value $\tilde{\mathsf{ls}}^{2'}_{L,j} \neq \tilde{\mathsf{ls}}^{2}_{L,j}$, where $\tilde{\mathsf{ls}}^{2}_{L,j}$ is the second round of LS_L that has been sent in the fourth round of NMZK by the adversary in the main thread. In summary, the expected polynomial-time extraction of $\tilde{w}_j$ can fail only when the adversary is able to open $\tilde{\mathtt{tcom}}_{0,j}$ to different values. We recall that the only hope to extract $\tilde{w}_j$ is to have two accepting transcript for LS_L such that $(\tilde{\mathsf{ls}}^{1}_{L,j}, \tilde{\mathsf{ls}}^{2}_{L,j}, \tilde{\mathsf{ls}}^{3}_{L,j}, \tilde{\mathsf{ls}}^{4}_{L,j})$ and $(\tilde{\mathsf{ls}}^{1}_{L,j}, \tilde{\mathsf{ls}}^{2}_{L,j}, \tilde{\mathsf{ls}}^{3'}_{L,j}, \tilde{\mathsf{ls}}^{4'}_{L,j})$

---

[12] We recall that we have already proven in Lemma 4.1 that the probabilities of $\mathcal{A}_{\mathsf{NMZK}}$ to complete a right session in $\mathcal{H}_0$ and $\mathcal{H}_7$ are negligible close.

[13] We assume that the adaptive-input PoK extractor of LS_L works by rewinding the adversary by sending randomly generated third round ls^3_L. See the beginning of the security proof (the part referred to *(Delayed-Input) NMZK)* of Theorem 4.1 for the precise description of $\mathsf{Sim}_{\mathsf{NMZK}}$.

with $\tilde{\mathsf{ls}}^3_{L,j} \neq \tilde{\mathsf{ls}}^{3'}_{L,j}$. If the adversary is able to open to different values of $\tilde{\mathsf{ls}}^2_{L,j}$ during the rewinding procedure then, by the Special Binding property of TC_0 it holds that the value committed in $\tilde{\mathtt{com}}_j$ is 0. Then, by the Instance-Dependent Binding property of TC_1, we obtain that $\tilde{\mathtt{tcom}}_{1,j}$ is statistically binding. This chain of implications in turn implies that during the rewinds the value opened with respect to $\tilde{\mathtt{tcom}}_{1,j}$ in the fourth round stays the same.

The crucial observation is that in this right session it is possible to run the adaptive-input PoK extractor of $\mathsf{LS}_{\mathsf{nm}}$ thus obtaining two accepting transcripts for $\mathsf{LS}_{\mathsf{nm}}$ that share the same first two rounds ($\tilde{\mathsf{ls}}^1_{\mathsf{nm},j}$ and $\tilde{\mathsf{ls}}^2_{\mathsf{nm},j}$). Therefore, with non-negligible probability, it is possible to extract the decommitment information of the non-malleable commitment NM and compute $\tilde{s}^j_0 \oplus \tilde{s}^j_1 = \tilde{\sigma}^j_1 || \tilde{\sigma}^j_2$, where $(\tilde{\sigma}^j_1, \tilde{\sigma}^j_2)$ are two valid signatures with respect to the verification key $\tilde{\mathsf{vk}}_j$. Thus we can conclude this part of the security proof claiming that if $\mathsf{Sim}_{\mathsf{NMZK}}$ fails in extracting $\tilde{w}_j$ then (1) two signatures for $\tilde{\mathsf{vk}}_j$ can be extracted with non-negligible probability and (2) the non-malleable commitment is well formed.

- In the hybrid experiment $\mathcal{H}_6$ the prover procedure is used instead of the Special HVZK simulator to compute $(\mathsf{ls}^1_L, \mathsf{ls}^2_L, \mathsf{ls}^3_L, \mathsf{ls}^4_L)$. We observe that, with non-negligible probability, there still exists a right session j where the signatures for the verification key $\tilde{\mathsf{vk}}_j$ can be extracted using the adaptive-input PoK extractor of $\mathsf{LS}_{\mathsf{nm}}$ and moreover the adaptive-PoK extractor of LS_L fails, otherwise a reduction to the adaptive Special HVZK of LS_L can be done.
  We now define a different extraction procedure $\mathtt{ExtCom}$ that works as follows.
  - In the **right sessions** $\mathtt{ExtCom}$ runs the adaptive-input PoK extractor for both LS_L and $\mathsf{LS}_{\mathsf{nm}}$. More precisely, $\mathtt{ExtCom}$ keeps fixed the first two rounds of the main thread and sends multiple random values $\tilde{\mathsf{ls}}^3_L$ and $\tilde{\mathsf{ls}}^3_{\mathsf{nm}}$.
  - In the **left session** $\mathtt{ExtCom}$ acts similarly to $\mathsf{Sim}_{\mathsf{NMZK}}$ differing only in the way ls^2_L is computed during the rewinds. More precisely, for any new message ls^3_L received by the adversary, $\mathtt{ExtCom}$ opens $\mathtt{tcom}_0$ always to the same ls^2_L and provides an accepting transcript $(\mathsf{ls}^1_L, \mathsf{ls}^2_L, \mathsf{ls}^3_L, \mathsf{ls}^4_L)$ using the honest prover procedure (as it has been done in the main thread).

We now show that $\mathtt{ExtCom}$ is able to extract the decommitment information of the non-malleable commitment that allows to compute two valid signatures. More precisely, we argue that during the rewinds the adversary is forced to open $\tilde{\mathtt{tcom}}_{1,j}$ always to the same 2nd round of $\mathsf{LS}_{\mathsf{nm}}$ ($\tilde{\mathsf{ls}}^2_{\mathsf{nm},j}$) in some right-session j. This holds because of the following chain of implications. In $\mathcal{H}_7$ we have showed that there exists a right session j where, with non-negligible probability, the adaptive-input PoK extractor for $\mathsf{LS}_{\mathsf{nm}}$ can compute a valid decommitment information for the non-malleable commitment such that two valid signatures can be extracted. Moreover, we have proved that in this session j the extractor for LS_L fails. As discussed above this implies that $\tilde{\mathtt{com}}_j$ contains 0 and that $\tilde{\mathtt{tcom}}_{1,j}$ is statistically binding. Since $\mathtt{ExtCom}$ keeps fixed the first two rounds of the main thread during the rewinds, the adversary has no way to use the trapdoor procedure to compute $\tilde{\mathtt{tcom}}_{1,j}$ once that $\tilde{\mathtt{com}}_j$ contains 0. Moreover, the adversary cannot selectively abort some of the right sessions since the values $(\mathsf{ls}^1_L, \mathsf{ls}^2_L, \mathsf{ls}^3_L, \mathsf{ls}^4_L)$ are identically distributed to values that are sent in the main thread of $\mathcal{H}_6$. These observations make us able to claim that ExtCom can extract, with non-negligible probability, a valid decommitment information of the non-malleable commitment that allows to compute two signatures for $\tilde{\mathsf{vk}}_j$. We observe that ExtCom could be able to extract $\tilde{w}_j$ as well in this case, but it would just ignore the problem.

- The next hybrid that we consider is $\mathcal{H}_5$. This hybrid experiment is the same as $\mathcal{H}_6$ with the difference that $\mathtt{tcom}_0$ is computed using the commitment procedure (and not the trapdoor procedure). We observe that the transcript for LS_L in $\mathcal{H}_6$ is computed using the honest prover procedure, therefore the trapdoor procedure is not needed anymore to provide an accepting transcript with respect to LS_L. We claim that the output of ExtCom for $\mathcal{H}_5$ is the same as the output of ExtCom for $\mathcal{H}_6$. If this is not true then a reduction to the trapdoorness of $\mathtt{tcom}_0$ can be done.
- The next hybrid that we consider is $\mathcal{H}_4$. The difference between $\mathcal{H}_5$ and $\mathcal{H}_4$ is that the value committed in com is 1. We observe that also in this case the output of ExtCom stays the same otherwise a reduction to the hiding of com can be done.
- The next hybrid that we consider is $\mathcal{H}_3$. The difference between $\mathcal{H}_4$ and $\mathcal{H}_3$ is that $\mathtt{tcom}_1$ is computed using the trapdoor procedure. We claim that the output of ExtCom is the same as the output of ExtCom for $\mathcal{H}_4$. If this is not true then a reduction to the trapdoorness of $\mathtt{tcom}_1$ can be done.
- The next hybrid that we consider is $\mathcal{H}_2$. The difference between $\mathcal{H}_3$ and $\mathcal{H}_2$ is that the transcript for $\mathsf{LS}_{\mathsf{nm}}$ is computed using the Special HVZK simulator instead of the honest prover procedure. We observe that the simulator of $\mathsf{LS}_{\mathsf{nm}}$ can be used in $\mathcal{H}_2$ because $\mathtt{tcom}_1$ is computed using the trapdoor procedure. So, upon receiving $\mathsf{ls}^3_{\mathsf{nm}}$ the Special HVZK simulator of $\mathsf{LS}_{\mathsf{nm}}$ is invoked thus obtaining $(\mathsf{ls}^2_{\mathsf{nm}}, \mathsf{ls}^4_{\mathsf{nm}})$, and $\mathsf{ls}^2_{\mathsf{nm}}$ will be the value to which $\mathtt{tcom}_1$ will be opened using the trapdoor procedure.

We now want to prove that there exists a right session j where the adversary is still computing a valid non-malleable commitment of two signatures for $\tilde{\mathsf{vk}}_j$. We recall that this statement is true for the hybrid experiment $\mathcal{H}_3$. Suppose by contradiction that this claim does not hold when considering $\mathcal{H}_2$, then we can construct a reduction to the Special HVZK of $\mathsf{LS}_{\mathsf{nm}}$. The reduction works as follows. Let $\mathcal{C}^{SHVZK}$ be the challenger for the Special HVZK of $\mathsf{LS}_{\mathsf{nm}}$.

1. The reduction interacts with the adversary in the left and in the right sessions according to $\mathcal{H}_3$ (and $\mathcal{H}_2$).
2. The reduction, upon receiving $\mathsf{ls}^1_{\mathsf{nm}}$ and $\mathsf{ls}^3_{\mathsf{nm}}$ in the left session forwards these messages to $\mathcal{C}^{SHVZK}$ together with $(x_{\mathsf{nm}}, w_{\mathsf{nm}})$.
3. The reduction, upon receiving $(\mathsf{ls}^2_{\mathsf{nm}}, \mathsf{ls}^4_{\mathsf{nm}})$ from $\mathcal{C}^{SHVZK}$, uses them to complete the left execution against the adversary.
4. When the adversary stops, the reduction rewinds the adversary in the j-th right session using the ExtCom's strategy, and upon receiving $\mathsf{ls}^{3'}_{\mathsf{nm}}$ in the left ses-

sion computes $(\mathsf{ls}^{2'}_{\mathsf{nm}}, \mathsf{ls}^{4'}_{\mathsf{nm}})$ using the honest prover procedure (so using w'_{nm}). Moreover, during all the rewinds $\mathtt{tcom}_1$ is always opened to the value $\mathsf{ls}^{2'}_{\mathsf{nm}}$.
5. The reduction now uses the output of $\mathtt{ExtCom}$ to check whether the non-malleable commitment computed in the main thread contains a value $\tilde{s}^j_0$ such that $\tilde{s}^j_0 \oplus \tilde{s}^j_1$ represents two signatures with respect to $\tilde{\mathsf{vk}}_j$.
6. If the non-malleable commitment of the main thread is well formed and two signatures are extracted then the reduction outputs 0 (to claim that the challenger has used the honest prover procedure for $\mathsf{LS}_{\mathsf{nm}}$), and a random bit otherwise.

We observe that the extractor will output the decommitment information for the non-malleable commitment computed in one of the rewinds made by $\mathtt{ExtCom}$ and not the decommitment information for the non-malleable commitment received in the main thread. Since we assume that the non-malleable commitment scheme fixes the decommitment information in the second round, then the decommitment information extracted can be used to check what is committed in the main thread as well. We recall that the extraction procedure used in the reduction corresponds exactly to the extraction procedure used in $\mathcal{H}_3$. Moreover, when $(\mathsf{ls}^2_{\mathsf{nm}}, \mathsf{ls}^4_{\mathsf{nm}})$ is computed using the honest prover procedure by the challenger, the view of the adversary in the main thread and during the rewinds is perfectly indistinguishable. Therefore the probability that the extractor is successful when $(\mathsf{ls}^2_{\mathsf{nm}}, \mathsf{ls}^4_{\mathsf{nm}})$ is computed using the honest prover procedure corresponds (except for a negligible difference) to the probability that the extractor succeeds in $\mathcal{H}_3$.

- The next hybrid that we consider is $\mathcal{H}_1$. The difference between $\mathcal{H}_2$ and $\mathcal{H}_1$ is that the non-malleable commitment contains a value s_0 such that $s_0 \oplus s_1$ is equal to a random string, whereas in the previous hybrid experiment it holds that $s_0 \oplus s_1 = \sigma_1||\sigma_2$. Since we are considering a synchronous adversary we can immediately rely on the security of the one-one synchronous non-malleable commitment NM to claim that the adversary in some session j, with non-negligible probability, is still computing a valid non-malleable commitment of a string $\tilde{s}^j_0$ such that $\tilde{s}^j_0 \oplus \tilde{s}^j_1 = \sigma^j_0||\sigma^j_1$ and $\sigma^j_0||\sigma^j_1$ represents two valid signatures for $\tilde{\mathsf{vk}}_j$. We recall that during the reduction to NM two signatures for two messages with respect to vk need to be extracted in the left session. Since NM is public coin the extraction of the signatures does not interfere with the reduction to the non-malleable commitment.
- The next hybrid that we consider is $\mathcal{H}_0$. The difference between $\mathcal{H}_1$ and $\mathcal{H}_0$ is that on the left session the procedure to extract two valid signatures for vk is not run anymore. Moreover, as proved in the first part of Lemma 4.1, the adversary aborting probabilities in $\mathcal{H}_0$ and $\mathcal{H}_1$ are negligibly close. From previous arguments it follows that in $\mathcal{H}_1$ there exists a session j where the adversary computes a valid commitment of two signatures using NM. Therefore, we can claim that also in $\mathcal{H}_0$ there exists a session j where, with non-negligible probability, the adversary is computing a well-formed non-malleable commitment such that the value extracted from it allows to compute two signatures for $\tilde{\mathsf{vk}}_j$. This implies that using the weak extractability of the non-malleable commitment NM we can extract from some right session j two signatures for the verification $\tilde{\mathsf{vk}}_j$ reaching a contradiction.

Indeed, it is possible to contradict the security of the signature scheme because no more rewinds are needed in the left session between the third and the second round. We just rewind from the fourth to the third round in the right session j to extract the signatures and this rewinding procedure does not interfere with the reduction that breaks the security of the signature scheme.

During the security proof we have assumed that the adversary is synchronous. We now briefly explain why the lemma holds also against asynchronous adversaries. In all the reductions that we have made for the synchronous case we have showed that there is always a procedure to extract the signatures from some j-th right session, thus reaching a contradiction in $\mathcal{H}_0$. This part of the proof follows mostly the same arguments used above for the synchronous case, with the major difference that we cannot rely on the security of the synchronous non-malleable commitment. In more detail, we first argue that in $\mathcal{H}_2$ the asynchronous $\mathcal{A}_{\mathsf{NMZK}}$ computes a valid commitment of two signatures with respect to the verification key vk_j in some $j-$th right session, and then we show an extractor for $\mathcal{H}_1$ relying on the adaptive hiding instead of the non-malleability property of NM.

In the reductions considered for the synchronous case the adversary is rewound to check the validity and the content of the non-malleable commitments computed by $\mathcal{A}_{\mathsf{NMZK}}$ in the right sessions. Any of these rewinding procedures, when applied to an asynchronous adversary, might completely rewind the left session. In this case, the adversary could send messages in the left session which are different from all the messages that appeared in the main thread. This is a problem when $\mathcal{A}_{\mathsf{NMZK}}$ is involved in a security reduction. Indeed, the reduction might need to ask the challenger to restart the security game from the beginning. This is the reason why we require the cryptographic primitives involved in our protocol to enjoy this notion of *multi* security. Therefore, the reductions described for the hybrids experiments $\mathcal{H}_7, \ldots, \mathcal{H}_2$ work almost as showed for the synchronous, but they rely on the *multi* security of the primitives involved in the reductions.

The only thing that is left to argue is the existence of an extraction procedure that outputs two valid signatures for vk_j in $\mathcal{H}_1$ and $\mathcal{H}_0$ even when $\mathcal{A}_{\mathsf{NMZK}}$ is asynchronous. Given that NM retains the non-malleability only against one-one *synchronous* adversary, we need to use a different strategy to prove the existence of such an extractor.

Since in $\mathcal{H}_2$ the adversary commits to two valid signatures in some session j with non-negligible probability, we can distinguish two cases: (1) $\mathcal{A}_{\mathsf{NMZK}}$ commits to those signatures in a *synchronous* right session of $\mathcal{H}_2$; (2) $\mathcal{A}_{\mathsf{NMZK}}$ commits to those signatures in an *asynchronous* right session of $\mathcal{H}_2$. If case 1 happens with non-negligible probability, then the proof is over since this case has been already discussed previously. So let us assume that only case 2 happens with non-negligible probability. We now prove that if this is the case then a reduction to the adaptive hiding of NM can be done as follows. Let C be the challenger for the adaptive hiding security game. The reduction picks two random challenge messages ($m_0 \leftarrow \{0,1\}^\lambda, m_1 \leftarrow \{0,1\}^\lambda$) and sends them to C. The reduction now computes all the messages as in $\mathcal{H}_1$ and $\mathcal{H}_2$ and acts as a proxy between C and $\mathcal{A}_{\mathsf{NMZK}}$ with respect to the left-session messages of NM. Moreover, in the last round of the left session the reduction sets $s_1 = m_0 \oplus \sigma_1 || \sigma_2$.

When the execution with $\mathcal{A}_{\mathsf{NMZK}}$ stops, the reduction runs the weak-extractor of NM on all the asynchronous right sessions. If there exists a right session j where the extracted value is a string $\tilde{s}_0^j$ such that $\tilde{s}_0^j \oplus \tilde{s}_1^j = \sigma_0^j||\sigma_1^j$ and $\sigma_0^j||\sigma_1^j$ represents two valid signatures for $\tilde{\mathsf{vk}}_j$ then the reduction outputs m_0, otherwise she outputs m_b, with $b \in \{0, 1\}$.

In this reduction there is an issue that we address by requiring NM to be adaptive hiding. Indeed, it could happen that the weak-extractor completely rewinds the left session. In this case the adversary might start a new session with C by sending a different first round of NM nm_1, and this is the reason why we require NM to be adaptive hiding.

We observe that what we have proved only guarantees that it is possible to extract valid signatures for vk_j for some j-th session of $\mathcal{H}_1$ with non-negligible probability. That is, we cannot claim that the non-malleable commitment computed by $\mathcal{A}_{\mathsf{NMZK}}$ in the j-th right session of $\mathcal{H}_1$ is well formed. Anyway, the extraction guarantee is sufficient to complete our security proof. Indeed, for the same arguments used for the synchronous case the probability that $\mathcal{A}_{\mathsf{NMZK}}$ aborts in $\mathcal{H}_0$ is negligibly close to the aborting probability of $\mathcal{A}_{\mathsf{NMZK}}$ in $\mathcal{H}_1$. Therefore the weak-extractor of NM can be used to extract two valid signatures from some j-th right section of $\mathcal{H}_0$ thus reaching a contradiction. □

Theorem 4.2 *If OWFs exists, then* NMZK *is a synchronous delayed-input many-many NMZK AoK for* $\mathcal{NP}$.

Proof The proof proceeds very similarly to the one showed for Theorem 4.1. The main difference between these two proofs is that we have to consider also polynomially many synchronous left sessions played in parallel. Therefore the only difference between this proof and the one of Theorem 4.1 is that in the reductions we need to rely on the security of a many-one non-malleable commitment scheme and on the security of the other primitives under parallel composition. We notice that using the same arguments of the security proof of Proposition 1 provided in [138], it is possible to claim that a synchronous (one-one) non-malleable commitment is also synchronous many-one non-malleable. Therefore no additional assumption are required in order to prove that NMZK is also many-many parallel delayed-input NMZK. Note also that the simulator needs to extract the trapdoor (the signatures of two different messages) in all the left (synchronous) sessions completed in the main thread. The extraction succeeds except with negligible probability for the same arguments used in the security proof of Theorem 4.1. □

4.3 Multi-party Coin-Tossing Protocol

4.3.1 4-Round Secure Multi-party Coin Tossing: Π_{MCF}

The high-level idea of our protocol Π_{MCF} significantly differs from the one of [84] (e.g., we use our 4-round delayed-input synchronous many-many NMZK instead of

3-round 3-robust parallel non-malleable commitment scheme). Our protocol simply consists of each party committing to a random string r, which is opened in the last round along with a simulatable proof of correct opening given to all parties independently. The output consists of the $\oplus$ of all opened strings. Let's see in more details how our Π_{MCF} works. For our construction we use the following tools.

1. A non-interactive perfectly binding computationally hiding commitment scheme $\mathsf{PBCOM} = (\mathsf{Com}, \mathsf{Dec})$.
2. A Σ-protocol $\mathsf{BL}_L = (\mathcal{P}_L, \mathcal{V}_L)$ for the $\mathcal{NP}$-language $L = \{\mathtt{com} : \exists\,(\mathtt{dec}, m) \text{ s.t. } \mathsf{Dec}(\mathtt{com}, \mathtt{dec}, m) = 1\}$ with Special HVZK simulator Sim_L. We use two instantiations of BL_L in order to construct the protocol for the OR of two statements Π_{OR} as described in Chap. 2. Π_{OR} is a proof system for the $\mathcal{NP}$-language $L_{\mathrm{com}} = \{(\mathtt{com}_0, \mathtt{com}_1) : \exists\,(\mathtt{dec}, m) \text{ s.t. } \mathsf{Dec}(\mathtt{com}_0, \mathtt{dec}, m) = 1 \text{ OR } \mathsf{Dec}(\mathtt{com}_1, \mathtt{dec}, m) = 1\}$.[14] Informally, by running Π_{OR}, one can prove the knowledge of the message committed in $\mathtt{com}_0$ or in $\mathtt{com}_1$.
3. A 4-round delayed-input synchronous many-many NMZK $\mathsf{NMZK} = (\mathcal{P}_{\mathsf{NMZK}}, \mathcal{V}_{\mathsf{NMZK}})$ for the following $\mathcal{NP}$-language

$$L_{\mathsf{NMZK}} = \{((\mathtt{com}_0, \mathtt{com}_1), m) :\ \forall i \in \{0, 1\}\ \exists\, \mathtt{dec}_i \text{ s.t. } \mathsf{Dec}(\mathtt{com}_i, \mathtt{dec}_i, m) = 1\}.$$

   Informally, by running NMZK, one can prove that 2 commitments contain the same message m.

4.3.2 Π_{MCF}: *Informal Description and Security Intuition*

The high level description of our protocol between just two parties (A_1, A_2) is given in Fig. 4.3. For a formal description of Π_{MCF} we refer the reader to Sect. 4.3.3. In Fig. 4.3 we consider an execution of Π_{MCF} that goes from A_1 to A_2 (the execution from A_2 to A_1 is symmetric). We recall that the protocol is executed simultaneously by both A_1 and A_2. The main idea is the following. Each party commits to his input using two instantiations of a non-interactive commitment. More precisely we have that A_1 computes two non-interactive commitments $\mathtt{com}_0$ and $\mathtt{com}_1$ (along with their decommitment information $\mathtt{dec}_0$ and $\mathtt{dec}_1$) of the message r_1. Each party also runs Π_{OR} for the $\mathcal{NP}$-language L_{com}, from the first to the third round, in order to prove knowledge of the message committed in $\mathtt{com}_0$ or in $\mathtt{com}_1$. In the last round each party sends his own input (i.e., r_1 for A_1 and r_2 for A_2) and proves, using a delayed-input synchronous many-many non-malleable ZK for the $\mathcal{NP}$-language L_{NMZK}, that messages committed using PBCOM were actually equal to that input (i.e., r_1 for A_1 and r_2 for A_2). That is, A_1 sends r_1 and proves that $\mathtt{com}_0$ and $\mathtt{com}_1$ are valid commitments of the message r_1.

---

[14] We use Π_{OR} in a non-black box way, but for ease of exposition sometimes we will refer to entire protocol Π_{OR} in order to invoke the proof of knowledge property enjoyed by Π_{OR}.

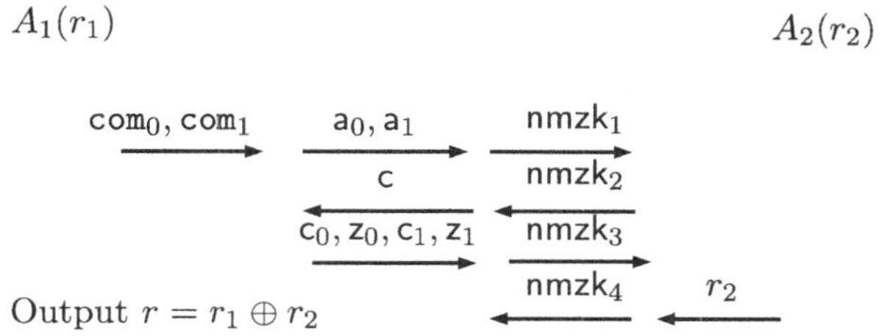

- com_0 and com_1 are two non-interactive commitments of the message r_1 computed using PBCOM.
- $(\mathsf{a}_0, \mathsf{a}_1, \mathsf{c}_0, \mathsf{c}_1, \mathsf{z}_0, \mathsf{z}_1)$ is the transcript generated from an execution of the WIPoK Π_{OR} in which $\mathcal{P}_{\mathsf{OR}}$ proves the knowledge of either the message committed in com_0 or in com_1.
- $(\mathsf{nmzk}_1, \mathsf{nmzk}_2, \mathsf{nmzk}_3, \mathsf{nmzk}_4)$ in the transcript generated from an execution of the delayed-input synchronous many-many NMZK NMZK in which $\mathcal{P}_{\mathsf{NMZK}}$ proves that both com_0 and com_1 are valid commitments of the message r_1.

Fig. 4.3 Π_{MCF}: Informal description of the execution from A_1 to A_2. The execution from A_2 to A_1 is symmetric

Intuition About the Security of Π_{MCF}.

Let A_1^* be the corrupted party.

Informally the simulator Sim works as follows. Sim starts an interaction against A_1^* using as input a random string y until the third round of Π_{MCF} is received by A_1^*. More precisely, in the first round he computes two commitments com_0 and com_1 (along with their decommitment information dec_0 and dec_1) of y, and runs $\mathcal{P}_{\mathsf{OR}}$ using as a witness (dec_1, y). After the 3rd round Sim extracts the input r_1^* of the corrupted party A_1^* using the extractor E_{OR} of Π_{OR} (that exists from the PoK property of Π_{OR}) and sends r_1^* to the ideal world functionality. At this point Sim receives r from the ideal-world functionality, and completes the execution of the 4th round by sending $r_2 = r \oplus r_1^*$. We observe that Sim, in order to send a string r_2 that differs from y in the 4th round, has to cheat in NMZK. This is done by simply running the simulator of NMZK. To prove the security of our scheme we will go through a sequence of hybrid experiments in order to show that the output view of the adversary in the real world can be simulated in the ideal world by Sim. The security proof strongly relies on the non-malleable zero knowledge property of NMZK. Indeed the aim of NMZK is to ensure that the adversary does not maul the messages received from Sim. That is, the behavior of A_1^* allows to extract, in every hybrid experiments that we will consider, the correct input of A_1^*. This holds even in case the commitments sent by Sim to A_1^* are commitments of a random string y, and the value sent in the 4th round is inconsistent with the value committed in the first round.

4.3.3 Formal Description

Let $P = \{P_1, \ldots, P_n\}$ be the set of parties. Furthermore, denote by $(\mathtt{id}_1, \ldots, \mathtt{id}_n)$[15] the unique identities of parties $\{P_1, \ldots, P_n\}$, respectively. Let us denote by $\mathsf{F}_{\mathsf{MCF}} : (1^\lambda)^n \rightarrow \{0, 1\}^\lambda$ the function $\mathsf{F}_{\mathsf{MCF}}(r_1, \ldots, r_n) = r_1 \oplus \cdots \oplus r_n$. The protocol starts with each party P_i choosing a random string r_i for $i = 1, \ldots, n$. It consists of four rounds, i.e., all parties send messages in each round and the messages of all executions are seen by every party. Following [84] we describe the protocol between two parties (A_1, A_2) observing that the real protocol actually consists of n simultaneous executions of a two-party coin-tossing protocol $\Pi_{\mathsf{MCF}} = (A_1, A_2)$ between parties (P_i, P_j) where P_i acts as A_1 with input r_i and P_j acts as A_2 with input r_j (both are symmetric). Let the input of A_1 be r_1, and the input of A_2 be r_2. The set of messages enabling A_1 to learn the output is denoted by (m_1, m_2, m_3, m_4) where (m_1, m_3) are sent by A_1 and (m_2, m_4) are sent by A_2. Likewise, the set of messages enabling A_2 to learn the output are denoted by $(\tilde{m}_1, \tilde{m}_2, \tilde{m}_3, \tilde{m}_4)$ where $(\tilde{m}_1, \tilde{m}_3)$ are sent by A_2 and $(\tilde{m}_2, \tilde{m}_4)$ are sent by A_1. Therefore, messages $(m_l, \tilde{m}_l)$ are simultaneously exchanged in the l-th round for $l = 1, \ldots, 4$.

Protocol Π_{MCF}.

Common input: security parameter λ, instances length: ℓ_{NMZK}, $\ell_{\mathtt{com}}$.
Round 1. We first describe how A_1 constructs m_1.

1. Compute $(\mathtt{com}_0, \mathtt{dec}_0) \leftarrow \mathsf{Com}(r_1)$ and $(\mathtt{com}_1, \mathtt{dec}_1) \leftarrow \mathsf{Com}(r_1)$.
2. Compute $\mathsf{a}_0 \leftarrow \mathcal{P}_L(1^\lambda, \mathtt{com}_0, (\mathtt{dec}_0, r_1))$.
3. Pick $\mathsf{c}_1 \leftarrow \{0, 1\}^\lambda$ and compute $(\mathsf{a}_1, \mathsf{z}_1) \leftarrow \mathsf{Sim}_L(1^\lambda, \mathtt{com}_1, \mathsf{c}_1)$.
4. Run $\mathcal{V}_{\mathsf{NMZK}}$ on input 1^λ and ℓ_{NMZK} thus obtaining the 1st round nmzk_1 of NMZK.
5. Message m_1 is defined to be $(\mathtt{com}_0, \mathtt{com}_1, \mathsf{a}_0, \mathsf{a}_1, \mathsf{nmzk}_1)$.

Likewise, A_2 performs the same action as A_1 in order to construct $\tilde{m}_1 = (\tilde{\mathtt{com}}_0, \tilde{\mathtt{com}}_1, \tilde{\mathsf{a}}_0, \tilde{\mathsf{a}}_1, \widetilde{\mathsf{nmzk}}_1)$.
Round 2. In this round A_2 sends message m_2 and A_1 sends $\tilde{m}_2$. We first describe how A_2 constructs m_2.

1. Run $\mathcal{P}_{\mathsf{NMZK}}$ on input 1^λ, $\mathtt{id}_2$, ℓ_{NMZK} and nmzk_1 thus obtaining the 2nd round nmzk_2 of NMZK.
2. Pick $\mathsf{c} \leftarrow \{0, 1\}^\lambda$.
3. Define message $m_2 = (\mathsf{c}, \mathsf{nmzk}_2)$.

Likewise, A_1 performs the same actions as A_2 in the previous step to construct the message $\tilde{m}_2 = (\tilde{\mathsf{c}}, \widetilde{\mathsf{nmzk}}_2)$.
Round 3. In this round A_1 sends message m_3 and A_2 sends $\tilde{m}_3$. A_1 prepares m_3 as follows.

1. Compute $\mathsf{c}_0 = \mathsf{c} \oplus \mathsf{c}_1$ and $\mathsf{z}_0 \leftarrow \mathcal{P}_L(\mathsf{c}_0)$.

---

[15] As discuss in the Definition 2.17 the use of the identifiers can be avoid, we use them, to uniformity of notation.

2. Run $\mathcal{V}_{\mathsf{NMZK}}$ on input nmzk_2 thus obtaining the 3rd round nmzk_3 of NMZK.
3. Define $m_3 = (\mathsf{nmzk}_3, \mathsf{c}_0, \mathsf{c}_1, \mathsf{z}_0, \mathsf{z}_1)$.

Likewise, A_2 performs the same actions as A_1 in the previous step to construct the message $\tilde{m}_3 = (\tilde{\mathsf{nmzk}}_3, \tilde{\mathsf{c}}_0, \tilde{\mathsf{c}}_1, \tilde{\mathsf{z}}_0, \tilde{\mathsf{z}}_1)$.

Round 4. In this round A_2 sends message m_4 and A_1 sends $\tilde{m}_4$. A_2 prepares m_4 as follows.

1. Check that the following conditions are satisfied: a) $\mathsf{c} = \mathsf{c}_0 \oplus \mathsf{c}_1$; b) the transcript $\mathsf{a}_0, \mathsf{c}_0, \mathsf{z}_0$ is accepting w.r.t. the instance $\mathtt{com}_0$; c) the transcript $\mathsf{a}_1, \mathsf{c}_1, \mathsf{z}_1$ is accepting w.r.t. the instance $\mathtt{com}_1$. If one of the check fails then output $\perp$, otherwise continue with the following steps.
2. Set $x_{\mathsf{NMZK}} = (\tilde{\mathtt{com}}_0, \tilde{\mathtt{com}}_1, r_2)$ and $w_{\mathsf{NMZK}} = (\tilde{\mathtt{dec}}_0, \tilde{\mathtt{dec}}_1)$.
3. Run $\mathcal{P}_{\mathsf{NMZK}}$ on input nmzk_3, the statement to be proved x_{NMZK} and the witness w_{NMZK} s.t. $(x_{\mathsf{NMZK}}, w_{\mathsf{NMZK}}) \in \mathsf{Rel}_{L_{\mathsf{NMZK}}}$, thus obtaining the 4th round nmzk_4 of NMZK.
4. Define $m_4 = (r_2, x_{\mathsf{NMZK}}, \mathsf{nmzk}_4)$.

Likewise, A_1 performs the same actions as A_2 in the previous step to construct the message $\tilde{m}_4 = (r_1, \tilde{x}_{\mathsf{NMZK}}, \tilde{\mathsf{nmzk}}_4)$.

Output computation of Π_{MCF}. Check, for each party, if $(\mathsf{nmzk}_1^i, \mathsf{nmzk}_2^i, \mathsf{nmzk}_3^i, \mathsf{nmzk}_4^i)$ is accepting for $\mathcal{V}_{\mathsf{NMZK}}$ with respect to the instance x^i_{NMZK} $(i = 1, \ldots, n)$ and that all pairs of parties used the same inputs $(r_1, \ldots, r_n)$. If so, output $r = r_1 \oplus \cdots \oplus r_n$.

Theorem 4.3 *If one-to-one OWFs exist, then the multi-party protocol* Π_{MCF} *securely computes the multi-party coin-tossing functionality with black-box simulation.*

Proof Let $P = \{P_1, \ldots, P_n\}$ be the set of parties participating in the execution of Π_{MCF}. Also let $P^* \subseteq P$ be the set of parties corrupted by the adversary $\mathcal{A}$. The simulator Sim only generates messages on behalf of parties $P \setminus P^*$. In particular, we show that for every adversary $\mathcal{A}$ there exists an "ideal" world adversary Sim such that

$$\mathsf{REAL}_{\Pi_{\mathsf{MCF}},\mathcal{A}(z)}(1^\lambda) \approx \mathsf{IDEAL}_{\mathsf{F}_{\mathsf{MCF}},\mathsf{Sim}(z)}(1^\lambda).$$

We prove this claim by considering hybrid experiments $\mathcal{H}_1, \ldots, \mathcal{H}_7$ as described below. Without loss of generality, we will assume that party P_1 is the only honest party since our protocol is secure against $n-1$ corruptions. We denote the output of the parties in the hybrid experiment $\mathcal{H}_i$ with $\{\mathsf{OUT}_{\mathcal{H}_i,\mathcal{A}(z)}(1^\lambda)\}$.

- The 1st hybrid experiment $\mathcal{H}_1$ is identical to the real execution. More specifically, $\mathcal{H}_1$ starts $\mathcal{A}$ with fresh randomness and interacts with it as P_1 would do using uniform randomness r_1 as input. The output of $\mathcal{H}_1$ consists of $\mathcal{A}$'s view. We observe that, by construction, the output of $\mathcal{A}$ in the real execution is identically distributed to $\mathcal{H}_1$. Moreover, all the messages generated on the behalf of P^* are honestly computed with overwhelming probability due to the soundness of NMZK.

- The 2nd hybrid experiment $\mathcal{H}_2$ is identical to $\mathcal{H}_1$ except that this hybrid experiment also extracts the P^*'s inputs $r_2^*, \ldots, r_n^*$. In order to obtain $r_2^*, \ldots, r_n^*$, $\mathcal{H}_2$ runs the extractor E_{OR} of Π_{OR} on each execution of Π_{OR} made by a malicious party. Note that the existence of E_{OR} is guaranteed from the Adaptive Proof of Knowledge property of Π_{OR}. If the extractor fails, then $\mathcal{H}_2$ aborts. At this point $\mathcal{H}_2$ completes the 4th round and prepares the output exactly as $\mathcal{H}_1$.[16]
  $\{\mathsf{OUT}_{\mathcal{H}_1,\mathcal{A}(z)}(1^\lambda)\}$ and $\{\mathsf{OUT}_{\mathcal{H}_2,\mathcal{A}(z)}(1^\lambda)\}$ are statistically close, and the extraction is successful in expected polynomial time, both claims follow from the PoK property of Π_{OR}. Observe that we are guaranteed that what E_{OR} outputs correspond to the input of the the malicious party, from the fact that with non-negligible probability $\mathcal{A}$ correctly computes all the steps of Π_{MCF}. More precisely the soundness of NMZK ensures that the extracted values correspond to the $r_2^*, \ldots, r_n^*$ received in the last round.
- The 3rd hybrid experiment $\mathcal{H}_3$ differs from $\mathcal{H}_2$ in the way the transcript for the delayed-input synchronous many-many NMZK NMZK is computed. More precisely in this hybrid experiment the simulator $\mathsf{Sim}^{\mathsf{NMZK}}$ for NMZK is used. Following [4, 84], the extraction of NMZK's trapdoor and the extraction of P^*'s input are performed during the same steps. Observe that these two extraction procedures do not interfere with each other, indeed they just rewind from the third to the second round by sending a freshly generated second round.

  The first property of $\mathsf{Sim}^{\mathsf{NMZK}}$ (see Definition 2.17) ensures that $\{\mathsf{OUT}_{\mathcal{H}_2,\mathcal{A}(z)}(1^\lambda)\}$ is computationally indistinguishable from $\{\mathsf{OUT}_{\mathcal{H}_3,\mathcal{A}(z)}(1^\lambda)\}$. Moreover the second property enjoyed by $\mathsf{Sim}^{\mathsf{NMZK}}$ (simulation-extraction) ensures that in $\mathcal{H}_3$ the witnesses can be extracted from $\mathcal{A}$ (one witness for every execution of NMZK made by every malicious P_i^*), therefore we are guaranteed that $\mathcal{A}$ correctly computes all the steps of Π_{MCF}. That is, the value $r_2^*, \ldots, r_n^*$ sent by the malicious party in the last round is actually committed in the second round sent by $\mathcal{A}$. It is important to observe that in this hybrid experiment the probability that $\mathcal{A}$ completes the third round is negligible close to the probability of completing the third round in $\mathcal{H}_2$ (otherwise the output of the two experiments would be distinguishable). Therefore the probability that E_{OR} works correctly in this experiment is negligibly close to the probability that E_{OR} works in $\mathcal{H}_2$. This holds because, following the Definition 2.3, the probability of E_{OR} to given in output a valid witness for the instance $(\mathtt{com}_0, \mathtt{com}_1)$ is negligible close to the probability that $\mathcal{A}$ completes an accepting third round.
- The 4th hybrid experiment $\mathcal{H}_4$ differs from $\mathcal{H}_3$ in the way $\mathtt{com}_1$ is computed. More precisely, instead of a committing to r_1 in $\mathtt{com}_1$ a commitment of a random string y is made. We claim that $\{\mathsf{OUT}_{\mathcal{H}_3,\mathcal{A}(z)}(1^\lambda)\}$ and $\{\mathsf{OUT}_{\mathcal{H}_4,\mathcal{A}(z)}(1^\lambda)\}$ are computationally indistinguishable due to the computationally hiding of PBCOM. We claim also that in $\mathcal{H}_4$ $\mathcal{A}$ still behaves correctly, indeed we can use the simulator extractor $\mathsf{Sim}^{\mathsf{NMZK}}$ in order to check whether the theorem proved by every party

[16] Also in this case we are considering an adversary that completes the execution of Π_{MCF} against Sim with non-negligible probability. In the case that the abort probability of the adversary is overwhelming then the security proof is already over.

controlled by $\mathcal{A}$ using NMZK are still true. If it is not the case, then we can make a reduction to the hiding of $\mathtt{com}_1$.[17]

- The 5th hybrid experiment $\mathcal{H}_5$ follows the same steps of $\mathcal{H}_4$ except that the honest prover procedure ($\mathcal{P}_L$), instead of the Special HVZK simulator (Sim_L), is used to compute the prover's messages $\mathsf{a}_1, \mathsf{z}_1$ of the transcript $\tau_1 = (\mathsf{a}_1, \mathsf{c}_1, \mathsf{z}_1)$ w.r.t. the instance $\mathtt{com}_1$.
  Suppose now by contradiction that the output distributions of the hybrid experiments are distinguishable, then we can show a malicious verifier $\mathcal{V}^\star$ that distinguishes between a transcript $\tau_1 = (\mathsf{a}_1, \mathsf{c}_1, \mathsf{z}_1)$ computed using Sim_L and one computed using the honest prover procedure. In more detail, let C_{SHVZK} be the challenger of the Special HVZK. $\mathcal{V}^\star$ picks $\mathsf{c}_1 \leftarrow \{0, 1\}^\lambda$ and sends c_1 to C_{SHVZK}. Upon receiving $\mathsf{a}_1, \mathsf{z}_1$ from C_{SHVZK} $\mathcal{V}^\star$ plays all the messages of Π_{MCF} as in $\mathcal{H}_4$ ($\mathcal{H}_5$) except for the messages of τ_1 where he $\mathcal{V}^\star$ acts as a proxy between C_{SHVZK} and $P^\star$. At the end of the execution $\mathcal{V}^\star$ runs the distinguisher D that distinguishes the output distribution of $\mathcal{H}_4$ from the output distribution of $\mathcal{H}_5$ and outputs what D outputs. We observe that if C_{SHVZK} sends a simulated transcript then $P_2^\star$ acts as in $\mathcal{H}_4$ otherwise he acts as in $\mathcal{H}_5$.
  There is a subtlety in the above reduction $\mathcal{V}^\star$ runs the $\mathsf{Sim}^{\mathsf{NMZK}}$ that rewinds from the third to the second round. This means that $\mathcal{V}^\star$ has to be able to complete during the rewinds the third round while receiving different challenges $\mathsf{c}^1, \ldots, \mathsf{c}^{\mathsf{poly}(\lambda)}$ w.r.t. Π_{OR}. Since we are splitting the challenge c, $\mathcal{V}^\star$ can just keep fixed the value c_1 reusing the same z_1 (sent by C_{SHVZK}) and computing an answer to a_0 using the knowledge of the decommitment information of $\mathtt{com}_0$. To argue that $\mathcal{A}$ correctly computes all the steps of Π_{MCF}, also in this hybrid experiment we can use the simulator-extractor $\mathsf{Sim}^{\mathsf{NMZK}}$ to check whether the theorem proved by $\mathcal{A}$ is still true. If it is not the case we can construct a reduction to the Special HVZK property of BL_L. Note that the rewinds of $\mathsf{Sim}^{\mathsf{NMZK}}$ from the fourth to the third round do not affect the reduction. Moreover, the fact that $\mathsf{Sim}^{\mathsf{NMZK}}$ extracts the witnesses for the theorems proved by every party controlled by $\mathcal{A}$ still ensures that $\mathcal{A}$ behaves honestly.
- $\mathcal{H}_6$ proceeds exactly as $\mathcal{H}_5$ except that the Special HVZK simulator (Sim_L), instead of honest procedure ($\mathcal{P}_L$), is used to compute the prover's messages $\mathsf{a}_0, \mathsf{z}_0$ of the transcript $\tau_0 = (\mathsf{a}_0, \mathsf{c}_0, \mathsf{z}_0)$ w.r.t. the instance $\mathtt{com}_0$.
  We claim that $\{\mathsf{OUT}_{\mathcal{H}_5,\mathcal{A}(z)}(1^\lambda)\}$ and $\{\mathsf{OUT}_{\mathcal{H}_6,\mathcal{A}(z)}(1^\lambda)\}$ are computationally indistinguishable due the same arguments used to prove that $\{\mathsf{OUT}_{\mathcal{H}_4,\mathcal{A}(z)}(1^\lambda)\} \approx \{\mathsf{OUT}_{\mathcal{H}_5,\mathcal{A}(z)}(1^\lambda)\}$. Furthermore we claim that $\mathcal{A}$ still behaves honestly for the same arguments given in $\mathcal{H}_5$.
- The 7th hybrid experiment $\mathcal{H}_7$ differs from $\mathcal{H}_6$ in the way $\mathtt{com}_0$ is computed. More precisely, instead of committing to r_1 in $\mathtt{com}_0$, a commitment of a random string y is computed. For the same arguments used to prove that $\{\mathsf{OUT}_{\mathcal{H}_3,\mathcal{A}(z)}(1^\lambda)\} \approx \{\mathsf{OUT}_{\mathcal{H}_4,\mathcal{A}(z)}(1^\lambda)\}$, we claim that $\{\mathsf{OUT}_{\mathcal{H}_6,\mathcal{A}(z)}(1^\lambda)\} \approx \{\mathsf{OUT}_{\mathcal{H}_7,\mathcal{A}(z)}(1^\lambda)\}$ and that $\mathcal{A}$ still behaves honestly. We observe that r_1 appears only in the 4th round. More

[17] In order to extract the witnesses for the theorems proved by every party controlled by $\mathcal{A}$, $\mathsf{Sim}^{\mathsf{NMZK}}$ needs to rewind also from the 4th to the 3rd round, but this does not affect the reduction.

precisely there is no relation between r_1 and the values committed in $\mathcal{H}_1$. Therefore the security proof is almost over. Indeed our simulator Sim proceeds as $\mathcal{H}_7$ until the 3rd round, then invokes the functionality thus obtaining a value r and completes the 4th round of $\mathcal{H}_7$ setting $r_1 = r \oplus \cdots \oplus r_n^*$. □

4.4 Special WIPoK

4.4.1 *Improving the Soundness of LS*

In this section, we consider the 3-round WIPoK for the $\mathcal{NP}$-complete language of graph Hamiltonicity (HC), provided in [76], and we will refer to this construction as the *LS protocol*. An interesting property of this WIPoK is that only the size of the statement needs to be known before the last round by both the prover and the verifier. We show that the LS protocol does not enjoy special soundness when the statement to be proved is adaptively chosen by the prover in the last round. That is, if two accepting transcripts (that share the first round) are provided w.r.t. to two different instances x_0 and x_1, then only the witness w for x_b is extracted (with $b \in \{0, 1\}$). More precisely, given the accepting transcript $(\mathsf{ls}^1, \mathsf{ls}_0^2, \mathsf{ls}_0^3)$ for the statement x_0 and $(\mathsf{ls}^1, \mathsf{ls}_1^2, \mathsf{ls}_1^3)$ for the statement x_1 (with $\mathsf{ls}_0^2 \neq \mathsf{ls}_1^2$) then it could be that only w_b can be extracted. We provide a construction that overcomes this issue, allowing the extraction of the witnesses for both x_0 and x_1 thus obtaining a Σ-protocol where the special soundness holds even when the two accepting transcripts refer to different theorems adaptively chosen in the last round. Following [53] we refer to this property as adaptive-input special soundness.

Before showing why LS is not already adaptive-input special sound and how our construction works, we briefly describe the LS protocol with one-bit challenge following [162].

Let $\mathcal{P}$ be prover and $\mathcal{V}$ the verifier. The common input of $\mathcal{P}$ and $\mathcal{V}$ is κ, that represents the number of vertexes of the instance G to be proved. The graph G is represented by a $\kappa \times \kappa$ adjacency matrix MG where $\mathsf{MG}[i][j] = 1$ if there exists an edge between vertexes i and j in G. A non-edge position i,j is a pair of vertexes that are not connected in G and for which $\mathsf{MG}[i][j] = 0$.

- $\mathcal{P}$ picks a random κ-vertex cycle graph C and commits bit-by-bit to the corresponding adjacency matrix using a statistically binding commitment scheme.
- $\mathcal{V}$ responds with a randomly chosen bit b.
- $\mathcal{P}$ on input the graph G and the Hamiltonian cycle w executes the following steps. If $b = 0$, $\mathcal{P}$ opens all the commitments, showing that the matrix committed in the first round is actually an κ-vertex cycle. If $b = 1$, $\mathcal{P}$ sends a permutation π mapping the vertex of C in G. Then it opens the commitment of the adjacency matrix of C corresponding to the non-edges of the graph G.

– $\mathcal{V}$ accepts (outputs 1) if what he receives in the third round is consistent with the bit b that he was sent in the second round.

Getting the answer for both $b = 0$ and $b = 1$ (w.r.t. to the same graph G) allows the extraction of the cycle for G. The reason is the following. For $b = 0$ one gets the random cycle C. Then for $b = 1$ one gets the permutation mapping the random cycle in the actual cycle that is given to $\mathcal{P}$ before the last message of the protocol.

We now observe that a malicious prover $\mathcal{P}^\star$ could gives the answer for $b = 0$ w.r.t. to the graph G_0 and the answer for $b = 1$ w.r.t. the graph G_1 (due to the delayed-input nature of LS). This means that even knowing two accepting transcripts that share the first round, the permutation that maps the vertexes of C in G_0 it is not known. Therefore an efficient algorithm can only compute the cycle w_1 of G_1 and gets no information about the Hamiltonian cycle of G_0. Summing up, given the accepting transcripts $(\mathsf{ls}^1, 0, \mathsf{ls}_0^3)$ for the graph G_0 and $(\mathsf{ls}^1, 1, \mathsf{ls}_1^3)$ for the graph G_1, only the Hamiltonian cycle for G_1 can be computed. That is, only the cycle for the graph proved by $\mathcal{P}^\star$ to be Hamiltonian using as a second round the challenge 1 can be efficiently computed. Starting from this observation, in order to allow an efficient algorithm to compute cycles for both G_0 and G_1, we construct an improved version of LS that we denoted with $\mathsf{LS}^{\mathsf{imp}} = (\mathcal{P}^{\mathsf{imp}}, \mathcal{V}^{\mathsf{imp}})$. $\mathsf{LS}^{\mathsf{imp}}$ uses LS in a black-box way. For ease of exposition we use the following notation. $\mathsf{ls}^1 \leftarrow \mathcal{P}(1^\lambda, \kappa; \rho)$ denotes that $\mathcal{P}$ is executed on input the security parameter (in unary) 1^λ, κ and the randomness ρ and gives in output the first round of LS ls^1. $\mathsf{ls}^3 \leftarrow \mathcal{P}(G, w, \mathsf{ls}^2, \rho)$ denotes that $\mathcal{P}$ has computed the third round of LS by running on input the graph G, the cycle w for the graph G, the bit ls^2 and the randomness used to compute ls^1. $\mathcal{V}(\mathsf{ls}^1, \mathsf{ls}^2, \mathsf{ls}^3, G)$ denotes the output of $\mathcal{V}$ on input $\mathsf{ls}^1, \mathsf{ls}^2, \mathsf{ls}^3$ and the graph G. Let κ be the number of vertexes of the graph G to be proved, our $\mathsf{LS}^{\mathsf{imp}} = (\mathcal{P}^{\mathsf{imp}}, \mathcal{V}^{\mathsf{imp}})$ works as follows.

1. $\mathcal{P}^{\mathsf{imp}}$ on input the security parameter λ, κ and the randomness $\rho_0||\rho_1$ computes $\mathsf{ls}_0^1 \leftarrow \mathcal{P}(1^\lambda, \kappa; \rho_0)$, $\mathsf{ls}_1^1 \leftarrow \mathcal{P}(1^\lambda, \kappa; \rho_1)$ and sends $(\mathsf{ls}_1^0, \mathsf{ls}_1^1)$ to $\mathcal{V}^{\mathsf{imp}}$.
2. $\mathcal{V}^{\mathsf{imp}}$ picks and sends a random bit b.
3. $\mathcal{P}^{\mathsf{imp}}$, upon receiving b, on input the graph G and the Hamiltonian cycle w for G computes $\mathsf{ls}_0^3 \leftarrow \mathcal{P}(G, w, b, \rho_0)$, $\mathsf{ls}_1^3 \leftarrow \mathcal{P}(G, w, 1-b, \rho_1)$ and sends $(\mathsf{ls}_0^3, \mathsf{ls}_1^3)$.
4. $\mathcal{V}^{\mathsf{imp}}$ accepts iff $\mathcal{V}(G, \mathsf{ls}_0^1, b, \mathsf{ls}_0^3) = 1$ and $\mathcal{V}(G, \mathsf{ls}_1^1, 1-b, \mathsf{ls}_1^3) = 1$.

Theorem 4.4 *Assuming one-to-one OWFs,* $\mathsf{LS}^{\mathsf{imp}}$ *is a* Σ*-protocol with adaptive-input Special HVZK simulator and adaptive-input special soundness. Moreover,* $\mathsf{LS}^{\mathsf{imp}}$ *is Zero Knowledge.*

Proof **(Delayed-input) Completeness**. The (delayed-input) completeness of $\mathsf{LS}^{\mathsf{imp}}$ comes from the (delayed-input) completeness of LS.
Adaptive-input special soundness. Let us consider two accepting transcripts that share the first round for $\mathsf{LS}^{\mathsf{imp}}$: $\big((\mathsf{ls}_0, \mathsf{ls}_1), 0, (\mathsf{ls}_0^3, \mathsf{ls}_1^3)\big)$ for the statement G and $\big((\mathsf{ls}_0, \mathsf{ls}_1), 1, (\mathsf{ls}_1^{3'}, \mathsf{ls}_1^{3'})\big)$ for the statement G'. We can isolate the sub-transcripts $(\mathsf{ls}_0, 0, \mathsf{ls}_0^3)$ and $(\mathsf{ls}_0, 1, \mathsf{ls}_0^{3'})$ and observe that $\mathcal{V}(G, \mathsf{ls}_0^1, 0, \mathsf{ls}_0^3) = 1 = \mathcal{V}(G'\mathsf{ls}_0^1, 1, \mathsf{ls}_0^{3'})$. From what we discussed before about LS we know that in this case the witness w for G' can be extracted. Also let us now consider the two sub-transcripts

$(\mathsf{ls}_1, 1, \mathsf{ls}_1^3)$ and $(\mathsf{ls}_1, 0, \mathsf{ls}_1^{3'})$. Also in this case, by observing that $\mathcal{V}(G, \mathsf{ls}_1, 1, \mathsf{ls}_1^3) = 1 = \mathcal{V}(G', \mathsf{ls}_1, 0, \mathsf{ls}_1^{3'})$, the cycle for G can be efficiently computed.
Adaptive-input Special HVZK. Following [151], we consider an adaptive-input Special HVZK simulator S associated to the LS's protocol. This is equal to a Special HVZK simulator with the additional property that the first round can be simulated without knowing the instance to be proved. In more detail S works in two phases. In the first phase just 1^λ, the challenge ls^2, the number of vertexes κ is used to output the first round ls^1. We denote this phase using: $\mathsf{ls}^1 \leftarrow S(1^\lambda, \mathsf{ls}^2, \kappa)$. In the second phase, S takes as input the instance and output the third round ls^3. We denote this phase using $\mathsf{ls}^3 \leftarrow S(G)$. The adaptive-input Special HVZK simulator S^{imp} for $\mathsf{LS}^{\mathsf{imp}}$ just internally runs S two times, once using b and once using $1-b$ as a challenge. In more details, the two phases of S^{imp} are the following.

1. S^{imp}, on input 1^λ, the challenge b, κ and the randomness $\rho_b||\rho_{1-b}$, computes $\mathsf{ls}_b^1 \leftarrow S(1^\lambda, b, \kappa; \rho_b)$, $\mathsf{ls}_{1-b}^1 \leftarrow S(1^\lambda, 1-b, \kappa; \rho_{1-b})$ and outputs $(\mathsf{ls}_b^1, \mathsf{ls}_{1-b}^1)$.
2. S^{imp}, on input the graph G, ρ_0 and ρ_1 computes $\mathsf{ls}_b^3 \leftarrow S(G, \rho_b)$, $\mathsf{ls}_{1-b}^3 \leftarrow S(G, \rho_{1-b})$ and outputs $(\mathsf{ls}_b^3, \mathsf{ls}_{1-b}^3)$.

The transcript $\left((\mathsf{ls}_b^1, \mathsf{ls}_{1-b}^1), b, (\mathsf{ls}_b^3, \mathsf{ls}_{1-b}^3)\right)$ output by S^{imp} is is computationally indistinguishable from a transcript computed by $\mathcal{P}^{\mathsf{imp}}$ (that uses as input an Hamiltonian cycle w of G) due to the security of the underlying adaptive-input Special HVZK simulator S.
Zero-Knowledge. The ZK simulator of $\mathsf{LS}^{\mathsf{imp}}$ just needs to guess the bit b chosen by the adversarial verifier and runs the adaptive-input Special HVZK simulator. □

It is easy to see that (as for LS) if we consider λ parallel executions of $\mathsf{LS}^{\mathsf{imp}}$ then we obtain a protocol LS^λ that still enjoys adaptive-input completeness, adaptive-input special soundness, adaptive-input Special HVZK. Moreover LS^λ is WI. Formally, we can claim the following theorems.

Theorem 4.5 *Assuming one-to-one OWFs,* LS^λ *is a* Σ*-protocol with adaptive-input Special HVZK, adaptive-input special soundness and WI.*

Proof Completeness, adaptive-input special soundness and adaptive-input Special HVZK come immediately from the adaptive-input special soundness and adaptive-input Special HVZK of $\mathsf{LS}^{\mathsf{imp}}$. The WI comes from the observation that $\mathsf{LS}^{\mathsf{imp}}$ is WI (due to the zero-knowledge property), and that WI is preserved under parallel (and concurrent) composition. □

Theorem 4.6 *Assuming OWFs,* LS^λ *is a 4-round public-coin interactive protocol with adaptive-input Special HVZK, adaptive-input special soundness and WI.*

Proof The proof of this theorem just relies on the observation that in order to instantiate a statistically binding commitment scheme using OWFs an additional round is required to compute the first round of Naor's commitment scheme [154]. □

Observe that since Hamiltonicity is an $\mathcal{NP}$-complete language, the above constructions work for any $\mathcal{NP}$ language through $\mathcal{NP}$ reductions. For simplicity, we will omit the $\mathcal{NP}$ reduction therefore assuming that the above scheme works directly on a given $\mathcal{NP}$-language L.

4.4.2 Combining (Adaptive-Input) Special HVZK PoK Through [57]

In this chapter, we instantiate Π_{OR} using as Π_0 and Π_1 Blum's protocol [22] for the $\mathcal{NP}$-complete language for graph Hamiltonicity (that also is a Σ-Protocol).

We also consider an instantiation of Π_{OR} using as $\Pi = (\mathcal{P}, \mathcal{V})$ our LS^λ. If we instantiate Π_{OR} using LS^λ and the corresponding adaptive-input Special HVZK simulator LS^λ, then Π_{OR} is adaptive-input special soundness. More formally we can claim the following theorem.

Theorem 4.7 *If Π_{OR} is instantiated using LS^λ (and the corresponding adaptive-input Special HVZK simulator S^λ), then Π_{OR} enjoys the delayed-input completeness and adaptive-input special sound for the $\mathcal{NP}$-relation $\mathsf{Rel}_{\mathsf{L_{OR}}}$.*

Proof The delayed-input completeness follows from the delayed-input completeness of LS^λ.

Adaptive-input special soundness. Let us consider two accepting transcripts that share the first round for Π_{OR}: $\big((\pi_0, \pi_1), \pi^2, (\pi_0^2, \pi_0^3, \pi_1^2, \pi_1^3)\big)$ for the statement (x_0, x_1) and $\big((\pi_0, \pi_1), \pi^{2'}, (\pi_0^{2'}, \pi_0^{3'}, \pi_1^{2'}\pi_1^{3'})\big)$ for the statement (x_0', x_1'), where $\pi^2 \neq \pi^{2'}$. We observe that since $\pi^2 \neq \pi^{2'}$, $\pi^2 = \pi_0^2 \oplus \pi_1^2$ and $\pi^{2'} = \pi_0^{2'} \oplus \pi_1^{2'}$ it holds that either $\pi_0^2 \neq \pi_0^{2'}$ or $\pi_1^2 \neq \pi_1^{2'}$. Suppose w.l.o.g. that $\pi_0^2 \neq \pi_0^{2'}$. Then we are guaranteed from the adaptive-input special soundness of LS^λ that using the transcripts $(\pi_0, \pi_0^2, \pi_0^3)$ and $(\pi_0, \pi_0^{2'}, \pi_0^{3'})$ the values (w_a, w_b) s.t. $(x_0, w_a) \in \mathsf{Rel}_{\mathsf{L}_0}$ and $(x_0', w_b) \in \mathsf{Rel}_{\mathsf{L}_0}$ can be extracted in polynomial-time. The same arguments can be used when $\pi_1^2 \neq \pi_1^{2'}$. □

Using a result of [53] (also presented in Chap. 2) we can claim the following theorem.

Theorem 4.8 *Π_{OR} instantiated using LS^λ is Adaptive Proof of Knowledge for the $\mathcal{NP}$-relation $\mathsf{Rel}_{\mathsf{L_{OR}}}$.*

It would be easy to prove that Π_{OR} is also WI, however, we are not going to rely directly on the WI property of Π_{OR}, in order to deal with the rewinding issue that we have described earlier. More precisely, in the two main contributions we will use Π_{OR} (the one instantiated from Blum's protocol and the one instantiated using LS^λ) in a non-black-box way in order to prove the security of our protocols. It will be crucial for our reduction to rely on the (adaptive-input) Special HVZK of Π_0 and Π_1 instead of using directly the WI property of Π_{OR}. The intuitive reason is that it is often easier in a reduction to rely on the security of a non-interactive primitive (like Special HVZK is) instead of an interactive primitive (like WI). This is the reason why we use the OR composition of [57, 82] combined with the Blum's protocol (or the LS protocol) instead of relying on the (adaptive-input) WI provided by a Blum's protocol (LS protocol).

To rely on OWFs only, we sometimes use a four-round version of Blum's and LS protocols. In this case, there is an additional initial round that goes from the verifier to the prover and corresponds to the first round of Naor's commitment scheme [154].

Chapter 5
Private Set-Membership in the Semi-Honest Setting

5.1 Introduction

There are many real-world applications in which parties are required to securely compute the intersection of their inputs. As an example, when mobile users install messaging apps, they need to discover who among their contacts (from their address book) is also using the app, in order to be able to start communicating seamlessly with them. Doing so requires users to learn the intersection of their contact list with the list of registered users of the service which is stored at the server side. This is typically done by having users send their contact list to the server, which can then compute the intersection and return the result to the user. Unfortunately, this solution is very problematic not only for the privacy of the user but for the privacy of the users' contacts as well. In particular, some of the people in the contact list might not want their phone numbers being transferred and potentially stored by the server, but they have no control over this.[1] PSI has many other applications, including computing intersections of suspect lists, private matchmaking (comparing interests), *testing human genome* [9], *privacy-preserving ride-sharing* [109], *botnet detection* [153], *advertisment conversion rate* [115], and many more.

History of PSI.

From a feasibility point of view, PSI is just a special case of 2PC and therefore any generic 2PC protocol (such as [90]) could be used to securely evaluate PSI instances as well. However, since PSI is a natural functionality that can be applied in numerous real-world applications, many efficient protocols for this specific functionality have been proposed, with early results dating back to the 80s [148, 186]. The problem was formally defined in [81] and follow up work increased the efficiency of PSI

[1] Some apps do not transfer the contact list in cleartext, but a hashed version instead. However, since the domain space of phone numbers is small enough to allow for brute forcing of the hashes, this does not guarantee any real privacy guarantee.

M. Ciampi and L. Siniscalchi, *Round and Computational Efficiency of Multi-party Protocols*, Information Security and Cryptography,
https://doi.org/10.1007/978-3-031-92374-6_5

protocols to have complexity only *linear* in the inputs of the parties [58, 120]. However, these protocols still require expensive public-key operations (e.g., exponentiations) for every element in the input sets. As public-key operations are orders of magnitudes more expensive than symmetric key operations, these protocols are not practically efficient for large input sets. In the meanwhile, generic techniques for 2PC had improved by several orders of magnitude and the question of whether special purpose protocols or generic protocols were most efficient has been debated in [59, 114]. Due to its practical relevance, PSI protocols in the *server-aided* model have been proposed as well [122].

OT-Based PSI.

The most efficient PSI protocols are those following the approach of Phasing [175, 176]. These protocols make extensive use of a cryptographic primitive known as *oblivious transfer (OT)*. While OT provably requires expensive public-key operation, OT can be "extended" as shown by [5, 118, 131] i.e., the few necessary expensive public-key operations can be amortized over a very large number of OT instances, and the marginal cost of OT is only a few (faster) symmetric key operations instead. In particular, improvements in OT-extension techniques directly imply improvements to PSI protocols as shown by e.g., [132, 157].

In a nutshell, the Phasing protocol introduced two important novel ideas to the state of the art of PSI. First, they give an efficient instantiation of the *private set membership protocol* (PSM) introduced in [80] based on OT. Second, they show how to efficiently implement PSI from PSM using hashing techniques. An overview of their techniques is provided below.

Chapter's Contribution.

The main contribution of this chapter is to give an efficient instantiation of PSM that provides output in encrypted format and can therefore be combined with further 2PC protocols. Our PSM protocol can be naturally combined with the hashing approach of Phasing to give a PSI protocol with encrypted output achieving the same favorable complexity in the input sizes. This enables to combine the efficiency of modern PSI techniques with the potentials of general 2PC. Combining our protocols with the right 2PC post-processing allows to more efficiently evaluate functionalities of the form $Z = f(X \cap Y)$ for any function f. To the best of our knowledge ours is the best special purpose PSI protocol which can be combined with 2PC techniques for post-processing, and therefore we propose the first alternative to *circuit-based PSI*.

Like in Phasing we only focus on semi-honest security. Using the protocol together with an actively secure OT-extension protocol such as [6, 126] would result in a protocol with *privacy* but not *correctness* (e.g., the view of the protocol *without* the output can be efficiently simulated), which is a meaningful notion of security in some settings. PSI protocols with security against malicious adversaries have been proposed in e.g., [111, 180]. Also, like in Phasing, we only focus on the two-party setting. The result of [113] has shown that multi-party set-intersection can be computed efficiently. Extending our result to the multi-party case is an interesting future research direction.

5.2 Technical Overview

Why Phasing and 2PC do not Mix

We start with a quick overview of the PSM protocol in Phasing [175, 176], to explain why their protocol inherently reveals the intersection to one of the parties. From a high-level point of view, the protocol is conceptually similar to the PSM protocol from OPRF of [80], except that the OPRF is replaced with a similar functionality efficiently implemented using OT. For simplicity, here we will use the OPRF abstraction.

The goal of a PSM protocol is the following: the receiver R has input x, and the sender S has input a set Y; at the end of the protocol the receiver learns whether $x \in Y$ or not while the sender learns nothing. The protocol starts by using the OPRF subprotocol, so that R learns $x^* = F_k(x)$ (where k is known to S), whereas S learns nothing about x. Now S evaluates the PRF on her own set and sends the set $Y^* = \{y^* = F_k(y) | y \in Y\}$ to R, who checks if $x^* \in Y^*$ and concludes that $x \in Y$ if this is the case. In other words, we map all inputs into pseudorandom strings and then let one of the parties test for membership "in the clear". Since the party performing the test doesn't have access to the mapping (e.g., the PRF key), this party can only check for the membership of x and no other points (i.e., all elements in $Y^* \setminus \{x^*\}$ are indistinguishable from random in R's view).

From the above description, it should be clear that the Phasing PSM inherently reveals the output to one of the parties. Turning this into a protocol that provides encrypted output is a challenging task. Here is an attempt at a "strawman" solutions: we change the protocol such that R still learns the pseudorandom string $x^* = F_k(x)$ corresponding to x, but now S sends a value *for every element in the universe*. Namely, for each i (in the domain of Y) S sends an encryption of whether $i \in Y$ "masked" using $F_k(i)$ e.g., S sends $c_i = F_k(i) \oplus E(i \in Y)$.[2] Now R can compute $c_x \oplus x^* = E(x \in Y)$ i.e., an encrypted version of whether $x \in Y$, which can be then used as input to the next protocol.

While this protocol produces the correct result, its complexity is exponential in the bit-length of $|x|$, which is clearly not acceptable.

Intuitively, we know that only a polynomial number of c_i's will contain encryptions of 1, and therefore we need to find a way to "compress" all the c_i corresponding to $i \notin Y$ into a single one, to bring the complexity of the protocol back to $O(|Y|)$. In the following, after defining some useful notation, we give an intuitive explanation on how to do that.

[2] The exact format of the "encryption" $E(\cdot)$ would depend on the subsequent 2PC protocol and is irrelevant for this high-level description.

5.2.1 The Protocol

Notation.

We introduce some useful (and informal) notation in order to make easier to understand the ideas behind our construction. We let $Y = \{y_1, \ldots, y_M\}$ be the input set of S, and we assume w.l.o.g., that $|Y| = M = 2^m$.[3] All strings have the same length e.g., $|x| = |y_i| = \lambda$.[4] We will use a special symbol $\perp$ such that $x \neq \perp$ $\forall x$. We use a function $\mathsf{Prefix}(x, i)$ that outputs the i most significant bits of x. ($\mathsf{Prefix}(x, i) \neq \mathsf{Prefix}(x, j)$ when $i \neq j$ independently of the value of x) and for simplicity we define $\mathsf{Prefix}(Y, i)$ to be the set constructed by taking the i most significant bits of every element in Y.

The protocol uses a symmetric key encryption scheme $\mathsf{Sym} = (\mathsf{Gen}, \mathsf{Enc}, \mathsf{Dec})$ with the additional property that given a key $k \leftarrow \mathsf{Gen}(1^s)$ it is possible to efficiently verify if a given ciphertext is in the range of k (see Sect. 5.3 for a formal definition).

Finally, the output of the protocol will be one of two strings γ_0, γ_1 chosen by S, respectively denoting $x \notin Y$ and $x \in Y$. The exact format of the two strings depends on the protocol used for post-processing. For instance if the post-processing protocol is based on: (1) *garbled circuits*, then γ_0, γ_1 will be the labels corresponding to some input wire; (2) *homomorphic encryption*, then $\gamma_b = \mathsf{Enc}(pk, b)$ for some homomorphic encryption scheme Enc; (3) *secret-sharing*, then $\gamma_b = s_2 \oplus b$ where s_2 is a uniformly random share chosen by S, so that if R defines its own share as $s_1 = \gamma_b$ then it holds that $s_1 \oplus s_2 = b$.[5]

In order to "compress" the elements of Y we start by considering an undirected graph with a level structure of $\lambda + 1$ levels. The vertices in the last level of this graph will correspond to the elements of Y. More precisely, we associate the secret key $k_{b_\lambda b_{\lambda-1} \ldots b_1}$ of a symmetric key encryption scheme Sym to each element $y = b_\lambda b_{\lambda-1} \ldots b_1 \in Y$. The main idea is to allow the receiver to obliviously navigate this graph in order to get the key $k_{b_\lambda b_{\lambda-1} \ldots b_1}$ if $x = y$, for some $y = b_\lambda b_{\lambda-1} \ldots b_1 \in Y$, or a special key $k^\star$ otherwise. Moreover we allow the receiver to navigate the graph efficiently, that is, every level of the graph is visited only once.

Once a key k is obtained by the receiver, the sender sends $O(|Y|)$ ciphertexts in a such a way that the key obtained by the receiver can decrypt only one ciphertext. Moreover the plaintext of this ciphertext will correspond to γ_0 or γ_1 depending on whether $x \in Y$ or not.

---

[3] Sets can always be padded with dummy elements, but the complexity of the protocol can match M that in practice can be $M \approx 2^{m-1}$.

[4] We can assume λ to be smaller than the (statistical) security parameter s and we will denote the bit decomposition of x by $x = x_\lambda \ldots x_1$.. Otherwise before running the protocol the parties can hash their input down and run the protocol with inputs $h(x)$ and $h(Y) = \{h(y_1), \ldots, h(y_M)\}$. Clearly if $x = y_i$ then $h(x) = h(y_i)$, and for correctness we need that $Pr[h(x) \in h(Y) \wedge x \notin Y] < 2^{-s}$.

[5] Here we use $\oplus$-secret sharing without loss of generality. Any 2-out-2 secret sharing would work here.

First Step: Construct the Graph G.

Each graph level $i \in \{0, \ldots, \lambda\}$ has size at most $|\mathsf{Prefix}(i, Y)| + 1$.

More precisely, for every $t = b_\lambda b_{\lambda-1} \ldots b_{\lambda-i} \in \mathsf{Prefix}(Y, i)$ there is a node in the level i of G that contains a key $k_{b_\lambda b_{\lambda-1} \ldots b_{\lambda-i}}$. In addition, in the level i there is a special node, called *sink node* that contains a key $k_i^\star$ (which we refer to as *sink key*). The aim of $k_i^\star$ is to represent all the values that do not belong to $\mathsf{Prefix}(i, Y)$.

Let us now describe how the graph G is constructed. First, for $i = 1, \ldots, \lambda$ the key (for a symmetric key encryption scheme) $k_j^\star$ is generated using the generation algorithm $\mathsf{Gen}(\cdot)$. As discussed earlier the aim of this keys is to represent the elements that do not belong to Y. More precisely, the sink key $k_i^\star$, with $i \in \{1, \ldots, \lambda\}$ represents all the values that do not belong to $\mathsf{Prefix}(Y, i)$ and the key $k_\lambda^\star$ (the last sink key) will be used to encrypt the output γ_0 corresponding to non-membership in the last step of our protocol. Note that if $\mathsf{Prefix}(x, i) \notin \mathsf{Prefix}(Y, i)$ then $\mathsf{Prefix}(x, j) \notin \mathsf{Prefix}(Y, j)$ for all $j > i$. Therefore, once entered in a sink node, the *sink path* is never abandoned and thus the final sink key $k_\lambda^\star$, will be retrieved (which allows to recover γ_0).

Let us now give a more formal idea of how G is constructed.

- The root of G is empty, and in the second level there are two vertices k_0 and k_1 where,[6] for $b = 0, 1$

$$k_b = \begin{cases} k \leftarrow \mathsf{Gen}(1^s), & \text{if } b \in \mathsf{Prefix}(Y, 1) \\ k_1^\star, & \text{otherwise} \end{cases}$$

- For each vertex k_t in the level $i \in \{1, \ldots, \lambda\}$ and for $b = 0, 1$ create the node $k_{t||b}$ as follows (if it does not exists) and connect k_t to it.

$$k_{t||b} = \begin{cases} k \leftarrow \mathsf{Gen}(1^s), & \text{if } t||b \in \mathsf{Prefix}(Y, i+1) \\ k_{i+1}^\star, & \text{if} t||b \notin \mathsf{Prefix}(Y, i+1) \\ k_{i+1}^\star, & \text{if } k_t = k_i^\star \end{cases} .$$

We observe that a new node $k_{t||b}$ is generated only when $t||b \in \mathsf{Prefix}(Y, i)$. In the other cases the sink node $k_{i+1}^\star$ is used.

In Fig. 5.1 we show an example of what the graph G looks like for the set $Y = \{010, 011, 110\}$. In this example it is possible to see how, in the 2nd level, all the elements that do not belong to $\mathsf{Prefix}(Y, 2)$ are represented by the sink node $k_2^\star$. Using this technique, we have that in the last level of G one node ($k_3^\star$ in this example) is sufficient to represent all the elements that do not belong to Y. Therefore, we have that the last level of G contains at most $|Y| + 1$ elements. We also observe that every level of G cannot contain more than $|Y| + 1$ nodes.

[6] In abuse of notation we refer to a vertex using the key represented by the vertex itself.

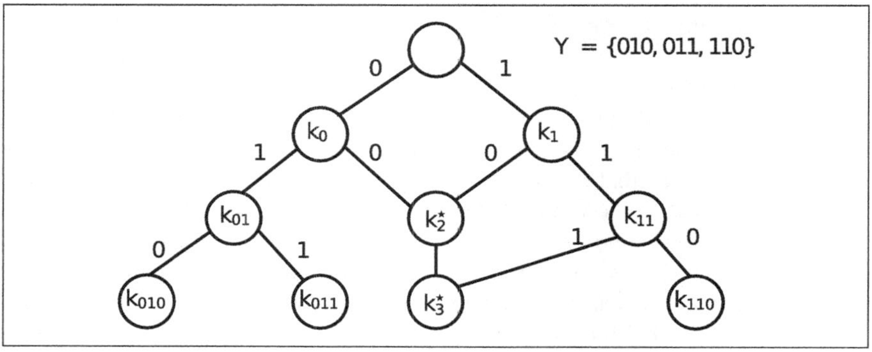

Fig. 5.1 Example of how the graph G appears when the sender holds the set Y

Second Step: Oblivious Navigation of G.

Let $x = x_\lambda x_{\lambda-1} \ldots x_1$ be the receiver's (R's) private input and Y be the sender's (S's) private input. After S constructs the graph G we need a way to allow R to obtain $k_{x_\lambda x_{\lambda-1} \ldots x_1}$ if $x \in Y$ and the sink key $k^\star_\lambda$ otherwise. All the computation has to be done in such a way that no other information about the set Y is leaked to the receiver, and as well that no information about x is leaked to the sender. In order to do so we use λ executions of 1-out-of-2 OT. The main idea is to allow the receiver to select which branch to explore in G depending on the bits of x. More precisely, in the first execution of OT, R will receive the key k_{x_λ} iff there exists an element in Y with the most significant bit equal to x_λ, the sink key $k^\star_1$ otherwise. In the second execution of OT, R uses $x_{\lambda-1}$ as input and S uses (c_0, c_1) where c_0 is computed as follows:

- For each key in the second level of G that has the form $k_{t||0}$, the key $k_{t||0}$ is encrypted using the key k_t.
- For every node v in the first level that is connected to a sink node $k^\star_2$ in the second level, compute an encryption of $k^\star_2$ using the key contained in v.
- Pad the input with random ciphertexts up to the upper bound for the size of this layer (more details about this step are provided later).
- Randomly permute these ciphertexts.

The procedure to compute the input c_1 is essentially the same (the only difference is that in this case we consider every key with form $k_{t||1}$ and encrypt it using k_t).

Roughly, in this step every key contained in a vertex u of the second level is encrypted using the keys contained in the vertex v of the previous level that is connected to u. For example, following the graph provided in Fig.5.1, c_0 would be equal to $\{\mathsf{Enc}(k_0, k^\star_2), \mathsf{Enc}(k_1, k^\star_2)\}$ and c_1 to $\{\mathsf{Enc}(k_0, k_{01}), \mathsf{Enc}(k_1, k_{11})\}$.

Thus, after the execution of OT R receives $c_{x_{\lambda-1}}$ that contains the ciphertexts described above where only one of these can be decrypted using the key k obtained in the first execution of OT. The obtained plaintext corresponds to the key $k_{x_\lambda x_{\lambda-1}}$ if

$\mathsf{Prefix}(x, 2) \in \mathsf{Prefix}(Y, 2)$, to the sink key $k_2^\star$ otherwise. The same process is iterated for all the levels of G. More generally if $\mathsf{Prefix}(x, j) \in \mathsf{Prefix}(Y, j)$ then after the jth execution of OT R can compute the key $k_{x_\lambda x_{\lambda-1} \ldots x_{\lambda-j}}$ using the key obtained in the previous phase. Conversely if $\mathsf{Prefix}(x, j) \notin \mathsf{Prefix}(Y, j)$ then the sink key $k_j^\star$ is obtained by R. We observe that after every execution of OT R does not know which ciphertext can be decrypted using the key obtained in the previous phase, therefore he will try to decrypt all the ciphertext until the decryption procedure is successful. To avoid adding yet more indexes to the (already heavy) notation of our protocol we deal with this using a private-key encryption scheme with efficiently verifiable range. We note that this is not necessary and that when implementing the protocol one can instead use the *point-and-permute technique* [14]. This, and other optimizations and extensions of our protocol, are described in Sect. 5.5.

Third Step: Obtain the Correct Share.

In this step S encrypts the output string γ_0 using the key $k_\lambda^\star$ and uses all the other keys in the last level of G to encrypt the output string γ_1.[7] At this point the receiver can only decrypt either the ciphertext that contains γ_0 if $x \notin Y$ or one (and only one) of the ciphertexts that contain γ_1 if $x \in Y$. In the protocol that we have described so far R does not know which ciphertext can be decrypted using the key that he has obtained. Also in this case we can use a point-and-permute technique to allow R to identify the only ciphertext that can be decrypted using his key.

On the Need for Padding.

As described earlier, we might need to add some padding to the OT sender's inputs. To see why we need this we made the following observation. We recall that in the ith OT execution the sender computes an encryption of the keys in the level i of the artificial graph G using the keys of the previous level $(i - 1)$.[8] As a result of this computation the sender obtains the couple (c_0^i, c_1^i), that will be used as input of the ith OT execution, where c_0^i (as well as c_1^i) contains a number of encryptions that depends upon the number of vertices on level $(i - 1)$ of G. We observe that this leaks informations about the structure of G to the receiver, and therefore leaks information about the elements that belong to Y. Considering the example in Fig. 5.1, if we allow the receiver to learn that the 2nd level only contains 3 nodes, then the receiver will learn that all the elements of Y have the two most significant bits equal to either t or t' for some $t, t' \in \{0, 1\}^2$ (in Fig. 5.1, for example, we have $t = 01$ and $t' = 11$). However, note that the receiver will not learn the actual values of t and t'.

We finally note that the technique described in this section can be seen as a special (and simpler) example of securely evaluating a branching program. Secure evaluation of branching programs has previously been considered in [119, 152]: unfortunately these protocols cannot be instantiated using OT-extension and therefore will not lead

---

[7] The key $k_\lambda^\star$ could not exists; e.g., if Y contains all the strings of λ bits.

[8] The only exception is the first OT execution where just two keys are using as input.

to practically efficient protocols (the security of these protocols is based on *strong* OT which, in a nutshell, requires the extra property that when executing several OTs in parallel, the receiver should not be able to correlate the answers with the queries beyond correlations which follow from the output).

5.3 Definitions and Tools

5.3.1 Semi-Honest Two-Party Computation

A two-party protocol problem is cast by specifying a random process that maps pairs of inputs to pairs of outputs (one for each party). We refer to such a process as a functionality and denote it as $F = (F_1, F_2)$. That is, for every pair of inputs $x, y \in \{0,1\}^s$, the output-pair is a random variable $(F_1(x, y), F_2(x, y))$ ranging over pairs of strings. The first party (with input x) wishes to obtain $F_1(x, y)$ and the second party (with input y) wishes to obtain $F_2(x, y)$. We often denote such a functionality by $(x, y) \to (F_1(x, y), F_2(x, y))$.

Let $F = (F_1, F_2)$ be a probabilistic polynomial-time functionality and let $\Pi = (P_1, P_2)$ be a two-party protocol for computing F where P_1 and P_2 denote the two parties. The view of the party P_i $(i \in \{1, 2\})$ during an execution of Π on (x, y) and security parameter s is denoted by $\mathsf{View}^{\Pi}_{P_i}(x, y, 1^s)$.

The output of the party P_i $(i \in \{1, 2\})$ during an execution of Π on (x, y) and security parameter s is denoted by $\mathsf{output}^{\Pi}_{P_i}(1^s, x, y)$ and can be computed from its own view of the execution. We denote the joint output of both parties by $\mathsf{output}^{\Pi}(1^s, x, y) = (\mathsf{output}^{\Pi}_{P_1}(1^s, x, y), \mathsf{output}^{\Pi}_{P_2}(1^s, x, y))$.

Definition 5.1 (*Semi-Honest Secure two-party computation [112]*) Let $F = (F_1, F_2)$ be a functionality. We say that Π securely computes F in the presence of static semi-honest adversaries if there exist probabilistic polynomial-time algorithms Sim_{P_1} and Sim_{P_2} called simulators, such that

$$\{(\mathsf{Sim}_{P_1}(1^s, x, F_1(x, y)), F(x, y))\}_{\{x,y,s\}} \approx \{\mathsf{View}^{\Pi}_{P_1}(1^s, x, y), \mathsf{output}^{\Pi}(1^s x, y)\}_{\{x,y,s\}}$$

and

$$\{(\mathsf{Sim}_{P_2}(1^s, y, F_2(x, y)), F(x, y))\}_{\{x,y,s\}} \approx \{\mathsf{View}^{\Pi}_{P_2}(1^s, x, y), \mathsf{output}^{\Pi}(1^s, x, y)\}_{\{x,y,s\}}$$

where $x, y \in \{0, 1\}^{\star}$ such that $|x| = |y|$, and $s \in \mathbb{N}$.

5.3.2 Special *Private-Key Encryption*

In our construction we use a private-key encryption scheme with two additional properties. The first is that given the key k, it is possible to efficiently verify if a given ciphertext is in the range of k. With the second property, we require that an encryption under one key will fall in the range of an encryption under another key with negligible probability

As discussed in [142], it is easy to obtain a private-key encryption scheme with the properties that we require. According to Definition 2 of [142] we give the following definition.

Definition 5.2 Let $\mathsf{Sym} = (\mathsf{Gen}, \mathsf{Enc}, \mathsf{Dec})$ be a private-key encryption scheme and denote the range of a key in the scheme by $\mathsf{Range}_s(k) = \{\mathsf{Enc}(k, x)\}_{x \in \{0,1\}^s}$. Then

1. We say that Sym has an *efficiently verifiable range* if there exists a PPT algorithm M such that $M(1^s, k, c) = 1$ if and only if $c \in \mathsf{Range}_s(k)$. By convention, for every $c \notin \mathsf{Range}_s(k)$, we have that $\mathsf{Dec}(k, c) = \perp$.
2. We say that Sym has an *elusive range* if for every probabilistic polynomial-time machine $\mathcal{A}$, there exists a negligible function $\nu(\cdot)$ such that

$$\mathrm{Prob}_{k \leftarrow \mathsf{Gen}(1^s)}[\mathcal{A}(1^s) \in \mathsf{Range}_s(k)] < \nu(s).$$

In order to make the security proof of our scheme easier, without loss of generality we assume Sym to be secure in the setting where the challenge messages $\mathbf{m}_0$ and $\mathbf{m}_1$ are lists of λ values. That is $\mathbf{m}_0 = \{m_0^1, \ldots, m_0^\lambda\}$ and $\mathbf{m}_1 = \{m_1^1, \ldots, m_1^\lambda\}$. The challenger, upon receiving these lists picks $b \leftarrow \{0, 1\}$, defines an empty list $\mathbf{cx}$ and for $i = 1, \ldots \lambda$ acts as follows:

1. computes $k_i \leftarrow \mathsf{Gen}(1^s)$;
2. computes $\mathsf{Enc}(k_i, m_b^i)$ and adds it to $\mathbf{cx}$.

The aim of the adversary is to guess the bit b having on input just $\mathbf{m}_0$, $\mathbf{m}_1$, $\mathbf{cx}$, and an auxiliary input z.

5.4 The Protocol $\Pi^{\in}$

In this section, we provide the formal description of our protocol $\Pi^{\in} = (\mathsf{S}, \mathsf{R})$ for the functionality $\mathcal{F}^{\in} = (\mathcal{F}_{\mathsf{S}}^{\in}, \mathcal{F}_{\mathsf{R}}^{\in})$ where

$$\mathcal{F}_{\mathsf{S}}^{\in}: \{\{0,1\}^\lambda\}^M \times \{\gamma^0, \gamma^1\} \times \{0,1\}^\lambda \longrightarrow \perp$$

and

$$\begin{aligned}\mathcal{F}_{\mathsf{R}}^{\in}\colon \{\{0,1\}^{\lambda}\}^{M} \times \{\gamma^0,\gamma^1\} \times \{0,1\}^{\lambda} &\longrightarrow \{\gamma^0,\gamma^1\}\\ (Y,x) &\longmapsto \begin{cases}\gamma^1 & \text{if } x \in Y\\ \gamma^0 & \text{otherwise}\end{cases}\end{aligned}$$

where γ^0 and γ^1 are arbitrary strings and are part of the sender's input. Therefore our scheme protects both Y and γ^{1-b}, when γ^b is received by R.

For the formal description of $\Pi^{\in}$, we collapse the first and the second step from the information description in Sect. 5.2 into a single one. That is, instead of constructing the graph G, we only compute the keys at level i in order to feed the ith OT execution with the correct inputs. The way in which the keys are computed is the same as the vertices for G are computed, we just do not need to physically construct G to allow S to efficiently compute the keys.

We use the following tools.

1. A protocol $\Pi_{\mathcal{OT}}^{\gamma} = (S_{\mathcal{OT}}, R_{\mathcal{OT}})$ that securely (according to Definition 5.1) computes the following functionality

$$\begin{aligned}F_{\mathcal{OT}}\colon (\{0,1\}^{\star} \times \{0,1\}^{\star}) \times \{0,1\} &\longrightarrow \{\bot\} \times \{0,1\}^{\star}\\ ((c_0,c_1),b) &\longmapsto (\bot, c_b).\end{aligned}$$

2. A symmetric key encryption scheme $\mathsf{Sym} = (\mathsf{Gen}, \mathsf{Enc}, \mathsf{Dec})$ with efficiently verifiable range and elusive range.
3. In our construction we make use of the following function

$$\begin{aligned}\delta\colon \mathbb{N} &\longrightarrow \mathbb{N}\\ i &\longmapsto \mathsf{min}\{2^i, |Y|\}.\end{aligned}$$

The function computes the maximum number of vertices that can appear in the level i of the graph G. As discussed before, the structure of G leaks information about Y. In order to avoid this information leakage about Y, it is sufficient to add some padding to the OT sender's input so that the input size becomes $|Y|$. Indeed, as observed above, every level contains at most $|Y|$ vertices. Actually, it is easy to see that $\mathsf{min}\{|Y|, 2^i\}$ represents a better upper bound on the number of vertices that the ith level can contain given Y. Therefore, in order to compute the size of the padding for the sender's input we use the function δ.

5.4.1 Formal Description

Common input: security parameter s and λ.
S's *input:* a set Y of size M, $\gamma^0 \in \{0,1\}^s$ and $\gamma^1 \in \{0,1\}^s$.
R's *input:* an element $x \in \{0,1\}^\lambda$.
First Stage

1. For i=1, ..., λ compute the sink key $k_i^\star \leftarrow \mathsf{Gen}(1^s)$.
2. S computes $k_0 \leftarrow \mathsf{Gen}(1^s)$, $k_1 \leftarrow \mathsf{Gen}(1^s)$. For $b = 0, 1$, if $b \notin \mathsf{Prefix}(Y, 1)$ then set $k_b = k_1^\star$.[9] Set $(c_0^1, c_1^1) = (k_0, k_1)$.
3. S and R execute $\Pi_{\mathcal{OT}}^{\gamma}$, where S acts as the sender $S_{\mathcal{OT}}$ using (c_0^1, c_1^1) as input and R acts as a receiver using x_λ as input. When the execution of $\Pi_{\mathcal{OT}}^{\gamma}$ ends R obtains $k_1 := c_{x_\lambda}^1$.

Second Stage
For $i = 2, \ldots, \lambda$:

1. S executes the following steps.
   1.1 Define the empty list c_0^i and for all $t \in \mathsf{Prefix}(Y, i-1)$ execute the following steps.

   If $t||0 \in \mathsf{Prefix}(Y, i)$ then compute $k_{t||0} \leftarrow \mathsf{Gen}(1^s)$ and add $\mathsf{Enc}(k_t, k_{t||0})$ to the list c_0^i. Otherwise, if $t||0 \notin \mathsf{Prefix}(Y, i)$ then compute and add $\mathsf{Enc}(k_t, k_i^\star)$ to the list c_0^i.

   1.2 If $|c_0^i| < \delta(i-1)$ then execute the following steps.

   - Compute and add $\mathsf{Enc}(k_{i-1}^\star, k_i^\star)$ to the list c_0^i.
   - For $i = 1, \ldots, \delta(i-1) - |c_0^i|$ compute and add $\mathsf{Enc}(\mathsf{Gen}(1^s), 0)$ to c_0^i.[10]

   1.3 Permute the elements inside c_0^i.
   1.4 Define the empty list c_1^i and for all $t \in \mathsf{Prefix}(Y, i-1)$ execute the following step.

   If $t||1 \in \mathsf{Prefix}(Y, i)$ then compute $k_{t||1} \leftarrow \mathsf{Gen}(1^s)$ and add $\mathsf{Enc}(k_t, k_{t||1})$ to the list c_1^i. Otherwise, if $t||1 \notin \mathsf{Prefix}(Y, i)$ compute and add $\mathsf{Enc}(k_t, k_i^\star)$ to the list c_1^i.

   1.5 If $|c_1^i| < \delta(i-1)$ then execute the following steps.

---

[9] We observe that if Y is not empty (like in our case) then there exists at most one bit b s.t. $b \notin \mathsf{Prefix}(Y, 1)$.

[10] In this step, as well as in the step 1.5 of this stage, the function δ is used to compute the right amount of fake encryption to be added to the list that will we used as input of $R_{\mathcal{OT}}$. The fake encryptions encrypts the value 0, but of course any other value could be used.

- Compute and add $\mathsf{Enc}(k^\star_{i-1}, k^\star_i)$ to the list c^i_1.
- For $i = 1, \ldots, \delta(i-1) - |c^i_1|$ compute and add $\mathsf{Enc}(\mathsf{Gen}(1^s), 0)$ to c^i_1.

1.6 Permute the elements inside c^i_1.

2. S and R execute $\Pi^{\gamma}_{\mathcal{OT}}$, where S acts as the sender $S_{\mathcal{OT}}$ using (c^i_0, c^i_1) as input. and R acts as a receiver using $x_{\lambda-i+1}$ as input. When the execution of $\Pi^{\gamma}_{\mathcal{OT}}$ ends, R obtains $c^i_{x_{\lambda-i+1}}$.

Third Stage

1. S executes the following steps.

   1.1 Define the empty list l.
   1.2 For every $t \in \mathsf{Prefix}(Y, \lambda)$ compute and add $\mathsf{Enc}(k_t, \gamma^1)$ to l.
   1.3 If $|l| < 2^\lambda$ then compute and add $\mathsf{Enc}(k^\star_\lambda, \gamma^0)$ to l.
   1.4 Permute the elements inside l and send l to R.

2 R, upon receiving l execute the following steps.

   2.1 For $i = 2, \ldots, \lambda$ execute the following step.

   For every element t in the list $c^i_{x_{\lambda-i+1}}$ compute $k \leftarrow \mathsf{Dec}(k_{i-1}, t)$. If $k \neq \perp$ then set $k_i = k$.

   2.2 For all $e \in l$ compute $\mathsf{out} \leftarrow \mathsf{Dec}(k_\lambda, e)$ and output out if and only if $\mathsf{out} \neq \perp$.

5.4.2 Complexity Analysis

We focus our analysis on the described protocol without taking into account the many possible optimizations that we will describe in Sect. 5.5. In $\Pi^{\in}$, sender and receiver run λ executions of a 1-out-of-2 OT; in addition, they perform some symmetric key operations. More precisely, in order to compute the inputs for the ith OT executions, with $i \in \{2, \ldots, \lambda\}$, S computes $2 \cdot \min\{2^{i-1}, |Y|\}$ encryptions using the private-key encryption scheme Sym. We now observe that each encryption could contain a different key, and that this key needs to be generated by running $\mathsf{Gen}(\cdot)$.[11] This means that $4M$ represents an upper bound on the number of symmetric key operations performed by S in every OT execution. Moreover, in the last interaction with R, S computes M encryptions. Therefore, an upper bound on the number symmetric key operation performed by S is $(\lambda - 1) \cdot 4M + M + 2 \approx \lambda \cdot 4M$, where 2 represents the cost of running $\mathsf{Gen}(\cdot)$ twice in order to compute the two keys required

[11] We recall that $|Y| = M$ and that λ is the bit size of a set element.

to feed the first OT execution.[12] In every OT execution i, with $i \in \{2, \ldots, \lambda\}$, R receives $\min\{2^{i+1}, |Y|\}$ encryptions, and tries to decrypt all of them. Moreover, in the last interaction with S, R receives M encryptions and tries to decrypt all of them as well. This means that the upper bound on the number of symmetric key operations made by R is $(\lambda - 1) \cdot M + M = \lambda \cdot M$. Following [177] we assume that 3 symmetric key operations are required for one OT execution. Therefore the total amount of symmetric key operations is $\lambda(4M + 3)$ for the sender and $\lambda(M + 3)$ for the receiver. In order to compare the efficiency of our protocol with the PSI protocols provided in [177] and to be consistent with their complexity analysis, we consider only the computation complexity for the party with the majority of the workload in the comparison.

Therefore we reach the conclusion that our protocol has better performance than all the circuit-based PSI approaches (which can be combined with further post-processing) proposed in [177]. We note that, as described in Sect. 4.4 of [177], the approach based on evaluating the OPRF inside circuit is faster than any other PSI protocols if one set is much smaller than the other (like in the case of PSM), but in this case the output will necessarily leak to the receiver, which prevents composition with further 2PC protocol. We refer the reader to Table 7 of [177] for a detailed efficiency comparison between different PSI protocols). Finally, we observe that the complexities analysis proposed in [177] is related to PSI protocols, while in this section we have only compared the efficiency of the PSM subprotocol.

Communication Complexity.

The communication complexity of our protocol is dominated by the communication complexity of the underlying OT protocol $\Pi^{\gamma}_{\mathcal{OT}} = (S_{\mathcal{OT}}, R_{\mathcal{OT}})$. Let $\mathsf{sOT}(D)$ be the amount of bit exchanged between $S_{\mathcal{OT}}$ and $R_{\mathcal{OT}}$ when $S_{\mathcal{OT}}$ uses an input of size D, and let $\mathsf{sSYM}(A)$ be the size of a ciphertext for the encryption scheme Sym when a plaintext of size A is used. Then the communication complexity of our protocol is

$$\lambda \cdot \mathsf{sOT}(2 \cdot M \cdot \mathsf{sSYM}(\lambda)) + M \cdot \mathsf{sSYM}(\lambda)$$

where $2 \cdot M$ is the number of ciphertexts used as input of OT and M is the amount of ciphertexts that are sent in the last interaction between S and R. If we assume that a chipertext for Sym is roughly of size λ, and that $\Pi^{\gamma}_{\mathcal{OT}}$ has a communication complexity that is approximately close to the size of the input used,[13] we obtain that the overall communication complexity of our protocol is well approximated by $M\lambda \cdot (2\lambda + 1)$.

Round Complexity: Parallelizability of our Scheme In the description of our protocol in Sect. 5.4.1 we have the sender and the receiver engaging λ sequential OT

[12] In this section, without loss of generality, we assume that λ is always greater than the security parameter s.

[13] This is actually true for the most common implementations of OT (OT extension).

executions. We now show that this is not necessary since the OT executions can be easily parallelized, given that each execution is independent from the other. That is, the output of a previous OT execution is not used in a later execution. For simplicity, we assume that Π^{γ}_{OT} consists of just two rounds, where the first round goes from the receiver to the sender, and the last goes in the opposite direction. We modify the description of the protocol of Sect. 5.4.1 as follows.

- The step 3 of the *first stage* and the step 2 of the *second stage* are moved to the beginning of the *third stage*.
- When S sends the last round of Π^{γ}_{OT}, he also performs the step 1 of the *third stage*. Therefore the list l is sent together with the last rounds of the λ Π^{γ}_{OT} executions.

Roughly, in this new protocol S first computes all the inputs $(k_0, k_1, c_0^1, c_1^1, \ldots, c_0^\lambda, c_1^\lambda)$ for the OTs. Then, upon receiving λ first rounds of Π^{γ}_{OT} computed by R using as input the bits of x, S sends λ second round of Π^{γ}_{OT} together with the list l.

5.4.3 Security Proof

Theorem 5.1 *Suppose Π^{γ}_{OT} securely computes the 1-out-of-2 OT functionality F_{OT} and* Sym *is a symmetric key encryption scheme with efficiently verifiable range and elusive range, then $\Pi^{\in}$ securely computes the functionality $\mathcal{F}^{\in}$.*

Proof In order to prove the security of $\Pi^{\in}$, according to Definition 5.1 we need show two probabilistic polynomial-time algorithms Sim_S and Sim_R called simulators, such that the following two conditions hold:

$$\begin{aligned}\{(\mathsf{Sim}_\mathsf{S}(1^s, Y, \gamma^0, \gamma^1, \mathcal{F}^{\in}_\mathsf{S}(Y, \gamma^0, \gamma^1, x)), \mathcal{F}^{\in}(Y, \gamma^0, \gamma^1, x))\}_{\{Y,x,s\}} \approx \\ \{\mathsf{View}^{\Pi^{\in}}_\mathsf{S}(1^s, Y, \gamma^0, \gamma^1, x), \mathsf{output}^{\Pi^{\in}}(1^s, Y, \gamma^0, \gamma^1, x)\}_{\{Y,x,s\}}\end{aligned} \tag{5.1}$$

$$\begin{aligned}\{(\mathsf{Sim}_\mathsf{R}(1^s, x, \mathcal{F}^{\in}_\mathsf{R}(Y, \gamma^0, \gamma^1, x)), \mathcal{F}^{\in}(Y, \gamma^0, \gamma^1, x))\}_{\{Y,x,s\}} \approx \\ \{\mathsf{View}^{\Pi^{\in}}_\mathsf{R}(1^s, Y, \gamma^0, \gamma^1, x), \mathsf{output}^{\Pi^{\in}}(1^s, Y, \gamma^0, \gamma^1, x)\}_{\{Y,x,s\}}\end{aligned} \tag{5.2}$$

where $Y \in \{\{0,1\}^\star\}^\star$, $x \in \{0,1\}^\star$, and $s \in \mathbb{N}$.

Therefore we divide our proof into two parts. In the former we show a PPT algorithm Sim_S that satisfies the property of the first point, and then a PPT algorithm Sim_R that satisfiy the requirment of the second point.

Sim_S description and proof of indistinguishability. Sim_S runs S with some randomness r and the input Y. At this point Sim_S needs a strategy to act as a receiver of OT in all the λ OT executions (without the receiver's input x). In order to do that, Sim_S runs the simulator of Π^{γ}_{OT}, that we call $\mathsf{Sim}_{\mathsf{S}_{OT}}$ (and that exists by assumption), in every OT execution. We observe that in order to run $\mathsf{Sim}_{\mathsf{S}_{OT}}$ in the ith OT execution the inputs c_0^i and c_1^i need to be known. Clearly those values can be efficiently computed since the randomness r and the input Y used to run S are known.

We now show more formally how Sim_S works. Let $\mathsf{Sim}_{\mathsf{S}_{\mathcal{OT}}}$ be such that

$$\{\mathsf{Sim}_{\mathsf{S}_{\mathcal{OT}}}(1^s, (c_0, c_1), \bot), F_{\mathcal{OT}}((c_0, c_1), b)\}_{\{c_0, c_1, b, s\}} \approx$$
$$\{\mathsf{View}_{\mathsf{S}_{\mathcal{OT}}}^{\Pi_{\mathcal{OT}}^{\gamma}}(1^s, (c_0, c_1), b), \mathsf{output}^{\Pi_{\mathcal{OT}}^{\gamma}}(1^s, (c_0, c_1), b)\}_{\{c_0, c_1, b, s\}}$$

where $c_0, c_1 \in \{0, 1\}^\star$, $b \in \{0, 1\}$, and $s \in \mathbb{N}$. Sim_S, on input Y and 1^s executes the following steps.

1. Pick a $r \leftarrow \{0, 1\}^s$ and runs S on input 1^s, Y using r as a randomness.
2. For every OT execution i, with $i = 1, \ldots, \lambda$, run $\mathsf{Sim}_{\mathsf{S}_{\mathcal{OT}}}$ on input 1^s, c_0^i and c_1^i, where c_0^i and c_1^i are computed using the same procedure that S uses.
3. Continue the execution against S as R would do.

In order to conclude this first part of the proof we just need to prove the following lemma.

Lemma 5.1

$$\{(\mathsf{Sim}_\mathsf{S}(1^s, Y, \mathcal{F}_\mathsf{S}^{\in}(Y, \gamma^0, \gamma^1, x)), \mathcal{F}^{\in}(Y, \gamma^0, \gamma^1, x))\} \approx$$
$$\{\mathsf{View}_\mathsf{S}^{\Pi^{\in}}(1^s, Y, \gamma^0, \gamma^1, x), \mathsf{output}^{\Pi^{\in}}(1^s, Y, \gamma^0, \gamma^1, x)\}$$

where $Y \in \{\{0, 1\}^\star\}^\star$, $x \in \{0, 1\}^\star$, *and* $s \in \mathbb{N}$.[14]

Proof The proof goes through hybrid arguments starting from the real execution of $\Pi^{\in}$. We gradually modify the execution until the input of R is not needed anymore in such a way that the final hybrid represents the simulator Sim_S. We denote with $\mathsf{OUT}_\mathsf{S}^{\mathcal{H}_i}(1^s)$ the view of S in the hybrid experiment $\mathcal{H}_i$ with $i \in \{0, \ldots, \lambda\}$. The hybrid experiments that we consider are the following.

1. $\mathcal{H}_0$ is identical to the real execution of $\Pi^{\in}$. More precisely $\mathcal{H}_0$ runs S using fresh randomness and interacts with him as R would do on input x.
2. $\mathcal{H}_i$ proceeds according to $\mathcal{H}_0$ with the difference that in the first i OT executions $\mathsf{Sim}_{\mathsf{S}_{\mathcal{OT}}}$ is used.

Since $\mathcal{F}^{\in}$ is a deterministic function we have that

$$\{\mathsf{View}_\mathsf{S}^{\Pi^{\in}}(1^s, Y, \gamma^0, \gamma^1, x), \mathcal{F}^{\in}(Y, \gamma^0, \gamma^1, x))\} \equiv$$
$$\{\mathsf{View}_\mathsf{S}^{\Pi^{\in}}(1^s, Y, \gamma^0, \gamma^1, x), \mathsf{output}^{\Pi^{\in}}(1^s, Y, \gamma^0, \gamma^1, x)\}\ .$$

Moreover we observe that

$$\{\mathsf{OUT}_{\mathcal{H}_0}(1^s), \mathcal{F}^{\in}(Y, \gamma^0, \gamma^1, x)\} =$$
$$\{\mathsf{View}_\mathsf{S}^{\Pi^{\in}}(1^s, Y, \gamma^0, \gamma^1, x), \mathcal{F}^{\in}(Y, \gamma^0, \gamma^1, x))\}$$

---

[14] To avoid overburdening the notation, here and in the rest of this chapter, we omit to specify the inputs domain when it is clear from the context.

and that

$$\{\mathsf{OUT}_{\mathcal{H}_\lambda}(1^s), \mathcal{F}^{\in}(Y,\gamma^0,\gamma^1,x)\} = \{(\mathsf{Sim}_{\mathsf{S}}(1^s,Y,\gamma^0,\gamma^1,\mathcal{F}^{\in}_{\mathsf{S}}(Y,\gamma^0,\gamma^1,x)), \mathcal{F}^{\in}(Y,\gamma^0,\gamma^1,x))\}\,.$$

Therefore the only thing that remains to argue is that

$$\{\mathsf{OUT}_{\mathcal{H}_{i-1}}(1^s), \mathcal{F}^{\in}(Y,\gamma^0,\gamma^1,x)\} \approx \{\mathsf{OUT}_{\mathcal{H}_i}(1^s), \mathcal{F}^{\in}(Y,\gamma^0,\gamma^1,x)\}$$

for $i = 1, \ldots, \lambda$. We now show that if this statement does not hold then we can construct an adversary $\mathcal{A}^S_{\mathcal{OT}}$ that breaks the security of $\Pi^{\gamma}_{\mathcal{OT}}$ against malicious sender. Let $\mathsf{Sen}^S_{\mathcal{OT}}$ be the challenger for the security game w.r.t. the security of $\Pi^{\gamma}_{\mathcal{OT}}$ against malicious sender; the reduction works as follows.

1. $\mathcal{A}^S_{\mathcal{OT}}$ runs S with randomness r and interacts with him according to $\mathcal{H}_{i-1}$ ($\mathcal{H}_i$) until the ith OT execution.
2. At this point $\mathcal{A}^S_{\mathcal{OT}}$ computes (c^i_0, c^i_1) and sends $((c^i_0, c^i_1), x_{\lambda-i+1})$ to $\mathsf{Sen}^S_{\mathcal{OT}}$.
3. $\mathcal{A}^{S_{\mathcal{OT}}}$ then acts as a proxy between $\mathsf{Sen}^S_{\mathcal{OT}}$ and S.
4. When the interaction between $\mathsf{Sen}^S_{\mathcal{OT}}$ and S is over, $\mathcal{A}$ continues the execution with S according to $\mathcal{H}_{i-1}$ ($\mathcal{H}_i$).

The security proof ends with the observation that if $\mathsf{Sen}^{S_{\mathcal{OT}}}$ has used the simulator $\mathsf{Sim}_{S_{\mathcal{OT}}}$ then the joint distribution of the view of S and $\mathcal{F}^{\in}(Y,\gamma^0,\gamma^1,x)$ corresponds to $\{\mathsf{OUT}^{\mathsf{R}}_{\mathcal{H}_i}(1^s), \mathcal{F}^{\in}(Y,\gamma^0,\gamma^1,x)\}$, to $\{\mathsf{OUT}^{\mathsf{R}}_{\mathcal{H}_{i-1}}(1^s), \mathcal{F}^{\in}(Y,\gamma^0,\gamma^1,x)\}$ otherwise. □

$\mathsf{Sim}_{\mathsf{R}}$ Description and proof of Indistinguishability.

At a very high level, $\mathsf{Sim}_{\mathsf{R}}$ runs R with some randomness r and the input x. $\mathsf{Sim}_{\mathsf{R}}$ then needs a strategy to acts as a sender of OT in all the λ OT executions (without sender's input Y). In order to do that, $\mathsf{Sim}_{\mathsf{R}}$ runs the simulator of $\Pi^{\gamma}_{\mathcal{OT}}$, that we call $\mathsf{Sim}_{\mathsf{R}_{\mathcal{OT}}}$ in every OT execution.[15] Moreover we need to feed the OT simulator with the correct input, depending on the value x. More precisely in the first OT execution $\mathsf{Sim}_{\mathsf{R}_{\mathcal{OT}}}$ is run by using as input a key k_1. In the ith OT execution (for $i = 2, \ldots, \lambda$) the simulator will run using $x_{\lambda-i+1}$ and c^i. c^i contains encryptions of a fixed value, let say 0, computed using a fresh secret key (different for every ciphertext) and one encryption of the key k_i using the key k_{i-1}. After the λ OT executions $\mathsf{Sim}_{\mathsf{R}}$ sends to R M encryptions of 0 using a randomly generated secret key (also in this case a different secret key is used for each encryption of 0) and the encryption of the message $\mathsf{out} = \mathcal{F}^{\in}_{\mathsf{S}}(Y,\gamma^0,\gamma^1,x)$ using the key k_λ. We now show more formally how $\mathsf{Sim}_{\mathsf{R}}$ works. Let $\mathsf{Sim}_{\mathsf{R}_{\mathcal{OT}}}$ be such that

$$\{\mathsf{Sim}_{\mathsf{R}_{\mathcal{OT}}}(1^s, b, c_b), F_{\mathcal{OT}}((c_0,c_1),b)\}_{\{c_0,c_1,b,s\}} \approx \{\mathsf{View}^{\Pi^{\gamma}_{\mathcal{OT}}}_{\mathsf{R}_{\mathcal{OT}}}(1^s,(c_0,c_1),b), \mathsf{output}^{\Pi^{\gamma}_{\mathcal{OT}}}(1^s,(c_0,c_1),b)\}_{\{c_0,c_1,b,s\}}$$

---

[15] We recall that $\mathsf{Sim}_{\mathsf{R}_{\mathcal{OT}}}$ exists by assumption.

where $c_0, c_1 \in \{0, 1\}^\star$, $b \in \{0, 1\}$, and $s \in \mathbb{N}$.

$\mathsf{Sim}_{\mathsf{R}}$, on input x, out and 1^s executes the following steps.

1. Compute $\mathsf{k}_1 \leftarrow \mathsf{Gen}(1^s)$ ad run $\mathsf{Sim}_{\mathsf{R}_{\mathcal{OT}}}$ on input $(1^s, x_\lambda, \mathsf{k}_1)$.
2. For $i = 2, \ldots, \lambda$ execute the following steps.
   2.1 Define the empty list c^i. For $j = 1, \ldots, \mathsf{min}\{2^i, |Y|\} - 1$ compute and add $\mathsf{Enc}(\mathsf{Gen}(1^s), 0))$ to c^i.
   2.2 Compute $\mathsf{k}_i \leftarrow \mathsf{Gen}(1^s)$, and add $\mathsf{Enc}(\mathsf{k}_{i-1}, \mathsf{k}_i)$ to the list c^i.
   2.3 Permute the elements inside c^i.
   2.4 Run $\mathsf{Sim}_{\mathsf{R}_{\mathcal{OT}}}$ on input $(1^s, x_{\lambda-i+1}, \mathsf{c}^i)$.
3. Define an empty list l.
4. For $i = 1, \ldots M - 1$ compute and add $\mathsf{Enc}(\mathsf{Gen}(1^s), 0)$ to l.
5. Add $\mathsf{Enc}(\mathsf{k}_\lambda, \mathsf{out})$ to l.
6. Permute the element inside l and send it.
7. Continue the execution according to R's description.

In order to conclude this latter part of the proof we need to prove the following lemma.

Lemma 5.2

$$\{(\mathsf{Sim}_{\mathsf{R}}(1^s, x, \mathsf{out}, \mathcal{F}^{\in}_{\mathsf{R}}(Y, \gamma^0, \gamma^1, x)), \mathcal{F}^{\in}(Y, \gamma^0, \gamma^1, x))\}_{\{Y,x,s\}} \approx$$
$$\{\mathsf{View}^{\Pi^{\in}}_{\mathsf{R}}(1^s, Y, \gamma^0, \gamma^1, x), \mathsf{output}^{\Pi^{\in}}(1^s, Y, \gamma^0, \gamma^1, x)\}_{\{Y,x,s\}}$$

where $Y \in \{\{0, 1\}^\star\}^\star$, $x \in \{0, 1\}^\star$, *and* $s \in \mathbb{N}$.

Proof The proof goes trough hybrid arguments starting from the real execution of $\Pi^{\in}$. We gradually modify the execution until the input of S (Y) is not needed anymore such that the final hybrid would represent the simulator $\mathsf{Sim}_{\mathsf{R}}$. We denote with $\mathsf{OUT}^{\mathsf{R}}_{\mathcal{H}_i}(1^s)$ the view of R in the hybrid experiment $\mathcal{H}_i$ with $i \in \{0, \ldots, \lambda\}$.

1. $\mathcal{H}_0$ is identical to the real execution of $\Pi^{\in}$. More precisely $\mathcal{H}_0$ runs R using fresh randomness and interacts with him as S would do on input Y.
2. $\mathcal{H}_1$ proceeds according to $\mathcal{H}_0$ with the difference that in the first OT executions $\mathsf{Sim}_{\mathsf{R}_{\mathcal{OT}}}$ is used on input $(1^s, x_\lambda, \mathsf{k}_1 \leftarrow \mathsf{Gen}(1^s))$.
3. $\mathcal{H}_i$ proceeds according to $\mathcal{H}_1$ with the difference that in the jth OT executions, with $2 \le j \le i$, $\mathsf{Sim}_{\mathsf{R}_{\mathcal{OT}}}$ is run on input $(1^s, x_{\lambda-j+1}, \mathsf{c}^j = c^j_{x_{\lambda-j+1}})$.
4. $\mathcal{H}^\star$ proceeds according to $\mathcal{H}_\lambda$ with the difference that in each OT execution i, with $2 \le i \le \lambda$, the input c^i for the simulator $\mathsf{Sim}_{\mathsf{R}_{\mathcal{OT}}}$ is computed as follows.
   - For $j = 1, \ldots, \mathsf{min}\{2^i, |Y|\} - 1$ compute and add $\mathsf{Enc}(\mathsf{Gen}(1^s), 0)$ to c^i.
   - Compute $\mathsf{k}_i \leftarrow \mathsf{Gen}(1^s)$, and add $\mathsf{Enc}(\mathsf{k}_{i-1}, \mathsf{k}_i)$ to the list c^i.
   - Permute the elements inside c^i.

   Moreover the first step of the third stage is performed as follows.

   - Define an empty list l.

- For $i = 1, \dots M-1$ compute and add $\mathsf{Enc}(\mathsf{Gen}(1^s), 0)$ to l.
- Add $\mathsf{Enc}(\mathsf{k}_\lambda, \mathsf{out})$ to l.
- Permute the element inside l and send it to R.

Since $\mathcal{F}^{\in}$ is deterministic we have that

$$\{\mathsf{View}_{\mathsf{R}}^{\Pi^{\in}}(1^s, Y, \gamma^0, \gamma^1, x), \mathcal{F}^{\in}(Y, \gamma^0, \gamma^1, x))\} \equiv \{\mathsf{View}_{\mathsf{R}}^{\Pi^{\in}}(1^s, Y, \gamma^0, \gamma^1, x), \mathsf{output}^{\Pi^{\in}}(1^s, Y, \gamma^0, \gamma^1, x)\}.$$

Moreover we observe that

$$\{\mathsf{OUT}_{\mathcal{H}_0}^{\mathsf{R}}(1^s), \mathcal{F}^{\in}(Y, \gamma^0, \gamma^1, x)\} = \{\mathsf{View}_{\mathsf{R}}^{\Pi^{\in}}(1^s, Y, \gamma^0, \gamma^1, x), \mathcal{F}^{\in}(Y, \gamma^0, \gamma^1, x))\}$$

and that

$$\{\mathsf{OUT}_{\mathcal{H}^\star}^{\mathsf{R}}(1^s), \mathcal{F}^{\in}(Y, \gamma^0, \gamma^1, x)\} = \{(\mathsf{Sim}_{\mathsf{R}}(1^s, x, \mathsf{out}, \mathcal{F}_{\mathsf{R}}^{\in}(Y, \gamma^0, \gamma^1, x)), \mathcal{F}^{\in}(Y, \gamma^0, \gamma^1, x))\}\,.$$

Therefore there are two things that remain to argue:

1. $\{\mathsf{OUT}_{\mathcal{H}_{i-1}}^{\mathsf{R}}(1^s), \mathcal{F}^{\in}(Y, \gamma^0, \gamma^1, x)\} \approx \{\mathsf{OUT}_{\mathcal{H}_i}^{\mathsf{R}}(1^s), \mathcal{F}^{\in}(Y, \gamma^0, \gamma^1, x)\}$ for $i = 1, \dots, \lambda$ and
2. $\{\mathsf{OUT}_{\mathcal{H}_\lambda}^{\mathsf{R}}(1^s), \mathcal{F}^{\in}(Y, \gamma^0, \gamma^1, x)\} \approx \{\mathsf{OUT}_{\mathcal{H}^\star}^{\mathsf{R}}(1^s), \mathcal{F}^{\in}(Y, \gamma^0, \gamma^1, x)\}$.

We now start by showing that if the first statement does not hold for $i = 1$, then we can construct a adversary $\mathcal{A}_{\mathcal{OT}}^{S}$ that breaks the security of $\Pi_{\mathcal{OT}}^{\gamma}$ against malicious receiver. Let $\mathsf{Sen}_{\mathcal{OT}}^{R}$ be the challenger for the security game w.r.t. the security of $\Pi_{\mathcal{OT}}^{\gamma}$ against malicious receiver. The reduction works as follows.

1. $\mathcal{A}_{\mathcal{OT}}^{R}$ runs R with randomness r, computes $k_0 \leftarrow \mathsf{Gen}(1^s)$, $k_1 \leftarrow \mathsf{Gen}(1^s)$ and sends $((k_0, k_1), x_\lambda)$ to $\mathsf{Sen}_{\mathcal{OT}}^{R}$.
2. $\mathcal{A}_{\mathcal{OT}}^{R}$ then acts as a proxy between $\mathsf{Sen}_{\mathcal{OT}}^{R}$ and R.
3. When the interaction between $\mathsf{Sen}_{\mathcal{OT}}^{S}$ and R is over, $\mathcal{A}_{\mathcal{OT}}^{R}$ continues the execution with R according to $\mathcal{H}_0$ ($\mathcal{H}_1$).

This part of the security proof ends with the observation that if $\mathsf{Sen}^{R_{\mathcal{OT}}}$ has used the simulator $\mathsf{Sim}_{R_{\mathcal{OT}}}$ then the joint distribution of the view of R and $\mathcal{F}^{\in}(Y, \gamma^0, \gamma^1, x)$ corresponds to $\{\mathsf{OUT}_{\mathcal{H}_0}^{\mathsf{R}}(1^s), \mathcal{F}^{\in}(Y, \gamma^0, \gamma^1, x)\}$, to $\{\mathsf{OUT}_{\mathcal{H}_1}^{\mathsf{R}}(1^s), \mathcal{F}^{\in}(Y, \gamma^0, \gamma^1, x)\}$ otherwise.

The proof that

$$\{\mathsf{OUT}_{\mathcal{H}_{i-1}}^{\mathsf{R}}(1^s), \mathcal{F}^{\in}(Y, \gamma^0, \gamma^1, x)\} \approx \{\mathsf{OUT}_{\mathcal{H}_i}^{\mathsf{R}}(1^s), \mathcal{F}^{\in}(Y, \gamma^0, \gamma^1, x)\}$$

for $i = 2, \dots, \lambda$ follows the same arguments.

In order to prove that

$$\{\mathsf{OUT}^{\mathsf{R}}_{\mathcal{H}_\lambda}(1^s), \mathcal{F}^{\in}(Y, \gamma^0, \gamma^1, x)\} \approx \{\mathsf{OUT}^{\mathsf{R}}_{\mathcal{H}^\star}(1^s), \mathcal{F}^{\in}(Y, \gamma^0, \gamma^1, x)\},$$

thus concluding the lemma's security proof, we need to consider the following intermediate hybrid experiment $\mathcal{H}^\star_y$ with $y \in \{1, \dots, \lambda\}$. The description of the hybrid experiment follows.

1. Compute $\mathsf{k}_1 \leftarrow \mathsf{Gen}(1^s)$ and run $\mathsf{Sim}_{\mathsf{R}_{\mathcal{OT}}}$ on input $(1^s, x_\lambda, \mathsf{k}_1)$.
2. For $i = 2, \dots, y$ execute the following steps.
   2.1 Define the empty list c^i. For $j = 1, \dots, \min\{2^i, |Y|\} - 1$ compute and add $\mathsf{Enc}(\mathsf{Gen}(1^s), 0))$ to c^i.
   2.2 Compute $\mathsf{k}_i \leftarrow \mathsf{Gen}(1^s)$, and add $\mathsf{Enc}(\mathsf{k}_{i-1}, \mathsf{k}_i)$ to the list c^i.
   2.3 Permute the elements inside c^i.
   2.4 Run $\mathsf{Sim}_{\mathsf{R}_{\mathcal{OT}}}$ on input $(1^s, x_{\lambda-i+1}, \mathsf{c}^i)$.
3. For each $t \in \mathsf{Prefix}(Y, y) - \{x_\lambda \dots x_{\lambda-y+1}\}$ compute $k_t \leftarrow \mathsf{Gen}(1^s)$.
   If $x_\lambda \dots x_{\lambda-y+1} \in \mathsf{Prefix}(Y, y)$ then set $k_{x_\lambda \dots x_{\lambda-y+1}} = \mathsf{k}_y$, otherwise $k^\star_y = \mathsf{k}_y$.
4. For $i = y + 1, \dots, \lambda$ execute the following steps.
   4.1 Define the empty list c^i and for each $t \in \mathsf{Prefix}(Y, i - 1)$ execute the following steps.

      If $t||x_{\lambda-i+1} \in \mathsf{Prefix}(Y, i)$ then compute $k_{t||x_{\lambda-i+1}} \leftarrow \mathsf{Gen}(1^s)$ and add $\mathsf{Enc}(k_t, k_{t||x_{\lambda-i+1}})$ to the list c^i. Otherwise, if $t||x_{\lambda-i+1} \notin \mathsf{Prefix}(Y, i)$ then compute and add $\mathsf{Enc}(k_t, k^\star_i)$ to the list c^i.

   4.2 If $|\mathsf{c}^i| < \delta(i - 1)$ then execute the following steps.
      - Compute and add $\mathsf{Enc}(k^\star_{i-1}, k^\star_i)$ to the list c^i.
      - For $i = 1, \dots, \delta(i - 1) - |\mathsf{c}^i|$ compute and add $\mathsf{Enc}(\mathsf{Gen}(1^s), 0)$ to c^i.

   4.3 Permute the elements inside c^i.
   4.4 Run $\mathsf{Sim}_{\mathsf{R}_{\mathcal{OT}}}$ on input $(1^s, x_{\lambda-i+1}, \mathsf{c}^i)$.
5. For every $t \in \mathsf{Prefix}(Y, \lambda)$ compute and add $\mathsf{Enc}(k_t, \gamma^1)$ to l.
6. If $|l| < 2^\lambda$ then compute and add $\mathsf{Enc}(k^\star_\lambda, \gamma^0)$ to l.
7. Permute the elements inside l and send l to R.

We now prove that

$$\{\mathsf{OUT}^{\mathsf{R}}_{\mathcal{H}^\star_{y-1}}(1^s), \mathcal{F}^{\in}(Y, \gamma^0, \gamma^1, x)\} \approx \{\mathsf{OUT}^{\mathsf{R}}_{\mathcal{H}^\star_y}(1^s), \mathcal{F}^{\in}(Y, \gamma^0, \gamma^1, x)\}$$

for $y = 2, \dots, \lambda$. The proof proceeds by contradiction. Suppose that there exists some $y \in \{2, \dots, \lambda\}$ such that

$$\{\mathsf{OUT}^{\mathsf{R}}_{\mathcal{H}^\star_{y-1}}(1^s), \mathcal{F}^{\in}(Y, \gamma^0, \gamma^1, x)\} \approx \{\mathsf{OUT}^{\mathsf{R}}_{\mathcal{H}^\star_y}(1^s), \mathcal{F}^{\in}(Y, \gamma^0, \gamma^1, x)\}$$

then we can construct ad adversary $\mathcal{A}^{\mathsf{Sym}}$ that breaks the security of the encryption scheme Sym. Let $\mathsf{Sen}^{\mathsf{Sym}}$ be the challenger for the security game w.r.t to Sym. Our adversary runs R with randomness r and executes the following steps.

1. Compute $\mathsf{k}_1 \leftarrow \mathsf{Gen}(1^s)$ and run $\mathsf{Sim}_{\mathsf{R}_{\mathcal{OT}}}$ on input $(1^s, x_\lambda, \mathsf{k}_1)$.
2. For $i = 2, \ldots, y-1$ execute the following steps.
   2.1 Define the empty list c^i. For $j = 1, \ldots, \mathsf{min}\{2^i, |Y|\} - 1$ compute and add $\mathsf{Enc}(\mathsf{Gen}(1^s), 0))$ to c^i.
   2.2 Compute $\mathsf{k}_i \leftarrow \mathsf{Gen}(1^s)$, and add $\mathsf{Enc}(\mathsf{k}_{i-1}, \mathsf{k}_i)$ to the list c^i.
   2.3 Permute the elements inside c^i.
   2.4 Run $\mathsf{Sim}_{\mathsf{R}_{\mathcal{OT}}}$ on input $(1^s, x_{\lambda-i+1}, \mathsf{c}^i)$.
3. Define two empty lists $\mathbf{m}_0$ and $\mathbf{m}_1$ that will represent the challenge messages to be sent to $\mathsf{Sen}^{\mathsf{Sym}}$.
4. For each $t \in \mathsf{Prefix}(Y, y) - \{x_\lambda \ldots x_{\lambda-y+1}\}$ compute $k_t \leftarrow \mathsf{Gen}(1^s)$ and add it to the list $\mathbf{m}_0$.
5. For $j = 1, \ldots, |\mathsf{Prefix}(Y, y) - \{x_\lambda \ldots x_{\lambda-y+1}\}|$ compute and add 0 to $\mathbf{m}_1$.
6. Send the challenge messages to $\mathsf{Sen}^{\mathsf{Sym}}$.
7. Upon receiving the challenge ciphertext $\mathbf{cx}$, set $\mathsf{c}^y = \mathbf{cx}$
8. For $j = 1, \ldots, \mathsf{min}\{2^i, |Y|\} - |\mathbf{cx}| - 1$ compute and add $\mathsf{Enc}(\mathsf{Gen}(1^s), 0))$ to c^i.
9. Compute $\mathsf{k}_y \leftarrow \mathsf{Gen}(1^s)$, and add $\mathsf{Enc}(\mathsf{k}_{y-1}, \mathsf{k}_y)$ to the list c^i.
10. Permute the elements inside c^i.
11. Run $\mathsf{Sim}_{\mathsf{R}_{\mathcal{OT}}}$ on input $(1^s, x_{\lambda-i+1}, \mathsf{c}^i)$.
12. If $x_\lambda \ldots x_{\lambda-y+1} \in \mathsf{Prefix}(Y, y)$ then set $k_{x_\lambda \ldots x_{\lambda-y+1}} = \mathsf{k}_y$, otherwise set $k^\star_y = \mathsf{k}_y$.
13. For $i = y+1, \ldots, \lambda$ execute the following steps.
    13.1 Define the empty list c^i and for each $t \in \mathsf{Prefix}(Y, i-1)$ execute the following steps.

    If $t||x_{\lambda-i+1} \in \mathsf{Prefix}(Y, i)$ then compute $k_{t||x_{\lambda-i+1}} \leftarrow \mathsf{Gen}(1^s)$ and add $\mathsf{Enc}(k_t, k_{t||x_{\lambda-i+1}})$ to the list c^i. Otherwise, if $t||x_{\lambda-i+1} \notin \mathsf{Prefix}(Y, i)$ then compute and add $\mathsf{Enc}(k_t, k^\star_i)$ to the list c^i.

    13.2 If $|\mathsf{c}^i| < \delta(i-1)$ then execute the following steps.

    - Compute and add $\mathsf{Enc}(k^\star_{i-1}, k^\star_i)$ to the list c^i.
    - For $i = 1, \ldots, \delta(i-1) - |\mathsf{c}^i|$ compute and add $\mathsf{Enc}(\mathsf{Gen}(1^s), 0)$ to c^i.

    13.3 Permute the elements inside c^i.
    13.4 Run $\mathsf{Sim}_{\mathsf{R}_{\mathcal{OT}}}$ on input $(1^s, x_{\lambda-i+1}, \mathsf{c}^i)$.
14. For every $t \in \mathsf{Prefix}(Y, \lambda)$ compute and add $\mathsf{Enc}(k_t, \gamma^1)$ to l.
15. If $|l| < 2^\lambda$ then compute and add $\mathsf{Enc}(k^\star_\lambda, \gamma^0)$ to l.
16. Permute the elements inside l and send l to R.

This part of the security proof ends with the observation that if $\mathsf{Sen}^{\mathsf{Sym}}$ has used $\mathbf{m}_0$ then the joint distribution of the view of R and $\mathcal{F}^{\in}(Y, \gamma^0, \gamma^1, x)$ corresponds to $\{\mathsf{OUT}^{\mathsf{R}}_{\mathcal{H}^\star_{y-1}}(1^s), \mathcal{F}^{\in}(Y, \gamma^0, \gamma^1, x)\}$, to $\{\mathsf{OUT}^{\mathsf{R}}_{\mathcal{H}^\star_y}(1^s), \mathcal{F}^{\in}(Y, \gamma^0, \gamma^1, x)\}$ otherwise.

Since the following two distributions coincide

$$\{\mathsf{OUT}^{\mathsf{R}}_{\mathcal{H}_\lambda}(1^s), \mathcal{F}^{\in}(Y, \gamma^0, \gamma^1, x)\} = \{\mathsf{OUT}^{\mathsf{R}}_{\mathcal{H}^\star_1}(1^s), \mathcal{F}^{\in}(Y, \gamma^0, \gamma^1, x)\}$$

to complete the entire security proof we just need to prove that $\{\mathsf{OUT}^{\mathsf{R}}_{\mathcal{H}^\star_\lambda}(1^s), \mathcal{F}^{\in}(Y, \gamma^0, \gamma^1, x)\} \approx \{\mathsf{OUT}^{\mathsf{R}}_{\mathcal{H}^\star}(1^s), \mathcal{F}^{\in}(Y, \gamma^0, \gamma^1, x)\}$. The indistinguishability between the two distributions can be proved by using arguments similar to the one used lately. That is, by proceedings by contradiction and constructing adversary that breaks the security of the encryption scheme Sym. □

5.5 Optimizations and Extension

Point and Permute.

In our protocol, the receiver must decrypt every ciphertext at every layer to identify the correct one. This is suboptimal both because of the number of decryptions and because encryptions that have efficiently verifiable range necessarily have longer ciphertexts. This overhead can be removed using the standard *point-and-permute technique* [14] which was introduced in the context of garbled circuits. Using this technique we can add to each key in each layer a *pointer* to the ciphertext in the next layer which can be decrypted using this key. This has no impact on security.

One-time Pad.

It is possible to reduce the communication complexity of our protocol by using *one-time pad encryption* in the last $\log s$ layers of the graph, in the setting where the output values γ^0, γ^1 are such that $|\gamma^b| < s$. For instance, if the output values are bits (in case we combine our PSM with a GMW-style protocol), then the keys (and therefore the ciphertexts) used in the last layer of the graph only need to be 1 bit long. Unfortunately, since the keys in the second to last layer are used to mask up to two keys in the last layer, the keys in the second to last layer must be of length 2 and so on, which is why this optimization only gives benefits in the last $\log s$ layer of the graph.

PSM with Secret Shared Input.

Our PSM protocol produces an output which can be post-processed using other 2PC protocol. It is natural to ask whether it is possible to design efficient PSM protocols that also work on encrypted or secret-shared inputs. We note here that our protocol can also be used in the setting in which the input string x is *bit-wise secret-shared* between the sender and the receiver i.e., the receiver knows a share r and the sender knows a share s s.t., $r \oplus s = x$. The protocol does not change for the receiver, who now inputs the bits of $r = r_\lambda, \ldots, r_1$ to the λ one-out-of-two OTs (instead of the bits of x as in the original protocol). The sender, at each layer i, will follow the protocol as described above if $s_i = 0$ and instead swap the inputs to the OT if $s_i = 1$. It can be easily verified that the protocol still produces the correct result and does not leak any extra information.

Keyword Search.

Our PSM protocol outputs an encryption of a bit indicating whether $x \in Y$ or not. The protocol can be easily modified to output a value dependent on x itself and therefore implement "encrypted keyword search". That is, instead of having only two output strings γ^1, γ^0 representing membership and non-membership respectively, we can have $|Y| + 1$ different output strings (one for each element $y \in Y$ and one for non-membership). This can be used for instance in the context where Y is a database containing id's y and corresponding values $v(y)$, and the output of the protocol should be an encryption of the value $v(x)$ if $x \in Y$ or a standard value $v(\perp)$ if $x \notin Y$. The modification is straightforward: instead of using all the keys in the last layer of the graph to encrypt the same value γ^1, use each key k_y to encrypt the corresponding value $v(y)$ and the sink key (which is use to encrypt γ^0 in our protocol) to encrypt the value $v(\perp)$.

PSI from PSM.

We can follow the same approach of Phasing [175, 176] to turn our PSM protocol into a protocol for PSI. Given a receiver with input X and a sender with input Y the trivial way to construct PSI from PSM is to run $|X|$ copies of PSM, where in each execution the receiver inputs a different x from X and where the sender always inputs her entire set Y. As described above, the complexity of our protocol (as the complexity of Phasing) is proportional in the size of $|Y|$, so this naïve approach leads to quadratic complexity $O(|X| \cdot |Y|)$. Phasing deals with this using *hashing* i.e., by letting the sender and the receiver locally preprocess their inputs X, Y before engaging in the PSM protocols. The different hashing techniques are explained and analyzed in [177, Sect. 3]. We present the intuitive idea and refer to their paper for details: in Phasing the receiver uses *Cuckoo hashing* to map X into a vector X' of size $\ell = O(|X|)$ such that all elements of X are present in X' and such that every $x'_i \in X'$ is either an element of X or a special $\perp$ symbol. The sender instead maps her set Y into $\ell = |X'|$ small buckets $Y'_1, \ldots, Y'_\ell$ such that every element $y \in Y$ is mapped into the "right bucket" i.e., the hashing has the property that if $y = x'_i$ for some i then y will end up in bucket Y'_i (and potentially in a few other buckets). Now Phasing uses the underlying PSM protocol to check whether x'_i is a member of Y'_i (for all i's), thus producing the desired result. The overall protocol complexity is now $O(|X'| \cdot |Y'_i|)$ which (by careful choice of the hashing parameters) can be made linear in input size i.e., the overall protocol has complexity $O(|X| + |Y|)$. Since this technique is agnostic of the underlying PSM protocol, we can apply the same technique to our PSM protocol to achieve a PSI protocol that produces encrypted output.

5.6 Applications

In this section, we provide two examples of how our protocol can be used to implement more complex secure set operations. The examples show some guiding principles that can be used to design other applications based on our protocol.

As we will see, the major advantage provided by $\Pi^{\in}$ is that the output of the receiver can be an arbitrary value chosen by the sender as a function of x for each value $x \in Y \cup \{\bot\}$. This is in contrast with most of the approaches for set membership, where the value obtained by the receiver is a fixed value (e.g., 0) when $x \in Y$, or some random value otherwise.

Without loss of generality in the following applications only the receiver will learn the output of the computation. Moreover we assume that the size of X and Y is equal to the same value M.[16] Also for simplicity we will describe our application using the naïve PSI from PSM construction with quadratic complexity, but using the Phasing approach, as described in Sect. 5.5, it is possible to achieve linear complexity using hashing techniques. Finally, in both our applications we exploit the fact that additions can be performed locally (and for free) using secret-sharing based 2PC. In applications in which round complexity is critical, the protocols can be redesigned using garbled circuits computing the same functionality, since the garbled circuit can be sent from the sender to the other messages of the protocol. However in this case additions have to be performed inside the garbled circuit.

5.6.1 Computing Statistics of the Private Intersection

Here we want to construct a protocol where sender and receiver have on input two sets, X and Y respectively, and want to compute some statistics on the intersections of their sets. For instance the receiver has a list of id's X and that the sender has a list of id's Y and some corresponding values $v(Y)$ (thus we use the variant of our protocol for *keyword search* described in Sect. 5.5). At the end of the protocol the receiver should learn the average of $v(X \cap Y)$ (and not $|X \cap Y|$).

The main idea is the following: the sender and the receiver run M executions of our protocol where the receiver inputs a different x_i from X in each execution. The sender always inputs the same set Y, and chooses the $|Y| + 1$ outputs γ_i^y for all $y \in Y \cup \{\bot\}$ for all $i = 1, \ldots, M$ in the following way: γ_i^y is going to contain

[16] We assume this only to simplify the protocol description, indeed our protocol can be easily instantiated when the two sets have different size.

two parts, namely an arithmetic secret sharing of the bit indicating whether $x_i \in Y$ and an arithmetic secret sharing of the value $v(y)$. The arithmetic secret sharing will be performed using a modulo N large enough such that $N > M$ and $N > M \cdot V$ where V is some upper bound on $v(y)$ so to be sure that no modular reduction will happen when performing the addition of the resulting shares. Concretely the sender sets $\gamma_i^y = (-u_i^2 + 1 \mod N, -v_i^2 + v(y) \mod N)$ for all $y \in Y$ and $\gamma_i^\perp = (-u_i^2 \mod N, -v_i^2 \mod N)$. After the protocol the receiver defines her shares u_i^1, v_i^1 to the shares contained in her output of the PSM protocol, and then both parties add their shares locally to obtain secret sharing of the size of the intersection and of the sum of the values i.e., $U^1 = \sum_i u_i^1$, $V^1 = \sum_i v_i^1$, $U^2 = \sum_i u_i^2$, and $V^2 = \sum_i v_i^2$. Now the parties check if (U^1, U^2) is a sharing of 0 and, if not, they compute and reveal the result of the computation $\frac{V^1+V^2}{U^1+U^2}$. Both these operations can be performed using efficient two-party protocols for comparison and division such as the one in [60, 187].

5.6.2 Threshold PSI

In this example, we design a protocol $\Pi^t = (P_1^t, P_2^t)$ that securely compute the functionality $\mathcal{F}^t = (\mathcal{F}^t_{P_1^t}, \mathcal{F}^t_{P_2^t})$ where

$$\mathcal{F}^t_{P_1^t} : \{\{0,1\}^\lambda\}^M \times \{\{0,1\}^\lambda\}^M \longrightarrow \perp$$

and

$$\mathcal{F}^t_{P_2^t} : \{\{0,1\}^\lambda\}^M \times \{\{0,1\}^\lambda\}^M \longrightarrow \{\{0,1\}^\lambda\}^\star$$
$$(S_1, S_2) \longmapsto \begin{cases} S_1 \cap S_2 & \text{if } |S_1 \cap S_2| \geq t \\ \perp & \text{otherwise} \end{cases} .$$

That is, the sender and the receiver have on input two sets, S_1 and S_2 respectively, and the receiver should only learn the intersection between these two sets if the size of the intersection is greater or equal than a fixed (public) threshold value t. In the case that the size of the intersection in smaller that t, then no information about S_1 is leaked to P_2^t and no information about S_2 is leaked to P_1^t. (This notion was also considered in [109] in the context of privacy-preserving ride-sharing).

As in the previous example, the sender and the receiver run M executions of our protocol where the receiver inputs a different x_i from S_2 in each execution. The sender always inputs the same set S_1, and chooses the two outputs γ_i^0, γ_i^1 in the following way: γ_i^b is going to contain two parts, namely an arithmetic secret sharing of 1 if $x_i \in Y$ or 0 otherwise, as well as encryption of the same bit using a key k. The arithmetic secret sharing will be performed using a modulo larger than M, so that the arithmetic secret sharings can be added to compute a secret-sharing of the value

$|S_1 \cap S_2|$ with the guarantee that no overflow will occur. Then, the sender and the receiver engage in a secure-two party computation of a function that outputs the key k to the receiver if and only if $|S_1 \cap S_2| > t$. Therefore, if the intersection is larger than the threshold now the receiver can decrypt the ciphertext part of the γ values and learn which elements belong to the intersection. The required 2PC is a simple comparison with a known value (the threshold is public) which can be efficiently performed using protocols such as [83, 143].

Part II
Non-malleable Primitives

Chapter 6
Three-Round Non-malleable Commitment

6.1 Introduction

A non-malleable commitment [70] is a type of cryptographic commitment that prevents an adversary, called man-in-the-middle (MiM), from creating a related commitment based on an existing one. In other words, given a commitment to a value x, it should be computationally infeasible for an attacker to produce another commitment that is meaningfully related to the original commitment.

We have a clear understanding of how to design one or two-round round commitment schemes under various assumptions [88, 108, 154, 155, 174], but for non-malleable commitments, provide a full characterization of assumptions and round complexity has proven to be an elusive task.

Starting from the construction of [70] that required a logarithmic number of rounds, various constant-round schemes were proposed [11, 28, 48, 94, 95, 99, 135, 136, 169–171, 173]. In [167], Pass proved that NM commitments[1] require at least 3 rounds [167] when security is proved through a black-box reduction to a falsifiable (polynomial) hardness assumption. In this chapter, we focus our attention on the setting where the adversary mounts a concurrent MiM attack: the adversary receives multiple commitments from honest senders, and generates multiple commitments for the honest receivers.

6.1.1 Towards 3-Round (Concurrent) NM Commitments

The existence of 3-round NM commitment schemes is an important question first, because 3 is the best possible constant (in light of the lower bound of [167]), and second, because 3 is the smallest number of rounds for a primitive that often makes use of commitment schemes: proofs of knowledge.

[1] We consider the notion of NM commitment w.r.t. commitment.

M. Ciampi and L. Siniscalchi, *Round and Computational Efficiency of Multi-party Protocols*, Information Security and Cryptography,
https://doi.org/10.1007/978-3-031-92374-6_6

Interestingly, the work of Goyal et al. [97], where the authors showed that 3 rounds are sufficient to obtain (non-concurrent) non-malleable commitments from one-way functions. In [128] the authors propose a 3-round concurrent non-malleable commitment under number theoretic assumptions.

In this chapter, we study the following question.

Main Question: Can we construct a 3-round concurrent non-malleable commitment scheme under standard generic assumptions, rather than specific number-theoretic assumptions?

6.1.2 Other 3-Round Challenges

In addition, we consider 3 additional interesting settings and propose protocols that are secure against concurrent MiM.

- Proofs of knowledge are very useful in Cryptography. They have been studied in particular when there are only 3 rounds and the verifier just sends random bits (e.g., Σ-protocols [57, 62], Blum's protocol for Hamiltonicity [22]). Despite their importance, there is no construction for 3-round proofs of knowledge (PoK) that is sufficiently secure under concurrent MiM attacks. This is due to the fact that such attacks are in general extremely difficult to deal with. Even though there exist constructions with a constant number of rounds, the case of just 3 rounds so far has remained unsolved.
- Lapidot and Shamir in [133] proposed a 3-round public-coin delayed-input WIPoK for NP: the LS protocol. As we mentioned already in this document, when a PoK is used as a sub-protocol, the delayed-input feature becomes instrumental in giving a better round complexity to the final protocol. An additional feature of delayed-input protocols is that they allow to shifting large part of the computation to an off-line phase. Unfortunately, the LS protocol and the PoKs of [52, 53] (that we also present in Chaps. 8 and 9 respectively) are not secure against concurrent MiM attacks and this penalizes those applications where both round complexity and security against concurrent MiM attacks are important.
- We notice that identification schemes have been often proposed (e.g., [75]) through the paradigm of proving "knowledge" of a secret.[2] Under this formulation there are constant-round constructions that are proven secure against concurrent MiM attacks [15]. However no 3-round scheme known in literature is proven secure in presence of a concurrent MiM adversary.

---

[2] Other notions based on signature or decryption capabilities are considered weaker since in some applications the verifier wants to make sure that the prover is the actual entity matching the announced identity. Indeed without a PoK a prover could give some partial information about his secret to others that can still succeed in convincing the verifier, even though they do not know the full secret.

6.1.3 This Chapter's Contribution

We study 3-round commitment scheme in the presence of concurrent MiM attacks and solve in the positive the above open problems.

3-Round concurrent NM commitment schemes and more. In the main result of this chapter, we show a transform that on input any 3-round NM commitment scheme[3] gives a 3-round concurrent NM commitment scheme. The construction of [97] can be used to instantiate our transformation, therefore obtaining a 3-round concurrent NM commitment scheme based on any one-way permutation secure against subexponential-time adversaries.

Our transform extends the security of the underlying commitment scheme to multiple receivers. It is known that this implies security also with multiple senders [138]. The crucial idea of our transform is to combine the underlying NM commitment scheme along with a one-time pad, to produce a commitment of a message that by itself, in case of a malleability attack, will have sufficient structure to be recognized by a distinguisher in the session in which it appears. Therefore a successful concurrent MiM even playing multiple commitments with multiple receivers will have to maul the underlying commitment scheme in at least one session. Since the message has sufficient structure with respect to that single session, we are able to translate the concurrent MiM attack into a non-concurrent MiM that violates the security of the underlying (non-concurrent) NM commitment scheme. We will implement the idea of committing to a message with structure by forcing a successful concurrent MiM to commit to the solution of a puzzle in at least one session. We will use complexity leveraging to show that the attack of the concurrent MiM is indistinguishable from the attack of a polynomial-time simulator that plays with receivers only.

Furthermore we show a different approach for 3-round one-one non-malleable commitments that can be instantiated with a limited form of non-malleability enjoyed by both a subprotocol of [99] and a subprotocol of [97] (therefore we can instantiate our result in two completely different ways). The main result of the chapter can still be instantiated using our 3-round one-one non-malleable commitment scheme.

Our 3-round one-one non-malleable commitment scheme combines some ideas of the first mentioned result of the chapter along with the concept of weak non-malleable commitment. In particular we start with a scheme that is one-one non-malleable only against synchronous adversaries that do not commit to $\perp$. Note that both a subprotocol of [99] and a subprotocol of [97] satisfy this security property. Considering this notion we construct a compiler that, on input a 3-round synchronous weak one-one NM commitment scheme, gives as output a 3-round extractable one-one NM commitment scheme assuming OWPs secure against subexponential-time adversaries.

3-round arguments of knowledge and ID schemes against concurrent MiM attacks. We notice that our 3-round concurrent NM commitment scheme is a commit-and-prove argument of knowledge (AoK). This means that one can see our scheme as

[3] We also require the scheme to be extractable. Extractability often comes for free since it is commonly used in the non-malleability proof.

a commitment followed by an AoK about the committed value. By applying a simple change to the statement of the underlying AoK we obtain a 3-round concurrent NM witness-indistinguishable AoK (concurrent NMWIAoK) a notion introduced in [159] and later on extended in [139]. We stress that the delayed-input and public-coin properties of our commitment scheme are preserved by our concurrent NMWIAoK.

Notice that AoKs under standard assumptions require at least 3 rounds. The simulation-based notion for concurrent non-malleable arguments of knowledge (i.e., concurrent NM zero knowledge) requires at least a polylogarithmic number of rounds [13, 33] when the simulator is black box. In [159] it is shown how to get concurrent NM zero knowledge (NMZK) in the bare public-key (BPK) model [30, 149] with just two executions of a concurrent NMWIAoK. Therefore here we directly obtain a round-efficient concurrent NMZKAoK in the BPK model. Notice also that by making use of the delayed-input feature the simulator can extend a main thread avoiding issues due to aborting adversaries as discussed in [160, 184].

Finally, we notice that one can get an identification scheme secure in the PoK sense in the concurrent[4] setting of [15] as well as under the stronger definition based on matching conversations of [17, 123] naturally extended to multiple concurrent sessions. Following [41, 159], the key idea consists in using an identity that has two possible secrets such that knowledge of one witness does not allow to compute the other one in polynomial time. Then, by using our implementation of a concurrent NMWIAoK for proving knowledge of a secret associated to such identity we obtain a 3-round identification scheme secure against concurrent MiM attacks.

Other applications.

In [84] it is showed that the existence of a 3-round 3-robust parallel non-malleable commitment scheme implies the existence of a 4-round protocol for secure multi-party coin tossing for polynomially many coins and of a 4-round secure two-party protocol for any functionality in the simultaneous channel. One of the candidate instantiations of such special commitment scheme is our 3-round concurrent non-malleable commitment scheme.

6.2 3-Round Concurrent Non-malleable Commitments

In this section we show the main result of this work, a transform that starting from a 3-round extractable one-one non-malleable commitment scheme outputs a 3-round concurrent non-malleable commitment scheme.

---

[4] In [15] a notion called CR2 is proposed to deal with concurrent MiM attacks and reset attacks. Reset attack were also considered in the notion CR1+ introduced in [25]. Since reset attacks are out of the scope here, we will focus on concurrent MiM attacks only.

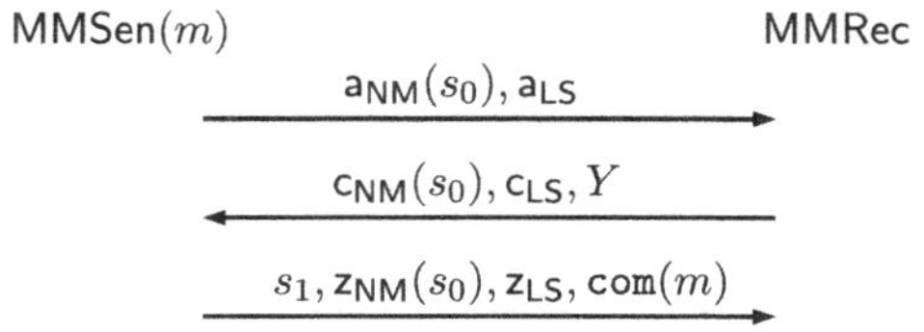

- Y is an element taken from the range of the OWP f.
- $\mathtt{com}(m)$ is the perfectly binding commitment of m computed using NI.
- $(\mathsf{a}_{\mathsf{nmc}}(s_0), \mathsf{c}_{\mathsf{nmc}}(s_0), \mathsf{z}_{\mathsf{nmc}}(s_0)) = \tau$ is the transcript of the execution of the NM commitment scheme Π_{nmc} when the sender commits to s_0.
- $(\mathsf{a}_{\mathsf{LS}}, \mathsf{c}_{\mathsf{LS}}, \mathsf{z}_{\mathsf{LS}}) = \pi$ is the transcript of LS proving knowledge of either m and the randomness used to compute $\mathtt{com}$, or of $(s_0, \mathtt{dec})$, s.t. $f(s_0 \oplus s_1) = Y$ and $\mathtt{dec}$ is a valid decommitment of s_0 w.r.t. τ.

Fig. 6.1 Informal description of our 3-round concurrent NM commitment scheme

6.2.1 Informal Description

The transform we consider stakes as input a 3-round extractable one-one NM commitment scheme Π_{nmc}, a OWP f, a non-interactive perfectly binding commitment scheme NI, the 3-round delayed-input adaptive WI/PoK LS and outputs a 3-round fully concurrent (i.e., many-many) NM commitment scheme $\Pi_{1-n} =$ (NMSen, NMRec). Let m be the message that NMSen wants to commit. The high-level idea of our compiler is depicted in Fig. 6.1. The sender NMSen, on input the session-id $\mathtt{id}$ and the message m, computes the 1st round of the protocol by running LS and sending the 1st round of nmc to commit to a random message s_0 using $\mathtt{id}$ as session-id. In the 2nd round the receiver NMRec sends the challenges of nmc and LS, also sends a random value Y in the range of the OWP f.[5] In the last round NMSen commits to message m using NI, therefore obtaining $\mathtt{com}$, then computes the last round of nmc, completes the transcript of LS, and finally sends a random string s_1. The protocol LS is used by NMSen to prove to NMRec that either she knows message m and the randomness used to compute $\mathtt{com}$, or she knows the values $(s_0, \mathtt{dec})$, such that $f(s_0 \oplus s_1) = Y$ and $\mathtt{dec}$ is a valid decommitment to s_0 w.r.t. the commitment computed using Π_{nmc}. We observe that NMSen needs m only when computing the 3rd round, therefore our construction enjoys delayed-input correctness.

[5] When sampling from the range of f corresponds to picking a random string, we have that our commitment scheme is public coin.

6.2.2 The Compiler

The compiler needs the following tools:

1. a OWP f that is secure against PPT adversaries and $\tilde{T}_f$-breakable;
2. a non interactive perfectly binding commitment scheme $\mathsf{NI} = (\mathsf{NISen}, \mathsf{NIRec})$ that is T_{NI}-hiding and $\tilde{T}_{\mathsf{NI}}$-breakable;
3. a 3-round extractable *one-one* NM commitment scheme $\Pi_{\mathsf{nmc}} = (\mathsf{Sen}_{\mathsf{nmc}}, \mathsf{Rec}_{\mathsf{nmc}})$ that is T_{nmc}-hiding/non-malleable, and $\tilde{T}_{\mathsf{nmc}}$-breakable;
4. the LS proof system [133] $\mathsf{LS} = (\mathcal{P}, \mathcal{V})$ for the language

$$\begin{aligned} L = \Big\{\big((a, c, z), Y, s_1, \mathtt{com}, \mathtt{id}\big) : \exists\, (m, \sigma) \text{ s.t.} \\ \mathtt{com} = \mathsf{NISen}(m; \sigma) \text{ OR} \\ \big(\exists(\rho, s_0)\text{s.t. } a = \mathrm{Sen}^1_{\mathsf{nm}}(\mathtt{id}, s_0; \rho) \text{ AND} \\ z = \mathrm{Sen}^2_{\mathsf{nm}}(\mathtt{id}, c, s_0; \rho) \text{ AND } Y = f(s_0 \oplus s_1)\big)\Big\} \end{aligned}$$

that is T_{LS}-WI for the corresponding relation $\mathsf{Rel}_{\mathsf{L}}$.

Let λ be the security parameter of our scheme. We will also use wlog λ also as a security parameter for the hardness to invert f with respect to polynomial time adversaries. Then, we consider the following hierarchy of security levels for the above tools: $T_f \ll T_{\mathsf{NI}} \ll \sqrt{T_{\mathsf{nmc}}} \ll T_{\mathsf{nmc}} \ll \sqrt{T_{\mathsf{LS}}} \ll T_{\mathsf{LS}}$ where by "$T \ll T'$" we mean that "$T \cdot \mathsf{poly}(\lambda) < T'$". We also require that:

- NI is T_{NI}-hiding, but is also $\tilde{T}_{\mathsf{NI}} = \sqrt{T_{\mathsf{nmc}}}$-breakable;
- Π_{nmc} is T_{nmc} hiding/non-malleable, but the hiding is also $\tilde{T}_{\mathsf{nmc}} = \sqrt{T_{\mathsf{LS}}}$-breakable.

Now, we need to define different security parameters, one for each tool involved in the security proof to be consistent with the hierarchy of security levels defined above (a similar use of security parameters has been proposed in [173]). Given the security parameter λ of our scheme, we will make use of the following security parameters (all polynomially related to λ and such that the above hierarchy of security levels holds): λ for f, λ_{NI} for NI, λ_{nmc} for Π_{nmc}, λ_{LS} for LS.

We denote by Params the function that on input λ outputs $(\lambda_{\mathsf{NI}}, \lambda_{\mathsf{nmc}}, \lambda_{\mathsf{LS}}, \ell)$ where ℓ is the size of the theorem to be proved using LS.[6] Our concurrent NM commitment scheme $\Pi_{1-n} = (\mathsf{NMSen}, \mathsf{NMRec})$ is fully described in Fig. 6.2 and an high-level overview is given in Fig. 6.1.

Theorem 6.1 *Suppose there exist OWPs secure against subexponential-time adversaries, then Π_{1-n} is a perfectly binding delayed-input commitment scheme.*

[6] To compute 1st and 2nd round of LS only the length ℓ of the instance is required.

Common input: Security parameters: λ, $(\lambda_{\mathsf{NI}}, \lambda_{\mathsf{nmc}}, \lambda_{\mathsf{LS}}, \ell) = \mathsf{Params}(\lambda)$.
NMSen's identity: $\mathtt{id} \in \{0,1\}^{\lambda}$.
Input to NMSen: $m \in \{0,1\}^{\mathsf{poly}\{\lambda\}}$.

Commitment Phase:

1. NMSen $\rightarrow$ NMRec
   1. Pick $s_0 \in \{0,1\}^{\lambda}$.
   2. Pick a randomness $\rho \in \{0,1\}^{\lambda_{\mathsf{nm}}}$ and compute $\mathsf{a}_{\mathsf{nmc}} = \mathsf{Sen}^1_{\mathsf{nm}}(\mathtt{id}, s_0; \rho)$.
   3. Pick a randomness $\alpha \in \{0,1\}^{\lambda_{\mathsf{LS}}}$ and compute $\mathsf{a}_{\mathsf{LS}} = \mathsf{P}^1(\ell; \alpha)$.
   4. Send $(\mathsf{a}_{\mathsf{nmc}}, \mathsf{a}_{\mathsf{LS}})$ to NMRec.
5. NMRec $\rightarrow$ NMSen
   1. Pick a randomness γ and run $\mathsf{Rec}_{\mathsf{nmc}}$ on input $(\mathtt{id}, \mathsf{a}_{\mathsf{nmc}}; \gamma)$ to obtain c_{nm}.
   2. Pick a randomness β and run $\mathcal{V}$ to obtain c_{LS}.
   3. Pick a random $y \in \{0,1\}^{\lambda}$ and compute $Y = f(y)$.
   4. Send $(\mathsf{c}_{\mathsf{nmc}}, \mathsf{c}_{\mathsf{LS}}, Y)$ to NMSen.
5. NMSen $\rightarrow$ NMRec
   1. Pick a randomness $\sigma \in \{0,1\}^{\lambda_{\mathsf{NI}}}$ and compute $(\mathtt{com}, \mathtt{dec}) = \mathsf{NISen}(m; \sigma)$.
   2. Pick $s_1 \leftarrow \{0,1\}^{\lambda}$.
   3. Compute $(\mathsf{z}_{\mathsf{nmc}}, \mathtt{dec}_{\mathsf{nmc}}) = \mathsf{Sen}^2_{\mathsf{nm}}(\mathtt{id}, \mathsf{c}_{\mathsf{nmc}}, s_0; \rho)$.
   4. Set $x = \big((\mathsf{a}_{\mathsf{nmc}}, \mathsf{c}_{\mathsf{nmc}}, \mathsf{z}_{\mathsf{nmc}}), Y, s_1, \mathtt{com}, \mathtt{id}\big)$ and $w = (m, \sigma, \bot, \bot)$ with $(|x| = \ell)$. Run $\mathsf{z}_{\mathsf{LS}} = \mathsf{P}^2(x, w, \mathsf{c}_{\mathsf{LS}}; \alpha)$ where x is the theorem to be proven and w is the witness.
   5. Send $(\mathsf{z}_{\mathsf{nmc}}, \mathtt{com}, \mathsf{z}_{\mathsf{LS}}, s_1)$ to NMRec.
6. NMRec: Set $x = \big((\mathsf{a}_{\mathsf{nmc}}, \mathsf{c}_{\mathsf{nmc}}, \mathsf{z}_{\mathsf{nmc}}), Y, s_1, \mathtt{com}, \mathtt{id}\big)$ and abort iff $(\mathsf{a}_{\mathsf{LS}}, \mathsf{c}_{\mathsf{LS}}, \mathsf{z}_{\mathsf{LS}})$ is not accepting for $\mathcal{V}$ with respect to x.

Decommitment Phase:

1. NMSen $\rightarrow$ NMRec: Send $(\mathtt{dec}, m, \mathtt{dec}_{\mathsf{nmc}}, s_0)$ to NMRec.
2. NMRec: Accept m as the committed message iff
   1. $\mathsf{NIRec}(\mathtt{dec}, \mathtt{com}, m) = 1$ and
   2. $\mathsf{Rec}_{\mathsf{nmc}}$ on input γ, $(\mathsf{a}_{\mathsf{nmc}}, \mathsf{c}_{\mathsf{nmc}}, \mathsf{z}_{\mathsf{nmc}}, \mathtt{id})$, s_0 and $\mathtt{dec}_{\mathsf{nmc}}$ outputs 1.

Fig. 6.2 Our 3-round concurrent NM commitment scheme

Before start the proof of security, we recall that LS and NI can be constructed from OWPs secure against subexponential-time adversaries as well as Π_{nmc} that can be constructed from OWPs secure against subexponential-time using the constructions of [97] or the construction showed in Sect. 6.4.1.

Proof **Correctness.** The delayed-input correctness of Π_{1-n} follows by inspection considering the delayed-input completeness of LS, and the correctness of Π_{nmc} and NI.

Binding. To prove the binding property we only observe that the message given in output in the decommitment phase of Π_{1-n} is the message committed using NI. Moreover the decommitment phase of Π_{1-n} coincides with the decommitment of NI and Π_{nmc}. Since they are both perfectly binding we have that therefore Π_{1-n} is perfectly binding too.

Hiding. The hiding property follows directly from the non-malleability property proved in Theorem 6.2. Indeed the proof of Theorem 6.2 does not rely on the hiding of Π_{1-n}. □

In this section we prove our main theorem.

Theorem 6.2 *Suppose there exist OWPs secure against subexponential-time adversaries, then Π_{1-n} is concurrent (i.e., many-many) non-malleable.*

Proof Since we can use Proposition 2.1, we only need to prove that our commitment enjoys one-many non-malleability. More formally with respect to a one-many adversary $\mathcal{A}$, we need to show that for all $m \in \{0,1\}^{\mathsf{poly}(\lambda)}$ it holds that:

$$\{\mathsf{mim}^{\mathcal{A},m}_{\Pi_{1-n}}(z)\}_{z\in\{0,1\}^\star} \approx \{\mathsf{sim}^{S}_{\Pi_{1-n}}(1^\lambda, z)\}_{z\in\{0,1\}^\star}$$

where S is the simulator depicted in Fig. 6.3.

This means that the real execution in which the sender runs NMSen to commit to a message m must be indistinguishable with respect to an execution in which a simulator Sim runs internally the MiM adversarial $\mathcal{A}$ sending a commitment of 0^λ, and then forwards the messages that $\mathcal{A}$ sends in the right sessions to receivers $\mathsf{NMRec}_1, \ldots, \mathsf{NMRec}_{\mathsf{poly}(\lambda)}$.

We remark that in the security proof we denote by $\tilde{\delta}_i$ a value associated with the i-th right session (where the adversary $\mathcal{A}$ plays with a receiver NMRec_i with $i \in \{1, \ldots, \mathsf{poly}(\lambda)\}$) where δ is the corresponding value in the left session. For example, the sender commits to v in the left session while $\mathcal{A}$ commits to $\tilde{v}_i$ in the i-th right session.

To prove the indistinguishability of the above two experiments we proceed by showing 3 hybrid experiments[7] $\mathcal{H}^m_i(z)$ with $i = 1, 2, 3$, where m is the message committed in the left session. Following [135] we denote by $\{\mathsf{mim}^{\mathcal{A}}_{\mathcal{H}^m_i}(z)\}_{z\in\{0,1\}^\star}$ the random variable describing the view of the MiM $\mathcal{A}$ combined with the value it commits in the right interaction in hybrid $\mathcal{H}^m_i(z)$ (as usual, the committed value is replaced by $\perp$ if the right interaction does not correspond to a commitment that can be successfully opened or if $\mathcal{A}$ has copied the identity of the left interaction).

The first hybrid is the experiment in which in the left session NMSen commits to m, while in the right session we run $\mathsf{NMRec}_1, \ldots, \mathsf{NMRec}_{\mathsf{poly}(\lambda)}$ for the rights sessions played by $\mathcal{A}$. We refer to this hybrid experiment as $\mathcal{H}^m_1(z)$, details follow below.

$\mathcal{H}^m_1(z)$.
Left session:

1. First round.

   1.1 Pick $s_0 \leftarrow \{0,1\}^\lambda$.
   1.2 Compute $\mathsf{a}_{\mathsf{nmc}} = \mathrm{Sen}^1_{\mathsf{nm}}(\mathtt{id}, s_0; \rho)$.

[7] We will describe the hybrid experiments in a succinct way focusing on the key steps (e.g., omitting sampling of randomness, generation of parameters $\lambda_{\mathsf{NI}}, \lambda_{\mathsf{nmc}}, \lambda_{\mathsf{LS}}, \ell$).

1.3 Compute $\mathsf{a}_{\mathsf{LS}} = \mathsf{P}^1(1^{\lambda_{\mathsf{LS}}}, \ell; \alpha)$.
1.4 Send $(\mathsf{a}_{\mathsf{nmc}}, \mathsf{a}_{\mathsf{LS}})$ to $\mathcal{A}$.

2. Third round, upon receiving $(\mathsf{c}_{\mathsf{nmc}}, \mathsf{c}_{\mathsf{LS}}, Y)$ from $\mathcal{A}$.

2.1 Compute $(\mathtt{com}, \mathtt{dec}) = \mathsf{NISen}(m; \sigma)$.
2.2 Pick $s_1 \leftarrow \{0, 1\}^{\lambda}$.
2.3 Compute $(\mathsf{z}_{\mathsf{nmc}}, \mathtt{dec}_{\mathsf{nmc}}) = \mathrm{Sen}^2_{\mathsf{nm}}(\mathtt{id}, \mathsf{c}_{\mathsf{nmc}}, s_0; \rho)$.
2.4 Set $x = \big((\mathsf{a}_{\mathsf{nmc}}, \mathsf{c}_{\mathsf{nmc}}, \mathsf{z}_{\mathsf{nmc}}), Y, s_1, \mathtt{com}, \mathtt{id}\big)$ and $w = (m, \sigma, \bot, \bot)$ with $(|x| = \ell)$. Run $\mathsf{z}_{\mathsf{LS}} = \mathsf{P}^2(x, w, \mathsf{c}_{\mathsf{LS}}; \alpha)$.
2.5 Send $(\mathsf{z}_{\mathsf{nmc}}, \mathtt{com}, \mathsf{z}_{\mathsf{LS}}, s_1)$ to $\mathcal{A}$.

Right sessions: act as a proxy between $\mathcal{A}$ and $\mathsf{NMRec}_1, \ldots, \mathsf{NMRec}_{\mathsf{poly}(\lambda)}$.

We have that for all $m \in \{0, 1\}^{\mathsf{poly}(\lambda)}$ $\{\mathsf{mim}^{\mathcal{A}}_{\mathcal{H}_1^m}(z)\}_{z\in\{0,1\}^\star}$ clearly corresponds to $\{\mathsf{mim}^{\mathcal{A},m}_{\Pi_{1-n}}(z)\}_{z\in\{0,1\}^\star}$. Before we move on with the sequence of hybrid experiments we need to prove that, for all $i \in \{1, \ldots, \mathsf{poly}(\lambda)\}$ $\mathcal{A}$ does not manage to invert any values $\tilde{Y}_i$ in the right sessions by sending a value $\tilde{s_1}_i$ such that $f(\tilde{s_0}_i \oplus \tilde{s_1}_i) = \tilde{Y}_i$ where $\tilde{s_0}_i$ is the message committed in the i-th right session through nmc.

Lemma 6.1 *Let p_i be the probability that in the i-th right session, for $i \in \{1, \ldots, \mathsf{poly}(\lambda)\}$, $\mathcal{A}$ sends a value $\tilde{s_1}_i$ such that $f(\tilde{s_1}_i \oplus \tilde{s_0}_i) = \tilde{Y}_i$ where $\tilde{s_0}_i$ is the value committed using* nmc. *Then $p_i < \nu(\lambda)$ for some negligible function ν.*

Proof Suppose by contradiction that for a right session i the claim does not hold. We can construct an adversary $\mathcal{A}_f$ that inverts the OWP f in polynomial time. Formally we consider a challenger C_f of f that chooses a random Y in the range of f and sends it to $\mathcal{A}_f$. $\mathcal{A}_f$ wins if it gives as output y such that $Y = f(y)$. Before describing the adversary we need to consider the augmented machine $\mathcal{M}$ that will be used by $\mathcal{A}_f$. $\mathcal{M}$ internally executes $\mathcal{A}$, and interacts with an external receiver $\mathsf{Rec}_{\mathsf{ext}}$ of the protocol Π_{nmc} acting as the sender. Formally $\mathcal{M}$ acts as follows.

$\mathcal{M}(Y, \varphi, z)$

1. Act in the left session with $\mathcal{A}$ (that runs using randomness φ) as in $\mathcal{H}_1^m(z)$.
2. For all $j \neq i \in \{1, \ldots \mathsf{poly}(\lambda)\}$ run NMRec_j as in $\mathcal{H}_1^m(z)$. Instead run NMRec_i as described in steps 3, 4 and 5.
3. Upon receiving the 1st round of the i-th right session $(\tilde{\mathsf{a}}_{\mathsf{nmc}_i}, \tilde{\mathsf{a}}_{\mathsf{LS}_i})$ from $\mathcal{A}$, send $\tilde{\mathsf{a}}_{\mathsf{nmc}_i}$ to $\mathsf{Rec}_{\mathsf{ext}}$.
4. Upon receiving $\tilde{\mathsf{c}}_{\mathsf{nm}_i}$ from $\mathsf{Rec}_{\mathsf{ext}}$, run as follows:

4.1 Run $\mathcal{V}$ to obtain $\tilde{\mathsf{c}}_{\mathsf{LS}_i}$.
4.2 Set $\tilde{Y}_i = Y$.
4.3 Send $(\tilde{\mathsf{c}}_{\mathsf{nmc}_i}, \tilde{\mathsf{c}}_{\mathsf{LS}_i}, \tilde{Y}_i)$ to $\mathcal{A}$.

5. Upon receiving the 3rd round of the i-th right session $(\tilde{\mathsf{z}}_{\mathsf{nmc}_i}, \tilde{\mathtt{com}}_i, \tilde{\mathsf{z}}_{\mathsf{LS}_i}, \tilde{s_1}_i)$, set $\tilde{x} = \big((\tilde{\mathsf{a}}_{\mathsf{nmc}_i}, \tilde{\mathsf{c}}_{\mathsf{nmc}_i}, \tilde{\mathsf{z}}_{\mathsf{nmc}_i}), \tilde{Y}, \tilde{s_1}_i, \tilde{\mathtt{com}}_i, \tilde{\mathtt{id}}\big)$ and abort iff $(\tilde{\mathsf{a}}_{\mathsf{LS}_i}, \tilde{\mathsf{c}}_{\mathsf{LS}_i}, \tilde{\mathsf{z}}_{\mathsf{LS}_i})$ is not accepting for $\mathcal{V}$ with respect to $\tilde{x}$.

6. Send $\tilde{\mathsf{z}}_{\mathsf{nmc}_i}$ to $\mathsf{Rec}_{\mathsf{ext}}$.

Notice that the above execution of $\mathcal{M}$ is distributed identically to $\mathcal{H}_1^m(z)$ when $\mathsf{Rec}_{\mathsf{ext}}$ plays identically as honest receiver. Now we can conclude the proof of this lemma by describing how $\mathcal{A}_f$ works. $\mathcal{A}_f$ runs the extractor of Π_{nmc} using $\mathcal{M}$ as sender (recall that an extractor of Π_{nmc} plays only having access to a sender of Π_{nmc}). We have that the extractor with non-negligible probability outputs the committed message of an execution that inverts f. By using the randomness φ, $\mathcal{A}_f$ can reconstruct the view of $\mathcal{A}$ and retrieve the value $\tilde{s_1}_i$. Therefore $\mathcal{A}$ running in polynomial time[8] outputs with non-negligible probability the value $y = \tilde{s_0}_i \oplus \tilde{s_1}_i$ such that $f(y) = Y$. □

We now consider the second hybrid experiment $\mathcal{H}_2^m(z)$ where in the left session, after receiving Y from $\mathcal{A}$, the sender in time T_f finds a value y such that $Y = f(y)$. Then the sender sets and sends $s_1 = y \oplus s_0$, where s_0 is the value committed using Π_{nmc}. The only difference between this hybrid experiment and $\mathcal{H}_1^m(z)$ is that $\mathcal{H}_2^m(z)$ runs in time sub-exponential in λ, and the value s_1 is equal to $y \oplus s_0$ where $Y = f(y)$. Formally $\mathcal{H}_2^m(z)$ is the following experiment.

$\mathcal{H}_2^m(z)$.

Left session:

1. First round.
   1.1 Pick $s_0 \leftarrow \{0, 1\}^\lambda$.
   1.2 Compute $\mathsf{a}_{\mathsf{nmc}} = \mathsf{Sen}^1_{\mathsf{nm}}(\mathtt{id}, s_0; \rho)$.
   1.3 Compute $\mathsf{a}_{\mathsf{LS}} = \mathsf{P}^1(1^{\lambda_{\mathsf{LS}}}, \ell; \alpha)$.
   1.4 Send $(\mathsf{a}_{\mathsf{nmc}}, \mathsf{a}_{\mathsf{LS}})$ to $\mathcal{A}$.
2. Third round. Upon receiving $(\mathsf{c}_{\mathsf{nmc}}, \mathsf{c}_{\mathsf{LS}}, Y)$ from $\mathcal{A}$.
   2.1 Compute $(\mathtt{com}, \mathtt{dec}) = \mathsf{NISen}(m; \sigma)$.
   2.2 <u>Run in time T_f to compute y such that $Y = f(y)$.</u>
   2.3 <u>Set $s_1 = y \oplus s_0$.</u>
   2.4 Compute $(\mathsf{z}_{\mathsf{nmc}}, \mathtt{dec}_{\mathsf{nmc}}) = \mathsf{Sen}^2_{\mathsf{nm}}(\mathtt{id}, \mathsf{c}_{\mathsf{nmc}}, s_0; \rho)$.
   2.5 Set $x = \big((\mathsf{a}_{\mathsf{nmc}}, \mathsf{c}_{\mathsf{nmc}}, \mathsf{z}_{\mathsf{nmc}}), Y, s_1, \mathtt{com}, \mathtt{id}\big)$ and $w = (m, \sigma, \perp, \perp)$ with $(|x| = \ell)$. Run $\mathsf{z}_{\mathsf{LS}} = \mathsf{P}^2(x, w, \mathsf{c}_{\mathsf{LS}}; \alpha)$.
   2.6 Send $(\mathsf{z}_{\mathsf{nmc}}, \mathtt{com}, \mathsf{z}_{\mathsf{LS}}, s_1)$ to NMRec.

Right sessions: Act as a proxy between $\mathcal{A}$ and $\mathsf{NMRec}_1, \ldots, \mathsf{NMRec}_{\mathsf{poly}(\lambda)}$.

[8] The extractor is an expected polynomial-time algorithm while $\mathcal{A}_f$ must be a strict polynomial-time algorithm. Therefore $\mathcal{A}_f$ will run the extractor up to a given upperbounded number of steps that depends on the distinguishing advantage of the adversary. This allows, with non-negligible probability, the *truncated* extraction procedure to be completed successfully and this is sufficient for $\mathcal{A}_f$ to invert f. The same standard argument about truncating the execution of an expected polynomial-time algorithm will be needed later but for simplicity, we will not repeat this discussion.

When switching from $\mathcal{H}_1^m(z)$ to $\mathcal{H}_2^m(z)$ we will make sure that the following two properties hold.

1. For all message $m \in \{0,1\}^{\mathsf{poly}(\lambda)}$ it holds that $\mathsf{mim}^{\mathcal{A}}_{\mathcal{H}_1^m}(z) \approx \mathsf{mim}^{\mathcal{A}}_{\mathcal{H}_2^m}(z)$.[9]
2. Let p_i be the probability that in the i-th right session of $\mathcal{H}_2$, for $i \in \{1,\dots,\mathsf{poly}(\lambda)\}$, $\mathcal{A}$ sends a value $\tilde{s_1}_i$ such that $f(\tilde{s_1}_i \oplus \tilde{s_0}_i) = \tilde{Y}_i$ where $\tilde{s_0}_i$ is the value committed using nmc. Then $p_i < \nu(\lambda)$ for some negligible function ν.

We now prove that the above two properties hold.

Lemma 6.2 *For all message $m \in \{0,1\}^{\mathsf{poly}(\lambda)}$ it holds that* $\mathsf{mim}^{\mathcal{A}}_{\mathcal{H}_1^m}(z) \approx \mathsf{mim}^{\mathcal{A}}_{\mathcal{H}_2^m}(z)$.

Proof Suppose by contradiction that the distribution of $\mathsf{mim}^{\mathcal{A}}_{\mathcal{H}_1^m}(z)$ is distinguishable from $\mathsf{mim}^{\mathcal{A}}_{\mathcal{H}_2^m}(z)$; this means that there exists a distinguisher $\mathcal{D}$ that can tell apart such two distributions. We now use $\mathcal{D}$ and $\mathcal{A}$ to construct an adversary $\mathcal{A}_{\mathsf{Hiding}}$ that breaks the hiding of Π_{nmc} in time $\mathsf{poly}(\lambda) \cdot T_{\mathsf{NI}}$ therefore reaching a contradiction.[10] Let $\mathcal{C}_{\mathsf{Hiding}}$ be the challenger of the hiding game, we consider two randomly chosen challenge messages (m_0, m_1) sent to $\mathcal{C}_{\mathsf{Hiding}}$. We now provide a formal description of the adversary $\mathcal{A}_{\mathsf{Hiding}}$.

$\mathcal{A}_{\mathsf{Hiding}}(m_0, m_1, z)$

1. Upon receiving the 1st round $\mathsf{a}_{\mathsf{nmc}}$ from $\mathcal{C}_{\mathsf{Hiding}}$, run as follows:
   1.1 Compute $\mathsf{a}_{\mathsf{LS}} = \mathsf{P}^1(1^{\lambda_{\mathsf{LS}}}, \ell; \alpha)$.
   1.2 Send $(\mathsf{a}_{\mathsf{nmc}}, \mathsf{a}_{\mathsf{LS}})$ to $\mathcal{A}$.
2. Upon receiving $(\mathsf{c}_{\mathsf{nmc}}, \mathsf{c}_{\mathsf{LS}}, Y)$ from $\mathcal{A}$, send $\mathsf{c}_{\mathsf{nmc}}$ to $\mathcal{C}_{\mathsf{nmc}}$.
3. Upon receiving the 3rd round $\mathsf{z}_{\mathsf{nmc}}$ from $\mathcal{C}_{\mathsf{Hiding}}$, run as follows:
   3.1 Compute y such that $Y = f(y)$, set $s_1 = m_0 \oplus y$.
   3.2 Compute $(\mathtt{com}, \mathtt{dec}) = \mathsf{NISen}(m; \sigma)$.
   3.3 Set $x = \big((\mathsf{a}_{\mathsf{nmc}}, \mathsf{c}_{\mathsf{nmc}}, \mathsf{z}_{\mathsf{nmc}}), Y, s_1, \mathtt{com}, \mathtt{id}\big)$ and $w = (m, \sigma, \bot, \bot)$ with $(|x| = \ell)$. Run $\mathsf{z}_{\mathsf{LS}} = \mathsf{P}^2(x, w, \mathsf{c}_{\mathsf{LS}}; \alpha)$.
   3.4 Send $(\mathsf{z}_{\mathsf{nmc}}, \mathtt{com}, \mathsf{z}_{\mathsf{LS}}, s_1)$ to $\mathcal{A}$.
4. Simulate $\mathsf{NMRec}_1, \dots, \mathsf{NMRec}_{\mathsf{poly}(\lambda)}$ with $\mathcal{A}$ when $\mathcal{A}$ plays as a sender.
5. Let M be an empty tuple. For all $i \in \{1,\dots,\mathsf{poly}(\lambda)\}$, consider $\tilde{\mathtt{com}}_i$, the non-interactive commitment received by NMRec_i, run in time T_{NI} to compute $\tilde{m}_i$ such that $\exists\, \tilde{\mathtt{dec}} : 1 = \mathsf{NIRec}(\tilde{\mathtt{com}}_i, \tilde{\mathtt{dec}}, \tilde{m}_i)$ and add $\tilde{m}_i$ to M.
6. Give M and the view of $\mathcal{A}$ to the distinguisher $\mathcal{D}$ and output what $\mathcal{D}$ outputs.

[9] To simplify the notation here, and in the rest of the proof, we will omit that the indistinguishability between two distributions must hold for every auxiliary input z.

[10] Recall that Π_{nmc} is secure against adversaries running in time $\mathsf{poly}(\lambda) \cdot T_{\mathsf{NI}} < T_{\mathsf{nmc}}$.

The proof ends with the observation that if C_{Hiding} has committed to m_0 then the xor of the committed value with s_1 is equal to y such that $f(y) = Y$, like in $\mathcal{H}_2^m(z)$. If instead C_{Hiding} has committed to m_1 then the xor of the committed value and s_1 is equal to a random value, like in $\mathcal{H}_1^m(z)$. □

Lemma 6.3 *Let p_i be the probability that in the i-th right session of $\mathcal{H}_2$, for $i \in \{1, \ldots, \mathsf{poly}(\lambda)\}$, $\mathcal{A}$ sends a value $\tilde{s}_{1i}$ such that $f(\tilde{s}_{1i} \oplus \tilde{s}_{0i}) = \tilde{Y}_i$ where $\tilde{s}_{0i}$ is the value committed using* nmc. *Then $p_i < \nu(\lambda)$ for some negligible function ν.*

Proof Suppose by contradiction that for a right session i the claim does not hold. We can construct a distinguisher $\mathcal{D}_{\mathsf{nmc}}$ and an adversary $\mathcal{A}_{\mathsf{nmc}}$ that break the non-malleability of Π_{nmc}. Let C_{nmc} be the challenger of the NM commitment and let (m_0, m_1) be two randomly chosen challenge messages given to C_{nmc}.

$\mathcal{A}_{\mathsf{nmc}}(m_0, m_1, z)$

Left session:

1. Act as $\mathcal{A}_{\mathsf{Hiding}}$ acts in the left session.

Right sessions:

1. For all $j \neq i \in \{1, \ldots, \mathsf{poly}(\lambda)\}$ run NMRec_j as in $\mathcal{H}_2^m(z)$. Instead run NMRec_i as described in steps 1.1, 1.2 and 1.3.
   1.1 Forward $\tilde{\mathsf{a}}_{\mathsf{nmc}_i}$ to $\mathsf{Rec}_{\mathsf{nmc}}$.
   1.2 Upon receiving $\tilde{\mathsf{c}}_{\mathsf{nmc}}$ from $\mathsf{Rec}_{\mathsf{nmc}}$, pick a random $\tilde{\mathsf{c}}_{\mathsf{LS}_i}$, pick a random $\tilde{Y}_i$ and send $(\tilde{\mathsf{c}}_{\mathsf{nmc}_i}, \tilde{\mathsf{c}}_{\mathsf{LS}_i}, \tilde{Y}_i)$ to $\mathcal{A}$.
   1.3 Upon receiving $\tilde{\mathsf{z}}_{\mathsf{nmc}_i}$ from $\mathcal{A}$, send it to $\mathsf{Rec}_{\mathsf{nmc}}$.

Let $\mathsf{mim}^{\mathcal{A}_{\mathsf{nmc}}}(z)$ be the view of $\mathsf{mim}^{\mathcal{A}_{\mathsf{nmc}}}(z)$ and the tuple of committed messages in the right session. The distinguisher $\mathcal{D}_{\mathsf{nmc}}$ takes as input $\mathsf{mim}^{\mathcal{A}_{\mathsf{nmc}}}(z)$ and acts as follows.

$\mathcal{D}_{\mathsf{nmc}}(\mathsf{mim}^{\mathcal{A}_{\mathsf{nmc}}}(z))$: Let $\tilde{s}_{0i}$ be the committed message sent in the i-right session by $\mathcal{A}_{\mathsf{nmc}}$ to NMRec. Reconstruct the output messages of $\mathcal{A}$ (using the same randomness of $\mathsf{mim}^{\mathcal{A}_{\mathsf{nmc}}}(z)$) to pick $\tilde{s}_{1i}$. If $f(\tilde{s}_{1i} \oplus \tilde{s}_{0i}) = \tilde{Y}_i$ output 1 and output 0 otherwise. The proof ends with the observation that if C_{nmc} has committed to m_0 then the xor of the committed value with s_{1i} is equal to y such that $f(y) = Y$ like in $\mathcal{H}_2^m$. If instead C_{Hiding} has committed to m_1 then the xor of the committed value with s_{1i} is equal to a random string as in $\mathcal{H}_1^m$. □

The third hybrid experiment that we consider is equal to $\mathcal{H}_2^m(z)$ with the difference that the LS proof system is executed using s_0 and the randomness of the non-malleable commitment of s_0. Recall that $f(s_0 \oplus s_1) = Y$. We observe that in the left session of $\mathcal{H}_2^m(z)$ it already holds that $f(s_0 \oplus s_1) = Y$, therefore we can switch the witness used in LS and complete the execution of the proof system. Formally $\mathcal{H}_3^m(z)$ is the following experiment.

$\mathcal{H}_3^m(z)$.

Left sessions:

1. First round.
   1.1 Pick $s_0 \leftarrow \{0,1\}^\lambda$.
   1.2 Compute $\mathsf{a}_{\mathsf{nmc}} = \mathsf{Sen}^1_{\mathsf{nm}}(\mathtt{id}, s_0; \rho)$.
   1.3 Compute $\mathsf{a}_{\mathsf{LS}} = \mathsf{P}^1(1^{\lambda_{\mathsf{LS}}}, \ell; \alpha)$.
   1.4 Send $(\mathsf{a}_{\mathsf{nmc}}, \mathsf{a}_{\mathsf{LS}})$ to $\mathcal{A}$.
2. Third round. Upon receiving $(\mathsf{c}_{\mathsf{nmc}}, \mathsf{c}_{\mathsf{LS}}, Y)$ from $\mathcal{A}$.
   2.1 Compute $(\mathtt{com}, \mathtt{dec}) = \mathsf{NISen}(m; \sigma)$.
   2.2 Run in time T_f to compute y such that $Y = f(y)$.
   2.3 Set $s_1 = s_0 \oplus y$.
   2.4 Compute $(\mathsf{z}_{\mathsf{nmc}}, \mathtt{dec}_{\mathsf{nmc}}) = \mathsf{Sen}^2_{\mathsf{nm}}(\mathtt{id}, \mathsf{c}_{\mathsf{nmc}}, s_0; \rho)$.
   2.5 Compute $(\mathtt{com}, \mathtt{dec}) = \mathsf{NISen}(1^{\lambda_{\mathsf{NI}}}, m; \sigma)$.
   2.6 Set $x = \big((\mathsf{a}_{\mathsf{nmc}}, \mathsf{c}_{\mathsf{nmc}}, \mathsf{z}_{\mathsf{nmc}}), Y, s_1, \mathtt{com}, \mathtt{id}\big)$ and $\underline{w = (\bot, \bot, s_0, \rho)}$ with $(|x| = \ell)$. Run $\mathsf{z}_{\mathsf{LS}} = \mathsf{P}^2(x, w, \mathsf{c}_{\mathsf{LS}}; \alpha)$.
   2.7 Send $(\mathsf{z}_{\mathsf{nmc}}, \mathtt{com}, \mathsf{z}_{\mathsf{LS}}, s_1)$ to $\mathcal{A}$.

Right sessions: Act as a proxy between $\mathcal{A}$ and $\mathsf{NMRec}_1, \ldots, \mathsf{NMRec}_{\mathsf{poly}(\lambda)}$.

Even in this case we need to prove the following two properties.

1. For all message $m \in \{0,1\}^{\mathsf{poly}(\lambda)}$ it holds that $\mathsf{mim}^{\mathcal{A}}_{\mathcal{H}_2^m}(z) \approx \mathsf{mim}^{\mathcal{A}}_{\mathcal{H}_3^m}(z)$.
2. Let p_i be the probability that in the i-th right session of $\mathcal{H}_3$, for any $i \in \{1, \ldots, \mathsf{poly}(\lambda)\}$, $\mathcal{A}$ sends a value $\tilde{s_1}_i$ such that $f(\tilde{s_1}_i \oplus \tilde{s_0}_i) = \tilde{Y}_i$ where $\tilde{s_0}_i$ is the value committed using nmc. Then $p_i < \nu(\lambda)$ for some negligible function ν.

Lemma 6.4 *For any message* $m \in \{0,1\}^{\mathsf{poly}(\lambda)}$ *it holds that* $\mathsf{mim}^{\mathcal{A}}_{\mathcal{H}_2^m}(z) \approx \mathsf{mim}^{\mathcal{A}}_{\mathcal{H}_3^m}(z)$.

Proof Suppose by contradiction that there exist a adversary $\mathcal{A}$ and a distinguisher $\mathcal{D}$ that can tell apart such two distributions. We can use this adversary and the associated distinguisher to construct an adversary $\mathcal{A}_{\mathsf{LS}}$ for the T_{LS}-witness-indistinguishable property of the LS protocol. Let C_{LS} be the WI challenger, the adversary works as follows. $\mathcal{A}_{\mathsf{LS}}(z)$

1. Pick $s_0 \leftarrow \{0,1\}^\lambda$.
2. Compute $\mathsf{a}_{\mathsf{nmc}} = \mathsf{Sen}^1_{\mathsf{nm}}(\mathtt{id}, s_0; \rho)$.
3. Upon receiving a_{LS} from C_{LS}, send $(\mathsf{a}_{\mathsf{nmc}}, \mathsf{a}_{\mathsf{LS}})$ to $\mathcal{A}$.
4. Upon receiving $(\mathsf{c}_{\mathsf{nmc}}, \mathsf{c}_{\mathsf{LS}}, Y)$ from $\mathcal{A}$ run as follows:
   4.1 Run in time T_f to compute y such that $Y = f(y)$.
   4.2 Set $s_1 = s_0 \oplus y$.

4.3 Compute $(\mathsf{z}_{\mathsf{nmc}}, \mathtt{dec}_{\mathsf{nmc}}) = \mathrm{Sen}^2_{\mathsf{nm}}(\mathtt{id}, \mathsf{c}_{\mathsf{nmc}}, s_0; \rho)$.
4.4 Compute $(\mathtt{com}, \mathtt{dec}) = \mathsf{NISen}(1^{\lambda_{\mathsf{NI}}}, m; \sigma)$.
4.5 Set $x = \big((\mathsf{a}_{\mathsf{nmc}}, \mathsf{c}_{\mathsf{nmc}}, \mathsf{z}_{\mathsf{nmc}}), Y, s_1, \mathtt{com}, \mathtt{id}\big)$, $w_0 = (\bot, \bot, s_0, \rho)$, $w_1 = (m, \sigma, \bot, \bot)$ and send $(x, \mathsf{c}_{\mathsf{LS}}, w_0, w_1)$ to C_{LS}.

5. Upon receiving z_{LS} from C_{LS}, send $(\mathsf{z}_{\mathsf{nmc}}, \mathtt{com}, \mathsf{z}_{\mathsf{LS}})$ to $\mathcal{A}$.
6. Simulate $\mathsf{NMRec}_1, \ldots, \mathsf{NMRec}_{\mathsf{poly}(\lambda)}$ with $\mathcal{A}$, when $\mathcal{A}$ plays as a sender.
7. Let M be an empty tuple. For all $i \in \{1, \ldots, \mathsf{poly}(\lambda)\}$, consider $\tilde{\mathtt{com}}_i$, the non-interactive commitment received by NMRec_i, and run in time $\tilde{T}_{\mathsf{NI}}$ to compute $\tilde{m}_i$ such that $\exists\, \tilde{\mathtt{dec}} : 1 = \mathsf{NIRec}(\tilde{\mathtt{com}}_i, \tilde{\mathtt{dec}}, \tilde{m}_i)$ and add $\tilde{m}_i$ to M.
8. Give M and the view of $\mathcal{A}$ to the distinguisher $\mathcal{D}$.
9. Output what $\mathcal{D}$ outputs.

□

The proof ends with the observation that if C_{LS} has has used as witness the randomness of the non-malleable commitment of the value s_0 such that $f(s_0 \oplus s_1) = Y$ then we are in the hybrid experiment $\mathcal{H}_3^m(z)$. If instead C_{LS} has used as a witness the randomness used to compute the non-interactive commitment NI then we are in the hybrid experiment $\mathcal{H}_2^m(z)$.

Lemma 6.5 *Let p_i be the probability that in the i-th right session of $\mathcal{H}_3^m$, for $i \in \{1, \ldots, \mathsf{poly}(\lambda)\}$, $\mathcal{A}$ sends a value $\tilde{s}_{1i}$ such that $f(\tilde{s}_{1i} \oplus \tilde{s}_{0i}) = \tilde{Y}_i$ where $\tilde{s}_{0i}$ is the value committed using* nmc. *Then $p_i < \nu(\lambda)$ for some negligible function ν.*

Proof Suppose by contradiction that for a right session i the claim does not hold, then we can construct an adversary $\mathcal{A}'_{\mathsf{LS}}$ for the T_{LS} witness-indistinguishable property of the LS protocol. Let C_{LS} be the WI challenger, the adversary works as follows.

$\mathcal{A}'_{\mathsf{LS}}(z)$

1. Pick $s_0 \leftarrow \{0, 1\}^{\lambda}$.
2. Compute $\mathsf{a}_{\mathsf{nmc}} = \mathrm{Sen}^1_{\mathsf{nm}}(\mathtt{id}, s_0; \rho)$.
3. Upon receiving a_{LS} from C_{LS}, send $(\mathsf{a}_{\mathsf{nmc}}, \mathsf{a}_{\mathsf{LS}})$ to $\mathcal{A}$.
4. Upon receiving $(\mathsf{c}_{\mathsf{nmc}}, \mathsf{c}_{\mathsf{LS}}, Y)$ from $\mathcal{A}$, run as follow:

4.1 Run in time T_f to compute y such that $Y = f(y)$.
4.2 Set $s_1 = s_0 \oplus y$.
4.3 Compute $(\mathsf{z}_{\mathsf{nmc}}, \mathtt{dec}_{\mathsf{nmc}}) = \mathrm{Sen}^2_{\mathsf{nm}}(\mathtt{id}, \mathsf{c}_{\mathsf{nmc}}, s_0; \rho)$.
4.4 Compute $(\mathtt{com}, \mathtt{dec}) = \mathsf{NISen}(1^{\lambda_{\mathsf{NI}}}, m; \sigma)$.
4.5 Set $x = \big((\mathsf{a}_{\mathsf{nmc}}, \mathsf{c}_{\mathsf{nmc}}, \mathsf{z}_{\mathsf{nmc}}), Y, s_1, \mathtt{com}, \mathtt{id}\big)$, $w_0 = (\bot, \bot, s_0, \rho)$, $w_1 = (m, \sigma, \bot, \bot)$ and send $(x, \mathsf{c}_{\mathsf{LS}}, w_0, w_1)$ to C_{LS}.

5. Upon receiving z_{LS} from C_{LS}, send $(\mathsf{z}_{\mathsf{nmc}}, \mathtt{com}, \mathsf{z}_{\mathsf{LS}})$ to $\mathcal{A}$.
6. Simulate $\mathsf{NMRec}_1, \ldots, \mathsf{NMRec}_{\mathsf{poly}(\lambda)}$ with $\mathcal{A}$, when $\mathcal{A}$ plays as a sender.
7. Run in time $\tilde{T}_{\mathsf{nmc}}$ to extract the value $\tilde{s}_{0i}$ from the non-malleable commitment sent by $\mathcal{A}$ in the i-th session. Output 1 if $f(\tilde{s}_{0i} \oplus \tilde{s}_{1i}) = \tilde{Y}_i$ and output 0 otherwise.

The proof ends with the observation that if C_{LS} has used $w_0 = (\perp, \perp, s_0, \rho)$ as a witness then $\mathcal{A}$ acts as in $\mathcal{H}_3^m(z)$, sending with non-negligible probability two shares such that the xor of them gives a puzzle solution. If C_{LS} has used $w_1 = (m, \sigma, \perp, \perp)$ then the xor of the two shares is with overwhelming probability different from a puzzle solution as in $\mathcal{H}_2^m(z)$. □

The next hybrid experiment that we consider is $\mathcal{H}_3^0(z)$. The only differences between this hybrid experiment and $\mathcal{H}_3^m(z)$ is that the sender, using NI, commits to a message 0^λ instead of m. Formally the hybrid experiment is the following.

$\mathcal{H}_3^0(z)$.

Left session:

1. First round.
   1.1 Pick $s_0 \leftarrow \{0,1\}^\lambda$.
   1.2 Compute $\mathsf{a}_{\mathsf{nmc}} = \mathsf{Sen}^1_{\mathsf{nm}}(\mathtt{id}, s_0; \rho)$.
   1.3 Compute $\mathsf{a}_{\mathsf{LS}} = \mathsf{P}^1(\ell; \alpha)$.
   1.4 Send $(\mathsf{a}_{\mathsf{nmc}}, \mathsf{a}_{\mathsf{LS}})$ to $\mathcal{A}$.
2. Third round. Upon receiving $(\mathsf{c}_{\mathsf{nmc}}, \mathsf{c}_{\mathsf{LS}}, Y)$ from $\mathcal{A}$, run as follows:
   2.1 Run in time T_f to compute y such that $Y = f(y)$.
   2.2 Set $s_1 = s_0 \oplus y$.
   2.3 Compute $(\mathsf{z}_{\mathsf{nmc}}, \mathtt{dec}_{\mathsf{nmc}}) = \mathsf{Sen}^2_{\mathsf{nm}}(\mathtt{id}, \mathsf{c}_{\mathsf{nmc}}, s_0; \rho)$.
   2.4 Compute $(\mathtt{com}, \mathtt{dec}) = \underline{\mathsf{NISen}(0^\lambda; \sigma)}$.
   2.5 Set $x = \big((\mathsf{a}_{\mathsf{nmc}}, \mathsf{c}_{\mathsf{nmc}}, \mathsf{z}_{\mathsf{nmc}}), Y, s_1, \mathtt{com}, \mathtt{id}\big)$ and $w = (\perp, \perp, s_0, \rho)$ with $(|x| = \ell)$. Run $\mathsf{z}_{\mathsf{LS}} = \mathsf{P}^2(x, w, \mathsf{c}_{\mathsf{LS}}; \alpha)$.
   2.6 Send $(\mathsf{z}_{\mathsf{nmc}}, \mathtt{com}, \mathsf{z}_{\mathsf{LS}}, s_1)$ to $\mathcal{A}$.

Right sessions: Act as a proxy between $\mathcal{A}$ and $\mathsf{NMRec}_1, \ldots, \mathsf{NMRec}_{\mathsf{poly}(\lambda)}$.

We now prove the following properties.

1. Let p_i be the probability that in the i-th right session of $\mathcal{H}_3^0$, for any $i \in \{1, \ldots, \mathsf{poly}(\lambda)\}$, $\mathcal{A}$ sends a value $\tilde{s_1}_i$ such that $f(\tilde{s_1}_i \oplus \tilde{s_0}_i) = \tilde{Y}_i$ where $\tilde{s_0}_i$ is the value committed using nmc. Then $p_i < \nu(\lambda)$ for some negligible function ν.
2. For any message $m \in \{0,1\}^{\mathsf{poly}(\lambda)}$ it holds that $\mathsf{mim}^{\mathcal{A}}_{\mathcal{H}_3^m}(z) \approx \mathsf{mim}^{\mathcal{A}}_{\mathcal{H}_3^0}(z)$.

Lemma 6.6 *Let p_i be the probability that in the i-th right session of $\mathcal{H}_3^0$, for $i \in \{1, \ldots, \mathsf{poly}(\lambda)\}$, $\mathcal{A}$ sends a value $\tilde{s_1}_i$ such that $f(\tilde{s_1}_i \oplus \tilde{s_0}_i) = \tilde{Y}_i$ where $\tilde{s_0}_i$ is the value committed using* nmc. *Then $p_i < \nu(\lambda)$ for some negligible function ν.*

Proof Suppose by contradiction that there exists a right session $i \in \{1, \ldots, \mathsf{poly}(\lambda)\}$ in which $\mathcal{A}$ commit to a string $\tilde{s_0}$ such that $f(\tilde{s_0}_i \oplus \tilde{s_1}_i) = \tilde{Y}_i$ using Π_{nmc}. Then we can construct an adversary $\mathcal{A}_{\mathsf{NI}}$ that breaks the hiding property of the non interactive commitment scheme NI. Let C_{NI} be the challenger that on input $m_0 = 0^\lambda$ and $m_1 = m$, picks a random bit b, computes $(\mathtt{com}, \mathtt{dec}) = \mathsf{NISen}(1^{\lambda_{\mathsf{NI}}}, m_b; \sigma)$ and sends $\mathtt{com}$ to $\mathcal{A}_{\mathsf{NI}}$.

Before describing $\mathcal{A}_{\mathsf{NI}}$ we need to consider, as in the proof of Lemma 6.1, a machine $\mathcal{M}$ that internally executes $\mathcal{A}$, and interacts with a receiver $\mathsf{Rec}_{\mathsf{ext}}$ of the protocol Π_{nmc} acting as the sender.

Formally $\mathcal{M}$ acts as follows.

$\mathcal{M}(\mathtt{com}, \varphi, z)$

Run $\mathcal{A}$ using randomness φ.

1. Pick $s_0 \leftarrow \{0, 1\}^\lambda$.
2. Compute $\mathsf{a}_{\mathsf{nmc}} = \mathsf{Sen}^1_{\mathsf{nm}}(\mathtt{id}, s_0; \rho)$.
3. Compute $\mathsf{a}_{\mathsf{LS}} = \mathsf{P}^1(1^{\lambda_{\mathsf{LS}}}, \ell; \alpha)$.
4. Send $(\mathsf{a}_{\mathsf{nmc}}, \mathsf{a}_{\mathsf{LS}})$ to $\mathcal{A}$.
5. Upon receiving $(\mathsf{c}_{\mathsf{nmc}}, \mathsf{c}_{\mathsf{LS}}, Y)$ from $\mathcal{A}$, run as follows:

   5.1 Run in time T_f to compute y such that $Y = f(y)$.
   5.2 Set $s_1 = s_0 \oplus y$.
   5.3 Compute $(\mathsf{z}_{\mathsf{nmc}}, \mathtt{dec}_{\mathsf{nmc}}) = \mathsf{Sen}^2_{\mathsf{nm}}(\mathtt{id}, \mathsf{c}_{\mathsf{nmc}}, s_0; \rho)$.
   5.4 Set $x = \big((\mathsf{a}_{\mathsf{nmc}}, \mathsf{c}_{\mathsf{nmc}}, \mathsf{z}_{\mathsf{nmc}}), Y, s_1, \mathtt{com}, \mathtt{id}\big)$ and $w = (\bot, \bot, s_0, \rho)$ with $(|x| = \ell)$. Run $\mathsf{z}_{\mathsf{LS}} = \mathsf{P}^2(x, w, \mathsf{c}_{\mathsf{LS}}; \alpha)$.
   5.5 Send $(\mathsf{z}_{\mathsf{nmc}}, \mathtt{com}, \mathsf{z}_{\mathsf{LS}}, s_1)$ to $\mathcal{A}$.

6. Let $i \in \{1, \ldots, \mathsf{poly}(\lambda)\}$ be the right session that contradicts the claim. For all $j \neq i \in \{1, \ldots \mathsf{poly}(\lambda)\}$ run NMRec_j as in $\mathcal{H}_4(m, z)$. Run NMRec_i as follows.

   6.1 Upon receiving the 1rd round of the i-th right session $(\tilde{\mathsf{a}}_{\mathsf{nmc}_i}, \tilde{\mathsf{a}}_{\mathsf{LS}_i})$ from $\mathcal{A}$, send $\tilde{\mathsf{a}}_{\mathsf{nmc}_i}$ to the external receiver $\mathsf{Rec}_{\mathsf{ext}}$.
   6.2 Upon receiving $\mathsf{c}_{\tilde{\mathsf{nm}}_i}$ from $\mathsf{Rec}_{\mathsf{ext}}$, run as follows:
      i. Run $\mathcal{V}$ to obtain $\mathsf{c}_{\tilde{LS}_i}$.
      ii. Pick a random $\tilde{Y}_i$.
      iii. Send $(\mathsf{c}_{\tilde{\mathsf{nmc}}_i}, \mathsf{c}_{\tilde{\mathsf{LS}}_i}, \tilde{Y}_i)$ to $\mathcal{A}$.
   6.3 Upon receiving the 3rd round of the i-th right session $(\tilde{\mathsf{z}}_{\mathsf{nmc}_i}, \tilde{\mathtt{com}}_i, \tilde{\mathsf{z}}_{\mathsf{LS}_i}, \tilde{s_1}_i)$, set $\tilde{x} = \big((\tilde{\mathsf{a}}_{\mathsf{nmc}_i}, \tilde{\mathsf{c}}_{\mathsf{nmc}_i}, \tilde{\mathsf{z}}_{\mathsf{nmc}_i}), \tilde{Y}, \tilde{s_1}_i, \tilde{\mathtt{com}}_i, \tilde{\mathtt{id}}\big)$ and abort iff $(\tilde{\mathsf{a}}_{\mathsf{LS}_i}, \tilde{\mathsf{c}}_{\mathsf{LS}_i}, \tilde{\mathsf{z}}_{\mathsf{LS}_i})$ is not accepted by $\mathcal{V}$ with respect to $\tilde{x}$.
   6.4 Send $\tilde{\mathsf{z}}_{\mathsf{nmc}_i}$ to $\mathsf{Rec}_{\mathsf{ext}}$.

Now we can conclude the proof of this lemma by describing how $\mathcal{A}_{\mathsf{NI}}$ works. $\mathcal{A}_{\mathsf{NI}}$ runs the extractor of the protocol Π_{nmc} using $\mathcal{M}$ as sender (recall that an extractor of Π_{nmc} plays only having access to a sender of Π_{nmc}). Since the extractor with non-negligible probability outputs the committed message we have that $\mathcal{A}_{\mathsf{NI}}$ retrieves $\tilde{s_0}_i$. Moreover $\mathcal{A}_{\mathsf{NI}}$ gets $\tilde{s_1}_i$ by reconstructing the view of $\mathcal{A}$ using the randomness φ.

Since by contradiction $\mathcal{A}$ contradicts the claim of this lemma, we have that $\mathcal{A}_{\mathsf{NI}}$ can break the hiding of NI because $f(\tilde{s_0}_i \oplus \tilde{s_1}_i) = \tilde{Y}$ with non-negligible probability in $\mathcal{H}_3^0(z)$ where $m_0 = 0^\lambda$ is committed in $\mathtt{com}$, while the same happens with negligible probability only in $\mathcal{H}_3^m(z)$ where $m_1 = m$. Therefore if this happens, $\mathcal{A}_{\mathsf{NI}}$ outputs 0, otherwise $\mathcal{A}_{\mathsf{NI}}$ outputs a random bit. □

Lemma 6.7 *For any message $m \in \{0,1\}^{\mathsf{poly}(\lambda)}$ it holds that $\mathsf{mim}^{\mathcal{A}}_{\mathcal{H}_3^m}(z) \approx \mathsf{mim}^{\mathcal{A}}_{\mathcal{H}_3^0}(z)$.*

Proof Suppose by contradiction that there exists a distinguisher $\mathcal{D}$ and an adversary $\mathcal{A}$ such that $\mathsf{mim}^{\mathcal{A}}_{\mathcal{H}_3^m}(z)$ is distinguishable from $\mathsf{mim}^{\mathcal{A}}_{\mathcal{H}_3^0}(z)$ then we can construct an adversary $\mathcal{A}_{\mathsf{NI}}$ that breaks the hiding property of the non-interactive commitment scheme NI. Let C_{NI} be the challenger that on input $m_0 = 0^\lambda$ and $m_1 = m$, picks a random bit b, computes $(\mathtt{com}, \mathtt{dec}) = \mathsf{NISen}(1^{\lambda_{\mathsf{NI}}}, m_b; \sigma)$ and sends $\mathtt{com}$ to $\mathcal{A}_{\mathsf{NI}}$. Before describing $\mathcal{A}_{\mathsf{NI}}$, we consider the following experiment $\mathcal{E}_{m_b}(\varphi, \mathtt{com}, z)$.

$\boldsymbol{\mathcal{E}_{m_b}(\varphi, \mathtt{com}, z)}$.
The randomness required from all next steps is take from φ.

Run $\mathcal{A}(z)$.
Left session:

1. First round.
   1.1 Pick $s_0 \leftarrow \{0,1\}^\lambda$.
   1.2 Compute $\mathsf{a}_{\mathsf{nmc}} = \mathsf{Sen}^1_{\mathsf{nm}}(\mathtt{id}, s_0; \rho)$.
   1.3 Compute $\mathsf{a}_{\mathsf{LS}} = \mathsf{P}^1(\ell; \alpha)$.
   1.4 Send $(\mathsf{a}_{\mathsf{nmc}}, \mathsf{a}_{\mathsf{LS}})$ to $\mathcal{A}$.
2. Third round. Upon receiving $(\mathsf{c}_{\mathsf{nmc}}, \mathsf{c}_{\mathsf{LS}}, Y)$ from $\mathcal{A}$, run as follows:
   2.1 Run in time T_f to compute y such that $Y = f(y)$.
   2.2 Set $s_1 = s_0 \oplus y$.
   2.3 Compute $(\mathsf{z}_{\mathsf{nmc}}, \mathtt{dec}_{\mathsf{nmc}}) = \mathsf{Sen}^2_{\mathsf{nm}}(\mathtt{id}, \mathsf{c}_{\mathsf{nmc}}, s_0; \rho)$.
   2.4 Set $x = \big((\mathsf{a}_{\mathsf{nmc}}, \mathsf{c}_{\mathsf{nmc}}, \mathsf{z}_{\mathsf{nmc}}), Y, s_1, \mathtt{com}, \mathtt{id}\big)$ and $w = (\bot, \bot, s_0, \rho)$ with $(|x| = \ell)$. Run $\mathsf{z}_{\mathsf{LS}} = \mathsf{P}^2(x, w, \mathsf{c}_{\mathsf{LS}}; \alpha)$.
   2.5 Send $(\mathsf{z}_{\mathsf{nmc}}, \mathtt{com}, \mathsf{z}_{\mathsf{LS}}, s_1)$ to $\mathcal{A}$.

Right sessions: Act as a proxy between $\mathcal{A}$ and $\mathsf{NMRec}_1, \ldots, \mathsf{NMRec}_{\mathsf{poly}(\lambda)}$.

Now we are ready to describe the adversary $\mathcal{A}_{\mathsf{NI}}$ for the hiding of NI. $\mathcal{A}_{\mathsf{NI}}$ executes the following steps.

1. Let M be an empty tuple. $\mathcal{A}_{\mathsf{NI}}$ runs $\boldsymbol{\mathcal{E}_{m_b}(\varphi, \mathtt{com}, z)}$.
2. For all $i \in \{1, \ldots, \mathsf{poly}(\lambda)\}$, $\mathcal{A}_{\mathsf{NI}}$ runs the extractor of LS on the i-th right session of the execution of $\boldsymbol{\mathcal{E}_{m_b}(\varphi, \mathtt{com}, z)}$ obtaining $\tilde{m}_i$ and adds it to M.

3. Using the randomness φ, $\mathcal{A}_{\mathsf{NI}}$ reconstructs the view of $\mathcal{A}$ in the execution of $\mathcal{E}_{m_b}(\boldsymbol{\varphi}, \mathbf{com}, z)$. Use such view and M as input to $\mathcal{D}$.
4. Output what $\mathcal{D}$ outputs.

The proof ends with the observation that if C_{NI} has committed to 0^λ then the view of $\mathcal{A}$ and the distribution of the committed messages coincide with $\mathcal{H}_3^0$, otherwise they coincide with $\mathcal{H}_3^m$. □

The entire security proof now is almost over because we have proved that for all $m \in \{0,1\}^{\mathsf{poly}(\lambda)}$ the following relation holds:

$$\begin{aligned}\{\mathsf{mim}^{\mathcal{A},m}_{\Pi_{1-n}}(z)\}_{z\in\{0,1\}^\star} &= \{\mathsf{mim}^{\mathcal{A}}_{\mathcal{H}_1^m}(z)\}_{z\in\{0,1\}^\star}\\ \approx \{\mathsf{mim}^{\mathcal{A}}_{\mathcal{H}_2^m}(z)\}_{z\in\{0,1\}^\star} &\approx \{\mathsf{mim}^{\mathcal{A}}_{\mathcal{H}_3^m}(z)\}_{z\in\{0,1\}^\star}\\ \approx \{\mathsf{mim}^{\mathcal{A}}_{\mathcal{H}_3^0}(z)\}_{z\in\{0,1\}^\star} &\approx \{\mathsf{mim}^{\mathcal{A}}_{\mathcal{H}_2^0}(z)\}_{z\in\{0,1\}^\star}\\ \approx \{\mathsf{mim}^{\mathcal{A}}_{\mathcal{H}_1^0}(z)\}_{z\in\{0,1\}^\star} &= \{\mathsf{sim}^{S}_{\Pi_{1-n}}(1^\lambda, z)\}_{z\in\{0,1\}^\star}.\end{aligned}$$

We show in Fig. 6.3 the simulator Sim.

We observe that in this proof we had to consider a delayed-input version of our commitment scheme. Indeed, the sender can choose the message m to be committed by sending the non-interactive commitment $\mathtt{com}$ of the message m in the third round. It is easy to see that the same security proof still works when the non-interactive commitment is sent in the 1st round, but then clearly the delayed-input property is lost. □

Common input: Security parameters: λ, $(\lambda_{\mathsf{NI}}, \lambda_{\mathsf{nmc}}, \lambda_{\mathsf{LS}}, \ell) = \mathsf{Params}(\lambda)$. Identity: $\mathtt{id} \in \{0,1\}^\lambda$.

Internal simulation of the left session:

1. Pick $s_0 \leftarrow \{0,1\}^\lambda$.
2. Pick a randomness ρ, and compute $(\mathsf{dec_{nmc}}, \mathsf{a_{nmc}}) = \mathsf{Sen}^1_{\mathsf{nm}}(\mathtt{id}, s_0; \rho)$.
3. Pick a randomness α and compute $\mathsf{a_{LS}} = \mathsf{P}^1(\ell; \alpha)$.
4. Send $(\mathsf{a_{nmc}}, \mathsf{a_{LS}})$ to $\mathcal{A}$.
5. Upon receiving $(\mathsf{c_{nmc}}, \mathsf{c_{LS}}, Y)$ from $\mathcal{A}$.
    1. Pick a randomness σ and compute $(\mathtt{com}, \mathsf{dec}) = \mathsf{NISen}(1^{\lambda_{\mathsf{NI}}}, 0^\lambda; \sigma)$.
    2. Pick $s_1 \leftarrow \{0,1\}^\lambda$.
    3. Compute $\mathsf{z_{nmc}} = \mathsf{Sen}^2_{\mathsf{nm}}(\mathtt{id}, \mathsf{c_{nmc}}, s_0; \rho)$.
    4. Set $x = \big((\mathsf{a_{nmc}}, \mathsf{c_{nmc}}, \mathsf{z_{nmc}}), Y, s_1, \mathtt{com}, \mathtt{id}\big)$ and $w = (0^\lambda, \sigma, \perp, \perp)$ with $(|x| = \ell)$. Run $\mathsf{z_{LS}} = \mathsf{P}^2(x, w, \mathsf{c_{LS}}; \alpha)$ where x is the theorem to be proven and w is the witness.
    5. Send $(\mathsf{z_{nmc}}, \mathtt{com}, \mathsf{z_{LS}}, s_1)$ to $\mathcal{A}$.

Stand-alone commitment:

1. Sim acts as a proxy between $\mathcal{A}$ and NMRec_i for $i = 1, \ldots, \mathsf{poly}(\lambda)$.

Fig. 6.3 The simulator Sim

6.3 More 3-Round Protocols Against Concurrent MiM Attacks

In this section we show how to obtain some forms of 3-round arguments of knowledge and of 3-round identification schemes that are secure against concurrent MiM attacks.

6.3.1 NMWI Argument Systems

The definition of non-malleable witness indistinguishability (NMWI) given in [159] requires that the witness *encoded in the proof* given by the MiM $\mathcal{A}$ be independent of the witness used by the honest prover in his proof. The concept of witness encoded in a proof becomes clear when considering *commit-and-prove* argument systems. In such arguments, the transcript includes a commitment that encodes in an unambiguous way the witness used by the prover. In a NMWI commit-and-prove argument system, the witness encoded in the proof produced by the $\mathcal{A}$ must be independent of the witness used (and thus encoded by the honest prover) in the proof in which $\mathcal{A}$ acts as a verifier. Similarly to the case of non-malleable commitments, one can give a definition with or without sessions ids. Here we use the one without sessions ids since it is more useful in the applications.

Let $\mathcal{A}$ be a MiM interacting in the left proof with $\mathcal{P}$ that is running on input x and witness w. In the right proof $\mathcal{A}$ interacts with $\mathcal{V}$ on common input $\tilde{x}$ chosen by $\mathcal{A}$. We denote by z the auxiliary information available to $\mathcal{A}$. NMWI is defined in terms of the random variable $\mathsf{wmim}^{\mathcal{A}}(x, w, z)$ that is the view of $\mathcal{A}$ that we denote by $\mathsf{View}^{\mathcal{P}}_{\mathcal{A}}(x, w, z)$ (i.e., the view of $\mathcal{A}$ when running with z as auxiliary input and playing with $\mathcal{P}$ that runs on input (x, w)) and the witness encoded in the right proof given by $\mathcal{A}$. If the right proof is not accepting or the transcript is identical to the one of the left proof then the witness encoded is $\perp$; otherwise the string w committed by $\mathcal{A}$ in the right proof is returned. In other words, $\mathsf{wmim}^{\mathcal{A}}(x, w, z)$ consists of the view of $\mathcal{A}$ and the witness encoded in the right proof unless the proof is not accepting.

Definition 6.1 (*NMWI argument system* [159]) A commit-and-prove argument system $\Pi = (\mathcal{P}, \mathcal{V})$ for an $\mathcal{NP}$-language L and corresponding relation Rel_L is a *non-malleable witness indistinguishable* argument if, for all PPT man-in-the-middle adversaries $\mathcal{A}$, for all $x \in L$ and all w, w' such that $\mathsf{Rel}_\mathsf{L}(x, w)$, $\mathsf{Rel}_\mathsf{L}(x, w')$ for all auxiliary information z it holds that $\{\mathsf{wmim}^{\mathcal{A}}(x, w, z)\} \approx \{\mathsf{wmim}^{\mathcal{A}}(x, w', z)\}$.

The above notion extends in a straight-forward way to the case of a concurrent MiM adversary trivially. Formally, the concurrent MiM $\mathcal{A}$ opens $\mathsf{poly}(\lambda)$ left and right proofs each with a common input of length $\mathsf{poly}(\lambda)$. $\mathcal{A}$ interacts in the i-th left proof with an instance of the honest prover $\mathcal{P}$ on common input "$x_i \in L$" and private input w_i such that $\mathsf{Rel}_\mathsf{L}(x_i, w_i)$. In the j-th right proof $\mathcal{A}$ is interacting with the honest verifier V on common input $\tilde{x}_j$ of its choice.

Let X, W be respectively the sequence of instances and witnesses in input to $\mathcal{P}$ in the left proofs. Now the distribution $\mathsf{wmim}^{\mathcal{A}}(X, W, z)$ consists of the view $\mathsf{View}^{\mathcal{P}}_{\mathcal{A}}(X, W, z)$ of $\mathcal{A}$ along with a sequence $(\tilde{w}_1, \ldots, \tilde{w}_{\mathsf{poly}(\lambda)})$ and it holds that: if the j-th right proof is not accepting or the transcript is identical to the one of a left proof then $\tilde{w}_j = \perp$; otherwise, $\tilde{w}_j$ is the witness encoded in the j-th right proof.

Definition 6.2 (*cNMWI argument* [159]) A commit-and-prove argument system $\Pi = (\mathcal{P}, \mathcal{V})$ for an $\mathcal{NP}$-language L and corresponding relation $\mathsf{Rel}_{\mathsf{L}}$ is *concurrent non-malleable witness indistinguishable* if, for all PPT concurrent man-in-the-middle adversaries $\mathcal{A}$, for all sequences X of $\mathsf{poly}(\lambda)$ elements of L of length $\mathsf{poly}(\lambda)$, for all sequences W and W' of witnesses for X, and for all auxiliary information z it holds that $\{\mathsf{wmim}^{\mathcal{A}}(X, W, z)\} \approx \{\mathsf{wmim}^{\mathcal{A}}(X, W', z)\}$.

6.3.2 Non-malleable WI Arguments of Knowledge

Our concurrent NM commitment scheme when instantiated without sessions ids, can be used to obtain almost directly a *commit-and-prove* AoK. Recall that in our scheme there is a non-interactive commitment $\mathtt{com}$ of m and then rest of the protocol is an AoK. This AoK is used by the sender to claim that either he knows the message committed in $\mathtt{com}$, or he committed through Π_{nmc} to a share s_0 that allows to compute the solution of the puzzle.

In order to be fully compliant with the notion of commit-and-prove AoK, we just need to make a trivial change to the statement of the LS subprotocol. Given an instance $x \in L$ and a witness w the prover of our commit-and-prove AoK uses the non-interactive commitment to commit to w, and uses the rest to prove that either he knows the committed message w that moreover is a witness for $x \in L$ or again, he committed through Π_{nmc} to a share s_0 that allows to compute the solution of the puzzle.

More formally, we define a commit-and-prove AoK $\Pi_{\mathsf{CaP}} = (\mathcal{P}_{\mathsf{CaP}}, \mathcal{V}_{\mathsf{CaP}})$ that corresponds to our concurrent NM commitment scheme with some minimal changes. First, $\mathcal{P}_{\mathsf{CaP}}$ and $\mathcal{V}_{\mathsf{CaP}}$ have as a common input an instance $x \in L$, where L is an NP-language. Second, $\mathcal{P}_{\mathsf{CaP}}$ has as private input w such that $(x, w) \in \mathsf{Rel}_{\mathsf{L}}$. Third, $\mathcal{P}_{\mathsf{CaP}}$ runs the sender NMSen having as input w, while $\mathcal{V}_{\mathsf{CaP}}$ runs the receiver NMRec with the exception of running the LS subprotocol LS for:

$$\begin{aligned} L_{\mathsf{CaP}} = \Big\{ &\big(x, (a, c, z), Y, s_1, \mathtt{com}, \mathtt{id}\big) : \\ &(\exists\, (w, \sigma) \text{ s.t. } \mathtt{com} = \mathsf{NISen}(w; \sigma) \text{ AND } (x, w) \in \mathsf{Rel}_{\mathsf{L}}) \\ &\text{OR } \big(\exists (\rho, s_0) \text{ s.t. } a = \mathsf{Sen}^1_{\mathsf{nm}}(\mathtt{id}, s_0; \rho) \\ &\text{AND} z = \mathsf{Sen}^2_{\mathsf{nm}}(\mathtt{id}, c, s_0; \rho) \text{ AND } Y = f(s_0 \oplus s_1)\big)\Big\} \end{aligned}$$

that is WI for the relation

$$\begin{aligned}\mathsf{Rel}_{\mathsf{L_{CaP}}} = \big\{\big((x, (a, c, z), Y, s_1, \mathtt{com}, \mathtt{id}), (w, \sigma, s_0, \rho)\big) : \\ (\mathtt{com} = \mathsf{NISen}(w; \sigma)\ \mathrm{AND}(x, w) \in \mathsf{Rel_L}) \\ \mathrm{OR}\ \big(a = \mathrm{Sen}^1_{\mathsf{nm}}(\mathtt{id}, s_0; \rho) \\ \mathrm{AND} z = \mathrm{Sen}^2_{\mathsf{nm}}(\mathtt{id}, c, y; \rho)\ \mathrm{AND}\ Y = f(s_0 \oplus s_1)\big)\big\}.\end{aligned}$$

We can now claim the following theorem.

Theorem 6.3 *Suppose there exist OWPs secure against subexponential-time adversaries, then Π_{CaP} is a 3-round concurrent NMWI argument of knowledge.*

Proof The proof of this theorem is pretty straightforward given the previous proof for the concurrent non-malleability of our commitment scheme, therefore here we just point out the main intuition.

First of all, Π_{CaP} is clearly a commit-and-prove AoK. Indeed, there exists a commitment of the witness and there is an AoK proving that the committed message is a witness. In order to see this, notice that for any PPT malicious prover succeeding with non-negligible probability in proving a statement $x \in L$, the extractor of LS (of course this needs to be run against an augmented machine) would return (in expected polynomial time and with overwhelming probability) the committed witness since otherwise it would return a share s_0 that combined with s_1 allows to invert the OWP in polynomial time.

We can now focus on the concurrent NMWI property, and we can assume (by contradiction) that the adversary succeeds in encoding in the right sessions witnesses that are related to the witnesses encoded in the left sessions. Notice that the proof is almost identical to the one of Theorem 6.2. We can indeed prove the case of one prover and multiple verifiers (i.e., one-many), and then we can apply the fact that any one-many NMWIAoK is also a concurrent NMWIAoK. Indeed this was used in [159] and follows similar arguments given in [138, 169]. For the one-many case we can therefore follow the proof of Theorem 6.2 with the following trivial change. Instead of running hybrid experiments starting with a message m and ending with a message 0, in the proof of one-many concurrent NMWI we start with a witness w_0 and end with a witness w_1. Everything else remains untouched and all the reductions work directly. □

We finally notice that Π_{CaP} can be instantiated to be public-coin and delayed-input, precisely as our concurrent non-malleable commitment scheme. While what we discussed above applies to arguments only, techniques to obtain proofs can be found in [35].

Instances with just one witness and non-transferability.

Recall that the definition of NMWI considers two experiments that differ only on the witness used by the prover. Therefore it is unclear which security is given by a NMWIAoK when the instance has only one witness. In order to understand the security guaranteed by Π_{CaP} in such a case, consider the proof of concurrent NMWI, and thus, in turn, consider the proof of concurrent non-malleability of our commitment scheme. Notice that while the sequence of hybrids goes from an experiment where the committed message is m to an experiment where the committed message is 0, there is an experiment $\mathcal{H}_3(\cdot, z)$ in which the committed message is irrelevant. Indeed, the entire execution is based on inverting the OWP, in encrypting it through the shares s_0 and s_1 and in using this witness in the execution of LS. This experiment can be seen as the execution of a quasi-polynomial time simulator that breaks the puzzle[11] following the approach of [165][12]. Therefore following the same observations of [165, 166] on the security offered by quasi-polynomial time simulation, our concurrent NMWIAoK even for instances with just one witness would not help the adversary in proving a statement whose witness is much harder to compute than breaking the puzzle.

The above discussion explains also the non-transferability flavor of Π_{CaP}. Indeed, at first sight, a MiM attack of an adversary $\mathcal{A}$ to an AoK should be an attempt of $\mathcal{A}$ to transfer the proof that it gets from the prover to a verifier. As such, an AoK that is secure against concurrent MiM attacks should provide some non-transferability guarantee. Since the success of $\mathcal{A}$ during a MiM attack can be replicated without a MiM attack by a quasi-polynomial time simulator, we have that Π_{CaP} guarantees non-transferability whenever computing the witnesses for the considered instances is assumed to be harder than breaking the puzzle.

Using NMWI for NMZK in the Bare Public-Key (BPK) model.

In [159] it is shown that a concurrent NMWIAoK Π gives directly a concurrent NMZKAoK in the BPK model. The construction is straightforward as it just consists of running Π twice, first from the verifier to the prover (proving knowledge of one out of two secrets) and then from the prover to the verifier (proving knowledge of either a witness for $x \in L$ or of one out of the two secrets of the verifier).

Our construction from Theorem 6.3 when combined with the construction of [159] gives a candidate round-efficient concurrent NMZKAoK in the BPK model.

6.3.3 Identification Schemes

Identification schemes represent one of the most successful real-world applications of cryptographic protocols. We show here a 3-round identification scheme secure against concurrent MiM attacks following the concept of proving knowledge of a secret.

Identification schemes based on proving knowledge of a secret.

[11] The puzzle can be implemented through a OWP that can be inverted in quasi-polynomial time.

[12] The work of Pass did not take into account MiM attacks.

The importance of this setting was for instance discussed in [41] mentioning the following example. Consider a verifier $\mathcal{V}$ that provides a service to restricted group of provers $\mathcal{P}$. A malicious prover $\mathcal{P}^\star$ could give to another party B that is not part of the group, some partial information about his secret that is sufficient for B to obtain the service from $\mathcal{V}$, while still B does not know $\mathcal{P}^\star$'s secret. The paradigm of proving knowledge of a secret in an identification scheme allows to prevent attacks like the one just described. When the identification scheme consists in proving knowledge of a secret the sole fact that B convinces $\mathcal{V}$ is sufficient to claim that one can extract the whole secret from B. This implies that B obtained $\mathcal{P}^\star$'s secret corresponding to his identity, and thus B is actually $\mathcal{P}^\star$.[13]

We now introduce a security definition that takes into account concurrent MiM attacks similarly to the definition CR2 (concurrent-reset on-line) of [15]. The definition of [15] also includes possible reset attacks in addition to allowing $\mathcal{A}$ to invoke multiple concurrent executions of the prover in the left sessions while $\mathcal{A}$ is interacting with the verifier. In the remaining part of this section we will ignore reset attacks since they are out of the purpose of our work. As described in [123] in most network-based settings reset attacks are not an issue. Following the notation of [123] we now give a formal security definitions for an identification scheme.

Definition 6.3 Let $\Pi = (\mathcal{K}, \mathcal{P}, \mathcal{V})$ be a tuple of PPT algorithms. We say Π is an identification scheme secure against man-in-the-middle attacks if the following conditions hold:

Correctness. For all $(\mathsf{pk}, \mathsf{sk})$ output by $\mathcal{K}(1^\lambda)$, we have

$$\text{Prob}\left[\ \langle \mathcal{P}(\mathsf{sk}), \mathcal{V}\rangle(\mathsf{pk}) = 1\ \right] = 1.$$

Security. For all PPT adversaries $\mathcal{A}$ there exists a negligible function ν such that

$$\text{Prob}\left[\ (\mathsf{pk}, \mathsf{sk}) \leftarrow \mathcal{K}(1^\lambda) : \langle \mathcal{A}^{\mathcal{P}(\mathsf{sk})}, \mathcal{V}\rangle(\mathsf{pk}) = 1 \ \text{ AND } \ \tau \notin T\ \right] < \nu(\lambda),$$

where $\mathcal{A}$ has oracle access to a stateful (i.e., non-resettable) $\mathcal{P}(\mathsf{sk})$, T is defined as the transcripts set of the interactions between $\mathcal{P}(\mathsf{sk})$ and $\mathcal{A}$, and τ is defined as the transcript of one of the interactions between $\mathcal{A}$ and $\mathcal{V}$. All interactions can be arbitrarily interleaved and $\mathcal{A}$ controls the scheduling of the messages.

Identification scheme from NMWI. Our construction $\Pi_{\mathsf{ID}} = (\mathcal{K}_{\mathsf{ID}}, \mathcal{P}_{\mathsf{ID}}, \mathcal{V}_{\mathsf{ID}})$ follows the approach of [41, 159]. Let $f : \{0,1\}^\lambda \rightarrow \{0,1\}^\lambda$ be a one-way permutation, let λ be the security parameter. The public key of $\mathcal{P}_{\mathsf{ID}}$ is the pair $(\mathsf{pk}_0, \mathsf{pk}_1)$, the secret key is sk_b for a randomly chosen bit b, such that $\mathsf{pk}_\mathsf{b} = f(\mathsf{sk}_b)$. Therefore the algorithm $\mathcal{K}_{\mathsf{ID}}$ takes as input the security parameter and outputs $((\mathsf{pk}_0, \mathsf{pk}_1), \mathsf{sk}_b)$ as described above. The protocol simply consists in $\mathcal{P}_{\mathsf{ID}}$ running our 3-round concurrent NMWIAoK Π_{CaP} with $\mathcal{V}_{\mathsf{ID}}$ to prove that it *knows* the pre-image of either pk_0 or pk_1. Formally, let $L_{\mathtt{id}}$ be the following language $L_{\mathtt{id}} = \{(y_0, y_1) : \exists x \in \{0,1\}^\lambda$ such that

[13] This is instead not likely to happen in scenarios where the same secret key is used for other critical tasks such as signatures of any type of document.

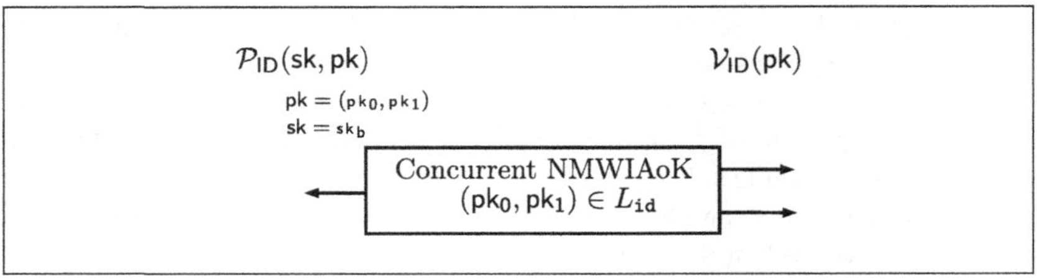

Fig. 6.4 Our 3-round identification scheme Π_{ID} from our 3-round concurrent NMWIAoK

$y_0 = f(x) \vee y_1 = f(x)\}$, then the identification scheme consists of $\mathcal{P}_{\mathsf{ID}}$ proving the statement $(\mathsf{pk}_0, \mathsf{pk}_1) \in L_{\mathtt{id}}$ using Π_{CaP}. Figure 6.4 summarizes our identification scheme. Now we can claim the following theorem.

Theorem 6.4 *Assume the existence of OWPs secure against subexponential-time adversaries then* Π_{ID} *is an identification scheme secure against concurrent MiM attacks.*

The proof is again straight-forward. If a PPT $\mathcal{A}$ succeeds then concurrent NMWI of Π_{CaP} guarantees that the witness that he encoded in the proof is independent of the one encoded in the proofs given by $\mathcal{P}$. Therefore by using the AoK property of Π_{CaP} we can invert f with non-negligible probability.

6.4 3-Round One-One NM Commitments

In this section we show our one-one non-malleable commitment scheme. In particular we construct a compiler that, on input a 3-round synchronous weak one-one NM commitment scheme, gives as output a 3-round extractable one-one NM commitment scheme assuming OWPs secure against subexponential-time adversaries.

6.4.1 The 3-Round One-One NM Commitment

Our construction is based on a compiler that takes as input a 3-round synchronous weak one-one NM commitment scheme $\Pi_{\mathsf{wsyn}} = (\mathsf{Sen}_{\mathsf{wsyn}}, \mathsf{Rec}_{\mathsf{wsyn}})$, a OWP f, a WI adaptive PoK for $\mathcal{NP}$ LS, and outputs a 3-round extractable one-one NM commitment scheme $\Pi_{\mathsf{NMCom}} = (\mathsf{NMSen}, \mathsf{NMRec})$.

In order to construct our compiler we consider the following tools:

1. a OWP f that is secure against PPT adversaries and that is $\tilde{T}_f$-breakable;
2. a 3-round one-one synchronous weak NM commitment scheme $\Pi_{\mathsf{wsyn}} = (\mathsf{Sen}_{\mathsf{wsyn}}, \mathsf{Rec}_{\mathsf{wsyn}})$ that is T_{wsyn}-hiding/NM, and $\tilde{T}_{\mathsf{wsyn}}$-breakable;

3. the LS PoK $\mathsf{LS} = (\mathcal{P}, \mathcal{V})$ for the language

$$L = \big\{(a, c, z, Y, \mathtt{id}) : \exists\, (m, \mathtt{dec}, y) \text{ s.t. } \big(\mathsf{Rec}_{\mathsf{wsyn}} \text{ on input } (a, c, z, m, \mathtt{dec}, \mathtt{id}) \text{ accepts } m \neq \perp \text{ as a decommitment of } (a, c, z, \mathtt{id}) \text{ OR } Y = f(y)\big)\big\}$$

that is T_{LS}-WI for the corresponding relation $\mathsf{Rel}_{\mathsf{L}}$.

Let λ be the security parameter of our scheme. We use w.l.o.g. λ also as security parameter for the one-wayness of f with respect to polynomial-time adversaries. We consider the following hierarchy of security levels: $\tilde{T}_f \ll T_{\mathsf{wsyn}} \ll \tilde{T}_{\mathsf{wsyn}} = \sqrt{T_{\mathsf{LS}}} \ll T_{\mathsf{LS}}$ where by "$T \ll T'$" we mean that "$T \cdot \mathsf{poly}(\lambda) < T'$".

Now, similarly to [46, 173], we define different security parameters, one for each tool involved in the security proof to be consistent with the hierarchy of security levels defined above. Given the security parameter λ of our scheme, we will make use of the following security parameters: (1) λ for the OWP f; (2) λ_{wsyn} for the synchronous weak one-one NM commitment scheme; (3) λ_{LS} for LS.

All of them are polynomially related to λ and they are such that the above hierarchy of security levels holds. In the construction we assume for simplicity to have a function Params that on input λ outputs $(\lambda_{\mathsf{wsyn}}, \lambda_{\mathsf{LS}}, \ell)$ where ℓ is the length of the theorem to be proved using LS.[14] The detailed scheme is described in Fig. 6.6 and a compact version is depicted in Fig. 6.5.

Roughly speaking our compiler works as follows. Let m be the message that NMSen wants to commit. The sender NMSen, on input the session-id $\mathtt{id}$ and the message m, computes the 1st round of the protocol by sending the 1st round a_{LS} of LS and the 1st round $\mathsf{a}_{\mathsf{wsyn}}$ of Π_{wsyn} (to commit to the message m using $\mathtt{id}$ as session-id). In the 2nd round the receiver NMRec sends challenges $\mathsf{c}_{\mathsf{wsyn}}$ and c_{LS} of Π_{wsyn} and LS, also picks and sends an element Y in the range of f. In the 3rd round NMSen computes the 3rd round of Π_{wsyn} and completes the transcript for LS by sending $\mathsf{z}_{\mathsf{wsyn}}$ and z_{LS}. Let $\tau = (\mathsf{a}_{\mathsf{wsyn}}, \mathsf{c}_{\mathsf{wsyn}}, \mathsf{z}_{\mathsf{wsyn}})$ be the transcript of the execution of Π_{wsyn}. LS is used by NMSen to prove knowledge of either a decommitment of τ to a message $\neq \perp$ or of a preimage of Y.

Theorem 6.5 *Suppose there exists a synchronous weak one-one NM commitment scheme and OWPs, both secure against subexponential-time adversaries, then* Π_{NMCom} *is a one-one NM commitment scheme.*

We are now ready to start the proof, that is divided in two parts. First we prove that Π_{NMCom} is a commitment scheme. Then we prove that Π_{NMCom} is a NM commitment scheme. Before that, we recall that LS can be constructed from OWPs secure against subexponential-time adversaries as well as Π_{wsyn} that can be constructed from OWPs secure against subexponential-time using the constructions of [97, 99].

---

[14] To compute 1st and 2nd round of LS only the length ℓ of the instance is required.

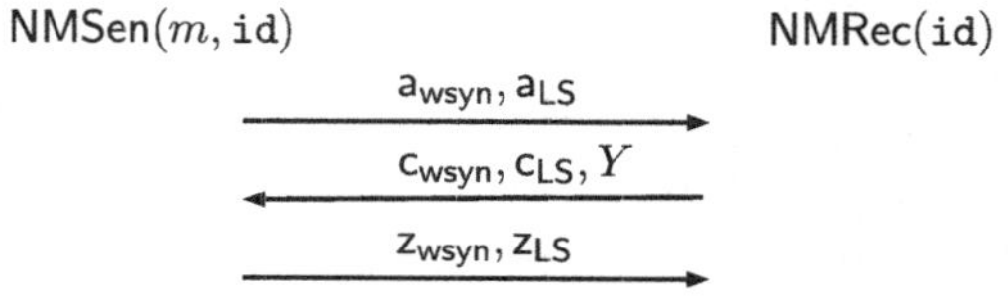

- Y is an element taken from the range of the OWP f.
- $\tau = (\mathsf{a}_{\mathsf{wsyn}}, \mathsf{c}_{\mathsf{wsyn}}, \mathsf{z}_{\mathsf{wsyn}})$ is the transcript of $\langle \mathsf{Sen}_{\mathsf{wsyn}}(m), \mathsf{Rec}_{\mathsf{wsyn}}\rangle(\mathtt{id})$.
- $(\mathsf{a}_{\mathsf{LS}}, \mathsf{c}_{\mathsf{LS}}, \mathsf{z}_{\mathsf{LS}})$ is the transcript of LS for proving knowledge of either the decommitment of τ to a message $\neq\perp$ or of the preimage of Y.

Fig. 6.5 Informal description of our 3-round NM commitment scheme Π_{NMCom}

Common input: security parameters: λ, $(\lambda_{\mathsf{wsyn}}, \lambda_{\mathsf{LS}}, \ell) = \mathsf{Params}(\lambda)$, $\mathtt{id} \in \{0,1\}^{\lambda}$.
Input to NMSen: $m \in \{0,1\}^{\mathsf{poly}\{\lambda\}}$.
Commitment phase:

1. NMSen $\rightarrow$ NMRec
   1. Run $\mathsf{Sen}_{\mathsf{wsyn}}$ on input $1^{\lambda_{\mathsf{wsyn}}}$, $\mathtt{id}$ and m thus obtaining the 1st round $\mathsf{a}_{\mathsf{wsyn}}$ of Π_{wsyn}.
   2. Run $\mathcal{P}$ on input $1^{\lambda_{\mathsf{LS}}}$ and ℓ thus obtaining the 1st round a_{LS} of LS.
   3. Send $(\mathsf{a}_{\mathsf{wsyn}}, \mathsf{a}_{\mathsf{LS}})$ to NMRec.
2. NMRec $\rightarrow$ NMSen
   1. Run $\mathsf{Rec}_{\mathsf{wsyn}}$ on input $\mathtt{id}$ and $\mathsf{a}_{\mathsf{wsyn}}$ thus obtaining the 2nd round $\mathsf{c}_{\mathsf{wsyn}}$ of Π_{wsyn}.
   2. Run $\mathcal{V}$ on input a_{LS} thus obtaining the 2nd round c_{LS} of LS.
   3. Pick a random $Y \in \{0,1\}^{\lambda}$.
   4. Send $(\mathsf{c}_{\mathsf{wsyn}}, \mathsf{c}_{\mathsf{LS}}, Y)$ to NMSen.
3. NMSen $\rightarrow$ NMRec
   1. Run $\mathsf{Sen}_{\mathsf{wsyn}}$ on input $\mathsf{c}_{\mathsf{wsyn}}$ thus obtaining the 3rd round $\mathsf{z}_{\mathsf{wsyn}}$ of Π_{wsyn} and the decommitment information $\mathsf{dec}_{\mathsf{wsyn}}$.
   2. Set $x = (\mathsf{a}_{\mathsf{wsyn}}, \mathsf{c}_{\mathsf{wsyn}}, \mathsf{z}_{\mathsf{wsyn}}, Y, \mathtt{id})$ and $w = (m, \mathsf{dec}_{\mathsf{wsyn}}, \perp)$ with $|x| = \ell$. Run $\mathcal{P}$ on input x, w, and c_{LS} thus obtaining the 3rd round z_{LS} of LS.
   3. Send $(\mathsf{z}_{\mathsf{wsyn}}, \mathsf{z}_{\mathsf{LS}})$ to NMRec.
4. NMRec: Set $x = (\mathsf{a}_{\mathsf{wsyn}}, \mathsf{c}_{\mathsf{wsyn}}, \mathsf{z}_{\mathsf{wsyn}}, Y, \mathtt{id})$ and abort iff $(\mathsf{a}_{\mathsf{LS}}, \mathsf{c}_{\mathsf{LS}}, \mathsf{z}_{\mathsf{LS}})$ is not accepted by $\mathcal{V}$ for $x \in L$.

Decommitment phase:

1. NMSen $\rightarrow$ NMRec: Send $(\mathsf{dec}_{\mathsf{wsyn}}, m)$ to NMRec.
2. NMRec: accept m as the committed message if and only if $\mathsf{Rec}_{\mathsf{wsyn}}$ on input $(m, \mathsf{dec}_{\mathsf{wsyn}})$ accepts m as a committed message of $(\mathsf{a}_{\mathsf{wsyn}}, \mathsf{c}_{\mathsf{wsyn}}, \mathsf{z}_{\mathsf{wsyn}}, \mathtt{id})$.

Fig. 6.6 Our 3-round NM commitment scheme Π_{NMCom}

Lemma 6.8 Π_{NMCom} *is a statistically-binding computationally-hiding commitment scheme.*

Proof **Correctness.** The correctness of Π_{NMCom} follows immediately from the delayed-input completeness of LS, and the correctness of Π_{wsyn}.

Perfect Binding. Observe that the message given in output in the decommitment phase of Π_{NMCom} is the message committed using Π_{wsyn}. Moreover the decommitment phase of Π_{NMCom} coincides with the decommitment phase of Π_{wsyn}. Since Π_{wsyn} is perfectly binding we have that the same holds for Π_{NMCom}.

Hiding. Following Definition 2.11 to prove the hiding of Π_{NMCom} we have to show that the experiment $\mathsf{ExpHiding}^0_{\mathcal{A},\Pi_{\mathsf{NMCom}}}(\lambda)$ in which NMSen commits to a message m_0 is computationally indistinguishable from the experiment $\mathsf{ExpHiding}^1_{\mathcal{A},\Pi_{\mathsf{NMCom}}}(\lambda)$ in which NMSen commits to a message m_1. In order to prove this indistinguishability we consider the following hybrid experiments.

- The 1st hybrid experiment $\mathcal{H}^0(\lambda)$ is equal to the real game experiment $\mathsf{ExpHiding}^0_{\mathcal{A},\Pi_{\mathsf{NMCom}}}(\lambda)$, with the difference that a value y s.t. $Y = f(y)$ is computed and used as a witness for LS. Observe that in order to compute y the commitment phase takes time $\tilde{T}_f$. The indistinguishability between $\mathcal{H}^0(\lambda)$ and $\mathsf{ExpHiding}^0_{\mathcal{A},\Pi_{\mathsf{NMCom}}}(\lambda)$ comes from the adaptive-input WI of LS, that holds against adversaries with running time bounded by $T_{\mathsf{LS}} \gg \tilde{T}_f$.
- The 2nd hybrid $\mathcal{H}^1(\lambda)$ differs from $\mathcal{H}^0(\lambda)$ in the message committed by the adversary using Π_{wsyn}. More precisely, Π_{wsyn} is used by NMSen to commit to the message m_1 instead of m_0. The indistinguishability between $\mathcal{H}^0(\lambda)$ and $\mathcal{H}^1(\lambda)$ comes from the hiding of Π_{wsyn} and noticing that the hiding of Π_{wsyn} still holds against adversaries with running time bounded by $T_{\mathsf{wsyn}} \gg \tilde{T}_f$.

The proof ends with the observation that $\mathcal{H}^1(\lambda) \approx \mathsf{ExpHiding}^1_{\mathcal{A},\Pi_{\mathsf{NMCom}}}(\lambda)$. The indistinguishability between $\mathcal{H}^1(\lambda)$ and $\mathsf{ExpHiding}^1_{\mathcal{A},\Pi_{\mathsf{NMCom}}}(\lambda)$ comes from the adaptive-WI property of LS and from the observation that, as before, the adaptive-input WI of LS still holds against adversaries with running time bounded by $T_{\mathsf{LS}} \gg \tilde{T}_f$. □

Lemma 6.9 Π_{NMCom} *is a one-one NM commitment scheme.*

The proof of security is divided in two cases, in the first case we consider an adversarial MiM $\mathcal{A}_{\mathsf{NMCom}}$ that acts in a synchronized way, while in the second case $\mathcal{A}_{\mathsf{NMCom}}$ is non-synchronized. In both cases we want to show that the committed value (and the view) of $\mathcal{A}_{\mathsf{NMCom}}$ when interacting with a prover NMSen that commits to a message m is indistinguishable from the committed value (and the view) of a simulator. The proof for the synchronous case goes through a series of hybrid experiments listed below.

- We consider the real game experiment $\mathcal{H}_1^m(z)$ in which in the left session NMSen commits to m, while in the right session NMRec interacts with $\mathcal{A}_{\mathsf{NMCom}}$. Now we prove that in the right session the MiM adversary $\mathcal{A}_{\mathsf{NMCom}}$ does not commit to a message $\tilde{m} = \perp$. By contradiction if $\mathcal{A}_{\mathsf{NMCom}}$ commits to $\tilde{m} = \perp$ then the witness used to complete an accepting transcript for LS is a value $\tilde{y}$ s.t. $f(\tilde{Y}) = \tilde{y}$. Then, by using the adaptive-input PoK property of LS we can reach a contradiction by inverting f in polynomial time.

- The 2nd hybrid is $\mathcal{H}_2^m(z)$ and it differs from $\mathcal{H}_1^m(z)$ only in the witness used to compute the LS transcript. The adversary $\mathcal{A}_{\mathsf{NMCom}}$, running in sub-exponential time, computes a value y s.t. $f(y) = Y$, and uses it as witness for the execution of LS. From the adaptive-input WI (that is stronger than inverting the OWP and of breaking Π_{wsyn}) of LS, the view and the committed message of $\mathcal{A}_{\mathsf{NMCom}}$ do not change between $\mathcal{H}_2^m(z)$ and $\mathcal{H}_1^m(z)$.
- We now consider the hybrid experiment $\mathcal{H}_1^0(z)$ that differs from the first hybrid experiment that we have considered $\mathcal{H}_1^m(z)$ in the committed message. Indeed in this case, the message committed in the left session is 0^λ. We observe that $\mathcal{H}_1^0(z)$ actually is the simulated game. As for the hybrid experiment $\mathcal{H}_1^m(z)$ 2e need to prove that in the right session, the MiM adversary $\mathcal{A}_{\mathsf{NMCom}}$ does not commit to a message $\tilde{m} =\perp$. By contradiction, if $\mathcal{A}_{\mathsf{NMCom}}$ commits to $\tilde{m} =\perp$ then the witness used to complete an accepting transcript for LS is a value $\tilde{y}$ s.t. $f(\tilde{Y}) = \tilde{y}$. Then, by using the adaptive-input PoK property of LS we can reach a contradiction by inverting f in polynomial time.
- The last hybrid experiment that we consider is $\mathcal{H}_2^0(z)$ and it differs from $\mathcal{H}_1^0(z)$ only in the witness used to compute the LS transcript. In more detail the adversary $\mathcal{A}_{\mathsf{NMCom}}$, running in sub-exponential time, computes a value y s.t. $f(y) = Y$, and uses it as witness for the execution of LS. From the adaptive-input WI (that is stronger than inverting the OWP and of breaking Π_{wsyn}) of LS, the view and the committed message of $\mathcal{A}_{\mathsf{NMCom}}$ do not change between $\mathcal{H}_2^0(z)$ and $\mathcal{H}_1^0(z)$.

To conclude this proof we show that the view and the committed message of $\mathcal{A}_{\mathsf{NMCom}}$ acting in $\mathcal{H}_1^m(z)$ are indistinguishable from the view and the committed message of $\mathcal{A}_{\mathsf{NMCom}}$ acting in $\mathcal{H}_1^0(z)$. For what has been argued above, it remains to show that the view and the committed message of $\mathcal{H}_2^m(z)$ are indistinguishable from the view and the committed message of $\mathcal{H}_2^0(z)$. This is ensured by the synchronous weak one-one non-malleability of Π_{wsyn}. Here we need only to use a *weak* synchronous one-one NM commitment since we are guaranteed, from the above arguments, that whenever $\mathcal{A}_{\mathsf{NMCom}}$ completes a commitment in a right session the underlying commitment computed through Π_{wsyn} corresponds to $\perp$ with negligible probability only both in $\mathcal{H}_2^m(z)$ and in $\mathcal{H}_2^0(z)$.

The proof for the asynchronous case is much simpler and relies on the hiding of Π_{NMCom}. More precisely we observe that in case of asynchronous scheduling it is possible to rewind the adversary $\mathcal{A}_{\mathsf{NMCom}}$ without rewinding the sender in the left session. This allows us to extract (in polynomial time) the witness used by the adversary in the execution of LS, that with overwhelming probability corresponds to the committed message. Therefore we contradict the hiding of Π_{NMCom}. Note that the only two possible schedules that are possible for a 3-round NM commitment scheme is the synchronous one or a one that allow the extraction of the message from the transcript of LS without rewinding the sender (i.e. asynchronous schedule). This observation concludes the proof.

Chapter 7
Four-Round Concurrent Non-malleable Commitments from One-Way Functions

7.1 Introduction

In the previous chapter, we obtained a non-malleable commitment scheme that requires only three rounds of communication. However, that scheme can be proven secure, assuming sub-exponential time assumptions. We now propose a different protocol that relies only on polynomial-time assumptions but adds an additional round of communication to the commitment phase.

To construct such a commitment scheme, we need to devise a novel approach that allows to break the multiple-slot barrier for concurrent NM commitments. While previous work relied on having either (1) stronger assumptions, (2) multiple rewind slots, (3) non-generic assumptions, or (4) do not achieve concurrency, in this chapter, we introduce techniques that allow to have just one rewind slot, minimal hardness assumptions, and full concurrency.

We recall the contributions that will be provided in this chapter.

Non-malleable commitments w.r.t. non-aborting adversaries. We prove that a subprotocol of [99] is a four-round statistically binding concurrent NM commitment scheme from OWFs (resp., a three-round perfectly binding concurrent NM commitment scheme from one-to-one OWFs), if the adversary is restricted to playing well-formed commitments in the right sessions when receiving well-formed commitments from the left sessions. We refer to this weaker security notion as concurrent weak non-malleability (wNM).

Simulation-Witness-Independence. We define a security notion for argument systems w.r.t. man-in-the-middle attacks that we refer to as simulation-witness-independence (SimWI). This security notion seemingly is not implied by previous notions as simulation extractability/soundness and strong non-malleable witness indistinguishability.

Four-Round One-Many SimWI from OWFs. We then construct a four-round one-many SimWI argument of knowledge for same specific languages by relying on OWFs only. This construction circumvents the major problem caused by the need

M. Ciampi and L. Siniscalchi, *Round and Computational Efficiency of Multi-party Protocols*, Information Security and Cryptography,
https://doi.org/10.1007/978-3-031-92374-6_7

to rewind on the left to simulate and on the right to extract when there is only one available slot.

Concurrent wNM + One-Many SimWI $\Rightarrow$ Four-Round Concurrent NM Commitments. We present our paradigm consisting in combining the above two notions in a protocol that runs in parallel the concurrent wNM commitment scheme and the one-many SimWI argument of knowledge. Therefore as the main result of this work, we upgrade concurrent wNM to full-fledged concurrent non-malleability without any penalization in rounds and assumptions.

We now discuss in more detail each of the above four contributions.

7.1.1 Weak Non-malleable Commitments

We define commitment schemes enjoying a limited form of non-malleability.[1]

Informally, we say that a commitment scheme is weak non-malleable (wNM) if it is non-malleable w.r.t. adversaries that never commit to $\perp$ when receiving honestly computed commitments. This form of non-malleability is significantly weaker than full-fledged non-malleability. Indeed, a full-fledged MiM $\mathcal{A}$ can, for instance, maul as follows: $\mathcal{A}$ creates a commitment of m_0 making use of messages computed by the sender in the left session so that if the sender commits to m_0 then the commitment of $\mathcal{A}$ is a well-formed commitment of m_0, while instead if the sender commits to $m_1 \neq m_0$ then the commitment of $\mathcal{A}$ is not well formed and therefore corresponds to $\perp$.

While by itself the wNM guarantee is certainly unsatisfying as protection against MiM attacks, the design of a wNM commitment scheme can be an easier task and schemes with such light non-malleability flavor might exist with improved round complexity, efficiency, and complexity assumptions compared to schemes achieving full-fledged non-malleability.

Concurrent wNM commitments. We show that a protocol due to [99] is a four-round statistically binding concurrent wNM commitment scheme requiring OWFs only (resp., a three-round perfectly binding concurrent wNM commitment scheme requiring one-to-one OWFs only). Moreover, their protocol can be instantiated to be public coin. The security proof consists of some pretty straightforward observations on top of various useful lemmas already proven in [99]. The chapter contribution on wNM commitments therefore consists of (1) introducing and formalizing this notion; (2) observing the existence of a secure construction in previous work; (3) using it as one of the two main building blocks of our paradigm allowing to obtain four-round concurrent (full-fledged) NM commitments from OWFs. A formal definition of weak NM commitments can be found in the definition section (see Definition 2.14). The proof that a scheme proposed in [99] satisfies this notion can be found in Sect. 7.5.

[1] We remark that Goyal in [94] defined a weaker notion of non-malleable commitments (non-malleability w.r.t. replacement) that also had the goal to deal with commitments of $\perp$. While the goal is similar to our definition, the actual formulation is quite different.

7.1.2 Simulation-Witness-Independence

We introduce a different security notion against MiM attacks to argument systems. We call our security notion *simulation-witness-independence* (SimWI) since it has similarities both with simulation extractability/soundness (see [170, 182]) and with (strong) non-malleable witness indistinguishability [139, 159] (sNMWI,NMWI). For simplicity we will discuss now the case of one prover and one verifier only, however our formal definition, construction, and application will focus on the one-many case (i.e., up to one prover and polynomially many verifiers).

The first security flavor that our notion tries to capture is the concept that the view of a MiM in the real game should be simulatable. Therefore we will have an experiment corresponding to the real game where the MiM plays with a honest prover and an honest verifier, and an experiment corresponding to the simulated game that simply consists of the output of a stand-alone simulator that emulates the prover and runs the code of honest verifiers when interacting internally with the MiM.[2]

While the above first security flavor guarantees that the statements proven by the MiM in the real-world experiment and in the simulated experiment are indistinguishable, there still is no guarantee that the MiM is unable to prove in the two experiments' statements that are associated to witnesses belonging to distinguishable distributions. In other words, as second flavor we want to capture the independence of the witnesses associated to the statements proven by the MiM with respect to the fact that the actual witness in the left session is used (this is the case of the real game) or is not used (this is the case of the simulated game). To avoid any ambiguity on which witness is associated to a statement, we associate to $\mathcal{NP}$ languages a non-negative integer γ. More precisely, for any $\mathcal{NP}$ language L we consider the largest non-negative integer γ such that for any $x \in L$ all witnesses of x have the same first γ bits.[3] The reason why we assign such a value γ to every $\mathcal{NP}$ language is that it fixes is some non-ambiguous way the input for the distinguisher of SimWI (indeed the input will be the first γ bits of any witness) and at same time the prefix of the witnesses of an instance can be recovered by extracting any witness.

The above second flavor makes our security definition non-trivial. Indeed standard zero knowledge is clearly insufficient and the definition has strong connections with the (hard to achieve) concept of committed message in NM commitments.[4] One might think that some heavy machinery could already imply our notion but instead, perhaps surprisingly, by taking into account all subtleties of the definitions, it turns out that SimWI is not implied by simulation extractability, simulation soundness and

---

[2] There is nothing surprising so far, this is just the concept of zero knowledge naturally augmented by extending the simulator with the behavior of honest verifiers to feed the MiM with messages belonging to the right sessions too.

[3] Note that when $\gamma = 0$ the second security flavor is cancelled and SimWI becomes equivalent to zero knowledge. Furthermore when γ is equal to the largest witness size then the subclass of languages corresponds to $\mathcal{UP}$.

[4] We stress that the main goal of this chapter is to construct four-round concurrent NM commitments from OWFs, and we will achieve it by making use of SimWI. As such, to avoid circularity, we cannot use concurrent NM commitments to construct SimWI.

sNMWI/NMWI. We stress that our goal is to get a *one-many four*-round construction under minimal assumptions.

Comparison with simulation extractability and simulation soundness. Simulation extractability requires the simulator to output a transcript and witnesses for the statements appearing in the right sessions of the transcript.

Simulation soundness requires the MiM to fail in proving false statements when receiving simulated proofs of false statements.

SimWI requires the simulator to output a transcript that includes statements proven in right sessions. The distribution of the instance/witness pairs associated to those statements is required to be indistinguishable from the distribution of the instance/witness pairs associated to the statements proved by the MiM in the real game. Instead, in simulation extractability there is no requirement on the witness given in output by the simulator beyond being valid witnesses. Simulation soundness does not have any requirement on the witnesses associated to the statements proven by the MiM.

Comparison with sNMWI/NMWI. sNMWI considers two indistinguishable distributions of instance/witnesses pairs. Very informally, the requirement of sNMWI/NMWI is that the instance/witness pairs associated to the arguments given by the MiM in the right sessions be independent of the distribution from which the instance/witness pair of the argument given to the MiM in the left session has been sampled.

SimWI requires the existence of a simulator while instead sNMWI/NMWI only considers experiments where the actual prover plays.

One-Many SimWI From OWFs in Four Rounds (i.e., in Just One Rewind Slot!). As discussed above, SimWI is an interesting security notions w.r.t. MiM attacks and similarly to all previous non-malleability notions is certainly non-trivial to achieve, especially when considering 1) the one-many case 2) only four rounds (i.e., one rewind slot), and 3) minimal assumptions. In this chapter we show how to construct a four-round one-many SimWI argument of knowledge (AoK) from OWFs, therefore avoiding multiple rewind slots.

A common approach to construct four-round zero-knowledge arguments (even without non-malleability requirements) relies on the FLS/FS paradigm [76, 133]. First there is a subprotocol useful to extract a trapdoor from the adversarial verifier. Then there is a witness-indistinguishable proof of knowledge (WIPoK) where the prover proves knowledge of either a witness for the statement or of the trapdoor. In order to save rounds the two subprotocols are parallelized.

The above common approach fails in presence of MiM attacks. The reason is that the MiM adversary can attack the witness indistinguishability (WI) of the WIPoK received in the left session in order to prove his statements (e.g., potentially false statement, statements with specific witnesses) in the right sessions. Using such an MiM to contradict the WI of the WIPoK is problematic since one should extract some useful information from the right session but this would require also to rewind the challenger of the WI of the WIPoK on the left.

We bypass the above difficulty as follows. Instead of relying on the WI of the WIPoK that requires two messages played by the challenger, we propose a construction where we essentially break the interactive challenger of WI into two non-interactive challengers. We implement this idea by relying on: (1) instance-dependent trapdoor commitments (IDTCom) and (2) special honest-verifier zero knowledge (Special HVZK). More in details, let $(\pi_1, \pi_2, \pi_3, \pi_4)$ be the transcript of a delayed-input[5] four-round Special HVZK adaptive-input proof of knowledge (PoK). We require the prover to send an IDTCom $\mathtt{com}$ of π_2 that is opened, sending the opening $\mathtt{dec}$, only in the last round, when π_4 is sent. The actual transcript therefore becomes $(\pi_1, \mathtt{com}, \pi_3, (\pi_2, \mathtt{dec}, \pi_4))$.

Consider now an experiment where the trapdoor is known and π_2 can be opened arbitrarily. If the output of the experiment deviates from the original one, we will have a reduction to the trapdoorness of the IDTCom. The reduction is not problematic since the challenger of the trapdoorness is non-interactive, sending a pair (commitment, decommitment) that is either computed using the regular procedure or through the use of the trapdoor. Next, in another experiment, we can replace the prover of the PoK with the Special HVZK simulator that will compute π_2 and π_4 after having as input π_1 and π_3. Again, the output of this experiment will not deviate from the previous one otherwise we can show an adversary for the Special HVZK property. The reduction again is not problematic since the challenger of Special HVZK is non-interactive.

We implement the trapdoor-extraction subprotocol through OWFs by using as trapdoor knowledge of two signatures under the same public key sent by the verifier in the first round. The verifier will send a signature of one message (chosen by the prover) in the third round. We will use a delayed-input Special HVZK adaptive-input PoK where the prover proves knowledge of either a witness for the statement or of signatures of messages. The IDTCom will have the public key of the signature scheme as instance, therefore the simulator after having extracted the signatures will be able to equivocate the commitments. The security proof presents one more caveat. Once the simulator rewinds on the left to obtain the trapdoor it is not clear how to argue that the extraction from the right is meaningful since the extractor might simply obtain the same trapdoor and this is useless. More specifically, the adversary might be able to equivocate on the right, therefore the extractor of the PoK would fail, and the best we can get from such a binding violation is the trapdoor of the IDTCom played in the right session. This does not give any contradiction since the trapdoor of the right session had to be already known in order to answer twice (before and after the rewind) in the right session to the MiM. We resolve this problem by relying on a specific proof approach where while the initial transcript is generated by the simulator, when the extractions are played in the right sessions, the transcript of the left session is re-completed by running the prover of the Special HVZK PoK. The reason why in this case the extraction on the right will succeed is that if we extract the trapdoor from the right session then this will also happen in the real game where the trapdoor is never used. In turn it would break the security of the signature scheme.

[5] By *delayed-input* we mean that the statement will be known only at the last round.

Caveat: adaptive-input selection. We will give a formal definition that allows the MiM to select the instance/witness pair for the left session only at the end, while the MiM must fix the statement for a right session already when playing his first round in that session. Our construction satisfies this notion and even a more important form of adaptiveness. We allow the MiM to specify the statement in the last round of a right session, as long as the witness is already fixed when playing his first round in that session. The reason why we prove such more sophisticated form of adaptive-input selection is that it is required in our application for concurrent NM commitments. Ideally one would like to satisfy the best possible adaptive-input selection, in order to make this primitive useful in a broader range of applications. However we cannot prove our construction secure with fully adaptive-input selection since we are not able to extract the witness from an MiM selecting a new statement (with possibly a new witness) in the last round of a right session. Indeed we would end up having a certain statement in the transcript of the simulator and then a witness for another statement obtained through rewinds. This would negatively affect our proof approach. We leave as a very interesting open question the construction of a four-round fully adaptive-input one-many SimWI AoK from OWFs.

7.1.2.1 Four-Round Concurrent NM Commitments from OWFs

We solve the problem left open by [99] by showing a four-round concurrent NM commitment scheme relying on OWFs only. The paradigm that we propose to obtain concurrent non-malleability consists in combining in parallel a four-round public-coin concurrent wNM commitment scheme from OWFs Π_0, and a one-many four-round SimWI argument of knowledge from OWFs Π_1.

The novel paradigm. Π_0 is run in order to commit to the message m. Π_1 is instead used to prove knowledge of a valid message and randomness explaining the transcript of Π_0. The power of the approach consists in using the above two tools that are in perfect synergy to defeat a concurrent MiM attack. The idea of the security proof is now quite simple. Since any one-many NM commitment is also many-many[6] NM, we focus the following discussion on the one-many case.

In the first experiment (the real game RG0) the sender commits to m_0. Clearly there cannot be a commitment to $\perp$ on the right otherwise the soundness of Π_1 is contradicted. Symmetrically there is an experiment RG1 where the sender commits to m_1 and there is no commitment to $\perp$ on the right. Then we consider a hybrid game H0 where the simulator of one-many SimWI of Π_1 is used. Observe that if (by contradiction) the distribution of the messages committed on the right changes w.r.t. RG0 we have that also the distribution of the witnesses corresponding to the statements proved in Π_1 on the right changes. However this clearly violates SimWI. Therefore it must still be the case that a commitment played on the right corresponds to $\perp$ with negligible probability only. Symmetrically, there is an experiment H1

[6] A many-many NM commitment scheme can be also indicated as a concurrent NM commitment scheme.

that is indistinguishable from RG1 and such that commitments played on the right are well formed (i.e., different from $\perp$). Therefore we can conclude that RG0 is indistinguishable from RG1 by noticing that H0 is indistinguishable from H1. Indeed, both H0 and H1 guarantee that the messages committed by the adversary on the right correspond to $\perp$ with negligible probability only. Summing up, a detectable deviation from H0 to H1 implies a contradiction of the concurrent wNM of Π_0.[7] This observation concludes the high-level overview of the security proof. However, some remarks are in order.

Remark 1: The required adaptive-input flavor. As specified in the previous section, our four-round one-many SimWI AoK Π_1 is fully adaptive on the left but instead on the right requires the witness to be fixed already in the first round of the MiM. The statements instead can be decided in the last round also in the right sessions. The flexibility with the statement is important since Π_0 is completed only in the last round and the entire transcript of Π_0 is part of the statement of Π_1. The lack of flexibility on the witness in the right sessions forces us to add one more requirement to Π_0. We need that message and randomness are already fixed in the second round of Π_0, since they will be the witness for Π_1. This property is satisfied by the construction of [99] that we prove in Sect. 7.5 to be concurrent wNM.

Remark 2: On the need of public coins in Π_0. In a reduction we will have to simulate the last round of the receiver of Π_0 without knowing the randomness he used to compute the previous round. Obviously public coins are easy to simulate.

7.2 Definition of Simulation-Witness-Independence (SimWI) for L^γ

We define SimWI for an $\mathcal{NP}$ language L associating to the language a non-negative integer γ. Roughly speaking all witnesses of an instance have in common the first γ bits, and this property holds for all instances of L. More formally we will consider γ as a non-negative integer such that for any $x \in L$ it holds that any witness w of x can be parsed as $w = \alpha|\beta$, where $|\alpha| = \gamma$, and α is the same for all witnesses of x. In order to easy the notation, we will note denote by L^γ the $\mathcal{NP}$ language having the above prefix γ. We will say that L^γ is γ-prefix language meaning that for any instance x of L^γ all witnesses of x have the same first γ bits.

When defining SimWI we will consider the one-many case since this is what we will use in the next part of this chapter. Adapting the definition to the one-one case and to the fully concurrent case is straightforward.

Discussion on adaptive-input selection and black-box simulation. Since our definition considers a real game where the MiM plays with at most one prover and polynomially many verifiers, and a simulated game that consists of an execution of a stand-alone simulator, a natural definition would require the indistinguishability of the two games for any $x \in L^\gamma$, giving to the prover as input also a witness. This

[7] This reduction needs extra help, see Remark 2.

definition however would be difficult to use when the argument of knowledge is played as a subprotocol of a larger protocol, especially if it is played in parallel with other subprotocols and the adversary contributes in selecting the statement for the left session. More specifically applications require a security definition that features a delayed-input property so that players start the protocol with the common input that is still undefined, and that will be defined later potentially with the contribution of the adversary. Therefore, in our definition, we will allow the adversary to explicitly select the statement, and as such the adversary will provide also the witness for the prover. The simulated game however will filter out the witness so that the simulator will receive only the instance. This approach strictly follows the one of [183] where adaptive-input selection is explicitly allowed and managed in a similar way. As final remark, our definition will require the existence of a black-box simulator since a non-black-box simulator could retrieve from the code of the adversary the witness for the adaptively generated statement. The non-black-box simulator could then run the honest prover procedure, therefore canceling completely the security flavor of the simulation paradigm.

Definition. Let $\Pi = (\mathcal{P}, \mathcal{V})$ be an argument system for an γ-prefix language L^γ and let $\mathsf{Rel}_{\mathsf{L}^\gamma}$ be the corresponding witness relation. Consider a PPT MiM adversary $\mathcal{A}$ that is simultaneously participating in one left session and $\mathsf{poly}(\lambda)$ right sessions. When the execution starts, all parties receive as a common input the security parameter 1^λ then $\mathcal{A}$ chooses the statement $x \in L^\gamma$ and witness w s.t. $(x, w) \in \mathsf{Rel}_{\mathsf{L}^\gamma}$ and sends them to $\mathcal{P}$, furthermore $\mathcal{A}$ receives as auxiliary input $z \in \{0, 1\}^\star$.

In the left session an honest prover $\mathcal{P}$ interacting with $\mathcal{A}$ proves the membership of x in L^γ. In the $\mathsf{poly}(\lambda)$ right sessions, $\mathcal{A}$ proves the membership in L^γ of instances $\tilde{x}_1, \ldots, \tilde{x}_{\mathsf{poly}(\lambda)}$ of his choice to the honest verifiers $\mathcal{V}_1, \ldots, \mathcal{V}_{\mathsf{poly}(\lambda)}$. For simplicity, in this definition we consider an adversary $\mathcal{A}$ that chooses the statement to be proved in the first round that he plays in every right sessions.[8]

Let $\{\mathsf{wimim}_\Pi(1^\lambda, z)\}_{\lambda \in \mathbb{N}, z \in \{0,1\}^\star}$ be a random variable that describes the following three values: 1) the view of $\mathcal{A}$ in the above experiment, 2) the output of $\mathcal{V}_i$ for $i = 1, \ldots, \mathsf{poly}(\lambda)$, and 3) the first γ-bits $\tilde{w}_1^\gamma, \ldots, \tilde{w}_{\mathsf{poly}(\lambda)}^\gamma$ of the corresponding witnesses $\tilde{w}_1, \ldots, \tilde{w}_{\mathsf{poly}(\lambda)}$ w.r.t. the instances $\tilde{x}_1, \ldots, \tilde{x}_{\mathsf{poly}(\lambda)}$ that are part of $\mathcal{A}$'s view except that $\tilde{w}_i^\gamma = \bot$ if $\mathcal{V}_i$ did not output 1, with $i = 1, \ldots, \mathsf{poly}(\lambda)$.

Let $\{\mathsf{sim}_\Pi^S(1^\lambda, z)\}_{\lambda \in \mathbb{N}, z \in \{0,1\}^\star}$ be a random variable that describes the following three values: 1) and 2) correspond to the output of S, 3) consists of the first γ-bits $\tilde{w}_1^\gamma, \ldots, \tilde{w}_{\mathsf{poly}(\lambda)}^\gamma$ of the corresponding witnesses $\tilde{w}_1, \ldots, \tilde{w}_{\mathsf{poly}(\lambda)}$ w.r.t. the instances $\tilde{x}_1, \ldots, \tilde{x}_{\mathsf{poly}(\lambda)}$ that appear in the MiM view of the output of S except that $w_i^\gamma = \bot$ if $b_i = 0$. The output of S is composed of the following two values: 1) an MiM view and 2) bits $b_1, \ldots, b_{\mathsf{poly}(\lambda)}$.

S has black-box access to $\mathcal{A}$ and has the goal to emulate the prover without having a witness, while perfectly emulating the verifiers of the right sessions. Therefore S

[8] Our construction will satisfy a much stronger notion where in the left session $\mathcal{A}$ can choose statement and witness in the last round, while in the right sessions $\mathcal{A}$ can choose the statement in the very last round, as long as the witness is already fixed in the second round.

rewinds only when playing as prover[9] and every instance/witness pair (x, w) given in output by $\mathcal{A}$ is replaced by $(x, \perp)$ and then returned to $\mathcal{S}$ (i.e., the simulator runs without the witness w for the instance x chosen by $\mathcal{A}$).

Definition 7.1 (SimWI) An argument system $\Pi = (\mathcal{P}, \mathcal{V})$ for an γ-prefix language L^{γ} with witness relation $\mathsf{Rel}_{L^{\gamma}}$ is *SimWI* if there exists an expected polynomial-time simulator $\mathcal{S}$ such that for every MiM adversary $\mathcal{A}$ that participates in one left session and $\mathsf{poly}(\lambda)$ right sessions the ensembles $\{\mathsf{wimim}_{\Pi}(1^{\lambda}, z)\}_{\lambda \in \mathbb{N}, z \in \{0,1\}^{\star}}$ and $\{\mathsf{sim}_{\Pi}^{\mathcal{S}}(1^{\lambda}, z)\}_{\lambda \in \mathbb{N}, z \in \{0,1\}^{\star}}$ are computationally indistinguishable over λ.

7.3 Four-Round One-Many SimWI from OWFs

We now show our construction of a four-round argument of knowledge $\mathsf{SWI} = (\mathcal{P}^{\mathsf{swi}}, \mathcal{V}^{\mathsf{swi}})$ for the γ-prefix language L^{γ} that is one-many SimWI and can be instantiated using any OWF. We will need the following tools:

1. a signature scheme $\Sigma = (\mathsf{Gen}, \mathsf{Sign}, \mathcal{V})$;
2. a two-round IDTC scheme $\mathsf{TC}_{\Sigma} = (\mathsf{Sen}_{\Sigma}, \mathsf{Rec}_{\Sigma}, \mathsf{TFake}_{\Sigma})$ for the following $\mathcal{NP}$-language

$$L_{\Sigma} = \big\{\mathsf{vk} : \exists\, (\mathtt{msg}_1, \mathtt{msg}_2, \sigma_1, \sigma_2) \text{ s.t. } \mathcal{V}(\mathsf{vk}, \mathtt{msg}_1, \sigma_1) = 1 \\ \text{AND } \mathcal{V}(\mathsf{vk}, \mathtt{msg}_2, \sigma_2) = 1 \text{ AND } \mathtt{msg}_1 \neq \mathtt{msg}_2\big\};$$

3. a four-round delayed-input public-coin Special HVZK proof system $\mathsf{LS} = (\mathcal{P}, \mathcal{V})$ for the γ-prefix language L^{γ} that is adaptive-input PoK for the corresponding relation $\mathsf{Rel}_{L^{\gamma}}$.

Let $x \in L^{\gamma}$ be the statement that $\mathcal{P}^{\mathsf{swi}}$ wants to prove, and w a witness s.t. $(x, w) \in \mathsf{Rel}_{L^{\gamma}}$. The high-level idea of our protocol is depicted in Fig. 7.1. In the first round the verifier $\mathcal{V}^{\mathsf{swi}}$ computes and sends the first round ls^1 of LS, computes a pair of signature and verification keys $(\mathsf{sk}, \mathsf{vk})$, sends the verification key vk to $\mathcal{P}^{\mathsf{swi}}$ and computes and sends the first round ρ of TC_{Σ} by running Rec_{Σ} on input 1^{λ} and the instance $\mathsf{vk} \in L_{\Sigma}$. Then $\mathcal{P}^{\mathsf{swi}}$ on input x, w and the received first round, computes the second round ls^2 of LS and runs Sen_{Σ} on input 1^{λ}, vk, ρ and message ls^2 thus obtaining a pair $(\mathtt{com}, \mathtt{dec})$. $\mathcal{P}^{\mathsf{swi}}$ sends $\mathtt{com}$ and a random message $\mathtt{msg}$ to $\mathcal{V}^{\mathsf{swi}}$.

[9] The motivation behind this definitional choice is that $\mathcal{S}$ is supposed to be not more than an extended zero-knowledge simulator that takes care also of the honest behavior of the verifiers since $\mathcal{A}$ expects to play with them. Instead allowing $\mathcal{S}$ to have any behavior on the right would hurt the power of SimWI in composing in parallel with other protocols. Indeed if $\mathcal{S}$ rewinds on the right as verifier, it would in turn rewind also the left player of the external protocol that is played in parallel. This would hurt the security of the overall scheme whenever the external protocol is not resettably secure. We will indeed compose a SimWI AoK with a weak NM commitment scheme that is not resettably secure.

$\mathcal{P}^{\mathsf{swi}}(x, w)$		$\mathcal{V}^{\mathsf{swi}}(x)$
	$\leftarrow$ $\rho, \mathsf{ls}^1, \mathsf{vk}$	sk
	$\mathtt{com}(\mathsf{ls}^2), \mathtt{msg}$ $\rightarrow$	
Upon receiving x and w s.t. $(x, w) \in \mathsf{Rel}_{\mathsf{L}^\gamma}$	$\leftarrow$ ls^3, σ	
	$\mathsf{dec}, \mathsf{ls}^2, \mathsf{ls}^4$ $\rightarrow$	

- $(\mathsf{sk}, \mathsf{vk}) \leftarrow \mathsf{Gen}(\lambda)$ and $\sigma \leftarrow \mathsf{Sign}(\mathsf{sk}, \mathtt{msg})$;
- $\mathtt{com}(\mathsf{ls}^2)$ is the commitment computed by running Sen_Σ for the language L_Σ and instance vk on input ρ (i.e., the 1st round of the commitment scheme), in order to commit to ls^2 (dec represents the decommitment information of $\mathtt{com}(\mathsf{ls}^2)$);
- $(\mathsf{ls}^1, \mathsf{ls}^2, \mathsf{ls}^3, \mathsf{ls}^4)$ is the transcript of LS for proving that $x \in L^\gamma$.

Fig. 7.1 Our SimWI AoK SWI from OWFs

In the third round $\mathcal{V}^{\mathsf{swi}}$ sends the third round ls^3 of LS and a signature σ (computed using sk) of the message $\mathtt{msg}$. In the last round $\mathcal{P}^{\mathsf{swi}}$ verifies whether or not σ is a valid signature for $\mathtt{msg}$. If σ is a valid signature, then $\mathcal{P}^{\mathsf{swi}}$, using x, w, and ls^3, computes the fourth round ls^4 of LS and sends $\mathtt{dec}$, ls^2, and ls^4 to $\mathcal{V}^{\mathsf{swi}}$. At this point $\mathcal{V}^{\mathsf{swi}}$ outputs 1 iff Rec_Σ on input vk, $\mathtt{com}$, $\mathtt{dec}$, ls^2 accepts $(\mathsf{ls}^2, \mathtt{dec})$ as a decommitment of $\mathtt{com}$ and the transcript for LS is accepting for $\mathcal{V}$ with respect to the instance x. We remark that to execute LS the instance is not needed until the last round but the instance length is required from the onset of the protocol.

Figure 7.2 describes in detail our SimWI AoK SWI.

Theorem 7.1 *Assuming OWFs,* $\mathsf{SWI} = (\mathcal{P}^{\mathsf{swi}}, \mathcal{V}^{\mathsf{swi}})$ *is a four-round one-many SimWI AoK for γ-prefix language.*

We divide the security proof in three parts, proving that SWI enjoys delayed-input completeness, adaptive-input AoK and SimWI. Before that, we recall that LS can be constructed from OWFs (see Sect. 2.11) as well as Σ using [181]. We also observe that if Σ relies on OWFs, then also TC_Σ can be constructed from OWFs (see Sect. 2.11).

Delayed-Input Completeness. The completeness follows directly from the completeness of LS, the correctness of TC_Σ and the validity of Σ. We observe that, due to the delayed-input property of LS, the statement x (and the respective witness w) is used by $\mathcal{P}^{\mathsf{swi}}$ only to compute the last round. Therefore SWI enjoys delayed-input completeness.

Adaptive-Input Argument of Knowledge. In order to prove that SWI enjoys adaptive-input AoK for $\mathsf{Rel}_{\mathsf{L}^\gamma}$, we need to show an efficient extractor E that outputs the witnesses for the statements proved by an adversarial prover $\mathcal{P}^{\mathsf{swi}\star}$. E simply runs ExtLS, the adaptive-input PoK extractor of LS, in every right session, and outputs what ExtLS outputs. More precisely E internally runs and interacts with a SWI prover $\mathcal{P}^{\mathsf{swi}}$ as $\mathcal{V}_i^{\mathsf{swi}}$ does, but acting as a proxy between $\mathcal{P}^{\mathsf{swi}\star}$ and ExtLS w.r.t. the messages of LS (for $i = 1, \ldots, \mathsf{poly}(\lambda)$). The important observation is that E could fail if the following event NoExt happens with non-negligible probability: $\mathcal{P}^{\mathsf{swi}\star}$

Common input: security parameter λ, instance $x \in L^{\gamma}$, instance length ℓ.
Input to $\mathcal{P}^{\mathsf{swi}}$: w s.t. $(x, w) \in \mathsf{Rel}_{L^{\gamma}}$, with x, w available only in the 4th round.
Commitment phase:

1. $\mathcal{V}^{\mathsf{swi}} \rightarrow \mathcal{P}^{\mathsf{swi}}$
   1. Run $(\mathsf{sk}, \mathsf{vk}) \leftarrow \mathsf{Gen}(1^{\lambda})$.
   2. Run $\mathcal{V}$ on input 1^{λ} and ℓ thus obtaining the 1st round ls^1 of LS.
   3. Run Rec_{Σ} on input 1^{λ} and vk thus obtaining ρ.
   4. Send $(\mathsf{vk}, \mathsf{ls}^1, \rho)$ to $\mathcal{P}^{\mathsf{swi}}$.
2. $\mathcal{P}^{\mathsf{swi}} \rightarrow \mathcal{V}^{\mathsf{swi}}$
   1. Run $\mathcal{P}$ on input 1^{λ}, ℓ and ls^1 thus obtaining the 2nd round ls^2 of LS.
   2. Run Sen_{Σ} on input 1^{λ}, vk, ρ and message ls^2 to compute the pair $(\mathtt{com}, \mathtt{dec})$.
   3. Pick a message $\mathtt{msg} \leftarrow \{0, 1\}^{\lambda}$.
   4. Send $(\mathtt{com}, \mathtt{msg})$ to $\mathcal{V}^{\mathsf{swi}}$.
3. $\mathcal{V}^{\mathsf{swi}} \rightarrow \mathcal{P}^{\mathsf{swi}}$
   1. Run $\mathcal{V}$ thus obtaining the 3rd round ls^3 of LS.
   2. Run $\mathsf{Sign}(\mathsf{sk}, \mathtt{msg})$ thus obtaining a signature σ of the message $\mathtt{msg}$.
   3. Send (ls^3, σ) to $\mathcal{P}^{\mathsf{swi}}$.
4. $\mathcal{P}^{\mathsf{swi}} \rightarrow \mathcal{V}^{\mathsf{swi}}$
   1. If $\mathcal{V}(\mathsf{vk}, \mathtt{msg}, \sigma) \neq 1$ then abort, continue as follows otherwise.
   2. Run $\mathcal{P}$ on input x, w and ls^3 thus obtaining the 4th round ls^4 of LS.
   3. Send $((\mathtt{dec}, \mathsf{ls}^2), \mathsf{ls}^4)$ to $\mathcal{V}^{\mathsf{swi}}$.
5. $\mathcal{V}^{\mathsf{swi}}$: output 1 iff the following conditions are satisfied.
   1. Rec_{Σ} on input $\mathsf{vk}, \mathtt{com}, \mathtt{dec}, \mathsf{ls}^2$ accepts $(\mathsf{ls}^2, \mathtt{dec})$ as a decommitment of $\mathtt{com}$.
   2. $(\mathsf{ls}^1, \mathsf{ls}^2, \mathsf{ls}^3, \mathsf{ls}^4)$ is accepting for $\mathcal{V}$ with respect to the instance x.

Fig. 7.2 Our SimWI AoK SWI from OWFs

opens the commitment $(\rho, \mathtt{com})$ to a different ls^2 during the rewinds. Indeed, in this case ExtLS could fail in obtaining a witness. We prove the following claim.

Claim There exists a negligible function ν such that $\text{Prob}\left[\ \mathsf{NoExt}\ \right] < \nu(\lambda)$.

Proof The proof is by contradiction, more specifically we now show an adversary $\mathcal{A}^{\Sigma}$ that extracts two signatures for two different messages in order to break the signature scheme Σ when $\text{Prob}\left[\ \mathsf{NoExt}\ \right]$ is non-negligible in λ.

If two decommitments of $(\mathtt{com}, \rho)$ w.r.t. two different messages ($\mathsf{ls}^{2'}$ and ls^2) are shown by $\mathcal{P}^{\mathsf{swi}\star}$ in the last round of SWI, $\mathcal{A}^{\Sigma}$ can extract two different signatures for two different messages by using the special binding of TC_{Σ}. More precisely, let vk be the verification key given by the challenger of the signature scheme, then our adversary $\mathcal{A}^{\Sigma}$ works as follows.

For all $i \in \{1, \ldots, \mathsf{poly}(\lambda)\} - \{j\}$, $\mathcal{A}^{\Sigma}$ interacts in the i-th session against $\mathcal{P}^{\mathsf{swi}\star}$ as $\mathcal{V}_i^{\mathsf{swi}}$ would do. Instead in the j-th session $\mathcal{A}^{\Sigma}$ runs as E would do, using vk to compute the first round, and the oracle $\mathsf{Sign}(\mathsf{sk}, \cdot)$ to compute a signature σ of a message m sent by $\mathcal{A}^{\Sigma}$ in the second round. Since we are assuming (by contradiction) that during the rewinds from the fourth round to the third round the commitment $(\rho, \mathtt{com})$ (sent in the second round by $\mathcal{P}^{\mathsf{swi}\star}$) is opened in more than one way, then, by using the special binding of TC_Σ, $\mathcal{A}^\Sigma$ extracts and outputs two signatures for two different messages. We conclude this proof with the following two observations. First, the signature oracle $\mathsf{Sign}(\mathsf{sk}, \cdot)$ is called only once since, by construction of E, the second round is played by $\mathcal{P}^{\mathsf{swi}\star}$ only once. Second, the extractor E is an expected polynomial-time algorithm while $\mathcal{A}^\Sigma$ must be a strict polynomial-time algorithm. This mean that the execution E has to be truncated. Obviously the running time of the extraction procedure can be truncated to a sufficiently long value so that with non-negligible probability the truncated extraction procedure will still yield the event NoExt to happen and this is sufficient for $\mathcal{A}^\Sigma$ to break the signature scheme.[10] □

SimWI. In order to prove that SWI is SimWI (Definition 7.1) for the γ-prefix language L^γ we prove the following lemma.

Lemma 7.1 $\{\mathsf{wimim}_{\mathsf{SWI}}(1^\lambda, z)\}_{\lambda\in\mathbb{N}, z\in\{0,1\}^\star} \approx \{\mathsf{sim}^{\mathcal{S}^{\mathsf{swi}}}_{\mathsf{SWI}}(1^\lambda, z)\}_{\lambda\in\mathbb{N}, z\in\{0,1\}^\star}$.

Proof Here we actually prove something stronger. Indeed we prove the security of SWI considering an MiM adversary $\mathcal{A}^{\mathsf{swi}}$ that has additional power both in the left and in the right sessions. More precisely in the left session $\mathcal{A}^{\mathsf{swi}}$ can choose the statement to be proved (and the related witness) in the third round. That is, in the last round that goes from $\mathcal{A}^{\mathsf{swi}}$ to $\mathcal{P}^{\mathsf{swi}}$.

Also, in all right sessions $\mathcal{A}$ chooses a family of statements $\mathcal{X}_w = \{x : (x, w) \in \mathsf{Rel}_{L^\gamma}$ or $x \notin L^\gamma\}$ in the second round, and then adaptively picks the statement to be proved from that family in the last round. Roughly speaking $\mathcal{X}_w$ is the family of statements that either share the same witness w, or do not belong to the γ-prefix language L^γ. In this way the MiM adversary has the power to adaptively choosing the statement to be proved in the last round of every right session conditioned on $\mathcal{X}_w$ that has to be fixed in the second round. We will refer to a SimWI protocol that is secure also in this setting as *adaptive-input* SimWI.

We start by showing the simulator $\mathcal{S}^{\mathsf{swi}}$ and giving an overview of the entire proof. The simulator is described in Fig. 7.3. Roughly, $\mathcal{S}^{\mathsf{swi}}$ interacts against $\mathcal{A}^{\mathsf{swi}}$ in both the left and right sessions. In the left session $\mathcal{S}^{\mathsf{swi}}$ runs TFake_Σ to compute and sends a commitment $\mathtt{com}$. $\mathcal{S}^{\mathsf{swi}}$ then rewinds $\mathcal{A}^{\mathsf{swi}}$ from the third to the second round, in order to obtain two valid signatures σ_1, σ_2 for two different messages $(\mathtt{msg}_1, \mathtt{msg}_2)$. These informations constitute the trapdoor $\mathtt{tk}$ for TC_Σ. After that $\mathtt{tk}$ is computed, $\mathcal{S}^{\mathsf{swi}}$ comes back to the main thread execution. Upon receiving ls^3 and x in the third round from $\mathcal{A}^{\mathsf{swi}}$, $\mathcal{S}^{\mathsf{swi}}$ computes an accepting transcript for LS $(\mathsf{ls}^1, \mathsf{ls}^2, \mathsf{ls}^3, \mathsf{ls}^4)$ running the Special HVZK simulator of LS on input ls^1, received in the first round from $\mathcal{A}^{\mathsf{swi}}$, and (x, ls^3). In the last round computes, by using $\mathtt{tk}$, the decommitment information $(\mathtt{dec}, \mathsf{ls}^2)$ for $\mathtt{com}$, and sends $(\mathtt{dec}, \mathsf{ls}^2, \mathsf{ls}^4)$ to $\mathcal{A}^{\mathsf{swi}}$. In the i-th right session, for $i = 1, \ldots, \mathsf{poly}(\lambda)$, $\mathcal{S}^{\mathsf{swi}}$ acts as $\mathcal{V}^{\mathsf{swi}}_i$ would do against $\mathcal{A}^{\mathsf{swi}}$. When the execution against $\mathcal{A}^{\mathsf{swi}}$ ends, $\mathcal{S}^{\mathsf{swi}}$ outputs the view of $\mathcal{A}^{\mathsf{swi}}$.

In the security proof we denote by $\{\mathsf{wimim}_{\mathcal{H}_i}(1^\lambda, z)\}_{\lambda\in\mathbb{N}, z\in\{0,1\}^\star}$ the random variable describing 1) the view of $\mathcal{A}^{\mathsf{swi}}$, 2) the output of $\mathcal{V}^{\mathsf{swi}}_i$ for $i = 1, \ldots, \mathsf{poly}(\lambda)$,

---

[10] The same arguments are used in [87]. The same standard argument about truncating the execution of an expected polynomial-time algorithm is used in other proofs but for simplicity we will not repeat this discussion.

Common input: security parameters λ and instance length ℓ.
Internal simulation of the left session:

1. Upon receiving $(\mathsf{vk}, \mathsf{ls}^1, \rho)$ from $\mathcal{A}^{\mathsf{swi}}$.
   1.1. Run TFake_Σ on input 1^λ, vk, ρ to compute the pair $(\mathtt{com}, \mathtt{aux})$.
   1.2. Pick a message $\mathtt{msg}_1 \leftarrow \{0,1\}^\lambda$.
   1.3. Send $(\mathtt{com}, \mathtt{msg}_1)$ to $\mathcal{A}^{\mathsf{swi}}$.
2. Upon receiving $(\mathsf{ls}^3, \sigma_1, x, \bot)$ from $\mathcal{A}^{\mathsf{swi}}$.
   2.1. If $\mathcal{V}(\mathsf{vk}, \mathtt{msg}_1, \sigma) \neq 1$ then abort, continue as follows otherwise.
   2.2. Repeat Step 1.3, 1.2 and follow-up right session message up to λ/p times[a] in order to obtain a signature σ_2 of a random message $\mathtt{msg}_2 \neq \mathtt{msg}_1$. Abort in case of failure in obtaining σ_2 in such λ/p attempts otherwise return to the main thread.
   2.3. Run the Special HVZK simulator of LS on input $(x, \mathsf{ls}^1, \mathsf{ls}^3)$ in order to obtain $(\mathsf{ls}^2, \mathsf{ls}^4)$.
   2.4. Run TFake_Σ on input $\mathtt{tk} = (\mathtt{msg}_1, \mathtt{msg}_2, \sigma_1, \sigma_2)$, vk, ρ, $\mathtt{com}$, $\mathtt{aux}$ and ls^2 to compute $\mathtt{dec}$.
   2.5. Send $((\mathtt{dec}, \mathsf{ls}^2), \mathsf{ls}^4)$ to $\mathcal{A}^{\mathsf{swi}}$.

Internal simulation of the right sessions:

1. For $i = 1, \ldots, \mathsf{poly}(\lambda)$ acts as $\mathcal{V}_i^{\mathsf{swi}}$ would do against $\mathcal{A}^{\mathsf{swi}}$.

Output: When the execution against $\mathcal{A}^{\mathsf{swi}}$ ends, outputs the view of $\mathcal{A}^{\mathsf{swi}}$ and the bits $b_1, \ldots, b_{\mathsf{poly}(\lambda)}$ where, for $i = 1, \ldots, \mathsf{poly}(\lambda)$, $b_i = 0$ iff $\mathcal{V}_i^{\mathsf{swi}}$ is rejecting, $b_i = 1$ otherwise[b].

[a] We refer with p as the probability that $\mathcal{A}^{\mathsf{swi}}$ sends in the Step 2 a valid signature for a randomly chosen message.
[b] Of course, if $\mathcal{A}^{\mathsf{swi}}$ ends during the step 2.2 the simulator continues to work until that step is completed.

Fig. 7.3 SimWI $\mathcal{S}^{\mathsf{swi}}$ for SWI

3) the first γ-bits $\tilde{w}_1^\gamma, \ldots, \tilde{w}_{\mathsf{poly}(\lambda)}^\gamma$ of the corresponding witnesses $\tilde{w}_1, \ldots, \tilde{w}_{\mathsf{poly}(\lambda)}$ w.r.t. the instances $\tilde{x}_1, \ldots, \tilde{x}_{\mathsf{poly}(\lambda)}$ that appear in $\mathcal{A}^{\mathsf{swi}}$'s view except that $\tilde{w}_i^\gamma = \bot$ if $\mathcal{V}_i^{\mathsf{swi}}$ rejected, with $i = 1, \ldots, \mathsf{poly}(\lambda)$.[11]

The proof makes use of the following main hybrid experiments:

- The first hybrid experiment is $\mathcal{H}_1(1^\lambda, z)$. In this hybrid in the left session $\mathcal{P}^{\mathsf{swi}}$ interacts with $\mathcal{A}^{\mathsf{swi}}$ in order to prove the validity of the instance x using the witness w, while in the right sessions $\mathcal{V}_i^{\mathsf{swi}}$ interacts with $\mathcal{A}^{\mathsf{swi}}$ for $i = 1, \ldots, \mathsf{poly}(\lambda)$. We want to prove that in the i-th right session $\mathcal{A}^{\mathsf{swi}}$ does not prove any false

[11] To ease the notation sometimes we will refer to $\{\mathsf{wimim}_{\mathcal{H}_i}(1^\lambda, z)\}_{\lambda \in \mathbb{N}, z \in \{0,1\}^\star}$ using just $\mathsf{wimim}_{\mathcal{H}_i}(1^\lambda, z)$.

instance $\tilde{x}_i$ for any $i = 1, \ldots, \mathsf{poly}(\lambda)$.[12] This property follows immediately from the adaptive-input AoK of SWI. We observe that in this case it is crucial that SWI is adaptive-input AoK, because we are considering an adversary $\mathcal{A}^{\mathsf{swi}}$ that can choose the instance to be proved in the last round of every right session.

- The second hybrid experiment is $\mathcal{H}_2(1^\lambda, z)$ and differs from $\mathcal{H}_1(1^\lambda, z)$ in the way the commitment $\mathtt{com}$ and the decommitment information $\mathtt{dec}$ are computed in the left session. More precisely, $\mathcal{P}^{\mathsf{swi}}$ runs TFake_Σ to compute a commitment $(\rho, \mathtt{com})$, and subsequently to compute a decommitment of $(\rho, \mathtt{com})$ to the value ls^2 (we remark that no trapdoor is needed to run TFake_Σ in order to compute $(\rho, \mathtt{com})$). In more detail, this experiment rewinds the adversary $\mathcal{A}^{\mathsf{swi}}$ from the third to the second round of the left session to extract two signatures σ_1, σ_2 of two different messages $(\mathtt{msg}_1, \mathtt{msg}_2)$ and uses them as trapdoor to run TFake_Σ. The indistinguishability between $\mathsf{wimim}_{\mathcal{H}_1}(1^\lambda, z)$ and $\mathsf{wimim}_{\mathcal{H}_2}(1^\lambda, z)$ comes from the hiding and the trapdoorness of TC_Σ.
- The third hybrid experiment is $\mathcal{H}_3(1^\lambda, z)$ and differs from $\mathcal{H}_2(1^\lambda, z)$ in the way the transcript for LS is computed. In more detail the Special HVZK simulator $\mathcal{S}$ of LS is used to compute the messages ls^2 and ls^4 instead of using the honest procedure $\mathcal{P}^{\mathsf{swi}}$. The indistinguishability between $\mathsf{wimim}_{\mathcal{H}_2}(1^\lambda, z)$ and $\mathsf{wimim}_{\mathcal{H}_3}(1^\lambda, z)$ comes from the Special HVZK of LS. We observe that the security proof ends with this hybrid experiment because $\mathsf{wimim}_{\mathcal{H}_3}(1^\lambda, z) \equiv \mathsf{sim}^{\mathcal{S}^{\mathsf{swi}}}_{\mathsf{SWI}}(1^\lambda, z)$.

□

The formal proof of the Theorem 7.1 can be found in Sect. 7.6.1.

7.4 Four-Round Concurrent NM Commitment Scheme

Our construction makes use of an adaptive-input SimWI AoK $\mathsf{SWI} = (\mathcal{P}^{\mathsf{swi}}, \mathcal{V}^{\mathsf{swi}})$ combined with a weak NM commitment scheme Π_{wom}. For our propose we consider a weak NM commitment scheme that with overwhelming probability for any accepting well-formed commitment can be opened to only one message. We recall that the weak NM commitment scheme of [99] enjoys this property when instantiated with Naor's commitment scheme [154].

We now consider the following language L based on the weak NM commitment scheme $\Pi_{\mathsf{wom}} = (\mathsf{Sen}_{\mathsf{wom}}, \mathsf{Rec}_{\mathsf{wom}})$:

$$L = \big\{(\tau, \mathtt{id}) : \exists\, (m, \mathtt{dec}) \text{ s.t. } \mathsf{Rec}_{\mathsf{wom}} \text{ on input } (m, \mathtt{dec}, \mathtt{id}) \text{ accepts } m \text{ as decommitment of } \tau\big\}$$

and the corresponding relation Rel_L.

[12] When we refer to a *proved instance* $\tilde{x}_i$ we implicitly assume that $\mathcal{V}^{\mathsf{swi}}_i$ is accepting, with $i = 1, \ldots, \mathsf{poly}(\lambda)$.

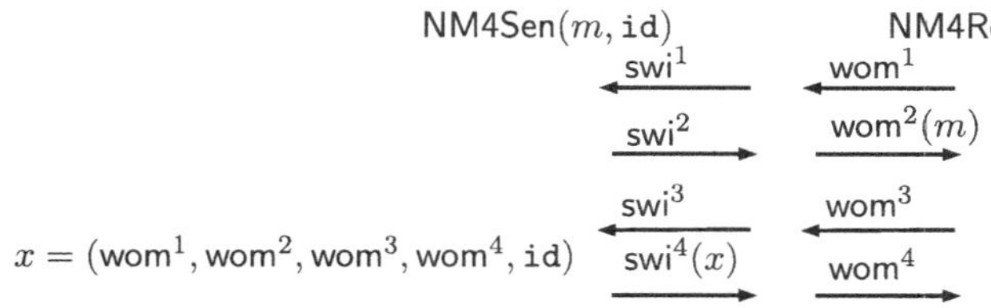

- $t = (\mathsf{wom}^1, \mathsf{wom}^2(m), \mathsf{wom}^3, \mathsf{wom}^4)$ is the transcript generated from the execution of the weak non-malleable commitment Π_{wom} in which $\mathsf{Sen}_{\mathsf{wom}}$ wishes to commit to the message m (using id $\mathtt{id}$).
- $(\mathsf{swi}^1, \mathsf{swi}^2, \mathsf{swi}^3, \mathsf{swi}^4(x))$ in the transcript generated from an execution of the SimWI AoK SWI in which $\mathcal{P}^{\mathsf{swi}}$ proves that the commitment $(t, \mathtt{id})$ computed using Π_{wom} is well formed (i.e, it is a commitment of a message $m \neq \perp$).

Fig. 7.4 Four-round concurrent NM commitment scheme from OWFs

We now use $\mathsf{SWI} = (\mathcal{P}^{\mathsf{swi}}, \mathcal{V}^{\mathsf{swi}})$ to upgrade a four-round public-coin concurrent weak NM commitment scheme Π_{wom} with the property that after the second round there is at most one valid message, to a concurrent NM commitment scheme. We will be able to invoke the security of SWI, since the language L is a γ-prefix language with overwhelming probability with $\gamma = |m|$. In fact, given an instance $(\tau, \mathtt{id})$ of L all the witnesses $w_1, \ldots, w_n$ of $(\tau, \mathtt{id})$ have the form $m|\mathtt{dec}_i$ for $i = 1, \ldots, n$ (i.e., all witnesses have the same prefix m).

Consider a SimWI AoK for L. Let m be the message that NM4Sen wants to commit and $\mathtt{id}$ be the ID for this session. The high-level idea of our protocol is depicted in Fig. 7.4.

In the first round the receiver NM4Rec computes and sends the first round swi^1 of SWI and the first round wom^1 of Π_{wom} using as input the $\mathtt{id}$. Then NM4Sen on input $\mathtt{id}$, the message m, and the received first round, computes the second round wom^2 of Π_{wom} in order to commit to the message m, using $\mathtt{id}$, furthermore he obtains $\mathtt{dec}_{\mathsf{wom}}$ s.t. $(m, \mathtt{dec}_{\mathsf{wom}})$ constitutes the decommitment information.[13] Moreover NM4Sen computes and sends the second round swi^2 of SWI. In the third round NM4Rec sends the third round wom^3 of Π_{wom} and the third round swi^3 of SWI. In the last round NM4Sen computes the fourth round wom^4 of Π_{wom}. Furthermore, NM4Sen, using $(\mathsf{wom}^1, \mathsf{wom}^2, \mathsf{wom}^3, \mathsf{wom}^4, \mathtt{id})$ as instance and $(m, \mathtt{dec}_{\mathsf{wom}})$ as a witness, computes the fourth round swi^4 of SWI and sends wom^4, swi^4 to NM4Rec. At this point NM4Rec accepts the commitment (i.e., the transcript of the protocol generated so far) iff the transcript for SWI is accepting for $\mathcal{V}^{\mathsf{swi}}$ with respect to the instance $(\mathsf{wom}^1, \mathsf{wom}^2, \mathsf{wom}^3, \mathsf{wom}^4, \mathtt{id})$. The decommitment phase of our scheme simply corresponds to the decommitment phase of Π_{wom}.

[13] In order to match the adaptive-input selection satisfied by SWI, message and randomness explaining the entire transcript are already fixed in this round.

Common input: security parameter λ, instance length ℓ, NM4Sen's identity $\mathtt{id} \in \{0,1\}^{\lambda}$.
Input to NM4Sen: $m \in \{0,1\}^{\mathsf{poly}(\lambda)}$.
Commitment phase:

1. NM4Rec $\rightarrow$ NM4Sen
   1. Run $\mathsf{Rec}_{\mathsf{wom}}$ on input 1^{λ}, $\mathtt{id}$ thus obtaining the 1st round wom^1 of Π_{wom}.
   2. Run $\mathcal{V}^{\mathsf{swi}}$ on input 1^{λ} and ℓ thus obtaining the 1st round swi^1 of SWI.
   3. Send $(\mathsf{swi}^1, \mathsf{wom}^1)$ to NM4Sen.
2. NM4Sen $\rightarrow$ NM4Rec
   1. Run $\mathcal{P}^{\mathsf{swi}}$ on input 1^{λ}, ℓ and swi^1 thus obtaining the 2nd round swi^2 of SWI.
   2. Run $\mathsf{Sen}_{\mathsf{wom}}$ on input 1^{λ}, $\mathtt{id}$, wom^1 and the message m thus obtaining the 2nd round wom^2 of Π_{wom} and $\mathsf{dec}_{\mathsf{wom}}$ s.t. $(m, \mathsf{dec}_{\mathsf{wom}})$ constitutes the decommitment information.
   3. Send $(\mathsf{swi}^2, \mathsf{wom}^2)$ to NM4Rec.
3. NM4Rec $\rightarrow$ NM4Sen
   1. Run $\mathsf{Rec}_{\mathsf{wom}}$ on input wom^2 thus obtaining the 3rd round wom^3 of Π_{wom}.
   2. Run $\mathcal{V}^{\mathsf{swi}}$ on input swi^2 thus obtaining the 3rd round swi^3 of SWI.
   3. Send $(\mathsf{wom}^3, \mathsf{swi}^3)$ to NM4Sen.
4. NM4Sen $\rightarrow$ NM4Rec
   1. Run $\mathsf{Sen}_{\mathsf{wom}}$ on input wom^3 thus obtaining the 4th round wom^4 of Π_{wom}.
   2. Set $x = (\mathsf{wom}^1, \mathsf{wom}^2, \mathsf{wom}^3, \mathsf{wom}^4, \mathtt{id})$ and $w = (m, \mathsf{dec}_{\mathsf{wom}})$ with $|x| = \ell$. Run $\mathcal{P}^{\mathsf{swi}}$ on input x, w and swi^3 thus obtaining the 4th round swi^4 of SWI.
   3. Send $(\mathsf{wom}^4, \mathsf{swi}^4)$ to NM4Rec.
5. NM4Rec : Set $x = (\mathsf{wom}^1, \mathsf{wom}^2, \mathsf{wom}^3, \mathsf{wom}^4, \mathtt{id})$ and accept the commitment iff $(\mathsf{swi}^1, \mathsf{swi}^2, \mathsf{swi}^3, \mathsf{swi}^4)$ is accepting for $\mathcal{V}^{\mathsf{swi}}$ with respect to the instance x.

Decommitment phase:

1. NM4Sen $\rightarrow$ NM4Rec: Send $(m, \mathsf{dec}_{\mathsf{wom}})$ to NM4Rec.
2. NM4Rec: accept m as the committed message if and only if $\mathsf{Rec}_{\mathsf{wom}}$, on input $(m, \mathsf{dec}_{\mathsf{wom}})$, accepts m as the committed message of $(\mathsf{wom}^1, \mathsf{wom}^2, \mathsf{wom}^3, \mathsf{wom}^4, \mathtt{id})$.

Fig. 7.5 Our four-round concurrent NM commitment scheme Π_{NM4Com} from OWFs

As described before, SWI $= (\mathcal{P}^{\mathsf{swi}}, \mathcal{V}^{\mathsf{swi}})$ is used by NM4Sen to prove knowledge of a message and randomness consistent with the transcript computed using Π_{wom}. To execute SWI the instance is not needed until the last round.

Figure 7.5 describes in detail our four-round concurrent NM commitment scheme Π_{NM4Com}.

Theorem 7.2 *Assuming OWFs,* $\Pi_{\mathsf{NM4Com}} = (\mathsf{NM4Sen}, \mathsf{NM4Rec})$ *is a four-round concurrent NM commitment scheme.*

The four-round concurrent NM commitment scheme $\Pi_{\mathsf{NM4Com}} = (\mathsf{NM4Sen}, \mathsf{NM4Rec})$ relies on OWFs, because the adaptive-input SimWI AoK SWI can be constructed using OWFs only (see Theorem 7.1) and Π_{wom} can be instantiated using the weak concurrent non-malleable commitment scheme proposed in Sect. 7.5 that relies on OWFs. Note that the construction of Sect. 7.5 has also the additional property that we require (i.e., after the second round the only valid message and the corresponding decommitment informations are fixed).

The security proof is divided into two parts. In the first part we prove that Π_{NM4Com} is indeed a commitment scheme. In the second part we prove that Π_{NM4Com} is a one-many NM commitment scheme, and then we go from one-many to concurrent non-malleability by using Proposition 2.1.

Lemma 7.2 $\Pi_{\mathsf{NM4Com}} = (\mathsf{NM4Sen}, \mathsf{NM4Rec})$ *is a statistically binding computationally hiding commitment scheme.*

Proof **Correctness.** The correctness follows directly from the delayed-input completeness of SWI and the correctness of Π_{wom}.

Statistically Binding. Observe that the message given in output in the decommitment phase of Π_{NM4Com} is the message committed using Π_{wom}. Moreover the decommitment of Π_{NM4Com} coincides with the decommitment of Π_{wom}. Since Π_{wom} is statistically binding then so is Π_{NM4Com}.

Computationally Hiding. Computational hiding follows immediately from Lemma 7.3.

□

Lemma 7.3 *For all* $m \in \{0,1\}^{\mathsf{poly}(\lambda)}$ $\{\mathsf{mim}_{\Pi_{\mathsf{NM4Com}}}^{\mathcal{A}_{\mathsf{NMCom}},m}(z)\}_{z\in\{0,1\}^\star} \approx \{\mathsf{sim}_{\Pi_{\mathsf{NM4Com}}}^{\mathsf{Sim}^{\mathsf{NM4Com}}}(1^\lambda, z)\}_{z\in\{0,1\}^\star}$.

We denote by $\{\mathsf{mim}_{\mathcal{H}_i^m}^{\mathcal{A}^{\mathsf{NM4Com}},m}(z)\}_{z\in\{0,1\}^\star}$ the random variable describing the view of the MiM $\mathcal{A}^{\mathsf{NM4Com}}$ combined with the values that it commits in the $\mathsf{poly}(\lambda)$ right sessions in hybrid $\mathcal{H}_i^m(z)$.

As required by the definition, we want to show that the distribution of the real game experiment (i.e., the view of the MiM $\mathcal{A}^{\mathsf{NM4Com}}$ when playing with $\mathsf{NM4Sen}$ committing m along with the messages committed in the right sessions) and one of the outputs of a simulator are computationally indistinguishable. We start by showing the simulator $\mathsf{Sim}^{\mathsf{NM4Com}}$ and giving an overview of the entire proof. The simulator is described in Fig. 7.6.

- The first hybrid experiment is $\mathcal{H}_1^m(z)$. In this hybrid in the left session $\mathsf{NM4Sen}$ commits to m, while in the right sessions $\mathsf{NM4Rec}_i$ interacts with $\mathcal{A}^{\mathsf{NM4Com}}$ for $i = 1, \ldots, \mathsf{poly}(\lambda)$. We prove that in the i-th right session $\mathcal{A}^{\mathsf{NM4Com}}$ does not commit to a message $\tilde{m}_i = \perp$ for any $i = 1, \ldots, \mathsf{poly}(\lambda)$. The proof follows immediately from the adaptive-input AoK of SWI. We observe that in this case it is crucial that SWI is adaptive-input AoK, because the theorem proved by $\mathcal{A}^{\mathsf{NM4Com}}$ is fully specified only in the last round of every right session. Clearly we have that $\mathsf{mim}_{\Pi_{\mathsf{NM4Com}}}^{\mathcal{A}^{\mathsf{NM4Com}},m}(z) = \mathsf{mim}_{\mathcal{H}_1^m}^{\mathcal{A}^{\mathsf{NM4Com}},m}(z)$.
- The second hybrid experiment is $\mathcal{H}_2^m(z)$ and differs from $\mathcal{H}_1^m(z)$ in the way the transcript of SWI is computed. In this hybrid the simulator $\mathcal{S}^{\mathsf{swi}}$ of SWI is used to compute the transcript of SWI. The indistinguishability between $\mathsf{mim}_{\mathcal{H}_1^m}^{\mathcal{A}^{\mathsf{NM4Com}},m}(z)$

Common input: Security parameters: λ. NM4Sen's identity: $\mathtt{id} \in \{0,1\}^\lambda$.
Internal simulation of the left session:

1. Upon receiving $(\mathsf{swi}^1, \mathsf{wom}^1)$ from $\mathcal{A}^{\mathsf{NM4Com}}$.
   1.1. Run $\mathcal{P}^{\mathsf{swi}}$ on input 1^λ, ℓ and swi^1 thus obtaining the 2nd round swi^2 of SWI.
   1.2. Run $\mathsf{Sen}_{\mathsf{wom}}$ on input 1^λ, $\mathtt{id}$, wom^1 and the message 0^λ thus obtaining the 2nd round wom^2 of Π_{wom} and $\mathtt{dec}_{\mathsf{wom}}$ s.t. $(0^\lambda, \mathtt{dec}_{\mathsf{wom}})$ constitutes the decommitment informations.
   1.3. Send $(\mathsf{swi}^2, \mathsf{wom}^2)$ to $\mathcal{A}^{\mathsf{NM4Com}}$.
2. Upon receiving $(\mathsf{wom}^3, \mathsf{swi}^3)$ from $\mathcal{A}^{\mathsf{NM4Com}}$.
   2.1. Run $\mathsf{Sen}_{\mathsf{wom}}$ on input wom^3 thus obtaining the 4th round wom^4 of Π_{wom}.
   2.2. Set $x = (\mathsf{wom}^1, \mathsf{wom}^2, \mathsf{wom}^3, \mathsf{wom}^4, \mathtt{id})$ and $w = (0^\lambda, \mathtt{dec}_{\mathsf{wom}})$ with $|x| = \ell$. Run $\mathcal{P}^{\mathsf{swi}}$ on input x, w and swi^3 thus obtaining the 4th round swi^4 of SWI.
   2.3. Send $(\mathsf{wom}^4, \mathsf{swi}^4)$ to $\mathcal{A}^{\mathsf{NM4Com}}$.

Stand-alone commitment:

1. $\mathsf{Sim}^{\mathsf{NM4Com}}$ acts as a proxy between $\mathcal{A}^{\mathsf{NM4Com}}$ and $\mathsf{NM4Rec}_i$, with $i = 1, \ldots, \mathsf{poly}(\lambda)$.

Fig. 7.6 The simulator $\mathsf{Sim}^{\mathsf{NM4Com}}$ of Π_{NM4Com}

and $\mathsf{mim}_{\mathcal{H}_2^m}^{\mathcal{A}^{\mathsf{NM4Com}},m}(z)$ comes from the adaptive-input SimWI property of SWI. It is important to observe that we can properly rely on the adaptive-input SimWI property of SWI since the committed message in Π_{wom} is fixed in the second round. Therefore also the family of statement $\mathcal{X}_w = \{x : (x, w) \in \mathsf{Rel}_{\mathsf{L}} \text{ or } x \notin L\}$ proved using SWI is implicitly fixed in the second round. Moreover we can rely on the security of SWI because the language L is a γ-prefix language for $\mathsf{prefix} = |m|$. Indeed, all witnesses of any instance of L have the same prefix (i.e., the committed message m). Therefore when using the simulator of SWI we are guaranteed that the distribution of the first γ bits of the witnesses corresponding to the statements proven by the adversary in the right sessions of SWI does not change. In turn, this implies that the distribution of the committed messages in the right sessions does not change since each message committed in a session is in the first γ bits of any witness corresponding to the statement proven in SWI in that session.

We also consider the hybrid experiments $\mathcal{H}_1^0(z)$, $\mathcal{H}_2^0(z)$ that are the same hybrid experiments described above with the difference that Π_{wom} is used to commit to a message 0^λ instead of m. From the same arguments described above we have that $\mathsf{mim}_{\mathcal{H}_1^0}^{\mathcal{A}^{\mathsf{NM4Com}},m}(z) \approx \mathsf{mim}_{\mathcal{H}_2^0}^{\mathcal{A}^{\mathsf{NM4Com}},m}(z)$ and that in the i-th right session of $\mathcal{H}_1^0(z)$ $\mathcal{A}^{\mathsf{NM4Com}}$ commits to a message $\tilde{m}_i = \perp$ with negligible probability (for any $i \in= 1, \ldots, \mathsf{poly}(\lambda)$). We also observe that $\mathsf{mim}_{\mathcal{H}_1^0}^{\mathcal{A}^{\mathsf{NM4Com}},m}(z) = \mathsf{sim}_{\Pi_{\mathsf{NM4Com}}}^{\mathsf{Sim}^{\mathsf{NM4Com}}}(1^\lambda, z)$.

The only thing that remains to argue to complete the proof is that the view of $\mathcal{A}^{\mathsf{NM4Com}}$, along with messages committed in the right sessions of the execution of $\mathcal{H}_2^m(z)$, is indistinguishable from the view of $\mathcal{A}^{\mathsf{NM4Com}}$ along with the messages committed in the right sessions of $\mathcal{H}_2^0(z)$. This is actually ensured by the weak concurrent non-malleability of Π_{wom}. Indeed, from the arguments given above, in both $\mathcal{H}_2^m(z)$ and $\mathcal{H}_2^0(z)$ the adversary $\mathcal{A}^{\mathsf{NM4Com}}$ commits to a message $\tilde{m}_i = \bot$ with negligible probability for $i = 1, \ldots, \mathsf{poly}(\lambda)$. Therefore we can use this $\mathcal{A}^{\mathsf{NM4Com}}$ to construct and adversary $\mathcal{A}^{\mathsf{wom}}$ that breaks the weak concurrent non-malleability of Π_{wom}. Roughly speaking, let $m, 0^\lambda$ be the challenge messages, then $\mathcal{A}^{\mathsf{wom}}$ works as following against the challenger C^{wom}. In the left session acts as a proxy for all the messages of Π_{wom} between C^{wom} and $\mathcal{A}^{\mathsf{NM4Com}}$ and executes the simulator $\mathcal{S}^{\mathsf{swi}}$ of SWI in parallel. In the i-th right session $\mathcal{A}^{\mathsf{wom}}$ interacts as $\mathsf{Rec}_{\mathsf{wom},i}$ would do w.r.t. the messages of Π_{wom} and as $\mathcal{V}_i^{\mathsf{swi}}$ for the messages of SWI, for all $i = 1, \ldots, \mathsf{poly}(\lambda)$. The distinguisher that breaks the concurrent weak non-malleability of Π_{wom} runs $\mathcal{D}^{\mathsf{NM4Com}}$ (that exists by contradiction) that distinguishes $\mathsf{mim}_{\mathcal{H}_2^0}^{\mathcal{A}^{\mathsf{NM4Com}},m}(z)$ from $\mathsf{mim}_{\mathcal{H}_2^m}^{\mathcal{A}^{\mathsf{NM4Com}},m}(z)$, and outputs what $\mathcal{D}^{\mathsf{NM4Com}}$ outputs.

A caveat that we have to address in this reduction is due to the rewinds made by $\mathcal{S}^{\mathsf{swi}}$ in the left session in order to compute the transcript of SWI. Indeed a rewind made in the left session could affect the reduction rewinding also the receivers of Π_{wom} involved in the reduction. More precisely could happen that in a session $j \in \{1, \ldots, \mathsf{poly}(\lambda)\}$ the third round of Π_{wom} has to be played multiple times because of the multiple values $\tilde{\mathsf{wom}}_j^2$ received in the j-th right session. We can avoid this problem by sending a random string as a third round of Π_{wom}. In this way for the first value $\tilde{\mathsf{wom}}_j^2$ received from $\mathcal{A}^{\mathsf{NM4Com}}$ the reduction interacts with the receiver of Π_{wom} and for all the other values the reduction sends a random string. This is the reason why in our construction we require Π_{wom} to be public coin. One additional issue is the following. The simulator of SWI could rewind the entire left session during the reduction, therefore requiring to compute a new commitment of m for the protocol Π_{wom}. Since we are assuming that Π_{wom} is concurrent, the reduction can request to receive multiple commitments for the same message.

The formal proof can be found in Sect. 7.6.2.

7.5 On the Weak Concurrent Property of [99]

In this section we consider the one-one eight-round NM commitment (from OWFs) $\Pi_{1\text{-}1}$ of [99] in order to show that one of the main tools used to construct $\Pi_{1\text{-}1}$ is actually a weak concurrent public-coin non-malleable commitment (see Definition 2.14). In this section we will refer to the full version of [99].

$\Pi_{1\text{-}1}$ is the result of the sequential execution of two protocols. The first one is a special four-round public-coin commitment scheme Π_{wom}. The second one is a four-round zero-knowledge AoK ZK that ensures that the commitment computed using Π_{wom} is well formed, that is, is not a commitment of a message $m = \bot$. We now prove that Π_{wom} is a weak concurrent NM commitment.

First of all it is easy to prove that if $\Pi_{\text{1-1}}$ is hiding then Π_{wom} so is. We assume by contradiction that there exists an adversary $\mathcal{A}^h$ for the hiding of Π_{wom} and use it to break the hiding of $\Pi_{\text{1-1}}$. The reduction simply acts as a proxy w.r.t. the messages of Π_{wom} between $\mathcal{A}^h$ and the challenge of the hiding of $\Pi_{\text{1-1}}$, and acts a verifier w.r.t. the message of ZK. The output of the reduction corresponds to the output of $\mathcal{A}^h$.

Since the decommitment informations of $\Pi_{\text{1-1}}$ correspond to the decommitment informations of Π_{wom}, and since $\Pi_{\text{1-1}}$ is statistically binding, then Π_{wom} is statistically binding as well. In this section we consider the definition of *adaptive hiding*. The only difference with the classical definition of hiding is the following. Let m_0 and m_1 be the challenge messages. The challenger of adaptive hiding picks a random bit b and computes the commitment of m_b. The adversary, upon receiving the commitment, either outputs his guess $b' \in \{0, 1\}$, or asks to receive another commitment of m_b (the latter step can be executed a polynomial number of times). The adversary is successful if $\text{Prob}\left[\ b = b'\ \right] - 1/2$ is non-negligible in the security parameter. It is easy to see that commitment scheme is hiding iff is adaptive hiding.

Now we are ready to prove the following lemma.

Lemma 7.4 *If OWFs exists then* Π_{wom} *is a four-round public-coin concurrent weak NM commitment scheme.*

Proof We start by proving that Π_{wom} is a four-round public-coin one-many and then we go though one-many to concurrent by using similar arguments used in the proof of Proposition 2.1. Therefore now we show that for every PPT one-many MiM adversary $\mathcal{A}^{\mathsf{wom}}$ that does not commit to $\bot$ when a well-formed commitment is received in the left session, there exists a PPT simulator S such that for every $m \in \{0, 1\}^{\mathsf{poly}(\lambda)}$ the following ensembles are computationally indistinguishable: $\{\mathsf{mim}^{\mathcal{A},m}_{\Pi_{\mathsf{wom}}}(z)\}_{z\in\{0,1\}^\star} \approx \{\mathsf{sim}^{S}_{\Pi_{\mathsf{wom}}}(1^\lambda, z)\}_{z\in\{0,1\}^\star}$.

For sake of contradiction we suppose that there exists an MiM adversary $\mathcal{A}^{\mathsf{wom}}$ and a distinguisher $\mathcal{D}^{\mathsf{wom}}$ that distinguishes between the above two ensembles with probability at least $2p$, for some non-negligible p. We now use $\mathcal{A}^{\mathsf{wom}}$ and $\mathcal{D}^{\mathsf{wom}}$ to break the adaptive hiding of Π_{wom}. More precisely we construct an extractor E that extracts the messages committed by $\mathcal{A}^{\mathsf{wom}}$ in all the right sessions. Then we construct an adversary $\mathcal{A}^h$ that uses E in order to break the adaptive hiding of Π_{wom}. Before showing how exactly the reduction works, we formally describe the extractor E.

We start by assuming that only one right session is computed during the execution of Π_{wom}, and that the probability that $\mathcal{A}^{\mathsf{wom}}$ completes the execution of Π_{wom} is at least p. In this way we show an extractor that extracts the message committed in that session with probability greater than $1 - p$ (that will be enough to break the hiding of Π_{wom}). Then, by using standard arguments (the same used in [94]) we show that the extractor works properly also in the case of $\mathsf{poly}(\lambda)$ right sessions. The extractor that we use is the same used in Fig. 3 of [99], but our purpose the only things to know about how E works are the following:

1. E takes as input a *well-formed* transcript T of an execution of Π_{wom}, and has oracle access to the MiM adversary. A transcript T is well formed if both the commitment computed in the left session and the commitment computed in the right session are correctly computed; that is, they are commitments of messages different from $\perp$.
2. The extraction procedure of E rewinds $\mathcal{A}^{\mathsf{wom}}$, in the right session, from the fourth to the second round $\mathsf{poly}(\lambda)$ times, feeding the MiM adversary with a random third round every time.
3. If the rewinds made in the right session require the fourth message of the left session to be played again, E answers by using a specific strategy.

Let's now focus on the item 1. As we described before, in the non-malleable commitment scheme $\Pi_{\mathsf{1\text{-}1}}$ of [99] a ZK argument is executed in order to ensure that the commitment computed with Π_{wom} is well formed. We observe that, by definition of weak non-malleable commitment, we are considering now an MiM adversary that never commits to $\perp$ in the right session if the commitment that he receives in the left session is well formed. For that reason we can properly use the extractor E (slightly modified as we will describe later) according to Theorem 2 of [99], that is the following.

Theorem 7.3 *(*[99, Theorem 2]*) Let T be the well-formed transcript that is given as input to E. Let $\tilde{m}$ be MiM's commitment in the right session of T. Then the probability that E outputs a message different from $\tilde{m}$ is at most p.*

Let's now see more formally how we can use E to construct an adversary $\mathcal{A}^h$ for the adaptive hiding of Π_{wom}. $\mathcal{A}^h$ picks m and 0^λ as challenge messages and sends them to the challenger of the adaptive hiding of Π_{wom} C^h. Then he acts as a proxy between C^h and $\mathcal{A}^{\mathsf{wom}}$ for all the messages of Π_{wom} of the left session. Instead, in the right session, $\mathcal{A}^h$ interacts against $\mathcal{A}^{\mathsf{wom}}$ as the receiver of Π_{wom} would do. When the execution ends, a transcript T for the execution of Π_{wom} is generated. At this point $\mathcal{A}^h$ runs the extractor E on input T in order to extract the messages committed in the right sessions. Then he feeds the distinguisher $\mathcal{D}^{\mathsf{wom}}$ with the extracted messages and the view of $\mathcal{A}^{\mathsf{wom}}$, and outputs what $\mathcal{D}^{\mathsf{wom}}$ outputs.

It is important to observe that the extractor E could rewind the left session, that is, could rewind the C^h. There are two messages scheduling that can cause this problem. The synchronized scheduling and the scheduling that require the entire left session to be played again (see Fig. 7.7 for an example of such scenario).

As described earlier in the item 2, E knows how to deal with the synchronized case. Indeed in that scheduling, because of how E works, can only happen that fourth message of the left session is required to be played again (in order to answer to a new third message). For the second case the behavior of E is not well defined, indeed in that case E has to compute another commitment of m_b without knowing m_b. This is not a problem since we are making a reduction to the adaptive hiding of Π_{wom}. Therefore, when E has to play again the entire left session in order to commit to m_b, $\mathcal{A}^h$ can ask to C^h to start another execution of Π_{wom} and acts as a proxy between C^h and E. We recall that the adversary has the power to ask multiple commitments for the

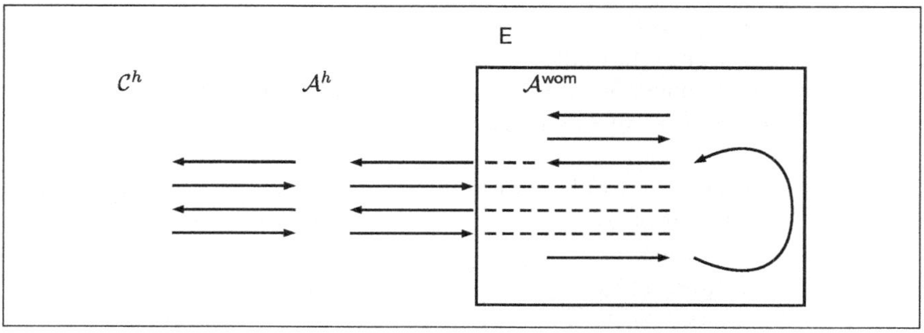

Fig. 7.7 During the reduction to the adaptive hiding of Π_{wom} could be required to play the left session multiple times because of the rewinds made by E. In general this happens when it is required to recompute the second round of the left session, due to a new first round received by $\mathcal{A}^{\mathsf{wom}}$ (in the left session)

same challenge message because C^h is the challenger of adaptive hiding. In this case the extractor is still able to extract $\tilde{m}$ from the right session since, in every rewind, $\mathcal{A}^{\mathsf{wom}}$ receives well-formed commitment on the left. Therefore, by the definition of weak non-malleable commitment, $\mathcal{A}^{\mathsf{wom}}$ is computing well-formed commitment in the right session. This ensures that $\tilde{m}$ is extracted with non-negligible probability (by construction of E).

We now consider an MiM adversary that opens $\mathsf{poly}(\lambda)$ right sessions. First we point out that the extractor we construct is able to extract $\tilde{m}$ from the right interaction with high probability, without rewinding the left execution.

Therefore we can follow [94], and run the extractor E one by one for all the right session. More precisely, for every right session $i = 1, \ldots, \mathsf{poly}(\lambda)$:

- define a machine $\mathcal{M}_i$ with emulates all the right sessions except session i on its own and expose the i-th session to an outside receiver;
- run the extractor on the machine $\mathcal{M}_i$ giving it as input the left view as in the main thread and the right view of the i-th session in the main thread.

As for [94], by the union bound our extractor will succeed in extracting from all of the right interactions with high probability.

In order to conclude the proof we now prove the following claim.

Claim Let Π_{1-n} be a weak one-many non-malleable, then Π_{1-n} is also weak concurrent non-malleable commitment.

Proof The security proof is similar to the security proof of Proposition 2.1 that is provided in [138], but for sake of completeness here we propose a full security proof of our claim.

Let $\mathcal{A}$ be a weak man-in-the-middle adversary that participates in at most $v = \mathsf{poly}(\lambda)$ concurrent executions. We provide a concurrent simulator S for $\mathcal{A}$. S proceeds as follows on input 1^λ and z. S incorporates $\mathcal{A}$ and internally emulates all the left interactions for $\mathcal{A}$ by simply honestly committing to the string 0^λ. Messages from the right interactions are instead forwarded externally to the receivers of Π_{1-n}. Finally S outputs the view of $\mathcal{A}$. We show that the values that S commits to are indistinguishable from the values that $\mathcal{A}$ commits to. Suppose, for contradiction, that this is not the case. Then, there exists a polynomial-time distinguisher $\mathcal{D}$ and a polynomial $p(\lambda)$ such that for infinitely many λ, there exist messages $m_0, m_1, \ldots, m_v$ and $z \in \{0,1\}^\star$ s.t. the distinguisher $\mathcal{D}$ distinguishes between $\mathsf{mim}_{\Pi_{1-n}}^{\mathcal{A},m_1,\ldots,m_v}(z)$ and $\mathsf{sim}_{\Pi_{1-n}}^{S}(1^\lambda, z)$ with probability $1/p(\lambda)$. Fix a generic λ for which this happens. Consider the hybrid simulator S_i that on input $1^\lambda, z' = m_1, \ldots, m_v, z$, proceeds just as S, with the exception that in left interactions $j \le i$, it instead commits to m_j. It directly follows that $\mathsf{mim}_{\Pi_{1-n}}^{\mathcal{A},m_1,\ldots,m_v}(z) = \mathsf{sim}_{\Pi_{1-n}}^{S_v}(1^\lambda, z')$ and $\mathsf{sim}_{\Pi_{1-n}}^{S}(1^\lambda, z) = \mathsf{sim}_{\Pi_{1-n}}^{S_0}(1^\lambda, z')$. By a standard hybrid argument there exists an $i \in \{1, \ldots, v\}$ such that

$$\mathrm{Prob}\left[\, a \leftarrow \mathsf{sim}_{\Pi_{1-n}}^{S_{i-1}}(1^\lambda, z') : \mathcal{D}(1^\lambda, z', a) = 1 \,\right] -$$
$$\mathrm{Prob}\left[\, b \leftarrow \mathsf{sim}_{\Pi_{1-n}}^{S_i}(1^\lambda, z') : \mathcal{D}(1^\lambda, z', b) = 1 \,\right] \ge 1/(p(\lambda)v).$$

Note that the only difference between the executions by $S_{i-1}(1^\lambda, z')$ and $S_i(1^\lambda, z')$ is that in the former $\mathcal{A}$ receives a commitment to 0^λ in session i, whereas in the latter it receives a commitment to m_i. Consider the one-many adversary $\tilde{\mathcal{A}}$ that on input $\tilde{z} = z', \lambda, i$ executes $S_{i-1}(1^\lambda, z')$ with the exception that the i-th left interaction is forwarded externally. Consider, the function $\mathsf{reconstruct}$ that on input $\mathsf{mim}_{\Pi_{1-n}}^{\tilde{\mathcal{A}},0^\lambda}(z)$, i.e., values $\tilde{m}'_1, \ldots, \tilde{m}'_v$ and the view of $\tilde{A}$, reconstructs the view view of $\mathcal{A}$ in the emulation by $\tilde{\mathcal{A}}$, and outputs $\tilde{m}'_1, \ldots, \tilde{m}'_v, \mathsf{view}$. By construction, it follows that

$$\mathsf{reconstruct}(\mathsf{mim}_{\Pi_{1-n}}^{\tilde{\mathcal{A}},0^\lambda}(z)) = \mathsf{sim}_{\Pi_{1-n}}^{S_{i-1}}(1^\lambda, z')$$

$$\mathsf{reconstruct}(\mathsf{mim}_{\Pi_{1-n}}^{\tilde{\mathcal{A}},m_i}(z)) = \mathsf{sim}_{\Pi_{1-n}}^{S_i}(1^\lambda, z').$$

Since $\mathsf{reconstruct}$ is polynomial-time computable, this contradicts the one-many non-malleability of Π_{1-n}. □

A useful property enjoyed by Π_{wom}, that is also used in this work, is that the decommitment informations $(\mathtt{dec}, m)$ are fixed in the second round of the Π_{wom}. We also observe that if the underling commitment scheme (the one used in the construction of Π_{wom}) is perfectly binding, so is Π_{wom}. We recall that the existence of one-to-one OWFs implies the existence of perfectly binding commitment scheme. Therefore we can consider an instantiation of the underling commitment of Π_{wom} using one-to-one OWFs, obtaining a three-round perfectly binding public-coin concurrent weak NM commitment scheme. The number of rounds goes from four to three because in Π_{wom} the first round from receiver to sender is just related to the underling commitment from OWFs (e.g., Naor's commitment).

7.6 Formal Proofs

7.6.1 Formal Proof of Theorem 7.1

In this section we give more details about the security proof. In order to simplify the security proof, here we actually consider the notion of *adaptive Special HVZK* and *adaptive trapdoorness* instead of Special HVZK and trapdoorness. The only differences with the classical definition of Special HVZK is the following. Let $(\mathsf{ls}^1, \mathsf{ls}^3, x)$ be a challenge. The challenger of adaptive Special HVZK picks a random bit b and computes an accepting transcript $t = (\mathsf{ls}^1, \mathsf{ls}^2, \mathsf{ls}^3, \mathsf{ls}^4)$ for x. If $b = 0$ then t has been computed by using $\mathcal{P}$, with the Special HVZK simulator otherwise. The adversary, upon receiving t, either outputs his guess $b' \in \{0, 1\}$, or asks to receive another transcript t according to a new challenge $(\mathsf{ls}^{1'}, \mathsf{ls}^{3'}, x')$. Note that the adversary can require a polynomial number of transcripts according to different challenges before he outputs b'. The adversary is successful if Prob $[\ b = b'\ ] - 1/2$ is non-negligible in the security parameter. It is easy to see that a protocol is Special HVZK iff is adaptive Special HVZK.

Analogously, the only difference with the definition of trapdoorness given in Definition 2.16 is the following. Let (x, ρ, m) and $\mathtt{tk}$ s.t. $(x, \mathtt{tk}) \in \mathsf{Rel}_{L_\Sigma}$ be the challenge messages used by the adversary to interact with the challenger. The challenger of adaptive trapdoorness picks a random bit b and computes a commitment $\mathtt{com}$ and the respectful decommitment information $(m, \mathtt{dec})$. If $b = 0$ then both $\mathtt{com}$ and $(m, \mathtt{dec})$ are computed using the trapdoor procedure TFake_Σ, using the honest procedure Sen_Σ otherwise. The adversary, upon receiving $\mathtt{com}$ and $(m, \mathtt{dec})$, either outputs his guess $b' \in \{0, 1\}$, or asks to start another interaction against the challenger by using different (x', ρ', m') and $\mathtt{tk}'$. Note that the adversary can start (in a sequential way) a polynomial number of other interactions using different (x', ρ', m') before he outputs b'. The adversary is successful if Prob $[\ b = b'\ ] - 1/2$ is non-negligible in the security parameter. It is easy to see that commitment scheme enjoys the adaptive trapdoorness property iff enjoys the trapdoor property.

Below we formally describe both the hybrid experiments and the reductions involved in the security proof.

- As described before, the first hybrid experiment is $\mathcal{H}_1(1^\lambda, z)$. In this hybrid in the left session $\mathcal{P}^{\mathsf{swi}}$ interacts with $\mathcal{A}^{\mathsf{swi}}$ in order to prove the validity of the instance x (adaptively chosen by $\mathcal{A}^{\mathsf{swi}}$) using the witness w, while in the right sessions $\mathcal{V}_i^{\mathsf{swi}}$ interacts with $\mathcal{A}^{\mathsf{swi}}$ for $i = 1, \ldots, \mathsf{poly}(\lambda)$. Also, we have already observed that in every right session the probability that $\mathcal{A}^{\mathsf{swi}}$ proves a false instance is negligible because of the property of adaptive-input AoK of SWI.
- We now consider an intermediate hybrid experiment $\mathcal{H}_1^{\mathsf{rew}}(1^\lambda, z)$ that differs from $\mathcal{H}_1(1^\lambda, z)$ as follows. In the left session, by rewinding the adversary $\mathcal{A}^{\mathsf{swi}}$ from the third to the second round, two signatures σ_1, σ_2 for two distinct messages $(\mathtt{msg}_1, \mathtt{msg}_2)$ are extracted. First of all we prove that in $\mathcal{H}_1^{\mathsf{rew}}(1^\lambda, z)$ two signatures are obtained with non-negligible probability. Let p the probability that a valid signature σ for the message $\mathtt{msg}$ is provided by $\mathcal{A}^{\mathsf{swi}}$, that is, $\mathcal{V}(\mathsf{vk}, \mathtt{msg}, \sigma) = 1$.

If a valid signature is received, then the steps 2.3, 2.4, and follow-up right session messages are repeated up to λ/p times. This implies that for a non-negligible p the probability that $\mathcal{A}^{\mathsf{swi}}$ does not give a second valid signature for two randomly chosen messages after λ/p rewinds is negligible in λ. For that reason the above deviation increases the abort probability of the experiment only by a negligible amount, therefore we can claim that $\mathsf{wimim}_{\mathcal{H}_1}(1^\lambda, z) \approx \mathsf{wimim}_{\mathcal{H}_1^{\mathsf{rew}}}(1^\lambda, z)$.
- We now consider the second hybrid experiment $\mathcal{H}_2(1^\lambda, z)$ that differs from $\mathcal{H}_1^{\mathsf{rew}}(1^\lambda, z)$ as follows. The value $\mathtt{com}$ is computed by running TFake_Σ instead of Sen_Σ. We recall that by Definition 2.16 no trapdoor information is required in order to compute $\mathtt{com}$ using the algorithm TFake_Σ. Then the hybrid experiment proceeds as $\mathcal{H}_1^{\mathsf{rew}}(1^\lambda, z)$ until signatures (σ_1, σ_2) for two different messages $(\mathtt{msg}_1, \mathtt{msg}_2)$ are extracted. At this point the extracted information is used as trapdoor to run TFake_Σ in order to compute a decommitment $(\mathtt{dec}, \mathsf{ls}^2)$ w.r.t. the commitment $(\rho, \mathtt{com})$. First, we prove that the probability of extracting two valid signatures for two different messages in this hybrid experiment is greater (or equal) than the probability that this event occurs in $\mathcal{H}_1^{\mathsf{rew}}(1^\lambda, z)$, and then we prove that $\mathsf{wimim}_{\mathcal{H}_2}(1^\lambda, z) \approx \mathsf{wimim}_{\mathcal{H}_1^{\mathsf{rew}}}(1^\lambda, z)$. The following claim is sufficient to prove the first part.

Claim Let $p_1(\lambda)$ be the (non-negligible) probability that a valid signature for $\mathtt{msg}$ is sent in the third round of $\mathcal{H}_1^{\mathsf{rew}}(1^\lambda, z)$ by $\mathcal{A}^{\mathsf{swi}}$, and let $p_2(\lambda)$ be the probability that event occurs in $\mathcal{H}_2(1^\lambda, z)$ then, for every polynomial $\mathsf{poly}(\cdot)$, $p_1(\lambda) \leq p_2(\lambda) + 1/\mathsf{poly}(\lambda)$.

Proof Suppose by contradiction that there exists polynomial $\mathsf{poly}(\cdot)$ s.t., for a sufficiently large security parameter λ, $p_1(\lambda) > p_2(\lambda) + 1/\mathsf{poly}(\lambda)$, then we can construct an adversary $\mathcal{A}^{\mathsf{TC}_\Sigma}$ that has non-negligible advantage in breaking the hiding of TC_Σ. Formally $\mathcal{A}^{\mathsf{TC}_\Sigma}$, interacting with the challenger for the hiding of TC_Σ, works as follows:

1. Upon receiving the first round from $\mathcal{A}^{\mathsf{swi}}$ in the left session, $\mathcal{A}^{\mathsf{TC}_\Sigma}$ computes ls^2 and sends it as the challenge message together with vk and ρ.
2. $\mathcal{A}^{\mathsf{TC}_\Sigma}$, upon receiving $\mathtt{com}$ from the challenger, uses it to compute and send the second round of SWI to $\mathcal{A}^{\mathsf{swi}}$ on the left session.
3. Let $\overline{p}(\lambda)$ be the probability that a valid signature w.r.t. to vk is received in the third message of the left session by $\mathcal{A}^{\mathsf{swi}}$.
4. If $\overline{p}(\lambda)$ is negligible close to $p_1(\lambda)$ then outputs 0, outputs 1 otherwise.[14]

We conclude the security proof by observing that the probability of $\mathcal{A}^{\mathsf{swi}}$ to send a pair $(x, w) \in \mathsf{Rel}_L$ in the third round of $\mathcal{H}_1^{\mathsf{rew}}(1^\lambda, z)$ is negligibly close to the probability to the probability of receiving a pair $(x, w) \in \mathsf{Rel}_L$ in the third round of $\mathcal{H}_2(1^\lambda, z)$. If it is not the case, then $\mathcal{A}^{\mathsf{swi}}$ can be used to break the hiding of TC_Σ. □

[14] The output values are computed according to Definition 2.16.

We recall that the transcript of an execution of $\mathcal{H}_2(1^\lambda, z)$ differs from $\mathcal{H}_1^{\mathsf{rew}}(1^\lambda, z)$ in the way the commitment $(\rho, \mathtt{com})$ of TC_Σ and the corresponding decommitment information are computed. To prove that $\mathsf{wimim}_{\mathcal{H}_2}(1^\lambda, z) \approx \mathsf{wimim}_{\mathcal{H}_1^{\mathsf{rew}}}(1^\lambda, z)$ we proceed by contradiction constructing an adversary $\mathcal{A}^{\mathsf{TC}_\Sigma}$ for the adaptive trapdoorness property of the two-round instance-dependent trapdoor commitment scheme TC_Σ. Roughly speaking, we are assuming by contradiction that there exists an adversary $\mathcal{A}^{\mathsf{swi}}$ and a distinguisher $\mathcal{D}^{\mathsf{swi}}$ that distinguishes $\mathsf{wimim}_{\mathcal{H}_2}(1^\lambda, z)$ from $\mathsf{wimim}_{\mathcal{H}_1^{\mathsf{rew}}}(1^\lambda, z)$. Therefore, we can construct an adversary $\mathcal{A}^{\mathsf{TC}_\Sigma}$ that interacts with $\mathcal{A}^{\mathsf{swi}}$ in the left and the right sessions according to both $\mathcal{H}_1^{\mathsf{rew}}(1^\lambda, z)$ and $\mathcal{H}_2(1^\lambda, z)$ for all messages except for the messages of TC_Σ. For these messages $\mathcal{A}^{\mathsf{TC}_\Sigma}$ acts as a proxy between $\mathcal{A}^{\mathsf{swi}}$ and the challenger (involved in the adaptive-trapdoor security game) in the left session.

Let $\tilde{x}_1, \ldots, \tilde{x}_{\mathsf{poly}(\lambda)}$ be the statements proved in the right sessions by $\mathcal{A}^{\mathsf{swi}}$. $\mathcal{A}^{\mathsf{TC}_\Sigma}$ extracts from all the right sessions the witnesses $\tilde{w}_1, \ldots, \tilde{w}_{\mathsf{poly}(\lambda)}$ for $\tilde{x}_1, \ldots, \tilde{x}_{\mathsf{poly}(\lambda)}$ relying on the adaptive-input PoK property of LS. Then $\mathcal{A}^{\mathsf{TC}_\Sigma}$ runs the distinguisher $\mathcal{D}^{\mathsf{swi}}$ on input the first γ-bits of each witnesses, namely, $\tilde{w}_1^\gamma, \ldots, \tilde{w}_{\mathsf{poly}(\lambda)}^\gamma$, and outputs what $\mathcal{D}^{\mathsf{swi}}$ outputs.

Formally, against the challenger of adaptive trapdoorness $\mathcal{C}^{\mathsf{TC}_\Sigma}$, $\mathcal{A}^{\mathsf{TC}_\Sigma}$ works as follows:

1. Upon receiving the first round from $\mathcal{A}^{\mathsf{swi}}$, $\mathcal{A}^{\mathsf{TC}_\Sigma}$ computes ls^2 and sends it as the challenge message together with ρ and vk to $\mathcal{C}^{\mathsf{TC}_\Sigma}$.
2. $\mathcal{A}^{\mathsf{TC}_\Sigma}$, upon receiving $\mathtt{com}$ from $\mathcal{C}^{\mathsf{TC}_\Sigma}$, uses it to compute and send the second round of SWI to $\mathcal{A}^{\mathsf{swi}}$ on the left.
3. $\mathcal{A}^{\mathsf{TC}_\Sigma}$ extracts two valid signatures of two different messages from the left session therefore obtaining the trapdoor $\mathtt{tk}$ for TC_Σ. Then $\mathcal{A}^{\mathsf{TC}_\Sigma}$ sends $\mathtt{tk}$ to $\mathcal{C}^{\mathsf{TC}_\Sigma}$.
4. Upon receiving $\mathtt{dec}$ from $\mathcal{C}^{\mathsf{TC}_\Sigma}$, $\mathcal{A}^{\mathsf{TC}_\Sigma}$ uses $\mathtt{dec}$ to complete the left session against $\mathcal{A}^{\mathsf{swi}}$.
5. $\mathcal{A}^{\mathsf{TC}_\Sigma}$ uses the extractor of LS to extract from the $\mathsf{poly}(\lambda)$ right sessions the witnesses used by $\mathcal{A}^{\mathsf{swi}}$ to compute the LS PoKs (the witnesses correspond to statements $\tilde{x}_i$ proved by $\mathcal{A}^{\mathsf{swi}}$ in the i-th right session, for $i = 1, \ldots, \mathsf{poly}(\lambda)$). We recall that the extractor of LS succeeds with non-negligible probability from the adaptive-input AoK property of LS. Indeed, since we have proved in the previous hybrid experiment that event NoExt happens with negligible probability, so is in this hybrid experiment. If it is not the case then we can construct another adversary that breaks the adaptive trapdoorness property of TC_Σ.
6. From what we argue above we can assume that the extraction succeeds with non-negligible probability, and thus $\mathcal{A}^{\mathsf{TC}_\Sigma}$ can run the distinguisher $\mathcal{D}^{\mathsf{swi}}$ on input the first γ-bits of each extracted witnesses to distinguish $\mathsf{wimim}_{\mathcal{H}_2}(1^\lambda, z)$ from $\mathsf{wimim}_{\mathcal{H}_1^{\mathsf{rew}}}(1^\lambda, z)$, thus breaking the trapdoorness property of TC_Σ.

We now argue that rewinds made on the right sessions (during the step 5) do not affect the reduction. We distinguish between three kinds of right sessions: $\mathsf{3Rewind}$, $\mathsf{AllRewind}$, and $\mathsf{NoRewind}$.

- A right session is 3Rewind if during the extraction procedure is required, in the left session, to play again *only* the fourth round having received a different third round (i.e., a different ls^3).
- A right session is AllRewind if during the extraction procedure is required, in the left session, to play again *the entire* left session due to a different first round $(\mathsf{vk}', \mathsf{ls}^{1'}, \rho')$ received from $\mathcal{A}^{\mathsf{swi}}$.
- A right session is NoRewind if it is neither 3Rewind nor AllRewind.

It is easy to see that NoRewind right sessions do not interfere with the reduction, that is, the left session is not actually rewound because both the first and the third rounds stay the same during the extraction. It is less trivial to deal with the 3Rewind and AllRewind sessions but still that sessions do not cause issue during the reduction. When the rewinds occur in the 3Rewind right session, to compute the fourth round it is possible to reuse $(\mathtt{dec}, \mathsf{ls}^2)$ in order to compute an accepting transcript for LS $(\mathsf{ls}^1, \mathsf{ls}^2, \mathsf{ls}^{3'}, \mathsf{ls}^{4'})$ w.r.t. $\mathsf{ls}^{3'}$ and a (potentially different) statement x' that is provided in the third round by $\mathcal{A}^{\mathsf{swi}}$. This is possible because of the delayed-input completeness property enjoyed by LS and because the witness for the theorem x' is provided by $\mathcal{A}^{\mathsf{swi}}$ in the third round of the left session. For the AllRewind right sessions, the adversary $\mathcal{A}^{\mathsf{TC}_\Sigma}$, upon receiving a new first round $(\mathsf{vk}', \mathsf{ls}^{1'}, \rho')$ from $\mathcal{A}^{\mathsf{swi}}$, starts a new interaction against the challenger of adaptive trapdoorness executing all steps described above starting from step 1 as summarized in Fig. 7.8.

- The third hybrid experiment is $\mathcal{H}_3(1^\lambda, z)$ and differs from $\mathcal{H}_2(1^\lambda, z)$ in the way the transcript for LS is computed. More precisely, the Special HVZK simulator $\mathcal{S}$ of LS is used to compute the messages ls^2 and ls^4 instead of using the honest prover

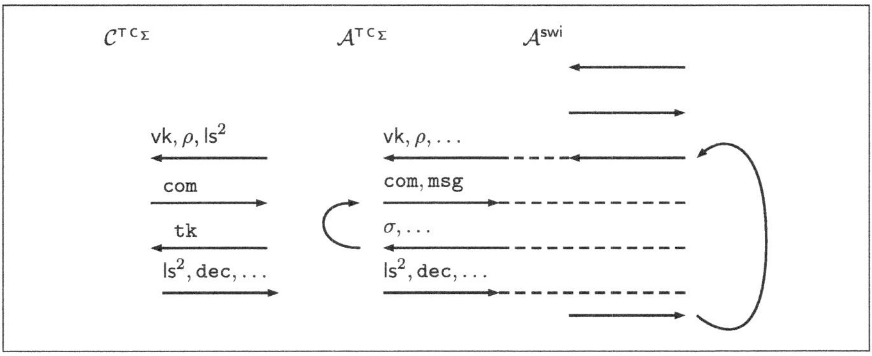

Fig. 7.8 During the reduction to the adaptive trapdoorness of TC_Σ could be required to play the left session multiple times because of the rewinds made in a AllRewind right session. In general this happens when it is required to recompute the second round of the left session, due to a new first round received by $\mathcal{A}^{\mathsf{swi}}$ (in the left session). In the figure it is also showed that, for every new interaction that $\mathcal{A}^{\mathsf{TC}_\Sigma}$ starts against C^{TC_Σ}, a new extraction of the trapdoor information $\mathtt{tk}$ is required in order to complete the reduction. We observe that the extraction of $\mathtt{tk}$ does not disturb the extraction made on the right session

procedure $\mathcal{P}$. We observe that this is possible because in this hybrid experiment the commitment $(\rho, \mathtt{com})$ can be opened to any value ls^2 due to the trapdoor property of TC_Σ. Therefore, after receiving ls^1 in the first round, and (ls^3, x, w) in the third round from $\mathcal{A}^{\mathsf{swi}}$, $(\mathsf{ls}^1, \mathsf{ls}^3, x)$ are given as input of $\mathcal{S}$ that will output $\mathsf{ls}^2, \mathsf{ls}^4$. These values are then used to compute the fourth round of the left session.
Before proving that $\mathsf{wimim}_{\mathcal{H}_2}(1^\lambda, z) \approx \mathsf{wimim}_{\mathcal{H}_3}(1^\lambda, z)$ we observe that the first three rounds of the left interaction in $\mathcal{H}_3(1^\lambda, z)$ are identically distributed to the first three rounds of $\mathcal{H}_2(1^\lambda, z)$. Therefore the probability of receiving a pair $(x, w) \in \mathsf{Rel}_L$ in the third round from $\mathcal{A}^{\mathsf{swi}}$ is the same in both $\mathcal{H}_2(1^\lambda, z)$ and $\mathcal{H}_3(1^\lambda, z)$. For the same arguments also the extraction of the signatures holds with the same probability in both $\mathcal{H}_2(1^\lambda, z)$ and $\mathcal{H}_3(1^\lambda, z)$.
We now prove that $\mathsf{wimim}_{\mathcal{H}_2}(1^\lambda, z) \approx \mathsf{wimim}_{\mathcal{H}_3}(1^\lambda, z)$ by contradiction constructing an adversary $\mathcal{A}^{\mathsf{SHVZK}}$ for the adaptive Special HVZK of LS. This adversary $\mathcal{A}^{\mathsf{SHVZK}}$ uses the adversary $\mathcal{A}^{\mathsf{swi}}$ and the distinguisher $\mathcal{D}^{\mathsf{swi}}$ that distinguishes $\mathsf{wimim}_{\mathcal{H}_2}(1^\lambda, z)$ from $\mathsf{wimim}_{\mathcal{H}_3}(1^\lambda, z)$ that exist by contradiction. Let $\mathcal{C}^{\mathsf{SHVZK}}$ be the challenger of adaptive Special HVZK. The reduction works as follows:

1. $\mathcal{A}^{\mathsf{SHVZK}}$ runs $\mathcal{A}^{\mathsf{swi}}$ (both on the left and on the right sessions) according to both $\mathcal{H}_2(1^\lambda, z)$ and $\mathcal{H}_3(1^\lambda, z)$ until the third round of the left session is received from $\mathcal{A}^{\mathsf{swi}}$.
2. $\mathcal{A}^{\mathsf{SHVZK}}$ extracts from the left session two valid signatures for two different messages (as described before), and then sends to the challenger of Special HVZK $\mathcal{C}^{\mathsf{SHVZK}}$ the statement x the witness w (provided in the third round of the left session by $\mathcal{A}^{\mathsf{swi}}$) and the pair $(\mathsf{ls}^1, \mathsf{ls}^3)$ received in the first and third round from $\mathcal{A}^{\mathsf{swi}}$.
3. $\mathcal{A}^{\mathsf{SHVZK}}$ upon receiving the messages $(\mathsf{ls}^2, \mathsf{ls}^4)$ from the $\mathcal{C}^{\mathsf{SHVZK}}$ uses them to compute and sends the last round of SWI.
4. $\mathcal{A}^{\mathsf{SHVZK}}$ extracts from the $\mathsf{poly}(\lambda)$ right sessions the witnesses for the statements proved by $\mathcal{A}^{\mathsf{swi}}$ as follows.
   For the $\mathsf{NoRewind}$ and $\mathsf{AllRewind}$ right sessions the extractor procedure is the same as described before. That is, we use the PoK extractor of LS to extract the witnesses for the statements proved in these sessions. Note that the extractor of LS succeeds with non-negligible probability due to the adaptive-input AoK property of LS and the adaptive Special HVZK of LS. In more detail if the extractor fails with non-negligible probability then the event NoExt holds with non-negligible probability, and it is possible to show an adversary $\mathcal{A}^{\mathsf{SHVZK}}$ that breaks the adaptive Special HVZK of LS. Indeed, if NoExt holds with non-negligible probability, then $\mathcal{A}^{\mathsf{SHVZK}}$ has a non-negligible advantage since we are proved earlier that NoExt holds with negligible probability when the values $\mathsf{ls}^2, \mathsf{ls}^4$ are computed using the honest prover procedure $\mathcal{P}$.
   In addition, for the $\mathsf{AllRewind}$ right sessions $\mathcal{A}^{\mathsf{SHVZK}}$ interacts against $\mathcal{A}^{\mathsf{swi}}$ executing the above steps, starting from step 1, every time that a first round is received in the left session, as showed in Fig. 7.9. We remark that this is possible because we are considering a challenger for adaptive Special HVZK.

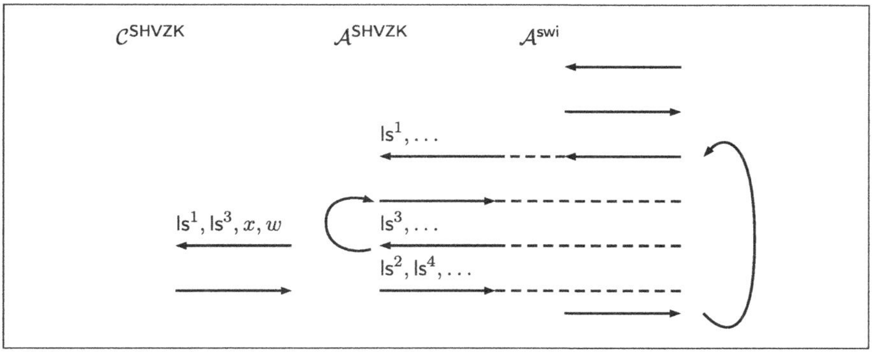

Fig. 7.9 During the reduction to the adaptive Special HVZK of LS could be required to play the left session multiple times because of the rewinds made in the right session. In general this happens when it is required to recompute the fourth round of the left session, due to a new first round received by $\mathcal{A}^{\mathsf{swi}}$ (in the left session). In the figure it is also showed that, for every new interaction that $\mathcal{A}^{\mathsf{SHVZK}}$ starts against $\mathcal{C}^{\mathsf{SHVZK}}$, a new extraction of the trapdoor information $\mathtt{tk}$ is required in order to complete the reduction. We observe that the extraction of $\mathtt{tk}$ does not disturb the extraction made on the right session

For the $\mathsf{3Rewind}$ sessions we need to use a different approach, due to fact that we cannot use reuse ls^2 in order to compute an accepting transcript for LS $(\mathsf{ls}^1, \mathsf{ls}^2, \mathsf{ls}^{3'}, \mathsf{ls}^{4'})$ with $\mathsf{ls}^3 \neq \mathsf{ls}^{3'}$. Therefore the extraction procedure of the witness for the statement $\tilde{x}_j$ proved by $\mathcal{A}^{\mathsf{swi}}$ in the j-th right session (with $j = 1, \ldots, \mathsf{poly}(\lambda)$) works as follows. The fourth round of the left session is played again by decommitting $(\rho, \mathtt{com})$ to a different value $\mathsf{ls}^{2'}$ generated by running $\mathcal{P}$ on input 1^λ, ℓ and ls^1. We remark that it is possible to open $(\rho, \mathtt{com})$ to a different value because we are using TFake_Σ to compute both commitment and decommitment informations. In order to end up in obtaining that session j is completed successfully, multiple rewinds trying with different polynomial values for $\mathsf{ls}^{2'}$ could be required, until a successful $\mathsf{ls}^{2'}$ is found. Let $\tilde{x}_j^*$ be the statement proved by $\mathcal{A}^{\mathsf{swi}}$ in the j-th right session when a successful $\mathsf{ls}^{2'}$ is found. $\mathcal{A}^{\mathsf{SHVZK}}$ runs the extractor of LS in the j-th right session in order to extract the witness for the theorem $\tilde{x}_j^*$ (the same argument discussed above need to be used here in order to ensure that the extractor of LS succeeds with non-negligible probability). Observe that when it is required to recompute the fourth round during the extraction procedure, now it is possible to reuse $(\mathtt{dec}, \mathsf{ls}^{2'})$ in order to compute an accepting transcript for LS $(\mathsf{ls}^1, \mathsf{ls}^{2'}, \mathsf{ls}^{3'}, \mathsf{ls}^{4'})$ by running $\mathcal{P}$, for every $\mathsf{ls}^{3'}$ received by $\mathcal{A}^{\mathsf{swi}}$. If the extraction is successful then $\mathcal{A}^{\mathsf{SHVZK}}$ has obtained a witness for $\tilde{x}_j^*$. The crucial observation is that $\tilde{x}_j^*$ has the same witness of $\tilde{x}_j$. Indeed, in the security proof of this lemma, we are assuming the $\mathcal{A}^{\mathsf{swi}}$ can choose the statement to be proved in the last round of every right session, but the family of statements $\mathcal{X}_w$ has to be fixed in the second round of every right sessions.

5. From what we argue above the extraction of the witnesses succeeds with non-negligible probability, and thus $\mathcal{A}^{\mathsf{SHVZK}}$ runs the distinguisher $\mathcal{D}^{\mathsf{swi}}$ on input the first γ-bits of each extracted witnesses to distinguish $\mathsf{wimim}_{\mathcal{H}_2}(1^\lambda, z)$ from $\mathsf{wimim}_{\mathcal{H}_3}(1^\lambda, z)$ in order to break the Special HVZK of LS.

The proof ends by observing that the following holds:

$$\mathsf{wimim}_{\mathsf{SWI}}(1^\lambda, z) = \mathsf{wimim}_{\mathcal{H}_1}(1^\lambda, z) \approx \mathsf{wimim}_{\mathcal{H}_1^{\mathsf{rew}}}(1^\lambda, z) \approx$$
$$\mathsf{wimim}_{\mathcal{H}_2}(1^\lambda, z) \approx \mathsf{wimim}_{\mathcal{H}_3}(1^\lambda, z) = \mathsf{sim}_{\mathsf{SWI}}^{\mathcal{S}^{\mathsf{swi}}}(1^\lambda, z).$$

7.6.2 *Formal Proof of Theorem 7.2*

In this section we give more detail on the hybrid experiments and on the security proof.

- The first experiment that we consider is $\mathcal{H}_1^m(z)$. In this, in the left session $\mathsf{NM4Sen}$ commits to m, while in the i-th right session, for $i = 1, \ldots, \mathsf{poly}(\lambda)$, $\mathsf{NM4Rec}_i$ interacts with $\mathcal{A}^{\mathsf{NM4Com}}$. For ease of exposition we consider that the messages of SWI are organized as a query. That is, an MiM adversary of an execution of SWI expects to receive a query query that contains both the queries of the left and the right sessions. Following [86, 105], we make the following assumptions about the queries:

- The same query is never asked twice.
- A query is a partial transcript $(b_1, a_1, \ldots, b_i)$ of the protocol. Moreover, whenever such query is made, all proper prefixes of this query were previously queried, namely, all sequences of the form $(b_1, a_1, \ldots, b_j)$ for $j < i$.

Therefore we can assume that a query has the following form $\mathsf{query} = (\mathsf{prefix}, \mathsf{q})$ where prefix are the messages of query previously queried, and q is a new message. The first message of a query is q^s and is the message sent to initiate new execution of SWI. Therefore when a query is composed only of the starting message $\mathsf{query} = (\mathsf{q}^s)$ the experiment starts $\mathcal{A}^{\mathsf{NM4Com}}$.

More formally the experiment $\mathcal{H}_1^m(z)$ is defined in the following way. The possible values of q w.r.t. the messages of $\mathcal{P}^{\mathsf{swi}}$ are as follows:

- Message $\mathsf{q}_2^{\mathsf{L}}$ is the message sent at the second round of SWI protocol in a left session.
- Message $\mathsf{q}_4^{\mathsf{L}}$ is the message sent at the fourth round of SWI protocol in a left session.

The possible values of q w.r.t. the messages of $\mathcal{V}_i^{\mathsf{swi}}$, with $i = 1, \ldots, \mathsf{poly}(\lambda)$, are as follows:

- Message $\mathsf{q}_1^{\mathsf{R},\mathsf{i}}$ is the message sent at the first round of SWI protocol in a i-th right session.
- Message $\mathsf{q}_3^{\mathsf{R},\mathsf{i}}$ is the message sent at the third round of SWI protocol in a i-th right session.

Let table be a lookup table, in which each row contains a query query and the messages (and the randomness used to compute these messages) of Π_{wom} computed when query was processed. We refer to that messages as τ_{wom}. When a query query $=$ (prefix, q) is received the experiment looks up in table for the query prefix in order to recover τ_{wom}. Then, the experiment reconstructs the partial transcript τ_{NM4Com} of Π_{NM4Com} computed according to the messages of prefix. We assume without loss of generality that $\mathcal{A}^{\mathsf{NM4Com}}$ is deterministic, therefore the experiment reconstructs τ_{NM4Com} interacting with $\mathcal{A}^{\mathsf{NM4Com}}$ using the messages of τ_{wom} contained in prefix. After that, the new message q is processed and depending on the value of q, the experiment acts in different way. More precisely, if q is a message of $\mathcal{P}^{\mathsf{swi}}$, the experiment interacts with $\mathcal{A}^{\mathsf{NM4Com}}$ acting as NM4Sen would do for the messages of Π_{wom} forwarding the messages contained in query in order to act as $\mathcal{P}^{\mathsf{swi}}$. Similarly, if q is a message of the right session, let us say, a message from $\mathcal{V}_i^{\mathsf{swi}}$, the experiment interacts with $\mathcal{A}^{\mathsf{NM4Com}}$ acting as $\mathsf{NM4Rec}_i$ would do for the messages of Π_{wom} and forwarding to $\mathcal{A}^{\mathsf{NM4Com}}$ q. When the execution against $\mathcal{A}^{\mathsf{NM4Com}}$ finishes a new entry in table is created in order to memorize the received query and τ'_{wom}, where τ'_{wom} contains the messages (and the randomness used to compute these messages) of Π_{wom} obtained when query is processed. Then the experiment collects the messages w.r.t. SWI received by $\mathcal{A}^{\mathsf{NM4Com}}$ in an answer answer that is the answer to the asked query. More formally, the experiment works as follows.

Upon receiving query $=$ (prefix, q), if query $= \mathsf{q}^s$ then start $\mathcal{A}^{\mathsf{NM4Com}}$, otherwise execute the following steps:

1. Look up in table for a query that correspond to prefix and recover τ_{wom}.
2. In the left session interact with $\mathcal{A}^{\mathsf{NM4Com}}$ forwarding the messages contained in prefix w.r.t. SWI in order to act as $\mathcal{P}^{\mathsf{swi}}$ would do. Use the messages of prefix of τ_{wom} in order to act as NM4Sen would do.
3. In the i-th right session, for $i = 1, \dots, \mathsf{poly}(\lambda)$, forwarding the messages contained in prefix w.r.t. SWI in order to act as $\mathcal{V}_i^{\mathsf{swi}}$ would do. Furthermore, interact with $\mathcal{A}^{\mathsf{NM4Com}}$ using the messages of prefix of τ_{wom} in order to act as $\mathsf{NM4Rec}_i$.
4. Set $\tau'_{\mathsf{wom}} = \tau_{\mathsf{wom}}$ and process q computing the following steps.

Left session.

- If $\mathsf{q} = \mathsf{q}_2^{\mathsf{L}}$ then computes the following steps. Upon receiving $\mathsf{wom}^1, \mathsf{swi}^1$ from $\mathcal{A}^{\mathsf{NM4Com}}$, run $\mathsf{Sen}_{\mathsf{wom}}$ on input 1^λ, $\mathtt{id}$, wom^1 and m thus obtaining the second round wom^2 of Π_{wom} and $\mathtt{dec}_{\mathsf{wom}}$ s.t. $(m, \mathtt{dec}_{\mathsf{wom}})$ constitutes the decommitment information. Add $(\mathsf{wom}^2, m, \mathtt{dec}_{\mathsf{wom}})$ (according to the randomness used to compute it) to τ'_{wom}. Recover swi^2 from $\mathsf{q}_2^{\mathsf{L}}$ and send $(\mathsf{wom}^2, \mathsf{swi}^2)$ to $\mathcal{A}^{\mathsf{NM4Com}}$.
- If $\mathsf{q} = \mathsf{q}_4^{\mathsf{L}}$ then compute the following steps. Upon receiving $\mathsf{wom}^3, \mathsf{swi}^3$ from $\mathcal{A}^{\mathsf{NM4Com}}$ run $\mathsf{Sen}_{\mathsf{wom}}$ on input wom^3 thus obtaining the fourth round wom^4 of

Π_{wom}. Add wom^4 (according to the randomness used to compute it) to τ'_{wom} and send $(\mathsf{wom}^4, \mathsf{swi}^4)$ to $\mathcal{A}^{\mathsf{NM4Com}}$.

i **-th right session.**

- If $\mathsf{q} = \mathsf{q}_1^{\mathsf{R},\mathsf{i}}$ compute the following steps. Run $\mathsf{Rec}_{\mathsf{wom}}$ on input 1^λ, $\tilde{\mathtt{id}}_i$ thus obtaining the first round $\tilde{\mathsf{wom}}_i^1$ of Π_{wom}. Update τ'_{wom} with $\tilde{\mathsf{wom}}_i^1$ and the randomness used to compute it. Recover $\tilde{\mathsf{swi}}_i^1$ from $\mathsf{q}_1^{\mathsf{R},\mathsf{i}}$ and send $(\tilde{\mathsf{wom}}_i^1, \tilde{\mathsf{swi}}_i^1)$ to $\mathcal{A}^{\mathsf{NM4Com}}$.
- If $\mathsf{q} = \mathsf{q}_3^{\mathsf{R},\mathsf{i}}$ computes the following steps. Upon receiving $(\tilde{\mathsf{wom}}_i^2, \tilde{\mathsf{swi}}_i^2)$ from $\mathcal{A}^{\mathsf{NM4Com}}$. Run $\mathsf{Rec}_{\mathsf{wom}}$ on input $\tilde{\mathsf{wom}}_i^2$ thus obtaining the third round $\tilde{\mathsf{wom}}_i^3$ of Π_{wom}. Update τ'_{wom} with $\tilde{\mathsf{wom}}_i^3$ and the randomness used to compute it. Recover $\tilde{\mathsf{swi}}_i^3$ from $\mathsf{q}_3^{\mathsf{R},\mathsf{i}}$ and send $(\tilde{\mathsf{wom}}_i^3, \tilde{\mathsf{swi}}_i^3)$ to $\mathcal{A}^{\mathsf{NM4Com}}$.

5. Construct the answer answer for the query query as follows.
   5.1. In the left session if $(\mathsf{swi}^1, \mathsf{wom}^1)$ is received add swi^1 to answer. Otherwise if $(\mathsf{swi}^3, \mathsf{wom}^3)$ is received recover $\mathsf{wom}^1, \mathsf{wom}^2, m, \mathtt{dec}_{\mathsf{wom}}$ from τ'_{wom}, set $x = (\mathsf{wom}^1, \mathsf{wom}^2, \mathsf{wom}^3, \mathsf{wom}^4, \mathtt{id})$ and $w = (m, \mathtt{dec}_{\mathsf{wom}})$, and add $(x, w, \mathsf{swi}^1, \mathsf{swi}^3)$ to answer.
   5.2. For the i-th right session add to answer the messages of SWI received from $\mathcal{A}^{\mathsf{NM4Com}}$ in i-th right session, for $i = 1, \ldots, \mathsf{poly}(\lambda)$.
6. Memorize query and τ'_{wom} in a new row of table and return answer.

Clearly we have that $\mathsf{mim}_{\Pi_{\mathsf{NM4Com}}}^{\mathcal{A}_{\mathsf{NMCom}},m}(z) = \mathsf{mim}_{\mathcal{H}_1^m}^{\mathcal{A}_{\mathsf{NMCom}},m}(z)$. We prove the following claim.

Claim Let $\bar{p}_i$ be the probability that for $i = 1, \ldots, \mathsf{poly}(\lambda)$ in the i-th right sessions of $\mathcal{H}_1^m(z)$ $\mathcal{A}^{\mathsf{NM4Com}}$ successfully commits to a message $\tilde{m}_i = \perp$, then $\bar{p}_i < \nu(\lambda)$ for some negligible function ν.

Proof We prove this claim by contradiction: we assume that there exists a right session i where $\mathcal{A}^{\mathsf{NM4Com}}$ commits to $\perp$, then the statement proved by SWI in the i-th right session is false, this contradicts the adaptive-input AoK property of SWI. In more detail, we can use the extractor of SWI in order to extract the witness $\tilde{w}_i$ s.t. $(\tilde{x}_i, \tilde{w}_i) \in \mathsf{Rel}_{\mathsf{L}}$, where $\tilde{x}_i$ is the statement proved by $\mathcal{A}^{\mathsf{NM4Com}}$ in i-th right session. Since the extractor of SWI succeeds with non-negligible probability we can recover with non-negligible probability the witness $\tilde{w}_i$ that corresponds to the decommitment informations of the well-formed commitment computed by $\mathcal{A}^{\mathsf{NM4Com}}$ in i-th right session. This implies that $\mathcal{A}^{\mathsf{NM4Com}}$ commits to a message $\tilde{m}_i = \perp$ in i-th right session with negligible probability. □

- We consider the experiment $\mathcal{H}_1^0(z)$ that corresponds to $\mathcal{H}_1^m(z)$ with the only difference that the message committed using Π_{wom} is 0^λ instead of m. We observe that $\mathsf{mim}_{\mathcal{H}_1^0}^{\mathcal{A}^{\mathsf{NM4Com}},m}(z) = \mathsf{sim}_{\Pi_{\mathsf{NM4Com}}}^{\mathsf{Sim}^{\mathsf{NM4Com}}}(1^\lambda, z)$ and we prove the following claim.

Claim Let $\bar{p}_i$ be the probability that for $i = 1, \ldots, \mathsf{poly}(\lambda)$ in the i-th right sessions of $\mathcal{H}_1^0(z)$ $\mathcal{A}^{\mathsf{NM4Com}}$ successfully commits to a message $\tilde{m}_i = \perp$, then $\bar{p}_i < \nu(\lambda)$ for some negligible function ν.

The security proof of this claim follows strictly the one of Claim 7.6.2.

- We now consider the second hybrid experiment $\mathcal{H}_2^m(z)$ that differs from $\mathcal{H}_1^m(z)$ in the way the transcript for SWI is computed. More precisely, in this case the transcript for SWI is computed by using the simulator $\mathcal{S}^{\mathsf{swi}}$[15] of SWI. In the hybrid experiment $\mathcal{H}_2^m(z)$ we process the queries query made by $\mathcal{S}^{\mathsf{swi}}$ in the same way as we described in the hybrid $\mathcal{H}_1^m(z)$. We prove the following claim.

Claim For all $m \in \{0,1\}^{\mathsf{poly}(\lambda)}$ it holds that $\mathsf{mim}_{\mathcal{H}_1^m}^{\mathcal{A}^{\mathsf{NM4Com}},m}(z) \approx \mathsf{mim}_{\mathcal{H}_2^m}^{\mathcal{A}^{\mathsf{NM4Com}},m}(z)$.

Suppose by contradiction that there exist adversary $\mathcal{A}^{\mathsf{NM4Com}}$ and a distinguisher $\mathcal{D}^{\mathsf{NM4Com}}$ that can tell apart such two distributions. We can use this adversary and the associated distinguisher to construct an MiM adversary $\mathcal{A}^{\mathsf{swi}}$ and a distinguisher $\mathcal{D}^{\mathsf{swi}}$ that breaks the adaptive-input SimWI property of SWI. Observe that this reduction is possible due to the adaptiveness of SWI; indeed, in every right sessions the statement proved by $\mathcal{A}^{\mathsf{NM4Com}}$ is fully defined only in the last round. We also recall that even if the statement to be proved is specified in the last round, the family of theorems $\mathcal{X}_w$ has to be fixed at second round. Since Π_{wom} fixes the decommitment informations in the second round, then also $\mathcal{X}_w$ is implicitly fixed at second round.

Let C^{swi} be the challenger of SimWI. $\mathcal{A}^{\mathsf{swi}}$ interacts with $\mathcal{A}^{\mathsf{NM4Com}}$ forwarding the messages of SWI that receive from C^{swi} and computing the messages of Π_{wom} on his own. In more detail $\mathcal{A}^{\mathsf{swi}}$ acts against C^{swi} processing his queries in the same way that is described in both the experiments $\mathcal{H}_1^m(z)$ and $\mathcal{H}_2^m(z)$. Let's now describe how $\mathcal{D}^{\mathsf{swi}}$ works. $\mathcal{D}^{\mathsf{swi}}$ takes as input the view $\mathcal{A}^{\mathsf{swi}}$ the first γ-bits of the witness $\tilde{w}_1, \ldots, \tilde{w}_{\mathsf{poly}(\lambda)}$, namely, $\tilde{w}_1^{\gamma}, \ldots, \tilde{w}_{\mathsf{poly}(\lambda)}^{\gamma}$, associated to the statement proved by $\mathcal{A}^{\mathsf{swi}}$ and the bits $b_1, \ldots, b_{\mathsf{poly}(\lambda)}$ s.t. $w_i^{\gamma} = \perp$ iff $b_i = 0$ with $i = 1, \ldots, \mathsf{poly}(\lambda)$.

Every $\tilde{w}_i^{\gamma} \neq \perp$ corresponds to the message $\tilde{m}_i$ of the commitment computed using Π_{wom} in i-th right session, for $i = 1, \ldots, \mathsf{poly}(\lambda)$. Therefore, $\mathcal{A}^{\mathsf{swi}}$ recovers the messages $\tilde{m}_1, \ldots, \tilde{m}_{\mathsf{poly}(\lambda)}$ committed in the right sessions setting $\tilde{m}_i = \perp$ if $\tilde{w}_i^{\gamma} = \perp$. Finally, $\mathcal{D}^{\mathsf{swi}}$ reconstructs the view of $\mathcal{A}^{\mathsf{NM4Com}}$ (by using the randomness of $\mathcal{A}^{\mathsf{swi}}$ contained in $\mathcal{A}^{\mathsf{swi}}$'s view) and gives it and the messages $\tilde{m}_1, \ldots, \tilde{m}_{\mathsf{poly}(\lambda)}$ as inputs of $\mathcal{D}^{\mathsf{NM4Com}}$ giving in output what $\mathcal{D}^{\mathsf{NM4Com}}$ outputs. Since by contradiction $\mathcal{D}^{\mathsf{NM4Com}}$ distinguishes between $\mathsf{mim}_{\mathcal{H}_1^m}^{\mathcal{A}^{\mathsf{NM4Com}},m}(z)$ and $\mathsf{mim}_{\mathcal{H}_2^m}^{\mathcal{A}^{\mathsf{NM4Com}},m}(z)$ we have that $\mathcal{D}^{\mathsf{swi}}$ tells apart whether $\mathcal{A}^{\mathsf{swi}}$ interacts with the simulator of SWI or not. The proof ends with the observation that if C^{swi} computes the transcript of SWI as the simulator for SWI does, then $\mathcal{A}^{\mathsf{NM4Com}}$ acts as in $\mathcal{H}_2^m(z)$, otherwise he acts as in $\mathcal{H}_1^m(z)$.

---

[15] Following [86, 105] we assume that if $(b_1, a_1, \ldots, b_m, a_m)$ is the transcript that appears in the final output of $\mathcal{S}^{\mathsf{swi}}$, then $\mathcal{S}^{\mathsf{swi}}$ has queried $\mathcal{A}^{\mathsf{swi}}$ on $(b_1, a_1, \ldots, b_m, a_m)$.

– We consider the experiment $\mathcal{H}_2^0(z)$ that corresponds to $\mathcal{H}_2^m(z)$ with the only difference that $\mathsf{NM4Sen}$ commits using Π_{wom} to a message 0^λ instead of m. We prove the following claims.

Claim For all $m \in \{0, 1\}^{\mathsf{poly}(\lambda)}$ it holds that $\mathsf{mim}_{\mathcal{H}_1^0}^{\mathcal{A}^{\mathsf{NM4Com}},m}(z) \approx \mathsf{mim}_{\mathcal{H}_2^0}^{\mathcal{A}^{\mathsf{NM4Com}},m}(z)$.

The security proof of this claim follows strictly the one of Claim 7.6.2.

Claim For all $m \in \{0, 1\}^{\mathsf{poly}(\lambda)}$ it holds that $\mathsf{mim}_{\mathcal{H}_2^m}^{\mathcal{A}^{\mathsf{NM4Com}},m}(z) \approx \mathsf{mim}_{\mathcal{H}_2^0}^{\mathcal{A}^{\mathsf{NM4Com}},m}(z)$.

The proof follows from the weak concurrent non-malleability property of Π_{wom}. Indeed observe that here it suffices to rely on the *weak* concurrent NM commitment because we are guaranteed (from the previous arguments) that whenever $\mathcal{A}^{\mathsf{NM4Com}}$ completes a commitment in the i-th right session, with $i = 1, \ldots, \mathsf{poly}(\lambda)$, the corresponding message committed through Π_{wom} is different from $\perp$ with overwhelming probability in both $\mathcal{H}_2^m(z)$ and $\mathcal{H}_2^0(z)$. To prove the indistinguishability between those two hybrids experiments, we proceed by contradiction constructing an adversary $\mathcal{A}^{\mathsf{wom}}$ that breaks the *weak* concurrent non-malleability property of Π_{wom}.

Let C^{wom} be the challenger of the weak concurrent NM commitment and let $m_1, \ldots, m_{\mathsf{poly}}(\lambda)$ with $m, 0^\lambda$ be the challenge messages. $\mathcal{A}^{\mathsf{wom}}$ processes the queries sent by $\mathcal{S}^{\mathsf{swi}}$ as described in both $\mathcal{H}_2^m(z)$ and $\mathcal{H}_2^0(z)$, with the following difference. In the left session, for the messages of Π_{wom}, $\mathcal{A}^{\mathsf{wom}}$ acts as a proxy between C^{wom} and $\mathcal{A}^{\mathsf{NM4Com}}$. The same happen in the right sessions, where $\mathcal{A}^{\mathsf{wom}}$ acts as a proxy between $\mathcal{A}^{\mathsf{NM4Com}}$ and the receiver $\mathsf{Rec}_{\mathsf{wom},i}$ for $i = 1, \ldots, \mathsf{poly}(\lambda)$. More precisely $\mathcal{A}^{\mathsf{wom}}$ manages the queries made by $\mathcal{S}^{\mathsf{swi}}$ as described in both $\mathcal{H}_2^m(z)$ and $\mathcal{H}_2^0(z)$, but instead of internally run $\mathsf{Sen}_{\mathsf{wom}}$ and $\mathsf{Rec}_{\mathsf{wom}}$, in order to compute the messages of Π_{wom}, C^{wom} and the external receivers $\mathsf{Rec}_{\mathsf{wom},1} \ldots, \mathsf{Rec}_{\mathsf{wom},\mathsf{poly}(\lambda)}$ involved in the reduction are used. In this setting there are two caveats that $\mathcal{A}^{\mathsf{wom}}$ needs to address in order to successfully complete the reduction.

The first one is that $\mathcal{S}^{\mathsf{swi}}$ could rewind the entire left session during the reduction, therefore requiring to compute a new commitment for the protocol Π_{wom}. Since we are assuming that Π_{wom} is concurrent, $\mathcal{A}^{\mathsf{wom}}$ can request to receive multiple commitments for the same message m during the reduction in order to interact against $\mathcal{A}^{\mathsf{NM4Com}}$ in such a scenario. The second one is that the rewinds made by $\mathcal{S}^{\mathsf{swi}}$ in the left session could rewind the right sessions. Without loss of generality we suppose that right session affected by the rewinds made in the left session is the j-th, with $j \in \{1, \ldots, \mathsf{poly}(\lambda)\}$. If the entire right session is rewound, then $\mathcal{A}^{\mathsf{wom}}$ simply asks to start another execution with a new receiver $\mathsf{Rec}_{\mathsf{wom}',j}$ of Π_{wom}. Could also happen that $\mathsf{Rec}_{\mathsf{wom},j}$ is rewound from the third to the second round, that is, a new $\mathsf{wom}_j^{2\prime}$ is sent by $\mathcal{A}^{\mathsf{NM4Com}}$ in the right session that we are considering. In that case $\mathcal{A}^{\mathsf{wom}}$ does not forward $\mathsf{wom}_j^{2\prime}$ to $\mathsf{Rec}_{\mathsf{wom},j}$, but compute a random $\mathsf{wom}_j^{3\prime}$ and use it to reply to $\mathcal{A}^{\mathsf{NM4Com}}$. We observe that it is possible to compute $\mathsf{wom}_j^{3\prime}$ without knowing the randomness used by $\mathsf{Rec}_{\mathsf{wom},j}$ so far because Π_{wom} is public coin.

Now we are ready to show how $\mathcal{D}^{\mathsf{wom}}$ works. $\mathcal{D}^{\mathsf{wom}}$, on input the messages $\tilde{m}_1, \ldots, \tilde{m}_{\mathsf{poly}(n)}$ committed by $\mathcal{A}^{\mathsf{NM4Com}}$ and the view of $\mathcal{A}^{\mathsf{wom}}$, reconstructs the view that $\mathcal{A}^{\mathsf{NM4Com}}$ has when he played in the execution that generated the transcript of SWI given in output by $\mathcal{S}^{\mathsf{swi}}$. Then, $\mathcal{D}^{\mathsf{wom}}$ uses the view of $\mathcal{A}^{\mathsf{NM4Com}}$ along with m, 0^λ and the messages $\tilde{m}_1, \ldots, \tilde{m}_{\mathsf{poly}(n)}$ as inputs of $\mathcal{D}^{\mathsf{NM4Com}}$ giving in output what $\mathcal{D}^{\mathsf{NM4Com}}$ outputs. Since by contradiction $\mathcal{D}^{\mathsf{NM4Com}}$ distinguishes between $\mathsf{mim}_{\mathcal{H}_2^m}^{\mathcal{A}^{\mathsf{NM4Com}},m}(z)$ and $\mathsf{mim}_{\mathcal{H}_2^0}^{\mathcal{A}^{\mathsf{NM4Com}},m}(z)$ also $\mathcal{D}^{\mathsf{wom}}$ can tell apart which message was committed by C^{wom}. The proof ends with the observation that if C^{wom} commits to m $\mathcal{A}^{\mathsf{NM4Com}}$ acts as in $\mathcal{H}_2^m(z)$, otherwise he acts as in $\mathcal{H}_2^0(z)$.

The proof ends by observing that for all $m \in \{0,1\}^{\mathsf{poly}(\lambda)}$ the following holds:

$$\mathsf{mim}_{\Pi_{\mathsf{NM4Com}}}^{\mathcal{A}_{\mathsf{NMCom}},m}(z) = \mathsf{mim}_{\mathcal{H}_1^m}^{\mathcal{A}_{\mathsf{NMCom}},m}(z) \approx \mathsf{mim}_{\mathcal{H}_2^m}^{\mathcal{A}^{\mathsf{NM4Com}},m}(z) \approx$$
$$\approx \mathsf{mim}_{\mathcal{H}_2^0}^{\mathcal{A}^{\mathsf{NM4Com}},m}(z) \approx \mathsf{mim}_{\mathcal{H}_1^0}^{\mathcal{A}^{\mathsf{NM4Com}},m}(z) = \mathsf{sim}_{\Pi_{\mathsf{NM4Com}}}^{\mathsf{Sim}^{\mathsf{NM4Com}}}(1^\lambda, z).$$

Part III
Efficient Proof Systems

Chapter 8
Improved OR Composition

8.1 Introduction

Witness-indistinguishable (WI) proofs are fundamental for the design of cryptographic protocols, particularly when they are also proofs of knowledge (PoK). In a WIPoK the prover $\mathcal{P}$ proves knowledge of a witness certifying the veracity of a statement $x \in L$ to a verifier $\mathcal{V}$. WIPoKs can be used directly in some applications (e.g., in identification schemes) or can be a building block for stronger security notions (e.g., for zero-knowledge proofs using the FLS [76] paradigm or for round-optimal secure computation [124]).

Round complexity of cryptographic protocols has been extensively studied both for its practical relevance and for its natural and conceptual interest. Regarding WIPoKs, we know from Blum's protocol [22] that three-round WIPoKs exist for all $\mathcal{NP}$ languages under the sole assumptions that one-way permutations exist. This result is obtained by designing a WIPoK for the language of Hamiltonian graphs and then by leveraging on the NP-completeness of the language of Hamiltonian graphs. Under stronger cryptographic assumptions, two-round WI proofs, called ZAPs, and non-interactive WI (NIWI) proofs have been shown in [21, 71, 102]. Neither ZAPs nor NIWI proofs are PoKs.

Since $\mathcal{NP}$ reductions are extremely expensive, several practical interactive PoKs have been designed for languages that are used in real-world cryptographic protocols (e.g., for proving knowledge of a discrete logarithm (DLog)). The study of such ad hoc protocols mainly concentrates on a standardized form of a three-round PoK referred to as Σ-protocol [62, 185].

Σ-protocols. A Σ-protocol for an $\mathcal{NP}$ language L with witness relation R_L is a three-round proof system jointly run by a prover $\mathcal{P}$ and a verifier $\mathcal{V}$ in which $\mathcal{P}$ proves knowledge of a witness w for $x \in L$. In a Σ-protocol the only message sent by $\mathcal{V}$ is a random string called challenge. Such proof systems have two very useful properties: special soundness, which is a strong form of proof of knowledge, and special honest-verifier zero knowledge (SHVZK). The latter property basically

M. Ciampi and L. Siniscalchi, *Round and Computational Efficiency of Multi-party Protocols*, Information Security and Cryptography,
https://doi.org/10.1007/978-3-031-92374-6_8

says the following: if the challenge is known in advance, then by just knowing also the theorem, it is possible to generate an accepting transcript without using the witness. This is formalized through the existence of a special simulator, called the SHVZK simulator that, on input *a theorem* x and a challenge c, will output (a, z) such that (a, c, z) is an accepting three-message transcript for x and is indistinguishable from the transcript produced by the honest prover when the challenge is c. Blum's protocol for graph Hamiltonicity is an example of a Σ-protocol. Another popular example of Σ-protocols is Schnorr's protocol [185] for proving knowledge of a discrete logarithm.

The security provided by the SHVZK property is clearly insufficient as it gives no immediate guarantees against verifiers who deviates from the protocol. Despite of this, the success of Σ-protocols and their impact in various constructions [1, 101, 136, 141, 178, 184] is a fact. This is due to a breakthrough of Cramer et al. [57] that adds WI to the security of Σ-protocol.

OR composition of Σ-protocols. Let L be a language that admits a Σ-protocol Π_L. In [57] it is shown how to use Π_L and its properties to construct a new Σ-protocol, Π_L^{OR}, for proving the OR composition of theorems in L *avoiding* the $\mathcal{NP}$ reduction by crucially exploiting the honest-verifier zero-knowledge (HVZK[1]) property of Π_L. The rationale behind the transformation can be informally explained as follows. The prover wishes to prove a statement of the form $((x_0 \in L) \vee (x_1 \in L))$. The naïve idea of simply running Π_L twice in parallel would not work because the prover knows only one of the witnesses, say w_b, and cannot compute two accepting transcripts without knowing w_{1-b}. However, due to the HVZK property, the prover can generate an accepting transcript for $x_{1-b} \in L$ even without knowing w_{1-b}, by running the HVZK simulator Sim associated with Π_L. Indeed, Sim "only" needs in input the theorem x_{1-b} and will output the entire transcript, challenge included. The trick is then to generate the challenges for the two executions of Π_L, in such a way that the prover can control the challenge of exactly one of them (but not both), and set it to the value generated by Sim. Note that, if running the algorithm of Sim is as efficient as running the algorithm of $\mathcal{P}$, then the composed protocol is efficient. We stress that this OR-composition technique preserves SHVZK and will refer to it as the CDS-OR technique.

A very interesting property of this transformation, besides the fact that it does not need $\mathcal{NP}$ reduction, is that if Sim is a simulator for perfect HVZK then Π_L^{OR} is WI (this was shown in [57]). This result was further extended by Garay et al. [82] that noted that the CDS-OR technique can be used also for Σ-protocols that are computational HVZK. In this case the relation proved is slightly different, namely, starting with a relation Rel_L and instances x_0 and x_1, the resulting Π_L^{OR} protocol is computational WI for the relation $\mathsf{Rel}_L^{\mathsf{OR}} = \{((x_0, x_1), w) : ((x_0, w) \in \mathsf{Rel}_L \wedge (x_1 \in L)) \vee ((x_1, w) \in \mathsf{Rel}_L \wedge (x_0 \in L))\}$.

---

[1] HVZK requires the existence of a simulator that by receiving in input the theorem gives in output an accepting triple (a, c, z). Clearly HVZK is implied by SHVZK.

Delayed-input proofs. Often in cryptographic protocols there is a preamble phase that has the purpose of establishing, at least in part, a statement to be proven with a WI proof. In such cases, since one of the statements is fully specified only when the preamble is completed, the WI proof can start only after the preamble ends. Hence, the overall round complexity of protocols that follow this paradigm amounts to the sum of the round complexity of the preamble and of the WI proof.

In [133],[2] Lapidot and Shamir (and later on Feige et al. in [76]) show a three-round proof of knowledge for Hamiltonian Graphs which has the special property that enjoys the *delayed-input* property. In more detail, the prover can compute the first round of the proof, *without* knowing the theorem to be proved (that is, the graph) but only needs to know its size (that is, the number of vertices). Such a three-round protocol is a Σ-protocol (and thus satisfies the SHVZK property) and is a WI proof. We will refer to this protocol as LS.

The delayed-input property directly improves the round complexity of all the cryptographic protocols that follow the paradigm described above. The reason is that now the WI proof can start even if the preamble that generates the statement is not completed yet. It is worthy to note that in many applications the preamble serves as a means to generate some trapdoor theorem that is used only in the security proof. The "honest" theorem instead is typically known already at the beginning of the protocol. This technique has been used extensively and, most notably, it led to the celebrated FLS paradigm that upgrades any WI proof system into a zero-knowledge (ZK) proof system.

The delayed-input property of LS has been instrumental to provide round-efficient constructions from general assumptions, such as: four-round (optimal) secure 2PC where only one player gets the output (five rounds when both players get the output) [124], four-round resettable WI arguments [184, 194], four-round (optimal) resettable ZK for $\mathcal{NP}$ in the BPK model [184, 194].

Despite being so influential to achieve round efficiency for cryptographic protocols, the power of LS unfortunately vanishes as soon as practical constructions are desired. Indeed, similar to Blum's protocol, LS is crucially based on specific properties of Hamiltonian graphs. Thus, when used to prove more natural languages, which is the case of most of the applications using WI proofs, it requires to perform rather inefficient $\mathcal{NP}$ reductions.

Efficient protocols and limits of the CDS-OR technique. A natural question is what happens if we want to avoid the $\mathcal{NP}$ reduction and we try to use the CDS-OR technique to construct delayed-input adaptive WI proofs. A bit more specifically, we know that there exist Σ-protocols that are delayed input. Schnorr's protocol [185] for DLog is such an example since the first message can be computed without knowing the instance, but only a group generator. Thus the question is what happens if we apply the CDS-OR technique to an delayed-input Σ-protocol. Do we obtain a WI Σ-protocol that is delayed input as well?

---

[2] See [162] for a detailed description of [133].

Unfortunately, the answer is negative. The CDS-OR technique does *not* preserve the delayed-input property, not even when used to compose two Σ-protocols that are both delayed input. To see why, recall that the CDS-OR composition technique when applied to Σ-protocol Π_L for language L requires the prover to compute two accepting transcripts, one of which is computed by running the HVZK simulator Sim. Recall that Sim needs in input the theorem to be proved. Hence, to prove knowledge of a witness for the compound theorem $(x_0 \in L \vee x_1 \in L)$, the prover, who knows one witness, say w_b, needs to know also x_{1-b} already at the first round to be able to run the simulator. Thus, in the CDS-OR technique the prover can successfully complete the protocol if and only if *both*[3] instances are specified already at the first round.

Because of this missing feature, the CDS-OR technique has limited power in allowing one to obtain round-efficient/optimal cryptographic protocols, compared to the number of rounds obtained by using LS. As such, in some cases when focusing on efficient constructions, the *best* round complexity that we can achieve using efficient Σ-protocols and avoiding $\mathcal{NP}$ reductions needs at least one additional round, therefore requiring at least five rounds if one wants to match the previously mentioned applications (e.g., five-round resettable ZK for $\mathcal{NP}$ in the BPK model [184, 194] and five-round resettable WI [184, 194]) argument systems.

Additionally, we note that the CDS-OR technique is the bottleneck in the round complexity of the four-round straight-line perfect simulatable in quasi-polynomial time argument shown by Pass in [165]. This argument uses quasi-polynomial time simulation and, potentially, it would only need three rounds as any Σ-protocol. The additional first round is required precisely to define the trapdoor theorem. Hence, the following natural question arises:

> *Given a language L with an delayed-input* Σ-protocol Π_L*, is it possible to design an efficient Witness Indistinguishable* Σ-protocol Π^L_{OR} *for proving knowledge of a witness certifying that* $(x_0 \in L \vee x_1 \in L)$ *that does* not *require knowledge of both* x_0 *and* x_1 *to play the first round?*

8.1.1 This Chapter's Contribution

In this chapter, we answer the above question positively for a large class of Σ-protocols that includes *all* Σ-protocols used in efficient constructions. Specifically, we show an OR-composition technique for Σ-protocols that relaxes the need to have both instances fixed before the Σ-protocol starts. Our technique allows the composition of Σ-protocols for different languages and leads to improved round complexity in previous efficient constructions based on CDS-OR technique. Namely, we describe the following two results that we obtain by making use this OR-composition technique:

---

[3] To see why, note that the WI property requires that the prover would be able to prove any of the two theorems, and thus potentially use the simulator on either x_0 or x_1.

- Efficient three-round straight-line perfect quasi-polynomial time simulatable argument system for a large class of useful languages. The previous construction required four rounds [165].
- Efficient four-round rWI argument system. Previous constructions required five rounds [184, 194].

This technique can also be used to replace LS toward obtaining efficient round-optimal resettable zero-knowledge arguments in the BPK model (using the constructions of [184, 194]).

Finally, we provide a precise classification of the Σ-protocols that can be used in our OR-composition technique. In the following paragraphs, we first provide a high-level description of our OR-composition technique, then we discuss the applications in more detail.

8.1.2 The Techniques

Overview. We start by defining the setting we are considering. Let L_0 and L_1 be any pair of languages admitting Σ-protocols Π_0 and Π_1. We want to construct a Σ-protocol Π_L^{OR} for the language $L = L_0 \vee L_1$. An instance of L is a pair (x_0, x_1) and we want only x_0 to be specified before Π_L^{OR} starts while x_1 is specified only upon the last round of the protocol.[4] We assume that Π_1 is an *delayed-input* Σ-protocol and thus the first prover message of Π_1 can be computed without knowing x_1. As mentioned earlier this property is satisfied by popular Σ-protocols such as the ones for Discrete Log, Diffie–Hellman triples, and, of course, LS itself.

Now, recall that the problem with the CDS-OR technique was that a prover needs to run Sim to compute the first round of the protocol, and this necessarily requires knowledge of *both* theorems before the protocol starts. We want instead the prover to use only knowledge of x_0.

We solve this problem by introducing an OR-composition technique that does not require the prover to run Sim on x_1 already in the first round. Instead, our technique allows the prover to wait and take action only in the third round when x_1 is finally defined.

Our starting point is the well-known fact that given any Σ-protocol there exists an instance-dependent trapdoor commitment (IBTC) scheme where the witness for the membership of the instance in the language can be used as a trapdoor to open a committed message as any desired message, as in [64]. Our next observation is that, instead of having the prover send the first round for protocol Π_1 in the clear, we can have him send a commitment to it, and such commitment can be computed using an instance-dependent trapdoor commitment based on Π_0 with respect to instance x_0. Recall that this is possible, as in our setting we assume that Π_1 is an delayed-input Σ-protocol, so the prover can honestly compute the first message of Π_1 without

---

[4] Like LS, we will just need the size of x_1 to be known when Π_L^{OR} starts.

knowing x_1. Therefore, the first round of our Π_L^{OR} protocol is simply an IBTC of a honest Π_1's first round.

Later on, upon receiving the challenge c from the verifier, and after the theorem x_1 is defined, the prover computes the third round as follows. If she has received a witness for x_0, then she will run Sim on input (x_1, c) to compute an accepting transcript of Π_1 for x_1. Then, using the witness w_0 she will equivocate the commitment sent in the first round, according to the message output by Sim. Otherwise, if she has received a witness for x_1 then she does not need to equivocate: she will honestly open the commitment, and honestly compute the third message of Π_1. Therefore, the third round of Π_L^{OR} simply consists of an opening of the IBTC together with the third message of Π_1.

Now note that this idea works only if we have a special IBTC scheme that has the following strong trapdoor property: a sender can equivocate even a commitment that has been computed honestly. Unfortunately, this property is not satisfied in general by any trapdoor commitment based on Σ-protocols, but only for some. This would restrict the class of Σ-protocols that we can use as L_0 in our technique. For example, this class would not contain Blum's protocol.

The next contribution is the construction of IBTC schemes that satisfy this strong trapdoor property, for a large class of Σ-protocols. Toward this goal, we define the notion of a t-IBTC scheme which are IBTCs for which the ability to open a commitment in t ways implies knowledge of a witness for the instance associated with the commitment. Next, we construct 2-IBTC and 3-IBTC schemes based on two different classes of Σ-protocols, the union of which includes all the Σ-protocols that are commonly used in cryptographic protocols. Finally, we provide a general OR-composition technique for any pair of languages L_0 and L_1 such that L_0 has a t-IBTC scheme and L_1 has an delayed-input Σ-protocol.

t-instance-dependent trapdoor commitment scheme. For integer $t \geq 2$, a t-IBTC scheme for a polynomial-time relation Rel admitting Σ-protocol Π_{Rel} is a triple $(T_{\mathsf{NI}}, \mathsf{TDec}, \mathsf{TFake})$ where T_{NI}, TDec are the honest commitment/decommitment procedures and TFake is the equivocation procedure that, given a witness for an instance x, equivocates any commitment with respect to x computed by T_{NI}. The crucial differences between a t-IBTC scheme and a regular trapdoor commitment scheme are: (a) the trapdoor property is strong in the sense that knowledge of the trapdoor (that is, the witness of the instance x) allows to equivocate even commitments that have been honestly computed; (b) the binding property is relaxed: in a t-IBTC scheme, the sender can open the same commitment in $t-1$ different ways, even without the trapdoor. This relaxation allows us to build an IBTC scheme from a wider class of Σ-protocols, which will cover all the Σ-protocols that have been used in literature.

Constructing a 2-IBTC scheme. A 2-IBTC scheme can be straightforwardly constructed from any Σ-protocol Π_0 that has the following property: even if the first message a_0 was computed by the SHVZK simulator Sim, an accepting z_0 can be efficiently computed, for every challenge c_0, by using knowledge of the witness and of the randomness used by Sim to produce a_0. We call the Σ-protocols that satisfy this property, *chameleon* Σ-protocols, and we denote by $\mathsf{P}_{\mathsf{sim}}$ the special prover strategy that can answer any challenge even starting from a simulated a_0.

More precisely, given a chameleon Σ-protocol Π_0 for a language L_0, one can construct a 2-IBTC scheme as follows. Let $x_0 \in L_0$. To commit to a message m, the sender runs $\mathsf{Sim}(x_0, m; r_0)$ and obtains a_0, z_0. The commitment is the value a_0. The opening is the pair m, z_0. The commitment is accepted iff (x_0, a_0, m, z_0) is accepting. To equivocate a_0, as a message m', run the special prover algorithm $\mathsf{P}_{\mathsf{sim}}((x_0, m, r_0), w_0, m')$ and obtain an accepting z_0.

Constructing a 3-IBTC scheme. We now discuss a different committing strategy that works for Σ-protocols in which the simulated first message a_0 can only be continued for the challenge specified by Sim, even if a witness is made available. Blum's protocol for Hamiltonicity is an example of a Σ-protocol with this property.

To commit to m, the sender sends a pair (a_0, a'_0) where, with probability $1/2$, a_0 is obtained by running $\mathsf{Sim}(x_0, m)$ while a'_0 is computed by running the prover of Π_0, and with probability $1/2$ the above order is inverted. One can think of a commitment as composed of two threads: a *simulated* thread and a *honest* thread. To open the commitment, the prover sends m and z^*, and the verifier accepts the decommitment if m, z^* are accepting for one of the threads; namely, the verifier checks that either (a_0, m, z^*) or (a'_0, m, z^*) is accepting for $x_0 \in L_0$. To equivocate (a_0, a'_0) to a message m', the sender simply continues the thread of the honest prover, using m' as challenge and computes z^* using the witness. Clearly, a malicious sender can open in two different ways even when $x_0 \notin L$. Nevertheless, three openings allow the extraction of the witness for x_0.

When our OR-composition technique is instantiated with a 3-IBTC scheme we have that the resulting protocol is still WI since no power is added to the verifier. However the protocol is *not* a Σ-protocol since the special-soundness property is not guaranteed. The reason is that, in a 3-IBTC scheme the sender can open the commitment in two different ways even without having the trapdoor (i.e., the witness for $x_0 \in L_0$). Therefore, for any challenge c sent by $\mathcal{V}$, the fact that the commitment of a_1 can be opened in two ways gives a malicious prover $\mathcal{P}^*$ two chances (a_1, c, z_1) and (a'_1, c, z'_1) to successfully complete the protocol for a false statement x_1. Nevertheless, this extra freedom does not hurt soundness as both openings (i.e., a_1 and a'_1) are fixed in advance, and thus when x_1 is not an instance of the language there exist only two challenges c' and c'' that would allow $\mathcal{P}^*$ to succeed. When the challenge is long enough the success probability of $\mathcal{P}^*$ is therefore negligible.

Our construction when starting from a 3-IBTC scheme is three-special sound (i.e., answering to three challenges allows one to compute a witness efficiently), and therefore it is a proof of knowledge when the challenge is long enough.

8.1.3 Discussion

What really matters. This OR-composition technique works only when the theorem that has not been defined yet (i.e., x_1 admits an delayed-input Σ-protocol). We stress that this is not a limitation for the applications that we have in mind. In fact, in all *efficient* protocols that make use of delayed-input proofs that we are aware of, the preamble has always the purpose of generating the trapdoor theorem. In practical scenarios[5] L_1 usually corresponds to DLog or DDH. The fact that we cannot have Blum's Σ-protocol for L_1 when L_1 is the language of Hamiltonian graphs is therefore not relevant as the actual language of interest is L_0.

Comparison with the CDS-OR technique. We remark that even in the extremely simplified case where:

1. the two instances x_0 and x_1 are for the same language L,
2. L admits an *delayed-input* Σ-protocol Π_L which is also SHVZK,
3. Π_L is chameleon and thus one can compute the first message using Sim and then continue with the prover to answer to arbitrary challenges,
4. the prover knows in advance the witness w and instance x_b for which she will be able to honestly complete the protocol,

the CDS-OR technique fails in obtaining a Σ-protocol (or a WIPoK) for the OR composition of instances of L if any one of the instances is not known when the protocol starts.

Beyond Schnorr's protocol. The works of Cramer [55], Cramer and Damgård [56], and Maurer [146, 147] showed that a protocol (referred to as the *Pre-Image Protocol*) for proving knowledge of a pre-image of a group homomorphism unifies and generalizes a large number of protocols in the literature. Classic Σ-protocols, such as Schnorr's protocol [185] and the Guillou-Quisquater protocol [104], are particular cases of this abstraction. We show that the *Pre-Image Protocol* is a chameleon Σ-protocol and can thus be used in our construction.

What is in and what is out. As mentioned previously, the Σ-protocol for L_1 can be any *delayed-input* Σ-protocol. We now discuss which Σ-protocols can be used to instantiate L_0 in our OR transform. For this purpose, we identify four classes of Σ-protocols and we prove that any Σ-protocol that falls in any of the first three classes can be used in our OR transform (by instantiating either a 2-IBTC or a 3-IBTC scheme).

We also identify a class of Σ-protocols that is not suitable for any of our techniques. Luckily, we have no example of natural Σ-protocols that fall in this class, and in order to prove the separation we had to construct a very contrived scheme. The four classes are listed below:

---

[5] These are the only scenarios of interest for our work since if practicality is not desired than one can just rely on the LS Σ-protocol and use $\mathcal{NP}$ reductions.

- *(Class 1)* Σ-protocols that *are* Chameleon and *do not* require the witness to compute the first round. This class of Σ-protocols can be used to construct both 2-IBTC and 3-IBTC schemes.
- *(Class 2)* Σ-protocols that *are* Chameleon and *require* the prover to use the witness already to compute the first round. This class of Σ-protocols can be used to construct a 2-IBTC scheme.
- *(Class 3)* Σ-protocols that *are not* Chameleon but *do not require* the prover to use the witness in the first round. This class of Σ-protocols can be used to construct a 3-IBTC scheme.
- *(Class 4)* Σ-protocols that *are not* Chameleon and *require* the witness to be used already in the first round. This class of Σ-protocols cannot be used in our techniques.

The delayed-input features. We stress here that our techniques allow to start and complete an efficient OR composition of two Σ-protocols (with the discussed restrictions) provided that one instance x_0 is known and another one x_1 will be known later. Having a witness for the first or the second instance always allows $\mathcal{P}$ to convince $\mathcal{V}$. This contrasts with the CDS-OR technique where knowing a witness for x_0 would block $\mathcal{P}$ immediately since $\mathcal{P}$ would need immediately x_1 to continue, but x_1 will not be available until the third round.

8.1.4 Applications

This OR-composition technique does not provide the full power of LS because it needs one theorem to be known before the protocol starts. However, as we show below, this seemingly weaker property suffices to improve the round complexity of some of the previous constructions based on the CDS-OR technique. Such constructions aim to efficiently[6] transform a Σ-protocol for a relation Rel into a *round-efficient* argument with more appealing features.

Efficient three-round straight-line perfect quasi-polynomial time simulatable argument system. We achieve this result directly, using the construction of Pass [165] and replacing the CDS-OR technique with our technique. As a result the first round of the verifier of [165] can be postponed, therefore reducing the round complexity from four to three rounds. Our construction works for all languages admitting a perfect chameleon Σ-protocol.

Efficient four-round resettable WI arguments. Security against reset attacks has been extensively studied in literature [30, 41, 43, 71, 162]. It is well known [30] how to transform a Σ-protocol into a resettable WI protocol: the verifier commits to the challenge c using a perfectly hiding commitment scheme and sends it to the prover in the first round; the prover then computes its messages with randomness derived by

[6] By *efficiently* we mean that no $\mathcal{NP}$ reduction is needed and only a constant number of modular exponentiations are added. We do not discuss the practicality of the resulting constructions.

applying a pseudo-random function (PRF) on the commitment received. Soundness follows directly from the soundness of the Σ-protocol due to the perfect hiding of the commitment. WI follows from the fact that the protocol is zero knowledge against a stand-alone verifier and thus concurrent WI. Then the use of the PRF and the fact that all messages of the verifier are committed in advance upgrades concurrent WI to resettable WI. This approach, however, generates a five-round protocol.

Achieving the same result *efficiently*, namely, avoiding $\mathcal{NP}$ reductions, in only four rounds is non-trivial. The reason is that if we attempt to replace the two-round perfectly hiding commitment with a non-interactive commitment, we lose the unconditional soundness property, and then it is not clear how to argue about computational soundness. More specifically, black-box extraction of the witness is not possible (black-box extraction and resettable WI cannot coexist) and the adversarial prover could try to maul the commitment of the verifier and adaptively generate the first round of the Σ-protocol. In fact, even allowing complexity-leveraging arguments (and thus straight-line extraction), constructing a four-round WI argument system that avoids $\mathcal{NP}$ reductions and adds only a few modular exponentiations to the underlying Σ-protocol has proven to be a challenging problem.

We solve this problem by using our OR-composition technique. We have the verifier commit to the challenge in the first round, but then later, instead of sending the decommitment, she will directly send the challenge and prove that either the challenge is the correct opening of the commitment or she solved some hard puzzle (in our construction, computing the Discrete Log of a random group element chosen by the prover). The puzzle is sent by the prover in the second round and it will be solved by the reduction in super-polynomial time in the proof of soundness.

This trick has been proposed in literature in various forms [67, 165] and we are using the form used in [67] where the puzzle is sent only in the second round. [67] must use the LS transform and therefore needs $\mathcal{NP}$-reduction. As explained earlier, going through LS *was* necessary as the CDS-OR transform can be applied only if both statements are fixed at the beginning.

Our OR transform solves precisely this problem, and it allows the verifier to start the proof before the puzzle is defined, and this proof can be done efficiently without $\mathcal{NP}$ reductions.

Resettable WI follows from the CGGM transformation and the WI property of the proof generated by the prover. The groups used for the commitment of the challenge and for the puzzle sent by the prover will be chosen appropriately so that the hardness of computing discrete logarithms is different and guarantees that our reductions work (i.e., we make use of complexity leveraging).

Four-round (optimal round) resettable ZK argument systems in the `BPK` **model.** Our OR-composition technique can find various other applications. Indeed, wherever there is a round-efficient (but otherwise inefficient) construction based on the use of LS without a corresponding efficient construction with the *same* round complexity, then our technique constitutes a powerful tool toward achieving computationally efficient and round-efficient constructions. For instance, the four-round (optimal round) resettable ZK argument systems in the `BPK` model provided in [184,

194] consists (roughly) of the parallel execution of a (resettable) WI protocol from the prover to the verifier, where the prover proves that either $x \in L$ or he knows the secret key associated to the public identity of the verifier, and a three-round (resettably sound) WI protocol from the verifier to the prover, where $\mathcal{V}$ proves knowledge of the secret key associate to its public key, or knowledge of the solution of a puzzle computed by the prover. When instantiated with efficient Σ-protocols, such construction requires five rounds, where the additional round, from the prover to the verifier, is used to send the puzzle necessary for the verifier to start a proof using the CDS-OR technique. We observe that this setting closely resembles the setting of the four-round resettable WI (rwi) protocol that we provide in this work. As such, one could directly instantiate the proof provided by the prover of the BPK model, with our four-round rwi protocol, and have the verifier just prove knowledge of its secret keys, thus avoiding the need of the additional first round.

Other applications.

In [10] the authors introduce a new two-party protocol called Proof of Work or Knowledge (PoWorK). In this setting a prover can convince a verifier that he has either performed a work or he knows a witness for a public theorem. Also, a malicious verifier is unable to distinguish which strategy has been used by the prover. As also mentioned in [10], our OR composition can be used to implement PoWorK based on discrete logarithm assumption.

8.2 Constructing t-IBTC Scheme

8.2.1 *Constructing a* 2-IBTC *Scheme from a Chameleon* Σ*-Protocol*

Let $\Pi = (\mathcal{P}, \mathcal{V})$ with associated algorithms $(P_1, P_2, \mathsf{V}, \mathsf{P}_{\mathsf{sim}})$ be a Chameleon Σ-protocol for polynomial-time relation Rel with a security parameter 1^λ. Let l be the challenge length of Π and let Sim be a SHVZK simulator associated to Π. We construct a 2-IBTC scheme $(\mathsf{TCom}_\Pi, \mathsf{TDec}_\Pi, \mathsf{TFake}_\Pi)$ for Rel with messages space $M = \{0, 1\}^l$ for $x \in \hat{L}_R$ as follows:

Protocol 1 2-IBTC *scheme from* Chameleon Σ-protocol Π.

- $\mathsf{TCom}_\Pi(1^\lambda, x, m_1)$: On input x and $m_1 \in M$, pick randomness R and compute $(a, z) \leftarrow \mathsf{Sim}(x, m_1; R)$. Output $\mathtt{com} = a$, $\mathtt{dec} = z$ and $\mathtt{rand} = R$.
- $\mathsf{TDec}_\Pi(x, \mathtt{com}, \mathtt{dec}, m_1)$: On input x, $\mathtt{com}$, $\mathtt{dec}$ and m_1, run $b = \mathsf{V}(x, \mathtt{com}, m_1, \mathtt{dec})$ and accept m_1 as the decommitted message iff $b = 1$.
- TFake_Π: On input $(x, w) \in \mathsf{Rel}$, messages $m_1, m_2 \in M$, commitment $\mathtt{com}$ for m_1 and $\mathtt{rand}$ for $\mathtt{com}$, output $z = \mathsf{P}_{\mathsf{sim}}((x, m_1, \mathtt{rand}), w, m_2)$.

Theorem 8.1 *If* Π *is a Chameleon* Σ*-protocol for* Rel *then Protocol 1 is a* 2-IBTC *scheme for* Rel. *Moreover, if* Π *is perfect then so is Protocol 1.*

Proof Correctness follows directly from the completeness property of Π.
2-Special Extract. Suppose $\mathtt{com}$ is a commitment with respect to instance x and let $\mathtt{dec}_1$ and $\mathtt{dec}_2$ be two openings of $\mathtt{com}$ as messages $m_1 \neq m_2$, respectively. Then, triplets $(\mathtt{com}, m_1, \mathtt{dec}_1)$ and $(\mathtt{com}, m_2, \mathtt{dec}_2)$ are accepting transcripts for Π on common input x with the same first round; that is, they constitute a collision for Π. Therefore, we define algorithm ExtractTCom to be the algorithm that runs algorithm Extract (that exists by the special soundness of Π) on input the collision. ExtractTCom returns the witness for x computed by Extract.
(Perfect) Trapdoorness. It follows from the (perfect)
delayed-indistinguishability property of Π as well as the (perfect) Hiding property. □

Theorem 8.2 *If* Π *is a Chameleon* Σ*-protocol for* Rel *that enjoys the (perfect) WI property, then the* 2-IBTC *scheme for* Rel *is (perfect) WI* 2-IBTC *for* Rel.

Proof We recall that if Π is (perfect) WI he is (perfect) WI even when the pair $(\mathsf{Sim}, \mathsf{P}_{\mathsf{sim}})$ is used (that is when 2-IBTC is playing in the trapdoor mode). If exists an adversary that can contradict the WI-Trapdorness of WI 2-IBTC it is possible to use it to make a reduction to the WI of Π. More in detail, let $x \in \hat{L}_R$ be the statement on input to the procedures of 2-IBTC. The reduction works as a proxy between the adversary and the challenger of the WI of Π ($\mathcal{CH}$). The reduction chooses at random a messages $m_1 \in M$ and sends it to $\mathcal{CH}$ receiving back a. Then the reduction sends $\mathtt{com} = a$ to the adversary. Upon receiving $m_2 \in M$ and the witnesses w_0, w_1 s.t. $(x, w_0) \in \mathsf{Rel}$ and $(x, w_1) \in \mathsf{Rel}$ from the adversary the reduction sends m_2, w_0, w_1 to $\mathcal{CH}$. The reduction obtains z from $\mathcal{CH}$ and he sets $\mathtt{dec} = z$. The reduction sends $\mathtt{dec}$ to the adversary and outputs the output of the adversary.

If Π is perfect WI then the WI 2-IBTC enjoys the perfect WI-Trapdorness property. □

Theorem 8.3 *If* Π *is a Chameleon* Σ*-protocol for* Rel, *then the* 2-IBTC *scheme for* Rel *is a perfect binding* 2-IBTC *for* Rel.

Proof The property of perfect binding follows from the special soundness of Π. □

8.2.2 Constructing a 3-IBTC *Scheme*

Let Rel be a polynomial-time relation as above admitting a delayed-witness Σ-protocol Π with associated algorithms (P_1, P_2, V) and security parameter 1^λ. Let l denote the challenge length of Π. We construct a 3-IBTC scheme for message space $M = \{0, 1\}^l$ for $x \in \hat{L}_R$, as follows.

Protocol 2 3-IBTC *scheme.*

- TCom_Π: On input 1^λ, x and $m_1 \in M$, pick randomness R and compute $(a_0, z) \leftarrow \mathsf{Sim}(x, m_1)$ and $a_1 \leftarrow P_1(x; R)$. Let $\mathtt{com}_0 = a_0$ and $\mathtt{com}_1 = a_1$. Output $\mathtt{com} = (\mathtt{com}_b, \mathtt{com}_{1-b})$ for a randomly selected bit b, $\mathtt{dec} = z$ and $\mathtt{rand} = R$.
- TDec_Π: On input x, $\mathtt{com} = (\mathtt{com}_0, \mathtt{com}_1)$, $\mathtt{dec}$ and m_1, accept m_1 if and only if either $\mathsf{V}(x, \mathtt{com}_0, m_1, \mathtt{dec}) = 1$ or $\mathsf{V}(x, \mathtt{com}_1, m_1, \mathtt{dec}) = 1$.
- TFake_Π: On input $(x, w) \in \mathsf{Rel}$, messages $m_1, m_2 \in M$, commitment $\mathtt{com}$ for m_1 and $\mathtt{rand}$ for $\mathtt{com}$, output $z \leftarrow P_2(x, w, \mathtt{rand}, m_2)$.

Theorem 8.4 *If* Π *is a delayed-witness* Σ*-protocol for* Rel, *with the associated algorithms* (P_1, P_2, V), *then Protocol 2 is a* 3-IBTC *scheme for* Rel. *Moreover, if* Π *is Perfect then so is Protocol 2.*

Proof Correctness follows from the completeness of Π.

3-*Special Extract.* It follows from the special soundness of Π. Assume that the committer generates three accepting openings $\mathtt{dec}_1$, $\mathtt{dec}_2$, and $\mathtt{dec}_3$, for distinct messages m_1, m_2, and m_3, for the same commitment $\mathtt{com}$ computed w.r.t. x. In this case, we have three accepting transcript for Π and therefore at least two of them must share the same first message, i.e., it is a collision. Thus we can run the extractor Extract for Π on the collision and obtain a witness for x.

Trapdoorness. It follows from the SHVZK property of Π. We prove this property via hybrid arguments.

The first hybrid $\mathcal{H}_1$ is the real execution, where a honest prover commits to a message following the honest commitment and decommitment procedure, without using the trapdoor. More formally, in the hybrid $\mathcal{H}_1$ the prover performs the following steps:

- On input x and $m_1, m_2 \in M$, the prover selects random coin tosses R and computes $(a_0, z) \leftarrow \mathsf{Sim}(x, m_2)$, $a_1 \leftarrow P_1(x; R)$. It picks $b \leftarrow \{0, 1\}$ and sends $\mathtt{com} = (a_b, a_{1-b})$, $\mathtt{dec} = z, m_2$.

The second hybrid $\mathcal{H}_2$ is equal to $\mathcal{H}_1$ with the difference that a_0 is computed using the algorithm P_1 and z using P_2. Formally:

- On input x and $m_1, m_2 \in M$, the prover selects random coin tosses $R = (r_1, r_2)$ and computes $a_0 \leftarrow P_1(x; r_1)$, $z \leftarrow P_2(x, w, r_1, m_2)$, and $a_1 \leftarrow P_1(x; r_2)$. It picks $b \leftarrow \{0, 1\}$ and sends $\mathtt{com} = (a_b, a_{1-b})$, $\mathtt{dec} = z, m_2$.

Due to the SHVZK property of Π, $\mathcal{H}_1$ is indistinguishable from $\mathcal{H}_2$. Now we consider the hybrid $\mathcal{H}_3$ in which a_1 is computed using $\mathsf{Sim}(x, m_2)$. Formally:

- On input x and $m_1, m_2 \in M$, the prover selects random coin tosses R and computes $a_0 \leftarrow P_1(x; R)$, $z \leftarrow P_2(x, w, R, m_2)$ and $(a_1, \overline{z}) \leftarrow \mathsf{Sim}(x, m_1)$. It picks $b \leftarrow \{0, 1\}$ and sends $\mathtt{com} = (a_b, a_{1-b})$, $\mathtt{dec} = z, m_2$.

Even in this case, we can claim that $\mathcal{H}_3$ is indistinguishable from $\mathcal{H}_2$ because of the SHVZK of Π. The proof ends with the observation that $\mathcal{H}_3$ is the experiment in which a sender commits to a message m_1 and opens to m_2 using the trapdoor.

If Π is a perfect SHVZK protocol, then the sequence of hybrids produces identical distributions. □

Theorem 8.5 *If, Π is a is a delayed-witness Σ-protocol for* Rel *that enjoys (perfect) WI property, with the associated algorithms* (P_1, P_2, V)*, then the* 3-IBTC *scheme for* Rel *is a (perfect) WI* 3-IBTC *for* Rel.

Proof If exists an adversary against the WI-Trapdorness property of WI 3-IBTC it is possible to use it to make a reduction to the WI of Π. More in details, let $x \in \hat{L}_R$ be the statement on input to the procedures of 3-IBTC. The reduction works as a proxy between the adversary and the challenger of the WI of Π ($\mathcal{CH}$). Upon receiving a_0 from $\mathcal{CH}$ the reduction chooses at random a messages $m_1 \in M$ and runs $(a_1, \overline{z}) \leftarrow \mathsf{Sim}(x, m_1)$ and forwards $\mathtt{com} = (a_b, a_{1-b})$ to the adversary, where $b \in \{0, 1\}$. Upon receiving the reduction $m_2 \in M$ and the witnesses w_0, w_1 s.t. $(x, w_0) \in \mathsf{Rel}$ and $(x, w_1) \in \mathsf{Rel}$ from the adversary sends m_2, w_0, w_1 to $\mathcal{CH}$. The reduction obtains z from $\mathcal{CH}$ and he sets $\mathtt{dec} = z$. The reduction sends $\mathtt{dec}$ to the adversary and he outputs the output of the adversary. If Π is perfect WI then the WI 3-IBTC enjoys the perfect WI-Trapdorness property. □

Theorem 8.6 *If Π is a delayed-witness Σ-protocol for* Rel*, with the associated algorithms* (P_1, P_2, V)*, then the* 3-IBTC *scheme for* Rel *is a perfect binding* 3-IBTC *for* Rel.

Proof The property of binding follows from the special soundness of Π. □

8.3 An Advanced OR-Composition Technique

In this section we formally describe the OR transform. Let Rel_0 be a relation admitting a t-IDBC scheme,
$I = (\mathsf{TCom}_{\Pi_0}, \mathsf{TDec}_{\Pi_0}, \mathsf{TFake}_{\Pi_0})$, with $t = 2$ or $t = 3$, and Rel_1 a relation admitting an delayed-input Σ-protocol Π_1 with associated algorithms $(P_1^1, P_2^1, \mathsf{V}^1)$ and simulator Sim^1. We show a Σ-protocol Π^{OR} for the OR relation:

$$\begin{aligned}\mathsf{Rel}_\vee = \{((x_0, x_1), w) : &((x_0, w) \in \mathsf{Rel}_0 \wedge x_1 \in \hat{L}_{\mathsf{Rel}_1})\\ &\vee ((x_1, w) \in \mathsf{Rel}_1 \wedge x_0 \in \hat{L}_{\mathsf{Rel}_0})\}.\end{aligned}$$

We denote by $(P_1^\vee, P_2^\vee, \mathsf{V}^\vee)$ the algorithms associated with Π^{OR}. We assume that the initial common input is x_0. The other input x_1 and the witness w for (x_0, x_1) are made available to the prover only after the challenge has been received. We let

$b \in \{0, 1\}$ be such that $(x_b, w) \in \mathsf{Rel}_b$ and assume that the message space of the t-IDBC scheme I includes all possible first-round messages of Π_1. Note that for the constructions of the t-IDBC scheme we provide, the message space coincides with the set of challenges of the underlying Σ-protocol and, in Sect. 2.3.2, we show that the challenge length of a Σ-protocol can be easily expanded/reduced.

We remind that prover algorithm $P_2^\vee$ receives as further input the randomness $(R_1, \mathtt{rand}_1)$ used by $P_1^\vee$ to produce the first-round message.

Protocol 3 *Protocol* $\Pi^\vee$ *for* $\mathsf{Rel}_\vee$.

Common input: $(x_0, 1^\lambda)$, where 1^λ is the security parameter.

1. $P_1^\vee(x_0, 1^\lambda)$. Pick random R_1 and compute $a_1 \leftarrow P_1^1(1^\lambda; R_1)$. Then commit to a_1 by running $(\mathtt{com}, \mathtt{dec}_1, \mathtt{rand}_1) \leftarrow \mathsf{TCom}_{\Pi_0}(1^\lambda, x_0, a_1)$. Output $\mathtt{com}$.
2. $P_2^\vee((x_0, x_1), c, (w, b), (\mathtt{rand}_1, R_1))$ (with $(x_b, w) \in \mathsf{Rel}_b$).
   If $b = 1$, compute $z_1 \leftarrow P_2^1(x_1, w, R_1, c)$ and output $(\mathtt{dec}_1, a_1, z_1)$.
   If $b = 0$, compute $(a_2, z_2) \leftarrow \mathsf{Sim}^1(x_1, c)$, $\mathtt{dec}_2 \leftarrow$
   $\mathsf{TFake}_{\Pi_0}(x_0, w, a_1, a_2, \mathtt{com}, \mathtt{rand}_1)$ and output $(\mathtt{dec}_2, a_2, z_2)$.
3. $\mathsf{V}^\vee$, on input (x_0, x_1), $\mathtt{com}$, c, and $(\mathtt{dec}, a, z))$ received from Π^{OR}, outputs 1 iff

$$\mathsf{TDec}_{\Pi_0}(x_0, \mathtt{com}, \mathtt{dec}, a) = 1 \text{ and } \mathsf{V}^1(x_1, a, c, z) = 1.$$

Theorem 8.7 *If* Rel_0 *admits a* 2-IBTC *(resp.,* 3-IBTC*) scheme and if* Rel_1 *admits an delayed-input* Σ*-protocol, then* $\Pi^\vee$ *is a* Σ*-protocol (resp., is a three-round public-coin SHVZK PoK) for relation* $\mathsf{Rel}_\vee$.

Proof Completeness follows by inspection. We next prove the properties of Protocol 3 when instantiated with a 2-IBTC and 3-IBTC schemes.

Proof for the construction based on the 2-IBTC scheme. *Special Soundness.* It follows from the special soundness of the underlying Σ-protocol Π_1 and the 2-Special Extract of the 2-IBTC scheme. More formally, consider a collision $(\mathtt{com}, c, (\mathtt{dec}, a, z))$ and $(\mathtt{com}, c', (\mathtt{dec}', a', z'))$ for input (x_0, x_1). We observe that:

- if $a = a'$ then (a, c, z) and (a', c', z') is a collision for Π_1 for input x_1; then we can obtain a witness w_1 for x_1 by the Special Soundness property of Π_1;
- if $a \neq a'$, then $\mathtt{dec}$ and $\mathtt{dec}'$ are two openings of $\mathtt{com}$ with respect to x_0 for messages $a \neq a'$; then we can obtain a witness w_0 by the 2-Special Extract of the 2-IBTC scheme.

SHVZK property. Consider simulator $\mathsf{Sim}^\vee$ that, on input (x_0, x_1) and challenge c, sets $(a, c, z) \leftarrow \mathsf{Sim}_1(x_1, c)$ and $(\mathtt{com}, \mathtt{dec}) \leftarrow \mathsf{TCom}_{x_0}(a)$, and outputs $(\mathtt{com}, c, (\mathtt{dec}, a, z))$. Next, we show that the transcript generated by $\mathsf{Sim}^\vee$ is indistinguishable from the one generated by a honest prover.

Let us first consider the case in which the prover of $\Pi^{\vee}$ receives a witness for x_1. In this case, if we sample a random distribution $(\mathtt{com}, c, (\mathtt{dec}, a, z))$ of $\Pi^{\vee}$ on input (x_0, x_1) constrained to c being the challenge we have that (a, c, z) has the same distribution as in random transcript of Π_1 on input x_1 constrained to c being the challenge; moreover, $(\mathtt{com}, \mathtt{dec})$ is a pair of commitment and decommitment of a with respect to x_0. By the property SHVZK of Π_1, this distribution is indistinguishable from (a, c, z) computed as $\mathsf{Sim}_1(x_1, c)$ which is exactly as in the output $\mathsf{Sim}^{\vee}$.

Let us now consider the case in which the prover of $\Pi^{\vee}$ receives a witness for x_0. If we sample a random distribution $(\mathtt{com}, c, (\mathtt{dec}, a, z))$ of $\Pi^{\vee}$ on input (x_0, x_1) constrained to c being the challenge we have that (a, c, z) are distributed exactly as in the output of $\mathsf{Sim}^{\vee}$ (that is by running Sim_1 on input x_1 and c). In addition, in the output of $\mathsf{Sim}^{\vee}$, $(\mathtt{com}, \mathtt{dec})$ are commitment and decommitment of a whereas in the view of $\Pi^{\vee}$ they are computed by means of TFake algorithm. However, the two distributions are indistinguishable by the trapdoorness of the Instance-Dependent Trapdoor Commitment.

Proof for the construction based on the 3-IBTC scheme.

3-*Special Soundness.* This property ensures that there exists an efficient algorithm that, given three accepting transcripts, (a, c_0, z_0), (a, c_1, z_1), (a, c_2, z_2) with $c_i \neq c_j$ for $1 \leq i < j \leq 3$, for the same common input, outputs a witness for x.

Consider three accepting transcripts for $\Pi^{\vee}$ and input (x_0, x_1):

$$(\mathtt{com}, c_1, (\mathtt{dec}_1, a_1, z_1)), \qquad (\mathtt{com}, c_2, (\mathtt{dec}_2, a_2, z_2))$$

and

$$(\mathtt{com}, c_3, (\mathtt{dec}_3, a_3, z_3)).$$

We observe that:

- if $a_i = a_j$ for some $i \neq j$ then (a_i, c_i, z_i) and (a_j, c_j, z_j) is a collision for Π_1 for input x_1; thus we can obtain a witness w_1 for x_1 by the Special Soundness property of Π_1;
- if $a_i \neq a_j$ for all $i \neq j$, then, $\mathtt{dec}_1$ and $\mathtt{dec}_2$ and $\mathtt{dec}_3$ are three openings of the same $\mathtt{com}$ with respect to x_0 for messages a_1, a_2, and a_3; then we can obtain a witness w_0 for x_0 by the 3-Special Extract of the 3-IBTC scheme.

We stress that having a long enough challenge, 3-special soundness implies the proof-of-knowledge property.

SHVZK property. This is similar to the proof for the construction based on 2-IBTC.

□

8.3.1 Witness Indistinguishability of Our Transform

In this section we discuss the *adaptive WI* property of Π^{OR}. Roughly speaking, adaptive WI means that in the WI experiment the adversary $\mathcal{A}$ is not forced to choose *both* theorems x_0 and x_1 at the onset of the experiment. Rather, she can choose theorem x_1 and witnesses w_0, w_1 adaptively, *after* seeing the first message of Π^{OR} played by the prover on input x_0. After x_1, w_0, w_1 have been selected by $\mathcal{A}$, the experiment randomly selects $b \leftarrow \{0, 1\}$. The prover then receives x_1 and w_b and proceeds to complete the protocol. The adversary wins the game if she can guess b with probability non-negligibly greater than $1/2$. More formally, we consider adaptive WI for polynomial-time relation

$$\begin{aligned}\mathsf{Rel}_{\vee}^{p} = ((x_0, x_1), w) : &((x_0, w) \in \mathsf{Rel}_0 \wedge x_1 \in \hat{L}_{\mathsf{Rel}_1}) \\ &\vee((x_1, w) \in \mathsf{Rel}_1 \wedge x_0 \in \hat{L}_{\mathsf{Rel}_0})\end{aligned}$$

and for the weaker relation

$$\begin{aligned}\mathsf{Rel}_{\vee}^{c} = ((x_0, x_1), w) : &((x_0, w) \in \mathsf{Rel}_0 \wedge x_1 \in L_{\mathsf{Rel}_1}) \\ &\vee((x_1, w) \in \mathsf{Rel}_1 \wedge x_0 \in L_{\mathsf{Rel}_0}).\end{aligned}$$

The adaptive WI experiment, $\mathsf{ExpWI}_{\Pi,\mathcal{A}}(x_0, \lambda, \mathsf{aux})$ with $\delta \in \{c, p\}$, is parameterized by PPT adversary $\mathcal{A}$ and has three inputs: instance x_0, security parameter λ, and auxiliary information aux for $\mathcal{A}$.

$\mathsf{ExpWI}_{\Pi,\mathcal{A}}(x_0, \lambda, \mathsf{aux})$:

1. $a = P_1^{\vee}(x_0, 1^{\lambda}; R_1)$, for random coin tosses R_1;
2. $\mathcal{A}(x_0, a, \mathsf{aux})$ outputs $((x_1, w_0, w_1), c, \mathtt{state})$ such that $((x_0, x_1), w_0), ((x_0, x_1), w_1) \in \mathsf{Rel}_{\vee}^{\delta}$;
3. $b \leftarrow \{0, 1\}$;
4. $z \leftarrow P_2^{\vee}((x_0, x_1), w_b, R_1, c)$;
5. $b' \leftarrow \mathcal{A}(z, \mathtt{state})$;
6. If $b = b'$ then output 1 else output 0.

We set

$$\mathsf{Adv}_{\mathcal{A}}^{\delta}(x_0, \lambda, \mathsf{aux}) = \left|\mathrm{Prob}\left[\ \mathsf{ExpWI}_{\Pi,\mathcal{A}}(x_0, \lambda, \mathsf{aux}) = 1\ \right] - \frac{1}{2}\right|$$

Definition 8.1 Π^{OR} is *Adaptive Witness Indistinguishable* (resp., *Adaptive Perfect Witness Indistinguishable*) if for every adversary $\mathcal{A}$ there exists a negligible function ν such that for all aux and x_0 it holds that $\mathsf{Adv}_{\mathcal{A}}^{c}(x_0, \lambda, \mathsf{aux}) \leq \nu(\lambda)$ (resp., $\mathsf{Adv}_{\mathcal{A}}^{p}(x_0, \lambda, \mathsf{aux}) = 0$).

Next, in Theorem 8.8, we prove the Adaptive Perfect WI of Π^{OR} when both Π_0 and Π_1 are perfect SHVZK. When one of Π_0 and Π_1 is not perfect, we would like to prove that Π^{OR} is Adaptive WI. In Theorem 8.9 we prove a weaker form of Adaptive WI in which the adversary is restricted in his choice of witnesses (w_0, w_1) for relation $\mathsf{Rel}^c_\vee$.

Theorem 8.8 *If Π_0 and Π_1 are perfect SHVZK then Π^{OR} is Adaptive Perfect Witness Indistinguishable.*

Proof The proof considers the following three cases:

Case 1. $(x_0, w_0) \in \mathsf{Rel}_0$ and $(x_1, w_1) \in \mathsf{Rel}_1$;
Case 2. $(x_1, w_0) \in \mathsf{Rel}_1$ and $(x_1, w_1) \in \mathsf{Rel}_1$;
Case 3. $(x_0, w_0) \in \mathsf{Rel}_0$ and $(x_0, w_1) \in \mathsf{Rel}_0$.

For each case we present a sequence of hybrids and prove that pairs of consecutive hybrids are perfectly indistinguishable.

Case 1.

The first hybrid experiment $\mathcal{H}_1(x_0, \lambda, \mathsf{aux})$ is the original experiment $\mathsf{ExpWI}_{\Pi_k,\mathcal{A}}(x_0, \lambda, \mathsf{aux})$ in which $b = 1$ (and thus $\mathcal{P}$ uses witness w_1). That is,

- In Step 1 of $\mathsf{ExpWI}_{\Pi_k,\mathcal{A}}(x_0, \lambda, \mathsf{aux})$, the following steps are executed:
  1. $a = P_1^1(1^\lambda; R_1)$, for random coin tosses R_1;
  2. set $a' = a$;
  3. $(\mathtt{com}, \mathtt{dec}, \mathtt{rand}) \leftarrow \mathsf{TCom}_{\Pi_0}(x_0, 1^\lambda, a)$ and outputs $\mathtt{com}$.
- In Step 4 of $\mathsf{ExpWI}_{\Pi_k,\mathcal{A}}(x_0, \lambda, \mathsf{aux})$, the following steps are executed:
  1. $z \leftarrow P_2^1(x_1, w_1, c, R_1)$;
  2. set $\mathtt{dec}' = \mathtt{dec}$;
  3. output $(\mathtt{dec}', a', z)$.

The second hybrid experiment $\mathcal{H}_2(x_0, \lambda, \mathsf{aux})$ differs from $\mathcal{H}_1(x_0, \lambda, \mathsf{aux})$ in the way a' and $\mathtt{dec}'$ are computed. More specifically,

- Step 1 of $\mathsf{ExpWI}_{\Pi_k,\mathcal{A}}(x_0, \lambda, \mathsf{aux})$ stays the same.
  1. $a = P_1^1(1^\lambda; R^*)$, for random coin tosses R^*;
  2. $a' = P_1^1(1^\lambda; R_1)$, for random coin tosses R_1;
  3. $(\mathtt{com}, \mathtt{dec}, \mathtt{rand}) \leftarrow \mathsf{TCom}_{\Pi_0}(x_0, 1^\lambda, a)$ and outputs $\mathtt{com}$.
- In Step 4 of $\mathsf{ExpWI}_{\Pi_k,\mathcal{A}}(x_0, \lambda, \mathsf{aux})$, the following steps are executed:
  1. $z \leftarrow P_2^1(x_1, w_1, c, R_1)$;
  2. $\mathtt{dec}' \leftarrow \mathsf{TFake}_{\Pi_0}(x_0, w_0, a, a', \mathtt{com}, \mathtt{rand})$;
  3. $(\mathtt{dec}', a', z)$.

The trapdoorness of the instance-dependent trapdoor commitment scheme based on Π_0 and perfect WI of Π_0 guarantee that $\mathcal{H}_1(x_0, \lambda, \mathsf{aux})$ and $\mathcal{H}_2(x_0, \lambda, \mathsf{aux})$ are perfectly indistinguishable for all λ.

The third hybrid experiment $\mathcal{H}_3(x_0, \lambda, \mathsf{aux})$ differs from $\mathcal{H}_2(x_0, \lambda, \mathsf{aux})$ in the way a' and z are computed. More specifically,

- Step 1 of $\mathsf{ExpWI}_{\Pi_k,\mathcal{A}}(x_0, \lambda, \mathsf{aux})$ stays the same.
  1. $a = P_1^1(1^\lambda; R_1)$, for random coin tosses R_1;
  2. $(\mathtt{com}, \mathtt{dec}, \mathtt{rand}) \leftarrow \mathsf{TCom}_{\Pi_0}(x_0, 1^\lambda, a)$ and outputs com.
- In Step 4 of $\mathsf{ExpWI}_{\Pi_k,\mathcal{A}}(x_0, \lambda, \mathsf{aux})$, the following steps are executed:
  1. $(a', z) \leftarrow \mathsf{Sim}^1(x_1, c)$;
  2. $\mathtt{dec}' \leftarrow \mathsf{TFake}_{\Pi_0}(x_0, w_0, a, a', \mathtt{com}, \mathtt{rand})$;
  3. $(\mathtt{dec}', a', z)$.

By the perfect SHVZK of Π_1, we have that $\mathcal{H}_2(x_0, \lambda, \mathsf{aux})$ and $\mathcal{H}_3(x_0, \lambda, \mathsf{aux})$ are perfectly indistinguishable for all λ. The proof ends with the observation that $\mathcal{H}_3(x_0, \lambda, \mathsf{aux})$ is exactly experiment $\mathsf{ExpWI}_{\Pi_k,\mathcal{A}}(x_0, \lambda, \mathsf{aux})$ when $b = 0$.

Case 2.

The first hybrid experiment $\mathcal{H}_1(x_0, \lambda, \mathsf{aux})$ is again the original experiment $\mathsf{ExpWI}_{\Pi_k,\mathcal{A}}(x_0, \mathsf{aux})$ in which $b = 1$ (and thus $\mathcal{P}$ uses witness w_1). The second hybrid experiment $\mathcal{H}_2(x_0, \lambda, \mathsf{aux})$ differs from $\mathcal{H}_1(x_0, \lambda, \mathsf{aux})$ in the way z is computed (using as input w_0 instead of w_1 when P_2 is executed). More specifically,

- In Step 1 of $\mathsf{ExpWI}_{\Pi_k,\mathcal{A}}(x_0, \lambda, \mathsf{aux})$, the following steps are executed:
  1. $a = P_1^1(1^\lambda; R_1)$, for random coin tosses R_1;
  2. $(\mathtt{com}, \mathtt{dec}, \mathtt{rand}) \leftarrow \mathsf{TCom}_{\Pi_0}(x_0, 1^\lambda, a)$ and outputs com.
- In Step 4 of $\mathsf{ExpWI}_{\Pi_k,\mathcal{A}}(x_0, \lambda, \mathsf{aux})$, the following steps are executed:
  1. $z \leftarrow P_2^1(x_1, w_0, c, R_1)$;
  2. output $(\mathtt{dec}, a, z)$.

The Perfect $\mathcal{WI}$ property of Π_1 implies that $\mathcal{H}_1(x_0, \lambda, \mathsf{aux})$ is perfectly indistinguishable from $\mathcal{H}_2(x_0, \lambda, \mathsf{aux})$. The proof ends with the observation that $\mathcal{H}_2(x_0, \lambda, \mathsf{aux})$ is exactly the experiment $\mathsf{ExpWI}_{\Pi_k,\mathcal{A}}(x_0, \lambda, \mathsf{aux})$ when $b = 0$. □

Case 3.

The first hybrid experiment $\mathcal{H}_1(x_0, \lambda, \mathsf{aux})$ is again the original experiment $\mathsf{ExpWI}_{\Pi_k,\mathcal{A}}(x_0, \lambda, \mathsf{aux})$ in which $b = 1$ (and thus $\mathcal{P}$ uses witness w_1). The second hybrid experiment $\mathcal{H}_2(x_0, \lambda, \mathsf{aux})$ differs from $\mathcal{H}_1(x_0, \lambda, \mathsf{aux})$ in the way TFake is executed (namely, using as input w_0 instead of w_1). More specifically,

- Step 1 of $\mathsf{ExpWI}_{\Pi_k,\mathcal{A}}(x_0, \lambda, \mathsf{aux})$ stays the same.
  1. $a = P_1^1(1^\lambda; R_1)$, for random coin tosses R_1;
  2. $(\mathtt{com}, \mathtt{dec}, \mathtt{rand}) \leftarrow \mathsf{TCom}_{\Pi_0}(x_0, 1^\lambda, a)$ and outputs $\mathtt{com}$.
- In Step 4 of $\mathsf{ExpWI}_{\Pi_k,\mathcal{A}}(x_0, \lambda, \mathsf{aux})$, the following steps are executed:
  1. $(a', z) \leftarrow \mathsf{Sim}^1(x_1, c)$;
  2. $\mathtt{dec}' \leftarrow \mathsf{TFake}_{\Pi_0}(x_0, w_0, a, a', \mathtt{com}, \mathtt{rand})$;
  3. $(\mathtt{dec}', a', z)$.

Note that Π_0 is perfect SHVZK which implies that Π_0 is perfect WI and from Theorems 8.2 and 8.5 we can conclude that the IDTC based on Π_0 is also WI-IDTC. Therefore the WI-Trapdorness of the WI-IDTC scheme based on Π_0 implies that $\mathcal{H}_1(x_0, \lambda\mathsf{aux})$ is perfectly indistinguishable from $\mathcal{H}_2(x_0, \lambda\mathsf{aux})$ for all λ. The proof ends with the observation that $\mathcal{H}_2(x_0, \lambda, \mathsf{aux})$ is exactly experiment $\mathsf{ExpWI}_{\Pi_k,\mathcal{A}}(x_0, \lambda, \mathsf{aux})$ when $b = 0$.

Next we consider the computational case in which one of Π_0 and Π_1 is not Perfect SHVZK (but they are both SHVZK).

Theorem 8.9 *If Π_0 and Π_1 are SHVZK then Π^{OR} is Adaptive Witness Indistinguishable with respect to adversaries that output (x_1, w_0, w_1) such that at least one of w_0 and w_1 is a witness for $x_1 \in L_{\mathsf{Rel}_1}$.*

Proof We prove this theorem by considering the following two cases:

Case 1. $(x_0, w_0) \in \mathsf{Rel}_0$ and $(x_1, w_1) \in \mathsf{Rel}_1$;
Case 2. $(x_1, w_0) \in \mathsf{Rel}_1$ and $(x_1, w_1) \in \mathsf{Rel}_1$.

Case 1.

In this case the proof follows closely the one of Case 1 of Theorem 8.8, with the difference that hybrids here are only computationally indistinguishable.

Case 2.

In this case we show that there exists $\mathcal{A}'$ for Case 1 that has the same success probability of $\mathcal{A}$. Suppose indeed that both w_0 and w_1 are witnesses for x_1 and that $\mathcal{A}$ breaks the Adaptive WI property of Π^{OR}. Then, by definition of $\mathsf{Rel}_\vee^c$ and by Definition 8.1, there exists $\mathcal{A}'$ that has in his description a witness w_2 for x_0. Indeed, the output of $\mathcal{A}$ interacting with $\mathcal{P}((x_0, x_1), w_2)$ would necessarily be distinguishable from the output of the interaction with either $\mathcal{P}((x_0, x_1), w_0)$ or $\mathcal{P}((x_0, x_1), w_1)$. Therefore $\mathcal{A}'$ would contradict Case 1 and thus there exists no successful $\mathcal{A}$ for Case 2. □

In Theorem 8.9 we force the adversary of the Adaptive WI to output two witnesses w_0 and w_1, where at least one of w_0 and w_1 is a witness, for instance, $x_1 \in L_{\mathsf{Rel}_1}$. In fact we cannot demonstrate the Adaptive WI of Π^{OR} when both witnesses are, for instance, $x_0 \in L_{\mathsf{Rel}_0}$, because Π_0 is SHVZK, so we are not guarantee that is WI (Theorem 8.15). Therefore we cannot rely on this property to demonstrate that Π^{OR} is adaptive WI. Furthermore, we cannot use the same idea of Case 2 of Theorem 8.9 because the instance x_1 is adaptively chosen. However, using the transformation described in Sect. 2.3.3 we can obtain from Π_0 a Σ-protocol $\overline{\Pi}_0$ for Rel_0 that is WI (note that in Case 3 we are guaranteed that $x_0 \in L_{\mathsf{Rel}_0}$). We can use $\overline{\Pi}_0$ to construct a WI-IDTC following Theorems 8.2 and 8.5. Finally we will apply our OR-transformation on the WI-IDTC constructed from $\overline{\Pi}_0$ and Π_1 obtaining an OR composition Π^{OR} that is adaptive WI with no restriction. In more detail, we have the following theorem.

Theorem 8.10 *If $\overline{\Pi}_0$ and Π_1 are SHVZK then Π^{OR} is Adaptive Witness Indistinguishable.*

Proof We prove this theorem by considering the following three cases:

Case 1 $(x_0, w_0) \in \mathsf{Rel}_0$ and $(x_1, w_1) \in \mathsf{Rel}_1$;
Case 2 $(x_1, w_0) \in \mathsf{Rel}_1$ and $(x_1, w_1) \in \mathsf{Rel}_1$;
Case 3 $(x_0, w_0) \in \mathsf{Rel}_0$ and $(x_0, w_1) \in \mathsf{Rel}_0$.

Case 1 and Case 2.

For these two cases the proofs are the same, respectively, of the Case 1 and Case 2 of Theorem 8.9.

Case 3.

In this case the proof follows closely the one of Case 3 of Theorem 8.8, with the difference that hybrid experiments $(\mathcal{H}_1(x_0, \lambda, \mathsf{aux})$ and $\mathcal{H}_2(x_0, \lambda, \mathsf{aux}))$ are only computationally indistinguishable. In more detail if it exists a distinguisher between these hybrid experiments we can make a reduction to the WI-Trapdorness of WI-IBTC construct from $\overline{\Pi}_0$. The reduction works as a proxy between the malicious verifier $\mathcal{V}^\star$ and the challenger of the WI of Π $(\mathcal{CH})$ w.r.t. the messages of the WI-IBTC and for all the other messages he follows the steps described in $\mathcal{H}_1(x_0, \lambda, \mathsf{aux})$ (that are equal to the steps of $\mathcal{H}_2(x_0, \lambda, \mathsf{aux})$). More in detail, the reduction obtains a commit $\mathtt{com}$ of a random message from $\mathcal{CH}$ that he sends to $\mathcal{V}^\star$. Then upon receiving x_1, c, w_0, w_1 from $\mathcal{V}^\star$ the reduction computes the step 3 of $\mathcal{H}_1$ obtaining (a', z) and forwards a' and the witnesses w_0, w_1 to $\mathcal{CH}$. Upon receiving $\mathtt{dec}$ from $\mathcal{CH}$ sent $\mathtt{dec}, a', z$ to $\mathcal{V}^\star$, and outputs the output of $\mathcal{V}^\star$. It easy to see that if $\mathcal{CH}$ uses the witness w_1 the reduction acts as described in $\mathcal{H}_1$, otherwise acts as described in $\mathcal{H}_2$. This observation concludes the proof. □

8.4 Applications

In this section, we describe the application of the OR-composition technique for constructing a three-round straight-line perfect quasi-polynomial time simulatable argument system, an efficient four-round resettable WI argument system and an efficient four-round resettable zero knowledge with concurrent soundness argument system in the BPK model. For the last application we provide only an informal protocol description.

8.4.1 A Three-Round Efficient Perfectly Simulatable Argument System

In [165], Pass introduced relaxed notion of zero knowledge and knowledge extraction in which the simulator and the extractor are allowed to run in quasi-polynomial time. Allowing the simulator to run in quasi-polynomial time typically dispenses with the need of rewinding the verifier; that is, the simulator is *straight line*. In [165], Pass first describes the following 2-round perfect ZK argument for any language L. The verifier $\mathcal{V}$ sends a value $Y = f(y)$ for a randomly chosen y where f is a sub-exponentially hard OWF and the first round of a ZAP protocol. The prover $\mathcal{P}$ then sends a commitment to $(y'|w')$ and uses the second round of the ZAP to prove that either $y' = f^{-1}(y)$ or w' is a witness for $x \in L$. If language L admits a Σ-protocol Π_L then the above construction can be implemented as an efficient four-round argument with quasi-polynomial time simulation. The function f is concretely instantiated to be an exponentiation in a group in which the Discrete Log problem is hard and the ZAP is replaced with the CDS-OR composition of Π_L and Schnorr's Σ-protocol for the Discrete Log.

Note that Schnorr's Σ-protocol is delayed input and thus we can use it as Σ-protocol Π_1 in our OR transform in conjunction with any Chameleon Σ-protocol Π_0. One drawback of reducing to three round the result of [165] is that we can use only a perfect Σ-protocol since our goal is to obtain perfect WI in just three rounds.

8.4.1.1 Preliminary Definitions

We start by providing some useful definitions.

Simulation in quasi-polynomial time.

Since the verifier in an interactive argument is often modeled as a PPT machine, the classical zero-knowledge definition requires that the simulator runs also in (expected) polynomial time. In [165], the simulator is allowed to run in time $\lambda^{\mathtt{poly}(\mathtt{log}(\lambda))}$.

Loosely speaking, we say that an interactive argument is $\lambda^{\texttt{poly}(\texttt{log}(\lambda))}$-perfectly simulatable if for any adversarial verifier there exists a simulator running in time $\lambda^{\texttt{poly}(\texttt{log}(\lambda))}$, where λ is the size of the statement being proved, whose output is identically distributed to the output of the adversarial verifier.

Definition 8.2 (One-way functions for sub-exponential circuits. [165]) A function $f : \{0, 1\}^* \rightarrow \{0, 1\}^*$ is called one way for sub-exponential circuits if there exists a constant α such that the following two condition holds:

- there exist a deterministic polynomial-time algorithm that on input y outputs $f(y)$;
- for every probabilistic algorithm $\mathcal{A}$ with running time bounded by $2^{\lambda^{\alpha}}$, all sufficiently large λ's, and every auxiliary input $z \in \{0, 1\}^{\mathsf{poly}(\lambda)}$

$$\text{Prob}\Big[\; y \overset{R}{\leftarrow} \{0, 1\}^* : \mathcal{A}(f(y), z) \in f^{-1}(f(y)) \;\Big] < \frac{1}{\mathsf{poly}(2^{\lambda^{\alpha}})}.$$

Now we define straight-line $T(\lambda)$-perfectly simulatable interactive arguments.

For our result we consider a one-way function for sub-exponential circuits that has an efficiently recognizable range (as in [165]).

Definition 8.3 (straight-line $T(\lambda)$ simulatability, Definition 31 of [166]) Let $T(\lambda)$ be a class of functions that is closed under composition with any polynomial. We say that an interactive argument (proof) $(\mathcal{P}, \mathcal{V})$ for the language $L \in \mathcal{NP}$, with the witness relation Rel_L, is straight-line $T(\lambda)$-simulatable if for every PPT machine $\mathcal{V}^\star$ there exists a probabilistic simulator S with running time bounded by $T(\lambda)$ such that the following two ensembles are computationally indistinguishable (when the distinguish gap is a function in $\lambda = |x|$):

- $\{(\langle \mathcal{P}(w), \mathcal{V}^\star(z)\rangle(x))\}_{z\in\{0,1\}^*, x\in L}$ for arbitrary w s.t. $(x, w) \in \mathsf{Rel}_L$
- $\{(\langle S, \mathcal{V}^\star(z)\rangle(x))\}_{z\in\{0,1\}^*, x\in L}$.

We note that the above definition is very restrictive. In fact, the simulator is supposed to act as a cheating prover, with its only advantage being the possibility of running in time $T(\lambda)$, instead of in polynomial time. Trivially, it does not exist a straight-line $T(\lambda)$-simulatable proof for non-trivial languages (this should be contrasted with straight-line simulatable interactive arguments, which instead does exist).

The following theorem shows the importance of straight-line $\lambda^{\texttt{poly}(\texttt{log}(\lambda))}$-perfect simulatability by connecting it to concurrent composition of arguments.

Theorem 8.11 *If the interactive argument $\Pi = (\mathcal{P}, \mathcal{V})$ is straight-line $\lambda^{\texttt{poly}(\texttt{log}(\lambda))}$-simulatable then it is also straight-line concurrent $\lambda^{\texttt{poly}(\texttt{log}(\lambda))}$-simulatable.*

8.4.1.2 The Protocol

For any $\mathcal{NP}$-language L we consider the perfect chameleon Σ-protocol Π_L for the relation R_L. Also we consider the Schnorr Σ-protocol Π^{DLOG} for the following relation $\mathsf{DLOG} = \{((\mathcal{G}, q, g, Y), y) : g^y = Y\}$ with the associated $\mathcal{NP}$-language L_{DLOG}, over groups $\mathcal{G}$ of prime-order q, and use our OR-composition technique to obtain a new perfect Σ-protocol $\Pi^{\vee} = (\mathcal{P}^{\vee}, \mathcal{V}^{\vee})$ for the relation: $\mathsf{Rel}_{\vee} = \{((x_L, x_{\mathsf{DLOG}}), w) : ((x_L, w) \in \mathsf{Rel}_L \wedge x_{\mathsf{DLOG}} \in \hat{L}_{\mathsf{DLOG}}) \vee \; ((x_{\mathsf{DLOG}}, w) \in \mathsf{DLOG} \wedge x_L \in \hat{L}_{\mathsf{Rel}_L})\}$ with challenge length $l = \lambda$ and associated algorithms $P_1^{\vee}$, $P_2^{\vee}$, and $\mathsf{V}^{\vee}$.

Let f be a sub-exponentially hard one-way function that has an efficiently recognizable range implemented using DLog as described before, with the only change that for some constant α s.t. $0 < \lambda < 1$, f is one way w.r.t. circuits of size $2^{\lambda^{\alpha}}$. Let $L \in \mathcal{NP}$ and $k = \frac{1}{\alpha} + 1$. Our three-round straight-line quasi-polynomial time simulatable argument system for $x \in L$ is the following.

Protocol 4 *A three-round straight-line quasi-polynomial time simulatable argument system.*
Common input: An instance x of a language $L \in \mathcal{NP}$ with witness relation R_L and a perfect chameleon Σ-protocol, and 1^{λ} as security parameter.
Private input: $\mathcal{P}$ has w as a private input, s.t. $(x, w) \in \mathsf{Rel}_L$.
Round 1. $\mathcal{P} \rightarrow \mathcal{V}$:

1. On input a randomness R_1, $\mathcal{P}$ uniformly chooses (p, q, g) where $p = 2q + 1$ is a safe prime and g is a generator of a group $\mathcal{G}_q$ of size q. We remark that (p, q, g) are parameters selected so that the function $f(y) = g^y$ is a one-way function for some constant α w.r.t circuits of size $2^{\lambda^{\alpha}}$.
2. $\mathcal{P}$ computes $a \leftarrow P_1^{\vee}((x, 1^{\lambda^{\alpha}}); R_1)$.
3. $\mathcal{P}$ sends (p, q, g) and a to $\mathcal{V}$.

Round 2. $\mathcal{V} \rightarrow \mathcal{P}$:

1. $\mathcal{V}$ chooses $y \leftarrow \mathbb{Z}_q$ and computes $Y = g^y$.
2. $\mathcal{V}$ chooses $c \leftarrow \{0, 1\}^l$.
3. $\mathcal{V}$ sends c and Y to $\mathcal{P}$.

Round 3. $\mathcal{P} \rightarrow \mathcal{V}$:

1. $\mathcal{P}$ computes $z \leftarrow P_2^{\mathsf{OR}}((x, ((p, q, g), Y)), w, c, R_1)$.
2. $\mathcal{P}$ sends z to $\mathcal{V}$.
3. $\mathcal{V}$ accepts if and only if $\mathsf{V}^{\vee}((x, ((p, q, g), Y)), a, c, z) = 1$.

We remark that we are using the same assumption of [29] that allows the adversary of DLog to generate the DLog parameters while the challenger selects the random element of the group.

Theorem 8.12 *If $\Pi^{\vee}$ is a perfect Σ-protocol for OR composition of* Rel_L *and* DLOG, *then Protocol 4 is a three-round straight line perfectly $\lambda^{O(\log^k \lambda)}$-simulatable argument of knowledge.*

Proof Completeness follows directly from the completeness of $\Pi^{\vee}$.

Soundness/knowledge extraction. We show that Π is an argument of knowledge; this directly implies soundness. The claim follows from the fact that the argument system $\Pi^{\vee}$ used is a proof of knowledge when the challenge is long enough, and from the fact that a PPT adversary only finds a pre-image to Y (for f) with negligible probability. More formally, we construct a polynomial-time extractor E for every polynomial-time $\mathcal{P}^\star$ for protocol Π. E internally incorporates $\mathcal{P}^\star$ and each time $\Pi^{\vee}$ proves a new theorem it proceeds as follows. E invokes the extractor $\mathsf{E}^{\vee}$ for $\Pi^{\vee}$. E outputs whatever $\mathsf{E}^{\vee}$ outputs. By the proof knowledge property of $\Pi^{\vee}$, the output of E will either be a witness w for the statement proved, or the pre-image of Y. If E outputs w, we are done. Otherwise, if it outputs y with non-negligible probability, then we can construct a reduction that breaks the DLog assumption (still in the form proposed by [29]).

Quasi-polynomial time perfect simulation. Consider a straight-line simulator Sim that computes the first round as the honest prover. This is possible because $\Pi^{\vee}$ does not need any witness to compute the first round. After the simulator receives Y it checks that Y has a pre-image. Sim thereafter performs an exhaustive search to find a pre-image y of a value Y for the function f. To perform this task Sim tries all possible values $y' \in \{0, 1\}^{\log^k \lambda}$ and checks if $f(y') = Y$. This thus takes time $\mathsf{poly}(2^{\log^k \lambda})$, since the time it takes to evaluate the function f is a polynomial in λ. After having found a value y such that $f(y) = Y$, Sim uses y as witness to complete the execution of $\Pi^{\vee}$ (instead of using a real witness for x, as the honest prover would do). Clearly the running time of Sim is bounded by $\lambda^{O(\log^k \lambda)}$. We proceed to show that the output of the simulator is identically distributed to the output of any adversarial verifier in a real execution with an honest prover. Note that the only difference between a real execution and a simulated execution is in the choice of the witness used in the last stage of the protocol. Therefore, from the perfect adaptive WI property of $\Pi^{\vee}$ we have that the output of the simulated execution is identically distributed to the output of the real execution. □

8.4.2 Efficient Resettable WI Argument System

In this section, we show how to efficiently transform *any* Σ-protocol Π into a resettable WI (rwi) argument system at the cost of adding only one extra round and a constant number of modular exponentiations.

Resettable witness indistinguishability was introduced in [30]. Very roughly, a resetting verifier is a PPT adversary that is able to interact with the prover polynomially many times with possibly distinct inputs forcing the prover to execute the protocol using the same randomness several times. Namely, we can think of a prover under a reset attack as being equipped with a vector of inputs $\bar{x}$ and a vector of random tapes $\boldsymbol{\omega}$. The malicious verifier can adaptively start a new interaction with the prover by specifying the input x_I and the randomness ω_J to be used in the interaction. Moreover, the malicious verifier has complete control over the schedule of the messages. A concurrent verifier is a restricted form of resetting verifier that cannot start two interactions with the same randomness. A formal definition is found in [30].

An informal description. Let Rel be a polynomial-time relation with Σ-protocol Π. Now we give a high-level overview of our four-round rwi argument system $\Pi^{\mathcal{WI}} = (\mathcal{P}, \mathcal{V})$ for Rel. The basic idea is to have $\mathcal{V}$ that commits to the challenge of Π in the first round of $\Pi^{\mathcal{WI}}$. Subsequently, $\mathcal{P}$ and $\mathcal{V}$ play Σ-protocol Π where at the second round (corresponding to the 3 round of $\Pi^{\mathcal{WI}}$), $\mathcal{V}$ decommits to the challenge. To prove rwi we need that the commitment computed in the first round to be perfectly binding for $\mathcal{V}^\star$ so that reset attacks are ineffective, then we can demonstrate the rwi of $\Pi^{\mathcal{WI}}$ relying on the WI of Π. Instead, to prove soundness against $\mathcal{P}^\star$ we need that the commitment computed in the first round enjoys the property of trapdoorness. In this way we can rewind $\mathcal{P}^\star$ and using the special soundness of Π to reach a contradiction.

In order to implement this aspect we use a perfectly binding 2-IBTC for the following relation:

$$\mathsf{DDH} = \left\{\left(((\mathcal{G}, q, g), A = g^a, B = g^b, C = g^{ab}), b\right) : A^b = C\right\}$$

over groups $\mathcal{G}$ of prime-order q.

The perfectly binding 2-IBTC is perfectly binding when an instance T is s.t. $T \notin L_{\mathsf{DDH}}$, and it enjoys the property of perfect trapdoorness when $T \in L_{\mathsf{DDH}}$. Therefore we need to ensure that $\mathcal{V}^\star$ to compute the commitment of the challenge cannot choose an instance T s.t. $T \in L_{\mathsf{DDH}}$. For this reason we add a protocol $\Pi^{1-\mathsf{DDH}}$ to ensure that $T \notin T_{\mathsf{DDH}}$. In more detail, the protocol $\Pi^{1-\mathsf{DDH}}$ proves that T has the following form $T = ((\mathcal{G}, q, g), A = g^a, B = g^b, C = g^{ab+1})$, and this implies that $T \notin L_{\mathsf{DDH}}$. On the other hand in the proof of soundness we want to cheat, in order to use the trapdoorness of perfectly binding 2-IBTC. We could use our OR-composition technique combining $\Pi^{1-\mathsf{DDH}}$ with Schnorr's protocol, obtaining Π^{OR} that $T \notin L_{\mathsf{DDH}}$ or it knows the DLog of a challenge sent by the receiver. Note that our OR composition is crucial because the instance for Schnorr's protocol is available only in the second round of $\Pi^{\mathcal{WI}}$. In the proof of soundness we can break the DLog challenge running in super-polynomial time therefore succeeding in equivocate the commitment in order to rewinding the malicious prover $\mathcal{P}^\star$. Rewinding $\mathcal{P}^\star$ we obtain a collision for a false statement x and therefore by the special soundness of Π, it is possible to extract a witness w for s.t $(x, w) \in \mathsf{Rel}_L$ and reaching a contradiction. Instead $\mathcal{V}^\star$ will not be able to decommit to a different message since otherwise we could use $\mathcal{V}^\star$ to break in polynomial time the DLog challenge.

Formal description of our four-**round efficient resettable WI.** Let Π^{DLOG} be a delayed-input Σ-protocol for the discrete log polynomial-time relation:

$$\mathsf{DLOG} = \{((\mathcal{G}, q, g, Y), y) : g^y = Y\}$$

over groups $\mathcal{G}$ of prime-order q, e.g., Schnorr's Σ-protocol [185].

Consider also the following polynomial-time relation

$$\mathsf{1DDH} = \left\{\left(((\mathcal{G}, q, g), A = g^a, B = g^b, C = g^{ab+1}), b+1\right) : A^{b+1} = C\right\}$$

over groups $\mathcal{G}$ of prime-order q. We will refer to a tuple $T = \left((\mathcal{G}, q, g), A = g^a, B = g^b, C = g^{ab}\right)$ as DH tuple and $T' = \left((\mathcal{G}, q, g), A = g^a, B = g^b, C = g^{ab+1}\right)$ a one-non-DH tuple.

Let Π^{DDH} be a Chameleon Σ-protocol for DDH [174], and the Chameleon Σ-protocol Π^{1DDH} for 1DDH described in Sect. 8.6.1.

From Theorem 8.3 follows that we can use Π^{DDH} to build a perfectly binding 2-IBTC scheme $(\mathsf{TCom}_{\Pi^{\mathsf{DDH}}}, \mathsf{TDec}_{\Pi^{\mathsf{DDH}}}, \mathsf{TFake}_{\Pi^{\mathsf{DDH}}})$ for DDH.

Note that Π^{1DDH} is Chameleon Σ-protocol and Π^{DLOG} is delayed-input Σ-protocol, therefore we can apply Theorem 8.7 and construct the protocol Π^{OR}, with the associated algorithms $(P_1^{\mathsf{OR}}, P_2^{\mathsf{OR}}, \mathsf{V}^{\mathsf{OR}})$, for the following polynomial-time relation:

$$\mathsf{Rel}_\vee = \Big\{((x_0, x_1), w) : \big((x_0, w) \in \mathsf{DLOG} \wedge x_1 \in \hat{L}_{\mathsf{1DDH}}\big) \vee \\ \big((x_1, w) \in \mathsf{1DDH} \wedge x_0 \in \hat{L}_{\mathsf{DLOG}}\big)\Big\}.$$

We denote by x the common input and by w the witness received by $\mathcal{P}$ s.t. $(x, w) \in \mathsf{Rel}$. We also consider a Σ-protocol Π, with the associated algorithm (P_1, P_2, V) for the polynomial-time relation Rel.

Security parameters are λ, $\hat{\lambda}$. Given the security parameter λ we choose $\hat{\lambda}$ s.t. $2^{\hat{\lambda}} < 2^{\lambda} \cdot \mathsf{poly}(\lambda)$, where an adversary that runs in time $2^{\hat{\lambda}}$ can compute the discrete log of an element $Y \in \mathbb{Z}_{\hat{q}}$ and the 1DDH assumption still holds against adversary that running in time $2^{\hat{\lambda}}$.

The security of our proposed rwi $\Pi^{\mathcal{WI}} = (\mathcal{P}, \mathcal{V})$ for Rel is based on the 1DDH assumption and on a strengthening of it.

Protocol 5
Public input: Instance x and security parameter 1^λ.
Private input to $\mathcal{P}$: Witness w such $(x, w) \in \mathsf{Rel}$.
Round 1: From $\mathcal{V}$ to $\mathcal{P}$.

1.1 Committing to the challenge c of Π
$\mathcal{V}$ randomly selects $(\mathcal{G}, q, g) \leftarrow \mathsf{GG}(1^\lambda)$ and $(\hat{\mathcal{G}}, \hat{q}, \hat{g}) \leftarrow \mathsf{GG}(1^{\hat{\lambda}})$ and sends them to $\mathcal{P}$;
$\mathcal{V}$ randomly selects $r_1, r_2, \leftarrow \mathbb{Z}_q$, computes $A = g^{r_1}$, $B = g^{r_2}$, $C = A^{r_2} \cdot g$, and sets $T = ((\mathcal{G}, q, g), A, B, C)$;
$\mathcal{V}$ randomly selects $c \leftarrow \mathbb{Z}_q$ and computes $(\texttt{com}, \texttt{dec}, \texttt{rand}) \leftarrow \mathsf{TCom}_{\Pi^{\mathsf{DDH}}}(1^\lambda, T, c)$;

$\mathcal{V}$ sends $((\hat{\mathcal{G}}, \hat{q}, \hat{g}), T, \mathtt{com})$ to $\mathcal{P}$;

1.2 Computing first round of $\Pi^{\vee}$.
$\mathcal{V}$ randomly selects coin tosses R_1, sets $a^{\vee} = P_1^{\vee}(T; R_1)$, and sends $a^{\vee}$ to $\mathcal{P}$;

Round 2: From $\mathcal{P}$ to $\mathcal{V}$.

2.1 Picking randomness.
$\mathcal{P}$ reads ω from its random tape, computes $\bar{R} = F_{\omega}(x, T, (\hat{\mathcal{G}}, \hat{q}, \hat{g}), \mathtt{com}, a^{\mathsf{OR}})$, and parses it as $\bar{R} = (R_2, R_3)$.

2.2 Computing first round of Π.
$\mathcal{P}$ sets $a = P_1(x, w; R_2)$ and sends it to $\mathcal{V}$.

2.3 Preparing second input for $\Pi^{\vee}$ and sending the challenge for $\Pi^{\vee}$.
$\mathcal{P}$ randomly selects $y \leftarrow \mathbb{Z}_{\hat{q}}$, sets $Y = \hat{g}^{y}$, and sends it to $\mathcal{V}$.
$\mathcal{P}$ randomly selects $c^{\vee} \leftarrow \{0, 1\}^{l^{\vee}}$ and sends it to $\mathcal{V}$.

Round 3: From $\mathcal{V}$ to $\mathcal{P}$.

3.1 Opening commitment of challenge for Π.
$\mathcal{V}$ sends $(c, \mathtt{dec})$ to $\mathcal{P}$.

3.2 Computing third round of $\Pi^{\vee}$.
$\mathcal{V}$ randomly selects coin tosses R_4 and sets $w^{\vee} = r_2$ and computes and sends $z^{\vee} = P_2^{\vee}((T, (\hat{\mathcal{G}}, \hat{q}, \hat{g}, Y), c^{\vee}, w^{\vee}, R_1; R_4)$.

Round 4: From $\mathcal{P}$ to $\mathcal{V}$.

4.1 Verification of $\Pi^{\vee}$.
If $\mathsf{V}^{\mathsf{OR}}((T, ((\hat{\mathcal{G}}, \hat{q}, \hat{g}, Y)), a^{\mathsf{OR}}, c^{\mathsf{OR}}, z^{\mathsf{OR}}) = 0$, $\mathcal{P}$ aborts.

4.2 Checking the decommitment.
If $\mathsf{TDec}_{\Pi^{\mathsf{DDH}}}(T, \mathtt{com}, \mathtt{dec}, c) = 0$ then $\mathcal{P}$ aborts.

4.3 Compute third round of Π.
$\mathcal{P}$ computes $z = P_2(x, w, c, R_2; R_3)$ and sends it to $\mathcal{V}$.

$\mathcal{V}$'s decision: $\mathcal{V}$ accepts if and only if $\mathsf{V}(x, a, c, z) = 1$.

Theorem 8.13 *If polynomial-time relation* Rel *admits a* Σ*-protocol* Π *then, under the DDH assumption against sub-exponential adversary,* $\Pi^{\mathcal{WI}} = (\mathcal{P}, \mathcal{V})$ *is an argument system* rwi *for* Rel.

Completeness is straightforward.

Soundness.

Let $\mathcal{P}^{\star}$ be an efficient algorithm that starts $\mathsf{poly}(\lambda)$ concurrent interactions with an honest verifier $\mathcal{V}$. We show that for any common input $x \in \{0, 1\}^{\lambda}$, if $\mathcal{P}^{\star}$, for $x \notin L_{\mathsf{Rel}}$, makes the honest verifier $\mathcal{V}$ accept with non-negligible probability in one of the $\mathsf{poly}(\lambda)$ concurrent interactions, then we can reach a contradiction using the special soundness of Π.

In order to do that we consider the following four hybrid experiments $\mathcal{H}_0$, $\mathcal{H}_1$, $\mathcal{H}_2$, and $\mathcal{H}_3$.

The first hybrid experiment $\mathcal{H}_0(\mathtt{aux})$ is simply the real game between $\mathcal{P}^\star$ and the honest verifier $\mathcal{V}$. Note that in $\mathcal{H}_0(\mathtt{aux})$ $\mathcal{P}^\star$ can convince $\mathcal{V}$ of a false statement, $x \notin L_{\mathsf{Rel}}$, in one of the $\mathsf{poly}(\lambda)$ concurrent interactions, it comes from the assumption.

In the second hybrid experiment, $\mathcal{H}_1(\mathtt{aux})$, $\mathcal{P}^\star$ interacts in $\mathsf{poly}(\lambda)$ concurrent interactions with a verifier $\mathcal{V}_1$ that, for every interactions, computes the following steps. Upon receiving Y, $\mathcal{V}_1$, running in time at most $2^{\hat{\lambda}}$, computes the discrete logarithm y of Y (i.e., $Y = g^y$). Then, $\mathcal{V}_1$ sets $w^\vee = y$ at Step 3.2. Therefore, $\mathcal{V}_1$ uses y instead of r_2 to compute message $z^\vee$. $\mathcal{H}_0(\mathtt{aux})$ and $\mathcal{H}_1(\mathtt{aux})$ are statistical indistinguishable because of the perfect adaptive WI of Π^{OR}, it still holds that $\mathcal{P}^\star$, for $x \notin L_{\mathsf{Rel}}$, makes the honest verifier $\mathcal{V}$ accept with non-negligible probability in one of the $\mathsf{poly}(\lambda)$ concurrent interactions. Therefore there exists a portion non-negligible of randomness used by $\mathcal{P}^\star$ for which he declares an x s.t. $x \notin L_{\mathsf{Rel}}$ in one of the $\mathsf{poly}(\lambda)$ concurrent interactions, and he makes the honest verifier accept with non-negligible probability in that interaction. Let $\mathtt{i}$ be the index of this interaction. Furthermore let $\mathtt{rand}$ be a prefix of the randomness for which $\mathcal{P}^\star$ declares an x s.t. $x \notin L_{\mathsf{Rel}}$ in the $\mathtt{i}$-th interaction.

The next hybrid $\mathcal{H}_2$ takes as auxiliary input ($\mathtt{aux}$) the prefix of randomness $\mathtt{rand}$ and the index $\mathtt{i}$. The verifier $\mathcal{V}_2$ interacts with $\mathcal{P}^\star$ that is executed using the randomness that have as a prefix $\mathtt{rand}$. Until the interaction with index $\mathtt{i}$ $\mathcal{V}_2$ acts as $\mathcal{V}_1$. In the $\mathtt{i}$-th interaction $\mathcal{V}_2$ modifies the Step 1.1 choosing T as a DH tuple. In more detail, in the Step 1.1 of the $\mathtt{i}$-th interaction $\mathcal{V}_2$ picks at random $r_1, r_2, \leftarrow \mathbb{Z}_q$, computes $A = g^{r_1}$, $B = g^{r_2}$, $C = A^{r_2}$, and sets $T = ((\mathcal{G}, q, g), A, B, C)$. $\mathcal{V}_2$ computes all the other steps as $\mathcal{V}_1$ does.

Lemma 8.1 *In the hybrid $\mathcal{H}_2(\mathtt{aux})$ $\mathcal{P}^\star$, for $x \notin L_{\mathsf{Rel}}$, makes the honest verifier $\mathcal{V}$ accept with non-negligible probability in the interaction with index $\mathtt{i}$.*

Proof From the hybrid $\mathcal{H}_1(\mathtt{aux})$ follows that $\mathcal{P}^\star$ fed with the randomness that have as a prefix $\mathtt{rand}$ in the interaction with index $\mathtt{i}$ declares statement x s.t. $x \notin L_{\mathsf{Rel}}$ and makes the honest verifier accept with non-negligible probability. We observe that x is chosen before the interaction with index $\mathtt{i}$ is started, and before that the hybrids $\mathcal{H}_1(\mathtt{aux})$ and $\mathcal{H}_2(\mathtt{aux})$ are identical distributed. Therefore, if in $\mathcal{H}_1(\mathtt{aux})$ $\mathcal{P}^\star$, running using the prefix of randomness $\mathtt{rand}$, chooses a statement x s.t. $x \notin L_{\mathsf{Rel}}$ in the interaction with index $\mathtt{i}$ it continues, with non-negligible probability, to do the same in $\mathcal{H}_2(\mathtt{aux})$.

Now, we can argue that the interaction with index $\mathtt{i}$ is completed by $\mathcal{P}^\star$ with non-negligible probability also in $\mathcal{H}_2(\mathtt{aux})$. Suppose by contradiction that is not the case, then we can construct an adversary $\mathcal{A}$ that breaks the assumption (i.e., 1DDH assumption). In more detail, let C_{1DDH} be the challenger of 1DDH game. $\mathcal{A}$ acts as $\mathcal{V}_2$ against $\mathcal{P}^\star$ (i$\mathcal{P}^\star$ is fed with the randomnesses of the form $r = \mathtt{rand}||r'$) except that in the interaction with index $\mathtt{i}$, for which he has the following behavior. Upon receiving $T^\star = ((\mathcal{G}, q, g), A^\star, B^\star, C^\star)$ from C_{1DDH} $\mathcal{A}$ sets $T = T^\star$, then he continues the interaction with $\mathcal{P}^\star$ computing all the other steps as $\mathcal{V}_2$ does. If $\mathcal{P}^\star$

completes that in the interaction with index $\mathtt{i}$ $\mathcal{A}$ outputs 1, otherwise he outputs a bit b, where $b \in \{0, 1\}$. Observe that if $T^\star$ is a one-non-DH tuple then $\mathcal{A}$ acts as $\mathcal{V}_1$ of $\mathcal{H}_1(\mathtt{aux})$ otherwise he acts as $\mathcal{V}_2$ of $\mathcal{H}_2(\mathtt{aux})$.

The running time of the adversary $\mathcal{A}$ is dominated by $2^{\hat{\lambda}}$ that is the time needed to compute the discrete logarithm of Y but the 1DDH assumption still holds against adversary that runs in time $2^{\hat{\lambda}}$, therefore we reach a contradiction.

These two observations conclude the proof. □

The next hybrid $\mathcal{H}_3(\mathtt{aux})$ takes as auxiliary input $(\mathtt{aux})$ the prefix of randomness $\mathtt{rand}$ and the index $\mathtt{i}$ of the interaction. The verifier $\mathcal{V}_3$ acts as the verifier $\mathcal{V}_2$ excepted that in the interaction with index $\mathtt{i}$. In the Step 3.1 of the $\mathtt{i}$-th interaction he runs the trapdoor procedure TFake in order to equivocate the opening of the commitment computed at first round.

It follows from the statistically trapdoorness of 2-IBTC that $\mathcal{H}_2$ and $\mathcal{H}_3$ are statistically close. Therefore $\mathcal{P}^\star$ feed with the randomness that have as a prefix $\mathtt{rand}$ in the $\mathtt{i}$-th interaction chooses a statement $x \notin L_{\mathsf{Rel}}$ and has a non-negligible probability of making the verifier accept in this interaction. $\mathcal{V}_3$ can rewind $\mathcal{P}^\star$ at the ending of the second round and equivocate the opening of the commitment made in the first round w.r.t. different values: c, and $\hat{c}$, respectively, before and after the rewind. Note that the distribution seen by $\mathcal{P}^\star$ before and after the rewind is statistical close therefore $\mathcal{V}_3$ obtains with non-negligible probability two transcripts (a, c, z) and $(a, \hat{c}, \hat{z})$ that are a collision for x. It follows from the special soundness of Π that is possible to extract (in super-polynomial time) a witness for $x \in L_{\mathsf{Rel}}$. Contradiction.

Proof of rWI.

The idea of the proof for rWI is very simple. We consider the prover $\mathcal{P}_1$ that, when instructed to use randomness with index J and input with index I and receives first message $\mathtt{msg}$, checks first if a tuple $(J, I, \mathtt{msg}, R)$ has been stored in a previous step. If such a tuple is found then R is used as source of randomness; otherwise, a fresh R is selected and tuple $(J, I, \mathtt{msg}, R)$ is stored. Clearly, by pseudo-randomness, $\mathcal{P}_1$ is indistinguishable from the honest prover $\mathcal{P}$.

Now we observe that the resetting verifier $\mathcal{V}^\star$ is performing an attack on $\mathcal{P}_1$ in which two distinct interactions use the same randomness iff they share J, the input and the first message. More precisely, we say that interactions t_1 and t_2 between $\mathcal{P}_1$ and $\mathcal{V}^\star$ are a *collision* if they share the input, the randomness used by $\mathcal{P}_1$ and the first message and $\mathcal{V}^\star$ opens the commitment in the first messages in two different ways. If $\mathcal{V}^\star$ has a non-negligible probability of producing a transcript then we can break the Strong DLog Assumption (see Assumption 2). Consider algorithm DL that receives as input $(\bar{x}, \bar{w}^0, \bar{w}^1)$ for which $\mathcal{V}^\star$ distinguishes $(\bar{x}, \bar{w}^0)$ from $(\bar{x}, \bar{w}^1)$. DL interacts with $\mathcal{V}^\star$ and at the start of the interaction guesses two interactions $t_1 < t_2$ (in the hope they constitute a collision). In all interactions other than t_1 and t_2, DL runs just like $\mathcal{P}_1$. When DL receives the discrete logarithm parameters from $\mathcal{V}^\star$ as part of the first message of interaction t_1, it forwards them to the challenger of the discrete logarithm and receives Y (and the task is to compute the discrete logarithm of Y) and uses it as part of the second message of interaction t_1. When interaction t_2 is activated DL checks if the first message is the same as the first message of interaction t_1. If this is the case (and this happens with non-negligible probability) DL continues and sends the same second message, including Y. Notice that $\mathcal{V}^\star$ expects to receive the same message since it thinks it is interacting with $\mathcal{P}_1$ that is using the same randomness. Otherwise, DL aborts. Then DL rewinds $\mathcal{V}^\star$ and sends a different challenge for the $\Pi^\vee$ protocol in each of the two interactions. In at least one of them $\mathcal{V}^\star$ has opened the commitment to a different message than the one committed in the first message. This means that $\mathcal{V}^\star$ has used knowledge of the discrete logarithm of Y to complete the interaction and thus DL can extract it.

Finally, let us consider the case in which $\mathcal{V}^\star$ produces a collision in his resetting attack only with negligible probability. This means that $\mathcal{V}^\star$ is conducting a successful concurrent WI attack on the argument system. Standard arguments show that this contradicts the WI of Π.[7]

8.4.3 *Efficient Four-Round Resettable Zero Knowledge in the BPK Model*

Let Rel be a polynomial-time relation with Σ-protocol $\Pi = (\mathcal{P}, \mathcal{V})$. In this section we give an informal description of an efficient four-round argument system (Π^{BPK}) for Rel, that is, resettable zero knowledge and concurrently sound in the BPK model.

In our protocol we consider that each entry of the verifier's identity file is an element of a group $\mathcal{G}$ in which it is hard to compute the discrete logarithm. $\Pi^{\mathsf{BPK}} = (\mathcal{P}, \mathcal{V})$ for Rel consists of the interleaved execution of two protocols: $\Pi^{\mathcal{WI}}$, in which $\mathcal{P}$ acts a prover, and $\Pi^\vee$, in which $\mathcal{V}$ acts as a prover. $\Pi^\vee$ is the Σ-protocol obtained from the OR composition of two Schnorr's Σ-protocols Π_0 and Π_1. $\Pi^\vee$ is used by the verifier $\mathcal{V}$ to prove that she knows either the discrete logarithm of a selected identity $\mathtt{id}$, or the discrete logarithm of an elements sent by the prover $\mathcal{P}$ at the second round of Π^{BPK}. $\Pi^{\mathcal{WI}}$ is the rWI argument system described in Sect. 8.4.2, and it is used by the prover $\mathcal{P}$ to show that she know either the witness for the theorem x to be proved or the discrete logarithm of $\mathtt{id}$.

To prove concurrent soundness of Π^{BPK} we use the same arguments of Sect. 8.4.2, with the difference that at the end of the proof we can extract (in sub-exponential time) the discrete logarithm of $\mathtt{id}$ (instead of a witness for x), and construct a reduction using complexity leveraging to break the assumption that it is hard to compute the discrete logarithm of an elements in $\mathcal{G}$.

To prove $\mathsf{r}\mathcal{ZK}$ we consider a simulator $\mathcal{B}$ that rewinds the verifier $\mathcal{V}$ to get the discrete logarithm of $\mathtt{id}$ (used as a witness by $\mathcal{V}$ to run $\Pi^\vee$) and uses this witness

[7] We are implicitly using the fact that the Σ-protocol Π is WI. This is certainly true if Π is perfect [57]. If Π is only computational then we consider self-OR composition of Π which by [82] is WI.

to complete the execution of the protocol $\Pi^{\mathcal{WI}}$. We observe that $\mathcal{B}$ works correctly only if the first round of $\Pi^{\mathcal{WI}}$ can be computed without using the witness. In this case we have no problem, because we can construct $\Pi^{\mathcal{WI}}$ starting form a Σ-protocol Π' that enjoys this property. More specifically, Π' is the result of an OR composition (using [57]) of Π and of a Schnorr's Σ-protocol that is delayed witness. It is easy to see that the property of delayed witness of Schnorr's Σ-protocol holds even in Π' and in turn in $\Pi^{\mathcal{WI}}$. The last observation makes us able to conclude the proof sketch.

8.4.4 Proof of Work of Knowledge

In [10] the authors introduce a new class of prover verifier protocol called Proof of Work or Knowledge (PoWorK). Following [10], a PoWorK protocol $\Pi = (\mathcal{P}, \mathcal{V})$ has two mode operations: (a) the Proof-of-Knowledge (PoK) mode, where $\mathcal{P}$ convinces $\mathcal{V}$ that he knows a witness for some instance, or (b) the Proof-of-WorK (PoW) mode, where $\mathcal{P}$ makes calls to the puzzle solving algorithm to solve a certain puzzle. Furthermore a malicious verifier $\mathcal{V}^\star$ does not distinguish between the PoK mode and PoW mode. As a counterpart if a malicious prover $\mathcal{P}^\star$ has a running time (in number of steps) less than a specified parameter f calibrated according to the hardness of the puzzle, then there exists a knowledge extractor that extract the witness for the instance proved by $\mathcal{P}^\star$ (f-soundness).

In order to formalize the work aspect in [10] the authors give the notion of puzzle system. A puzzle system PuzSys is a tuple of algorithms $\mathsf{PuzSys} = (\mathsf{Sample}, \mathsf{Solve}, \mathsf{Verify})$ that are defined in the following way. Sample on input the security parameter 1^λ and the hardness factor h outputs a puzzle $\texttt{puz}$; Solve on input the security parameter 1^λ, a hardness factor h and a puzzle instance $\texttt{puz}$ outputs a potential solution $\texttt{sol}$; Verify on input the security parameter 1^λ, a hardness factor h a puzzle instance $\texttt{puz}$, and solution $\texttt{sol}$ outputs 0 or 1.

Loosely speaking in [10] require that the algorithms Sample and Verify are efficient. Furthermore, it is difficult to compute a solution for a sampled puzzle, that is, if puzzle system is f-hard, then the Solve algorithm cannot take less of f-steps of computation.

Using our OR composition we can also implement PoWorK protocol, where the prover proves either the knowledge of a witness for some instance or a solution for a puzzle.

More formally, let Π be a Chameleon Perfect Σ-protocol (or a delayed-witness Perfect Σ-protocol) for Rel, and let $\mathsf{PuzSys} = (\mathsf{Sample}, \mathsf{Solve}, \mathsf{Verify})$ a puzzle system that has an associated delayed-input Perfect Σ-protocol Π^{P} for the relation $\mathsf{Puzzle} = \{\texttt{puz} \leftarrow \mathsf{Sample}(1^\lambda, h) : \exists\ \texttt{sol} \text{ s.t. } \mathsf{Verify}(1^\lambda, h, \texttt{puz}, \texttt{sol}) = 1\}$.

We can use Π^{P} and Π as input of our OR composition and obtaining a $\Pi^{\mathsf{OR}} = (\mathcal{P}^{\mathsf{OR}}, \mathcal{V}^{\mathsf{OR}})$ for the following relation:

$$\mathsf{Rel}_\vee = \Big\{((x_0, x_1), w) : \big((x_0, w) \in L \wedge x_1 \in \hat{L}_{\mathsf{Puzzle}}\big) \vee \big((x_1, w) \in \mathsf{Puzzle} \wedge x_0 \in \hat{L}\big)\Big\}$$

where the statement x_1 (the puzzle) is sent by $\mathcal{V}$ at the second round.

First of all we observe that $\mathcal{P}^{\mathsf{OR}}$ can work in PoK mode and PoW mode. When $\mathcal{P}^{\mathsf{OR}}$ works in PoK mode he computes the third round of Π^{OR} using the witness w_0 s.t. $(x_0, w_0) \in \mathsf{Rel}_L$. Instead when $\mathcal{P}^{\mathsf{OR}}$ works in the PoW mode, he runs Solve obtaining a witness w_1 s.t. $(x_1, w_1) \in \mathsf{Puzzle}$ and he computes the third round of Π^{OR} using the witness w_1 (i.e., a solution for the puzzle). The perfect indistinguishability follows from the perfect adaptive WI property of Π^{OR}, and f-soundness follows from the PoK of Π^{OR}.

As the PoWorK protocols constructed in [10], also our contraction is three-round and public coin. Note, also, that we do not require the additional feature for the puzzle system that in [10] is called "density" and it is needed in [10].

Instantiation of the puzzle system. In [10] one of the constructions of the puzzle system is based on discrete logarithm problem. In that case we need a delayed-input Σ-protocol for Puzzle relation that corresponds to the DLog relation, therefore we can use Schnorr's Σ-protocol.

8.5 More About OR Composition

In this section we give some more details about our OR composition. In particular we show that the pre-image protocol described in [55, 146] is a Chameleon Σ-Protocol, therefore can be used to instantiate our OR composition. Then, we provide a precise classification of the Σ-Protocols that can be used in the OR-composition technique we showed. Finally, we discuss the efficiency of our technique.

8.5.1 More About Chameleon Σ-Protocols

Here we described the pre-image protocol for proving knowledge of a pre-image of a value in the range of a homomorphic function. This protocol is an abstraction of a large class of protocols like Schnorr's [185] protocol and Guillou-Quisquater [104]. This abstraction is first described in [55, 56] and later observed in [146].

Let $(\mathcal{G}, \star)$ and $(\mathcal{H}, \otimes)$ be two groups whose operations are efficiently computable, and let $f : \mathcal{G} \rightarrow \mathcal{H}$ be a one-way homomorphism from $\mathcal{G}$ to $\mathcal{H}$. That is, $f(x \star y) = f(x) \otimes f(y)$.

The pre-image protocol Π for relation $\mathsf{Rel} = \{(x, w) : x = f(w)\}$ with associated algorithm $(P_1, P_2, \mathsf{V}))$ and with challenge length l is described below:

Common input: (description of) $\mathcal{G}$ and $\mathcal{H}$ and $x \in \mathcal{H}$.

Prover's private input: w such that $x = f(w)$.

- Algorithm P_1.
  On input $(x, w) \in \mathsf{Rel}$ and random coin tosses R_1, P_1 picks $k \leftarrow \mathcal{G}$, sets $a \leftarrow f(k)$, and outputs a.
- Algorithm P_2.
  On input $(x, w) \in \mathsf{Rel}$, k, and challenge c, P_2 computes and outputs $z = k \star w^c$.
- Algorithm V.
  On input (x, a, c, z), V outputs 1 iff $f(z) = a \otimes x^c$.

The simulator Sim of Π on input instance x and challenge c works as follows:

- randomly pick $z \leftarrow \mathcal{G}$;
- compute $a = f(z) \otimes x^{-c}$;
- return (a, z).

Theorem 3 of [146] describes the two conditions under which the pre-image protocol is a Σ-protocol. Specifically, for integer y, $u \in \mathcal{G}$ and $(x, w) \in \mathsf{Rel}$ we have

- $\gcd(c_1 - c_2, y) = 1$, for all challenges $c_1 \neq c_2 \in \{0, 1\}^l$;
- $f(u) = x^y$.

Theorem 8.14 *The pre-image protocol is a Chameleon Σ-protocol.*

Proof We describe algorithm $\mathsf{P_{sim}}$. Let $(a, \tilde{z})$ be the output of Sim on input x and challenge $\tilde{c}$. PPT algorithm $\mathsf{P_{sim}}$ on input x, $\tilde{c}$ and the witness w for x and challenge c computes and outputs $z = \tilde{z} \star w^{-\tilde{c}} \star w^c$.

The triple (a, c, z) is an accepting transcript because the test $(f(z) = a \otimes x^c)$ of V is successful. Indeed we have

$$a \otimes x^c = f(\tilde{z}) \otimes x^{-\tilde{c}} \otimes x^c = f(\tilde{z}) \otimes f(w)^{-\tilde{c}} \otimes f(w)^c = f(\tilde{z} \star w^{-\tilde{c}} \star w^c) = f(z).$$

We show now the property of indistinguishability for Chameleon Σ-protocols. We prove that for all pairs of challenges $\tilde{c}$ and c and for all $(x, w) \in \mathsf{Rel}$ the two following distributions are indistinguishable:

- (a, c, z), where $a = f(z) \otimes x^{-c}$;
- (a, c, z), where $a = f(\tilde{z}) \otimes x^{-\tilde{c}}$ $z = \tilde{z} \star w^{-\tilde{c}} \star w^c$.

From the SHVZK property follows that the first distribution is perfect indistinguishable from a real transcript $a = f(k), c, z = k \star w^c$ (where k is a random element of $\mathcal{G}$) produced by Π.

We note that $\tilde{z}$ is a random element of $\mathcal{G}$, so $\tilde{z} \star w^{-\tilde{c}}$ is also a random element of $\mathcal{G}$, for this reason we can set $\bar{k} = \tilde{z} \star w^{-\tilde{c}}$, and obtain that the second distribution $a = f(\bar{k})$, c, $z = \bar{k} \star w^c$ is identically distributed to a transcript given in output by Π. □

Table 8.1 Class of Σ-protocols

	(Class 1)	(Class 2)	(Class 3)	(Class 4)
2-IBTC	Yes	Yes	No	No
3-IBTC	Yes	No	Yes	No

8.5.2 *Classification of Σ-Protocols*

We provide examples for the four classes of Σ-protocols mentioned in Sect. 8.1. Table 8.1 summarizes the classes of Σ-protocols that can be used to construct either a 2-IBTC scheme or a 3-IBTC scheme, or both, and the class of Σ-protocols that cannot be used to instantiate any of our IBTC schemes.

Examples of Class 1 and Class 3 Σ-protocols.

The Class 1 is the class of Σ-protocols that are Chameleon and that are delayed-witness Σ-protocols. Schnorr's Σ-protocol for DLog is an example of Class 1 Σ-protocol. Indeed, its first round consists of the prover sending a random group element. Moreover, even if this value is computed by a simulator, knowledge of the witness and of the randomness used by the simulator suffices for the prover to answer any challenge.

The Class 3 is the class of Σ-protocols that are not Chameleon and that are delayed-witness Σ-protocols. For instance, Blum's Σ-protocol for Hamiltonian graphs belongs to Class 3. In fact this Σ-protocol requires the prover only to know the graph to compute the first round.

An example of a Class 2 Σ-protocol.

Recall that Class 2 is the class of Σ-protocols that are Chameleon and that are not delayed-witness Σ-protocols. We construct a Class 2 Σ-protocol $\Pi = (\mathcal{P}, \mathcal{V})$ for the relation $\mathsf{DLOG} = \{((\mathcal{G}, q, g, Y), y) : g^y = Y\}$ by using Pedersen's commitment scheme [174] as a 2-IBTC scheme. The T_{NI} algorithm of the 2-IBTC scheme for DLOG based on Pedersen's commitment takes as input the description of a cyclic group $\mathcal{G}$ of order q, a generator g of $\mathcal{G}$, and an element $Y \in \mathcal{G}$. To commit to m, T_{NI} selects $r \leftarrow \mathbb{Z}_q$ uniformly at random and returns $\mathtt{com} = g^r \cdot Y^m$, $\mathtt{dec} = r$, $\mathtt{rand} = r$. The decommitment algorithm TDec is straightforward and the trapdoor algorithm TFake, knowing the discrete log of Y, can open the commitment $\mathtt{com}$ as any message m'.

We are now ready to describe our proposed Class 2 Σ-protocol for DLOG with common input $(\mathcal{G}, q, g, Y)$. In the first round, $\mathcal{P}$ computes $(\mathtt{com}_p, \mathtt{dec}_p^0, \mathtt{rand}) \leftarrow T_{\mathsf{NI}}(\mathcal{G}, g, Y, 0)$ and then uses TFake to compute an opening $\mathtt{dec}_p^1$ of $\mathtt{com}_p$

as 1. Finally, $\mathcal{P}$ computes $(\mathtt{com}_0, \mathtt{dec}_0, \mathtt{rand}_0) \leftarrow T_{\mathsf{NI}}(\mathcal{G}, g, Y, \mathtt{dec}_p^0)$ and $(\mathtt{com}_1, \mathtt{dec}_1, \mathtt{rand}_1) \leftarrow T_{\mathsf{NI}}(\mathcal{G}, g, Y, \mathtt{dec}_p^1)$ and sends $(\mathtt{com}_p, \mathtt{com}_0, \mathtt{com}_1)$ to $\mathcal{V}$ that replies with a one bit challenge b. $\mathcal{P}$ answers by sending $\mathtt{dec}_p^b$ and $\mathtt{dec}_b$. The simulator Sim for the SHVZK receives an instance $(\mathcal{G}, q, g, Y)$ and a bit b and computes $(\mathtt{com}_p, \mathtt{dec}_p^b, \mathtt{rand}) \leftarrow T_{\mathsf{NI}}((\mathcal{G}, q, g, Y), b)$. Commitment $\mathtt{dec}_p^b$ is committed twice obtaining $\mathtt{com}_0$ and $\mathtt{com}_1$ and only $\mathtt{com}_b$ is opened. Notice that, since Pedersen's commitment is perfectly hiding, then the simulation of Sim is perfect. Clearly, $\mathcal{P}$ needs the witness of Y for computing the first round. Moreover, the proposed protocol is Chameleon since Sim commits twice to the same opening of the commitment $\mathtt{com}_p$ but then $\mathcal{P}$, once the discrete log of Y becomes available, can computed $\mathtt{dec}_p^{1-b}$ and then open $\mathtt{com}_{1-b}$ as $\mathtt{dec}_p^{1-b}$.

Examples of Class 4 Σ-protocols.

Recall that Class 4 is the class of Σ-protocols that are not Chameleon and that are not delayed-witness Σ-protocols.

As an example of a Class 4 Σ-protocol we consider the protocol obtained from the Class 2 Σ-protocol described in the previous paragraph in which $\mathtt{dec}_p^0$ and $\mathtt{dec}_p^1$ are committed by using a (non-interactive) commitment scheme that is perfectly binding e computationally hiding instead of a Pedersen's commitment scheme. For example, the ElGamal encryption scheme can be used to construct such a commitment scheme. In this case, the Σ-protocol obtained is only computational HVZK.

8.5.3 *Efficiency*

We now give a briefly comparison our OR transform and the CDS-OR transform in terms of number of modular exponentiations that they involve.

For this comparison we consider a protocol Π^{OR} that proves the knowledge of one out of two discrete logarithms. Therefore the OR transforms have on input Π_0 and Π_1 both corresponding to Schnorr's Σ-protocol.

We consider two cases:

- First case: Π_0 is Schnorr's Σ-protocol for relation $\mathsf{DLOG} = \{((\mathcal{G}', q', g', Y'), y') : g^{y'} = Y'\}$, where q' is prime and $\mathcal{G}'$ is a group of order q' of the quadratic residues modulo p' s.t. $p' = 2q' + 1$, where $|p'| = 2048$ and $|q'| = 2047$. Π_1 is Schnorr's Σ-protocol for relation $\mathsf{DLOG} = \{((\mathcal{G}, q, g, Y), y) : g^y = Y\}$, where q is prime and G is a group of order q of the quadratic residues modulo p s.t. $p = 2q + 1$, where $|p| = 1024$ and $|q| = 1023$.
- Second case: Π_0 and Π_1 are both like Π_1 described in the first case.

In both cases we instantiate t–IDBC from Π_0.

The execution of Schnorr's Σ-protocol costs one modular exponentiation, while the execution of the simulator of Schnorr's Σ-protocol costs two modular exponentiations. By exponentiation mod p or exponentiation mod p', we indicate, respectively, the exponentiation modulo a prime of 1024 bits and the exponentiation modulo a prime of 2048 bits.

To evaluate the cost of our OR transform, we first note that the number of modular exponentiations of our OR transform are different when it is instantiated using a 2–IBTC scheme or 3–IBTC scheme, even when the 2–IBTC and 3–IBTC schemes are constructed from the same Σ-protocol. In particular if the schemes are constructed from Schnorr's Σ-protocol run the algorithm T_{NI} costs two modular exponentiations in the case of 2–IBTC and it costs three modular exponentiations in the case of a 3–IBTC.

From this observation follows that to compute the first round of our OR transform we need one exponentiation mod p to compute the first round of Schnorr's Σ-protocol plus the cost to execute T_{NI}.

To compute the third round of our OR transform we need two exponentiations mod p when we run equivocal procedure TFake, because we need to execute again a simulator of Π_1. Otherwise no other exponentiations are required. Therefore in the worst case to compute the third round of our OR transform we need two exponentiations mod p.

Summing up:

- In the first case our OR transform costs three exponentiations mod p plus two exponentiations mod p' if we use a 2–IBTC scheme (or three exponentiations mod p' if we use a 3–IBTC scheme).
- In the second case our OR transform costs three exponentiations mod p plus four exponentiations mod p if we use a 2–IBTC scheme (or six exponentiations mod p if we use a 3–IBTC scheme). Note that in this case to commit to a first round of Schnorr's Σ-protocol where $|a| = 1024$ bits, we need to run twice the T_{NI} procedure.

The CDS-OR transform costs in both cases three modular exponentiations. In the first case the two exponentiations are mod p and one exponentiation is mod p', in the second case all the exponentiations are mod p.

8.6 More About Σ-Protocols

In this last section, we will give some additional theorems on Σ-protocolthat have been used in the chapter. Furthermore, we will described a Σ-protocol for the 1DDH relation.

Theorem 8.15 *For every relation* Rel *such that* $L_{\mathsf{Rel}} \notin \mathtt{BPP}$ *there exist Σ-protocols that are not WI.*

Proof Let $\Pi' = (\mathcal{P}', \mathcal{V}')$ be a Σ-protocol for the relation Rel with challenge length l and let $(P_1', P_2', \mathsf{V}')$ be the triple of PPT algorithms associated to Π'. We use these algorithms to describe a Σ-protocol Π with associated algorithms (P_1, P_2, V) that is not WI. Consider $(x, w) \in \mathsf{Rel}$.

1. P_1 on input (x, w) and randomness R_1 parses it as (r_1, c_p) where c_p is an l-bit string, computes $a' \leftarrow P_1'(x, w; r_1)$, and outputs $a = (a', c_p)$.
2. P_2, on input (x, w), R_1, a challenge c computes $z' \leftarrow P_2'(x, w, r_1, c)$ and if $c = c_p$ then it also sets $z = w$ otherwise it sets $z = z'$; finally it outputs z.
3. V, on input x, $a = a'$, c_p, c and z, makes the following steps: in case c is different from c_p it outputs $\mathsf{V}'(x, a', c, z)$ otherwise it outputs 1 iff $(x, z) \in \mathsf{Rel}$.

We now check that Π is a Σ-protocol.

- **Completeness**: The completeness of Π follows from the completeness of Π' except when c is equal to c_p. In this case $\mathcal{P}$ has a witness and sends it to $\mathcal{V}$ that still accepts.
- **Special Soundness**: $\mathsf{Extract}$ on input a collision $(a = (a', c_p), c_1, z_1)$ $(a = (a', c_p), c_2, z_2)$ works as follows:
  - if c_1 and c_2 are different from c_p then it runs the extractor $\mathsf{Extract}'$ of Π' on input x and a collision (a', c_1, z_1) (a', c_2, z_2) returning its output.
  - If c_1 is equal to c_p, it outputs z_1 while instead if c_2 is equal to c_p it outputs z_2.
- **SHVZK** $\mathsf{Sim}(x, c)$ of Π works as follows:
  - Computes $(a', z') \leftarrow \mathsf{Sim}'(x, c)$, where $\mathsf{Sim}'(x, c)$ is the simulator of Π';
  - Picks $c_p \leftarrow \{0, 1\}^l$.
  - If c_p is equal to c then it aborts, otherwise it outputs $(a = (a', c_p), z')$.

We prove that Π is computational SHVZK, namely: for any l-bit string c, the transcript given in output by $\mathsf{Sim}(x, c)$ is computationally indistinguishable from a honest transcript where the challenge is c and $\mathcal{P}$ runs on common input x and private input w such that $(x, w) \in \mathsf{Rel}$.

Suppose there exists a distinguisher $\mathcal{A}$ for the SHVZK of Π, then we can show a distinguisher $\mathcal{A}'$ for the SHVZK of Π'.

$\mathcal{A}'$ runs $\mathcal{A}$ that outputs a pair (x, w) and a challenge c. $\mathcal{A}'$ then asks the challenger of SHVZK to produce a transcript (either honest or simulated) for instance x, witness w and challenge c. $\mathcal{A}'$ obtains from the challenger a pair (a', z') such that (a', c, z') is an accepting transcript. $\mathcal{A}'$ picks randomly an l-bit string c', sets $a = a'|c'$, $z = z'$, feeds (a, z) to $\mathcal{A}$, and outputs what $\mathcal{A}$ outputs.

We note that the success probability of $\mathcal{A}'$ is statistically close to the one of $\mathcal{A}$ since the probability that c is equal to c' is negligible and this case is the only deviation among the two distributions.

We finally note that Π' is not WI since an adversarial verifier $\mathcal{V}^\star$ can obtain a witness by just sending a challenge c that is equal to c_p. As a consequence $\mathcal{V}^\star$ can get and output a witness for $x \in L$ during an execution with $\mathcal{P}$. Clearly no PPT simulator can produce the same output unless $L \in \texttt{BPP}$. $\square$

8.6.1 Chameleon Σ-Protocol for the 1DDH Relation

Let 1DDH be the following relation:

$$\mathsf{1DDH} = \left\{\left(((\mathcal{G}, q, g), A = g^a, B = g^b, C = g^{ab+1}), b+1\right) : A^{b+1} = C\right\}$$

and let Π^{DDH} be a Chameleon Σ-protocol for DDH [174]. We can use Π^{DDH} to build a Chameleon Σ-protocol Π^{1DDH} for 1DDH in the following way. $\mathcal{P}$ and $\mathcal{V}$ on common input $T = \left((\mathcal{G}, q, g), A, B, C\right)$ construct the tuple $T' = \left((\mathcal{G}, q, g), A', B', C'/g\right)$, then they engage Π^{DDH} on input T'.

Theorem 8.16 Π^{1DDH} *is a Chameleon Σ-protocol for* 1DDH.

It is easy to observe that if T is a one-non-DH tuple, then T' is a DH tuple and $\mathcal{P}$ has a witness for it. Furthermore the completeness, the SHVZK and the special soundness of Π^{1DDH} follow from the completeness, the SHVZK and the special soundness of Π^{DDH}. Finally, Π^{1DDH} is a Chameleon Σ-protocol because Π^{DDH} is a Chameleon Σ-protocol.

Chapter 9
Delayed-Input Witness Indistinguishable Proofs of Knowledge

9.1 Introduction

As we highlighted in the previous chapter, the construction is shown in [57], although efficient, does not provide any form of adaptivity, as all the n instances must be fully specified before the protocol starts. As a consequence, in comparison to [133], the improved efficiency of the PoKs of [57] is often balanced by a worse round complexity of the larger protocol that uses those PoKs.

In the previous chapter we made a first preliminary step toward closing the gap between [57, 133]. Indeed, we have shown a different transform for WI proofs of partial knowledge that gives some adaptivity at the price of generality. Namely, we have shown a technique that yields a $(1, 2)$-proof of partial knowledge where the knowledge of one of the two instances can be postponed to the last round. In more detail, they show a PoK for a statement "$x_0 \in L_0 \vee x_1 \in L_1$" in which x_0 and x_1 are not immediately needed (in contrast to [57]). The honest prover needs x_0 to run the first round while x_1 is needed only in the 3rd round along with a witness for either one of x_0 and x_1. The verifier needs to see x_0 and x_1 only at the end, in order to accept/reject the proof.

We stress that a delayed-input protocol is not necessarily secure against inputs that have been adaptively chosen. Indeed, the technique shown in Chap. 8 yields a proof of partial knowledge that is delayed input for one of the two instances, is adaptive-input WI but it is not adaptively secure against a malicious prover. The achieved security is sufficient for their target applications as we have seen.

The above preliminary progress leaves open the following fascinating question: Can we design an efficient transform that yields an adaptive-input WI (k, n)-proof of partial knowledge where *all* n instances are known only in the last round?

Previous efficient transforms require the a-priori knowledge of all instances or of one out of two instances, even if the corresponding languages admit efficient delayed-input Σ-protocols. For the sake of concreteness, consider the well known Σ-protocol Σ^{dl}, due to Schnorr [185] for proving knowledge of discrete log. Schnorr's protocol

M. Ciampi and L. Siniscalchi, *Round and Computational Efficiency of Multi-party Protocols*, Information Security and Cryptography,
https://doi.org/10.1007/978-3-031-92374-6_9

is easily seen to be delayed-input as the prover needs not to know the instance $y = g^x$ in order to compute the first round. Now suppose one wants to prove knowledge of the discrete logarithm of at least one of $y_0 = g^{x_0}$ and $y_1 = g^{x_1}$. When we apply known transforms, the resulting protocol loses the delayed-input property. More specifically, both y_0 and y_1 are needed by [57], and at least one of y_0 and y_1 is needed for the approach of Chap. 8.

In this chapter, we study the above question and give various positive answers.

Σ-protocols and adaptive-input selection.

We shed light on the relationship between delayed-input Σ-protocols (in which honest parties not need to know the input statement at the onset of the protocol) and adaptive-input Σ-protocols (that retain their security properties even if the input statement is adaptively chosen after seeing the first messages of the protocol). Recall that a Σ-protocol enjoys a special soundness property, which means that, given two accepting transcripts[1] for the same statement having the same first round, there exists an efficient extractor that outputs a witness for that statement.

We show that delayed-input Σ-protocols are not necessarily adaptive-input sound; that is, they are not sound if the malicious prover can choose the statements adaptively. Indeed, in Sect. 9.3.1 we show how a malicious prover, based on the second round played by the verifier, can craft a false statement that will make the verifier accept. The attack applies to the most commonly used Σ-protocols, such as Schnorr's protocol for discrete logarithm, the protocol for Diffie-Hellman (DH) tuples and the protocol of [150] for proving knowledge of committed messages, and to all Σ-protocols in the well known class proposed by Cramer in [56] and Maurer in [146].

The loss of soundness with respect to provers that adaptively choose their inputs was already noticed in [19] for non-interactive zero-knowledge arguments obtained from Σ-protocols by means of the Fiat-Shamir transform [79]. Indeed there are in the literature some incorrect uses of the Fiat-Shamir transform in which an adversarial prover can first create a transcript and then can try to find an instance not in the language such that the transcript is accepting. In the random-oracle model the above issue can be easily addressed by using also the instance as input to the random oracle to generate the challenge. This fix is meaningless in the standard model that is the focus of our work.

We then analyze the transform of Chap. 8 that is delayed-input with respect to one instance only. We observe that when such a construction combines protocols belonging to the class of [56, 146], it is not secure with respect to a malicious prover that is allowed to adaptively choose his input. Therefore the transform of Chap. 8 is not adaptive-input sound. We stress however, that in the applications targeted in Chap. 8 he input that is specified only in the last round is chosen by the verifier. As such, for their applications they do not need any form of adaptive-input soundness, but only adaptive-input witness-indistinguishability (which they achieve). Summing

[1] In the literature special soundness is often generalized to $\ell > 2$ accepting transcripts with the bound of ℓ being polynomial in the security parameter.

up, in Chap. 8 we have correctly defined and achieved delayed-input Σ-protocols and adaptive-input WI and use it in the applications. However, adaptive-input soundness is not defined and not achieved in their work.

Adaptive-input special-sound Σ-protocols.

In light of the above discussion, a natural question is whether we can upgrade the security of the class of Σ-protocols that are delayed-input, but not adaptive-input sound.

Towards this, we first clarify the conceptual gap between adaptive-input selection and the adaptivity considered in Chap. 8, by formally defining *adaptive-input special soundness*. The notion of adaptive-input special soundness strengthens the notion of special-soundness in the following sense. The extractor on input two accepting transcripts, one for the statement x_0 and one for the statement x_1, should be able to extract the witnesses for both x_0 and x_1 if those transcripts share the same first round but have different second rounds.

In this work we show a compiler that takes as input any delayed-input Σ-protocol belonging to the class specified in [56, 146], and outputs a Σ-protocol that is adaptive-input special sound. The main idea behind this compiler is to force the prover to correctly send the first round of the Σ-protocol through another parallel run of the Σ-protocol. Intuitively, this allows for the extraction of the witness because the first round of the starting Σ-protocol is used as a theorem for another Σ-protocol, but this time the theorem is fixed in the first round. Therefore, it is possible to extract the randomness used to compute the first round, which yields to the extraction of the witnesses for the theorem chosen in the third round[2]. The compiler is shown in Sect. 9.3.2.

Adaptive-input (k, n)-proofs of partial knowledge.

The main contribution of this chapter is a transformation that yields an efficient (k, n)-proofs of partial knowledge where *all* n instances can be specified in the last round.

Our new transform takes as input a delayed-input Σ-protocol for a relation Rel, and outputs a 3-round public-coin WI (k, n)-proof of partial knowledge for the relation $(\mathsf{Rel} \vee \cdots \vee \mathsf{Rel})$ where no instance is known at the beginning. The security of our transform is based on the DDH assumption. The WI property of the resulting protocol holds also with respect to adaptive-input selection, while the PoK property holds also in case of adaptive-input selection only if the underlying Σ-protocol is adaptive-input special sound.

We also show a transform that admits instances taken from different relations. Interestingly, this construction makes use as subprotocol of the first construction where instances are taken from the same relation.

[2] This is a property enjoyed by a large class of commonly used Σ-protocols.

We also show that the construction of Chap. 8 preserves the adaptivity of the Σ-protocols that are combined. Namely, when applied to Σ-protocols that are already adaptive-input special sound and WI, Chap. 8's transform outputs a $(1, 2)$-proof of partial knowledge that is an adaptive-input proof of knowledge as well.

9.1.1 Our Techniques

We provide a technique for composing a delayed-input Σ-protocol for a relation Rel in a delayed-input Σ-protocol for the (k, n)-proof of partial knowledge for relation $(\mathsf{Rel} \vee \ldots \vee \mathsf{Rel})$.

For better understanding our technique, it is instructive to see why the previous transformation requires that all n (resp., 1 out of 2) instances are specified before the protocol starts.

Limitations of previous transforms.

Let Σ_{Rel} be a delayed-input Σ-protocol, and let $(\mathsf{Rel} \vee \ldots \vee \mathsf{Rel})$ be the relation for which we would like to have a (k, n)-proof of partial knowledge. The technique of [57] works as follows. The prover P, on input the instances $(x_1 \in \mathsf{Rel} \vee \ldots \vee x_n \in \mathsf{Rel})$, runs protocols $\Sigma_{\mathsf{Rel}}, \ldots, \Sigma_{\mathsf{Rel}}$ in parallel. P gets only k witnesses for k different instances but it needs to somehow generate an accepting transcript for *all* instances. How to prove the remaining $n - k$ instances without having the witness? The idea of [57] consists simply in letting the prover generate the $n - k$ transcripts (corresponding to the instances for which he did not get the witnesses) using the HVZK simulator Sim associated to the Σ-protocol. Additionally [57] introduces a mechanism that allows the prover to control the value of exactly $(n - k)$ of the challenges played by V, so that the prover runs the HVZK simulator in $(n - k)$ positions.

So, why does the transform of [57] need *all* instances to be known already in the 1st round? The answer is that P needs to run Sim already in the 1st round, and Sim expects the instance as input. Every instance could be needed as input by Sim depending on the k witnesses of the prover. Therefore, all instances must be known already at the first round. Similar but relaxed arguments apply for the construction of Chap. 8 where it is required that 1 instance out of 2 is known already in the 1st round.

The core idea of our technique.

Previous transforms fail because the prover runs the HVZK simulator to compute the 1st round of some of the transcripts of Σ_{Rel}. Our core idea is to provide mechanisms allowing P to postpone the use of the simulator to the 3rd round. The main challenge is to implement mechanisms that are very efficient and preserve soundness and WI of the original Σ-protocol. We stress that we want to solve the open problems in full, and thus none of the instances are known at the beginning of the protocol. To be more explicit, in the 1st round, the prover starts with the following statement $(? \in L_{\mathsf{Rel}} \vee \ldots \vee ? \in L_{\mathsf{Rel}})$.

Assume we have a (k, n)-equivocal commitment scheme that allows the prover to compute n commitments such that k of them are binding and the remaining $n - k$ are equivocal, and the verifier cannot distinguish between the two types of commitment, where the k commitments that are binding must be chosen already in the commitment phase (a similar tool was constructed in [161]). With this gadget in hand, we can construct a delayed-input (k, n)-proof of partial knowledge $\Sigma^{\mathsf{OR}}_{k,n}$ as follows. Let (a, c, z) denote generically the 3 messages exchanged during the execution of a Σ-protocol Σ_{Rel}.

In the 1st round, P honestly computes a_i for the i-th execution of Σ_{Rel}. Here we are using the fact that Σ_{Rel} is delayed-input, and thus a_i can be computed without using the instance. Then he commits to $a_1, \ldots, a_n$ using the (k, n)-equivocal commitment scheme discussed above, where the k binding positions are randomly chosen. Thus, the 1st round of protocol $\Sigma^{\mathsf{OR}}_{k,n}$ consists of n commitments. In the 2nd round V simply sends a single challenge c according to Σ_{Rel}. In the 3rd round, P obtains the n instances $x_1, \ldots, x_n$ and k witnesses. At this point, for the instances x_i for which he did not receive the witness, he will use the HVZK simulator to compute an accepting transcript $(\tilde{a}_i, c, \tilde{z}_i)$ and then equivocate the $(n - k)$ equivocal commitments so that they decommit to the new generated $\tilde{a}_i$. For the k remaining instances he will honestly compute the 3rd round using the committed input a_i.

Note that it is not an issue that the binding commitments are chosen at the first round, since we are composing the *same* Σ-protocol so that P can use any of the a_i committed in the 1st round to compute an honest transcript with respect to any theorem x (if P has the witness for x). Furthermore, P randomly permutes the binding and the equivocal commitments before sending them. This technique thus falls short as soon as we want to compose arbitrary Σ-protocols together. Nevertheless, we show how to modify this approach to also accommodate the case of different Σ-protocols (more about this will follow).

Intuitively, soundness follows from the fact that k commitments are binding, and from the soundness of Σ_{Rel}. WI follows from the hiding of the equivocal commitment scheme, the HVZK property of Σ_{Rel} and from the fact that the binding and the equivocal commitments are sent in a randomly chosen order.

(k, n)-equivocal commitment scheme.

A (k, n)-equivocal commitment scheme allows a sender to compute n commitments $\mathtt{com}_1, \ldots, \mathtt{com}_n$ such that k of them are binding and $n - k$ are equivocal. Moreover, the commitments are computed in such a way that the malicious receiver does not know which one is binding and which one it is not. We will use the language DH of DH tuples and we will implement a (k, n)-equivocal commitment scheme very efficiently under the DDH assumption as follows. In the commitment phase, the sender computes n tuples $T_1 = (g_1, A_1, B_1, X_1), \ldots, T_n = (g_n, A_n, B_n, X_n)$ and proves that k out of n tuples are *not* in DH.[3] We show that this can be done using the classical [57] (k, n)-proof of partial knowledge that can be obtained starting with a Σ-protocol Σ^{DDH} for DH.

We then use the well known fact that Σ-protocols can be used to construct an instance-dependent trapdoor commitment scheme [37, 38, 64, 112], where the sender can equivocate if he knows the witness for the instance. Thus, each tuple T_i can be used to compute an instance-dependent trapdoor commitment $\mathtt{com}_i$ using Σ^{DDH}. $\mathtt{com}_i$ will be equivocal if T_i was indeed a DH tuple, it will be binding otherwise. Because the sender proves that k tuples are not in DH, it holds that there are at least k binding commitments.

The fact that k commitments can be equivocated in such a way that the adversary does not know which of the commitments have been equivocated comes from the trapdoorness of the trapdoor commitment scheme, the WI property of [57] and the HVZK of Σ^{DDH}.

Since the trapdoor commitment that we will use has both the commitment and the decommitment phase non-interactive, and since Σ^{DDH} requires just 3-round of communication, we parallelize the commitment phase of the trapdoor commitment with the first round of Σ^{DDH}, and the opening phase with the third round of Σ^{DDH} thus obtaining a 3-round (k, n)-equivocal commitment scheme. We remark that in order to make easier the security proof of our scheme, we will use a (k, n)-equivocal commitment scheme in a non-black-box way.

The case of different Σ-protocols.

We now consider the case where we want to compose $\Sigma_1, \ldots, \Sigma_n$ for possibly different relations. Our (k, n)-equivocal commitment scheme does not help here because each a_i is specific to protocol Σ_i, and cannot be arbitrarily mixed and matched once the k witnesses are known.

For this case we thus use a different trick. We ask the prover to commit to each a_i twice, once using a binding commitment and once using an equivocal commitment. This again can be very efficiently implemented from the DDH assumption as follows. For each i, P generates tuples T_i^0 and T_i^1, that are such that at most one can be a DH tuple. It then commits to a_i twice using the instance-dependent trapdoor commitment associated to tuple T_i^0 and tuple T_i^1. Because at most one of the two tuples is a DH tuple, at most one of the commitments of a_i can be later equivocated. Thus the 1st round of our transformation consists of 2 commitments of a_i for $1 \leq i \leq n$.

In the 3rd round, when P receives instances $x_1, \ldots, x_n$ and k witnesses, he proceeds as follows. For each i, if P knows the witness for x_i, he will open the binding commitment for position i, and computes z_i using the honest prover procedure of Σ_i. Instead, if P does not have a witness for x_i, he will compute a new $\tilde{a}_i, z_i$ using the simulator on input x_i, c and open the equivocal commitment in position i. At the end, for each position i, one commitment has remained unopened.

[3] The tuples are sent in a random order to avoid that the malicious receiver could figure out something just by looking at the order of the tuples that he receives.

This mechanism allows an honest prover to complete the proof with the knowledge of only k witnesses. However, what stops a malicious prover to always open the equivocal commitments and thus complete the proof without knowing any of the witnesses?

We avoid this problem by requiring P to prove that, among the n tuples corresponding to the unopened commitments, at least k out of n tuples are DH tuples. This directly means that k of the opened commitments were constructed over tuples that are not DH, and therefore are binding.

Now note that proving this theorem requires an (k, n)-proof of partial knowledge where the instance to prove, i.e., the tuple that will be unopened, is known only in the 3rd round when P knows for which instances he is able to open a binding commitment. Here we crucially use the delayed-input (k, n)-proof of partial knowledge for the same Σ-protocol developed above.

9.1.2 Comparison with the State of the Art

In Table 9.1 we compare our results with the relevant related work. We consider [133], a 3-round public-coin WIPoK that is *fully adaptive-input* and that works for any $\mathcal{NP}$ language. We also consider [57] that proposed efficient 3-round public-coin WI proofs of partial knowledge (though, without supporting any adaptivity). Finally, we consider [52] since it was the only work that faced the problem of combining together efficiency and some form of delayed-input instances.

The last row refers to our main result that allows to postpone knowledge of all the instances to the last round.

The second column refers to the computational assumptions needed by [133] (i.e., one-way permutations) and our main result (i.e., DDH assumption). The third column specifies the type of WI depending on the adaptive selection of the instances from the adversarial verifier. The fourth column specifies the soundness depending on the adaptive selection of the instances from the adversarial prover.

Table 9.1 Comparison with previous work

	Assumption	Adaptive WI	Adaptive PoK	$\mathcal{NP}$ Reduction
LaSh90 [133]	OWP	k out of n (all adaptive)	k out of n (all adaptive)	Yes
CDS94 [57]	None	Not achieved	Not achieved	No
Chapter 8	None	1 out of 2 (1 adaptive)	Not achieved	No
This Work (main result)	DDH	k out of n (all adaptive)	k out of n (all adaptive)	No

Table 9.2 Prover's computational effort for the online phase in proofs of partial knowledge of discrete logarithms

	(1, 2) DLogs	(k, n) DLogs
LaSh [133]	$\mathcal{NP}$-reduction	$\mathcal{NP}$-reduction
[57]	3 exps	$2n - k$ exps
Chapter 8	4 exps	Not achieved
Our PoK and Adaptive-Input WI	2 exps	$2(n - k)$ exps
Our Adaptive-Input PoK and Adaptive-Input WI	4 exps	$4(n - k)$ exps

9.1.3 Online/Offline Computation

The main feature of our constructions is the property of being delayed-input and thus the prover can compute the first round without knowing instances in an *offline phase*. When interacting with the verifier (the *online phase*), the prover sends the precomputed first round and computes only the third round of the protocol thus greatly improving the efficient of the protocol. As we have already pointed out, the LaSh construction enjoys a similar property and, instead, the construction of [57] requires knowledge of the instances from the start of the protocol and so there is no offline phase.

In Table 9.2, we compare the computational effort of the prover in the online phase of our constructions with the computational effort of [57, 133] and the of the online phase of the construction of Chap. 8. for proofs of partial knowledge of discrete logarithms. In the online phase of LaSh, the prover computes an $\mathcal{NP}$ reduction. For the remaining constructions, we report the number of modular[4] exponentiations that are computed by the prover in the online phase.

As far as the construction of [57] is concerned, it is easy to see that $2n - k$ exponentiations are performed by the prover for the (n, k)-proof of partial knowledge.

For the construction of Chap. 8, we remind the reader that one instance, called the *original* instance, is known from the start of the protocol and the other, called the *adaptive* instance, is made available to the prover only after the first round has been completed along with the witness for one of the instances. In the (1, 2)-proof of partial knowledge of Chap. 8, the first round requires three exponentiations as the prover needs to run the simulator and the prover's algorithm of Schnorr's Σ-protocol. If the witness for the original instance is received, the prover needs to perform two extra exponentiations whereas if the witness received is for the adaptive instance then the prover can compute the third round by performing only one exponentiation. Out of the five exponentiations required in the worst case, one can be precomputed (the one relative to the prover's algorithm of Schnorr's Σ-protocol) and thus the prover of needs to compute four exponentiations in the online phase. The last two rows of the table report on the number of exponentiations performed by the prover in two

[4] We will omit the word *modular* from now on.

instantiations of the general construction of Sect. 9.4: the first is obtained by plugging in Schnorr's protocol (this only gives PoK) and the second is obtained by plugging in the adaptive-input 2-special sound protocol for discrete logarithm resulting by applying the compiler of Sect. 9.3.2 to Schnorr's protocol. For a detailed analysis on the number of exponentiations required by our two instantiations we refer the reader to Sect. 9.4.3.

9.2 Threshold Relation

A *polynomial-time* relation Rel is a relation for which membership of (x, w) to Rel can be decided in time polynomial in $|x|$. If $(x, w) \in \mathsf{Rel}$ then we say that w is a *witness* for *instance* x. A polynomial-time relation Rel is naturally associated with the $\mathcal{NP}$ language L_{Rel} defined as $L_{\mathsf{Rel}} = \{x | \exists w : (x, w) \in \mathsf{Rel}\}$. Similarly, an $\mathcal{NP}$ language is naturally associated with a polynomial-time relation. Following [82], we define $\hat{L}_{\mathsf{Rel}}$ to be the *input language* that includes both L_{Rel} and all well formed instances that do not have a witness. It follows that $L_{\mathsf{Rel}} \subseteq \hat{L}_{\mathsf{Rel}}$ and membership in $\hat{L}_{\mathsf{Rel}}$ can be tested in polynomial time. We consider the notion of *threshold relation*. Let $\mathsf{Rel}_1, \ldots, \mathsf{Rel}_n$ be polynomial-time relations. A threshold relation with threshold k is a polynomial-time relation as well, with the following form

$$\begin{aligned}\mathsf{Rel}_k = \{&(x_1, \ldots, x_n), ((w_1, d_1) \ldots, (w_k, d_k)) : \\ &1 \leq d_1 < \cdots < d_k \leq n \text{ and } (x_{d_i}, w_i) \in \mathsf{Rel}_i, \text{ for } i = 1, \ldots, k\big\}.\end{aligned}$$

Roughly, a threshold relation with threshold k contains a set of n $\mathcal{NP}$ statements $x_1, \ldots, x_n$, and a set of witnesses $w_1, \ldots, w_k$ with $k \leq n$, in which each w_i represents a valid witness for one and only one statement $x_{d_i} \in \hat{L}_{\mathsf{Rel}_{d_i}}$ with $d_i \in \{1, \ldots, n\}$.

Given two interactive machines M_0 and M_1, we denote by $\langle M_0(x_0), M_1(x_1)\rangle(x_2)$ the output of M_1 when running on input x_1 and interacting with M_0 running on input x_0 and common input x_2.

9.2.1 *Instance-Dependent Binding Commitment*

We define the notion of an Instance-Dependent Binding Commitment scheme associated with a polynomial-time relation Rel and describe a construction for all Rel admitting a Σ-protocol.

Definition 9.1 (*Instance-Dependent Binding Commitment scheme*) An *Instance-Dependent Binding Commitment* scheme (an *IDBC*, in short) for polynomial-time relation Rel with message space M is a quadruple of PPT algorithms $(\mathsf{Com}, \mathsf{Dec}, \mathsf{Fake}_1, \mathsf{Fake}_2)$ where:

- Com is the randomized *commitment* algorithm that takes as input an instance $x \in \hat{L}_{\mathsf{Rel}}$ and a message $m \in M$ and outputs *commitment* $\mathtt{com}$ and *decommitment* $\mathtt{dec}$;
- Dec is the *verification* algorithm that takes as input $x \in \hat{L}_{\mathsf{Rel}}$, $\mathtt{com}, \mathtt{dec}$ and $m \in M$ and decides whether m is the decommitment of $\mathtt{com}$;
- Fake_1 takes as input $(x, w) \in \mathsf{Rel}$ and outputs *commitment* $\mathtt{com}$, and *equivocation information* $\mathtt{rand}$;
- Fake_2 takes as input $(x, w) \in \mathsf{Rel}$, message $m \in M$, and pair $(\mathtt{com}, \mathtt{rand})$ and outputs $\mathtt{dec}$;

that enjoy the following properties:

- *Correctness*: for all $x \in \hat{L}_{\mathsf{Rel}}$, all $m \in M$, it holds that

$$\text{Prob}\left[\ (\mathtt{com}, \mathtt{dec}) \leftarrow \mathsf{Com}(x, m) : \mathsf{Dec}(x, \mathtt{com}, \mathtt{dec}, m) = 1\ \right] = 1.$$

- *Binding*: for all $x \notin L_{\mathsf{Rel}}$ and for every commitment $\mathtt{com}$ there exists at most one message $m \in M$ for which there exists a valid decommitment $\mathtt{dec}$; that is, such that $\mathsf{Dec}(x, \mathtt{com}, \mathtt{dec}, m) = 1$.
- *Hiding*: for every receiver $\mathcal{A}$, for every auxiliary information aux, for all $x \in L_{\mathsf{Rel}}$ and all for $m_0, m_1 \in M$, it holds that

$$\text{Prob}\left[\ b \leftarrow \{0, 1\}; (\mathtt{com}, \mathtt{dec}) \leftarrow \mathsf{Com}(1^\lambda, x, m_b) : b = \mathcal{A}(\mathsf{aux}, x, \mathtt{com}, m_0, m_1)\ \right] \leq \frac{1}{2}.$$

- *Trapdoorness*: for all $(x, w) \in \mathsf{Rel}$ and $m \in M$ the following two distributions coincide

$$\{(\mathtt{com}, \mathtt{rand}) \leftarrow \mathsf{Fake}_1(x, w); \mathtt{dec} \leftarrow \mathsf{Fake}_2(x, w, m, \mathtt{com}, \mathtt{rand}) : (\mathtt{com}, \mathtt{dec})\}$$

$$\{(\mathtt{com}, \mathtt{dec}) \leftarrow \mathsf{Com}(x, m) : (\mathtt{com}, \mathtt{dec})\}.$$

IDBC from Σ-protocol. Our construction follows similar constructions of [62, 65, 112]. Let $\Pi = (\mathcal{P}, \mathcal{V})$ be a Σ-protocol for the polynomial-time relation Rel challenge length λ, and simulator S. We define IDBC $\mathsf{CS}^\Pi = (\mathsf{Com}^\Pi, \mathsf{Dec}^\Pi, \mathsf{Fake}_1^\Pi, \mathsf{Fake}_2^\Pi)$ with message space $\{0, 1\}^\lambda$ as follows.

- Com^Π takes as input x and $m \in \{0, 1\}^\lambda$ and computes $(\mathtt{com}, \mathtt{dec})$ by running S on input (x, m).
- Dec^Π takes as input $x, \mathtt{com}, \mathtt{dec}, m$, runs $\mathcal{V}$ on instance x and transcript $(\mathtt{com}, m, \mathtt{dec})$ and outputs $\mathcal{V}$'s output.
- Fake_1^Π takes as input $(x, w) \in \mathsf{Rel}$, samples a random string ρ and runs $\mathcal{P}$ on input (x, w) and randomness ρ to get the 1st message a of Π. Fake_1^Π sets $\mathtt{com} = \mathsf{a}$ and $\mathtt{rand} = \rho$ and outputs $(\mathtt{com}, \mathtt{rand})$.

- Fake_2^{Π} takes as input $(x, w) \in \mathsf{Rel}$, message $m \in M$, and commitment $\mathtt{com}$ and equivocation information $\mathtt{rand}$ and runs $\mathcal{P}$ to get third-round message z of Π corresponding to first message $\mathsf{a} = \mathtt{com}$ produced with randomness $\rho = \mathtt{rand}$ and challenge $\mathsf{c} = m$. Fake_1^{Π} sets $\mathtt{dec} = \mathsf{z}$ and outputs $\mathtt{dec}$.

Theorem 9.1 *[62, 65, 112]* CS^{Π} *is an IDBC for the polynomial-time relation* Rel.

9.3 Adaptive-Input Special-Soundness of Σ-Protocols

In this section we start by describing classical Σ-protocols that are not secure when the adversarial prover can choose the statement adaptively after seeing the verifier's challenge. We then give an efficient compiler that, on input a Σ-protocol belonging to the general class considered in [56, 146] and that includes our examples, outputs a Σ-protocol that is adaptive-input special sound.

9.3.1 Adaptive-Input Insecure Delayed-Input Σ-Protocols

We start with the following well-known Σ-protocol $\Pi^{\mathsf{DH}} = (\mathcal{P}, \mathcal{V})$ for relation DH. On common input $T = (g, A, B, X)$ and private input α such that $A = g^{\alpha}$ and $X = B^{\alpha}$, the prover $\mathcal{P}$ sends $a = g^r$ and $x = B^r$ for randomly chosen $r \in Z_q$ (q denotes the size of the group $\mathcal{G}$). Upon receiving challenge c, $\mathcal{P}$ replies by sending $z = r + \alpha \cdot c$ to $\mathcal{V}$. $\mathcal{V}$ accepts if and only if $g^z = a \cdot A^c$ and $B^z = x \cdot X^c$.

We construct two accepting transcripts for Π^{DH}, one for each of two non-DH tuples. The two transcripts have the same first-round message and two different challenges (thus they constitute a collision) but, obviously, no witness can be extracted. Specifically, consider tuples $T_1 = (g, A = g^{\alpha}, B, X_1 = B^{\gamma_1})$ and $T_2 = (g, A = g^{\alpha}, B, X_2 = B^{\gamma_2})$ with $\gamma_1, \gamma_2 \neq \alpha$ (this guarantees that neither tuple is DH). We constructs the two transcripts by setting the common first-round message to $(a = g^r, x = B^s)$, for arbitrary $r \neq s$. Then we compute challenges c_1 and c_2 by setting $c_i = \frac{r-s}{\gamma_i - \alpha}$, for $i = 1, 2$; clearly, the two transcripts have different challenges. We complete the transcripts by computing the third-round messages z_1 and z_2 as $z_i = r + \alpha \cdot c_i$, for $i = 1, 2$. It is then easily see that both transcripts are accepting.

We remark that essentially the same reasoning can be used to prove that also adaptive-input soundness can be violated by a prover that is allowed to pick T after seeing c. Specifically, consider a malicious prover that first sends $(a = g^r, x = B^s)$, with $r \neq s$, and then it completes the protocol for adaptively chosen tuple $T = (g, A = g^{\alpha}, B, X = B^{\gamma})$ with $\gamma = \alpha + \frac{r-s}{c}$ by sending $z = r + \alpha \cdot c$. Tuple T is non-DH (as $\gamma \neq \alpha$ by the choice of r and s) and the verifier is easily seen to accept. Similar arguments apply for the Σ-protocol of [150] for relation $\mathsf{Com} = \{((g, h, G, H, m), r) : G = g^r \text{ and } H = h^{r+m}\}$.

We next consider Schnorr's Σ-protocol [185] for relation $\mathsf{DLog} = \{((\mathcal{G}, g, Y), y) : g^y = Y\}$. In Schnorr's protocol, the prover on input $(Y, y) \in \mathsf{DLog}$ starts by sending $a = g^r$, for a randomly chosen $r \in Z_q$ (q denotes the size of the group $\mathcal{G}$). Upon receiving challenge c, $\mathcal{P}$ replies by computing $z = r + yc$. $\mathcal{V}$ accepts (a, c, z) if and only if $g^z = a \cdot Y^c$. We show an efficient procedure that on input $Y_1 \in \mathcal{G}$ and challenges $c_1 \neq c_2$, outputs $Y_2 \in \mathcal{G}$ and accepting transcripts (a, c_1, z_1) and (a, c_2, z_2) for Y_1 and Y_2, respectively. This implies that, unless computing discrete log is easy, it is not possible to extract the discrete log of Y_1 from the two transcripts.

The first transcript (a, c_1, z_1) is constructed by running the SHVZK simulator of Schnorr's protocol. Then we set $Y_2 = Y_1^{\beta} \cdot g^{\gamma}$, where $\beta = c_1/c_2$ and γ is arbitrary in Z_q, and complete the second transcript by setting $z_2 = z_1 + c_2 \cdot \gamma$. We have that

$$\begin{aligned} g^{z_2} &= g^{z_1} \cdot g^{c_2 \cdot \gamma} \\ &= a \cdot Y_1^{c_1} \cdot g^{c_2 \cdot \gamma} \\ &= a \cdot Y_1^{c_2 \cdot \beta} \cdot g^{c_2 \cdot \gamma} \\ &= a \cdot [Y_1^{\beta} \cdot g^{\gamma}]^{c_2} \\ &= a \cdot Y_2^{c_2} \end{aligned}$$

and thus the second transcript is also accepting for Y_2.

9.3.2 A Compiler for Adaptive-Input Special Soundness

In this section we construct an adaptive-input special sound Σ-protocol Π_f^{a} for proving knowledge of the pre-image of a homomorphic function f. Our construction is based on the Σ-protocol $\Pi_f = (\mathcal{P}_f, \mathcal{V}_f)$ given in [56, 146] that generalizes and subsumes several Σ-protocols, including the ones by Schnorr [185] and Guillou-Quisquater [104], and the Σ-protocol for DH tuples [69]. Our construction works for the same class of *canonical* homomorphic functions f used in [56, 146].

More precisely, let $(\mathcal{G}, \star)$ and $(\mathcal{H}, \otimes)$ be two groups with efficient operations and let $f : \mathcal{G} \rightarrow \mathcal{H}$ be a one-way homomorphism from $\mathcal{G}$ to $\mathcal{H}$; that is, for all $x, y \in \mathcal{G}$, we have that $f(x \star y) = f(x) \otimes f(y)$ and, on input $x = f(w)$ for a randomly chosen w, it is infeasible to compute w' such that $f(w') = x$. We next describe Σ-protocol $\Pi_f = (\mathcal{P}_f, \mathcal{V}_f)$ for relation $\mathsf{Rel}_f = \{(x, w) : x = f(w)\}$. Here prover $\mathcal{P}_f$ and verifier $\mathcal{V}_f$ receive as input the descriptions of groups $\mathcal{G}$ and $\mathcal{H}$ along with $x \in \mathcal{H}$. In addition, $\mathcal{P}_f$ receives w such that $x = f(w)$ as a private input. The first-round message a is computed by $\mathcal{P}_f$ by randomly picking $r \in \mathcal{G}$ and by setting $a = f(r)$. The verifier's challenge is randomly selected from a subset C_f of $\{0, \ldots, |\mathcal{G}| - 1\}$. The last message z is computed by $\mathcal{P}_f$ by setting $z = r \star w^c$. Finally, $\mathcal{V}_f$ accepts if and only if $f(z) = a \otimes x^c$.

Completeness is easily seen to hold and it is also easy to see that Schnorr's [185] and Guillou-Quisquater [104] Σ-protocols as well as the one for DH tuples are special cases of Π_f. Therefore, since Schnorr's protocol is a special case, protocol Π_f does not enjoy adaptive-input special soundness. For special soundness, Theorem 3 of [146] gives necessary conditions for witness w such that $x = f(w)$ to be extracted from a a collision (a, c_1, z_1) and (a, c_2, z_2) for common input x. Specifically, this is possible provided that integer y and $u \in \mathcal{G}$ such that $\gcd(c_1 - c_2, y) = 1$ and $f(u) = x^y$ can be efficiently computed. We call a homomorphic function with the above property *canonical*.

From Π_f to Π_f^{a}.

By looking back at the proof that the Σ-protocol for DH does not enjoy adaptive-input special soundness, we notice that it was crucial for the malicious prover to be able to pick the first message (a, x) so that (g, a, B, x) was a non-DH tuple. Indeed, if the prover was forced to pick a DH-tuple then it could not have made the honest verifier accept. We next show that this holds in general: if we force the prover to correctly compute the first message then Π_f is adaptive-input special soundness; for Π_f this means to prove knowledge of r such that $a = f(r)$. This is easily achieved by having a second parallel instance of Π_f run on input a. We observe that the second instance of Π_f is not subject to an adaptive-input attack since in a collision the two transcripts share the first message a of the first instance of Π_f thus fixing the input of the second instance. Thus, in sums, protocol Π_f^{a} on common input x consists of the parallel execution of two instances of Π_f: the first with common input x and the second with common input the first-round message a of the first instance. The verifier of Π_f^{a} sends the same challenge to both instances and accepts if and only if, in both instances, the verifier of Π_f accepts. For reasons that will be clear in the proof, we set the challenge space of Π_f^{a} to $\mathsf{C}_f^{\mathsf{a}} = \mathsf{C}_f \setminus \{0\}$. The following observations are straightforward.

1. If the challenge space C_f consists of only one challenges then Π_f is vacuously adaptive-input 2-special sound and thus we consider $\Pi_f^{\mathsf{a}} = \Pi_f$.
2. If the challenge space C_f consists of two challenges and one of them is 0 then we have $\Pi_f^{\mathsf{a}} = \Pi_f$ and $\mathsf{C}_f^{\mathsf{a}} = \mathsf{C}_f - \{0\}$. We observe that, by definition, Π_f^{a} enjoys the property of adaptive-input special soundness.
3. In general, if C_f contains 0, then the output protocol of the compiler has challenge space smaller than C_f, and therefore has also worst knowledge error than the starting protocol. This can be easily avoided by amplifying the challenge space of Π_f before using our compiler. We recall that it is important to preserve the knowledge error to preserve the PoK property of the input protocol.[5]

Let us now prove that Π_f^{a} enjoys adaptive-input special soundness whenever Π_f enjoys special soundness (and we are not in Case 1 or 2 described before). Suppose

[5] We observe that the Theorem 2.2 cannot be directly applied to the Σ-protocol described in this section because of the different notation used to describe the challenge space of a Σ-protocol.

we have two accepting transcripts (a, c_1, z_1) and (a, c_2, z_2) of Π_f^{a} for inputs x_1 and x_2 with $c_1 \neq c_2$. By special soundness of the second instance of Π_f, we can extract the randomness r used to compute the first message a of the first instance of Π_f from the two sub-transcripts of the second instance of Π_f. We conclude the proof by showing that it is possible to compute w such that for $x = f(w)$ from one accepting transcript (a, c, z) of Π_f for x, provided that r such that $f(r) = a$ is available. We also assume that, y and u such that $f(u) = x^y$ and $\gcd(y, c) = 1$ are available (we use the same hypothesis of Theorem 3 of [146]). Note that this is the main reason why we require $c \neq 0$. By using the extended GCD algorithm, we can compute α and β such that $y \cdot \alpha + c \cdot \beta = 1$. Finally, we set $w = u^\alpha \star (r^{-1} \star z)^\beta$. Now observe that $f(z) = a \otimes x^c$ and this implies that $f(r^{-1} \star z) = x^c$. Therefore, $f(w) = f(u^\alpha \star (r^{-1} \star z)^\beta) = f(u)^\alpha \otimes f(z \star r^{-1})^\beta = x^{y\alpha} \otimes x^{\beta c} = x$ that proves that $f(w) = x$.

We have thus proved the following theorem.

Theorem 9.2 *Let f be a canonical one-way homomorphism. Then there exists a Σ-protocol Π_f^{a} for Rel_f that enjoys adaptive-input special soundness.*

9.3.3 On the Adaptive-Input Special Soundness of Chapter 8's Transform

Chapter 8 gives a compiler that takes as input two Σ-protocols, Π_0 and Π_1 for languages L_0 and L_1, and constructs a new Σ-protocol Π^{OR} for $L_0 \vee L_1$ in which the instance for language L_1 is needed by the prover only in the 3rd round. The compiler requires Π_1 to be delayed input. In this section we show that if Π_1 enjoys adaptive-input special soundness, then so does Π^{OR}. We briefly recall the main building blocks used in the construction of Chap. 8.

t-Instance-Dependent Binding Commitment.

Let t be a non-negative integer. In a t-Instance-Dependent Binding Commitment (a t-IDBC) scheme for polynomial-time relation Rel, one party can commit a message m from a predefined message space M with respect to an instance x. The commitment produced is hiding and binding unless a witness w such that $(x, w) \in \mathsf{Rel}$; in this case, the commitment can be equivocated.

More precisely, a t-IDBC scheme consists of a triple of PPT algorithms $(T_{\mathsf{NI}}, \mathsf{TDec}, \mathsf{TFake})$ with the following syntax. The *commitment* algorithm T_{NI} takes as input an instance x and a message m and returns a commitment $\mathtt{com}$ of m with respect to x along with a decommitment $\mathtt{dec}$. The decommitment algorithm TDec takes as input $\mathtt{com}$, $\mathtt{dec}$ and m and x and verifies whether $\mathtt{dec}$ is an opening of $\mathtt{com}$ as m with respect to x. TFake is the *equivocation* procedure that, given a witness for an instance x, a commitment $\mathtt{com}$ of message m with respect to x along with the random coin tosses used to produce it and message m' outputs a decommitment $\mathtt{dec}'$ of $\mathtt{com}$ as m'. It is required that a t-IDBC is *correct* (honestly computed commitments are correctly decommitted), *hiding* (honestly computed commitments hide the message), *trapdoor* (a fake commitment is indistinguishable from an honestly computed commitment) and *t-Special Extractable*. The property of t-Special Extractability informally says that if the sender opens the same commitment in t different ways, then it is possible to efficiently extract the witness w.

9.3.3.1 The Construction

Let Rel_0 be a relation admitting a t-IDBC scheme with $t = 2$ and let Rel_1 be a relation admitting an delayed-input Σ-protocol Π_1; we denote by S_1 the associated simulator for the honest verifier zero knowledge. We recall how the protocol Σ-protocol $\Pi^{\mathsf{OR}} = (\mathcal{P}^{\mathsf{OR}}, \mathcal{V}^{\mathsf{OR}})$ of Chap. 8 for the OR relation:

$$\mathsf{Rel}^{\mathsf{OR}} = \left\{((x_0, x_1), w) : ((x_0, w) \in \mathsf{Rel}_0 \wedge x_1 \in \hat{L}_{\mathsf{Rel}_1}) \text{ OR } ((x_1, w) \in \mathsf{Rel}_1 \wedge x_0 \in \hat{L}_{\mathsf{Rel}_0})\right\}$$

works.

We assume that x_0 and the length of x_1 in unary are available from the onset of the protocol whereas x_1 and the witness w such that $((x_0, x_1), w) \in \mathsf{Rel}^{\mathsf{OR}}$ are given before the 3rd round. Obviously, the verifier does not get to learn w.

1. $\mathcal{P}^{\mathsf{OR}}$ executes the following steps:

   1.1 pick random r_1 and compute the 1st round a_1 of the delayed-input Σ-protocol Π_1 using r_1 as random coin tosses;
   1.2 compute a pair $(\mathtt{com}, \mathtt{dec}_1)$ of commitment and decommitment of a_1 with respect to x_0.
   1.3 send $\mathtt{com}$ to $\mathcal{V}^{\mathsf{OR}}$;

2. $\mathcal{V}^{\mathsf{OR}}$ sends a random challenge c.
3. $\mathcal{P}^{\mathsf{OR}}$ on input $((x_0, x_1), c, (w, b))$ s.t. $(x_b, w) \in \mathsf{Rel}_b$ executes the following steps:

   3.1 If $b = 1$,
   compute the 3rd round of Π_1, z_1, using as input (x_1, w, c);
   3.2 send $(\mathtt{dec}_1, a_1, z_1)$ to $\mathcal{V}^{\mathsf{OR}}$;
   3.3 If $b = 0$,
   run simulator S_1 on input x_1 and c obtaining (a_2, z_2);
   use trapdoor to compute decommitment $\mathtt{dec}_2$ of $\mathtt{com}$ as a_2;
   3.4 send $(\mathtt{dec}_2, a_2, z_2)$ to $\mathcal{V}^{\mathsf{OR}}$.

4. $\mathcal{V}^{\mathsf{OR}}$ receives (a, z) and $\mathtt{dec}$ from $\mathcal{P}^{\mathsf{OR}}$ and accepts if and only if the following conditions are satisfied:

   4.1 (a, c, z) is an accepting conversation for x_1;
   4.2 $\mathtt{dec}$ is a valid decommitment of $\mathtt{com}$ for a message a.

9.3.3.2 On the Adaptive-Input Special Soundness of Π^{OR}

We now show that Π^{OR} preserves the adaptive-input special soundness of the underlying Σ-protocol.

Theorem 9.3 *If* Rel_0 *admits a* 2-IBTC *and* Rel_1 *admits a delayed-input adaptive-input special-sound* Σ*-protocol, then* Π^{OR} *is an adaptive-input special-sound* Σ*-protocol.*

Proof The claim follows from the adaptive-input special soundness of the underlying Σ-protocol Π_1 and from the 2-Special Extractability property of the 2-IBTC scheme. More formally, consider an accepting transcript $(\mathtt{com}, c, (a, z, \mathtt{dec}))$ for input (x_0, x_1) and an accepting transcript $(\mathtt{com}, c', (a', z', \mathtt{dec}'))$ for input (x_0, x_1'), where $c' \neq c$ and x_1 is potentially different from x_1'. We observe that:

- if $a = a'$ then, by adaptive-input special soundness of Π_1, there exists an efficient extractor $\mathsf{AExtract}$ that, given as input $((a, c, z), x_1)$ and $((a', c', z'), x_1')$, outputs w_1 and w_1' s.t. $(x_1, w_1) \in \mathsf{Rel}_1$ and $(x_1', w_1') \in \mathsf{Rel}_1$;
- if $a \neq a'$, then $\mathtt{dec}$ and $\mathtt{dec}'$ are two openings of $\mathtt{com}$ with respect to x_0 for messages $a \neq a'$; then we can obtain a witness w_0 for x_0 by the 2-Special Extractability of the 2-IBTC scheme. □

A similar arguments can be used to show that if Rel_0 admits a 3-IBTC and Rel_1 admits a delayed-input Σ-protocol with adaptive-input special soundness, then Π^{OR} enjoys the adaptive-input proof of knowledge property.

9.4 Delayed-Input Three-Round Protocols for the Threshold Relation

In this section we show that if a relation Rel has a delayed-input Σ-protocol Π, then we can construct a delayed-input 3-round public-coin PoK Π_k for the k-threshold relation. Also, under the DDH assumption, Π_k is adaptive-input WI. If, in addition, Π is *adaptive-input 2-special sound*, then Π_k is an adaptive-input proof of knowledge. Let us now proceed more formally.

For a polynomial-time relation Rel, we define the *k-threshold* relation Rel_k as follows

$$\mathsf{Rel}_k = \Big\{\Big(\big(x_1, \dots, x_n\big), \big((w_1, d_1), \dots, (w_k, d_k)\big)\Big) : 1 \le d_1 < \cdots < d_k \le n \\ \text{and } (x_{d_i}, w_i) \in \mathsf{Rel}, \ \text{for } i = 1, \dots, k\Big\}.$$

Let us give the intuition behind our construction of protocol Π_k for Rel_k. The prover of Π_k starts by randomly selecting k 1-non-DH tuples and $n - k$ DH tuples. Each tuple is used to commit to a random and independently selected first message of protocol Π by using the IDTC $\mathsf{CS} = (\mathsf{Com}, \mathsf{Dec}, (\mathsf{Fake}_1, \mathsf{Fake}_2))$ for the polynomial time relation $\mathsf{1nDH}$ (defined in Sect. 2.7.2). More specifically, algorithm Com is used to compute the commitments w.r.t. the DH tuples and algorithm Fake_1 to compute the commitments w.r.t. the 1-non-DH tuples. Note that Π is a delayed-input Σ-protocol and thus the inputs are not needed to complete this step. All commitments and tuples are sent to the verifier.

The verifier's challenge c and n inputs along with the witnesses for k of them are then made available to the prover that executes the following for each input, distinguishing between inputs for which a witness is available and inputs for which no witness has been provided. For each of the former, the prover associates one of the commitment computed with respect to a 1-non-DH tuple and opens it by using Dec thus revealing a first-round message. The corresponding third-round message is computed by the prover by using the witness. Instead, for each input for which no witness is available, the prover runs the SHVZK simulator of Π on input the challenge c and obtains an accepting transcript (a, c, z). The prover then associates to the input a commitment computed with respect to a DH tuple and computes, by using the algorithm Fake_2, an opening of it as a. The opening and z are then sent to the verifier.

In sums, for each input, the verifier receives an accepting transcript whose first message is shown to have been committed to in the first round. To ensure that the prover cannot cheat and choose n DH tuples (that will allow him to open all commitments produced at the first round at his will) the prover and the verifier engage in parallel an execution of Σ-protocol Π_k^{1nDH}.

1st round. $\mathcal{P}_k \Rightarrow \mathcal{V}_k$:

1. Set $(\mathcal{G}, p, g) \leftarrow \mathsf{GG}(1^\lambda)$.
2. Randomly select tuples $T_1 = (g_1, A_1, B_1, X_1), \ldots, T_n = (g_n, A_n, B_n, X_n)$ of elements of $\mathcal{G}$ under the constraint that exactly k are 1-non-DH and $n - k$ are DH, along with $\alpha_1, \ldots, \alpha_n$ such that $A_i = g_i^{\alpha_i}$, for $i = 1, \ldots, n$.
3. Let $b_1 < \ldots < b_k$ denote the indices of the k 1-non-DH tuples and $\widetilde{b}_1, \ldots, \widetilde{b}_{n-k}$ denote the indices of the $n - k$ DH tuples.
4. Randomly select coin tosses ρ and run the prover of Π_k^{1nDH} on input $\mathcal{T} = (T_1, \ldots, T_n)$, witness $((\alpha_{b_1}, b_1), \ldots, (\alpha_{b_k}, b_k))$ and randomness ρ thus obtaining message a^{1nDH}. Send a^{1nDH} to $\mathcal{V}_k$.
5. For $i = 1, \ldots, k$:
   Randomly select coin tosses r_{b_i} and compute first-round message a_{b_i} of Π by running $\mathcal{P}$ on input r_{b_i}.
   Compute the pair $(\mathtt{com}_{b_i}, \mathtt{dec}_{b_i})$ of commitment and decommitment of the message a_{b_i} using the 1-non-DH tuple T_{b_i}.
6. For $i = 1, \ldots, n - k$:
   Compute the equivocal commitment $\mathtt{com}_{\tilde{b}_i}$ using the DH tuple $T_{\tilde{b}_i}$.
7. Send $(T_1, \mathtt{com}_1), \ldots, (T_n, \mathtt{com}_n)$ to $\mathcal{V}_k$.

2nd round. $\mathcal{V}_k \Rightarrow \mathcal{P}_k$: randomly select a challenge c and send it to $\mathcal{P}_k$.

3rd round. $\mathcal{P}_k \Rightarrow \mathcal{V}_k$:

1. Receive inputs $(x_1, \ldots, x_n)$ and witnesses $(w_{d_1}, \ldots, w_{d_k})$ for inputs $x_{d_1}, \ldots, x_{d_k}$ (we denote by $\widetilde{d}_1, \ldots, \widetilde{d}_{n-k}$ the indices of the inputs for which no witness has been provided).
2. Compute the third round of Π^{1nDH} using c as challenge to get z^{1nDH} and send it to $\mathcal{V}_k$.
3. Randomly select permutation σ of $\{1, \ldots, k\}$ and, for $i = 1, \ldots, k$, associate 1-non-DH tuple T_{b_i} with input $x_{d_{\sigma(i)}}$.
4. For $i = 1, \ldots, k$:
   Use j as a shorthand for $d_{\sigma(i)}$.
   Compute z_j by running $\mathcal{P}$ on input (x_j, w_j), a_{b_i}, randomness r_{b_i} and challenge c.
   Set $M_j = (j, b_i, \mathtt{dec}_{b_i}, a_{b_i}, z_{b_i})$.
5. Randomly select permutation τ of $\{1, \ldots, n-k\}$ and, for $i = 1, \ldots, n-k$, associate DH tuple $T_{\widetilde{b}_i}$ with input $x_{\widetilde{d}_{\tau(i)}}$.
6. For $i = 1, \ldots, n-k$:
   Use j as a shorthand for $\widetilde{d}_{\tau(i)}$.
   Run simulator S on input x_j and c obtaining (a_j, z_j).
   Use trapdoor $\alpha_{\widetilde{b}_i}$ to compute decommitment $\mathtt{dec}_{\widetilde{b}_i}$ of $\mathtt{com}_{\widetilde{b}_i}$ as a_j.
   Set $M_j = (j, \widetilde{b}_i, \mathtt{dec}_{\widetilde{b}_i}, a_j, z_j)$.
7. For $j = 1, \ldots, n$: send M_j to $\mathcal{V}_k$.

$\mathcal{V}_k$, for $j = 1, \ldots, n$ parses $M_j = (j, i, \mathtt{dec}_i, a_j, z_j)$ and accepts if and only the following conditions are satisfied:

1. $(a^{\mathsf{1nDH}}, c, z^{\mathsf{1nDH}})$ is an accepting transcript for $\mathcal{V}^{\mathsf{1nDH}}$ with input $\mathcal{T}$;
2. for $j = 1, \ldots, n$: $(\mathtt{dec}_i, a_j)$ is a valid decommitment of $\mathtt{com}_i$ with respect to T_i, where i is the index associate to M_j;
3. for $j = 1, \ldots, n$: (a_j, c, z_j) is an accepting transcript for $\mathcal{V}$ with input x_j;

We observe that, clearly, Π_k is a delayed-input 3-round public coin and that Π_k has the same challenge length as Π. In the next sections we prove its security properties.

9.4.1 Proof of Knowledge

In this section we start by proving that Π_k is a proof of knowledge with knowledge error negligible in the length of the challenge. Then we prove that if Π is adaptive-input special soundness then Π_k is an adaptive-input proof of knowledge.

Theorem 9.4 *Protocol Π_k is a proof of knowledge for Rel_k with knowledge error negligible in the length of the challenge.*

Proof The completeness property is straightforward from the completeness of Π_k^{1nDH} and Π and from the correctness and trapdoor properties of the Instance-Dependent Binding Commitment scheme used.

Now we proceed to prove that Π_k is N-special sound with $N = k(n - k + 1) + 1$. Therefore, since $n = \mathsf{poly}(\lambda)$ and $k \leq n$, we can invoke Theorem 2.2 to conclude the security proof. Specifically, we show that there exists an efficient extractor that, for any sequence $(x_1, \ldots, x_n)$ of n inputs and for any set of N accepting transcripts of Π_k that share the same first message and have different challenges, outputs the k witnesses of the n inputs. The extractor is based on the following observations.

From any two (out of the N) accepting transcripts of Π_k, we can extract a collision for Π_k^{1nDH}. By the special soundness of Π_k^{1nDH}, the collision gives us the witnesses that k of the tuples used in the N transcripts are 1-non-DH. Without loss of generality, we assume that we obtain witnesses for $T_1, \ldots, T_k$ and we call them the *good* tuples. This implies that commitments $\mathtt{com}_1, \ldots, \mathtt{com}_k$ that appear in the shared first round of the N transcripts are opened to the same strings $a_1, \ldots, a_k$ in all the N transcripts. The k good tuples can be associated in each of the N transcripts to different inputs; however, if the same good tuple is associated with the same input x_i in two different transcripts then we obtain a collision for Π with input x_i and thus, by the special soundness of Π, it is possible to extract a witness for x_i. We call such inputs *good* as well. Notice that we have N transcripts and k good tuples and thus we have $k \cdot N$ associations of good tuple to inputs.

We next prove that the N transcripts contain collisions of protocol Π with good tuples for at least k inputs and thus at least k witnesses can be extracted. For the sake of contradiction, suppose that there are only $m \leq k - 1$ good inputs and let us count the good-tuple-to-input association (which we know to be $k \cdot N$) by counting the contributions of the good inputs and of the non-good inputs, separately. Clearly, each of the m good inputs is associated with at most one good tuple for each of the N transcripts thus contributing $m \cdot N$ associations. Each of the remaining $n - m$ inputs is associated with each of the k good tuples in at most *one* of the N transcripts thus contributing an extra $(n - m) \cdot k$ associations. We have thus counted a total of $m \cdot N + (n - m) \cdot k$ associations. Since the number of associations is an increasing function of m and since $m \leq k - 1$, we have

$$\begin{aligned} m \cdot N + (n - m) \cdot k &= m \cdot (N - k) + n \cdot k \\ &\leq (k - 1) \cdot (N - k) + n \cdot k \\ &\leq k \cdot N - N + k \cdot (n - k + 1) \\ &= k \cdot N - 1 \end{aligned}$$

Contradiction. □

Next we prove that if that adaptive-input security of Π is preserved by our construction. More precisely,

Theorem 9.5 *If Π is adaptive-input 2-special sound for* Rel *then Π_k is an adaptive-input proof of knowledge for* Rel_k *with knowledge error negligible in the length of the challenge.*

Proof The delayed-input completeness of Π_k follows from the delayed-input completeness of protocol Π, the correctness and trapdoor property of the Instance-Dependent Binding Commitment scheme used and from the completeness of Π_k^{1nDH}. In order to conclude the security proof we just need to show that Π_k is adaptive-input 2-special sound which, by Theorem 2.3, is sufficient to prove that Π_k is an adaptive-input PoK with knowledge error $\kappa(\lambda) = 2^{-\lambda}$.

Lemma 9.1 *If Π is adaptive-input 2-special sound for* Rel, *then Π_k is adaptive-input 2-special sound for* Rel_k.

Proof Let $T_1 = (a, c_1, z_1)$ and $T_2 = (a, c_2, z_2)$ with $c_1 \neq c_2$ be two accepting transcripts for input $(x_1^1, \ldots, x_n^1)$ and $(x_1^2, \ldots, x_n^2)$, respectively. First of all, observe that, by the special soundness of protocol Π_k^{1nDH}, it is possible to extract the witness certifying that k of the tuples $T_1, \ldots, T_n$ appearing in the first message are 1-non-DH. Let us denote by $b_1, \ldots, b_k$ the indices of the 1-non-DH tuples. This implies that commitments $\mathtt{com}_{b_1}, \ldots, \mathtt{com}_{b_k}$ that appear in the common first round of the two transcripts are binding and are thus opened to the same strings $a_{b_1}, \ldots, a_{b_k}$ in the two transcripts. Therefore, for $i = 1, \ldots, k$, we can extract from T_1 and T_2 two transcripts of Π: (a_{b_i}, c_1, z_{b_i}) for input $x_{b_i}^1$ and (a_{b_i}, c_2, z'_{b_i}) for input $x_{b_i}^2$. Each pair of transcripts gives, by the adaptive-input special soundness of Π, a witness for $x_{b_i}^1$ and one for $x_{b_i}^2$. □

9.4.2 *Adaptive-Input Witness Indistinguishability*

Here we prove that Π_k is WI with respect to a PPT adversary $\mathcal{A}$ that is allowed to select the instance and the witnesses after receiving the first round. We have the following theorem.

Theorem 9.6 *Under the DDH assumption, if Π is SHVZK for* Rel *then Π_k is adaptive-input WI for relation* Rel_k.

Proof For sake of contradiction, let $\mathcal{A}$ be a PPT adversary and aux an auxiliary information for which $\mathsf{AdvAWI}_{\Pi_k,\mathcal{A}}(\lambda, \mathsf{aux})$ is a non-negligible function of λ. We let $X = (x_1, \ldots, x_n)$ denote the instance output by $\mathcal{A}$ at Step 2 of $\mathsf{ExpAWI}_{\Pi_k,\mathcal{A}}$ and we let $W^0 = ((w_1^0, d_1^0), \ldots (w_k^0, d_k^0))$ and $W^1 = ((w_1^1, d_1^1), \ldots (w_k^1, d_k^1))$ denote the witnesses output. We remark that $(x_{d_i^b}, w_i^b) \in \mathsf{Rel}$ for $i = 1, \ldots, k$ and $b = 0, 1$ and that $i \neq j$ implies that $d_i^0 \neq d_j^0$ and $d_i^1 \neq d_j^1$. Let $m \leq k$ be the number of instances of Π in X for which W^1 contains a witness but W^0 does not. Obviously, since W^0 and W^1 contain witnesses for the same number k of instances of Π in X, it must be the case that m is also the number of instances of Π in X for which W^0 contains a witness and W^1 does not. We call m the number of *unique* instances (these are instances for which a witness appears in exactly one of W^0 and W^1).

For integer $0 \leq m \leq k$ for which $\mathcal{A}$ has a positive probability of outputting X, W^0, W^1 with m unique instances, we define $\mathsf{AdvAWI}(\lambda, \mathsf{aux}|m)$ to be the advantage of $\mathcal{A}$ conditioned on the event that there are m unique instances. Notice that we dropped the indices $\mathcal{A}$ and Π_k not to overburden the notation. Since $\mathsf{AdvAWI}(\lambda, \mathsf{aux})$ is non-negligible in λ there must exist integer $0 \leq m \leq k$ such that $\mathsf{AdvAWI}(\lambda, \mathsf{aux}|m)$ is defined and non-negligible and the probability of having m unique instances is also non-negligible. Notice that the value of m depends solely on the adversary $\mathcal{A}$ and we consider it fixed throughout the proof. In designing the reductions to the problem of distinguishing DH tuples from 1-non-DH tuples (which, by Lemma 2.4, is hard under the DDH assumption), we shall assume that $\mathcal{A}$ would output X, W^0 and W^1 with m unique instances. When this is actually the case, which by our choice of m has a non-negligible probability of occurring, we will have a non-negligible advantage in solving the problem; when instead the number of unique instances is other than m, we will output a random guess. This is sufficient to prove that a non-negligible advantage in distinguishing DH tuples from 1-non-DH tuples is obtained.

We rename the instances of X output by $\mathcal{A}$, so that W^0 and W^1 can be written as

$$W^0 = \big((w_1^0, m+1), \ldots, (w_m^0, 2m), (w_{m+1}^0, 2m+1), (w_k^0, m+k)\big)$$

and

$$W^1 = \big((w_1^1, 1), \ldots, (w_m^1, m), (w_{m+1}^1, 2m+1), \ldots, (w_k^1, m+k)\big);$$

that is, we sort the instances of X so that the first m instances, $x_1, \ldots, x_m$, have a witness only in W^1; the next m instances, $x_{m+1}, \ldots, x_{2m}$, have a witness only in W^0; and the last $k - m$ instances, $x_{2m+1}, \ldots, x_{m+k}$, have witnesses in the both. For any two such W^0 and W^1, we define the following intermediate sequences of witnesses $W_1, \ldots, W_k$:

1. For $i = 0, \ldots, m$: W_i consists of witnesses $W_i = \big((w_1^1, 1), \ldots, (w_i^1, i), (w_{i+1}^0, m+i+1), \ldots, (w_m^0, 2m), (w_{m+1}^0, 2m+1), \ldots, (w_{m+k}^0, m+k)\big)$. Note that W_i contains witnesses for $(x_1, \ldots, x_i, x_{m+1+i}, \ldots, x_{2m})$. Moreover, W_0 coincides with W^0 and in W_m the first m witnesses are from W^1 and the remaining are from W^0.
2. For $i = m+1, \ldots, k$: W_i consists of witnesses

$$W_i = \big((w_1^1, 1), \ldots, (w_m^1, m), (w_{m+1}^1, 2m+1), \ldots$$
$$\ldots, (w_{m+i}^1, m+i), (w_{m+i+1}^0, m+i+1), \ldots, (w_{m+k}^0, m+k)\big).$$

It is easy to see that W_k coincides with W^1.

For $i = 0, \ldots, k$, we define hybrid experiment $\mathcal{H}_i$ as the experiment in which the challenger C uses sequence of witnesses W_i to complete the third step of the experiment $\mathsf{ExpAWI}_{\Pi_k,\mathcal{A}}$. Clearly, $\mathcal{H}_0$ is the experiment $\mathsf{ExpAWI}_{\Pi_k,\mathcal{A}}$ when C picks $b = 0$ and $\mathcal{H}_k$ is the same experiment when C picks $b = 1$.

We start by proving indistinguishability of $\mathcal{H}_i$ and $\mathcal{H}_{i+1}$ for $i = 0, \ldots, m-1$. We will then argue about the indistinguishability of $\mathcal{H}_{m+i}$ and $\mathcal{H}_{m+i+1}$ for $i = 0, \ldots, k-m-1$. We assume inductively that in $\mathcal{H}_i$ the probability that there will be m unique instances is non-negligible and prove that this is still the case in $\mathcal{H}_{i+1}$. We remind the reader that, in $\mathcal{H}_i$ and $\mathcal{H}_{i+1}$, the challenger C uses witnesses for the following k instances:

$$\begin{array}{lllll} \mathcal{H}_i & x_1 \cdots x_i & & x_{m+i+1}\ x_{m+i+2} \cdots x_{2m}\ x_{2m+1} \cdots x_{m+k} \\ \mathcal{H}_{i+1} & x_1 \cdots x_i\ x_{i+1} & & \quad\quad\quad\ x_{m+i+2} \cdots x_{2m}\ x_{2m+1} \cdots x_{m+k} \end{array}$$

The differences between the two hybrid experiments are relative to instances x_{i+1} and x_{m+i+1} and to the witness used by the prover to complete the proof that at least k tuples are 1-non-DH. Specifically,

1. the transcript of Π for x_{i+1} is produced by the simulator in $\mathcal{H}_i$ and by the prover in $\mathcal{H}_{i+1}$;
2. the first messages of the transcript of Π for x_{i+1} is committed to with a DH tuple in $\mathcal{H}_i$ and with a 1-non-DH tuple in $\mathcal{H}_{i+1}$;
3. the transcript of Π for x_{m+i+1} is produced by the prover in $\mathcal{H}_i$ and by the simulator in $\mathcal{H}_{i+1}$;
4. the first messages of the transcript of Π for x_{m+i+1} is committed to with a 1-non-DH tuple in $\mathcal{H}_i$ and with a DH tuple in $\mathcal{H}_{i+1}$;
5. protocol Π^{1nDH} is completed by using the witnesses for the 1-non-DH tuples associated with $x_1, \cdots, x_i, x_{m+i+2}, \cdots, x_{2m}, x_{2m+1}, \cdots, x_{m+k}$. In addition, the witness for the 1-non-DH tuple associated with x_{m+i+1} is used by $\mathcal{H}_i$ and the witness for the 1-non-DH tuple associated with x_{i+1} is used by $\mathcal{H}_{i+1}$.
6. in addition, in both hybrid experiments exactly k of the tuples are 1-non-DH and exactly $n-k$ are DH.

To prove indistinguishability of $\mathcal{H}_i$ and $\mathcal{H}_{i+1}$ we consider four intermediate hybrids: $\mathcal{H}_i^1, \ldots, \mathcal{H}_i^4$.

$\mathcal{H}_i^1$ differs from $\mathcal{H}_i$ in the way the transcript of Π instance x_{i+1} is computed. Specifically, instead of using the SHVZK simulator of Π, $\mathcal{H}_i^1$ uses the algorithm of the prover of Π run with w_{i+1} as input. Indistinguishability of $\mathcal{H}_i^1$ and $\mathcal{H}_i$ follows directly from the following two observations. First, observe that x_{i+1} is associated in both $\mathcal{H}_i$ and $\mathcal{H}_i^1$ with a DH tuple and therefore the commitment is perfectly hiding. Moreover, Π's simulator is perfect.

$\mathcal{H}_i^2$ differs from $\mathcal{H}_i^1$ in the way the tuples used to compute the commitments are chosen. Specifically, $\mathcal{H}_i^2$ chooses $k+1$ 1-non-DH tuples, $n-k-1$ DH tuples (as opposed to k 1-non-DH tuples and $n-k$ DH tuples). The extra 1-non-DH tuple is used by $\mathcal{H}_i^2$ to compute the commitment of the first message of Π that will be associated to x_{i+1} in the third round. As a sanity check, notice that in this case the commitment associated with x_{i+1} is binding but this is not a problem as an accepting transcript of Π for x_{i+1} can be computed by using witness w_{i+1}.

We observe that Lemma 2.4 implies that the probability that, in $\mathcal{H}_i^2$, $\mathcal{A}$ produces two sequences W^0 and W^1 of witnesses with m unique instances is still non-negligible.[6]

Indistinguishability of $\mathcal{H}_i^1$ and $\mathcal{H}_i^2$ follows by Lemma 2.4. Let $T = (g, A, B, X)$ be either a random 1-non-DH tuple or a random DH tuple and consider the following simulator algorithm S that on input T produces the view of $\mathcal{A}$ in $\mathcal{H}_i^1$ or in $\mathcal{H}_i^2$ depending on whether T is DH or non-DH. The n tuples selected by S consist in k randomly selected 1-non-DH tuples, $n - k - 1$ randomly selected DH tuples and T. Then, S executes the same steps as in $\mathcal{H}_i^1$ and will associate tuple T with x_{i+1}. Notice that S does not need a witness for T being DH to complete the execution as the accepting transcript of Π for x_{i+1} is computed using the witness w_{i+1} and the prover's algorithm and thus there is no need of a trapdoor to change the first message committed in the 1st round.

$\mathcal{H}_i^3$ differs from $\mathcal{H}_i^2$ as protocol Π^{1nDH} is completed by using the witness of the tuple associated with x_{i+1} and not the tuple associated with x_{m+i+1} (along, obviously, the tuples associated with $x_1, \ldots, x_i$ and with $x_{m+i+2}, \ldots, x_{m+k}$). Indistinguishability of $\mathcal{H}_i^3$ and $\mathcal{H}_i^2$ follows from the perfect WI of Π^{1nDH}. Notice also that the only change intervenes after $\mathcal{A}$ has output the instances and the witnesses and therefore the probability of having m unique instances does not change.

$\mathcal{H}_i^4$ differs from $\mathcal{H}_i^3$ in the way the tuples used to compute the commitments are chosen. Specifically, $\mathcal{H}_i^4$ chooses k 1-non-DH tuples, $n - k$ DH tuples (as opposed to $k + 1$ 1-non-DH tuples and $n - k - 1$ DH tuples). The extra DH tuple is used by $\mathcal{H}_i^4$ to compute the commitment of the first message of Π that will be associated to x_{m+i+1} in the third round. Indistinguishability of $\mathcal{H}_i^3$ and $\mathcal{H}_i^4$ follows by the same argument used for the indistinguishability of $\mathcal{H}_i^2$ and $\mathcal{H}_i^1$ and also by the same argument the probability of having m unique instances stays non-negligible.

Finally, we observe that $\mathcal{H}_i^4$ differs from $\mathcal{H}_{i+1}$ in the way the transcript of Π instance x_{m+i+1} is computed. Specifically, instead of using the prover of Π, $\mathcal{H}_i^4$ uses the simulator of Π. Indistinguishability of $\mathcal{H}_i^4$ and $\mathcal{H}_{i+1}$ follows by the same argument used for the indistinguishability of $\mathcal{H}_i$ and $\mathcal{H}_i^1$. Notice also that the only change intervenes after $\mathcal{A}$ has output the instances and the witnesses and therefore the probability of having m unique instances does not change.

We have thus proved that $\mathcal{H}_0$ is indistinguishable from $\mathcal{H}_m$. To complete the proof, we need to prove that $\mathcal{H}_{m+i}$ and $\mathcal{H}_{m+i+1}$ are indistinguishable for $i = 0, \ldots, k - m - 1$. This follows directly from the observation that $\mathcal{H}_{m+i}$ and $\mathcal{H}_{m+i+1}$ only differ in the witness used for x_{2m+i+1}: $\mathcal{H}_{m+i}$ uses the witness from W^0 whereas $\mathcal{H}_{m+i+1}$ uses the witness from W^1. Indistinguishability then follows directly from the Perfect WI of Π.

---

[6] Actually, the probability is, up to a negligible additive factor, the same as in $\mathcal{H}_i^1$ which in turn is exactly the same as in $\mathcal{H}_i$.

9.4.3 Online Performances

In Table 9.2 of Sect. 9.1.3 we have compared the number of exponentiations made by the prover in the online phase of [57, 133] and of the construction of Chap. 8, with the exponentiations require by the prover of Π_k. More precisely, the third row of Table 9.2 refers to the case where Π_k is compiled by using a Σ-protocol for the logarithm discrete relation, and the last row refers to the case where an adaptive-input 2-special sound[7] protocol is used instead. Let us now show why we obtain $2(n-k)$ for the forme case, and $4(n-k)$ for the latter.

In the first case our construction involves $10n-k$ exponentiations in total, considering both the offline and the online phases. In our construction in the 1st round we sample $n-k$ DH tuples and k 1-non-DH, sampling a 1-non-DH/DH tuple costs 3 exponentiations, so this operation costs $3n$. Given that a commitment computed according to the commitment scheme described previously based on DH tuples costs 4 exponentiations and that in the 1st round we compute $n-k$ equivocal commitments and k binding commitments, this sums up to $2n+2k$ modular exponentiations. Furthermore the prover computes the 1st round of Schnorr's Σ-protocol n times and this costs n exponentiations. Moreover it has to run [57] to prove knowledge of witnesses for k instances out of n instances, and this costs $2n-k$ exponentiations. The only operations that involve exponentiations at the third round are the $n-k$ executions of the simulator of Schnorr's Σ-protocol. Therefore the online phase costs $2(n-k)$.

The Adaptive Proof of Knowledge version of our construction costs $13n-3k$ exponentiations in total. We first observe that in the adaptive-input 2-special sound version of Schnorr's Σ-protocol an execution of the simulator costs 4 exponentiations and that computing the 1st round using just the honest prover procedure involves 2 exponentiations. Hence the first round of our Adaptive Proof of Knowledge construction involves $6n+k$ exponentiations and the online phase costs $4(n-k)$ exponentiations. The analysis for the case of 1 out of 2 is similar with $k=1$ and $n=2$ but in this case, in the offline phase, we do not consider the cost of [57] since the correctness of the pair of tuples can be self-verified. □

9.5 Extension to Multiple Relations

In this section, we generalize the result of Sect. 9.4 to the case of different relations. More specifically, given delayed-input Σ-protocols $\Sigma_1, \ldots, \Sigma_n$ for polynomial-time relations $\mathsf{Rel}_1, \ldots, \mathsf{Rel}_n$, we construct an Adaptive-Input Proof of Partial Knowledge $\Gamma_k^{\mathsf{Rel}_1,\ldots,\mathsf{Rel}_n} = (\mathcal{P}_{\Gamma_k}{}^{\mathsf{Rel}_1,\ldots,\mathsf{Rel}_n}, \mathcal{V}_{\Gamma_k}^{\mathsf{Rel}_1,\ldots,\mathsf{Rel}_n})$ for the k-threshold polynomial-time relation

[7] We recall that by Theorem 9.5, when an adaptive-input 2-special sound protocol is used as input of our compiler we obtain that Π_k is Adaptive Proof of Knowledge.

$$\mathsf{Rel}^k(\mathsf{Rel}_1, \ldots, \mathsf{Rel}_n) = \Big\{\Big((x_1, \ldots, x_n), ((w_1, d_1) \ldots, (w_k, d_k))\Big) : 1 \le d_1 < \cdots < d_k \le n \text{ and } (x_{d_i}, w_i) \in \mathsf{Rel}_{d_i} \text{ for } i = 1, \ldots, k\Big\}.$$

Not to overburden our notation, we will just write Rel^k, Γ_k, $\mathcal{P}_{\Gamma_k}$, and $\mathcal{V}_{\Gamma_k}$, whenever $\mathsf{Rel}_1, \ldots, \mathsf{Rel}_n$ are clear from the context.

Let us start by providing some intuition on Γ_k. For $j = 1, \ldots, n$, the prover of Γ_k computes two first-round messages for Σ_j and commits to each one using a different tuple. Note that Σ_j is delayed-input so this step can be performed without knowing the instances (nor the witnesses). The two tuples, T_j^0 and T_j^1, used to compute the commitments for j are chosen so that they share the first three components and T_j^1 is DH and, consequently, T_j^0 is non-DH. Therefore, the verifier is guaranteed that, for each j, at most one of the commitments of the tuple is DH (and thus at most one commitment can be equivocated). For each j, the tuples T_j^0 and T_j^1 and the relative commitments $\mathtt{com}_j^0$ and $\mathtt{com}_j^1$ are sent in random order to the verifier. The prover then receives the n instances, witnesses for k of them and the verifier's challenge. Then, for each instance x_j for which a witness is available, the prover decommits the commitment computed using T_j^0 (the non-DH tuple) and computes the third round message by running the prover of Σ_j. On the other hand, for each instance x_j for which no witness is provided, the prover runs the simulator of Σ_j and produces an accepting transcript; then the commitment computed using T_j^1 (the DH tuple) is opened as the first message of the simulated transcript, by using equivocation. In both cases, the decommitment and the accepting transcript are sent to the verifier.

The verifier expects to receive an accepting transcript for each instance with the first message coming (through equivocation for $n - k$ of them) from a commitment sent as part of the first round. Moreover, to ensure that the prover has not cheated by equivocating too many commitments, the prover and the verifier engage in parallel in a protocol by which the prover proves that from among the n unopened commitments at least k are associated with DH tuples; this implies, by the way the pairs of tuples have been constructed, that at least k of the opened commitments are associated with non-DH tuples. We denote the resulting protocol by $\mathsf{ThresDDH} = (\mathcal{P}_{\mathsf{TDDH}}, \mathcal{V}_{\mathsf{TDDH}})$. Notice that when $\mathsf{ThresDDH}$ starts, the prover does not know which commitment will be opened (since this depends on the witnesses received after the challenge); this can be handled by our protocol described in Sect. 9.4, since it only needs the instances and witnesses before the third round starts.

More formally, we use the following tools to construct Γ_k.

1. We use as a commitment scheme an IDTC for the polynomial time relation $\mathsf{DH} = \{((g, A, B, X), \alpha) : A = g^\alpha \text{ and } X = B^\alpha\}$.
2. A delayed-input, adaptive-input 2-special sound, adaptive-input WI protocol for the relation

$$\mathsf{Rel}_{\mathsf{TDDH}} = \Big\{\Big((T_1, \ldots, T_n), \big((\alpha_1, d_1), \ldots, (\alpha_k, d_k)\big)\Big) : 1 \le d_1 < \cdots < d_k \le n \text{ and } (T_{d_i}, \alpha_i) \in \mathsf{DH}, \text{ for } i = 1, \ldots, k\Big\}.$$

We observe that this protocol can be obtained relying on Theorem 9.6, and by combining the fact that the well known Σ-protocol for DH tuple [69] can be converted into one that enjoys adaptive-input special soundness (see Sect. 9.3.2) with Lemma 9.4.1.

1st round. $\mathcal{P}_{\Gamma_k} \Rightarrow \mathcal{V}_{\Gamma_k}$:
$\mathcal{P}_{\Gamma_k}$ receives as unary inputs the security parameter λ, the number n of theorems that will be given as input at the beginning of the third round, and the number k of witnesses that will be provided.

1. Set $(\mathcal{G}, p, g) \leftarrow \mathsf{GG}(1^\lambda)$.
2. For $j = 1, \ldots, n$
   - 2.1 Randomly sample a non-DH tuple $T_j^0 = (g_j, A_j, B_j, X_j)$ over $\mathcal{G}$, along with α_j such that $A_j = g_j^{\alpha_j}$.
   - 2.2 Set $Y_j = B_j^{\alpha_j}$ and $T_j^1 = (g_j, A_j, B_j, Y_j)$ (note that, by construction, T_j^1 is a DH tuple).
3. Select random string R and use it to compute the first round message a^{ThresDDH} of $\mathsf{ThresDDH}$ by running prover $\mathcal{P}_{\mathsf{TDDH}}$.
   Send a^{ThresDDH} to $\mathcal{V}_{\Gamma_k}$.
4. For $j = 1, \ldots, n$
   - 4.1 Select random strings R_j^0 and R_j^1 and use them to compute the first-round messages a_j^0 and a_j^1 of Σ_j by running the prover of Σ_j.
   - 4.2 Compute the pair $(\mathtt{com}_j^0, \mathtt{dec}_j^0)$ of commitment and decommitment of the message a_j^0 using non-DH tuple T_j^0.
   - 4.3 Compute the commitment $\mathtt{com}_j^1$ (of the message a_j^1) using the DH tuple T_j^1.
   - 4.4 Send pairs $(T_j^0, \mathtt{com}_j^0)$ and $(T_j^1, \mathtt{com}_j^1)$ in random order to $\mathcal{V}_{\Gamma_k}$.

2nd round. $\mathcal{V}_{\Gamma_k} \Rightarrow \mathcal{P}_{\Gamma_k}$: $\mathcal{V}_{\Gamma_k}$ randomly selects a challenge c and sends it to $\mathcal{P}_{\Gamma_k}$.
3rd round. $\mathcal{P}_{\Gamma_k} \Rightarrow \mathcal{V}_{\Gamma_k}$:
$\mathcal{P}_{\Gamma_k}$ receives theorems $x_1, \ldots, x_n$ and, for $d_1 < \ldots < d_k$, witnesses $w_1, \ldots, w_k$ for theorems $x_{d_1}, \ldots, x_{d_k}$, respectively. We let $\widetilde{d}_1 < \ldots < \widetilde{d}_{n-k}$ denote the indices of the theorems for which no witness has been provided.

1. For $l = 1, \ldots, k$
   - 1.1 Use j as a shorthand for d_l.
   - 1.2 Set $U_j = T_j^1$ and $\hat{U}_j = T_j^0$.

1.3 Compute z_j by running prover of Σ_j on input (x_j, w_l), randomness R_j^0 used to compute the first round a_j^0, and challenge c.
1.4 Set $M_j = (a_j^0, z_j, \texttt{dec}_j^0, \hat{U}_j)$.

2. For $l = 1, \ldots, n-k$

2.1 Use j as a shorthand for $\widetilde{d}_l$.
2.2 Set $U_j = T_j^0$ and $\hat{U}_j = T_j^1$.
2.3 Run the simulator of Σ_j on input x_j and c therefore obtaining $(\widetilde{a}_j^1, z_j)$.
2.4 Use the trapdoor α_j to compute the decommitment $\texttt{dec}_j^1$ of $\texttt{com}_j^1$ as $\widetilde{a}_j^1$.
2.5 Set $M_j = (\widetilde{a}_j^1, z_j, \texttt{dec}_j^1, \hat{U}_j)$.

3. For $l = 1, \ldots, n$ send M_l to $\mathcal{V}_{\Gamma_k}$.
4. Compute the third round z^{ThresDDH} of ThresDDH by running $\mathcal{P}_{\mathsf{TDDH}}$ on input tuples $(U_1, \ldots, U_n)$, witnesses $\alpha_{d_1}, \ldots, \alpha_{d_k}$ and randomness R used to compute the first round a^{ThresDDH}.

$\mathcal{V}_{\Gamma_k}$ accepts if and only if the following conditions are satisfied.

1. For $j = 1, \ldots, n$
Check that the two tuples sent for j in the first round share the first three components.
Write M_j as $M_j = (a_j, z_j, \texttt{dec}_j, \hat{U}_j)$.
Check that (a_j, c, z_j) is an accepting conversation of Σ_j for instance x_j.
Check that $\texttt{dec}_j$ is a decommitment as a_j with respect to tuple $\hat{U}_j$ of one of $\texttt{com}_j^0$ and $\texttt{com}_j^1$ and that tuple $\hat{U}_j$ was associated with j in the first round. Denote by U_j the other tuple associated with j.
2. Check that $(a^{\mathsf{ThresDDH}}, c, z^{\mathsf{ThresDDH}})$ is an accepting conversation of $\mathcal{V}_{\mathsf{TDDH}}$ for instances $U_1, \ldots, U_n$.

9.5.1 Adaptive-Input Proof of Knowledge

In this section, we study the PoK properties of Γ_k. We start by proving in Theorem 9.7 that Γ_k is a PoK. Then, in Theorem 9.8, we prove that, under the additional assumption that $\Sigma_1, \ldots, \Sigma_n$ are adaptive-input 2-special sound, Γ_k is an adaptive-input PoK.

Theorem 9.7 *Γ_k is a proof of knowledge for* $\mathsf{Rel}^k(\mathsf{Rel}_1, \ldots, \mathsf{Rel}_n)$ *with knowledge error negligible in the length of the challenge.*

Proof The completeness property follows from the completeness of protocols ThresDDH and $\Sigma_1, \ldots, \Sigma_n$, and from the correctness and the trapdoor property of the Instance-Dependent Binding Commitment scheme used. We next prove that Γ_k is t-special sound, with $t = n - k + 2$. The theorem then follows by Theorem 2.2.

To prove that Γ_k is t-special sound we describe an algorithm that takes t accepting transcripts of Γ_k for the same input $(x_1, \ldots, x_n)$ that share the first message and outputs a witness for $(x_1, \ldots, x_n)$. We remind the reader that the first message contains n binding commitments to the first message of each of protocols $\Sigma_1, \ldots, \Sigma_n$. The last message of each transcript instead contains the openings of k of the binding commitments.[8]

The algorithm examines the t transcripts $\tau^1, \ldots, \tau^t$ one at the time looking for a revealing transcript. We say that transcript τ^j is *revealing* if each of the k binding commitments opened in the last message of τ^j has been opened at least once in one of the preceding $j - 1$ transcripts. Once the algorithm has found a revealing transcript, it can obtain a collision for k of the n Σ-protocols $\Sigma_1, \ldots, \Sigma_n$ from which, by special soundness, it obtains the witness for k of the inputs of transcript τ^j. We observe that the special soundness of $\Sigma_1, \ldots, \Sigma_n$ is sufficient to extract k witness since in τ^j every accepting transcript for Σ_i is with respect to the same theorem x_i for all $i \in \{1, \ldots, n\}$.

We conclude the proof by showing that any set of $t = n - k + 2$ transcripts contains at least one revealing transcript. Clearly, the k binding commitments opened in the last message of the first transcript are all opened for the first time. In each subsequent transcript that is not revealing there exists at least one binding commitment that is opened for the first time. Therefore, if, after $n - k + 1 = t - 1$ transcripts have been examined, no revealing transcript has been found then the t-th transcript must be a revealing transcript. □

We now look at adaptive-input PoK.

Theorem 9.8 *If $\Sigma_1, \ldots, \Sigma_n$ enjoy adaptive-input special soundness then Γ_k is an adaptive-input proof of knowledge for $\mathsf{Rel}^k(\mathsf{Rel}_1, \ldots, \mathsf{Rel}_n)$ with knowledge error negligible in the length of the challenge.*

Proof The delayed-input completeness of Γ_k follows from the delayed-input completeness of protocol ThresDDH, the correctness and trapdoor property of the Instance-Dependent Binding Commitment scheme used and from the delayed-input completeness of Σ_i for $i = 1, \ldots, n$. In order to prove that Γ_k enjoys the property of adaptive-input PoK we need to show an extractor AExtract that, given oracle access to $\mathcal{P}_{\Gamma_k}{}^{\star}$, outputs a couple (x, w) according to Definition 2.9. Before that, we prove the following lemma.

Lemma 9.2 *There exists an algorithm that, on input $m = n - k + 2$ accepting transcripts of protocol Γ_k with the same first message and distinct challenges, outputs in time polynomial in λ a witness for the input of one of the m transcripts.*

[8] Since $t > 1$ and ThresDDH is adaptive-input 2-special sound, then we can claim that at least k of the opened commitments in the last round are binding.

Proof This proof follows the same approach used in the proof of Theorem 9.7. The main difference is that in this case we rely on the adaptive-input special soundness instead of the special-soundness of $\Sigma_1, \ldots, \Sigma_n$ to extract the witnesses. The reason why special-soundness is not sufficient in this case is due to the additional power given to the malicious prover to choose different inputs for different transcripts.

We remind the reader that the m accepting transcripts share the first message that contains n binding commitments to the first messages of protocols $\Sigma_1, \ldots, \Sigma_n$. The last message of each transcript instead contains the openings of k of the binding commitments. The algorithm examines the m transcripts $\tau^1, \ldots, \tau^m$ one at the time looking for a revealing transcript. Once the algorithm has found a revealing transcript, it can obtain a collision for k of the n Σ-protocol $\Sigma_1, \ldots, \Sigma_n$ from which, by adaptive-input special soundness, it obtains the witness for k of the inputs of transcript τ^j. We conclude the proof by showing that any set of m transcripts contains at least one revealing transcript. Clearly, the k binding commitments opened in the last message of the first transcript are all opened for the first time. In each subsequent transcript that is not revealing there exists at least one binding commitment that is opened for the first time. Therefore, if, after $n - k + 1 = m - 1$ transcripts have been examined, no revealing transcript has been found then the m-th transcript must be a revealing transcript. □

Now we are ready to show how our extractor AExtract works when given access to malicious prover $\mathcal{P}^\star$.

1. Upon receiving a from $\mathcal{P}^\star$, AExtract randomly selects challenge $c^1 \leftarrow \{0,1\}^\lambda$ and sends it to $\mathcal{P}^\star$.
2. Upon receiving z^1 and the theorem x^1, AExtract runs $\mathcal{V}_{\Gamma_k}$ to check if (a, c^1, z^1) is accepting with respect to x^1. If $\mathcal{V}_{\Gamma_k}$ rejects, AExtract outputs $\perp$ and stops, otherwise it continues as follows.
3. For $i = 2, \ldots, t$

   $\mathcal{P}^\star$ rewinds $\mathcal{P}^\star$ by sending a new randomly selected challenge $c_i \leftarrow \{0,1\}^\lambda$ different from all previous challenges, and stops when either an accepting transcript (a, c^i, z^i) with respect to some input x^i is received, or 2^λ rewinds have been performed.

4. If t accepting transcripts have been computed then AExtract continues; otherwise, it stops and outputs $\perp$.
5. Relying on Lemma 9.2, AExtract uses the t accepting conversations to compute and output a witness for one of the inputs $x^1, \ldots, x^t$.

We now analyze the running time of AExtract. Let $p^\star(\lambda)$ be the probability that $\mathcal{P}^\star$ provides an accepting transcript for a challenge of length λ. We next show that if $p^\star > (n - k + 1)2^{-\lambda}$ then AExtract is an extractor for Γ_k. The probability that in the step 3, for a randomly selected challenge c_i, with $c_1 \neq \ldots \neq c_{i-1} \neq c_i$, $\mathcal{P}^\star$ provides an accepting transcript is $p^\star(\lambda) - (i-1)2^{-\lambda}$. Therefore the expected number of rewinds that have to be made in step 3, for some $i \in \{2, \dots, t\}$ is $\frac{1}{p^\star(\lambda)-(i-1)2^{-\lambda}}$. This means that the expected number of steps made by $\mathsf{AExtract}^{\mathcal{P}^\star}$ is

$$\sum_{i=2}^{t} \frac{1}{p^\star(\lambda) - (i-1)2^{-\lambda}} < \frac{t-1}{p^\star(\lambda) - (t-1)2^{-\lambda}}.$$

□

9.5.2 Adaptive-Input Witness Indistinguishability

Theorem 9.9 *If relations* $\mathsf{Rel}_1, \dots, \mathsf{Rel}_n$ *admit a SHVZK* Σ*-protocol then, under the DDH assumption,* Γ_k *is adaptive-input WI for* $\mathsf{Rel}^k(\mathsf{Rel}_1, \dots, \mathsf{Rel}_n)$.

Proof We adopt the same framework of the proof for the case of one relation. Specifically, we have the same definition of hybrid witness sequence W_i and of hybrid experiment $\mathcal{H}_i$, for $i = 0, \dots, k$. We start by proving indistinguishability of $\mathcal{H}_i$ and $\mathcal{H}_{i+1}$ for $i = 0, \dots, m-1$. The differences between the two hybrids are relative to inputs x_{i+1} and x_{m+i+1} and the witness used to complete protocol $\mathsf{ThresDDH}$. We consider the following intermediate hybrids.

$\mathcal{H}_i^1$ differs from $\mathcal{H}_i$ in the way the transcript of Σ_{i+1} for instance x_{i+1} is computed. Specifically, instead of using the SHVZK simulator of Σ_{i+1}, $\mathcal{H}_i^1$ uses the algorithm of the prover of Σ_{i+1} run with w_{i+1} as input. Notice that in both hybrids the tuple $\widehat{U}_{i+1}$ used to commit the first-round message of Σ_{i+1} is a DH tuple whereas U_{i+1} is a non-DH tuple. In $\mathcal{H}_i^1$ however the equivocability of the commitment is not used and the transcript is completed using the witness and the prover's algorithm for Σ_{i+1}. Indistinguishability of $\mathcal{H}_i^1$ and $\mathcal{H}_i$ follows directly from the perfect SHVZK.

$\mathcal{H}_i^2$ differs from $\mathcal{H}_i^1$ in the fact that tuple $\widehat{U}_{i+1}$ is a non-DH tuple and U_{i+1} is a DH tuple. In other words, in $\mathcal{H}_i^2$ the first-round message of the transcript relative to x_{i+1} shown at the third round has been committed to by a non-DH tuple.

Suppose now, for sake of contradiction, that there exists a PPT distinguisher D and a polynomial $\mathsf{poly}(\cdot)$ such that, for sufficiently large security parameters λ,

$$p_1(\lambda) \geq p_2(\lambda) + 1/\mathsf{poly}(\lambda),$$

where $p_1(\lambda)$ and $p_2(\lambda)$ are, respectively, the probabilities that D outputs 1 on input the view of $\mathcal{A}$ in $\mathcal{H}_i^1$ and in $\mathcal{H}_i^2$. We use D and $\mathcal{A}$ to design an algorithm $\mathcal{B}$ that has a non-negligible advantage in the DDH game. Algorithm $\mathcal{B}$ receives as input a challenge tuple $T = (g, A, B, X)$, randomly selects Y and constructs the tuple $\widehat{T} = (g, A, B, Y)$ that shares the first three components with T. Then $\mathcal{B}$ simulates the view of $\mathcal{A}$ in $\mathcal{H}_1^i$ with the following two modifications: T and $\widehat{T}$ are the tuples associated with $i+1$; in the third round, $\mathcal{B}$ selects one of the two at random and the commitment computed at the first round with respect to the selected tuple is opened.

$\mathcal{B}$ feeds D with the view generated by interacting with $\mathcal{A}$ and records D's output. Finally, $\mathcal{B}$ outputs 1 if and only if it had selected T and D has output 1 or it had selected $\widehat{T}$ and D has output 0.

Now, let us compute the probability that $\mathcal{B}$ outputs 1 when T is DH tuple. Notice that if T is selected (and this happens with probability $1/2$) then $\mathcal{B}$ has produced the view of $\mathcal{H}_i^1$ and thus the probability that D outputs 1 is p_1. On the other hand, if $\widehat{T}$ is selected then $\mathcal{B}$ has produce the view of $\mathcal{H}_i^2$ and thus the probability that D outputs 0 is $1 - p_2$. Therefore, it T is DH tuple, $\mathcal{B}$ outputs 1 with probability $1/2 \cdot (1 + p_1 - p_2)$.

Consider now the case in which T is non-DH. In this case, both T and $\widehat{T}$ are non-DH and thus the view received by D is independent from which one of the two is selected by $\mathcal{B}$. We thus denote by p the probability that D outputs 1 when the view contains two non-DH tuples. As in the previous case, $\mathcal{B}$ outputs 1 if T is selected and D outputs 1 (this event has probability $1/2p$) and $\widehat{T}$ is selected and D outputs 0 (this event has probability $1/2 \cdot (1 - p)$). Therefore $\mathcal{B}$ has probability $1/2$ of outputting 1 when it receives a non-DH tuple in input.

We thus conclude that $\mathcal{B}$ breaks the DDH assumption. Contradiction.

$\boldsymbol{\mathcal{H}_i^3}$ differs from $\mathcal{H}_i^2$ in the witness used to compute an accepting transcript for ThresDDH. More specifically α_{i+1} is used instead of α_{m+i+1} in the tuple that define the witness for ThresDDH. Observe that this is possible because U_{i+1} is a DH tuple. Suppose now, for sake of contradiction, that there exists a PPT distinguisher D and a polynomial $\mathsf{poly}(\cdot)$ such that, for sufficiently large security parameters λ,

$$p_1(\lambda) \geq p_2(\lambda) + 1/\mathsf{poly}(\lambda),$$

where $p_1(\lambda)$ and $p_2(\lambda)$ are, respectively, the probabilities that D outputs 1 on input the view of $\mathcal{A}$ in $\mathcal{H}_i^2$ and in $\mathcal{H}_i^3$. We use D and $\mathcal{A}$ to design an algorithm $\mathcal{B}$ that has a non-negligible advantage in break the adaptive WI property of ThresDDH. Algorithm $\mathcal{B}$ receives as input the first round challenge a^{ThresDDH} and computes all the other information needed to compute the first round of the protocol of Γ_k. $\mathcal{B}$, upon receiving the challenge c computes the challenge theorem and witnesses as following:

$$\begin{aligned}
X_{\mathsf{ThresDDH}} &= (U_1, \ldots, U_n);\\
W^0_{\mathsf{ThresDDH}} &= (\alpha_1, \ldots, \alpha_i, \alpha_{m+i+1}, \alpha_{m+i+2}, \ldots, \alpha_{2m}, \alpha_{2m+1}, \ldots \alpha_{m+k});\\
W^1_{\mathsf{ThresDDH}} &= (\alpha_1, \ldots, \alpha_{i+1}, \alpha_{m+i+2}, \ldots, \alpha_{2m}, \alpha_{2m+1}, \ldots \alpha_{m+k}).
\end{aligned}$$

Then sends them, with the challenge c, to the challenger. $\mathcal{B}$, upon receiving z^{ThresDDH}, completes the third round protocol using z^{ThresDDH}, and sends it to $\mathcal{A}$. $\mathcal{B}$ feeds D with the view generated by interacting with $\mathcal{A}$ and records D's output. Finally, $\mathcal{B}$ outputs 1 if and only if the witness W^0_{ThresDDH} has been used by the challenger and D has output 1 or has been used W^1_{ThresDDH} and D has output 0.

$\boldsymbol{\mathcal{H}_i^4}$ differs from $\mathcal{H}_i^3$ in the fact that tuple $\widehat{U}_{m+i+1}$ is a DH tuple and U_{m+i+1} is a non-DH tuple. In other words, in $\mathcal{H}_i^4$ the first-round message of the transcript relative to x_{m+i+1} shown at the third round has been committed to by a DH tuple.

The indistinguishability between $\mathcal{H}_i^3$ and $\mathcal{H}_i^4$ follows the same arguments of the indistinguishability between $\mathcal{H}_i^2$ and $\mathcal{H}_i^1$.

Finally, we observe that $\mathcal{H}_i^4$ differs from $\mathcal{H}_{i+1}$ in the way the transcript of Σ_{m+i+1} for the instance x_{m+i+1} is computed. Specifically, instead of using the prover of Σ_{m+i+1}, $\mathcal{H}_i^4$ uses the simulator of Σ_{m+i+1}. Indistinguishability of $\mathcal{H}_i^4$ and $\mathcal{H}_{i+1}$ follows by the same argument used for the indistinguishability of $\mathcal{H}_i$ and $\mathcal{H}_i^1$.

We have thus proved that $\mathcal{H}_0$ is indistinguishable from $\mathcal{H}_m$. To complete the proof, we need to prove that $\mathcal{H}_{m+i}$ and $\mathcal{H}_{m+i+1}$ are indistinguishable for $i = 0, \ldots, k - m - 1$. This follows directly from the observation that $\mathcal{H}_{m+i}$ and $\mathcal{H}_{m+i+1}$ only differ in the witness used for x_{2m+i+1}: $\mathcal{H}_{m+i}$ uses the witness from W^0 whereas $\mathcal{H}_{m+i+1}$ uses the witness from W^1. Indistinguishability then follows directly from the Perfect WI of Π. $\square$

Chapter 10
Non-interactive Zero-Knowledge Without Programmable Random Oracles

10.1 Introduction

In this chapter, we will still study and use sigma-protocols, but with the goal of designing efficient *Non-interactive zero-knowledge (NIZK)* proofs. Non-interactive zero-knowledge (NIZK) proofs introduced in [23, 24, 66] are widely used in Cryptography. Such proofs allow a prover to convince a verifier with just one message about the membership of an instance x in a language L without leaking any additional information. NIZK proofs are not possible without a setup assumption and the one proposed initially in [23] is the existence of a *Common Reference String* (CRS) received as input both by the prover and the verifier. The CRS model has been so far the standard setup for NIZK. Another setup that has been proposed in literature is the existence of registered public keys in [12, 39, 63, 188].

Starting with the breakthrough of [76, 77] we know that NIZK proofs in the CRS model exist for any $\mathcal{NP}$ language with the additional appealing feature of using just one CRS for any polynomial number of proofs. Moreover NIZK proofs and their stronger variations [102, 182, 183] have been shown to be not only interesting for their original goal of being a non-interactive version of classic zero-knowledge (ZK) proofs [92, 93], but also because they are powerful building blocks in many applications (e.g., for CCA encryption [156], ZAPs [71, 72]).

Efficient NIZK.

Generic constructions of NIZK proofs are rather inefficient since they require to first compute an $\mathcal{NP}$ reduction and then to apply the NIZK proof for a given $\mathcal{NP}$-complete language to the instance given in output by the reduction. A significant progress in efficiency has been proposed in [103] where several techniques have been proposed to obtain efficient NIZK proofs that can be used in bilinear groups.

The most popular use of NIZK proofs in real-world scenarios consists in taking an efficient *interactive* constant-round public-coin honest-verifier zero-knowledge

M. Ciampi and L. Siniscalchi, *Round and Computational Efficiency of Multi-party Protocols*, Information Security and Cryptography,
https://doi.org/10.1007/978-3-031-92374-6_10

(HVZK) proof system and in making it a NIZK argument through the so called *Fiat-Shamir (FS) transform* [79]. The FS transform replaces the verifier by calls to a hash function on input the transcript so far. In the random oracle [18] (RO) model the hash function can only be evaluated through calls to an oracle that answers as a random function. The security proof allows the simulator for HVZK to program the RO (i.e., the simulator decides how to answer to a query) and this allows to convert the entire transcript of a public-coin HVZK proof into a single message that is indistinguishable from the single message computed by a honest NIZK prover. The efficiency of the FS transform led to many practical applications. The transform is also a method to obtain signatures of knowledge, as discussed in [40].

In [100], Groth showed an efficient transform for NIZK where soundness is proved requiring a programmable RO while no random oracle is needed to prove zero knowledge.

The Risks of the FS Transform.

The main disadvantage of the FS transform is the fact that the random oracle methodology has been proved to be unsound both in general [31] and for the specific case [20, 91] of turning identification schemes into signatures as considered in [79]. Nevertheless, the examples of constructions proved secure in the RO model and insecure for any concrete hash function are seemingly artificial. Interestingly in [96] it is shown that the FS transform can be used to obtain (non-artificial) information-theoretic NIZK arguments that are not sound when knowledge of the description of the hash functions is used by the adversarial prover.

A slight modification of the FS transform gives as input to the hash function only the first round of a three-round protocol, without the instance to be proved. Despite the fact that this approach, called *weak FS transform*, has been used is literature, [19] showed the insecurity of the transform when the some HVZK protocols are used (similar issues have been discussed in [52, 53] in the standard model). Other weaknesses about the non-malleability of the FS transform are discussed in [74]. In contrast, there are some positive results [121, 151] based on obfuscation.

The FS transform applied to 3-round HVZK proofs is still one of the major uses of the RO model for real-world protocols, therefore any progress in this research direction (either on the security of the transform, or on its efficiency, or on its generality) is of extreme interest.

Efficient NIZK with Designated/Registered Verifiers.

A first attempt to get efficient NIZK arguments from some restricted class of 3-round public-coin HVZK proofs without ROs was done by [63] (the proof of soundness required complexity leveraging) and later on by [39, 188] that achieved a weaker form of soundness in the registered public-key model. The limitation of this model is that a NIZK proof can be verified only by a designated verifier (i.e., the proof requires a secret known to the verifier). Moreover, there is an inconvenient preliminary registration phase where the verifier has to register her public key.

Lindell's Transform.

In [141], Lindell proposed a very interesting transform that can be seen as an attempt toward obtaining efficient constructions without random oracles. Starting from a Σ-protocol for a language L (i.e., a special type of 3-round public-coin HVZK proof used already in several efficient constructions of zero knowledge [3, 36, 61, 68, 150, 158, 184, 189, 194]), Lindell shows how to construct an efficient NIZK[1] argument system for L in the CRS model. Two are the major advantages of Lindell's transform with respect to the FS transform. First, in Lindell's transform the proof of ZK does not need the existence of a random oracle and this allows to avoid some issues due to protocol composition [190]. We remark that the proof of ZK for Lindell's transform needs a CRS but this is unavoidable as one-round ZK in the plain model is possible only for trivial languages. Second, the soundness of Lindell's transform can be proved by relying on a *non-programmable random oracle* (NPRO). An NPRO is a RO that in the protocol and in the security proofs can be used only as a black box and cannot be programmed by a simulator or by the adversary of a reduction. This is a considerable advantage compared to the FS transform since replacing a RO by an NPRO is a step toward removing completely the need of ROs in a cryptographic construction. Indeed the work of Lindell goes precisely in the direction of solving a major open problem in Cryptography: obtaining an efficient RO-free transform for NIZK arguments to be used in place of the FS transform.

The main drawback of Lindell's transform is that it requires extra computation on top of the one needed to run the Σ-protocol for the language L. In contrast, the FS transform does not incur into any overhead on top of a 3-round public-coin HVZK proof for L. In addition, since 3-round public-coin HVZK proofs are potentially less demanding than Σ-protocols, we have that requiring a Σ-protocol as starting protocol for a transform instead of a public-coin HVZK proof may already result in an efficiency loss.

Lindell's transform is based on a primitive named *dual-mode* (DM) commitment scheme (DMCS). A DMCS is based on a membership-hard language Λ and each specific commitment takes as input an instance ρ of Λ and has the following property: if $\rho \notin \Lambda$, the DM commitment is perfectly binding; on the other hand, if $\rho \in \Lambda$, the DM commitment can be arbitrarily equivocated if a witness for $\rho \in \Lambda$ is known. Moreover, the two modes are indistinguishable.[2] Lindell showed that DMCSs can be constructed efficiently from Σ-protocols for membership-hard languages and also provided a concrete example based on the language of Diffie-Hellman tuples (DH). Then, Lindell's transform shows how to combine DM commitments and Σ-protocols along with a hash function[3] to obtain an efficient NIZK argument.

[1] Lindell's NIZK argument is a not an argument of knowledge in contrast to the NIZK argument obtained through an FS transform.

[2] A similar notion was introduced in [37, 38] and a scheme with similar features was proposed in [64].

[3] In the proof of soundness this function will be modeled as an NPRO.

10.1.1 This Chapter's Results

In this work, we continue the study of generic and efficient transforms from 3-round public-coin HVZK proofs to NIZK arguments.

We start by studying the generality and efficiency of Lindell's transform in terms of the Σ-protocol used for instantiating the DMCS (and in turn instantiating the CRS) and the Σ-protocol to which the transform is applied. As a result, we point out a significant gap in generality and efficiency of Lindell's transform compared to the FS transform.

Then we show an improved transform that is based on weaker requirements. Specifically, our transform only requires computational HVZK and optimal soundness instead of perfect special HVZK and special soundness. More interestingly and surprisingly despite being based on weaker requirements, our transform is also significantly more efficient than Lindell's transform and very close to the efficiency of the FS transform. We next discuss the contributions of the chapter in more detail.

The Classes of Σ-protocols Needed in [141].

Lindell defines Σ-protocols as 3-round public-coin proofs that enjoy *perfect* special HVZK and special soundness. The former property means that the simulator on input any valid statement x and challenge e can compute (a, z) such that the triple (a, e, z) is perfectly indistinguishable from an accepting transcript where the verifier sends e as challenge. Special soundness instead means that from any two accepting transcripts (a, e, z) and (a, e', z') for the same statement x that shares the first message but have different challenges $e \neq e'$, one can efficiently compute a witness w for $x \in L$. Lindell in [140] shows a construction of a DMCS from any (defined as above) Σ-protocol for a membership-hard language.

The Efficiency of Lindell's Transform.

Lindell's transform uses a DMCS derived from a Σ-protocol $\Pi_\Lambda = (\mathcal{P}_\Lambda, \mathcal{V}_\Lambda)$ for language Λ whose commitment algorithm $\mathtt{com}$ works by running the simulator of Π_Λ. The CRS contains an instance ρ of Λ along with the description of a hash function h. The argument produced by the NIZK $\Pi = (\mathcal{P}, \mathcal{V})$ for $x \in L$ starting from a Σ-protocol $\Pi_L = (\mathcal{P}_L, \mathcal{V}_L)$ for L is computed as a tuple (a', e, z, r) where $a' = \mathtt{com}(a, r), e = h(x|a')$, and z is the 3rd round of Π_L answering to the challenge e and having a as first round. The verifier checks that a' is a commitment of a with randomness r, that e is the output of $h(x|a')$ and that (a, e, z) is accepted by $\mathcal{V}_L$.

As an example, in [141] Lindell discussed the use of the Σ-protocol for the language DH for which the transform produces a very efficient NIZK proof; Indeed the additional cost is of only 8 modular exponentiations: 4 to be executed by the prover and 4 by the verifier.

We notice, however, that for certain Σ-protocol the Lindell's transform may suffer in terms of performances. The caveat is due to the message space of the DMCS. Indeed, once the CRS is fixed the max length of a message that can be committed to with only one execution of $\mathtt{com}$ is limited to the challenge length l_Λ of Π_Λ. Therefore in case the first round a of Π_L is much longer than l_Λ, the transform of Lindell requires multiple executions of $\mathtt{com}$ therefore suffering of a clear efficiency loss.[4]

We show indeed in Tables 10.2 and 10.3 that Lindell's transform can generate in the resulting NIZK argument a blow up of the computations compared to what $\mathcal{P}_L$ and $\mathcal{V}_L$ actually do, and therefore compared to the FS transform.

10.1.2 Our Transform

In this chapter, we present a different transform that is closer to the FS transform both on generality and on efficiency.

Our transform can be used to obtain a NIZK for any language L with a 3-round HVZK proofs enjoying optimal soundness (i.e., a weaker soundness requirement compared to special soundness). The CRS can be instantiated based on any membership-hard language Λ with a 3-round HVZK proofs enjoying optimal soundness. More specifically, we do not require perfect HVZK nor special HVZK for the involved Σ-protocols. Moreover, instead of special soundness, we will just require that, for any false statement and any first round message a, there is at most one challenge c that can be answered correctly. This is clearly a weaker requirement than special soundness and was already used by [150].

Essentially we just need that both protocols Π_L and Π_Λ are 3-round public-coin HVZK proofs with optimal soundness. Our transform produces a NIZK argument $\Pi = (\mathcal{P}, \mathcal{V})$ that does not require multiple executions of Π_L and Π_Λ and, therefore, it remains efficient under any scenario without suffering of the previously discussed issue about challenge spaces in Lindell's transform.

Techniques.

We start by considering the FS transform in the NPRO model and by noticing that, as already claimed and proved in [193], if the original 3-round public-coin HVZK proof is witness indistinguishable (WI),[5] then the transformed protocol is still WI, and of course the proof of WI is RO free.

Notice that as in [141], $\mathcal{P}$ and $\mathcal{V}$ need a common hash function (modeled as an NPRO in the soundness proof) to run the protocol and this can be enforced through

---

[4] As suggested by an anonymous reviewer of TCC 2016-A, to reduce the overhead of the Lindell's construction one could use the approach proposed in Groth's PhD thesis [100], thus committing to a secret share of the challenge instead of the first round of the Σ-protocol.

[5] We use WI both to mean witness indistinguishable and witness indistinguishability.

a setup (i.e., a non-programmable CRS [164], or a global hash function [34]). The use of the FS transform in the NPRO model is not sufficient for our purposes. Indeed we want generality and the HVZK proof might not be witness indistinguishable. Moreover we should make a witness available to the simulator. We solve this problem by using the OR composition of 3-round perfect HVZK proofs proposed in [57]. We will let the prover $\mathcal{P}$ for NIZK to prove that either $x \in L \vee \rho \in \Lambda$. We notice that in [57] the proposed OR composition is proved to guarantee WI only when applied to two instances of the same language having a public-coin *perfect* HVZK proof. We can avoid this limitation using a generalization discussed already in [82] that allows the OR composition of different protocols for different languages relying on *computational HVZK* only.

10.1.3 Comparison

Here we compare the computational effort, both for the prover and the verifier, required to execute Lindell's NIZK argument, our NIZK argument and the FS one. The properties of the three transforms are summarized in Table 10.1. The cost for the prover can be found in Table 10.2, while the one for the verifier can be found in Table 10.3. The comparison of the computational effort is performed with respect to three Σ-protocols.[6] Roughly speaking, in the comparisons, we consider the CRS to contain an instance of the the language DH of Diffie-Hellman triples with respect to 1024-bit prime p_{CRS} and consider two Σ-protocols: the one to prove that a triples is Diffie-Hellman[7] with respect to a prime p, for which we consider the cases in which p is 1024-bit and 2048-bit long,[8] and the Σ-protocol for graph isomorphism (GI). For the Σ-protocol for graph isomorphism, we count only the modular exponentiations and do not count other operations (e.g., random selection of a permutation and generation of the adjacency matrix of permuted graphs) since they are extremely efficient and clearly dominated by the cost of modular exponentiations. A detailed description of the Σ-protocols and of the way we measure the computational effort is found in Sect. 10.6.

The tables give evidence of the fact that while Lindell's transform on some specific cases can replace the FS transform by paying a small overhead, in other cases there is a significant loss in performance. Our transform instead remains very close to the FS transform both when considering the amount of computation and when considering the generality of the protocols that can be given as input to the transform.

---

[6] We consider the same Σ-protocol discussed in [141] and in addition we consider the one for Graph Isomorphism since it has the special property of having a very long first round that can be computed very efficiently.

[7] See Sect. 10.6 for a formal definition of the polynomial relation and the respective Σ-protocols.

[8] Clearly, in case p is such that $|p| < |p_{\mathsf{CRS}}|$, then Lindell's transform has a slightly smaller number of exponentiations with respect to the number of exponentiations that we count in the tables.

Table 10.1 Requirements for the proofs in input to the three transforms

Transform	$HVZK$ for Λ	$HVZK$ for L	Soundness	Model
Lindell [140]	Special + Perfect	Special + Perfect	Special	NPRO+CRS
This result	Computational	Computational	Optimal	NPRO+CRS
FS	/	Computational	Classic	PRO

Table 10.2 Efficiency of the three transforms: modular exponentiations for the prover

	DH		GI
Transform	$\|p\| = 1024$	$\|p\| = 2048$	n vertices
Lindell [140]	$2 \mod p + 12 \mod p_{\mathrm{CRS}}$	$2 \mod p + 20 \mod p_{\mathrm{CRS}}$	$4n^2 \mod p_{\mathrm{CRS}}$
This work	$2 \mod p + 4 \mod p_{\mathrm{CRS}}$	$2 \mod p + 4 \mod p_{\mathrm{CRS}}$	$4 \mod p_{\mathrm{CRS}}$
FS	$2 \mod p$	$2 \mod p$	/

Table 10.3 Efficiency of the three transforms: modular exponentiations for the verifier

	DH		GI
Transform	$\|p\| = 1024$	$\|p\| = 2048$	n vertices
Lindell [140]	$4 \mod p + 12 \mod p_{\mathrm{CRS}}$	$4 \mod p + 20 \mod p_{\mathrm{CRS}}$	$4n^2 \mod p_{\mathrm{CRS}}$
This work	$4 \mod p + 4 \mod p_{\mathrm{CRS}}$	$4 \mod p + 4 \mod p_{\mathrm{CRS}}$	$4 \mod p_{\mathrm{CRS}}$
FS	$4 \mod p$	$4 \mod p$	/

Which Protocols can be Given in Input to the Transform?

We stress that our transform allows for additional proof systems to be used for instantiating the CRS and for obtaining a NIZK argument system. This is not only a theoretical progress. Indeed there exist efficient constructions such as the one of [189] that is a variation of the one of [150]. The construction of [189] is an efficient 3-round HVZK proof system with optimal soundness for a language L and is not a Σ-protocol for the corresponding relation Rel_L. For further details, see Sect. 10.7.

10.2 Challenge Lengths of 3-Round HVZK Proofs with Optimal Soundness

Challenge-Length Amplification.

The challenge of a 3-round public-coin proof system with HVZK and optimal soundness can be extended through parallel repetition. This result is similar to the one shown in Chap. 2 but here we show this result for 3-round public-coin proof system with HVZK and optimal soundness.

Lemma 10.1 *Let Π_L be a 3-round public-coin proof system with optimal soundness for $\mathcal{NP}$-language L that enjoys perfect HVZK and has challenge length l. The protocol Π_L^k consisting of k parallel instances of Π_L is a 3-round public-coin proof system for relation L that enjoys perfect HVZK has optimal soundness and has challenge length $k \cdot l$.*

Proof The HVZK it is preserved by Π_L^k for the same arguments of [57]. About the optimal soundness of Π_L^k, it is simple to see that if the protocol Π_L^k in not optimal sound then also Π_L is not optimal sound. □

Challenge-Length Reduction.

It is also possible to show that starting from any 3-round public-coin proof system that enjoys HVZK and has optimal soundness with challenge length l, one can construct a 3-round public-coin proof system that still enjoys HVZK, has optimal soundness but works with a shorter challenge. Moreover perfect HVZK is preserved. A similar transformation was shown in [62] and reported in Chap. 2 for the case of Σ-protocol that are special perfect HVZK.

Lemma 10.2 *Let Π_L be a HVZK 3-round public-coin proof system for L with optimal soundness and challenge length l. Then for every $l' < l$, there exists a 3-round public-coin proof system Π'_L for L with HVZK and optimal soundness and challenge length l'. Protocol Π'_L has the same efficiency as Π_L and, moreover, if Π_L is perfect HVZK so is Π'_L.*

Proof We now give a description of Π'_L.

Common input: instance x for an $\mathcal{NP}$-language L.
Private input of $\mathcal{P}'_L$: w s.t. $(x, w) \in \mathsf{Rel}_L$.
The protocol Π'_L:

1. $\mathcal{P}'_L$ computes $a \leftarrow \mathcal{P}_L(x, w)$ and sends it to $\mathcal{V}'_L$[9];
2. $\mathcal{V}'_L$ randomly chooses challenge $e \leftarrow \{0, 1\}^{l'}$ and sends it to $\mathcal{P}'_L$;
3. $\mathcal{P}'_L$ randomly chooses $pad \leftarrow \{0, 1\}^{(l-l')}$, sets $e' = e|pad$, computes $z \leftarrow \mathcal{P}_L(x, w, a, e')$ and sends $z' = (z, pad)$ to $\mathcal{V}'_L$;
4. $\mathcal{V}'_L$ outputs the output of $\mathcal{V}_L(x, a, e|pad, z)$.

Completeness follows directly from the completeness of Π.

To prove the HVZK we can consider the simulator Sim', that on input x runs as follows:

---

[9] Because all the protocols of this chapter are public coin, we do not make a distinction between the verifier algorithm and the algorithm that decides whether to accept or not at the end of the interaction with the prover.

1. run $(a, e', z) \leftarrow \mathsf{Sim}(x)$;
2. set *pad* equal to the last $l - l'$ bits of e', and set e equal to the fist l' bits of e';
3. output $(a, e, (z, pad))$.

To conclude the proof we only observe that the optimal soundness follows directly from the optimal soundness of Π. □

The following theorem follows from Lemmas 10.1 and 10.2.

Theorem 10.1 *Suppose $\mathcal{NP}$-language L admits a HVZK 3-round public-coin proof system Π_L that has optimal soundness and challenge length l. Then for any $l' > 0$ there exists HVZK 3-round public-coin proof system Π'_L that has optimal soundness and challenge length l'. If $l' \leq l$ then Π'_L is as efficient as Π_L. Otherwise the communication and computation complexities of Π'_L are at most $\lceil l'/l \rceil$ times the ones of Π_L. Moreover, perfect HVZK is preserved.*

10.3 Non-interactive Argument Systems

Some definitions presented in this section are taken from [141].

Definition 10.1 A *non-interactive argument system* for an $\mathcal{NP}$-language L consists of three PPT machines $(\mathcal{CRS}, \mathcal{P}, \mathcal{V})$, that have the following properties:

- Completeness: for all $(x, w) \in \mathsf{Rel}_L$, it holds that

$$\text{Prob}\left[\ \sigma \leftarrow \mathcal{CRS}(1^n);\ \mathcal{V}(\sigma, x, \mathcal{P}(\sigma, x, w)) = 1\ \right] = 1.$$

- Adaptive Soundness: for every PPT function $f : \{0,1\}^{poly(n)} \rightarrow \{0,1\}^n \setminus L$ for all PPT prover $\mathcal{P}^\star$, there exists a negligible function ν, such that for all n:

$$\text{Prob}\left[\ \sigma \leftarrow \mathcal{CRS}(1^n);\ \mathcal{V}^{O}(\sigma, f(\sigma), \mathcal{P}^{\star O}(\sigma)) = 1\ \right] \leq \nu(n)$$

  where $O : \{0,1\}^* \rightarrow \{0,1\}^n$ is a random function.

Definition 10.2 A non-interactive argument system is *adaptive unbounded zero knowledge* (NIZK) for an $\mathcal{NP}$-language L if there exists a probabilistic PPT simulator S such that for every PPT function

$$f : \{0,1\}^{\texttt{poly(n)}} \rightarrow \left(\{0,1\}^n \times \{0,1\}^{\texttt{poly(n)}}\right) \cap \mathsf{Rel}_L,$$

and for every PPT malicious verifier $\mathcal{V}^\star$, there exists a negligible function ν such that,

$$\left|\text{Prob}\left[\ \mathcal{V}^\star\left(R_f(\mathcal{P}^f(n, p))\right) = 1\ \right] - \text{Prob}\left[\ \mathcal{V}^\star\left(S_f(n, p)\right) = 1\ \right]\right| \leq \nu(n)$$

where f_1 and f_2 denote the first and second output of f, respectively, and $R_f(\mathcal{P}^f(n, p))$ and $S_f(n, p)$ denote the output from the following experiments:

Real proofs $R_f(\mathcal{P}^f(n, p))$:

- $\sigma \leftarrow \mathcal{CRS}(1^n)$ a common reference string is sampled.
- For $i = 1, \ldots, p(n)$ (initially $\mathbf{x}$ and $\boldsymbol{\pi}$ are empty):
  - $x_i \leftarrow f_1(\sigma, \mathbf{x}, \boldsymbol{\pi})$: the next statement x_i to be proven is chosen.
  - $\pi_i \leftarrow \mathcal{P}(\sigma, f_1(\sigma, \mathbf{x}, \boldsymbol{\pi}), f_2(\sigma, \mathbf{x}, \boldsymbol{\pi}))$: the ith proof is generated.
  - set $\mathbf{x} = x_1 \ldots x_i$ and $\boldsymbol{\pi} = \pi_1 \ldots \pi_i$.
- output $(\sigma, \mathbf{x}, \boldsymbol{\pi})$.

Simulation $S_f(n, p)$:

- $\sigma \leftarrow S(1^n)$ a common reference string is sampled.
- For $i = 1, \ldots, p(n)$ (initially $\mathbf{x}$ and $\boldsymbol{\pi}$ are empty):
  - $x_i \leftarrow f_1(\sigma, \mathbf{x}, \boldsymbol{\pi})$: the next statement x_i to be proven is chosen.
  - $\pi_i \leftarrow S(x_i)$: simulator S generates a simulated proof π_i that $x_i \in L$.
  - set $\mathbf{x} = x_1 \ldots x_i$ and $\boldsymbol{\pi} = \pi_1 \ldots \pi_i$.
- output $(\sigma, \mathbf{x}, \boldsymbol{\pi})$.

Definition 10.3 A non-interactive argument system is *adaptive unbounded witness indistinguishable* (NIWI) for an $\mathcal{NP}$-language L if for every PPT adversary $\mathcal{V}^\star$, for every PPT function

$$f : \{0,1\}^{\mathtt{poly(n)}} \rightarrow \left(\{0,1\}^n \times \{0,1\}^{\mathtt{poly(n)}} \times \{0,1\}^{\mathtt{poly(n)}}\right) \cap \mathsf{Rel}_L^\wedge,$$

and for every polynomial $p(\cdot)$, there exists a negligible function ν such that

$$\left|\text{Prob}\left[\ \mathcal{V}^\star(R_0^{\mathcal{P},f}(n,p)) = 1\ \right] - \text{Prob}\left[\ \mathcal{V}^\star(R_1^{\mathcal{P},f}(n,p)) = 1\ \right]\right| \leq \nu(n),$$

where $\mathsf{Rel}_L^\wedge = \{(x, w^0, w^1) : (x, w^0) \in \mathsf{Rel}_L \wedge (x, w^1) \in \mathsf{Rel}_L\}$ and $R_b^{\mathcal{P},f}$ is the following experiment. $R_b^{\mathcal{P},f}(n, p)$:

- $\sigma \leftarrow \mathcal{CRS}(1^n)$.
- For $i = 1, \ldots, p(n)$ (initially $\mathbf{x}$ and $\boldsymbol{\pi}$ are empty):
  - $(x_i, w_i^0, w_i^1) \leftarrow f(\sigma, \mathbf{x}, \boldsymbol{\pi})$:
    statement x_i to be proven and witnesses w_i^0, w_i^1 for x_i are generated.
  - $\pi_i \leftarrow \mathcal{P}(\sigma, x_i, w_i^b)$: the ith proof is generated.
  - set $\mathbf{x} = x_1 \ldots x_i$ and $\boldsymbol{\pi} = \pi_1 \ldots \pi_i$.
- output $(\sigma, \mathbf{x}, \boldsymbol{\pi})$.

10.4 NIWI Argument Systems from 3-Round HVZK Proofs

In this section, we discuss the FS transform in the NPRO model in order to obtain a NIWI argument system $\Pi = (\mathcal{P}, \mathcal{V})$ for a polynomial relation Rel_L. We start from a 3-round public-coin WI HVZK proof system with optimal soundness $\Pi_L = (\mathcal{P}_L, \mathcal{V}_L)$ for the $\mathcal{NP}$ language L. $\mathcal{P}$ and $\mathcal{V}$ have access to an NPRO $H : \{0, 1\}^* \rightarrow \{0, 1\}^n$. We describe Π below and we assume that the challenge length of Π_L is the security parameter n.

Common input: instance x for $\mathcal{NP}$-language L.
Private input to $\mathcal{P}$: w s.t. $(x, w) \in \mathsf{Rel}_L$.
Common reference string: $\mathcal{CRS}$ samples a key s for a hash function family H and sets $\sigma = s$.

1. $\mathcal{P} \rightarrow \mathcal{V}$: The prover $\mathcal{P}$ executes the following steps:
   1.1. $a \leftarrow \mathcal{P}_L(x, w)$;
   1.2. $e \leftarrow H_s(x, a)$;
   1.3. $z \leftarrow \mathcal{P}_L(x, w, a, e)$;
   1.4. send $\pi = (a, e, z)$ to $\mathcal{V}$.
2. $\mathcal{V}$'s output: $\mathcal{V}$ outputs 1 if and only if $\mathcal{V}_L(x, a, e, z) = 1$ and $e = H_s(x, a)$.

The following theorem was proved by Yung and Zhao in [193] (see Claim 1, page 4). For sake of completeness, we provide a proof of the claim below.

Theorem 10.2 **([193])** *Let Π_L be a 3-round public-coin WI proof system for the polynomial relation Rel_L. Then Π is adaptive WI for Rel_L in the CRS model.*

Proof We show that Π is adaptive WI for Rel_L through the following hybrids.

1. $\mathcal{H}_1$ is the experiment $R_0^{\mathcal{P}, f}(n, p)$ (Definition 10.3), where $\mathcal{P}$ for $j = 1, \ldots, p(n)$ executes Π and outputs π_j using the first of the two witnesses given in output by f.
2. $\mathcal{H}_i$ (with $i > 0$) differs from $\mathcal{H}_1$ in the first i interactions, where $\mathcal{P}$ executes Π using the second witness given in output by f. Namely: $\mathcal{P}$ on input (x_j, w_j^1) executes Π and outputs π_j using w_j^1 for all $j : 1 \leq j < i$. Instead, for the interactions $i \leq j < p(n) + 1$, $\mathcal{P}$ on input (x_j, w_j^0) executes Π using w_j^0 as a witness and outputs π_j.
3. $\mathcal{H}_{p(n)+1}$ is the experiment $R_1^{\mathcal{P}, f}(n, p)$ (Definition 10.3), where $\mathcal{P}$ for $j = 1, \ldots, p(n)$ executes Π and outputs π_j using the second witness given in output by f.

$\mathcal{H}_i \approx \mathcal{H}_{i+1}$:

Suppose there exists a malicious adversary $\mathcal{V}^\star$ that distinguishes between the experiments $\mathcal{H}_i$ and $\mathcal{H}_{i+1}$ with $1 \leq i \leq p(n)$, then we can show that there exists an adversary $\mathcal{A}$ that breaks the WI property of Π_L. The reduction works as follows.

1. For $j = 1, \ldots, i-1$, $\mathcal{A}$ on input (x_j, w_j^1) executes Π using w_j^1 to obtain π_j.
2. For $j = i$, $\mathcal{A}$ interacts with the WI challenger of Π_L as follows:

    2.1 $\mathcal{A}$ has on input (x_j, w_j^0, w_j^1) and sends it to the challenger of WI;
    2.2 the challenger computes and sends the first message a_j to $\mathcal{A}$;
    2.3 $\mathcal{A}$ computes $e_j = H_s(a_j)$ and sends it to the challenger of WI;
    2.4 the challenger computes and sends z_j to $\mathcal{A}$;
    2.5 $\mathcal{A}$ sends $\pi_j = (a_j, e_j, z_j)$ to $\mathcal{V}^\star$;
    2.6 $\mathcal{A}$ adds to $\mathbf{x}$ the theorem x_j and to $\boldsymbol{\pi}$ the proof π_j.

3. $\forall j = i+1, \ldots, p(n)$ $\mathcal{A}$ on input (x_j, w_j^0) executes Π using w_j^0 to obtain π_j.
4. Set $\mathbf{x} = x_1, \ldots, x_{p(n)}$ and $\boldsymbol{\pi} = \pi_1, \ldots, \pi_{p(n)}$.

$\mathcal{A}$ sends $\mathbf{x}$ and $\boldsymbol{\pi}$ to $\mathcal{V}^\star$ and outputs what $\mathcal{V}^\star$ outputs.

We now observe that if the challenger of WI has used the first witness we are in $\mathcal{H}_i$ otherwise we are in $\mathcal{H}_{i+i}$. The security proof ends with the observation that $R_0^{\mathcal{P},f}(n,p) \equiv \mathcal{H}_1 \approx \cdots \approx \mathcal{H}_{p(n)} \approx \mathcal{H}_{p(n)+1} \equiv R_1^{\mathcal{P},f}(n,p)$. □

Adaptive Soundness.

To prove soundness, we follow [141] and use the fact that, for every function g, with a sufficiently large co-domain, relation $\mathsf{Rel} = \{(x, g(x))\}$ is evasive [32] in the NPRO model. A relation Rel is *evasive* if, given access to a random oracle $\mathcal{O}$, it is infeasible to find a string x so that the pair $(x, \mathcal{O}(x)) \in \mathsf{Rel}$.

Theorem 10.3 *Let Π_L be a 3-round public-coin proof system with optimal soundness for the $\mathcal{NP}$-language L, and let H be a non-programmable random oracle. Then, Π is a non-interactive argument system with (adaptive) soundness for L in the NPRO model.*

Proof Completeness of Π follows from the completeness of Π_L. Let $\mathcal{O}$ be an NPRO. In order to prove the soundness of Π we use the fact that for any function g, the relation $\mathsf{Rel} = \{(x, g(x))\}$ is evasive. We define the function g s.t. $g(x, a) = e$, where there exists z such that the transcript (a, e, z) is accepting for the instance x. If $x \notin L$ by the optimal soundness property we have that for every a there is a single e for which there is some z so that (a, e, z) is accepting. Therefore g is a function, as required and it follows that the relation $\mathsf{Rel} = \{((x, a), g(x, a))\}$ is evasive.

Suppose that there exists a polynomial function f and a malicious prover $\mathcal{P}^\star$ such that $\mathcal{P}^\star$ proves a false statement (i.e., $\mathcal{V}^{\mathcal{O}}(\sigma, f(\sigma), \mathcal{P}^{\star\mathcal{O}}(\sigma)) = 1$, where $\sigma \leftarrow \mathcal{CRS}(1^n)$) with non-negligible probability, then there is an adversary $\mathcal{A}$ that finds (x, a) s.t. $\mathcal{O}(x, a) = g(x, a)$ with non-negligible probability. The adversary $\mathcal{A}$ works as follows. First, it runs $\sigma \leftarrow \mathcal{CRS}(1^n)$. Then it runs $(x, a, e, z) \leftarrow \mathcal{P}^\star(\sigma)$. Finally it outputs $(x, \mathcal{O}(x, a))$. From the contradicting assumption we know that $\mathcal{V}^{\mathcal{O}}(\sigma, f(\sigma), (a, e, z)) = 1$ with non-negligible probability. This implies that the transcript $(a, \mathcal{O}(x, a), z)$ is accepting with non-negligible probability. Since $x \notin L$ there exists only one e for which $(a, \mathcal{O}(x, a), z)$ is accepting. Therefore we have that with non-negligible probability it holds that $\mathcal{O}(x, a) = e$ (i.e., $\mathcal{O}(x, a) = g(x, a)$) and this contradicts the fact that any function g is evasive for an NPRO. □

10.5 Our Transform: Non-interactive Zero Knowledge from HVZK

From the previous section we know that if we have a 3-round HVZK proof system with optimal soundness $\Pi_{L\vee\Lambda} = (\mathcal{P}_{L\vee\Lambda}, \mathcal{V}_{L\vee\Lambda})$ for polynomial relation

$$\hat{\mathsf{Rel}}_{L\vee\Lambda} = \{((x,\rho),w) : ((x,w) \in \mathsf{Rel}_L \wedge \rho \in \hat{\Lambda}) \vee ((\rho,\omega) \in \mathsf{Rel}_\Lambda \wedge x \in \hat{L})\}$$

that is also WI for polynomial relation

$$\mathsf{Rel}_{L\vee\Lambda} = \{((x,\rho),w) : ((x,w) \in \mathsf{Rel}_L \wedge \rho \in \Lambda) \vee ((\rho,w) \in \mathsf{Rel}_\Lambda \wedge x \in L)\},$$

then we can apply the FS transform to make it non-interactive while preserving WI and soundness.[10]

Here we make use of the above result in order to transform a 3-round HVZK proof system with optimal soundness for an $\mathcal{NP}$-language L into a NIZK argument for L in the CRS model using an NPRO in the proof of soundness. First, we recall the notion of Membership-hard languages with efficient sampling that will be used in our final construction.

Membership-hard languages with efficient sampling.

Lindell defines a membership-hard language Λ as a language such that one can efficiently sample both instances that belong to the language and instances that do not belong to the language. Still distinguishing among these two types of instances is hard. This is formalized through a sampling algorithm S_Λ that on input a bit b outputs an instance $\rho \in \Lambda$ along with a witness ω when $b = 0$, and outputs an instance $\rho \notin \Lambda$ otherwise. No polynomial-time distinguisher on input ρ can guess b with probability non-negligibly better than $1/2$. Let S^ρ_Λ denote the instance part of the output (i.e., without the witness when b is 0).

Definition 10.4 ([141]) Let Λ be a language. We say that Λ is membership-hard with efficient sampling if there exists a PPT sampler S_Λ such that for every PPT distinguisher $\mathcal{D}$ there exists a negligible function μ such that $|\mathrm{Probl}\big[\mathcal{D}(S^\rho_\Lambda(0,1^n),1^n) = 1\big] - \mathrm{Prob}\,[\,\mathcal{D}(S_\Lambda(1,1^n),1^n) = 1\,]\,| \leq \mu(n)$.

Now we are ready to show our NIZK argument $\Pi = (\mathcal{P}, \mathcal{V})$.

Common input: instance x for an $\mathcal{NP}$-language L.
Private input of $\mathcal{P}$: w s.t $(x,w) \in \mathsf{Rel}_L$.
Common reference string: $\mathcal{CRS}$ on input 1^n runs $\rho \leftarrow S_\Lambda(1,1^n)$ where Λ is an membership-hard language and samples a key s for a hash function family H. Then it sets $\sigma = (\rho, s)$.

---

[10] We recall that the common hash function is modeled as a NPRO only in the proof of soundness.

$\mathcal{P} \rightarrow \mathcal{V}$: $\mathcal{P}$ executes the following steps:

1. $a \leftarrow \mathcal{P}_{L\vee\Lambda}((x, \rho), w)$;
2. $e \leftarrow H_s(x, a)$;
3. $z \leftarrow \mathcal{P}_{L\vee\Lambda}((x, \rho), w, a, e)$;
4. send $\pi = (a, e, z)$ to $\mathcal{V}$.

$\mathcal{V}$*'s* output: $\mathcal{V}$ accepts if and only if $\mathcal{V}_{L\vee\Lambda}((x, \rho), a, e, z) = 1$ and $e = H_s(x, a)$.

In our construction we suppose that the challenge length of Π_Λ is n, where n denotes the security parameter. Therefore to use the OR composition of [57] we need to consider a 3-round public-coin proof system with HVZK and optimal soundness Π_L for Rel_L that has challenge length n (and therefore soundness error 2^{-n}). This is not a problem because we can use Theorem 10.1 to transform every 3-round public-coin proof system with HVZK and optimal soundness with challenge n' (where $n' \neq n$) to another one with challenge length n. More precisely, if $n' > n$ we can use Lemma 2.3 to reduce n' to n almost for free. If $n' < n$ we need to use Lemma 2.1, therefore we have to run multiple executions of Π_L to apply the OR composition of [57]. Notice that this potential computational effort is implicit also for the FS transform and for Lindell's transform. Indeed if the original 3-round public-coin proof system with HVZK and optimal soundness has just a one-bit (or in general a short) challenge then clearly the resulting NIZK is not sound. Therefore the parallel repetition of the 3-round public-coin proof system with HVZK and optimal soundness is required before applying the transform in order to reduce the soundness error (see Sect. 10.2).

Theorem 10.4 *Let* $\Pi_{L\vee\Lambda}$ *be a 3-round public-coin proof system for polynomial relation* $\hat{\mathsf{Rel}}_{L\vee\Lambda}$ *that is WI for polynomial relation* $\mathsf{Rel}_{L\vee\Lambda}$*. Then* Π *is zero knowledge for* Rel_L *in the CRS model.*

Proof The simulator S works as follows:

1. S on input 1^n, runs $(\rho, \omega) \leftarrow S_\Lambda(0, 1^n)$; samples a key s for a hash function and sets $\sigma = \{\rho, s\}$ and outputs σ.
2. S on input σ, ω and x_i (for every $i = 1, \ldots, p(n)$) computes $a \leftarrow \mathcal{P}_{L\vee\Lambda}((x_i, \rho), \omega)$, $e \leftarrow H_s(x_i, a)$ and $z \leftarrow \mathcal{P}_{L\vee\Lambda}((x_i, \rho), \omega, a, e)$. It outputs $\pi_i = (a, e, z)$.

We show that the output of S is computationally indistinguishable from a real transcript given in output by $\mathcal{P}$ in a real execution of Π through the following hybrids games.

1. $\mathcal{H}_0$ is the experiment $R_f(\mathcal{P}^f(n, p))$ (Definition 10.2).
2. $\mathcal{H}_1$ differs from $\mathcal{H}_0$ in the way that ρ is generated. Indeed in $\mathcal{H}_1$ we have that σ is computed by running $S_\Lambda(0, 1^n)$. The second output ω of S_Λ is not used. Clearly $\mathcal{H}_0$ and $\mathcal{H}_1$ are indistinguishable otherwise the membership-hard property of Λ would be contradicted. More details on this reduction will be given below.

3. $\mathcal{H}_2$ differs from $\mathcal{H}_1$ just on the witness used by $\mathcal{P}_{L\vee\Lambda}$. Indeed now ω is used as witness. The WI property of $\Pi_{L\vee\Lambda}$ guarantees that $\mathcal{H}_2$ cannot be distinguished from $\mathcal{H}_1$. More details on this reduction will be given below. Notice that $\mathcal{H}_2$ corresponds to the simulation.

$\mathcal{H}_0 \approx \mathcal{H}_1$:

If there exists a malicious verifier $\mathcal{V}^\star$ that distinguishes between $\mathcal{H}_0$ and $\mathcal{H}_1$, then there exists an adversary $\mathcal{A}$ that breaks the membership-hard property of Λ. The reduction works as follows.

1. $\mathcal{A}$ queries the challenger of S_Λ that sends back ρ.
2. $\mathcal{A}$ samples a key s for a hash function family H and sets $\sigma = \{\rho, s\}$.
3. $\mathcal{A}$ on input $(x_i, w_i) \in \mathsf{Rel}_L$ for $i = 1, \ldots, p(n)$ computes the following steps:
   3.1. compute $a_i \leftarrow \mathcal{P}_{L\vee\Lambda}((x_i, \rho), w_i)$;
   3.2. compute $e_i \leftarrow H_s(x_i, a_i)$;
   3.3. compute $z_i \leftarrow \mathcal{P}_{L\vee\Lambda}((x_i, \rho), w_i, a_i, e_i)$;
   3.4. set $\pi_i = (a_i, e_i, z_i)$;
   3.5. set $\mathbf{x} = x_1, \ldots, x_i$ and $\boldsymbol{\pi} = \pi_1, \ldots, \pi_i$.
4. $\mathcal{A}$ sends $\sigma, \mathbf{x}, \boldsymbol{\pi}$ to $\mathcal{V}^\star$.
5. $\mathcal{A}$ outputs the output of $\mathcal{V}^\star$.

We now observe that if the challenger of a sampling algorithm S_Λ sends $\rho \notin \Lambda$ we are in $\mathcal{H}_0$ otherwise we are in $\mathcal{H}_1$. This implies that $\mathcal{H}_0 \approx \mathcal{H}_1$.

$\mathcal{H}_1 \approx \mathcal{H}_2$:

If there exists a distinguisher $\mathcal{V}^\star$ that distinguishes between $\mathcal{H}_1$ and $\mathcal{H}_2$, then there exists an adversary $\mathcal{A}$ against the adaptive NIWI property of $\Pi_{L\vee\Lambda}$, therefore contradicting Theorem 10.2. The reduction works as follows.

1. $\mathcal{A}$ runs $(\rho, \omega) \leftarrow S_\Lambda(0, 1^n)$, samples a key s for a hash function and sets $\sigma = \{\rho, s\}$.
2. $\mathcal{A}$ has on input a PPT function $f = (f_1, f_2)$ and defines $f' = (f_1', f_2')$ as follows: $f'(\sigma, \mathbf{t}, \boldsymbol{\pi})$ on input a CRS σ, a vector of theorems $\mathbf{t} = (x_1, \rho), \ldots, (x_{p(n)}, \rho)$ and a vector of proofs $\boldsymbol{\pi} = \pi_1, \ldots, \pi_{p(n)}$ returns $(f_1(\sigma, \mathbf{x}, \boldsymbol{\pi}), \rho), (f_2(\sigma, \mathbf{x}, \boldsymbol{\pi}), \omega)$.
3. $\mathcal{A}$ interacts with the challenger of adaptive NIWI, using f', in order to obtain x_i, $\pi_i = \{a_i, e_i, z_i\}$, for $i = 1, \ldots, p(n)$.
4. $\mathcal{A}$ sets $\mathbf{x} = x_1, \ldots, x_{p(n)}$ and $\boldsymbol{\pi} = \pi_1, \ldots, \pi_{p(n)}$.
5. $\mathcal{A}$ sends $\sigma, \mathbf{x}, \boldsymbol{\pi}$ to $\mathcal{V}^\star$ and outputs the output of $\mathcal{V}^\star$.

We now observe that if the challenger of NIWI uses the first witness w_i we are in $\mathcal{H}_1$ otherwise we are in $\mathcal{H}_2$. This implies that $\mathcal{H}_1 \approx \mathcal{H}_2$.

We can thus conclude that $\mathcal{H}_0 \approx \mathcal{H}_1 \approx \mathcal{H}_2$ and therefore the output of S is computational indistinguishable from a real transcript. □

Theorem 10.5 *Let $\Pi_{L\vee\Lambda}$ be a 3-round public-coin HVZK proof system with optimal soundness for relation $\mathsf{Rel}_{L\vee\Lambda}$, and WI for relation $\hat{\mathsf{Rel}}_{L\vee\Lambda}$, and let H be an NPRO. Then, Π is a non-interactive argument system with adaptive soundness for the relation Rel_L in the CRS model using the NPRO model for soundness.*

Proof The completeness of Π follows from the completeness of $\Pi_{L\vee\Lambda}$. In order to prove adaptive soundness we notice that an adversarial prover proving a false statement $x \notin L$ can be directly reduced to an adversarial prover proving a false statement for $\Pi_{L\vee\Lambda}$ in the NPRO model. This contradicts Theorem 10.3. Indeed the only subtlety that is worthy to note is that when the adversarial prover runs the protocol, we have that the statement "$\rho \in \Lambda$" stored in the CRS is false, therefore if also the instance "$x \notin L$" proved by the prover is false then the OR composition of the two statements is also false. □

10.6 Efficiency Comparison

In this section we illustrate in details now the values in Tables 10.2 and 10.3 of Sect. 10.1.3 have been calculated. First of all we need to briefly introduce two Σ-protocols, one to prove that a tuple is $DH(\Pi_{\mathcal{DDH}}$ [112]), and the other one to prove that two graphs are isomorphic ($\Pi_{\mathcal{GH}}$ [89]). Our comparison assumes that the CRS is a DH tuple $((G_{\text{CRS}}, q_{\text{CRS}}, p_{\text{CRS}}, g_{\text{CRS}}), A_{\text{CRS}}, B_{\text{CRS}}, C_{\text{CRS}})$ with p_{CRS} and q_{CRS} primes such that $p_{\text{CRS}} = 2q_{\text{CRS}} + 1$ and $|p_{\text{CRS}}| = 1024$. We distinguish two cases. In the first one the prover wants to prove that a tuple $((G, q, p, g), A, B, C)$ is a DH tuple, and in the other one the prover tries to convince the verifier that two graphs G_0 and G_1 with n vertices each are isomorphic.

A Σ-protocol for Diffie-Hellman tuples.

We consider the following polynomial-time relation

$$\mathsf{Rel}_{\mathcal{DDH}} = \left\{\left(((G, q, g), A = g^r, B = h, C = h^r), r\right) : B^r = C\right\}$$

over cyclic groups G of prime-order q. Typically, G is the subgroup of quadratic residues of $\mathbb{Z}_p$ for prime $p = 2q + 1$. We next briefly describe Σ-protocol $\Pi_{\mathcal{DDH}} = (\mathcal{P}_{\mathcal{DDH}}, \mathcal{V}_{\mathcal{DDH}})$ for $\mathsf{Rel}_{\mathcal{DDH}}$.

Common input: instance x and language DH.
Private input of $\mathcal{P}_{\mathcal{DDH}}$: r.
The protocol $\Pi_{\mathcal{DDH}}$:

1. $\mathcal{P}_{\mathcal{DDH}}$ picks $t \in \mathbb{Z}_q$ at random, computes and sends $a = g^t$, $b = h^t$ to $\mathcal{V}_{\mathcal{DDH}}$;
2. $\mathcal{V}_{\mathcal{DDH}}$ chooses a random challenge $e \in \mathbb{Z}_q$ and sends it to $\mathcal{P}_{\mathcal{DDH}}$;

3. $\mathcal{P}_{\mathcal{DDH}}$ computes and sends $z = t + er$ to $\mathcal{V}_{\mathcal{DDH}}$;
4. $\mathcal{V}_{\mathcal{DDH}}$ accepts iff:
$$g^z = a \cdot A^e \text{ AND } h^z = b \cdot C^e.$$

We show the special HVZK simulator Sim for $\Pi_{\mathcal{DDH}}$. Sim, on input x and a challenge e of length $|q| - 1$ executes the following steps:

1. randomly chooses $z \in \mathbb{Z}_q$;
2. computes $a = g^z \cdot A^{-e}$;
3. computes $b = h^z \cdot C^{-e}$.

Graph Isomorphism.

We show a Σ-protocol $\Pi_{\mathcal{GH}} = (\mathcal{P}_{\mathcal{GH}}, \mathcal{V}_{\mathcal{GH}})$ to prove that two graphs are isomorphic. Given two graphs G_0 and G_1, prover $\mathcal{P}_{\mathcal{GH}}$ wants to convince verifier $\mathcal{V}_{\mathcal{GH}}$ that he knows a permutation ϕ such that $\phi(G_0) = G_1$.

Common input: theorem $x = (G_0, G_1)$.
Private input of $\mathcal{P}_{\mathcal{GH}}$: ϕ.
The protocol $\Pi_{\mathcal{GH}}$:

1. $\mathcal{P}_{\mathcal{GH}}$ randomly chooses a permutation ψ and a bit $b \in \{0, 1\}$, computes and sends $P = \psi(G_b)$;
2. $\mathcal{V}_{\mathcal{GH}}$ chooses and sends a random bit $b' \in \{0, 1\}$ $\mathcal{P}_{\mathcal{GH}}$;
3. $\mathcal{P}_{\mathcal{GH}}$ sends the permutation τ to $\mathcal{V}_{\mathcal{GH}}$, where

$$\tau = \begin{cases} \psi & if\ b = b' \\ \psi\phi^{-1} & if\ b = 0, b' = 1 \\ \psi\phi & if\ b = 1, b' = 0 \end{cases}$$

4. $\mathcal{V}_{\mathcal{GH}}$ accepts if and only if $P = \tau(G_{b'})$.

Computational Effort: Two Cases.

We show a summary of the comparison among our transform and Lindell's transform in Tables 10.2 and 10.3. The cost is measured by considering the computations in terms of number of exponentiations made by $\mathcal{P}$ and of $\mathcal{V}$. In our comparison we consider that a CRS contains a DH tuple $((G_{\text{CRS}}, q_{\text{CRS}}, p_{\text{CRS}}, g_{\text{CRS}}), A_{\text{CRS}}, B_{\text{CRS}}, C_{\text{CRS}})$ with $|p_{\text{CRS}}| = n = 1024$, with security parameter n (therefore $|q_{\text{CRS}}| = 1023$). We consider two cases. In the first one we use the NIZK argument to prove that a tuple $((G, q, p, g), A, B, C)$ is a DH tuple; in particular we take in account two sub-cases: when $p = 1024$ and when $p = 2048$. In the second case we use the NIZK argument to prove the isomorphism between two graphs G_0 and G_1, and we assume that $k = n^2$ bits are needed to represent a graph with n vertices. We stress that Lindell's transform needs to commit the first round of a Σ-protocol (plus the instance to be proved, but for our comparison we ignore that the instance has to be committed) associated to the language that we take into account (the language of the DH tuples or the language of the isomorphic graphs). Therefore, using the described CRS, to commit to a string of 1023 bit, 4 exponentiations are required. This is a consequence of the fact that the commitment is made by executing the simulator associated with $\Pi_{\mathcal{DDH}}$ (with $|q_{\text{CRS}}| = 1023$).

Case 1: Proving that a Tuple is a DH Tuple.

- [141]. When the instance to be proved is $((G, q, p, g), A, B, C)$ with $p = 1024$, the prover $\mathcal{P}$ needs to compute $a = g^t$, $b = h^t$ (as describe before) and needs to commit to them. The total size of a and b is 2048 bits, therefore to commit to 2048 bits we need to execute the DM commitment 3 times. This implies that the prover needs to compute $3 \cdot 4$ exponentiations mod p_{CRS} and 2 exponentiations mod p. The verifier $\mathcal{V}$ needs to check if open of the DM commitments was correct, and also needs to compute $g^z = a \cdot A^e p$ and $h^z = b \cdot C^e$. For this reason the verifier needs to compute $3 \cdot 4$ exponentiations mod p_{CRS} plus 4 exponentiations mod p. With the same arguments we can count the amount of exponentiations needed to prove that the instance is a DH tuple with $p = 2048$.
- Our transform. When $|p| = 1024$ (resp., $|p| = 2048$) the prover need to run the simulator Sim of $\Pi_{\mathcal{DDH}}$ with the instance $((G_{\text{CRS}}, q_{\text{CRS}}, p_{\text{CRS}}, g_{\text{CRS}}), A_{\text{CRS}}, B_{\text{CRS}}, C_{\text{CRS}})$ (this costs 4 exponentiations), also we need to compute $a = g^t$, $b = h^t$. The total number of exponentiations is 6 (2 exponentiations mod p, and 4 exponentiations mod p_{CRS}). The verifier needs to perform two times the verifier's algorithm for $\Pi_{\mathcal{DDH}}$, one with the instance $((G_{\text{CRS}}, q_{\text{CRS}}, p_{\text{CRS}}, g_{\text{CRS}}), A_{\text{CRS}}, B_{\text{CRS}}, C_{\text{CRS}})$, the other one with the instance $((G, q, p, g), A, B, C)$, for a total amount of 4 exponentiations mod p_{CRS}, and 4 exponentiations mod p.

Case 2: Graph Isomorphism.

- [141]. We consider that the instance to be proved is composed by two graphs (G_0, G_1). Also we assume that to represent one graph with n vertices $k = n^2$ bits are necessary. In this case we remark that because the security parameter is $n = 1024$ we need to execute n times the protocol $\Pi_{\mathcal{GH}}$ described before. For the described assumptions we have that the first round of $\Pi_{\mathcal{GH}}$ is $P = \sigma(G_b)$ and $|P| = n^2$. Therefore the prover needs to run n executions of the DM commitment function to commit to P, where each of them costs 4 exponentiations. Also we need to execute n iteration of this process, for a total amount of $4n^2$ exponentiations mod p_{CRS}. Even in this case the verifier needs to check if all opens with respect to the n commitments are correctly computed for a total amount of $4n^2$ exponentiations mod p_{CRS}.
- Our transform. In this case the prover $\mathcal{P}$ computes only 4 exponentiations mod p to compute the first round of $\Pi_{\mathcal{DDH}}$. The verifier runs the verifier's algorithm of $\Pi_{\mathcal{DDH}}$ and this requires 4 exponentiations mod p.

10.7 An Optimal-Sound (and Not Special Sound) 3-Round Perfect Special HVZK Proof

In this section, we show a 3-round public-coin perfect special HVZK proof system that is optimal sound and not special sound. First of all we briefly describe the Σ-protocol of [150] to prove that, given a commitment $\mathtt{com}$ and a message m, m is committed in $\mathtt{com}$. Then we show the protocol of [189], that is a modification of [150], where given a commitment $\mathtt{com}$ and a value Ψ, allows to prove that the discrete logarithm of Ψ is committed in $\mathtt{com}$.

In order to describe the protocol of [150, 189] we consider two prime p and q s.t. $p = 2q + 1$, a group of order $\mathcal{G}$ of order q such that the DDH assumption is hard. Also we consider two random elements, g and h, taken from $\mathcal{G}$.

We next describe Σ-protocol $\Pi_{Com} = (\mathcal{P}_{Com}, \mathcal{V}_{Com})$ of [150] for relation

$$\mathsf{Rel}_{Com} = \left\{\left(\left((\mathcal{G}, q, g, h), v, \mathtt{com} = (\hat{g}, \hat{h})\right), w\right) : \hat{g} = g^{w}, \hat{h} = h^{w+v}\right\}.$$

Common Input: $(\mathcal{G}, g, v, h, \mathtt{com} = (\hat{g}, \hat{h}), q)$ and relation Rel_{Com}.
Input of $\mathcal{P}_{Com}$: w s.t. $((\mathcal{G}, v, g, h, \mathtt{com} = (\hat{g}, \hat{h}), q), w) \in \mathsf{Rel}_{Com}$.
The protocol Π_{Com}:

1. The prover $\mathcal{P}_{Com}$ chooses r from $\mathcal{Z}_q$ and sends $(\widetilde{g} = g^r, \widetilde{h} = h^r)$ to $\mathcal{V}_{Com}$;
2. The verifier $\mathcal{V}_{Com}$ chooses a random challenge $e \leftarrow \mathcal{Z}_q$ and sends e to $\mathcal{P}_{Com}$;
3. $\mathcal{P}_{Com}$ sends $z = ew + r$ to $\mathcal{V}_{Com}$;
4. $\mathcal{V}_{Com}$ checks that $\hat{g}^e \widetilde{g} = g^z$ and $\left(\frac{\hat{h}}{h^v}\right)^e \widetilde{h} = h^z$ accepts if and only if the checks are successful.

In [189], a similar protocol was used to prove that $\mathtt{com}$ is a commitment of the discrete logarithm of a value $\Psi \in \mathcal{G}$ with $h^{\psi} = \Psi$. Formally the protocol is for the $\mathcal{NP}$ language

$$L = \left\{\left(\Psi = h^{\psi}, \mathtt{com} = (\hat{g} = g^{w}, \hat{h} = h^{w+\psi})\right) : g, h \leftarrow \mathcal{G}, \psi \in \mathbb{Z}_q, w \in \mathbb{Z}_q\right\}$$

and for the corresponding relation

$$\mathsf{Rel}_L = \left\{\left((\Psi = h^{\psi}, \mathtt{com} = (\hat{g} = g^{w}, \hat{h} = h^{w+\psi})), (w, \psi)\right) : g, h \leftarrow \mathcal{G}, \psi \in \mathbb{Z}_q, w \in \mathbb{Z}_q\right\}$$

The protocol follows Π_{Com} with the differences that the common input is $(\mathcal{G}, q, g, \Psi = h^{\psi}, h, \mathtt{com} = (\hat{g}, \hat{h}))$ and that the verifier decide whether to accept or not checking if it holds that $\hat{g}^e \widetilde{g} = g^z$ and $\left(\frac{\hat{h}}{\Psi}\right)^e \widetilde{h} = h^z$. While this protocol preserves the perfect special HVZK property, it is not a proof of knowledge for Rel_L neither special sound even though it still enjoys optimal soundness. We now proceed more formally.

Optimal Soundness.

We now consider an instance that is not in the $\mathcal{NP}$ language L, and show that, once the first round of the protocol is fixed, there exists only one challenge e s.t. the prover can answer successfully computing the third round z of the protocol. Consider the instance $\left(\Psi = h^{\psi}, \mathsf{com} = (\hat{g} = g^{w}, \hat{h} = h^{w+\psi'})\right) \notin L$ (with $\psi \neq \psi'$). Assume by contradiction that given the first round of the protocol $(\widetilde{g}, \widetilde{h})$ there exist two distinct challenges e_0 and e_1 for which the prover can make the verifier accept with answers z_0, z_1 respectively. In the end we prove that $\psi = \psi'$.

Proof Since the verifier accepts, it must be that for all $i \in \{0, 1\}$, the following checks are successful:

- $\hat{g}^{e_i}\widetilde{g} = g^{z_i}$;
- $\left(\frac{\hat{h}}{\Psi}\right)^{e_i}\widetilde{h} = h^{z_i}$.

It follows that $\hat{g}^{e_0-e_1} = g^{z_0-z_1}$ and $\left(\frac{\hat{h}}{\Psi}\right)^{e_0-e_1} = h^{z_0-z_1}$. Suppose that $h = g^{\omega}$, we get

$$g^{w\omega(e_0-e_1)} = \hat{g}^{(e_0-e_1)\omega} = g^{(z_0-z_1)\omega} = h^{(z_0-z_1)} = \left(\frac{\hat{h}}{\Psi}\right)^{e_0-e_1} = h^{z_0-z_1} = g^{\omega(w+\psi'-\psi)(e_0-e_1)}.$$

Therefore, if $e_0 \neq e_1$ we get the contradiction that $\psi = \psi'$. □

Π_{Com} is not special sound for Rel_L.

To argue that the protocol of [189] is not special sound, we note that in order to compute a commitment com of the discrete logarithm of Ψ, knowledge of this discrete logarithm is not necessary since it is possible to compute $\mathsf{com} = (\hat{g}, h^{w} \cdot \Psi)$ with $w \in \mathbb{Z}_q$. Indeed, notice that the discrete logarithm ψ of Ψ is never used in the proof. Formally, we suppose that the protocol is special sound for the polynomial relation Rel_L and then construct an adversary $\mathcal{A}$ that, given $Y = g^{y} \in \mathcal{G}$, returns the discrete logarithm y of Y.

We have shown that there exist 3-round public-coin proof systems that are optimal sound and not special sound. It is also easy to observe that special soundness implies optimal soundness.

Indeed, consider an $\mathcal{NP}$-Language L. All Σ-protocols for Rel_L must also be 3-round HVZK proofs for L with optimal soundness. If not, than the violation of optimal soundness ($\mathcal{P}^{\star}$ for a false statement can generate (a, c, z) and (a, c', z') with c' different from c and both accepting) implies directly also a violation of special soundness.

References

1. Abe, M., Okamoto, T., Suzuki, K.: Message recovery signature schemes from sigma-protocols. IEICE Transactions **96-A**(1), 92–100 (2013)
2. Aggarwal, D., Dodis, Y., Lovett, S.: Non-malleable codes from additive combinatorics. In: D.B. Shmoys (ed.) Symposium on Theory of Computing, STOC 2014, New York, NY, USA, May 31 - June 03, 2014, pp. 774–783. ACM (2014)
3. Almeida, J.B., Bangerter, E., Barbosa, M., Krenn, S., Sadeghi, A., Schneider, T.: A certifying compiler for zero-knowledge proofs of knowledge based on sigma-protocols. In: Computer Security - ESORICS 2010, 15th European Symposium on Research in Computer Security, Athens, Greece, September 20-22, 2010. Proceedings, *Lecture Notes in Computer Science*, vol. 6345, pp. 151–167. Springer (2010)
4. Ananth, P., Choudhuri, A.R., Jain, A.: A new approach to round-optimal secure multiparty computation. In: Advances in Cryptology - CRYPTO 2017 - 37th Annual International Cryptology Conference, Santa Barbara, CA, USA, August 20-24, 2017, Proceedings, Part I, pp. 468–499 (2017). DOI https://doi.org/10.1007/978-3-319-63688-7_16. URL https://doi.org/10.1007/978-3-319-63688-7_16
5. Asharov, G., Lindell, Y., Schneider, T., Zohner, M.: More efficient oblivious transfer and extensions for faster secure computation. In: 2013 ACM SIGSAC Conference on Computer and Communications Security, CCS'13, Berlin, Germany, November 4-8, 2013, pp. 535–548 (2013). DOI https://doi.org/10.1145/2508859.2516738. URL http://doi.acm.org/10.1145/2508859.2516738
6. Asharov, G., Lindell, Y., Schneider, T., Zohner, M.: More efficient oblivious transfer extensions with security for malicious adversaries. In: Advances in Cryptology - EUROCRYPT 2015 - 34th Annual International Conference on the Theory and Applications of Cryptographic Techniques, Sofia, Bulgaria, April 26-30, 2015, Proceedings, Part I, pp. 673–701 (2015). DOI https://doi.org/10.1007/978-3-662-46800-5_26. URL https://doi.org/10.1007/978-3-662-46800-5_26
7. Badrinarayanan, S., Goyal, V., Jain, A., Kalai, Y.T., Khurana, D., Sahai, A.: Promise zero knowledge and its applications to round optimal mpc. Cryptology ePrint Archive, Report 2017/1088 (2017). https://eprint.iacr.org/2017/1088
8. Badrinarayanan, S., Goyal, V., Jain, A., Kalai, Y.T., Khurana, D., Sahai, A.: Promise zero knowledge and its applications to round optimal MPC. In: H. Shacham, A. Boldyreva (eds.) Advances in Cryptology – CRYPTO 2018, Part II, *Lecture Notes in Computer Science*, vol. 10992, pp. 459–487. Springer, Cham, Switzerland, Santa Barbara, CA, USA (2018). DOI https://doi.org/10.1007/978-3-319-96881-0_16

M. Ciampi and L. Siniscalchi, *Round and Computational Efficiency of Multi-party Protocols*, Information Security and Cryptography,
https://doi.org/10.1007/978-3-031-92374-6

9. Baldi, P., Baronio, R., Cristofaro, E.D., Gasti, P., Tsudik, G.: Countering GATTACA: efficient and secure testing of fully-sequenced human genomes. In: Proceedings of the 18th ACM Conference on Computer and Communications Security, CCS 2011, Chicago, Illinois, USA, October 17-21, 2011, pp. 691–702 (2011). DOI https://doi.org/10.1145/2046707.2046785. URL http://doi.acm.org/10.1145/2046707.2046785
10. Baldimtsi, F., Kiayias, A., Zacharias, T., Zhang, B.: Indistinguishable proofs of work or knowledge. In: J.H. Cheon, T. Takagi (eds.) Advances in Cryptology - ASIACRYPT 2016 - 22nd International Conference on the Theory and Application of Cryptology and Information Security, Hanoi, Vietnam, December 4-8, 2016, Proceedings, Part II, *Lecture Notes in Computer Science*, vol. 10032, pp. 902–933 (2016)
11. Barak, B.: Constant-round coin-tossing with a man in the middle or realizing the shared random string model. In: 43rd Symposium on Foundations of Computer Science (FOCS 2002), 16-19 November 2002, Vancouver, BC, Canada, Proceedings, pp. 345–355 (2002)
12. Barak, B., Canetti, R., Nielsen, J.B., Pass, R.: Universally composable protocols with relaxed set-up assumptions. In: 45th Symposium on Foundations of Computer Science (FOCS 2004), 17-19 October 2004, Rome, Italy, Proceedings, pp. 186–195 (2004). DOI https://doi.org/10.1109/FOCS.2004.71. URL http://dx.doi.org/10.1109/FOCS.2004.71
13. Barak, B., Prabhakaran, M., Sahai, A.: Concurrent non-malleable zero knowledge. In: 47th Annual IEEE Symposium on Foundations of Computer Science (FOCS 2006), 21-24 October 2006, Berkeley, California, USA, Proceedings, pp. 345–354 (2006)
14. Beaver, D., Micali, S., Rogaway, P.: The round complexity of secure protocols (extended abstract). In: Proceedings of the 22nd Annual ACM Symposium on Theory of Computing, May 13-17, 1990, Baltimore, Maryland, USA, pp. 503–513 (1990). DOI https://doi.org/10.1145/100216.100287. URL http://doi.acm.org/10.1145/100216.100287
15. Bellare, M., Fischlin, M., Goldwasser, S., Micali, S.: Identification protocols secure against reset attacks. In: Advances in Cryptology - EUROCRYPT 2001, International Conference on the Theory and Application of Cryptographic Techniques, Innsbruck, Austria, May 6-10, 2001, Proceeding, pp. 495–511 (2001)
16. Bellare, M., Jakobsson, M., Yung, M.: Round-optimal zero-knowledge arguments based on any one-way function. In: Advances in Cryptology - EUROCRYPT '97, International Conference on the Theory and Application of Cryptographic Techniques, Konstanz, Germany, May 11-15, 1997, Proceeding, *Lecture Notes in Computer Science*, vol. 1233, pp. 280–305. Springer (1997)
17. Bellare, M., Rogaway, P.: Entity authentication and key distribution. In: D.R. Stinson (ed.) Advances in Cryptology - CRYPTO '93, 13th Annual International Cryptology Conference, Santa Barbara, California, USA, August 22-26, 1993, Proceedings, *Lecture Notes in Computer Science*, vol. 773, pp. 232–249. Springer (1993)
18. Bellare, M., Rogaway, P.: Random oracles are practical: A paradigm for designing efficient protocols. In: CCS '93, Proceedings of the 1st ACM Conference on Computer and Communications Security, Fairfax, Virginia, USA, November 3-5, 1993., pp. 62–73 (1993). DOI https://doi.org/10.1145/168588.168596. URL http://doi.acm.org/10.1145/168588.168596
19. Bernhard, D., Pereira, O., Warinschi, B.: How not to prove yourself: Pitfalls of the fiat-shamir heuristic and applications to helios. In: Advances in Cryptology - ASIACRYPT 2012 - 18th International Conference on the Theory and Application of Cryptology and Information Security, Beijing, China, December 2-6, 2012. Proceedings, pp. 626–643 (2012)
20. Bitansky, N., Dachman-Soled, D., Garg, S., Jain, A., Kalai, Y.T., López-Alt, A., Wichs, D.: Why "Fiat-Shamir for ProofsâŁž Lacks a Proof, pp. 182 – 201. Lecture Notes in Computer Science. Springer Berlin Heidelberg (2013)
21. Bitansky, N., Paneth, O.: Zaps and non-interactive witness indistinguishability from indistinguishability obfuscation. In: Y. Dodis, J.B. Nielsen (eds.) Theory of Cryptography - 12th Theory of Cryptography Conference, TCC 2015, Warsaw, Poland, March 23-25, 2015, Proceedings, Part II, *Lecture Notes in Computer Science*, vol. 9015, pp. 401–427. Springer (2015)
22. Blum, M.: How to prove a theorem so no one else can claim it. In: In Proceedings of the International Congress of Mathematicians, p. 444–451 (1986)

23. Blum, M., De Santis, A., Micali, S., Persiano, G.: Noninteractive zero-knowledge. SIAM J. Comput. **20**(6), 1084–1118 (1991). DOI https://doi.org/10.1137/0220068. URL http://dx.doi.org/10.1137/0220068
24. Blum, M., Feldman, P., Micali, S.: Non-interactive zero-knowledge and its applications (extended abstract). In: Proceedings of the 20th Annual ACM Symposium on Theory of Computing, May 2-4, 1988, Chicago, Illinois, USA, pp. 103–112 (1988). DOI https://doi.org/10.1145/62212.62222. URL http://doi.acm.org/10.1145/62212.62222
25. Blundo, C., Persiano, G., Sadeghi, A., Visconti, I.: Improved security notions and protocols for non-transferable identification. In: Computer Security - ESORICS 2008, 13th European Symposium on Research in Computer Security, Málaga, Spain, October 6-8, 2008. Proceedings, pp. 364–378 (2008)
26. Botta, V., Ciampi, M., Orsini, E., Siniscalchi, L., Visconti, I.: Black-box (and fast) non-malleable zero knowledge. In: L. Reyzin, D. Stebila (eds.) Advances in Cryptology – CRYPTO 2024, Part IX, *Lecture Notes in Computer Science*, vol. 14928, pp. 458–490. Springer, Cham, Switzerland, Santa Barbara, CA, USA (2024). DOI https://doi.org/10.1007/978-3-031-68400-5_14
27. Brakerski, Z., Halevi, S., Polychroniadou, A.: Four round secure computation without setup. In: Y. Kalai, L. Reyzin (eds.) TCC 2017: 15th Theory of Cryptography Conference, Part I, *Lecture Notes in Computer Science*, vol. 10677, pp. 645–677. Springer, Cham, Switzerland, Baltimore, MD, USA (2017). DOI https://doi.org/10.1007/978-3-319-70500-2_22
28. Brenner, H., Goyal, V., Richelson, S., Rosen, A., Vald, M.: Fast non-malleable commitments. In: Proceedings of the 22nd ACM SIGSAC Conference on Computer and Communications Security, Denver, CO, USA, October 12-6, 2015, pp. 1048–1057 (2015)
29. Canetti, R., Dakdouk, R.R.: Extractable perfectly one-way functions. In: Automata, Languages and Programming, 35th International Colloquium, ICALP 2008, Reykjavik, Iceland, July 7-11, 2008, Proceedings, Part II - Track B: Logic, Semantics, and Theory of Programming & Track C: Security and Cryptography Foundations, pp. 449–460 (2008). DOI https://doi.org/10.1007/978-3-540-70583-3_37. URL http://dx.doi.org/10.1007/978-3-540-70583-3_37
30. Canetti, R., Goldreich, O., Goldwasser, S., Micali, S.: Resettable zero-knowledge (extended abstract). In: F.F. Yao, E.M. Luks (eds.) Proceedings of the Thirty-Second Annual ACM Symposium on Theory of Computing, May 21-23, 2000, Portland, OR, USA, pp. 235–244. ACM (2000)
31. Canetti, R., Goldreich, O., Halevi, S.: The random oracle methodology, revisited (preliminary version). In: Proceedings of the Thirtieth Annual ACM Symposium on the Theory of Computing, Dallas, Texas, USA, May 23-26, 1998, pp. 209–218 (1998). DOI https://doi.org/10.1145/276698.276741. URL http://doi.acm.org/10.1145/276698.276741
32. Canetti, R., Goldreich, O., Halevi, S.: The random oracle methodology, revisited. J. ACM **51**(4), 557–594 (2004). DOI https://doi.org/10.1145/1008731.1008734. URL http://doi.acm.org/10.1145/1008731.1008734
33. Canetti, R., Kilian, J., Petrank, E., Rosen, A.: Black-box concurrent zero-knowledge requires omega (log n) rounds. In: Proceedings on 33rd Annual ACM Symposium on Theory of Computing, July 6-8, 2001, Heraklion, Crete, Greece, pp. 570–579 (2001)
34. Canetti, R., Lin, H., Paneth, O.: Public-coin concurrent zero-knowledge in the global hash model. In: TCC, pp. 80–99 (2013). DOI https://doi.org/10.1007/978-3-642-36594-2_5. URL http://dx.doi.org/10.1007/978-3-642-36594-2_5
35. Cao, Z., Visconti, I., Zhang, Z.: On constant-round concurrent non-malleable proof systems. Inf. Process. Lett. **111**(18), 883–890 (2011)
36. Catalano, D., Dodis, Y., Visconti, I.: Mercurial commitments: Minimal assumptions and efficient constructions. In: Theory of Cryptography, Third Theory of Cryptography Conference, TCC 2006, New York, NY, USA, March 4-7, 2006, Proceedings, pp. 120–144 (2006)
37. Catalano, D., Visconti, I.: Hybrid trapdoor commitments and their applications. In: Automata, Languages and Programming, 32nd International Colloquium, ICALP 2005, Lisbon, Portugal, July 11-15, 2005, Proceedings, pp. 298–310 (2005)

38. Catalano, D., Visconti, I.: Hybrid commitments and their applications to zero-knowledge proof systems. Theor. Comput. Sci. **374**(1-3), 229–260 (2007)
39. Chaidos, P., Groth, J.: Making sigma-protocols non-interactive without random oracles. In: Public-Key Cryptography - PKC 2015 - 18th IACR International Conference on Practice and Theory in Public-Key Cryptography, Gaithersburg, MD, USA, March 30 - April 1, 2015, Proceedings, pp. 650–670 (2015). DOI https://doi.org/10.1007/978-3-662-46447-2_29. URL http://dx.doi.org/10.1007/978-3-662-46447-2_29
40. Chase, M., Lysyanskaya, A.: On signatures of knowledge. In: C. Dwork (ed.) Advances in Cryptology - CRYPTO 2006, *Lecture Notes in Computer Science*, vol. 4117, pp. 78–96. Springer Berlin Heidelberg (2006). DOI https://doi.org/10.1007/11818175_5. URL http://dx.doi.org/10.1007/11818175_5
41. Cho, C., Ostrovsky, R., Scafuro, A., Visconti, I.: Simultaneously resettable arguments of knowledge. In: Theory of Cryptography - 9th Theory of Cryptography Conference, TCC 2012, Taormina, Sicily, Italy, March 19-21, 2012. Proceedings, pp. 530–547 (2012)
42. Choudhuri, A.R., Ciampi, M., Goyal, V., Jain, A., Ostrovsky, R.: Round optimal secure multiparty computation from minimal assumptions. In: R. Pass, K. Pietrzak (eds.) TCC 2020: 18th Theory of Cryptography Conference, Part II, *Lecture Notes in Computer Science*, vol. 12551, pp. 291–319. Springer, Cham, Switzerland, Durham, NC, USA (2020). DOI https://doi.org/10.1007/978-3-030-64378-2_11
43. Chung, K., Ostrovsky, R., Pass, R., Venkitasubramaniam, M., Visconti, I.: 4-round resettably-sound zero knowledge. In: Y. Lindell (ed.) Theory of Cryptography - 11th Theory of Cryptography Conference, TCC 2014, San Diego, CA, USA, February 24-26, 2014. Proceedings, *Lecture Notes in Computer Science*, vol. 8349, pp. 192–216. Springer (2014)
44. Ciampi, M., Orlandi, C.: Combining private set-intersection with secure two-party computation. In: D. Catalano, R.D. Prisco (eds.) Security and Cryptography for Networks - 11th International Conference, SCN 2018, Amalfi, Italy, September 5-7, 2018, Proceedings, *Lecture Notes in Computer Science*, vol. 11035, pp. 464–482. Springer (2018). DOI https://doi.org/10.1007/978-3-319-98113-0_25. URL https://doi.org/10.1007/978-3-319-98113-0_25
45. Ciampi, M., Orsini, E., Siniscalchi, L.: Four-round black-box non-malleable schemes from one-way permutations. In: E. Kiltz, V. Vaikuntanathan (eds.) TCC 2022: 20th Theory of Cryptography Conference, Part II, *Lecture Notes in Computer Science*, vol. 13748, pp. 300–329. Springer, Cham, Switzerland, Chicago, IL, USA (2022). DOI https://doi.org/10.1007/978-3-031-22365-5_11
46. Ciampi, M., Ostrovsky, R., Siniscalchi, L., Visconti, I.: Concurrent non-malleable commitments (and more) in 3 rounds. In: M. Robshaw, J. Katz (eds.) Advances in Cryptology - CRYPTO 2016 - 36th Annual International Cryptology Conference, Santa Barbara, CA, USA, August 14-18, 2016, Proceedings, Part III, *Lecture Notes in Computer Science*, vol. 9816, pp. 270–299. Springer (2016). DOI https://doi.org/10.1007/978-3-662-53015-3_10. URL http://dx.doi.org/10.1007/978-3-662-53015-3_10. Full version http://eprint.iacr.org/2016/566
47. Ciampi, M., Ostrovsky, R., Siniscalchi, L., Visconti, I.: Delayed-input non-malleable zero knowledge and multi-party coin tossing in four rounds. In: Y. Kalai, L. Reyzin (eds.) Theory of Cryptography - 15th International Conference, TCC 2017, Baltimore, MD, USA, November 12-15, 2017, Proceedings, Part I, *Lecture Notes in Computer Science*, vol. 10677, pp. 711–742. Springer (2017). DOI https://doi.org/10.1007/978-3-319-70500-2_24. URL https://doi.org/10.1007/978-3-319-70500-2_24. Full version http://eprint.iacr.org/2017/931
48. Ciampi, M., Ostrovsky, R., Siniscalchi, L., Visconti, I.: Four-round concurrent non-malleable commitments from one-way functions. In: Advances in Cryptology - CRYPTO 2017 - 37th Annual International Cryptology Conference, Santa Barbara, CA, USA, August 20-24, 2017, Proceedings, Part II, pp. 127–157 (2017). DOI https://doi.org/10.1007/978-3-319-63715-0_5. URL https://doi.org/10.1007/978-3-319-63715-0_5. Full version http://eprint.iacr.org/2016/621
49. Ciampi, M., Ostrovsky, R., Siniscalchi, L., Visconti, I.: Round-optimal secure two-party computation from trapdoor permutations. In: Y. Kalai, L. Reyzin (eds.) Theory of Cryptography - 15th International Conference, TCC 2017, Baltimore, MD, USA, November 12-15, 2017,

Proceedings, Part I, *Lecture Notes in Computer Science*, vol. 10677, pp. 678–710. Springer (2017). DOI https://doi.org/10.1007/978-3-319-70500-2_23. URL https://doi.org/10.1007/978-3-319-70500-2_23
50. Ciampi, M., Ostrovsky, R., Siniscalchi, L., Waldner, H.: List oblivious transfer and applications to round-optimal black-box multiparty coin tossing. In: H. Handschuh, A. Lysyanskaya (eds.) Advances in Cryptology – CRYPTO 2023, Part I, *Lecture Notes in Computer Science*, vol. 14081, pp. 459–488. Springer, Cham, Switzerland, Santa Barbara, CA, USA (2023). DOI https://doi.org/10.1007/978-3-031-38557-5_15
51. Ciampi, M., Ostrovsky, R., Siniscalchi, L., Waldner, H.: Round-optimal black-box multiparty computation from polynomial-time assumptions. Cryptology ePrint Archive, Report 2023/1742 (2023). URL https://eprint.iacr.org/2023/1742
52. Ciampi, M., Persiano, G., Scafuro, A., Siniscalchi, L., Visconti, I.: Improved or-composition of sigma-protocols. In: E. Kushilevitz, T. Malkin (eds.) Theory of Cryptography - 13th International Conference, TCC 2016-A, Tel Aviv, Israel, January 10-13, 2016, Proceedings, Part II, *Lecture Notes in Computer Science*, vol. 9563, pp. 112–141. Springer (2016). Full version http://eprint.iacr.org/2015/810
53. Ciampi, M., Persiano, G., Scafuro, A., Siniscalchi, L., Visconti, I.: Online/offline OR composition of sigma protocols. In: M. Fischlin, J. Coron (eds.) Advances in Cryptology - EUROCRYPT 2016 - 35th Annual International Conference on the Theory and Applications of Cryptographic Techniques, Vienna, Austria, May 8-12, 2016, Proceedings, Part II, *Lecture Notes in Computer Science*, vol. 9666, pp. 63–92. Springer (2016). Full version http://eprint.iacr.org/2016/175
54. Ciampi, M., Persiano, G., Siniscalchi, L., Visconti, I.: A transform for NIZK almost as efficient and general as the fiat-shamir transform without programmable random oracles. In: E. Kushilevitz, T. Malkin (eds.) Theory of Cryptography - 13th International Conference, TCC 2016-A, Tel Aviv, Israel, January 10-13, 2016, Proceedings, Part II, *Lecture Notes in Computer Science*, vol. 9563, pp. 83–111. Springer (2016). DOI https://doi.org/10.1007/978-3-662-49099-0_4. URL https://doi.org/10.1007/978-3-662-49099-0_4
55. Cramer, R.: Modular design of secure yet practical cryptographic protocols. Ph.D. thesis, University of Amsterdam (1996)
56. Cramer, R., Damgård, I.: Zero-knowledge proofs for finite field arithmetic; or: Can zero-knowledge be for free? In: H. Krawczyk (ed.) Advances in Cryptology - CRYPTO '98, 18th Annual International Cryptology Conference, Santa Barbara, California, USA, August 23-27, 1998, Proceedings, *Lecture Notes in Computer Science*, vol. 1462, pp. 424–441. Springer (1998)
57. Cramer, R., Damgård, I., Schoenmakers, B.: Proofs of partial knowledge and simplified design of witness hiding protocols. In: Y. Desmedt (ed.) Advances in Cryptology — CRYPTO '94, *Lecture Notes in Computer Science*, vol. 839, pp. 174–187. Springer Berlin Heidelberg (1994). DOI https://doi.org/10.1007/3-540-48658-5_19. URL http://dx.doi.org/10.1007/3-540-48658-5_19
58. Cristofaro, E.D., Tsudik, G.: Practical private set intersection protocols with linear complexity. In: Financial Cryptography and Data Security, 14th International Conference, FC 2010, Tenerife, Canary Islands, January 25-28, 2010, Revised Selected Papers, pp. 143–159 (2010). DOI https://doi.org/10.1007/978-3-642-14577-3_13. URL https://doi.org/10.1007/978-3-642-14577-3_13
59. Cristofaro, E.D., Tsudik, G.: Experimenting with fast private set intersection. In: Trust and Trustworthy Computing - 5th International Conference, TRUST 2012, Vienna, Austria, June 13-15, 2012. Proceedings, pp. 55–73 (2012). DOI https://doi.org/10.1007/978-3-642-30921-2_4. URL https://doi.org/10.1007/978-3-642-30921-2_4
60. Dahl, M., Ning, C., Toft, T.: On secure two-party integer division. In: Financial Cryptography and Data Security - 16th International Conference, FC 2012, Kralendijk, Bonaire, Februray 27-March 2, 2012, Revised Selected Papers, pp. 164–178 (2012). DOI https://doi.org/10.1007/978-3-642-32946-3_13. URL https://doi.org/10.1007/978-3-642-32946-3_13

61. Damgård, I.: Efficient concurrent zero-knowledge in the auxiliary string model. In: Advances in Cryptology - EUROCRYPT 2000, International Conference on the Theory and Application of Cryptographic Techniques, Bruges, Belgium, May 14-18, 2000, Proceeding, *Lecture Notes in Computer Science*, vol. 1807, pp. 418–430. Springer (2000)
62. Damgård, I.: On Σ-protocol. http://www.cs.au.dk/~ivan/Sigma.pdf (2010)
63. Damgård, I., Fazio, N., Nicolosi, A.: Non-interactive zero-knowledge from homomorphic encryption. In: Theory of Cryptography, Third Theory of Cryptography Conference, TCC, 2006, New York, NY, USA, March 4-7, 2006, Proceedings, pp. 41–59 (2006). DOI https://doi.org/10.1007/11681878_3. URL http://dx.doi.org/10.1007/11681878_3
64. Damgård, I., Groth, J.: Non-interactive and reusable non-malleable commitment schemes. In: Proceedings of the 35th Annual ACM Symposium on Theory of Computing, June 9-11, 2003, San Diego, CA, USA, pp. 426–437 (2003)
65. Damgård, I., Nielsen, J.B.: Perfect hiding and perfect binding universally composable commitment schemes with constant expansion factor. In: Advances in Cryptology - CRYPTO 2002, 22nd Annual International Cryptology Conference, Santa Barbara, California, USA, August 18-22, 2002, Proceedings, pp. 581–596 (2002)
66. De Santis, A., Micali, S., Persiano, G.: Non-interactive zero-knowledge proof systems. In: Advances in Cryptology - CRYPTO '87, A Conference on the Theory and Applications of Cryptographic Techniques, Santa Barbara, California, USA, August 16-20, 1987, Proceedings, pp. 52–72 (1987). DOI https://doi.org/10.1007/3-540-48184-2_5. URL http://dx.doi.org/10.1007/3-540-48184-2_5
67. Di Crescenzo, G., Persiano, G., Visconti, I.: Improved setup assumptions for 3-round resettable zero knowledge. In: Advances in Cryptology - ASIACRYPT 2004, 10th International Conference on the Theory and Application of Cryptology and Information Security, Jeju Island, Korea, December 5-9, 2004, Proceedings, *Lecture Notes in Computer Science*, vol. 3329, pp. 530–544. Springer (2004)
68. Di Crescenzo, G., Visconti, I.: Concurrent zero knowledge in the public-key model. In: Automata, Languages and Programming, 32nd International Colloquium, ICALP 2005, Lisbon, Portugal, July 11-15, 2005, Proceedings, *Lecture Notes in Computer Science*, vol. 3580, pp. 816–827. Springer (2005)
69. Diffie, W., Hellman, M.E.: New Directions in Cryptography. IEEE Transactions on Information Theory **22** (1976)
70. Dolev, D., Dwork, C., Naor, M.: Non-malleable cryptography (extended abstract). In: Proceedings of the 23rd Annual ACM Symposium on Theory of Computing, May 5-8, 1991, New Orleans, Louisiana, USA, pp. 542–552 (1991)
71. Dwork, C., Naor, M.: Zaps and their applications. In: 41st Annual Symposium on Foundations of Computer Science, FOCS 2000, 12-14 November 2000, Redondo Beach, California, USA, pp. 283–293 (2000). DOI https://doi.org/10.1109/SFCS.2000.892117. URL http://dx.doi.org/10.1109/SFCS.2000.892117
72. Dwork, C., Naor, M.: Zaps and their applications. SIAM J. Comput. **36**(6), 1513–1543 (2007). DOI https://doi.org/10.1137/S0097539703426817. URL http://dx.doi.org/10.1137/S0097539703426817
73. Even, S., Goldreich, O., Lempel, A.: A randomized protocol for signing contracts. In: Advances in Cryptology: Proceedings of CRYPTO '82, Santa Barbara, California, USA, August 23-25, 1982., pp. 205–210. Plenum Press, New York (1982)
74. Faust, S., Kohlweiss, M., Marson, G.A., Venturi, D.: On the non-malleability of the fiat-shamir transform. In: Progress in Cryptology - INDOCRYPT 2012, 13th International Conference on Cryptology in India, Kolkata, India, December 9-12, 2012. Proceedings, pp. 60–79 (2012)
75. Feige, U., Fiat, A., Shamir, A.: Zero knowledge proofs of identity. In: Proceedings of the 19th Annual ACM Symposium on Theory of Computing, 1987, New York, New York, USA, pp. 210–217 (1987)
76. Feige, U., Lapidot, D., Shamir, A.: Multiple non-interactive zero knowledge proofs based on a single random string (extended abstract). In: 31st Annual Symposium on Foundations

of Computer Science, St. Louis, Missouri, USA, October 22-24, 1990, Volume I, pp. 308–317. IEEE Computer Society (1990). URL http://ieeexplore.ieee.org/xpl/mostRecentIssue.jsp?punumber=310
77. Feige, U., Lapidot, D., Shamir, A.: Multiple non-interactive zero knowledge proofs under general assumptions. SIAM J. on Computing **29**(1), 1–28 (1999)
78. Feige, U., Shamir, A.: Zero knowledge proofs of knowledge in two rounds. In: Advances in Cryptology - CRYPTO '89, 9th Annual International Cryptology Conference, Santa Barbara, California, USA, August 20-24, 1989, Proceedings, pp. 526–544 (1989). DOI https://doi.org/10.1007/0-387-34805-0_46. URL http://dx.doi.org/10.1007/0-387-34805-0_46
79. Fiat, A., Shamir, A.: How to prove yourself: Practical solutions to identification and signature problems. In: Advances in Cryptology - CRYPTO '86, Santa Barbara, California, USA, 1986, Proceedings, pp. 186–194 (1986)
80. Freedman, M.J., Ishai, Y., Pinkas, B., Reingold, O.: Keyword search and oblivious pseudorandom functions. In: Theory of Cryptography, Second Theory of Cryptography Conference, TCC 2005, Cambridge, MA, USA, February 10-12, 2005, Proceedings, pp. 303–324 (2005). DOI https://doi.org/10.1007/978-3-540-30576-7_17. URLhttps://doi.org/10.1007/978-3-540-30576-7_17
81. Freedman, M.J., Nissim, K., Pinkas, B.: Efficient private matching and set intersection. In: Advances in Cryptology - EUROCRYPT 2004, International Conference on the Theory and Applications of Cryptographic Techniques, Interlaken, Switzerland, May 2-6, 2004, Proceedings, pp. 1–19 (2004). DOI https://doi.org/10.1007/978-3-540-24676-3_1. URL https://doi.org/10.1007/978-3-540-24676-3_1
82. Garay, J.A., MacKenzie, P., Yang, K.: Strengthening zero-knowledge protocols using signatures. Journal of Cryptology **19**(2), 169–209 (2006)
83. Garay, J.A., Schoenmakers, B., Villegas, J.: Practical and secure solutions for integer comparison. In: Public Key Cryptography - PKC 2007, 10th International Conference on Practice and Theory in Public-Key Cryptography, Beijing, China, April 16-20, 2007, Proceedings, pp. 330–342 (2007). DOI https://doi.org/10.1007/978-3-540-71677-8_22. URL https://doi.org/10.1007/978-3-540-71677-8_22
84. Garg, S., Mukherjee, P., Pandey, O., Polychroniadou, A.: The exact round complexity of secure computation. In: M. Fischlin, J. Coron (eds.) Advances in Cryptology - EUROCRYPT 2016 - 35th Annual International Conference on the Theory and Applications of Cryptographic Techniques, Vienna, Austria, May 8-12, 2016, Proceedings, Part II, *Lecture Notes in Computer Science*, vol. 9666, pp. 448–476. Springer (2016)
85. Goldreich, O.: Foundations of cryptography: volume 2, basic applications. Cambridge university press (2009)
86. Goldreich, O., Kahan, A.: How to construct constant-round zero-knowledge proof systems for NP. J. Cryptology **9**(3), 167–190 (1996)
87. Goldreich, O., Krawczyk, H.: On the composition of zero-knowledge proof systems. SIAM J. Comput. **25**(1), 169–192 (1996). DOI https://doi.org/10.1137/S0097539791220688. URL http://dx.doi.org/10.1137/S0097539791220688
88. Goldreich, O., Levin, L.A.: A hard-core predicate for all one-way functions. In: Proceedings of the 21st Annual ACM Symposium on Theory of Computing, May 14-17, 1989, Seattle, Washigton, USA, pp. 25–32 (1989)
89. Goldreich, O., Micali, S., Wigderson, A.: Proofs that yield nothing but their validity and a methodology of cryptographic protocol design (extended abstract). In: 27th Annual Symposium on Foundations of Computer Science, Toronto, Canada, 27-29 October 1986, pp. 174–187 (1986). DOI https://doi.org/10.1109/SFCS.1986.47. URL http://dx.doi.org/10.1109/SFCS.1986.47
90. Goldreich, O., Micali, S., Wigderson, A.: How to play any mental game or A completeness theorem for protocols with honest majority. In: A.V. Aho (ed.) Proceedings of the 19th Annual ACM Symposium on Theory of Computing, 1987, New York, New York, USA, pp. 218–229. ACM (1987). DOI https://doi.org/10.1145/28395.28420. URL http://doi.acm.org/10.1145/28395.28420

91. Goldwasser, S., Kalai, Y.T.: On the (in)security of the fiat-shamir paradigm. In: 44th Symposium on Foundations of Computer Science (FOCS 2003), 11-14 October 2003, Cambridge, MA, USA, Proceedings, pp. 102–113 (2003)
92. Goldwasser, S., Micali, S., Rackoff, C.: The knowledge complexity of interactive proof-systems (extended abstract). In: Proceedings of the 17th Annual ACM Symposium on Theory of Computing, May 6-8, 1985, Providence, Rhode Island, USA, pp. 291–304 (1985). DOI https://doi.org/10.1145/22145.22178. URL http://doi.acm.org/10.1145/22145.22178
93. Goldwasser, S., Micali, S., Rackoff, C.: The knowledge complexity of interactive proof systems. SIAM J. Comput. **18**(1), 186–208 (1989). DOI https://doi.org/10.1137/0218012. URL http://dx.doi.org/10.1137/0218012
94. Goyal, V.: Constant round non-malleable protocols using one way functions. In: Proceedings of the 43rd ACM Symposium on Theory of Computing, STOC 2011, San Jose, CA, USA, 6-8 June 2011, pp. 695–704 (2011)
95. Goyal, V., Lee, C., Ostrovsky, R., Visconti, I.: Constructing non-malleable commitments: A black-box approach. In: 53rd Annual IEEE Symposium on Foundations of Computer Science, FOCS 2012, New Brunswick, NJ, USA, October 20-23, 2012, pp. 51–60 (2012)
96. Goyal, V., Ostrovsky, R., Scafuro, A., Visconti, I.: Black-box non-black-box zero knowledge. In: Symposium on Theory of Computing, STOC 2014, New York, NY, USA, May 31 - June 03, 2014, pp. 515–524. ACM (2014)
97. Goyal, V., Pandey, O., Richelson, S.: Textbook non-malleable commitments. In: Proceedings of the 48th Annual ACM SIGACT Symposium on Theory of Computing, STOC 2016, Cambridge, MA, USA, June 18-21, 2016, pp. 1128–1141 (2016). Full version: Cryptology ePrint Archive, Report 2015/1178
98. Goyal, V., Richelson, S.: Non-malleable commitments using Goldreich-Levin list decoding. In: D. Zuckerman (ed.) 60th Annual Symposium on Foundations of Computer Science, pp. 686–699. IEEE Computer Society Press, Baltimore, MD, USA (2019). DOI https://doi.org/10.1109/FOCS.2019.00047
99. Goyal, V., Richelson, S., Rosen, A., Vald, M.: An algebraic approach to non-malleability. In: 55th IEEE Annual Symposium on Foundations of Computer Science, FOCS 2014, Philadelphia, PA, USA, October 18-21, 2014, pp. 41–50 (2014)
100. Groth, J.: Honest verifier zero-knowledge arguments applied. Dissertation Series DS-04-3, BRICS. PhD thesis. xii+119 pp (2004)
101. Groth, J., Kohlweiss, M.: One-out-of-many proofs: Or how to leak a secret and spend a coin. In: E. Oswald, M. Fischlin (eds.) Advances in Cryptology - EUROCRYPT 2015 - 34th Annual International Conference on the Theory and Applications of Cryptographic Techniques, Sofia, Bulgaria, April 26-30, 2015, Proceedings, Part II, *Lecture Notes in Computer Science*, vol. 9057, pp. 253–280. Springer (2015)
102. Groth, J., Ostrovsky, R., Sahai, A.: Perfect non-interactive zero knowledge for NP. In: S. Vaudenay (ed.) Advances in Cryptology - EUROCRYPT 2006, 25th Annual International Conference on the Theory and Applications of Cryptographic Techniques, St. Petersburg, Russia, May 28 - June 1, 2006, Proceedings, *Lecture Notes in Computer Science*, vol. 4004, pp. 339–358. Springer (2006)
103. Groth, J., Sahai, A.: Efficient non-interactive proof systems for bilinear groups. In: Advances in Cryptology - EUROCRYPT 2008, 27th Annual International Conference on the Theory and Applications of Cryptographic Techniques, Istanbul, Turkey, April 13-17, 2008. Proceedings, pp. 415–432 (2008). DOI https://doi.org/10.1007/978-3-540-78967-3_24. URL http://dx.doi.org/10.1007/978-3-540-78967-3_24
104. Guillou, L.C., Quisquater, J.: A practical zero-knowledge protocol fitted to security microprocessor minimizing both transmission and memory. In: C.G. Günther (ed.) Advances in Cryptology - EUROCRYPT '88, Workshop on the Theory and Application of of Cryptographic Techniques, Davos, Switzerland, May 25-27, 1988, Proceedings, *Lecture Notes in Computer Science*, vol. 330, pp. 123–128. Springer (1988)
105. Haitner, I., Reingold, O., Vadhan, S.P., Wee, H.: Inaccessible entropy. In: M. Mitzenmacher (ed.) Proceedings of the 41st Annual ACM Symposium on Theory of Computing, STOC

2009, Bethesda, MD, USA, May 31 - June 2, 2009, pp. 611–620. ACM (2009). DOI https://doi.org/10.1145/1536414.1536497. URL http://doi.acm.org/10.1145/1536414.1536497
106. Halevi, S., Hazay, C., Polychroniadou, A., Venkitasubramaniam, M.: Round-optimal secure multi-party computation. Cryptology ePrint Archive, Report 2017/1056 (2017). https://eprint.iacr.org/2017/1056
107. Halevi, S., Hazay, C., Polychroniadou, A., Venkitasubramaniam, M.: Round-optimal secure multi-party computation. In: H. Shacham, A. Boldyreva (eds.) Advances in Cryptology – CRYPTO 2018, Part II, *Lecture Notes in Computer Science*, vol. 10992, pp. 488–520. Springer, Cham, Switzerland, Santa Barbara, CA, USA (2018). DOI https://doi.org/10.1007/978-3-319-96881-0_17
108. Halevi, S., Micali, S.: Practical and provably-secure commitment schemes from collision-free hashing. In: Advances in Cryptology - CRYPTO '96, 16th Annual International Cryptology Conference, Santa Barbara, California, USA, August 18-22, 1996, Proceedings, pp. 201–215 (1996)
109. Hallgren, P., Orlandi, C., Sabelfeld, A.: Privatepool: Privacy-preserving ridesharing. In: IEEE 30th Computer Security Foundations Symposium, CSF 2017, Santa Barbara, CA, USA, August 21-25, 2017, pp. 276–291 (2017)
110. Hao, F., Kreeger, M.N., Randell, B., Clarke, D., Shahandashti, S.F., Lee, P.H.: Every vote counts: Ensuring integrity in large-scale electronic voting. USENIX Journal of Election Technology and Systems **2**(3) (2014)
111. Hazay, C., Lindell, Y.: Efficient protocols for set intersection and pattern matching with security against malicious and covert adversaries. In: Theory of Cryptography, Fifth Theory of Cryptography Conference, TCC 2008, New York, USA, March 19-21, 2008., pp. 155–175 (2008). DOI https://doi.org/10.1007/978-3-540-78524-8_10. URL https://doi.org/10.1007/978-3-540-78524-8_10
112. Hazay, C., Lindell, Y.: Efficient Secure Two-Party Protocols - Techniques and Constructions. Information Security and Cryptography. Springer (2010)
113. Hazay, C., Venkitasubramaniam, M.: Scalable multi-party private set-intersection. In: Public-Key Cryptography - PKC 2017 - 20th IACR International Conference on Practice and Theory in Public-Key Cryptography, Amsterdam, The Netherlands, March 28-31, 2017, Proceedings, Part I, pp. 175–203 (2017). DOI https://doi.org/10.1007/978-3-662-54365-8_8. URL https://doi.org/10.1007/978-3-662-54365-8_8
114. Huang, Y., Evans, D., Katz, J.: Private set intersection: Are garbled circuits better than custom protocols? In: 19th Annual Network and Distributed System Security Symposium, NDSS 2012, San Diego, California, USA, February 5-8, 2012 (2012). URL http://www.internetsociety.org/private-set-intersection-are-garbled-circuits-better-custom-protocols
115. Ion, M., Kreuter, B., Nergiz, E., Patel, S., Saxena, S., Seth, K., Shanahan, D., Yung, M.: Private intersection-sum protocol with applications to attributing aggregate ad conversions. Cryptology ePrint Archive, Report 2017/738 (2017). http://eprint.iacr.org/2017/738
116. Ishai, Y., Khurana, D., Sahai, A., Srinivasan, A.: On the round complexity of black-box secure MPC. In: T. Malkin, C. Peikert (eds.) Advances in Cryptology – CRYPTO 2021, Part II, *Lecture Notes in Computer Science*, vol. 12826, pp. 214–243. Springer, Cham, Switzerland, Virtual Event (2021). DOI https://doi.org/10.1007/978-3-030-84245-1_8
117. Ishai, Y., Khurana, D., Sahai, A., Srinivasan, A.: Round-optimal black-box MPC in the plain model. In: H. Handschuh, A. Lysyanskaya (eds.) Advances in Cryptology – CRYPTO 2023, Part I, *Lecture Notes in Computer Science*, vol. 14081, pp. 393–426. Springer, Cham, Switzerland, Santa Barbara, CA, USA (2023). DOI https://doi.org/10.1007/978-3-031-38557-5_13
118. Ishai, Y., Kilian, J., Nissim, K., Petrank, E.: Extending oblivious transfers efficiently. In: Advances in Cryptology - CRYPTO 2003, 23rd Annual International Cryptology Conference, Santa Barbara, California, USA, August 17-21, 2003, Proceedings, pp. 145–161 (2003). DOI https://doi.org/10.1007/978-3-540-45146-4_9. URL https://doi.org/10.1007/978-3-540-45146-4_9
119. Ishai, Y., Paskin, A.: Evaluating branching programs on encrypted data. In: Theory of Cryptography, 4th Theory of Cryptography Conference, TCC 2007, Amsterdam, The Netherlands,

February 21-24, 2007, Proceedings, pp. 575–594 (2007). DOI https://doi.org/10.1007/978-3-540-70936-7_31. URL https://doi.org/10.1007/978-3-540-70936-7_31
120. Jarecki, S., Liu, X.: Fast secure computation of set intersection. In: Security and Cryptography for Networks, 7th International Conference, SCN 2010, Amalfi, Italy, September 13-15, 2010. Proceedings, pp. 418–435 (2010). DOI https://doi.org/10.1007/978-3-642-15317-4_26. URL https://doi.org/10.1007/978-3-642-15317-4_26
121. Kalai, Y.T., Rothblum, G.N., Rothblum, R.D.: From obfuscation to the security of fiat-shamir for proofs. In: J. Katz, H. Shacham (eds.) Advances in Cryptology - CRYPTO 2017 - 37th Annual International Cryptology Conference, Santa Barbara, CA, USA, August 20-24, 2017, Proceedings, Part II, *Lecture Notes in Computer Science*, vol. 10402, pp. 224–251. Springer (2017). DOI https://doi.org/10.1007/978-3-319-63715-0_8. URL https://doi.org/10.1007/978-3-319-63715-0_8
122. Kamara, S., Mohassel, P., Raykova, M., Sadeghian, S.S.: Scaling private set intersection to billion-element sets. In: Financial Cryptography and Data Security - 18th International Conference, FC 2014, Christ Church, Barbados, March 3-7, 2014, Revised Selected Papers, pp. 195–215 (2014). DOI https://doi.org/10.1007/978-3-662-45472-5_13. URL https://doi.org/10.1007/978-3-662-45472-5_13
123. Katz, J.: Efficient cryptographic protocols preventing "man-in-the-middle" attacks. Ph.D. thesis, Columbia University (2002)
124. Katz, J., Ostrovsky, R.: Round-optimal secure two-party computation. In: Advances in Cryptology - CRYPTO 2004, 24th Annual International CryptologyConference, Santa Barbara, California, USA, August 15-19, 2004, Proceedings, pp. 335–354 (2004). DOI https://doi.org/10.1007/978-3-540-28628-8_21. URL http://dx.doi.org/10.1007/978-3-540-28628-8_21
125. Katz, J., Ostrovsky, R., Smith, A.D.: Round efficiency of multi-party computation with a dishonest majority. In: E. Biham (ed.) Advances in Cryptology - EUROCRYPT 2003, International Conference on the Theory and Applications of Cryptographic Techniques, Warsaw, Poland, May 4-8, 2003, Proceedings, *Lecture Notes in Computer Science*, vol. 2656, pp. 578–595. Springer (2003). DOI https://doi.org/10.1007/3-540-39200-9_36. URL http://dx.doi.org/10.1007/3-540-39200-9_36
126. Keller, M., Orsini, E., Scholl, P.: Actively secure OT extension with optimal overhead. In: Advances in Cryptology - CRYPTO 2015 - 35th Annual Cryptology Conference, Santa Barbara, CA, USA, August 16-20, 2015, Proceedings, Part I, pp. 724–741 (2015). DOI https://doi.org/10.1007/978-3-662-47989-6_35. URL https://doi.org/10.1007/978-3-662-47989-6_35
127. Khurana, D.: Round optimal concurrent non-malleability from polynomial hardness. In: Y. Kalai, L. Reyzin (eds.) TCC 2017: 15th Theory of Cryptography Conference, Part II, *Lecture Notes in Computer Science*, vol. 10678, pp. 139–171. Springer, Cham, Switzerland, Baltimore, MD, USA (2017). DOI https://doi.org/10.1007/978-3-319-70503-3_5
128. Khurana, D.: Round optimal concurrent non-malleability from polynomial hardness. In: Y. Kalai, L. Reyzin (eds.) Theory of Cryptography - 15th International Conference, TCC 2017, Baltimore, MD, USA, November 12-15, 2017, Proceedings, Part II, *Lecture Notes in Computer Science*, vol. 10678, pp. 139–171. Springer (2017)
129. Khurana, D., Sahai, A.: How to achieve non-malleability in one or two rounds. In: C. Umans (ed.) 58th IEEE Annual Symposium on Foundations of Computer Science, FOCS 2017, Berkeley, CA, USA, October 15-17, 2017, pp. 564–575. IEEE Computer Society (2017)
130. Kim, A., Liang, X., Pandey, O.: A new approach to efficient non-malleable zero-knowledge. In: Y. Dodis, T. Shrimpton (eds.) Advances in Cryptology – CRYPTO 2022, Part IV, *Lecture Notes in Computer Science*, vol. 13510, pp. 389–418. Springer, Cham, Switzerland, Santa Barbara, CA, USA (2022). DOI https://doi.org/10.1007/978-3-031-15985-5_14
131. Kolesnikov, V., Kumaresan, R.: Improved OT extension for transferring short secrets. In: Advances in Cryptology - CRYPTO 2013 - 33rd Annual Cryptology Conference, Santa Barbara, CA, USA, August 18-22, 2013. Proceedings, Part II, pp. 54–70 (2013). DOI https://doi.org/10.1007/978-3-642-40084-1_4. URL https://doi.org/10.1007/978-3-642-40084-1_4
132. Kolesnikov, V., Kumaresan, R., Rosulek, M., Trieu, N.: Efficient batched oblivious PRF with applications to private set intersection. In: Proceedings of the 2016 ACM SIGSAC

Conference on Computer and Communications Security, Vienna, Austria, October 24-28, 2016, pp. 818–829 (2016). DOI https://doi.org/10.1145/2976749.2978381. URL http://doi.acm.org/10.1145/2976749.2978381
133. Lapidot, D., Shamir, A.: Publicly verifiable non-interactive zero-knowledge proofs. In: Advances in Cryptology - CRYPTO (1990)
134. Lin, H., Pass, R.: Concurrent non-malleable zero knowledge with adaptive inputs. In: Y. Ishai (ed.) Theory of Cryptography - 8th Theory of Cryptography Conference, TCC 2011, Providence, RI, USA, March 28-30, 2011. Proceedings, *Lecture Notes in Computer Science*, vol. 6597, pp. 274–292. Springer (2011)
135. Lin, H., Pass, R.: Constant-round non-malleable commitments from any one-way function. In: L. Fortnow, S.P. Vadhan (eds.) Proceedings of the 43rd ACM Symposium on Theory of Computing, STOC 2011, San Jose, CA, USA, 6-8 June 2011, pp. 705–714. ACM (2011)
136. Lin, H., Pass, R.: Constant-round nonmalleable commitments from any one-way function. J. ACM **62**(1), 5:1–5:30 (2015)
137. Lin, H., Pass, R., Soni, P.: Two-round and non-interactive concurrent non-malleable commitments from time-lock puzzles. In: C. Umans (ed.) 58th IEEE Annual Symposium on Foundations of Computer Science, FOCS 2017, Berkeley, CA, USA, October 15-17, 2017, pp. 576–587. IEEE Computer Society (2017)
138. Lin, H., Pass, R., Venkitasubramaniam, M.: Concurrent non-malleable commitments from any one-way function. In: R. Canetti (ed.) Theory of Cryptography, Fifth Theory of Cryptography Conference, TCC 2008, New York, USA, March 19-21, 2008., *Lecture Notes in Computer Science*, vol. 4948, pp. 571–588. Springer (2008)
139. Lin, H., Pass, R., Venkitasubramaniam, M.: A unified framework for concurrent security: universal composability from stand-alone non-malleability. In: Proceedings of the 41st Annual ACM Symposium on Theory of Computing,STOC 2009, Bethesda, MD, USA, May 31 - June 2, 2009, pp. 179–188 (2009)
140. Lindell, Y.: An efficient transform from Sigma Protocols to NIZK with a CRS and non-programmable random oracle. Cryptology ePrint Archive, Report 2014/710 (2014). http://eprint.iacr.org/2014/710/20150906:203011
141. Lindell, Y.: An efficient transform from Sigma protocols to NIZK with a CRS and non-programmable random oracle. In: Theory of Cryptography - 12th Theory of Cryptography Conference, TCC 2015, Warsaw, Poland, March 23-25, 2015, Proceedings, Part I, pp. 93–109 (2015)
142. Lindell, Y., Pinkas, B.: A proof of security of yao's protocol for two-party computation. J. Cryptology **22**(2), 161–188 (2009). DOI https://doi.org/10.1007/s00145-008-9036-8. URL https://doi.org/10.1007/s00145-008-9036-8
143. Lipmaa, H., Toft, T.: Secure equality and greater-than tests with sublinear online complexity. In: Automata, Languages, and Programming - 40th International Colloquium, ICALP 2013, Riga, Latvia, July 8-12, 2013, Proceedings, Part II, pp. 645–656 (2013). DOI https://doi.org/10.1007/978-3-642-39212-2_56. URL https://doi.org/10.1007/978-3-642-39212-2_56
144. M, D.: Cryptography of the ancient sparta (2013). www.australianscience.com.au/technology/a-scytale-cryptography-of-the-ancient-sparta/ A Scytale.
145. Mahmoody, M., Pass, R.: The curious case of non-interactive commitments - on the power of black-box vs. non-black-box use of primitives. In: R. Safavi-Naini, R. Canetti (eds.) Advances in Cryptology - CRYPTO 2012 - 32nd Annual Cryptology Conference, Santa Barbara, CA, USA, August 19-23, 2012. Proceedings, *Lecture Notes in Computer Science*, vol. 7417, pp. 701–718. Springer (2012)
146. Maurer, U.: Zero-knowledge proofs of knowledge for group homomorphisms. Designs, Codes and Cryptography pp. 1–14 (2015). DOI https://doi.org/10.1007/s10623-015-0103-5. URL http://dx.doi.org/10.1007/s10623-015-0103-5
147. Maurer, U.M.: Unifying zero-knowledge proofs of knowledge. In: B. Preneel (ed.) Progress in Cryptology - AFRICACRYPT 2009, Second International Conference on Cryptology in Africa, Gammarth, Tunisia, June 21-25, 2009. Proceedings, *Lecture Notes in Computer Science*, vol. 5580, pp. 272–286. Springer (2009)

148. Meadows, C.A.: A more efficient cryptographic matchmaking protocol for use in the absence of a continuously available third party. In: Proceedings of the 1986 IEEE Symposium on Security and Privacy, Oakland, California, USA, April 7-9, 1986, pp. 134–137 (1986). DOI https://doi.org/10.1109/SP.1986.10022. URL https://doi.org/10.1109/SP.1986.10022
149. Micali, S., Reyzin, L.: Soundness in the public-key model. In: Advances in Cryptology - CRYPTO 2001, 21st Annual International Cryptology Conference, Santa Barbara, California, USA, August 19-23, 2001, Proceedings, pp. 542–565 (2001)
150. Micciancio, D., Petrank, E.: Simulatable commitments and efficient concurrent zero-knowledge. In: Advances in Cryptology - EUROCRYPT 2003, International Conference on the Theory and Applications of Cryptographic Techniques, Warsaw, Poland, May 4-8, 2003, Proceedings, pp. 140–159 (2003). DOI https://doi.org/10.1007/3-540-39200-9_9. URL http://dx.doi.org/10.1007/3-540-39200-9_9
151. Mittelbach, A., Venturi, D.: Fiat-shamir for highly sound protocols is instantiable. In: V. Zikas, R.D. Prisco (eds.) Security and Cryptography for Networks - 10th International Conference, SCN 2016, Amalfi, Italy, August 31 - September 2, 2016, Proceedings, *Lecture Notes in Computer Science*, vol. 9841, pp. 198–215. Springer (2016). DOI https://doi.org/10.1007/978-3-319-44618-9_11. URL https://doi.org/10.1007/978-3-319-44618-9_11
152. Mohassel, P., Niksefat, S.: Oblivious decision programs from oblivious transfer: Efficient reductions. In: Financial Cryptography and Data Security - 16th International Conference, FC 2012, Kralendijk, Bonaire, Februray 27-March 2, 2012, Revised Selected Papers, pp. 269–284 (2012). DOI https://doi.org/10.1007/978-3-642-32946-3_20. URL https://doi.org/10.1007/978-3-642-32946-3_20
153. Nagaraja, S., Mittal, P., Hong, C., Caesar, M., Borisov, N.: Botgrep: Finding P2P bots with structured graph analysis. In: 19th USENIX Security Symposium, Washington, DC, USA, August 11-13, 2010, Proceedings, pp. 95–110 (2010). URL http://www.usenix.org/events/sec10/tech/full_papers/Nagaraja.pdf
154. Naor, M.: Bit commitment using pseudorandomness. J. Cryptology **4**(2), 151–158 (1991)
155. Naor, M., Yung, M.: Universal one-way hash functions and their cryptographic applications. In: Proceedings of the 21st Annual ACM Symposium on Theory of Computing, May 14-17, 1989, Seattle, Washigton, USA, pp. 33–43 (1989)
156. Naor, M., Yung, M.: Public-key cryptosystems provably secure against chosen ciphertext attacks. In: Proceedings of the 22nd Annual ACM Symposium on Theory of Computing, May 13-17, 1990, Baltimore, Maryland, USA, pp. 427–437 (1990). DOI https://doi.org/10.1145/100216.100273. URL http://doi.acm.org/10.1145/100216.100273
157. Orrù, M., Orsini, E., Scholl, P.: Actively secure 1-out-of-n OT extension with application to private set intersection. In: Topics in Cryptology - CT-RSA 2017 - The Cryptographers' Track at the RSA Conference 2017, San Francisco, CA, USA, February 14-17, 2017, Proceedings, pp. 381–396 (2017). DOI https://doi.org/10.1007/978-3-319-52153-4_22. URL https://doi.org/10.1007/978-3-319-52153-4_22
158. Ostrovsky, R., Pandey, O., Visconti, I.: Efficiency preserving transformations for concurrent non-malleable zero knowledge. In: D. Micciancio (ed.) Theory of Cryptography, 7th Theory of Cryptography Conference, TCC 2010, Zurich, Switzerland, February 9-11, 2010. Proceedings, *Lecture Notes in Computer Science*, vol. 5978, pp. 535–552. Springer (2010)
159. Ostrovsky, R., Persiano, G., Visconti, I.: Constant-round concurrent non-malleable zero knowledge in the bare public-key model. In: Automata, Languages and Programming, 35th International Colloquium, ICALP 2008, Reykjavik, Iceland, July 7-11, 2008, Proceedings, Part II - Track B: Logic, Semantics, and Theory of Programming & Track C: Security and Cryptography Foundations, pp. 548–559 (2008)
160. Ostrovsky, R., Rao, V., Scafuro, A., Visconti, I.: Revisiting lower and upper bounds for selective decommitments. In: TCC, pp. 559–578 (2013)
161. Ostrovsky, R., Richelson, S., Scafuro, A.: Round-optimal black-box two-party computation. In: R. Gennaro, M. Robshaw (eds.) Advances in Cryptology - CRYPTO 2015 - 35th Annual Cryptology Conference, Santa Barbara, CA, USA, August 16-20, 2015, Proceedings, Part II, *Lecture Notes in Computer Science*, vol. 9216, pp. 339–358. Springer (2015). DOI https://

doi.org/10.1007/978-3-662-48000-7_17. URL http://dx.doi.org/10.1007/978-3-662-48000-7_17
162. Ostrovsky, R., Visconti, I.: Simultaneous resettability from collision resistance. Electronic Colloquium on Computational Complexity (ECCC) **19**, 164 (2012)
163. Pandey, O., Pass, R., Vaikuntanathan, V.: Adaptive one-way functions and applications. In: Advances in Cryptology - CRYPTO 2008, 28th Annual International Cryptology Conference, Santa Barbara, CA, USA, August 17-21, 2008. Proceedings, pp. 57–74 (2008)
164. Pass, R.: On deniability in the common reference string and random oracle model. In: Advances in Cryptology - CRYPTO 2003, 23rd Annual International Cryptology Conference, Santa Barbara, California, USA, August 17-21, 2003, Proceedings, pp. 316–337 (2003). DOI https://doi.org/10.1007/978-3-540-45146-4_19. URL http://dx.doi.org/10.1007/978-3-540-45146-4_19
165. Pass, R.: Simulation in quasi-polynomial time, and its application to protocol composition. In: E. Biham (ed.) Advances in Cryptology - EUROCRYPT 2003, International Conference on the Theory and Applications of Cryptographic Techniques, Warsaw, Poland, May 4-8, 2003, Proceedings, *Lecture Notes in Computer Science*, vol. 2656, pp. 160–176. Springer (2003)
166. Pass, R.: Bounded-concurrent secure multi-party computation with a dishonest majority. In: L. Babai (ed.) Proceedings of the 36th Annual ACM Symposium on Theory of Computing, Chicago, IL, USA, June 13-16, 2004, pp. 232–241. ACM (2004). DOI https://doi.org/10.1145/1007352.1007393. URL http://doi.acm.org/10.1145/1007352.1007393
167. Pass, R.: Unprovable security of perfect NIZK and non-interactive non-malleable commitments. In: TCC, pp. 334–354 (2013)
168. Pass, R., Rosen, A.: Bounded-concurrent secure two-party computation in a constant number of rounds. In: 44th Symposium on Foundations of Computer Science (FOCS 2003), 11-14 October 2003, Cambridge, MA, USA, Proceedings, pp. 404–413. IEEE Computer Society (2003)
169. Pass, R., Rosen, A.: Concurrent non-malleable commitments. In: 46th Annual IEEE Symposium on Foundations of Computer Science (FOCS 2005), 23-25 October 2005, Pittsburgh, PA, USA, Proceedings, pp. 563–572 (2005)
170. Pass, R., Rosen, A.: New and improved constructions of non-malleable cryptographic protocols. In: H.N. Gabow, R. Fagin (eds.) Proceedings of the 37th Annual ACM Symposium on Theory of Computing, Baltimore, MD, USA, May 22-24, 2005, pp. 533–542. ACM (2005)
171. Pass, R., Rosen, A.: Concurrent nonmalleable commitments. SIAM J. Comput. **37**(6), 1891–1925 (2008)
172. Pass, R., Rosen, A.: New and improved constructions of nonmalleable cryptographic protocols. SIAM J. Comput. **38**(2), 702–752 (2008)
173. Pass, R., Wee, H.: Constant-round non-malleable commitments from sub-exponential one-way functions. In: Advances in Cryptology - EUROCRYPT 2010, 29th Annual International Conference on the Theory and Applications of Cryptographic Techniques, French Riviera, May 30 - June 3, 2010. Proceedings, pp. 638–655 (2010)
174. Pedersen, T.P.: Non-interactive and information-theoretic secure verifiable secret sharing. In: Advances in Cryptology - CRYPTO '91, 11th Annual International Cryptology Conference, Santa Barbara, California, USA, August 11-15, 1991, Proceedings, pp. 129–140 (1991). DOI https://doi.org/10.1007/3-540-46766-1_9. URL http://dx.doi.org/10.1007/3-540-46766-1_9
175. Pinkas, B., Schneider, T., Segev, G., Zohner, M.: Phasing: Private set intersection using permutation-based hashing. In: 24th USENIX Security Symposium, USENIX Security 15, Washington, D.C., USA, August 12-14, 2015., pp. 515–530 (2015). URL https://www.usenix.org/conference/usenixsecurity15/technical-sessions/presentation/pinkas
176. Pinkas, B., Schneider, T., Zohner, M.: Faster private set intersection based on OT extension. In: Proceedings of the 23rd USENIX Security Symposium, San Diego, CA, USA, August 20-22, 2014., pp. 797–812 (2014). URL https://www.usenix.org/conference/usenixsecurity14/technical-sessions/presentation/pinkas

177. Pinkas, B., Schneider, T., Zohner, M.: Scalable private set intersection based on ot extension. Cryptology ePrint Archive, Report 2016/930 (2016). http://eprint.iacr.org/2016/930
178. Pointcheval, D., Stern, J.: Security proofs for signature schemes. In: U.M. Maurer (ed.) Advances in Cryptology - EUROCRYPT '96, International Conference on the Theory and Application of Cryptographic Techniques, Saragossa, Spain, May 12-16, 1996, Proceeding, *Lecture Notes in Computer Science*, vol. 1070, pp. 387–398. Springer (1996)
179. Polychroniadou, A.: On the communication and round complexity of secure computation. Ph.D. thesis, Aarhus University (2016)
180. Rindal, P., Rosulek, M.: Improved private set intersection against malicious adversaries. In: Advances in Cryptology - EUROCRYPT 2017 - 36th Annual International Conference on the Theory and Applications of Cryptographic Techniques, Paris, France, April 30 - May 4, 2017, Proceedings, Part I, pp. 235–259 (2017). DOI https://doi.org/10.1007/978-3-319-56620-7_9. URL https://doi.org/10.1007/978-3-319-56620-7_9
181. Rompel, J.: One-way functions are necessary and sufficient for secure signatures. In: Proceedings of the 22nd Annual ACM Symposium on Theory of Computing, May 13-17, 1990, Baltimore, Maryland, USA, pp. 387–394 (1990). DOI https://doi.org/10.1145/100216.100269. URL http://doi.acm.org/10.1145/100216.100269
182. Sahai, A.: Non-malleable non-interactive zero knowledge and adaptive chosen-ciphertext security. In: 40th Annual Symposium on Foundations of Computer Science, FOCS '99, 17-18 October, 1999, New York, NY, USA, pp. 543–553. IEEE Computer Society (1999). DOI https://doi.org/10.1109/SFFCS.1999.814628. URL http://dx.doi.org/10.1109/SFFCS.1999.814628
183. Santis, A.D., Crescenzo, G.D., Ostrovsky, R., Persiano, G., Sahai, A.: Robust non-interactive zero knowledge. In: J. Kilian (ed.) Advances in Cryptology - CRYPTO 2001, 21st Annual International Cryptology Conference, Santa Barbara, California, USA, August 19-23, 2001, Proceedings, *Lecture Notes in Computer Science*, vol. 2139, pp. 566–598. Springer (2001)
184. Scafuro, A., Visconti, I.: On round-optimal zero knowledge in the bare public-key model. In: D. Pointcheval, T. Johansson (eds.) Advances in Cryptology - EUROCRYPT 2012 - 31st Annual International Conference on the Theory and Applications of Cryptographic Techniques, Cambridge, UK, April 15-19, 2012. Proceedings, *Lecture Notes in Computer Science*, vol. 7237, pp. 153–171. Springer (2012)
185. Schnorr, C.: Efficient identification and signatures for smart cards. In: G. Brassard (ed.) Advances in Cryptology — CRYPTO' 89 Proceedings, *Lecture Notes in Computer Science*, vol. 435, pp. 239–252. Springer New York (1989)
186. Shamir, A.: On the power of commutativity in cryptography. In: Automata, Languages and Programming, 7th Colloquium, Noordweijkerhout, The Netherland, July 14-18, 1980, Proceedings, pp. 582–595 (1980). DOI https://doi.org/10.1007/3-540-10003-2_100. URL https://doi.org/10.1007/3-540-10003-2_100
187. Toft, T., et al.: Primitives and applications for multi-party computation. PhD Thesis, University of Aarhus, Denmark (2007)
188. Ventre, C., Visconti, I.: Co-sound zero-knowledge with public keys. In: Progress in Cryptology - AFRICACRYPT 2009, Second International Conference on Cryptology in Africa, Gammarth, Tunisia, June 21-25, 2009. Proceedings, *Lecture Notes in Computer Science*, vol. 5580, pp. 287–304. Springer (2009)
189. Visconti, I.: Efficient zero knowledge on the internet. In: Automata, Languages and Programming, 33rd International Colloquium, ICALP 2006, Venice, Italy, July 10-14, 2006, Proceedings, Part II, pp. 22–33 (2006)
190. Wee, H.: Zero knowledge in the random oracle model, revisited. In: Advances in Cryptology - ASIACRYPT 2009, 15th International Conference on the Theory and Application of Cryptology and Information Security, Tokyo, Japan, December 6-10, 2009. Proceedings, pp. 417–434 (2009). DOI https://doi.org/10.1007/978-3-642-10366-7_25. URL http://dx.doi.org/10.1007/978-3-642-10366-7_25
191. Wee, H.: Black-box, round-efficient secure computation via non-malleability amplification. In: 51th Annual IEEE Symposium on Foundations of Computer Science, FOCS 2010, October 23-26, 2010, Las Vegas, Nevada, USA, pp. 531–540. IEEE Computer Society (2010)

192. Yao, A.C.: Protocols for secure computations (extended abstract). In: 23rd Annual Symposium on Foundations of Computer Science, Chicago, Illinois, USA, 3-5 November 1982, pp. 160–164. IEEE Computer Society (1982). DOI https://doi.org/10.1109/SFCS.1982.38. URL https://doi.org/10.1109/SFCS.1982.38
193. Yung, M., Zhao, Y.: Interactive zero-knowledge with restricted random oracles. In: Theory of Cryptography, Third Theory of Cryptography Conference, TCC 2006, New York, NY, USA, March 4-7, 2006, Proceedings, pp. 21–40 (2006). DOI https://doi.org/10.1007/11681878_2. URL https://doi.org/10.1007/11681878_2
194. Yung, M., Zhao, Y.: Generic and practical resettable zero-knowledge in the bare public-key model. In: M. Naor (ed.) Advances in Cryptology - EUROCRYPT 2007, 26th Annual International Conference on the Theory and Applications of Cryptographic Techniques, Barcelona, Spain, May 20-24, 2007, Proceedings, *Lecture Notes in Computer Science*, vol. 4515, pp. 129–147. Springer (2007)

The manufacturer's authorised representative in the EU is Springer Nature Customer Service Centre GmbH, Europaplatz 3, 69115 Heidelberg, Germany. If you have any concerns regarding our products, please contact ProductSafety@springernature.com

Printed and bound by CPI Group (UK) Ltd, Croydon, CR0 4YY
30/09/2026
02225570-0007